Logic Programming

Logic Programming

Proceedings of the 1998 Joint International Conference and Symposium on Logic Programming

edited by Joxan Jaffar

The MIT Press
Cambridge, Massachusetts
London, England

ISSN 1061-0464

ISBN 978-0-262-60031-6 (pb. : alk. paper)

Contents

Poster Abstracts

Committees

General Chair
Kung-Kiu Lau, *University of Manchester*

Program Chair
Joxan Jaffar, *National University of Singapore*

Workshop and Tutorial Chair
Pat Hill, *University of Leeds*

Local Arrangements Chair
Ian Pratt, *University of Manchester*

Program Committee

Krzysztof Apt	CWI, Amsterdam, Netherlands
Maurice Bruynooghe	Katholieke Universiteit Leuven, Belgium
Mats Carlsson	SICS, Stockholm, Sweden
Philippe Codognet	INRIA, Rocquencourt, France
Veronica Dahl	Simon Fraser University, Canada
Saumya Debray	University of Arizona, Tucson, USA
Jürgen Dix	University of Koblenz, Germany
Koichi Furukawa	Keio University, Tokyo, Japan
Michael Gelfond	University of Texas, El Paso, USA
Nevin Heintze	Bell Labs, Murray Hill, USA
Joxan Jaffar	National University of Singapore, Singapore
Kung-Kiu Lau	University of Manchester, UK
Giorgio Levi	University of Pisa, Italy
John Lloyd	University of Bristol, UK
Shan-Hwei Nienhuys-Cheng	University of Rotterdam, Netherlands
Catuscia Palamidessi	Pennsylvania State University, USA
Shuky Sagiv	Hebrew University, Jerusalem, Israel
Peter Stuckey	University of Melbourne, Australia
V. S. Subrahmanian	University of Maryland, College Park, USA
Paul Tarau	Louisiana Tech University, USA
Kazunori Ueda	Waseda University, Tokyo, Japan
David S. Warren	State University of New York, Stony Brook, USA

The Association for Logic Programming

The Association for Logic Programming (ALP) was founded in 1986. In addition to this conference (JICSLP'98) held in Manchester, UK from 15–19 June, 1998, the ALP has sponsored International Conferences and Symposia in Melbourne (1987), Seattle (1988), Lisbon (1989), Cleveland (1989), Jerusalem (1990), Austin (1990), Paris (1991), San Diego (1991), Washington D.C. (1992), Budapest (1993), Vancouver (1993), Santa Margherita Ligure (1994), Ithaca, New York (1994), Kanagawa (1995), Portland, Oregon (1995), Bad Honnef (1996), Leuven (1997), and Port Jefferson, New York (1997). The proceedings of all these meetings are published by The MIT Press.

The Association sponsors workshops, contributes support to other meetings related to logic programming, and provides limited support for attendance at its sponsored conferences and workshops by participants in financial need. Members receive the Association's newsletter quarterly and can subscribe to *the Journal of Logic Programming* at a reduced rate.

The affairs of the Association are overseen by the Executive Council. Current members are Mats Carlsson, Veronica Dahl, Danny De Schreye, Joxan Jaffar, Maurizio Martelli, Lee Naish, and Peter Szeredi; Association President: Krzysztof Apt; and Past President: David Scott Warrent. The current officers of the Association are: Robert Kowalski, Secretary; Francesca Toni, Treasurer and Conference Budget Auditor; Veronica Dahl, Conference Coordinator; and Pat Hill, Newsletter Editor.

Further information about the Association may be obtained from:

Cheryl Anderson-Deakin
ALP Administrative Secretary
ICSTM, DOC
180 Queen's Gate
London SW7 2BZ

Tel: +44 (171) 594 8226
Fax: +44 (171) 589 1552
e-mail: alp@doc.ic.ac.uk

Series Foreword

The logic programming approach to computing investigates the use of logic as a programming language and explores computational models based on controlled deduction.

The field of logic programming has seen a tremendous growth in the last several years, both in depth and in scope. This growth is reflected in the number of articles, journals, theses, books, workshops, and conferences devoted to the subject. The MIT Press Series in Logic Programming was created to accommodate this development and to nurture it. It is dedicated to the publication of high-quality textbooks, monographs, collections, and proceedings in logic programming.

Ehud Shapiro
The Weizmann Institute of Science
Rehovot, Israel

Preface

This volume contains the papers presented at the 1998 International Conference and Symposium on Logic Programming (JICSLP'98) held at the University of Manchester, U.K., 16–19 June, 1998. This is the fourth joint event for the International Conference on Logic Programming (ICLP) and the International Logic Programming Symposium (ILPS), and it is the fifteenth conference in each of the two series of premier international conferences on Logic Programming. All of these are sponsored by the Association for Logic Programming.

JICSLP'98 coincides with the celebration of the fiftieth anniversary of the world's first stored-program computer, the Baby, built in Manchester in June 1948. It is also co-located with the Eighth International Workshop on Logic-based Program Synthesis and Transformation (LOPSTR'98), with parallel sessions between the two meetings. JICSLP'98 also coincides with the Industrial Day organised by PAP/PACT and CompulogNet. There were a total of 90 papers submitted. The program committee meeting was held on 20–21 February, 1998, at the University of Manchester. Twenty-one papers were selected for presentation and publication. A number of other papers were selected for poster presentations. Abstracts of these posters appear at the end of this volume. In addition, the program committee also selected for presentation 4 tutorials and 8 postconference workshops.

The number of papers accepted may seem low, but in fact the acceptance rate (23%) is comparable with earlier conferences (for example, 28% for JICSLP'92 and JICSLP'96). This program committee decided to accept only those papers that had strong reviews, though it acknowledged there were many other acceptable papers.

Finally, the organisation of this conference benefited from having a great support team: Kung-Liu Lau, for all general matters including PC reviewing and organizing the PC meeting; Pat Hill, for coordinating the solicitation and determination of tutorials and workshops; Roland Yap, who helped me automate the reviewing process; Julie Grimaldi of MIT Press, who was responsive and informative; and many others.

Joxan Jaffar

Referees

Christophe Aillaud
Jamie Andrews
Roberto Bagnara
Richard Banach
Chitta Baral
Jonas Barklund
Peter Baumgartner
R. Ben-Eliyahu-Zohary
Annalisa Bossi
Meo Maria Chiara
Takashi Chikayama
Wei-Ngan Chin
Nicoletta Cocco
Bruce Davey
Danny De Schreye
Bart Demoen
Marc Denecker
Yves Deville
Daniel Diaz
Wlodzimierz Drabent
Phan Minh Dung
Kerstin Eder
Jesper Eskilson
François Fages
Moreno Falaschi
Gilberto Filé
Peter Flach
Pierre Flener
Maurizio Gabbrielli
John Gallagher
M. Garcia de la Banda
Roberto Giacobazzi
Roberta Gori
John Hannan
Michael Hanus
James Harland
Pieter Hartel
Warwick Harvey
Fergus Henderson
Martin Henz
Manuel Hermenegildo
Joshua S. Hodas
Christian Holzbaur
Yan-Nong Huang
Katsumi Inoue
Gerda Janssens
Bharat Jayaraman
David Kemp
Siau Cheng Khoo
Andy King
Naoki Kobayashi
François Laburthe
Laura Lafave
Christophe Leclere
Baudouin Le Charlier
Michael Leuschel
Renwei Li
Thomas Lindgren
Bing Liu
Ewing Lusk
Michael Maher
Kim Marriott
Maurizio Martelli
Bern Martens
Andrea Masini
Norm McCain
Dale Miller
Eric Monfroy
Gínes Moreno Valverde
Lee Naish
Dino Oliva
Eugenio Omodeo
Mario Ornaghi
Alberto Pettorossi
Andreas Podelski
Maurizio Proietti
C. R. Ramakrishnan
Rafael Ramirez
Femke van Raamsdonk
Antoine Rauzy
Philippe Refalo
Sophie Renault
Jean-Hugues Réty
Salvatore Ruggieri
Konstantinos Sagonas
Chiaki Sakama
Ken Satoh
Andrea Schaerf
Dietmar Seipel
Patrik Simons
Gert Smolka
Zoltan Somogyi
Harald Søndergaard
Fausto Spoto
Robert Stärk
Frieder Stolzenburg
Terrence Swift
Peter Szeredi
Vincent Tam
Michael Thielscher
Hudson Turner
Kristof Van Belleghem
Henk Vandecasteele
Sofie Verbaeten
Razvan Voicu
Paolo Volpe
Ralf Wastl
Richard Watson
Rong Yang
Roland Yap
Jia-Huai You

Invited Talks

The Pi Calculus and its Applications

Robin Milner
The Computer Laboratory
University of Cambridge
Cambridge, U.K. CB2 3QG

Abstract

The pi calculus [2, 3] was defined by Milner, Parrow and Walker as a "Calculus of Mobile Processes", extending work by Engberg and Nielsen [1]. It provides an underlying formal model for interactive systems which can change their configuration on the fly; this spans a large spectrum from mobile telephone networks to Java-like languages. The calculus aims to be a model for interactive behaviour as basic as is the lambda calculus for sequential computation. In fact, the lambda calculus can be modelled straightforwardly within it, and thus sequential computation can be seen as a special case of interaction.

The pi calculus is very simple; in my talk I shall presume no previous knowledge of it, but I shall not need to spend long in describing its primitive constructions. I shall focus on how it can be applied; in particular, how it admits a pleasant type system in which "type" can be understood to mean "pattern of interaction". In particular, I shall show how properties like "each mobile agent (ambulance? ..) will never be connected to more than one transmitter station at a time" are statically checkable types.

If time allows, I shall briefly discuss the language Pict (for distributed interactive systems) based upon pi calculus by Pierce and Turner [4], and the application of pi calculus to model authentication protocols by Abadi and Gordon [5].

References

[1] Engberg, U. and Nielsen, M. A calculus of communicating systems with label-passing. Report DAIMI PB-208, Computer Science Department, University of Aarhus, Denmark, 1986.

[2] Milner, R., Parrow, J. and Walker, D. A calculus of mobile processes, Parts I and II. *Information and Computation*, 100:1–77, 1992.

[3] Milner, R. The polyadic pi-calculus: a tutorial. *Logic and Algebra of Specification*, ed. F.L. Bauer, W. Brauer and H. Schwichtenberg, Springer Verlag, 203–246, 1993.

[4] Pierce, B. and Turner, D. Pict: a programming language based on the pi calculus. Technical Report, Computer Science Department, Indiana University, USA, 1997.

[5] Abadi, M. and Gordon, A. A calculus for cryptographic protocols: the spi calculus. Technical Report 414, Computer Laboratory, University of Cambridge, UK, 1997.

Disjunctive Linear Programming: At the Intersection of Operations Research and Logic Programming

Ken McAloon
ILOG Inc.
1901 Landings Drive
Mountain View CA 94043
mcaloon@ilog.com

Abstract

There are two basic themes in constraint logic programming (CLP). One is discrete or finite domain constraint programming based on the constraint satisfaction model (CSP). The other is continuous constraint programming based on linear programming (LP) and its extensions such as integer programming (IP). LP and IP are the mainstays of operations research (OR) and constitute a spectacularly successful set of implementations of deep mathematical algorithms. In this talk, we will discuss a family of problems known as *disjunctive linear programs* (DLPs) and consider how these applications are candidates for a combined attack.

The precise definition of DLP is as follows: In R^n, half-spaces and hyperplanes are defined by linear constraints. An intersection of half-spaces in R^n is called a *polyhedral set.* A *disjunctive set* is a finite union of polyhedral sets. A DLP is the problem of determining whether the intersection of a family of disjunctive sets is nonempty. This is the decision problem formulation. It is NP-Complete. (There is an obvious formal similarity with SAT.) The optimization problem with linear objective function is both NP-Hard and co-NP-Hard.

Interestingly, the DLP problem class, which constitutes an extension of IP, leads one to try to generalize many classical theorems of OR. This serves to pinpoint the distinction in IP between the role of integers as discrete points and their role as 0-1 Booleans. Some open and some solved problems in this area will be presented.

Addressing DLP applications requires an elegant collaboration among constraint-solving engines. Although this is not a new theme in CLP, going back as it does to work on CHIP, CLP(R), Prolog III and other systems, it is one which has returned with a new urgency because of the growing industrial interest in rapid solution of complex constraint problems. In this context, current CLP systems which are oriented towards OR such as ILOG Planner and 2LP will be discussed.

Some of the issues for CLP that these developments raise are (1) the need for progress on the implementation of cooperating solver engines, (2) the need for modeling frameworks to bridge the gap between mathematicians and programmers, (3) the need for research into meta-analysis of the most appropriate algorithmic solution to an application presented through a high-level API, (4) the need to make design decisions on languages vs librairies, and more.

References

[1] DeBacker, B.; Beringer, H.: Combinatorial Problem Solving in Constraint Logic Programming with Cooperating Solvers, *Logic Programming: Formal Methods and Practical Applications*, edited by C. Beierle and L. Plümer,

[2] Bockmayr, A.; Kasper, T.: A Unifying Framework for Integer and Finite Domain Constraint Programming, Max-Planck-Institut Technical Report MPI-I-97-2-008, 1997

[3] *ILOG Planner User's Manual*, 1997

[4] Mackworth, A. K.; Freuder, E. C.: The complexity of constraint satisfaction revisited. *Artificial Intelligence* **25** (1993) 65–74

[5] McAloon, K.; Tretkoff, C.: *Optimization and Computational Logic.* John Wiley & Sons 1996

[6] McAloon, K.; Tretkoff, C.: Logic, Modeling and Programming. *Annals of Operations Research* **71** (1997) 335-372

[7] McAloon, K.; Tretkoff, C., G. Wetzel: Disjunctive Programming and Cooperating Solvers, *Advances in Computational and Stochastic Optimization, Logic Programming and Heuristic Search*, edited by D.L. Woodruff, Kluwer 1997

Inductive Logic Programming for Relational Knowledge Discovery

Nada Lavrač
J. Stefan Institute
Jamova 39, 1000 Ljubljana, Slovenia
nada.lavrac@ijs.si

Abstract

Inductive logic programming (ILP) is concerned with the induction of logic programs from examples and background knowledge. In ILP, the shift of attention from program synthesis to knowledge discovery resulted in advanced techniques that are practically applicable for discovering knowledge in relational databases. This paper gives a brief introduction to ILP and presents selected ILP techniques for relational knowledge discovery.

1 Introduction

Inductive logic programming (ILP) [23, 27, 19] is a research area that has its backgrounds in inductive machine learning and logic programming. ILP research aims at a formal framework as well as practical algorithms for inductive learning of relational descriptions that typically have the form of logic programs. From logic programming, ILP has inherited its sound theoretical basis, and from machine learning, an experimental approach and orientation towards practical applications. ILP research has been strongly influenced also by Computational learning theory, and recently, by Knowledge Discovery in Databases (KDD) [11] which led to the development of new techniques for relational data mining.

In general, an ILP learner is given an initial theory B (background knowledge) and some evidence E (examples), and its aim is to induce a theory H (hypothesis) that together with B *explains* some properties of E. In most cases the hypothesis H has to satisfy certain restrictions, which we shall refer to as the *bias*. Bias includes prior expectations and assumptions, and can therefore be considered as the logically unjustified part of the background knowledge. Bias is needed to reduce the number of candidate hypotheses. It consists of the language bias L, determining the hypothesis space, and the search bias which restricts the search of the space of possible hypotheses.

The background knowledge used to construct hypotheses is a distinctive feature of ILP. It is well known that relevant background knowledge may substantially improve the results of learning in terms of accuracy, efficiency and the explanatory potential of the induced knowledge. On the other hand, irrelevant background knowledge will have just the opposite effect. Consequently, much of the art of inductive logic programming lies in the appropriate selection and formulation of background knowledge to be used by the selected ILP learner.

This paper gives a brief introduction to ILP and presents selected ILP techniques for relational knowledge discovery. The overview is restricted to techniques satisfying the strong criterion formulated for machine learning by Michie [20] that requires explicit symbolic form of induced descriptions.

2 ILP problems and applications

Let us present some of the tasks that ILP can address. Some illustrated tasks concern *predictive knowledge discovery* where the goal is to induce classification and prediction rules from the given data and background knowledge. Others concern *descriptive knowledge discovery* where the goal is to induce a theory that describes properties of the data, but may have a form that can not be used for prediction and classification.

2.1 Sample ILP problems

A logic programming problem. Let the training set E consist of positive and negative examples for the predicate `sort/2`. A positive example $e \in E^+$ provides information known to be true and should be entailed by the induced hypothesis. A negative example $e \in E^-$ provides information that is known not to be true and should not be entailed.

$$E^+ = \{\texttt{sort([2,1,3],[1,2,3])}\}$$
$$E^- = \{\texttt{sort([2,1],[1])},\ \texttt{sort([3,1,2],[2,1,3])}\}$$

Let the background knowledge B contain correct definitions of predicates `permutation/2`, which is true if the second argument is a permuted list of the first argument, and `sorted/1`, which is true if its list-argument is sorted in ascending order. If the hypothesis language L contains all definite clauses using the predicate and functor symbols appearing in the examples and background knowledge, an ILP system can induce the following hypothesis:

```
sort(X,Y) ← permutation(X,Y), sorted(Y).
```

The above logic program can be used to answer queries about the `sort` predicate, e.g. `?- sort([4,3],[3,4])`. Hence, the illustrated program synthesis task belongs to predictive knowledge discovery.

In descriptive knowledge discovery, using E^+ and B only, an induced theory could contain the following clauses:

```
sorted(Y) ← sort(X,Y).
permutation(X,Y) ← sort(X,Y).
```

```
sorted(X) ← sort(X,X).
```

Whereas predictive knowledge discovery results in a program for sorting lists, descriptive knowledge discovery results in uncovered regularities and relations among the involved predicates.

While it is impractical at present to induce real-world logic programs from examples and background knowledge predicates only, ILP techniques have shown their potential as programming aids that can produce fully specified procedures when given examples, background predicates, and a partial specification of the target program as bias [1].

A knowledge discovery problem. Consider a problem of learning family relations where the predictive knowledge discovery task is to define the target relation `daughter(X,Y)`, which states that person `X` is a daughter of person `Y`, in terms of relations defined in background knowledge B.

E^+ = {`daughter(mary,ann)`, `daughter(eve,tom)`}
E^- = {`daughter(tom,ann)`, `daughter(eve,ann)`}
B = {`mother(ann,mary)`, `mother(ann,tom)`, `father(tom,eve)`, `father(tom,ian)`, `female(ann)`, `female(mary)`, `female(eve)`, `parent(X,Y) ← mother(X,Y)`, `parent(X,Y) ← father(X,Y)`, `male(pat)`, `male(tom)`}

In the hypothesis language of definite clauses, given E^+, E^- and B, a predictive ILP system can induce the following clause:

```
daughter(X,Y) ← female(X), parent(Y,X).
```

Alternatively, a learner could have induced a set of clauses:

```
daughter(X,Y) ← female(X), mother(Y,X).
daughter(X,Y) ← female(X), father(Y,X).
```

In descriptive knowledge discovery, given E^+ and B only, an induced theory could contain the following clauses:

```
← daughter(X,Y), mother(X,Y).
female(X) ← daughter(X,Y).
mother(X,Y); father(X,Y) ← parent(X,Y).
```

One can see that in the predictive knowledge discovery setting classification rules are generated, whereas in the descriptive setting database regularities are derived.

2.2 ILP applications

Most of the current real-world ILP applications involve predictive knowledge discovery, in particular the induction of classification and prediction rules from a given database of examples and the available background knowledge. Successful ILP applications include drug design [17], protein secondary structure prediction [25], mutagenicity prediction [32], carcinogenesis prediction [33], medical diagnosis [21], discovery of qualitative models in medicine [15], finite-element mesh design [7], telecommunications [31], natural language processing [22], recovering software specifications [3], and many others.

A sample ILP application, describing both predictive and descriptive knowledge discovery, is outlined.

River water quality evaluation. Given a list of biological indicators present at a river water sampling site and their abundance levels (300 samples), the predictive knowledge discovery task is to classify the sample into one of the five classes $B1a$, $B1b$, $B2$, $B3$ and $B4$ [8]. Knowledge about biological indicators (families of macro-benthis invertebrates) consisted of eighty predicates of the form `family(X,A)`, each denoting that `family` is present in sample `X` with aboundance level `A` (e.g., `tipulidae(X,A)`, `asellidae(X,A)`, etc.) and the background knowledge about the relations between abundance levels was applied.

The ILP system Golem [26] induced three rules for class $B1a$, fourteen for $B1b$, sixteen for $B2$, two for $B3$ and none for $B4$. According to river ecologist expert evaluation, many of the rules were interesting and agreed with the expert knowledge. Here are two examples of such rules.

```
b1a(X) ← leuctridae(X,A).
b1b(X) ← ancylidae(X,A), gammaridae(X,B), hydropsychidae(X,C),
   rhyacophilidae(X,D), greater_than(B,A), greater_than(B,D).
```

The first rule, covering forty-three positive and four negative examples, states that a sample belongs to the best water quality class $B1a$ if Leuctridae is present. Indeed, according to the expert, Leuctridae is an indicator of good water quality. The second rule states that Gammaridae in abundance is a good indicator of class $B1b$, along with the other families present.

The same data was used for descriptive knowledge discovery by an ILP system Claudien [6]. Claudien checks all possible clauses, within a given language bias, for consistency w.r.t. the given examples. For instance, the first clause below specifies more than one quality class for which the family Perlodidae is indicative. If, in addition, Rhyacophilidae are also present, then this indicates best water quality class $B1a$, as shown in the second rule.

```
b1a(X); b1b(X) ← perlodidae(X,A).
b1a(X) ← perlodidae(X,A), rhyacophilidae(X,A).
```

The river quality experts particularly liked the clauses induced by Claudien due to the coverage of more than one class by a single clause; this is important since the classification results were achieved by a discretization of the originally continuous clasification problem.

3 Problem specification

An inductive logic programming task can be formally defined as follows:

Given:
- a set of examples E
- a background theory B
- a language bias L that defines the clauses allowed in hypotheses
- a notion of *explanation*

Find: a hypothesis $H \subset L$ which explains the examples E with respect to the theory B.

This definition needs to be instantiated for different types of ILP tasks [27]. The instantiation will concern the representation of training examples, the choice of a hypothesis language and an appropriate notion of explanation. By explanation we here refer to an acceptance criterion of hypotheses: the hypothesis explains the data if it satisfies a certain user-defined criterion w.r.t. the data. We will discuss some formal acceptance criteria used in different ILP settings, but we also need to bear in mind that ILP aims at the induction of hypotheses that are expressed in an explicit symbolic form, that can be easily interpreted by the user/expert and may contribute to the better understanding of the problem addressed, ideally forming a piece of new knowledge discovered from the data.

Predictive ILP is the most common ILP setting, ofter referred to as *normal ILP*, *explanatory induction*, *discriminatory induction*, or *strong ILP*. Predictive ILP is aimed at learning of classification and prediction rules. This ILP setting typically restricts E to ground facts, and H and B to sets of definite clauses. The strict notion of explanation in this setting usually denotes coverage and requires global completeness and consistency.

Global completeness and consistency implicitly assume the notion of *intensional coverage* defined as follows. Given background theory B, hypothesis H and example set E, an example $e \in E$ is (intensionally) covered by H if $B \cup H \models e$. Hypothesis H is (globally) complete if $\forall e \in E^+ : B \cup H \models e$. Hypothesis H is (globally) consistent if $\forall e \in E^- : B \cup H \not\models e$.

Given the restriction to definite theories $T = H \cup B$, for which there exists a unique least Herbrand model $M(T)$,[1] and to ground atoms as examples,

[1] The least Herbrand model $M(T)$ of a definite theory T is a set of ground facts $M(T) = \{a \mid a \in$ Herbrand base of T and $T \models a\}$, where the Herbrand base of T is the set of

this is equivalent to requiring that all examples in E^+ are true in $M(B \cup H)$ [27].

By relaxing the notion of explanation to allow incomplete and inconsistent theories that satisfy some other acceptance criteria (predictive accuracy, significance, compression), the predictive ILP setting can be extended to include learning of classification and prediction rules from imperfect data, as well as *learning of logical decision trees* [2]. In a broader sense, predictive ILP incorporates also *first-order regression* [16] and *constraint inductive logic programming* [30] for which again different acceptance criteria apply.

Descriptive ILP is sometimes referred to as *confirmatory induction*, *non-monotonic ILP*, *description learning*, or *weak ILP*. Descriptive ILP is usually aimed at learning of clausal theories [6]. This ILP setting typically restricts B to a set of definite clauses, H to a set of (general) clauses, and E to positive examples. The strict notion of explanation used in this setting requires that all clauses c in H are true in some preferred model of $T = B \cup E$, where the preferred model of T may be, for instance, the least Herbrand model $M(T)$. (One may also require the completeness and minimality of H, where completeness means that a maximally general hypothesis H is found, and minimality means that the hypothesis does not contain redundant clauses.)

By relaxing the strict notion of explanation used in clausal discovery [6] to allow for theories that satisfy some other acceptance criteria (similarity, associativity, interestingness), descriptive ILP can be extended to incorporate *learning of association rules* [4], *first-order clustering* [5, 9], *database restructuring* [12, 31] *subgroup discovery* [35], *learning qualitative models* [15] and *equation discovery* [34].

Other ILP settings have also been investigated, the most important being *relational instance-based learning* [10]. Excellent predictive results have been achieved by the relational instance-based learner RIBL [10] in numerous classification and prediction tasks. Recently, *first-order reinforcement learning* has also been studied by De Raedt and Džeroski. Since these two ILP settings do not involve hypothesis formation in explicit symbolic form, the developed techniques do not qualify as techniques for relational knowledge discovery.

4 Dimensions of the problem

The computational difficulty of an ILP learning problem depends on how its primary components are instantiated, i.e., which languages are allowed for

all ground atoms which can be formed using the predicate, functor and constant symbols occuring in T. From a practical point of view, logical entailment of fact a by theory T can be verified using a Prolog interpreter with knowledge base T and query ?-a. Thus, roughly speaking, the least Herbrand model of T is the set of all facts that are logically entailed by theory T.

the specification of examples, background knowledge, and hypothesis, and which notion of explanation is used. In the most general case, full first-order logic could be used as a language, and as stated above for predictive ILP, explanation would be identified with general logical entailment. Due to the undecidability of first-order logic, in this case it is not even decidable whether a hypothesis is a solution to the learning problem. One of the central goals of ILP is thus to find restrictions of the various components of the learning problem that on the one hand make the problem easier while on the other still allow interesting concepts to be learned.

4.1 Choice of the learning setting and acceptance criteria

The nature of the problem indicates what is the appropriate ILP setting and the corresponding acceptance criteria for hypotheses.

When learning from real-life data which is imperfect, the strict notions of explanation need to be relaxed in order to deal with noise (random errors) in the examples E and background knowledge B, sparseness of the training set E, and inappropriateness of B that may contain predicates that are not relevant or are insufficient for reliably solving a learning task.

Due to these reasons, and also due to the difference in the nature of various learning tasks, the strict notion of explanation needs to be replaced by a less strict, and typically different acceptance criteria for hypotheses. Section 5 gives an indication of the variety of tasks and criteria used in relational knowledge discovery.

4.2 Choice of the hypothesis language

All ILP systems use a language bias to restrict the set of clauses allowed in the hypotheses, thus limiting the search space of hypotheses. Of course, an inappriopriate bias can prevent the learner from finding a hypothesis explaining the given examples.

Most ILP systems in use today employ clausal first-order logic as their representation, usually concentrating on Horn clauses, i.e., clauses with one positive literal (head). Entailment in these languages is still undecidable, so many systems in addition assume *function-free* languages which are decidable and have turned out to be adequate for many practical problems. Furthermore, it is possible to automatically transform a clausal representation with function symbols into a function-free representation using a technique known as *flattening* [29]. However, the answer set of the transformed function-free program is equivalent to the original program with functions only under certain conditions.

4.3 Structuring the hypothesis space

ILP can be regarded as a search problem, where the space of possible solutions is determined by the syntactic (language) bias L. Searching the whole hypothesis space is clearly inefficient, therefore structuring the search space is necessary. Nearly all ILP learners structure the search by means of the dual notions of generalization and specialization.

There is also a decision criterion, e.g., global completeness and consistency in predictive ILP, to check whether a candidate hypothesis H is a solution to a problem. However, even for a Horn clause program consisting of one ground fact, one ground query and two Horn clauses with two literals, the ILP problem defined above remains undecidable. Therefore, almost all ILP approaches have chosen to replace (semantic) logical entailment ($\models$) by (syntactic) θ-subsumption ($\geq_\theta$), first used for learning by Plotkin.

Semantic generalization. A hypothesis H_1 is semantically more general than a hypothesis H_2 with respect to theory B if and only if $B \cup H_1 \models H_2$.

Syntactic generalization or θ-subsumption. A clause c_1 (a set of literals) is syntactically more general than a clause c_2 if and only if there exists a substitution θ such that $c_1\theta \subseteq c_2$. In this ca e we say that clause c_1 θ-subsumes c_2 ($c_1 \geq_\theta c_2$). A hypothesis H_1 is syntactically more general than a hypothesis H_2 if and only if for each clause c_2 in H_2 there exists a clause c_1 in H_1 such that c_1 is syntactically more general than c_2.

Plotkin has proved that the syntactic *is more general than* relation induces a lattice on the set of all clauses, up to equivalence classes and variable renamings, i.e., a lattice on the set of *reduced* clauses. Equivalence classes consist of clauses that are θ-subsumption equivalent ($\equiv_\theta$): $c \equiv_\theta d$ if and only if $c \geq_\theta d$ and $d \geq_\theta c$. A clause is reduced if it is not θ-subsumption equivalent to any proper subset of itself. In a lattice, any two clauses have a least upper bound (*lub*) and a greatest lower bound (*glb*) which are unique up to renaming of variables.

Notice that when a clause c_1 (resp. hypothesis) is syntactically more general than a clause c_2 it is also semantically more general: i.e., if $c_1 \geq_\theta c_2$, then $c_1 \models c_2$.

The converse is not true, as shown by the examples in Figure 1. As illustrated by the last example in Figure 1, the incompleteness of θ-subsumption is due to clauses that can resolve with themselves. If these self-resolving clauses are not allowed, θ-subsumption is complete with respect to $\models$. Checking θ-subsumption is an NP-complete problem, but in many cases it is possible to exploit structural properties of the data (determinacy and locality) to greatly reduce the combinatorial matching problem and runtime when compared to a blind matching approach.

Both *is more general than* relations are useful for induction because:

- when generalizing a hypothesis H_1 to H_2, all formulae f entailed by the hypothesis H_1 and background theory B will also be entailed by hypothesis H_2 and theory B, i.e. $(B \cup H_1 \models f) \rightarrow (B \cup H_2 \models f)$.

c_1:=daughter(X,Y) ← parent(Y,X)
c_2:=daughter(mary,ann) ← parent(ann,mary)
c_3:=daughter(mary,ann) ← female(mary), parent(ann,mary), parent(tom,mary)
$c_1 \geq_\theta c_2$ and $c_1 \geq_\theta c_3$, both with $\theta = \{X/mary, Y/ann\}$.

c_4:=daughter(X,Y) ← parent(Y,X), parent(U,V)
$c_1 \equiv_\theta c_4$; c_1 is reduced, c_4 is not reduced.

c_5:=q(Y,Z,X) ← q(X,Y,Z), c_6:=q(Z,X,Y) ← q(X,Y,Z)
$c_5 \not\geq_\theta c_6$ and $c_6 \not\geq_\theta c_5$, but $c_5 \models c_6$ and $c_6 \models c_5$.

Figure 1: θ-subsumption examples.

- when specializing a hypothesis H_1 to H_2, all formulae f logically not entailed by hypothesis H_1 and background theory B will not be entailed by hypothesis H_2 and theory B either, i.e. $(B \cup H_1 \not\models f) \rightarrow (B \cup H_2 \not\models f)$.

The two properties can be used to prune large parts of the search space.

4.4 Searching the hypothesis space

In the θ-subsumption lattice of reduced clauses, an ILP learner can search the hypothesis space systematically, either top-down or bottom-up.

Specialization techniques search the hypothesis space top-down, from the most general to specific hypotheses, using a specialization/refinement operator, which ideally computes the set of all minimal (most general) specializations of the currently considered clause.

Generalization techniques search the hypothesis space in a bottom-up manner: they start from the training examples (most specific hypotheses) and search the hypothesis space by employing a generalization operator. Ideally, generalizations are the *least general generalizations* of the given examples ("cautious generalization").

In predictive ILP, both techniques repeat their procedure on a reduced example set if the found clause by itself does not entail all positive examples. They use thus an iterative process to compute disjunctive hypotheses consisting of more than one clause (often called the "covering" approach).

Specialization techniques are better suited for empirical learning in the presence of noise since top-down search can easily be guided by heuristics. On the other hand, generalization techniques are best suited for interactive and incremental learning from few examples.

4.5 Advanced search techniques

One of the key problems in ILP is how to search the space of logic programs efficiently. Existing ILP algorithms use variants of greedy search to explore the space of logic programs. Due to myopic behavior, a greedy search algorithm is easily trapped in a local minimum. To alleviate the problem of myopic greedy search, several advanced search techniques have been developed, such as beam search, bi-directional search, stochastic search and genetic search. The simplest is beam search in which a beam of literals is searched in order to find the best literals or conjunctions of literals needed in clause construction.

Bi-directional search is used in the Progol algorithm [24], combining the advantages of top-down and bottom-up search. The algorithm (1) randomly selects an example e_i, (2) uses (depth-bounded) inverse resolution to construct the most specific clause $c(e_i, B)$ that explains e_i (such that $c(e_i, B) \models e_i$), (3) by top-down search of the θ-subsumption lattice finds a clause c_i which subsumes $c(e_i, B)$, is consistent w.r.t. the current example set E and maximally compresses a set of examples subsumed by c_i, (4) adds c_i to the current hypothesis H. It repeats the process with the examples that are still not covered until no more compression is possible. Bi-directional search results in a substantial reduction of the search space.

Stochastic search in the state space of logic programs can be used to alleviate the problem of myopic greedy search. In a stochastic ILP system MILP [18], based on ideas from simulated annealing, transitions in the state space are probabilistic; the probability of a transition to a state is proportional to the (heuristically evaluated) quality of the state.

Genetic search is performed on a population of hypotheses. In each iteration, hypotheses are mutated and recombined, and the best n hypotheses are kept. To use such a strategy for ILP, a representation of hypotheses must be found that allows effective mutation and recombination operators to be formulated. In the GA-Smart system [14], a restricted hypothesis space based on clause templates was selected to allow for an appropriate bitstring representation. In the system Gilp by Varšek, a genetic algorithm operating on a population of Prolog clauses was employed in conjunction with the covering principle.

4.6 Other dimensions

Empirical versus incremental learning. This dimension describes the way the examples E are obtained. In empirical ILP, the evidence is given at the start and not changed afterwards. In incremental ILP, the user supplies the examples one by one, in a piecewise fashion.

Interactive versus non-interactive learning. In interactive ILP, the learner is allowed to pose questions to the user about the intended interpretation. Usually these questions query for the intended interpretation of examples or clauses.

Theory revision. In addition to examples E and background knowledge B, an existing theory may be given to the learner as a starting point for hypothesis construction, often requiring that it be minimally modified to arrive at a hypothesis. Incremental and interactive learning approaches require theory revision.

Predicate invention. Predicate invention denotes the process whereby entirely new predicates (not present in E and B) are induced. Predicate invention results in extending the vocabulary of the learner and may therefore facilitate the learning task.

Single versus multiple predicate learning. In single predicate learning, the evidence contains examples for only one predicate and the aim is to induce a definition for this predicate; in multiple predicate learning, the aim is to learn a set of possibly interacting predicate definitions or properties that hold among various predicates. Descriptive ILP tasks involving multiple predicates are handled easier and more naturally, due to overcoming the order dependency problem of multiple predicate learning in predictive ILP.

5 Techniques for relational knowledge discovery

5.1 Predictive ILP

Learning of classification rules. This is the standard ILP setting that has been used in numerous successful predictive knowledge discovery applications. The well-known systems for classification rule induction include Foil [28][2], Golem [26] and Progol [24]. Foil is efficient and best understood due to its similarity to Clark and Niblett's CN2. On the other hand, Golem and Progol are champions concerning successful ILP applications, despite the fact that they are substantially less efficient. Foil is a top-down learner, Golem is a bottom-up learner, and Progol uses a combined search strategy. All are mainly concerned with single predicate learning from positive and negative examples and background knowledge; in addition, Progol can also be used to learn from positive examples only. They use different acceptance criteria: compression, coverage/accuracy and minimal description length, respectively.

Induction of logical decision trees. The system Tilde [2] belongs to Top-down induction of decision tree algorithms. It can be viewed as a first-order upgrade of Quinlan's C4.5, employing logical queries in tree nodes which involves appropriate handling of variables. The main advantage of Tilde is its efficiency and capability of dealing with large numbers of training examples, which are the well-known properties of Tilde's propositional ancestors. Hence Tilde currently represents one of the most appropriate systems for predictive knowledge discovery. Besides the language bias, Tilde

[2] The successor of Foil, the system Ffoil, can successfully be used for inducing relational definitions of functions.

allows for lookahead and prepruning (according to the minimal number of examples covered) defined by parameter setting.

First-order regression. The relational regression task can be defined as follows: Given training examples as positive ground facts for the target predicate $r(Y, X_1, ..., X_n)$, where the variable Y has real values, and background knowledge predicate definitions, find a definition for $r(Y, X_1, ..., X_n)$, such that each clause has a literal binding Y (assuming that $X_1, ..., X_n$ are bound). Typical background knowledge predicates include less-or-equal tests, addition, subtraction and multiplication. An approach to relational regression is implemented in the system FORS (First Order Regression System) [16] which performs top-down search of a refinement graph. In each clause, FORS can predict a value for the target variable Y as the output value of a background knowledge literal, as a constant, or as a linear combination of variables appearing in the clause (using linear regression).

Inductive Constraint Logic Programming. It is well known that Constraint Logic Programming (CLP) can successfully deal with numerical constraints. The idea of Inductive Constraint Logic Programming (ICLP) [30] is to benefit from the number-handling capabilities of CLP, and to use the constraint solver of CLP to do part of the search involved in inductive learning. To this end a maximally discriminant generalization problem in ILP is transformed to an equivalent constraint satisfaction problem (CSP). The solutions of the original ILP problem can be constructed from the solutions of CSP, which can be obtained by running a constraint solver on CSP.

5.2 Descriptive ILP

Learning of clausal theories and association rules. In discovering full clausal theories, as done in the system Claudien [6], each example is a Herbrand model, and the system searches for the most general clauses that are true in all the models. Clauses are discovered independently from each other, which is a substantial advantage for data mining, as compared to the learning of classification rules (particularly learning of mutually dependent predicates in multiple predicate learning). In Claudien, search of clauses is limited by the language bias. Its acceptance criterion can be modified by setting two parameters: the requested minimal accuracy and minimal number of examples covered. In another clausal discovery system, Primus [13], the best-first search for clauses is guided by heuristics measuring the "confirmation" of clauses. The Claudien system was further extended to Warmr [4] that enables learning of association rules from multiple relations.

First-order clustering. Top-down induction of decision trees can be viewed as a clustering method since nodes in the tree correspond to sets of examples with similar properties, thus forming concept hierarchies. This view was adopted in C0.5 [5], an upgrade of the Tilde logical decision tree learner. An approach combining learning and conceptual clustering techniques was implemented in the system Cola [9]. Given a small (sparse) set of classified training instances and a set of unclassified instances, Cola uses Bisson's conceptual clustering algorithm KBG on the entire set of instances, climbs the hierarchy tree and uses the classified instances to identify (single or disjunctive) class descriptions.

Database restructuring. The system Fender [31] searches for common parts of rules describing a concept, thus forming subconcept definitions to be used in the refurmulation of original rules. The result is a knowledge base with new intermediate concepts and deeper inferential structure than the initial "flat" rulebase. The system Index [12] is concerned with the problem of determining which attribute dependencies (functional or multivalued) hold in the given relational database. The induced attribute dependencies can be used to obtain a more structured database. Both approaches can be viewed as doing predicate invention, where (user selected) invented predicates are used for theory restructuring.

Subgroup discovery. The subgroup discovery task is defined as follows: given a population of individuals and a property of those individuals we are interested in, find the subgroups of the population that are statistically "most interesting", i.e., are as large as possible and have the most unusual statistical (distributional) characteristics with respect to the property of interest. The system Midos [35] guides the top-down search of potentially interesting subgroups using numerous user-defined parameters.

Learning qualitative models of dynamic systems. The automated construction of models of dynamic system may be aimed at qualitative model discovery. A recent qualitative model discovery system [15], using a Qsim-like representation, is based on Coiera's Genmodel to which signal processing capabilities have been added.

Equation discovery. The system LAGRANGE [34] discovers a set of differential equations from an example behavior of a dynamic system. Example behaviors are specified by lists of measurements of a set of system variables, and background knowledge predicates enable the introduction of new variables as time derivatives, sines or cosines of system variables. New variables can be further introduced by multiplication.

Acknowledgements

This work reflects some of the research results achieved in the EU funded projects no. 6020 ILP (1992–95) and no. 20237 ILP2 (1996–98), and ILP related projects funded by the Slovenian Ministry of Science and Technology. The author is grateful to Luc De Raedt, Sašo Džeroski, Peter Flach and Stefan Wrobel for their collaboration and previous joint overviews of ILP that strongly influenced this work and its presentation.

References

[1] F. Bergadano, D. Gunetti. *Inductive Logic Programming: From Machine Learning to Software Engineering.* The MIT Press, 1995.

[2] H. Blockeel and L. De Raedt. Top-down induction of logical decision trees. Submitted to *DAMI, Special Issue on Inductive Logic Programming*, 1998.

[3] W. Cohen. Recovering software specifications with inductive logic programming. *Proc. Twelfth National Confeernce on Artificial Intelligence*, The MIT Press, 1994.

[4] L. Dehaspe, L. De Raedt. Mining association rules in multiple relations. *Proc. Seventh Int. Workshop on Inductive Logic Programming*, Springer, LNAI 1297, pp. 125–132, 1997.

[5] L. De Raedt, H. Blockeel. Using logical decision trees for clustering. *Proc. Seventh Int. Workshop on Inductive Logic Programming*, Springer, LNAI 1297, pp. 133–140, 1997.

[6] L. De Raedt, L. Dehaspe. Clausal discovery. *Machine Learning*, 26(2/3): 99–146, 1997.

[7] B. Dolšak, S. Muggleton. The application of inductive logic programming to finite-element mesh design. In S. Muggleton, ed., *Inductive Logic Programming*, pp. 453–472. Academic Press, 1992.

[8] S. Džeroski, L. De Haspe, B. Ruck, W. Walley. Classification of river water quality data using machine learning. *Proc. Fifth Int. Conference on the Development and Application of Computer Technologies to Environmental Studies, Vol. I: Pollution Modelling.*, pp. 129–137. Computational Mechanics Publications, Southampton, 1994.

[9] W. Emde. Learning of characteristic concept descriptions from small sets to classified examples. *Proc. Seventh European Conference on Machine Learning*, LNAI 784, pp. 103–121, Springer, 1994.

Inductive learning of characteristic concept descriptions. *Proc. Fourth Int. Workshop on Inductive Logic Programming*, GMD-Studien 237, pp. 51–70, 1994.

[10] W. Emde, D. Wettschereck. Relational instance-based learning. *Proc. Thirteenth Int. Conference on Machine Learning*, pp. 122–130, Morgan Kaufmann, 1996.

[11] U. Fayyad, G. Piatetsky-Shapiro, P. Smyth, R. Uthurusamy, eds. *Advances in Knowledge Discovery and Data Mining.* The MIT Press, 1995.

[12] P.A. Flach. Predicate invention in inductive data engineering. *Proc. Sixth European Conference on Machine Learning*, Springer, LNAI 667, pp. 83-94, 1993.

[13] P. Flach, N. Lachiche. Cooking up integrity constraints with Primus. Technical report, University of Bristol, 1998.

[14] A. Giordana, C. Sale. Learning structured concepts using genetic algorithms. *Proc. Ninth Int. Workshop on Machine Learning*, pp. 169–178, 1992.

[15] D.T. Hau, E.W.Coiera. Learning qualitative models of dynamic systems. *Machine Learning*, 26(2/3): 177–212, 1997.

[16] A. Karalič, I. Bratko. First order regression. *Machine Learning*, 26(2/3): 147–176, 1997.

[17] R.D. King, S. Muggleton, R. Lewis, M.J.E. Sternberg. Drug design by machine learning: The use of inductive logic programming to model the structure-activity relationships of trimethoprim analogues binding to dihydrofolate reductase. *Proc. of the National Academy of Sciences of the USA* 89(23): 11322–11326, 1992.

[18] M. Kovačič. MILP - A stochastic approach to inductive logic programming. *Proc. Fourth Int. Workshop on Inductive Logic Programming*, GMD-Studien 237, pp. 123–138, 1994.

[19] N. Lavrač, S. Džeroski. *Inductive Logic Programming: Techniques and Applications.* Ellis Horwood, 1994.

[20] D. Michie. Machine learning in the next five years. *Proc. Third European Working Session on Learning*, pp. 107–122. Pitman, 1988.

[21] F. Mizoguchi, H. Ohwada, M. Daidoji, S. Shirato. Using inductive logic programming to learn classification rules that identify glaucomatous eyes. In N. Lavrač, E. Keravnou, B. Zupan, eds., *Intelligent Data Analysis in Medicine and Pharmacology*, Kluwer, pp. 227–242, 1997.

[22] R.J. Mooney, M.E. Califf. Induction of first-order decision lists: Results on learning the past tense of English verbs. *Journal of Artificial Intelligence Research* 3: 1–24, 1995.

[23] S. Muggleton, ed. *Inductive Logic Programming.* Academic Press, 1992.

[24] S. Muggleton. Inverse Entailment and Progol. *New Generation Computing, Special issue on Inductive Logic Programming*, 13(3-4), 1995.

[25] S. Muggleton, R.D. King, M.J.E. Sternberg. Protein secondary structure prediction using logic. *Protein Engineering* 7: 647–657, 1992.

[26] S. Muggleton, C. Feng. Efficient induction of logic programs. *Proc. First Conference on Algorithmic Learning Theory*, pp. 368–381. Ohmsha, Tokyo, 1990.

[27] S. Muggleton, L. De Raedt. Inductive logic programming: Theory and methods. *Journal of Logic Programming* 19/20: 629–679, 1994.

[28] J.R. Quinlan. Learning logical definitions from Relations. *Machine Learning* 5:239-266, 1990.

[29] C. Rouveirol, J-F.Puget. A simple solution for inverting resolution. *Proc. Fourth European Working Session on Learning*, pp. 201–210, Pitman, 1989.

[30] M. Sebag, C. Rouveirol. Constraint Inductive Logic Programming. In L. De Raedt, ed., *Advances in Inductive Logic Programming*, pp. 277–294, IOS Press, 1996.

[31] E. Sommer. Rulebase stratifications: An approach to theory restructuring. *Proc. Fourth Int. Workshop on Inductive Logic Programming*, GMD-Studien 237, pp. 377-390, 1994.

[32] A. Srinivasan, S. Muggleton, R.D. King, M.J.E. Sternberg. Mutagenesis: ILP experiments in a non-determinate biological domain. *Proc. Fourth Int. Workshop on Inductive Logic Programming*, GMD-Studien 237, pp. 217–232, 1994.

[33] A. Srinivasan, R.D. King, S. Muggleton, M.J.E. Sternberg. Carcinogenesis prediction using inductive logic programming. In N. Lavrač, E. Keravnou, B. Zupan, eds., *Intelligent Data Analysis in Medicine and Pharmacology*, Kluwer, pp. 243–260, 1997.

[34] S. Džeroski, L. Todorovski. Discovering dynamics: From inductive logic programming to machine discovery. *Proc. Tenth Int. Conference on Machine Learning*, pp. 97–103, Morgan Kaufmann, 1993.

[35] S. Wrobel. An algorithm for multi-relational discovery of subgroups. *Proc. First European Symposium on Principles of Data Mining and Knowledge Discovery*, pp. 78–87. Springer, 1997.

Refereed Papers

Co-definite Set Constraints with Membership Expressions

Philippe Devienne, Jean-Marc Talbot, Sophie Tison [1]
Laboratoire d'Informatique Fondamentale de Lille
Université des Sciences et Technologies de Lille
59655 Villeneuve d'Ascq - France
{devienne,talbot,tison}@lifl.fr

Abstract

Set constraints express inclusion and non-inclusion relationships between sets of trees using boolean connectives, functional composition and "projections". It is a suitable formalism for program-analysis (set-based analysis) and typing. Complexity of satisfiability of the general class is NEXPTIME-complete, and lots of works deal with subclasses, trying to get more tractable algorithms.

Recently, Podelski and Charatonik introduce the class of co-definite set constraints for analysis of reactive logic programs. They give an algorithm for deciding satisfiability - and "computing" the greatest solution - for this class interpreted over sets of infinite and finite trees. In this paper, we extend this result by adding membership expressions: they are more expressive and we show how they provide an easy abstraction mechanism of the T_P operator. We think that our method improves previous works also by its simplicity. We use the tree automaton framework both for computation and representation of the greatest solution. The algorithm we obtain is rather simple and concepts that we introduce for the proof seem to be interesting on their own rights.

1 Introduction

Set constraints enable to express inclusion and non-inclusion relationships between sets of (finite) trees using boolean connectives such as intersection, union and complementation, functional composition and projections f_i^{-1} (applied on a set of trees S, f_i^{-1} is the set of trees $\{t_i\}$ such that $f(t_1, .., t_m) \in S$). They are mainly involved in program analysis (set-based analysis [13]) [12] [14] and typing. It turns out that the complexity of satisfiability and entailment problems for the general class is very high (*NEXPTIME*-complete [4, 2, 20]). This leads to search for more tractable subclasses by restricting either the arity of considered function symbols [1], or the different used set

[1] A long version of this work appears in the proceedings of the french workshop "Journées du GDR Programmation [8]"

operations.

Historically, the first class for which the satisfiability has been proven decidable is the class of definite set constraints [15]; this class consists in inclusions of the form $sexp_1 \subseteq sexp_2$, where $sexp_1$ is a set expression without complementation and $sexp_2$ is built only with variables and function symbols. The main property of this class is that if such a conjunction of set constraints is satisfiable, then it has a least solution.

Recently, Charatonik and Podelski [5] have proven the equivalence of this class with the class of (positive) set constraints with intersection (that is inclusions between set expressions built with function symbols and intersection), providing a proof of the *EXPTIME*-completeness of the satisfiability problem of definite set constraints.

In [9], the authors have extended this class by considering so-called "membership expressions": those expressions can be viewed as a generalization of projections and appeared as quantified set expressions in [16]. Their shape is $\{x \mid \phi\}$, where ϕ is a (implicitly existentially quantified) conjunction of membership test between a tree (with first-order variables) and a set expressions. It has been proven that considering "membership expressions" instead of projections does not change the complexity of the satisfiability problem, that is, for definite set constraints with membership expressions this problem remains *EXPTIME*-complete and that if it is satifiable, such constraints have a least solution.

Definite set constraints (with membership expressions) are used in the framework of program analysis to compute an accurate upper approximation of the success set of a logic program [16] [12] that is, the least fixpoint of the well-known operator T_P [17]. Similar results for program analysis have been obtained by [10] using logic program transformations, which in fact simulate tree automata transformations.

A *reactive logic program* is a definite logic program for which the behaviours of interest (w.r.t. the SLD-resolution) are the terminating as well as the nonterminating ones [17]. Their semantics is captured by the greatest model of the Clark' completion of the program over the complete Herbrand base (that is, atoms built over finite and infinite terms). This model is also defined (from a computational point of view) as the greatest fixpoint of the operator T_P computed on the complete Herbrand base.

Motivated by the computation of an approximation of this semantics, Podelski and Charatonik introduced in [6, 7] the class of co-definite set constraints. This class is not exactly the dual class of definite set constraints. Although it consists in inclusions of the form $sexp_1 \supseteq sexp_2$ such that $sexp_1$ is a set expression without complementation, the right-hand side $sexp_2$ is restricted to variables, constant and unary function symbols. They showed that a satisfiable system of set constraints of this class interpreted over sets of finite and infinite trees has a greatest solution. Their approach mixed syntactic transformations and automata constructions and built a tree automaton representation of the greatest solution (if the set constraints are satisfiable); finally, they proved the *EXPTIME*-completeness of the satisfiability problem for this class. A direct application of this method is used for inferring conservative approximations of temporal properties of infinite-states systems [18].

In this paper, we extend the class of co-definite set constraints (in a similar way than [9] w.r.t. [15]) by adding "membership expressions". This improves also previous work of the authors on another point since the case of sets of finite and infinite trees is now addressed. We will prove that this extension preserves the "greatest solution" property and does not change the complexity of the satisfiability problem (and so, of the construction of the greatest solution).

We claim that tree automata provide a homogeneous framework both for computing and representing the greatest solution (if there is one). It leads also to a simple algorithm described as a system of inference rules transforming a tree automaton into another one according to set constraints. This terminates either with a special value if the system of set constraints is not satisfiable or with an irreducible tree automaton (w.r.t. the system of inference rules) recognizing the greatest solution of the system of set constraints.

The class introduced here allows both an easy abstraction mechanism (computing from the program the suitable system of set contraints) and an easy safeness proof for this latter. Moreover, it provides a more accurate approximation that the one proposed in [6]. Finally, this approach points out the duality between the computation of an approximation of the least and the greatest fixpoint of T_P both for abstraction mechanism and for computation [16].

In Section 2, we recall definitions concerning (infinite) trees, set constraints and tree automata. The Section 3 presents a motivation of this work: we show how set constraints can be used for computing an (upper) approximation of the semantics of reactive logic programs. The Section 4 introduces formally the class of set constraints this paper addresses. In Section 5, we describe our algorithm for satisfiability and prove its correctness and its complexity.

2 Preliminaries

This part is devoted to basic definitions and notations concerning the three main notions used in this paper, respectively (generalized) trees, set constraints and tree automata.

2.1 Trees and Subtrees

Let Σ be a finite set of function symbols and ρ a mapping called *arity* from Σ into the set of natural numbers $\mathbb{N}$. Symbols having 0 (resp. n) for arity will be called nullary or constant symbols (resp. n-ary symbols). A signature *Sig* will be defined as a pair (Σ, ρ).
A tree t is a partial mapping from $\mathbb{N}_+^*$ (the free monoid over $\mathbb{N}\backslash\{0\}$ generated by concatenation "." and the empty word ϵ) to Σ such that the domain of t, denoted $dom(t)$, is non-empty and satisfies: $\forall d \in dom(t)$,

- $d.i \in dom(t) \Rightarrow d \in dom(t)$ ($dom(t)$ is prefix-closed)
- $(d.i \in dom(t) \ \wedge j \leq i) \Rightarrow d.j \in dom(t)$
- $(\rho(t(d)) = n \ \wedge n > 0) \Leftrightarrow (d.n \in dom(t) \wedge d.(n+1) \notin dom(t))$.

For a tree t, elements of $dom(t)$ will be called positions. A position d such that $d.1 \notin dom(t)$ is a leaf. One should notice that this definition implies that d is a leaf iff $t(d)$ is a constant. We will denote $TREE^*(Sig)$ (resp. $TREE(Sig)$) the set of trees (resp. the set of finite trees, that is those having a finite domain).
For any tree t, the subtree of t at position d, where $d \in dom(t)$ is the tree denoted $t|_d$ and defined by $dom(t|_d) = \{u \mid d.u \in dom(t)\}$ and for any u in $dom(t|_d)$, $t|_d(u) = t(d.u)$.

We will also consider finite trees with variables. Let $\mathcal{V}$ be a set of (first-order) variables (assumed to be disjoint from Σ). We denote $TREE(Sig \cup \mathcal{V})$, the set of finite trees built over Σ and $\mathcal{V}$, where variables are viewed as constant symbols. The set of variables occurring in a tree t will be denoted $var(t)$. The notion of (ground) substitution, that is a mapping from a finite set of variables into $TREE^*(Sig)$ is the obvious generalization of the standard one (see [17] for a formal definition) and is extended in a canonical way to a mapping from $TREE(Sig \cup \mathcal{V})$ into $TREE^*(Sig)$.

2.2 Set Constraints

Set constraints enable to express inclusion and non-inclusion relations between set expressions and are interpreted over sets of trees[2]. Those set expressions are built over a set V of set variables (denoted by X,Y,..), a signature $Sig = (\Sigma, \rho)$, boolean connectives ($\cup$,$\cap$,$\complement$) and projection symbols f_i^{-1} (with $f \in \Sigma$ and $1 \leq i \leq \rho(f)$).

$$sexp ::= X \mid f(sexp_1, .., sexp_m) \mid sexp \cup sexp' \mid sexp \cap sexp' \mid \complement sexp \mid f_i^{-1}(sexp)$$

Moreover, inspired by [16] and [10], the authors have added in [9] an operator, called *membership expression* of the form: $\{x \mid s_1 \in sexp_1, .., s_l \in sexp_l\}$, where $s_1, .., s_l \in TREE(Sig \cup \mathcal{V})$, $sexp_1, .., sexp_l$ are set expressions, and the

[2]In fact, most works deal only with set of finite trees.

variables occurring in the s_i's (except x) are implicitly existentially quantified.
A set (or system) of set constraints is interpreted as a conjunction of its set constraints.

An interpretation $\mathcal{I}$ is a valuation which maps (set) variables into sets of trees and is extended to set expressions in the following way:

- $\mathcal{I}(f(sexp_1, .., sexp_m)) = \{f(s_1, .., s_m) \mid s_1 \in \mathcal{I}(sexp_1), .., s_m \in \mathcal{I}(sexp_m)\}$
- $\cup$, $\cap$ and $\complement$ are interpreted in a canonical way.
- $\mathcal{I}(f_i^{-1}(sexp)) = \{s_i \mid \exists s_1, .., s_{i-1}, s_{i+1}, .., s_m,\ f(s_1, .., s_m) \in \mathcal{I}(sexp)\}$
- $\mathcal{I}(\{x \mid s_1 \in sexp_1, .., s_l \in sexp_l\})$ is the set of trees t for which there exists a substitution α defined on bound variables of the s_i's such that for any i, $([x/t] \circ \alpha)(s_i) \in \mathcal{I}(sexp_i)$.

An interpretation $\mathcal{I}$ is said to be a solution of $sexp_1 \subseteq sexp_2$ (resp. of $sexp_1 \not\subseteq sexp_2$) iff $\mathcal{I}(sexp_1) \subseteq \mathcal{I}(sexp_2)$ (resp. $\mathcal{I}(sexp_1) \not\subseteq \mathcal{I}(sexp_2)$). $\mathcal{I}$ is a solution for a system of set constraints $\mathcal{SC}$ iff it is a solution of each set constraint. A (system of) set constraint(s) is said to be satisfiable if it has a solution. $SOL(\mathcal{SC})$ will denote the set of solutions of $\mathcal{SC}$.

2.3 Tree Automata

In this section, we introduce tree automata which are the basic tool of our method. Those tree automata will recognize a tuple of sets of finite and infinite trees.

Definition 1 An n-ranked tree automaton (TA) $\mathcal{A}$ is a tuple $(Sig, \mathcal{Q}, \mathcal{F}, \mathcal{S})$ where $Sig = (\Sigma, \rho)$ is a signature, $\mathcal{Q}$ is a finite set of states, $\mathcal{F} = (F_1, .., F_n)$ is a tuple of sets of final states ($F_i \subseteq \mathcal{Q}$) and $\mathcal{S}$ is a set of transition rules of the form $f(q_1, .., q_m) \to q$, where $f \in \Sigma$ is a m-ary symbol and $\{q, q_1, .., q_m\} \subseteq \mathcal{Q}$

Definition 2 For an n-ranked tree automaton $\mathcal{A} = (Sig, \mathcal{Q}, \mathcal{F}, \mathcal{S})$ and a tree t, a run $r_t^{\mathcal{A}}$ is a mapping from $dom(t)$ into $\mathcal{Q}$ compatible with the transition rules of $\mathcal{A}$ *i.e.* for every $d \in dom(t)$,

$$f(r_t^{\mathcal{A}}(d.1), .., r_t^{\mathcal{A}}(d.\rho(f))) \to r_t^{\mathcal{A}}(d) \ \in \mathcal{S} \textit{ with } t(d) = f$$

The set of runs for a tree t and an n-ranked tree automaton $\mathcal{A}$ will be denoted $Run_{\mathcal{A}}(t)$.
A tree t is recognized for the ith component by an n-ranked tree automaton $\mathcal{A}$ iff there exists a run $r_t^{\mathcal{A}}$ for t in $\mathcal{A}$ such that $r_t^{\mathcal{A}}(\epsilon) \in F_i$ The language recognized by an n-ranked tree automaton $\mathcal{A}$ is the tuple $(L_1, .., L_n)$, where the L_i's are the sets of trees recognized by $\mathcal{A}$ for the ith component.

In fact, in this paper, we deal only with a particular class of tree automata, the class of deterministic and complete ones. Those properties are defined as:

Definition 3 An n-ranked tree automaton is said to be *bottom-up deterministic* (resp. *complete*) if for all left-hand sides *lhs*, there exists at most (resp. at least) one state q such that $lhs \to q \in \mathcal{S}$.

From now, "tree automaton" will stand for "n-ranked deterministic and complete tree automaton". It is easy to see that in such a tree automaton, for every finite tree, there exists a unique run. However this property is not true for infinite trees as shown in the example below.

Example 1 Let us consider the following (one-ranked) tree automaton $\mathcal{A}$ such that $Sig = \{(a,0),(f,1)\}$, $\mathcal{Q} = \{q_1,q_2\}$, $\mathcal{F} = (\{q_1,q_2\})$ and
$\mathcal{S} = \{a \to q_1,\ f(q_1) \to q_1,\ f(q_2) \to q_2\}$.
Let us consider the tree t such that $dom(t) = \{1\}^*$ and for any $d \in dom(t)$, $t(d) = f$. It is obvious to see that both mappings $r1_t^{\mathcal{A}}$ and $r2_t^{\mathcal{A}}$ defined as $\forall d \in dom(t)$, $r1_t^{\mathcal{A}}(d) = q_1$ and $r2_t^{\mathcal{A}}(d) = q_2$ are runs for the tree t in $\mathcal{A}$.

This comes from the fact that the notion of determinism used here is an bottom-up determinism [11]. One should also notice that this particular class of deterministic and complete automata does not modify the expressiveness of the language recognized by the automaton. In particular, for a rank equal to 1, this class has the same expressive power as Rabin's tree automata without accepting states [19, 21].
We introduce the important notion of reachability for a state in a tree automaton.

Definition 4 A state q is said to be reachable in a tree automaton $\mathcal{A}$ iff there exists a tree t for which there exists a run $r_t^{\mathcal{A}}$ such that $r_t^{\mathcal{A}}(\epsilon) = q$.

Testing whether a state is reachable in a tree automaton can be proved decidable by a simple reduction to the emptiness problem of Büchi automata. We will denote by $Reach(\mathcal{A})$ the set of reachable states for a tree automaton $\mathcal{A}$.
Finally, the notion of run is extented to $TREE(Sig \cup \mathcal{V})$. A run for such a tree will depend on the "run" values of variables.

Definition 5 Let $\mathcal{A}$ be a tree automaton, $t \in TREE(Sig \cup \mathcal{V})$ and σ be an mapping from $var(t)$ into $\mathcal{Q}$, a run $r_{t,\sigma}^{\mathcal{A}}$ for t and σ in $\mathcal{A}$ is defined as for "usual" trees except that for any d in $dom(t)$, if $t(d) \in \mathcal{V}$ then $r_{t,\sigma}^{\mathcal{A}}(d) = \sigma(t(d))$.

One should notice that for a finite tree t with variables and a mapping σ, this run is unique.

3 Set-based Analysis of Reactive Logic Programs

A reactive logic program is a definite logic program for which the behaviours of interest are not only the terminating ones. A suitable semantics for those kind of programs has been introduced in [17], using the notions of *complete* Herbrand universe and base.
The signature of a logic program is defined using a set of function symbols Σ and a set of predicate symbols *Pred*. The Herbrand universe (*HU*) corresponds to the set of trees $TREE^*(\Sigma)$. The elements of *HU* are called terms. The Herbrand base (*HB*) is the subset of $TREE^*(\Sigma \cup Pred)$ satisfying $A \in HB$ iff $A(d) \in Pred \Leftrightarrow d = \epsilon$ (the ϵ-position is the only one labelled with a predicate symbol). The elements of *HB* are called atoms.

The semantics of reactive logic programs is defined as the greatest model of the Clark's completion of the program over the complete Herbrand base and is proved to be equal to the greatest fixpoint of the immediate logical consequence operator T_p [17], defined for a logic program P as:

$$T_p(I) = \{H \mid H \leftarrow B_1, .., B_l \in Ground(P) \text{ and } B_1, .., B_l \in I\}$$

where *Ground*(P) is the set of ground instances (using substitution ranging over *HU*) of clauses of P and I is a subset of *HB*.

In [6], in the dual way of [12], Charatonik and Podelski used co-definite set constraints for computing a safe approximation of this semantics. They have used an algorithm of abstraction for achieving syntactically this approximation and proved the safeness of this latter. In this paper, we are going to follow the approach taken in [16]. It yields a simple abstraction method for which correctness can be addressed only with set-theoretical properties.

Let us reformulate the definition of the T_P operator. For this, let us consider a "functional" generalization of membership expressions, that are expressions of the form $\{t | s_1 \in X_1, .., s_l \in X_l\}$, where t and the s_i's are finite trees with variables. The semantics of this kind of expressions is similar to membership expressions presented above. It is interpreted as the set of trees $\alpha(t)$ such that α is a substitution from $var(t) \cup \bigcup_l var(s_l)$ to $TREE^*(Sig)$. Using this, we can define T_P as:

$$T_p(I) = \bigcup_{1 \leq i \leq n} \{H^i \mid B_1^i \in I, .., B_{l_i}^i \in I, x_1 \in HU, .., x_{m_i} \in HU\}$$

where $H^i \leftarrow B_1^i, .., B_{l_i}^i$ is the ith clause of the program and the x_j are the variables occurring in this clause for which the expression $x_j \in HU$ ensures that the instantiation used corresponds to a tree representing a term.

Starting from this, one can claim that the solutions (for the set variable I) of the following set equations are exactly the fixpoints of the T_p operator:

$$\begin{cases} I = \bigcup_{1 \leq i \leq n} \{H^i \mid B_1^i \in I, .., B_{l_i}^i \in I, x_1 \in HU, .., x_{m_i} \in HU\} \\ HU = \bigcup_{f \in \Sigma} f(HU, .., HU) \end{cases}$$

We can now give the abstraction mechanism: for a finite atom H^i with variables, let us replace the variables x_j of this tree by the expression $\{x_j \mid B_1^i \in I, .., B_{l_i}^i \in I, x_1 \in HU, .., x_{m_i} \in HU\}$, one obtain then set equations with membership expressions.

Example 2 Let P be the following logic program:

$$\begin{array}{ll} p(a,a) & p(b,c) \\ p(c,b) & q(c) \\ p(f(x),f(x)) \leftarrow p(x,x), q(y) & \end{array}$$

The system of set constraints having the fixpoints of T_P for solutions will be:

$$\begin{cases} I = p(a,a) \cup p(b,c) \cup p(c,b) \cup q(c) \cup \left\{ p(f(x),f(x)) \;\middle|\; \begin{array}{l} p(x,x) \in I, q(y) \in I \\ , x \in HU, y \in HU \end{array} \right\} \\ HU = a \cup b \cup c \cup f(HU) \end{cases}$$

The abstraction yields a system of set constraints, for which by using the monotonicity of the considered set operators, the equality symbol "$=$" can be replaced by an inclusion "$\subseteq$", preserving the greatest solution :

$$\begin{cases} I \subseteq p(a,a) \cup p(b,c) \cup p(c,b) \cup q(c) \cup \\ \quad p(f(\left\{ x \;\middle|\; \begin{array}{l} p(x,x) \in I, q(y) \in I, \\ x \in HU, y \in HU \end{array} \right\}), f(\left\{ x \;\middle|\; \begin{array}{l} p(x,x) \in I, q(y) \in I, \\ x \in HU, y \in HU \end{array} \right\})) \\ HU \subseteq a \cup b \cup c \cup f(HU) \end{cases}$$

One can easily prove that this abstraction gives an upper approximation; the safeness of this approximation goes by showing that the greatest solution of the first system (for the variable I), that is the greatest fixpoint of T_P, is a solution of the last system of inclusion set constraints and so, smaller than the greatest solution of this latter.

One can point out that the abstraction mechanism, described in [6], will yield the approximation defined as the greatest solution (for the variable I) of the grammar below :

$$\begin{array}{lcl} I & = & q(c) \mid p(a,a) \mid p(b,c) \mid p(c,b) \mid p(f(X),f(X)) \\ X & = & f(X) \mid a \mid b \mid c \end{array}$$

whereas for the mechanism, proposed in this paper, one obtains a more accurate approximation :

$$\begin{array}{lcl} I & = & q(c) \mid p(a,a) \mid p(b,c) \mid p(c,b) \mid p(f(X),f(X)) \\ X & = & f(X) \mid a \end{array}$$

4 Co-Definite Set Constraints with Membership Expressions

The form of the constraints extracted from a logic program (as done in the previous section) leads us to extend the class of co-definite set constraints [7] using membership expressions.
Hence, we investigate the class of co-definite set constraints with membership expressions, of the form $sexp_1 \subseteq sexp_2$, where $sexp_1$ is built over set variables, constant and unary function symbols [3] and union connectives and $sexp_2$ is a set expression (including membership expressions) without complementation.
As for co-definite set constraints, if a system of such constraints is satisfiable, then it has a greatest solution.

In fact, we are going to consider those set constraints in shallow form, that is of one of the following shape:

$$a \subseteq X_i$$
$$X_i \subseteq f(X_{i_1}, ..., X_{i_m})$$
$$X_i \subseteq X_{i_1} \cup X_{i_2}$$
$$X_i \subseteq \{x \mid s_1 \in X_{i_1}, ..., s_l \in X_{i_l}\}$$

It is easy to transform a system of co-definite set constraints with membership expressions into an equivalent shallow one using a polynomial algorithm: the size of functional compositions can be reduced by introducing "fresh" variables, unary function symbols and union connectives in the left-hand side of inclusions can be cancelled. For the right-hand, intersection connectives can also be cancelled and projections replaced by membership expressions. It comes from $g(X) \subseteq Y \Leftrightarrow X \subseteq g_1^{-1}(Y)$, $X \cup Y \subseteq Z \Leftrightarrow (X \subseteq Z \ \wedge Y \subseteq Z)$ and $X \subseteq Y \cap Z \Leftrightarrow (X \subseteq Y \wedge X \subseteq Z)$, $f_i^{-1}(X) = \{x \mid \exists y_1, .., y_{i-1}, y_{i+1}, .., y_m,\ f(y_1, .., y_{i-1}, x, y_{i+1}, .., y_m) \in X\}$.

4.1 Set Constraints and Tree Automata

We define in this section the form of considered tree automata. Let $\mathcal{SC}$ be a system of co-definite set constraints with membership expressions (in shallow form) and $\{X_1, ..., X_n\}$ be the set of (set) variables occurring in $\mathcal{SC}$. We will consider the set of tree automata $\mathcal{A} = (Sig, \mathcal{Q}, \mathcal{F}, \mathcal{S})$ s.t. $Sig = (\Sigma, \rho)$ is the signature of $\mathcal{SC}$, $\mathcal{Q} = \{0,1\}^n$ (the vectors of size n of boolean values) and $\mathcal{F} = (F_1, .., F_n)$ where F_i is the set of states having 1 on the ith component. The idea of our method is to compute (if the system of constraints is satisfiable) such a tree automaton, for which the recognized language $(L_1, .., L_n)$

[3] As pointed out in [7], considering function symbols with arities greater that 1 in this part of the inclusion implies that such systems of constraints do not have a greatest solution. However, for set-based analysis purpose, variables are sufficient in the left hand-sides of inclusion

is exactly the greatest solution of the system of set constraints.

Finally, we introduce a natural ordering relation over states by $q \preceq q'$ iff $\forall i,\ q \in F_i \Rightarrow q' \in F_i$.

5 An algorithm for satisfiability test

Our algorithm is described by a system of inference rules $\mathcal{R}$ (defining a relation over tree automata[4]) handled with a specific strategy ($\vdash_{\mathcal{R}}$ will denote the one-step relation of our algorithm). Starting from the automaton $\mathcal{S}_1$ (the tree automaton having each right-hand side of its transition rules set to $\{1\}^n$), our algorithm computes either a final tree automaton $\mathcal{S}_f$ ($\mathcal{S}_1 \vdash^*_{\mathcal{R}} \mathcal{S}_f$ and $\forall \mathcal{S}, \mathcal{S}_f \not\vdash_{\mathcal{R}} \mathcal{S}$) or a special value $\perp$.
The rules of the system $\mathcal{R}$ transform the transition rules of tree automata, by switching a "1" into "0" in right-hand side under some conditions defined according to the constraints of the system. The strategy consists in selecting among the convenient transition rules (for some inference rule) having an element of F_i for right-hand side, one transition rule having a minimal left-hand side[5].

We define the notation $switch_0(q,i)$ as the state equal to q except on the ith component which is set to "0" in $switch_0(q,i)$. More formally, $switch_0(q,i) \notin F_j$ iff $q \notin F_j \vee i = j$.

- (Compose)

$$\frac{\mathcal{S} \cup \{f(q_1,..,q_m) \to q\}}{\mathcal{S} \cup \{f(q_1,..,q_m) \to switch_0(q,i)\}} \ if \begin{cases} X_i \subseteq g(X_{i_1},..,X_{i_l}) \in \mathcal{SC} \ and \\ either\ g \neq f \\ or\ g = f\ and\ \exists k, q_k \notin F_{i_k} \end{cases}$$

- (Union)

$$\frac{\mathcal{S} \cup \{lhs \to q\}}{\mathcal{S} \cup \{lhs \to switch_0(q,i)\}} \ if \begin{cases} X_i \subseteq X_{i_1} \cup X_{i_2} \in \mathcal{SC} \ and \\ q \notin F_{i_1},\ q \notin F_{i_2} \end{cases}$$

- (Clash)

$$\frac{\mathcal{S} \cup \{a \to q\}}{\perp} \ if \begin{cases} a \subseteq X_i \in \mathcal{SC} \ and \\ q \notin F_i \end{cases}$$

- (Member)

$$\frac{\mathcal{S} \cup \{lhs \to q\}}{\mathcal{S} \cup \{lhs \to switch_0(q,i)\}} \ if \begin{cases} X_i \subseteq \{x \mid s_1 \in X_{i_1}, \dots, s_l \in X_{i_l}\} \in \mathcal{SC} \ and \\ for\ any\ mapping\ \sigma\ from\ \cup_l\ var(s_l)\ to\ \mathcal{Q}\ s.t. \\ \sigma(x) = q\ and\ for\ y \neq x,\ \sigma(y) \in Reach(\mathcal{S}), \\ \exists k\ s.t.\ r^{\mathcal{S}}_{s_k,\sigma}(\epsilon) \notin F_{i_k} \end{cases}$$

[4]Since the signature, the set of states and the tuple of sets of final states have been fixed, a tree automaton will be defined as its set of transition rules

[5]For two rules $f(q_1,..,q_m) \to q, f(q'_1,..,q'_m) \to q'$ the first one has a smaller left-hand side if $q_1 \preceq q'_1,.., q_m \preceq q'_m$

We recall that we expect the language recognized by the computed tree automaton to be the greatest solution of the system of set constraints (if it is satisfiable). In other words, for a tree t in the final computed automaton $\mathcal{S}_f$, there exists a run $r_t^{\mathcal{S}_f}$ such that $r_t^{\mathcal{S}_f}(\epsilon) \in F_i$ iff there exists a solution $\mathcal{I}$ such that $t \in \mathcal{I}(X_i)$.
Intuitively, according to the constraint, the first rule means that a term t of the form $f(t_1,..,t_m)$, which does not belong to $\mathcal{I}(g(X_{i_1},..,X_{i_l}))$ for any solution $\mathcal{I}$ (either because $g \neq f$ or because there exists some k such that $t_k \notin X_{i_k}$) could not belong to $\mathcal{I}(X_i)$. For the second rule, according to the constraint, if for any solution t does not belong to neither $\mathcal{I}(X_{i_1})$ nor $\mathcal{I}(X_{i_2})$, then it could not belong to X_i. The third rule is easy: according to the constraint, a has to belong to $\mathcal{I}(X_i)$ for any solution $\mathcal{I}$. But the conditions of the rule tell us that for any solution, $a \notin \mathcal{I}(X_i)$, which contradicts the previous claim. The last rule means that if for any substitution replacing x with a tree t and existentially quantified variables with arbitrary trees ("represented" by reachable states) and for any solution $\mathcal{I}$, there exists a membership test which is not satisfied, then t does not belong to $\mathcal{I}(X_i)$.

Finally, we introduce an important notion for proving correctness of our algorithm, the notion of *rule monotonicity property*. It is defined for tree automata of the form introduced above and based on the order $\preceq$ introduced in the previous section.

Definition 6 A tree automaton $\mathcal{A} = (\Sigma, \mathcal{Q}, \mathcal{F}, \mathcal{S})$ satisfies the *rule monotonicity property* (rmp) if for all $f(q_1,..,q_m) \to q$, $f(q'_1,..,q'_m) \to q' \in \mathcal{S}$, $(\forall i,\ q_i \preceq q'_i) \Rightarrow q \preceq q'$.

One can prove that this property holds for every considered tree automaton, that is $\vdash_{\mathcal{R}}$ preserves the rule monotonicity property (see theorem 1 below). Since $\mathcal{S}_1$ obviously satisfies *rmp*, at each step of the algorithm, the computed automaton does so.

Theorem 1 If the rule monotonicity property holds for $\mathcal{S}$, $\mathcal{S} \vdash_{\mathcal{R}} \mathcal{S}'$ and $\mathcal{S}' \neq \bot$ then it holds also for $\mathcal{S}'$.
Proof : The proof goes by case inspection of the different inference rules, taking into account the specific strategy. □

5.1 Correctness

5.1.1 Soundness

For soundness, we are going to prove that our algorithm, when it successfully terminates, computes a solution.
Let $\mathcal{S}_f$ be the final computed automaton ($\mathcal{S}_f \neq \bot$) and $(L_1,..,L_n)$ be the language recognized by $\mathcal{S}_f$. Let $\mathcal{I}_f$ be the interpretation defined by $\forall X_i,\ \mathcal{I}_f(X_i) = L_i$.

Theorem 2 $\mathcal{I}_f$ is a solution of $\mathcal{SC}$.
Proof : If $\mathcal{I}_f$ was not a solution, then there would be a violated constraint. By case inspection, we prove that in this case some inference rule could be applied on $\mathcal{S}_f$ leading to a contradiction. □

5.1.2 Completeness

The proof of completeness is more involved and uses additional notions. We start by introducing the notion of pre-runs based on $\preceq$.

Definition 7 A pre-run in a tree automaton $\mathcal{A}$ for a tree t is a mapping $pr_t^{\mathcal{A}}$ from $dom(t)$ into $\mathcal{Q}$ such that for every d in $dom(t)$, if for the rule $t(d)(pr_t^{\mathcal{A}}(d.1), .., pr_t^{\mathcal{A}}(d.\rho(f))) \to q$ belonging to $\mathcal{A}$, $pr_t^{\mathcal{A}}(d) \preceq q$.

The set of pre-runs for a tree t and a tree automaton $\mathcal{A}$ will be denoted $PRun_{\mathcal{A}}(t)$. One should notice that $Run_{\mathcal{A}}(t) \subseteq PRun_{\mathcal{A}}(t)$. A partial order $\trianglelefteq$ is defined over pre-runs (and so, over runs) using $\preceq$.

Definition 8 $pr1_t^{\mathcal{A}} \trianglelefteq pr2_t^{\mathcal{A}}$ iff $\forall d \in dom(t),\ pr1_t^{\mathcal{A}}(d) \preceq pr2_t^{\mathcal{A}}(d)$

The first key idea of the proof of completeness is to show that in any considered automaton, there exists for every pre-run a greater run, that is

Proposition 1 For any tree t, for any considered tree automaton $\mathcal{A}$ satisfying the rule monotonicity property,

$$\forall pr_t^{\mathcal{A}} \in PRUN_{\mathcal{A}}(t),\ \exists r_t^{\mathcal{A}} \in RUN_{\mathcal{A}}(t),\ pr_t^{\mathcal{A}} \trianglelefteq r_t^{\mathcal{A}}$$

Proof : The key idea of the proof is the following one: we define a function $Lift_{\mathcal{A}}$ mapping a pre-run (for a tree t in a tree automaton $\mathcal{A}$ satisfying *rmp*) to a greater one. Then, we prove that $\sup_{n \in \mathbb{N}} Lift_{\mathcal{A}}^n(pr_t^{\mathcal{A}})$ exists and that this limit is a run for t in $\mathcal{A}$.
□

For any tree t, a solution $\mathcal{I}$ defines a unique mapping $pr_t^{\mathcal{I}}$ from $dom(t)$ to $\mathcal{Q}$ such that $pr_t^{\mathcal{I}}(d) = q$ iff $\forall i\ q \in F_i \Leftrightarrow t|_d \in \mathcal{I}(X_i)$. The second key idea of the proof is only to prove that $pr_t^{\mathcal{I}}$ is a pre-run in every considered automaton.

Lemma 1 If, for every tree t, $pr_t^{\mathcal{I}}$ is a pre-run in $\mathcal{S}$ and $\mathcal{S} \vdash_{\mathcal{R}} \mathcal{S}'$ (with $\mathcal{S}' \neq \perp$), then for every t $pr_t^{\mathcal{I}}$ is a pre-run in $\mathcal{S}'$.

One can easily deduce that if $\mathcal{SC}$ has solutions, then the language recognized by the computed tree automaton $\mathcal{S}_f$ is greater than any of those solutions and that if $\mathcal{S}_f$ is equal to $\perp$, then $\mathcal{SC}$ has no solution.

Theorem 3

(i) if $\mathcal{S}_f \neq \perp$, then $(\exists \mathcal{I} \in SOL(\mathcal{SC})\ such\ that\ t \in \mathcal{I}(X_i)) \Longrightarrow t \in \mathcal{I}_f(X_i)$

(ii) if $\mathcal{S}_f = \perp$, then $\mathcal{SC}$ *has no solution*

Proof : For any solution $\mathcal{I}$ and for any tree t, it is obvious to see that $pr_t^{\mathcal{I}}$ is a pre-run for t in $\mathcal{S}_1$. By the lemma 1, one can deduce that for any $\mathcal{S}$ such that $\mathcal{S}_1 \vdash^*_{\mathcal{R}} \mathcal{S}$ ($\mathcal{S} \neq \perp$), $pr_t^{\mathcal{I}}$ is a pre-run for t in $\mathcal{S}$. Since $\mathcal{S}$ satisfies the rule monotonicity property, by proposition 1, there exists a run $r_t^{\mathcal{S}}$ s.t. $pr_t^{\mathcal{I}} \trianglelefteq r_t^{\mathcal{S}}$. Since $t \in \mathcal{I}(X_i)$, that is $pr_t^{\mathcal{I}}(\epsilon) \in F_i$, $r_t^{\mathcal{S}}(\epsilon) \in F_i$.
For (i): The previous remark obviously holds for $\mathcal{S}_f$, and thus $t \in \mathcal{I}_f(X_i)$.
For (ii): Let $\mathcal{S}$ be a tree automaton ($\mathcal{S} \neq \perp$) such that $\mathcal{S}_1 \vdash^*_{\mathcal{R}} \mathcal{S}$ and $\mathcal{S} \vdash_{\mathcal{R}} \perp$. Using the remark above, we can claim that if for any run $r_t^{\mathcal{S}}$, $r_t^{\mathcal{S}}(\epsilon) \notin F_i$, then for any solution $\mathcal{I}$, $t \notin \mathcal{I}(X_i)$. According to the inference rule for (Clash), for any solution $\mathcal{I}$, $a \notin \mathcal{I}(X_i)$. Therefore, no such a solution can exist.
□

We can conclude from soundness and completeness that $\mathcal{S}_f$ is equal to $\perp$ iff $\mathcal{SC}$ is not satisfiable and that if $\mathcal{SC}$ is satisfiable, then the language recognized by $\mathcal{S}_f$ is exactly the greatest solution of $\mathcal{SC}$.

Remarks:

• Due to the unicity of the result of the computation, confluency issue is trivial.

• It turns out that in fact there is for any tree t in every computed automaton $\mathcal{S}$ (in particular, $\mathcal{S}_f$) a greatest run $\hat{r}_t^{\mathcal{S}}$, that is: $\forall r_t^{\mathcal{S}}$, $r_t^{\mathcal{S}} \trianglelefteq \hat{r}_t^{\mathcal{S}}$
This could be closely related to the notion of greatest solution in the following sense : $t \in \mathcal{I}_f(X_i) \Leftrightarrow \hat{r}_t^{\mathcal{S}_f}(\epsilon) \in F_i$

• One should notice that this algorithm can also address interpretation over sets of finite trees. It is sufficient to restrict the definition of reachability to finite trees, that is a state q is reachable if there exists a *finite* tree t such that $r_t^{\mathcal{A}}(\epsilon) = q$. It comes from the fact that definitions and proofs are suitable for infinite trees as well as for the restriction to finite trees.

5.2 Complexity

In [7], Charatonik and Podelski prove the *EXPTIME*-completeness for the satisfiability problem of co-definite set constraints by reduction of the emptiness problem of tree automata intersection. It is clear that this result gives a lower bound for our problem, that is *EXPTIME*-hardness.

Proposition 2 The satisfiability problem for co-definite set constraints with memberhip expressions is *EXPTIME*-complete.
Proof : Because of the form and the size of the automaton, one can easily prove that each application of a rule can be achieved in an exponential time w.r.t. the size of the system and that the maximal number of steps is bounded by an exponential way w.r.t. the size of the system. Hence, the presented algorithm is in *EXPTIME*.
□

6 Conclusion

We have proposed in this paper an extension of the class of co-definite set constraints by considering membership expressions. For this extension, the "greatest solution" property is preserved and the (theoretical) complexity results remain the same.
Tree automaton approach allows to keep the same framework both for computation and representation of the greatest solution. Furthermore, it yields a rather simple algorithm and an easy characterization of this complexity. From a practical point of view, we have showed that this class provides an elegant and more accurate method for semantics approximation of reactive logic program than the one proposed in [6].

The method can be extended for reactive semantics of logic programs built over rational terms. We claim that our method is "dual" to the one presented in [16]. Recently, a dual of technics of [10] (shown equivalent to [16]) has been proposed in [3] using logic programs transformations giving results similar to those presented in this paper. However, if logic programs are a good formalism for representing "simple" tree automata, it may not be true when global acceptance conditions are needed (as it seems to be for computing an approximation of the least fixpoint of programs built over rational terms).

Acknowledgements

This work was supported in part by the European Project Esprit-CCL II. The authors thanks the anonymous referees for helpful comments.

References

[1] A. Aiken, D. Kozen, M. Vardi, and E. Wimmers. The Complexity of Set Constraints. In *Proceedings of Computer Science Logic*, pages 1–17, 1993.

[2] L. Bachmair, H. Ganzinger, and U. Waldmann. Set Constraints are the Monadic Class. In *Proceedings of the 8th IEEE Symposium on Logic in Computer Science*, pages 75 – 83, 1993.

[3] W. Charatonik, D. McAllester, and A. Podelski. The Greatest Fixed Point of the τ_P abstraction is Regular. Seminar on Applications of Tree Automata in Rewriting, Logic and Programming, oct 1997.

[4] W. Charatonik and L. Pacholski. Set Constraints with Projections are in NEXPTIME. In *Proceedings of the 35th Symposium on Foundations of Computer Science*, pages 642–653, 1994.

[5] W. Charatonik and A. Podelski. Set Constraints with Intersection. In *Proceedings of the 12th IEEE Symposium on Logic in Computer Science*, 1997.

[6] W. Charatonik and A. Podelski. Solving Set Constraints for Greatest Models. Technical Report MPI-I-97-2004, Max-Planck-Institut für Informatik, 1997.

[7] W. Charatonik and A. Podelski. Co-definite Set Constraints. In *Proceedings of the 9th International Conference on Rewriting techniques and applications*, LNCS, 1998.

[8] P. Devienne, JM. Talbot, and S. Tison. Co-definite Set Constraints with Membership Expressions. Actes des Journées du GDR Programmation, nov 1997.

[9] P. Devienne, JM. Talbot, and S. Tison. Solving Classes of Set Constraints with Tree Automata. In G. Smolka, editor, *Proceedings of the 3rd International Conference on Principles and Practice of Constraint Programming*, LNCS 1330, pages 62–76, oct 1997.

[10] T. Frühwirth, E. Shapiro, M.Y. Vardi, and E. Yardeni. Logic Programs as Types for Logic Programs. In *Proceedings of the 6th IEEE Symposium on Logic in Computer Science*, pages 300–309, jun 1991.

[11] F. Gécseg and M. Steinby. *Tree Automata*. Akadémiai Kiadó, Budapest, 1984.

[12] N. Heintze. Practical Aspects of Set Based Analysis. In *Proceedings of the Joint International Conference and Symposium on Logic Programming*. MIT-Press, nov 1992.

[13] N. Heintze. *Set Based Program Analysis*. PhD thesis, Carnegie Mellon University, sep 1992.

[14] N. Heintze. Set-based Analysis of ML Programs. In *Lisp and Functional Programming*, pages 306–317. ACM, 1994.

[15] N. Heintze and J. Jaffar. A Decision Procedure for a Class of Herbrand Set Constraints. In *Proceedings of the 5th IEEE Symposium on Logic in Computer Science*, pages 42–51, jun 1990.

[16] N. Heintze and J. Jaffar. A Finite Presentation Theorem for Approximating Logic Programs. In *Proceedings of the 17th ACM SIGPLAN-SIGACT Symposium on Principles of Programming Languages*, pages 197–209, jan 1990.

[17] J. Lloyd. *Foundations of Logic Programming*. Springer-Verlag, 1987.

[18] A. Podelski, W. Charatonik, and Martin Müller. Set-based Analysis of Reactive Infinite-state Systems. submitted for publication, 1997.

[19] M.O. Rabin. Decidability of Second-order Theories and Automata on Infinite Trees. In *Transactions of American Mathematical Society*, volume 141, pages 1–35, 1969.

[20] K. Stefansson. Systems of Set Constraints with Negative Constraints are NEXPTIME-Complete. In *Proceedings of the 9th IEEE Symposium on Logic in Computer Science*, 1994.

[21] W. Thomas. Automata on Infinite Objects. In *Handbook of Theoretical Computer Science*, volume B. Elsevier, 1990.

On the Representation and Management of Finite Sets in CLP languages

Agostino Dovier
Università di Verona, Italy
dovier@sci.univr.it

Carla Piazza and **Gianfranco Rossi**
Università di Parma, Dipartimento di Matematica
Via M. D'Azeglio 85/A, 43100 Parma, Italy
gianfr@prmat.math.unipr.it

Enrico Pontelli
New Mexico State University, USA
epontell@cs.nmsu.edu

Abstract

We review and compare the main techniques considered to represent finite sets in logic languages. We present a technique that combines the benefits of the previous techniques, avoiding their drawbacks. We show how to verify satisfiability of any conjunction of (positive and negative) literals based on $=, \subseteq, \in$, and $\cup, \cap, \setminus$, and $||$, viewed as predicate symbols, in a (hybrid) universe of finite sets. We also show that $\cup$ and $||$ (i.e., disjointness of two sets) are sufficient to represent all the above mentioned operations.

1 Introduction

We consider the problem of representing and manipulating *hereditarily finite well-founded sets* in the framework of CLP languages. *Hereditarily finite* means containing a *finite* number of elements that can be either memberless objects or *hereditarily finite* sets. *Hybrid* means that they can involve free Herbrand functors, i.e., distinct from the set constructor and the empty-set symbol $\emptyset$.

In the literature two main approaches have been adopted for the (extensional) representation of sets: ACI-terms [2, 5, 21], and list-like terms [4, 15, 7, 13]. Each has advantages and disadvantages over the other.

Regarding operations on sets, they include primarily the ability to *compare* sets. This, when considering the most general case of non-ground and partially specified sets, amounts to solving a (non trivial) *set unification problem* [2, 7, 1, 26]. Besides equality, a number of other basic set operations are usually required for dealing with sets, like membership ($\in$), inclusion and strict inclusion ($\subseteq$, $\subset$), union ($\cup$), intersection ($\cap$), and difference ($\setminus$). These operations are conveniently viewed as *constraints*. According to this view, systems of (set) constraints are tested as a whole for satisfiability by suitable *constraint solvers* [14]. The need to adopt a constraint-based management of set operations derives from the impossibility or impracticality of producing extensional representations of the solutions of such operations. Which operations are provided as constraints and which are programmed in the language is also an important language design decision.

In this paper we present a technique for representing hereditarily well-founded sets which combines the benefits of the two above mentioned techniques, avoiding their drawbacks. This technique is based on the use of the function symbol $\{\cdot\,|\,\cdot\}$, interpreted as the element insertion operation, used as set constructor, along with two predicate symbols, $\cup_3$ and $||$, respectively interpreted as union and disjointness, as the only primitive constraints directly supported by the language. We show that this choice allows to represent nested sets of any depth (not allowed when sets are represented as ACI-terms) as well as to represent complex unification problems involving more than one set variable, such as $X_1 \cup X_2 \cup X_3 = \{a, b\}$ (not allowed when using the list-like representation). Moreover, it allows all other basic set operation (such as $\cap$, $\subseteq$) to be expressed in a quite straightforward way.

The paper is organized as follows. In Sect. 2 we review the main techniques employed to represent finite sets in logic languages. In Sect. 3 we describe the syntax and semantics of the language we have chosen for our proposal. In Sect. 4 we show how to implement in the language itself the main set-theoretical operations. In Sect. 5 we describe in detail the constraint solver for our language, first dealing only with non-colored sets, and then extending the algorithms to the more general case of colored sets.

2 Set representations

We assume all the definitions and notations usually employed in unification theory (e.g., [18, 22]). $\Sigma = \Pi \cup \mathcal{F}$ will be used to denote a signature with *arity* function $ar : \Sigma \longrightarrow \mathbb{N}$. $\mathcal{V}$ is a denumerable set of logical variables disjoint from Σ. If t is a term, then $vars(t)$ denote the set of variables occurring in t. Capital letters X, Y, Z, etc. are used to represent variables; f, g, etc. stand for function symbols (i.e., elements of $\mathcal{F}$). We assume the usual notions (e.g., [11]) of T-unifier, complete set of T-unifiers, and related notions involved in the general theory of unification w.r.t. an equational theory T.

There are three main ways of representing sets as terms:[1]

- using the binary union symbol $\cup$ as the set constructor, as done, for instance, in [2, 5, 21];
- using the binary element insertion operator $\{\cdot\,|\,\cdot\}$ as the set constructor, as done, for instance, in [4, 15, 7, 13];

[1] A few other proposals for logic programming with sets can be hardly classified as following one of these approaches. In CLPS [19] all three approaches appear viable, as no choice is explicitly made. In [12], instead, sets are intended as subsets of a finite domain D of objects. At the language level, each ground set is represented as an individual constant (where all constants are partially ordered to reflect the $\subseteq$ lattice).

- using an infinite collection of function symbols of different arity [17, 25]—the set $\{a_1, \ldots, a_n\}$ is encoded by the term $\{_n(a_1, \ldots, a_n)$, using the n-ary functor $\{_n$.

We will concentrate on the first two methods only. The third one, in fact, does not suit to our purposes. In particular, stating equality in axiomatic form would require a non-trivial axiom schema like the following one: *for each pair of natural numbers m and n,*

$$\{_m(X_1, \ldots, X_m) = \{_n(Y_1, \ldots, Y_n) \leftrightarrow \bigwedge_{i=1}^{m} \bigvee_{j=1}^{n} X_i = Y_j \wedge \bigwedge_{j=1}^{n} \bigvee_{i=1}^{m} X_i = Y_j.$$

The two considered methods are compared as concerns the key problem of (set) unification: given any two $\mathcal{F} \cup \mathcal{V}$ terms ℓ and r, find a complete set of T-unifiers of $\ell = r$, where T is an equational theory describing the relevant properties of the set constructor symbols.

2.1 The $\cup$-based representation

$\mathcal{F}$ contains the binary function symbol $\cup$ and the constant symbol $\emptyset$. $\cup$ fulfills the equational axioms:

$$\begin{array}{lrcl} (A) & (X \cup Y) \cup Z & = & X \cup (Y \cup Z) \\ (C) & X \cup Y & = & Y \cup X \\ (I) & X \cup X & = & X \end{array}$$

while $\emptyset$ is the *identity* of the operation $\cup$:

$$(1) \quad X \cup \emptyset \;=\; X\,.$$

Intuitively, $\cup$ and $\emptyset$ have the meaning of the set union operator and empty-set, respectively.

2.1.1 Set unification algorithm: Flat sets

When $\mathcal{F}$ is composed by $\cup$, $\emptyset$, and by an arbitrary number of constant symbols, the unification problem falls into *ACI1-unification with constants.* Various solutions to this problem have been studied in the literature [2, 5, 21]. A viable solution is, for example, the one proposed by Baader and Büttner [2], based on the use of *ACI-matrices.* An ACI-matrix is a boolean matrix which describes a most general unifier (mgu) for a given ACI problem. The columns of the matrix are associated with the variables present in the original problem, while the rows are associated with the constants present in the unification problem as well as to a set of new variables. Mechanical procedures can be devised [2] to generate a finite collection of ACI-matrices representing a minimal and complete set of unifiers.

Example 2.1 *The matching problem $X_1 \cup X_2 \cup X_3 = a \cup b$ can be associated with $(2^3 - 1)^2 = 49$ ACI-matrices (in each row there must be at least one 1). Two of them, for example, are:*

X_1	X_2	X_3	
0	1	1	a
1	0	1	b

X_1	X_2	X_3	
0	0	1	a
0	1	0	b

yielding, resp., the unifiers: $[X_1/b, X_2/a, X_3/a \cup b]$, $[X_1/\emptyset, X_2/b, X_3/a]$.

In [2] the number of mgu's needed to cover the solution space (actually, exactly the unifiers generated by the algorithm) is made explicit.

2.1.2 Set unification algorithm: Nested sets

$ACI1$-unification with constants does not distinguish explicitly between sets and elements of sets. This makes it difficult to handle set unification when sets are defined by enumerating their elements, especially when elements are allowed to be variables. For example, the problem

$$\{X_1, X_2, X_3\} = \{a, b\} \quad (1)$$

(which admits 6 distinct solutions) is difficult to handle using $ACI1$-unification. In fact, one could map this into the $ACI1$-unification problem of Example 2.1, by interpreting the constants a and b as the singleton sets $\{a\}$ and $\{b\}$ (both in the formulation and in the unifiers), and then "filtering" the 49 distinct $ACI1$-unifiers, removing the solutions in which (at least) one of the X_i's is mapped to $\emptyset$ or to $a \cup b$ (in general to the union of more than one distinct constant). This is an impractical way of solving this problem in the general case.[2] Furthermore, this technique does not allow nested sets to be taken into account at all.

A viable solutions to these problems, still using the $\cup$-based representation, is obtained by assuming that a unary (free) operator $\{\cdot\}$ is present in Σ. The set $\{s_1, \ldots, s_m\}$ can be described as $\{s_1\} \cup \ldots \cup \{s_m\}$. To our knowledge, the only proposals that have addressed this problem so far are [20, 16, 3]. In particular, [3] shows how to combine unification algorithms for equational theories with disjoint signatures and theories. A *general* $ACI1$ unification algorithm (namely, $ACI1$ dealing also with free symbols, such as $\{\cdot\}$) can be obtained by combining $ACI1$-unification for $\emptyset$, $\cup$ and constants (as in Sect. 2.1.1), with unification in the free theory for all other symbols.

The generality of the combination procedure of [3], however, leads to the generation of a large number of non-deterministic choices.[3] In [3] some optimizations are proposed that allow to take advantage of certain features of the equational theories involved (e.g., certain non-deterministic choices can be avoided if one of the theory is a free theory), but it is unclear whether these optimizations can make the approach more practical.

2.2 The $\{\cdot \mid \cdot\}$-based representation

The $\{\cdot \mid \cdot\}$-based representation (or list-like representation) is the approach used in most papers dealing with sets in logic programming languages, such as [4, 7, 13, 15, 26].

[2] E.g., the problem $X_1 \cup \ldots \cup X_7 = a \cup b$ admits 16129 unifiers instead of the 126 of $\{X_1, \ldots, X_7\} = \{a, b\}$ [1].

[3] The non-deterministic selection of a partition of the variables in the problem generates $O((\frac{n}{2})^n)$ number of choices, while the selection of a given indexing ordering of the variables is of the order $O(n! \times 2^n)$.

$\mathcal{F}$ contains the binary function symbol $\{\cdot\,|\,\cdot\}$, the empty-set constant symbol $\emptyset$, and an arbitrary number of constant and function symbols. The function symbol $\{\cdot\,|\,\cdot\}$ fulfills the equational axioms [6, 7]:

$$\begin{array}{lrcl} (Ab) & \{X\,|\,\{X\,|\,Z\}\} & = & \{X\,|\,Z\} \\ (C\ell) & \{X\,|\,\{Y\,|\,Z\}\} & = & \{Y\,|\,\{X\,|\,Z\}\}. \end{array}$$

Intuitively, $\{\cdot\,|\,\cdot\}$ is interpreted as the *element insertion* operation and $\emptyset$ as the empty set. For the sake of simplicity, we denote by $\{t_0, \ldots, t_n\,|\,t\}$ the term $\{t_0\,|\ldots\{t_n\,|\,t\}\ldots\}$; in particular, if $t = \emptyset$, then we write it as $\{t_0, \ldots, t_n\}$.

2.2.1 Set unification algorithms

General (i.e., dealing also with free functors) $(Ab)(C\ell)$*-unification algorithms* have been proposed in [15, 7, 26, 1].

The algorithm in [15] is weaker than the others since its aim is that of solving matching problems instead of unification problems. [7] basically extends it by covering (nested) set unification problems of the form:

$$\{s_1, \ldots, s_m\,|\,s\} = \{t_1, \ldots, t_n\,|\,t\}$$

where $m, n \geq 0$, s_i and t_j can be generic terms and s, t can be either variables (possibly identical) or non-set terms (i.e., terms with an outermost symbol different from $\{\cdot\,|\,\cdot\}$, including $\emptyset$). [26] solves exactly the same problem using an elegant algorithm based on (temporarily generated) membership constraints. Moreover, the algorithm reduces the generation of redundant (namely, repetitions, instances) solutions of [7]. Finally, the algorithm in [1], though less elegant than that of [26], further reduces the number of redundancies. In particular, it is proved to be minimal for a number of sample set unification problems that are proposed as 'benchmarks'.

Differently from the $\cup$-based representation, the $\{\cdot\,|\,\cdot\}$-based representation naturally accommodates for *nested* sets. Thus, for instance, problem (1) can be rendered directly as $\{X_1, X_2, X_3\} = \{a, b\}$ (that is, using the internal notation, $\{X_1\,|\,\{X_2\,|\,\{X_3\,|\,\emptyset\}\}\} = \{a\,|\,\{b\,|\,\emptyset\}\}$), and all the proposed algorithms [15, 7, 26, 1] return exactly the 6 mgu's:

$$\begin{array}{lll} [X_1/a, X_2/a, X_3/b] & [X_1/b, X_2/b, X_3/a] & [X_1/a, X_2/b, X_3/b] \\ [X_1/b, X_2/a, X_3/a] & [X_1/a, X_2/b, X_3/a] & [X_1/b, X_2/a, X_3/b] \end{array}$$

without the need of any filtering of solutions.

Therefore, the $\{\cdot\,|\,\cdot\}$-based representation allows to solve set unification problems which cannot be expressed using $ACI1$-unification with constants. On the other hand, the $\cup$-based representation allows to write set terms that cannot be directly expressed using a list-like representation, as for instance the term $X \cup a \cup Y$ (as well as the terms involved in Example 2.1). The $\{\cdot\,|\,\cdot\}$-based representation, in fact, can only represent the union of a sequence of singletons with, eventually, a single variable.

Thus, the two different representations offer opposite advantages and disadvantages. One of the main contribution of this work is to define a representation of sets which allows to capture the benefits of both the approaches.

3 A (new) proposal for set representation

In this section we propose a new language for representing sets which combines the two approaches of Sect. 2.1 and 2.2, as it uses a $\{\cdot \mid \cdot\}$-based representation and it provides $\cup_3$ as a primitive constraint.

3.1 The language

The language is based on a signature $\Sigma = \Pi \cup \mathcal{F}$, which includes

- the predicate symbols $\cup_3$ (ternary) and $||$ (binary);
- the binary function symbol $\{\cdot \mid \cdot\}$, and the constant symbol $\emptyset$.

In view of the intended interpretation, variables and any terms whose outermost symbol is $\{\cdot \mid \cdot\}$ are called *set terms*, whereas all other terms, including $\emptyset$, are called *non-set terms*. As shown in Sect. 2.2, terms denoting sets can be *nested* at any depth—e.g., $\{a, \{X, \{\emptyset, f(\emptyset)\}\} \mid Y\}$. Observe that sets can be constructed by adding elements to any arbitrary (non-set) term: we call this term the *color* of the set. Sets constructed starting from a non-variable term different from $\emptyset$ are called *colored sets* [7].[4]

The *primitive constraints* are the (positive and negative) literals based on the predicate symbols $\cup_3$ and $||$. A *constraint* is any conjunction of primitive constraints. We will use $\not\pi(t_1, \ldots, t_n)$ to denote $\neg\pi(t_1, \ldots, t_n)$, for $\pi \in \Pi$.

3.2 The Semantics

Different proposals for an axiomatic semantics of terms denoting sets, suitable for CLP languages, have been recently presented (e.g., [7, 10, 6, 9]). In this paper we follow the approach of [9] which has been shown to be well suited for a parametric approach to the design of CLP languages which integrates different kinds of aggregate data objects (namely, sets, multi-sets, lists, and compact-lists).

The set theory, named *Set*, includes, besides the standard equality axioms, the axioms for the existence of the empty set (K), the axioms for the element insertion operation (W), the Clark Equality Theory axioms for the non-set terms (F_1', F_2), along with a weak form of the foundation axiom (F_3^s), and a suitable version of the extensionality axiom (E_k^s). *Set* is now augmented with the axioms for $\cup_3$ and $||$ (see the table below), which pro-

[4] Colored sets are motivated primarily by "technical" reasons. Actually, we could avoid considering colored sets by introducing two sorts, "terms" and "set terms", where the latter is a sub-sort of the former. This would allow us to restrict admissible solutions to well-sorted substitutions only. However, we prefer to take the opposite approach, which does not distinguish between different sorts, allowing colored sets to come into play. Thus the user can take advantage of the additional expressive power of colors (whose potentialities, however, still need to be further investigated).

vides the following intuitive meaning for the two new predicates: $\cup_3(r,s,t)$ means $t = r \cup s$, whereas $s||t$ stands for $s \cap t = \emptyset$.[5]

for all m, n, k and for all $x_0 \cdots x_m y_0 \cdots y_n z_0 \cdots z_k$:	
$(\cup)$	$\left(\begin{array}{l} \cup_3(\{x_1,\dots,x_m \mid x_0\},\{y_1,\dots,y_n \mid y_0\},\{z_1,\dots,z_k \mid z_0\}) \wedge \\ \forall w\,(w \notin x_0 \wedge w \notin y_0 \wedge w \notin z_0) \end{array}\right) \leftrightarrow$ $(\{z_1,\dots,z_k\} = \{x_1,\dots,x_m,y_1,\dots,y_n\} \wedge x_0 = y_0 \wedge x_0 = z_0)$
$(\|\|)$	$\left(\begin{array}{l} \{x_1,\dots,x_m \mid x_0\} \| \{y_1,\dots,y_n \mid y_0\} \wedge \\ \forall w\,(w \notin x_0 \wedge w \notin y_0) \end{array}\right) \leftrightarrow$ $(\forall z\,(z \in \{x_1,\dots,x_m\} \rightarrow z \notin \{y_1,\dots,y_n\}) \wedge x_0 = y_0)$

The interpretation domain is the ordinary Herbrand Universe H_Σ (or, equivalently, the set of finite trees over Σ), modulo the smallest congruence relation $\cong$ induced by the (Ab) and $(C\ell)$ axioms (denoted $H_\Sigma/\cong$).

The interpretation of $\cup_3$ and $||$ on the domain $H_\Sigma/\cong$ is strictly forced by their axioms. The axiom allows to unite (resp., verify disjointness of) two sets only if they are based on the same color (note that the colors are those terms that are forced by axiom (K) to not contain any elements.)

The interpretation $H_\Sigma/\cong$ can be proved to be a model of the simple theory of sets considered above. Therefore:

Proposition 3.1 *The axiomatic theory* $KWE^s_kF'_1F_2F^s_3 \cup ||$ *and the interpretation* $H_\Sigma/\cong$ *correspond [14] on the class of formulae constituted by conjunctions of literals based on* $=, \in, \cup_3, ||$.

Finally, it must be observed that the possibility to deal with non-set terms allows one to build (nested) sets with the same elements but different *colors*. This fact naturally induces the introduction of a predicate dealing with colors. Although the theory has been defined without making use of this predicate, the binary predicate symbol $\mathsf{c^{of}}$ (read 'color of') is useful to implement the constraint manager. As a matter of fact, if the color of a term is not a variable, then it is easy to make it explicit. On the contrary, a constraint of the form $\cup_3(X,Y,Z)$ is satisfiable only if X, Y, and Z have the same color. We could make this fact explicit by stating $\mathsf{c^{of}}(X,K) \wedge \mathsf{c^{of}}(Y,K) \wedge \mathsf{c^{of}}(Z,K)$. For this reason, we will make use of the predicate symbol $\mathsf{c^{of}}$, to be handled as a constraint. As our aim is to make the axioms work properly for finite sets only, we do not need to insert directly $\mathsf{c^{of}}$ into the theory, but we expand the language with the definition axioms ($f, g \not\equiv \{\cdot \mid \cdot\}$):

$$\mathsf{c^{of}}(f(s_1,\dots,s_m), g(t_1,\dots,t_n)) \text{ iff } f(s_1,\dots,s_m) = g(t_1,\dots,t_n)$$
$$\mathsf{c^{of}}(\{t \mid s\}, k) \text{ iff } \mathsf{c^{of}}(s,k).$$

The interpretation above can be easily completed to model $\mathsf{c^{of}}$ as well.

[5] The theory deals also with equality ($=$) and membership ($\in$). Actually, it would be possible to restate the theory using only $\cup_3$ and $||$ (see Prop. 4.1 and 4.2): for the sake of readability, however, we prefer to use this enlarged signature.

4 Set operations

In this section we show that the $\cup_3$ constraint, along with the other primitive constraint, $||$, if properly managed, allows to express most of the other usual set operations in a quite straightforward way (in particular, without having to resort to any universal quantification).

Proposition 4.1 *Literals based on the predicate symbols $\in$, $=$, $\subseteq$, can be equivalently replaced by literals based only on $\cup_3$.*

Proof. (sketch) $s \in t$ iff $\cup_3(t, t, \{s \mid t\})$; $s \subseteq t$ iff $\cup_3(s, t, t)$; $s = t$ iff $\cup_3(s, s, t)$. For the corresponding negative literals, it is enough to replace $\cup_3$ with $\not\cup_3$. □

The operation $\cap$ (viewed as ternary predicate symbol) could be easily programmed using (recursive) clauses in the language itself. However, this approach may cause problems when using $\cap_3$ with insufficiently instantiated arguments. For this reason, we have introduced the operation $||$ as a basic constraint symbol; in fact, $||$ allows to express $\cap_3$ literals (and other interesting operations) as simple combination of basic constraints, as shown by the following proposition.[6]

Proposition 4.2 *Literals based on predicate symbols: $\cap$, $\setminus$, and $\triangle$ can be equivalently replaced by conjunctions of literals based on $\cup_3$ and $||$.*

Proof. (sketch) $\setminus(x, y, z)$ denotes $z = x \setminus y$.

$$\begin{array}{rcl} \cap_3(r,s,t) & \text{iff} & \exists R, S(\cup_3(R,t,r) \wedge \cup_3(S,t,s) \wedge R||S) \\ \not\cap_3(r,s,t) & \text{iff} & \exists T(\cap_3(r,s,T) \wedge T \neq t) \\ \setminus(r,s,t) & \text{iff} & \exists W\,(\cup_3(t,r,r) \wedge \cup_3(s,t,W) \wedge \cup_3(r,W,W) \wedge s||t) \\ \not\setminus(r,s,t) & \text{iff} & \exists T(\setminus(r,s,T) \wedge T \neq t) \end{array}$$

Similarly for $\triangle$ ($s \triangle t = s \setminus t \cup t \setminus s$). □

5 Constraint solver

Like in *CLP*(*Set*) [7], in order to check satisfiability of a given constraint C, we transform C to an equivalent disjunction of constraints in *solved form*, guaranteed to be satisfiable.

The problem we tackle here extends the satisfiability problem for set unification, shown to be NP-complete in [16]. Thus, it is an NP-hard problem. NP-completeness ensues from [23]. The algorithm we propose here clearly does not belong to NP since it is non-deterministic and it applies syntactic substitutions. However, one could devise implementations of the algorithm adopting standard techniques (e.g., those of [22]) to avoid problems originated by substitutions, in order to achieve better complexity results.

[6] It can be proved that having only $\cup_3$ in the language one cannot define $\cap_3$ in the same "direct" way as done for $=$, $\subseteq$, and $\in$ in Prop. 4.1. Moreover, it can be proved that to express $\cup$ (as well as $\subseteq, \cap$) in the language of $\{\emptyset, \{\cdot \mid \cdot\}, =, \in\}$ universal quantifiers are *needed*. This implies that constraints based on $\cup_3$ are more expressive than those of *CLP*(*Set*).

In the algorithms (see Fig. 1) s, s_i, t, t_i denote generic terms, f, g function symbols different from $\{\cdot \mid \cdot\}$, and $X, X_i, Y, Y_i, W, W_i, Z, Z_i$ variables. $\{\_ \mid \_\}$ denotes a generic term which has $\{\cdot \mid \cdot\}$ as its outermost function symbol. The symbol $\equiv$ denotes syntactic equality. If a variable occurs only in the r.h.s. of a rewriting rule, then it must be intended as a 'newly generated' variable, distinct from all the others.

Although Prop. 4.1 allows one to forget '$=$' and '$\in$' literals, we prefer, for the sake of simplicity, to assume that the constraint solver is capable of managing also this kind of constraints. Thanks to Prop. 4.1, however, one can think of them as special cases of the $\cup_3$ constraint handler. Rewriting procedures for them can be obtained immediately from those of [10, 7] and are omitted due to lack of space.

Moreover, in order to make the presentation more readable we find it convenient to split it into two parts. In the first part, we deal only with non-colored sets, that is, we assume that in $\{t \mid s\}$, s is necessarily either $\emptyset$ or a set term, and, that in $\cup_3(r, s, t)$ and in $s||t$, r, s and t are necessarily either $\emptyset$ or set terms. In the second part, this assumption is relaxed and notions and algorithms presented in the first part are extended to the more general case of colored sets. This extension allows us to prove correctness and completeness of the proposed satisfiability checking procedure, without the restriction on the kind of sets considered.

5.1 Non-colored sets

5.1.1 Solved form

A constraint C, different from false, can be conveniently seen as the conjunction of the constraints $C_= \wedge C_{\neq} \wedge C_{\in} \wedge C_{\notin} \wedge C_{\cup_3} \wedge C_{\not\cup_3} \wedge C_{||} \wedge C_{\not||}$, where each C_π ($C_{\not\pi}$) is composed by the positive (negative) literals based on the predicate symbol π, π belonging to $\{=, \in, \cup_3, ||\}$. A primitive constraint c of C is in *solved form* if it is in one of the following forms:

(i) $X = t$, and X does not occur neither in t nor in the rest of C;

(ii) $X \neq t$, and X does not occur in t;

(iii) $t \notin X$, and X does not occur in t;

(iv) $\cup_3(X_1, X_2, X_3)$, $X_1 \not\equiv X_2$, and $X_1 \neq t_1$, $X_2 \neq t_2$, $X_3 \neq t_3$, t_1, t_2, t_3 any terms, do not occur in C;

(v) $X_1||X_2$, $X_1 \not\equiv X_2$.

A constraint C (C_π) is in solved form if it is empty or all its components are simultaneously in solved form (observe that the primitive constraints based on $\in$, $\not\cup_3$, and $\not||$ are completely eliminated; hence, $C_{\in}$, $C_{\not\cup_3}$, and $C_{\not||}$ are empty whenever C is in solved form).

For $C_=, C_{\neq}, C_{\in}$, and $C_{\notin}$ the conditions for the solved forms are the same as in [7, 10], as they capture the notion of a constraint which cannot be further simplified. The conditions for $C_{\cup_3}$ are aimed at avoiding situations like $\cup_3(X, Y, Z) \wedge \cup_3(X, Y, W) \wedge Z \neq W$, which are not satisfiable. The condition for $C_{||}$ are aimed at avoiding a situation like $X||X \wedge X \neq \emptyset$, which is also clearly not satisfiable in the context of non-colored sets.

The notion of solved form plays a fundamental role in the definition of the constraint satisfiability procedure, as emerges from the following theorem.

Theorem 5.1 *Let C be a constraint in solved form. Then C is satisfiable in $H_\Sigma/\cong$.*

Proof. (sketch) The proof is basically the construction of a mapping for the variables of C into H_Σ. The construction is divided into two parts. In the first part, $C_=$ is not considered. A solution for the other constraints is computed by looking for mappings of the form

$$X_i \mapsto \underbrace{\{\cdots\{\emptyset\}\cdots\}}_{n_i}$$

fulfilling all $\neq, ||, \notin$, and $\cup_3$ constraints. In particular, the variables appearing in $\cup_3$ are mapped into $\emptyset$ ($n_i = 0$) and the numbers n_i for the other variables are computed choosing one possible solution of a trivial integer system of inequations obtained by analyzing the "depth" of the occurrences of the variables in terms (to this aim, $||$ and $\neq$ constraints are treated in the same way). Then, all the variables occurring only in r.h.s. of equations of $C_=$ are bound to $\emptyset$ and the mappings for the variables of the l.h.s. are bound to the uniquely induced (ground) substitution. Complete proof can be found in [24]. A proof for the simpler cases, $C_=, C_{\neq}, C_{\in}, C_{\notin}$, can be found in [6]. □

5.1.2 Rewriting rules

The constraint satisfiability test is performed by a procedure, $SAT_{\mathcal{SET}}$, which uses a distinct (non-deterministic) rewriting algorithm for each distinct C_π. Algorithms for $C_=$, $C_{\neq}$, $C_{\in}$, $C_{\notin}$ can be found in [10, 6]. In this paper we present the algorithms union for $\cup_3$, disj for $||$, not_union for $\not\cup_3$, and not_disj for $\not||$ (see Figure 1).

5.1.3 Constraint satisfiability

For any given constraint C, the combination of the rewriting procedures of the previous section allows to compute, through non-determinism, either false or a finite collection of constraints in solved form, whose disjunction is equi-satisfiable to C in the theory presented (provided we restrict to non-colored sets). The constraint satisfiability procedure $SAT_{\mathcal{SET}}$ uses the following function STEP to call, in the proper order, the rewriting procedures:

STEP(C) : not_union(C); not_disj(C); member(C);
union(C); disj(C); equal(C); not_member(C); not_equal(C).

$SAT_{\mathcal{SET}}$ repeatedly calls STEP until a fix-point is reached (i.e., the resulting constraint is in solved form and no further rewriting applies to it):

$SAT_{\mathcal{SET}}(C)$: while (STEP(C) $\neq C$) do $C :=$ STEP(C).

Correctness and completeness of $SAT_{\mathcal{SET}}$ is stated by the following theorem:

union(C) :

while $C_{\cup_3}$ is not in solved form and $C \neq$ false do
apply any of the following rules to any
(conjunction of) primitive constraint(s) of C:

(1) $\cup_3(s, s, t) \mapsto s = t$

(2) $\cup_3(s, t, \emptyset) \mapsto s = \emptyset \wedge t = \emptyset$

(3) $\cup_3(s_1, s_2, \{t_1 \mid t_2\}) \mapsto$

$\{t_1 \mid t_2\} = \{t_1 \mid X\} \wedge t_1 \notin X \wedge$ *any of*

(i) $s_1 = \{t_1 \mid Z\} \wedge \cup_3(Z, s_2, X)$

(ii) $s_2 = \{t_1 \mid Z\} \wedge \cup_3(s_1, Z, X)$

(iii) $s_1 = \{t_1 \mid Z\} \wedge s_2 = \{t_1 \mid W\} \wedge \cup_3(Z, W, X)$

(4) $\cup_3(\emptyset, t, X)$ or $\cup_3(t, \emptyset, X) \mapsto X = t$

(5) $\cup_3(\{t_1 \mid t_2\}, t, X)$ or $\cup_3(t, \{t_1 \mid t_2\}, X) \mapsto$

$\{t_1 \mid t_2\} = \{t_1 \mid Z\} \wedge t_1 \notin Z \wedge X = \{t_1 \mid Y\} \wedge t_1 \notin Y \wedge$ *any of*

(i) $\cup_3(Z, t, Y)$

(ii) $t = \{t_1 \mid W\} \wedge t_1 \notin W \wedge \cup_3(Z, W, Y)$

(6) $\cup_3(X, Y, Z) \wedge Z \neq t \mapsto \cup_3(X, Y, Z) \wedge$ *any of*

(i) $Z = \{Z_1 \mid Z_2\} \wedge Z_1 \notin t$

(ii) $t = \{Z_1 \mid Z_2\} \wedge Z_1 \notin Z$

(iii) $Z = \emptyset \wedge t \neq \emptyset$

(7) $\cup_3(X, Y, Z) \wedge X \neq t$ or $\cup_3(Y, X, Z) \wedge X \neq t \mapsto \cup_3(X, Y, Z) \wedge$ *any of*

(i) $X = \{Z_1 \mid Z_2\} \wedge Z_1 \notin t$

(ii) $t = \{Z_1 \mid Z_2\} \wedge Z_1 \notin X$

(iii) $X = \emptyset \wedge t \neq \emptyset$

disj(C) :

while $C_{\|}$ is not in solved form and $C \neq$ false do
apply any of the following rules to any primitive constraint of C:

(1) $\emptyset \| t$ or $t \| \emptyset \mapsto$ *true*

(2) $\{t_1 \mid t_2\} \| X$ or $X \| \{t_1 \mid t_2\} \mapsto t_1 \notin X \wedge X \| t_2$

(3) $\{t_1 \mid s_1\} \| \{t_2 \mid s_2\} \mapsto t_1 \neq t_2 \wedge t_1 \notin s_2 \wedge t_2 \notin s_1 \wedge s_1 \| s_2$

(4) $X \| X \mapsto X = \emptyset$

not_union(C) :

while $C_{\not\cup_3}$ is not in solved form and $C \neq$ false do
apply the following rule to any primitive constraint of C:

(1) $\not\cup_3(s_1, s_2, s_3) \mapsto$ *any of* (i) $X \in s_3 \wedge X \notin s_1 \wedge X \notin s_2$

(ii) $X \in s_1 \wedge X \notin s_3$

(iii) $X \in s_2 \wedge X \notin s_3$

not_disj(C) :

while $C_{\not\|}$ is not in solved form and $C \neq$ false do
apply the following rule to any primitive constraint of C:

(1) $s \not\| t \mapsto X \in s \wedge X \in t$

Figure 1: Rewriting Procedures

Theorem 5.2 *Let C be a constraint not involving any colored sets and C'_i be a constraint in solved form returned by $SAT_{\mathcal{SET}}(C)$ other than* false. *Then $Set \models C \leftrightarrow \vec{\exists} \bigvee_i C'_i$.*

Proof. (sketch) The proof is by case analysis of all rules of all the algorithms presented. For the procedures equal, not_equal, member, and not_member, the result follows from the corresponding proofs in [10].

Let us analyze briefly the other procedures. Correctness (and completeness) of rule (1) of union follows directly from Prop. 4.1. Rules (2) and (4) are the cases in which at least one of the arguments is $\emptyset$. Rules (3) and (5) are the cases in which at least one of the arguments is surely non-empty. Rules (5), (6), and (7) are needed to reach solved form. Their correctness and completeness derive from axioms $(\cup), (K), (E_k^s), (W)$. The same holds for the single rule of not_union. Correctness and completeness of rules (2) and (3) of disj follow immediately from axiom $(||)$. The same consideration holds for the unique rule of not_disj. Correctness and completeness of rules (1) and (4) of disj follow from axiom $(||)$ and from (K), instantiated to the constant symbol $\emptyset$. □

The termination of $SAT_{\mathcal{SET}}$ and the finiteness of the number of non-deterministic choices generated during its computation ensure the finiteness of the number of constraints non-deterministically returned by $SAT_{\mathcal{SET}}$.

Theorem 5.3 *The $SAT_{\mathcal{SET}}$ procedure terminates for every constraint C.*

Proof. In [7] it is shown that the iteration of the procedures member, not_member, equal, and not_equal on a system of $\{=, \neq, \in, \notin\}$-constraints always terminates. We can use this result to provide an argument for the termination of the $SAT_{\mathcal{SET}}$ procedure proposed here. The proof is divided into two parts:

(i) show that each individual rewriting procedure terminates;
(ii) show that $SAT_{\mathcal{SET}}$ globally terminates.

Step (i) is straightforward. In step (ii), we can safely ignore not_union and not_disj, as they are going to be applied only once. Let us assume that an infinite computation can occur; for the time being let us ignore rules (6), (7) of the procedure union. The body of $SAT_{\mathcal{SET}}$ is organized as union(disj(equal(not_member(not_equal(C))))).

From [7] we know that the sequence equal(not_member(not_equal(C))) cannot lead to non-terminating executions. Thus, a non-terminating execution must contain infinite activations of at least one of union and disj. The disj by itself cannot cause infinite executions. This case can be easily ruled out observing that:

- since no new $||$ are ever created, an infinite computation must originate from infinite reductions of one $||$-constraint;
- the two rules which can be applied repeatedly (without removing the constraint from the system) are the rule (2) and (3). They both create only negative knowledge which cannot further feed the production of bindings.

Thus an infinite computation will require infinite activations of union. This implies that there is a $\cup_3$-constraint which is reduced infinite times, using either rule (3) or (5). But, if this is the case, then it will be possible to produce (by fixing one argument) a constraint system not involving any $\cup_3$-constraints which will involve the same infinite computation, and which would contradict the results in [7].

In the previous discussion we have ignored the rules (6) and (7) of the union procedure. It can be shown [24] that their presence does not endanger the global termination. □

5.2 Colored sets

In order to deal with colored sets, we first need to update the notion of solved form, in order to properly reflect the presence of colored sets. This is obtained by adding, in cases *(iv)* and *(v)*, the further condition that all the involved sets must have the *same color* t. This means that C must contain the primitive constraints $\mathsf{c}^{\mathsf{of}}(X_i, t)$, $i = 1, 2, (3)$, t term not of the form $\{\_ \mid \_\}$.

Moreover, a new solved form for c^{of} constraints must be introduced. This solved form requires the verification of two special conditions, the *sufficient wideness of $\mathcal{F}$* condition and the *acyclicity* condition. The first condition, formally introduced in [24], is used to guarantee the ability of the language to generate a sufficient number of distinct colors to satisfy all the c^{of} atoms and $\neq$ literals present in the constraint. For example, assume $\mathcal{F} = \{\{\cdot \mid \cdot\}, \emptyset, c_1, \dots, c_{n-1}\}$ and C has the form:

$$\textstyle\bigwedge_{i=0}^{n} \mathsf{c}^{\mathsf{of}}(X_i, Y_i) \wedge \bigwedge_{j,k=0, j \neq k}^{n} Y_j \neq Y_k \, .$$

This constraint is not satisfiable, as $\mathcal{F}$ allows the creation of at most n different colors. A single function symbol of arity greater or equal to 1 guarantees the sufficient wideness of $\mathcal{F}$.

The *acyclicity condition* represents a generalization of the concept of occur-check. Testing the acyclicity condition means checking that C does not contain any chain of the form $\mathsf{c}^{\mathsf{of}}(X_1, f_1(X_2)) \wedge \mathsf{c}^{\mathsf{of}}(X_2, f_2(X_3)) \wedge \dots \wedge \mathsf{c}^{\mathsf{of}}(X_n, f_n(X_1))$ which is clearly unsatisfiable. Therefore, the following case is added to the definition of a constraint C in solved form:

(vi) $\mathsf{c}^{\mathsf{of}}(X, t)$, $X \notin \mathit{vars}(t)$, $t \not\equiv \{\_ \mid \_\}$, and $\mathsf{c}^{\mathsf{of}}(X, s)$, $s \not\equiv t$, does not occur in C, and the sufficient wideness and the acyclicity conditions hold.

A constraint in solved form involving c^{of} primitive constraints is still satisfiable. To prove this fact one can extend proof of Theorem 5.1 to deal with this kind of constraints. In the second part of the proof, the solution computed in the first part is refined by mapping the variables occurring in $C_{\mathsf{c^{of}}}, C_{\not{\mathsf{c}}^{\mathsf{of}}}$ in different colors fulfilling the constraints and modifying the colors of the images of the mappings computed in the first step.

A new constraint rewriting algorithm, called colors, is developed for dealing with the $C_{\mathsf{c^{of}}}$ and the $C_{\not{\mathsf{c}}^{\mathsf{of}}}$ parts of a given constraint C. Accordingly, the STEP function is extended by including a call to colors after the call to not_equal. The colors procedure reduces c^{of} and $\not{\mathsf{c}}^{\mathsf{of}}$ constraints, possibly generating some $=$ and $\neq$ constraints, and possibly returning false if $\mathcal{F}$ is not wide enough.

Algorithms of Sect. 5 must be revised in order to correctly manipulate the colors of sets. For instance, rule (4) of union is modified as follows:

(4.1)	$\cup_3(f(s_1, \dots, s_m), g(t_1, \dots, t_n), X)$	$\mapsto$	$f(s_1, \dots, s_m) = g(t_1, \dots, t_n) \wedge X = f(s_1, \dots, s_m)$
(4.2)	$\cup_3(f(s_1, \dots, s_m), t, X)$ or $\cup_3(t, f(s_1, \dots, s_m), X)$ $t \equiv \{\_ \mid \_\}$ or $t \in \mathcal{V}$	$\mapsto$	$X = t \wedge \mathsf{c}^{\mathsf{of}}(t, f(s_1, \dots, s_m))$

Similar technical variations are applied to rules (2), (6), and (7) of the union, and for rules (1) and (4) of disj. A new rule (rule (8)) is added to union for imposing that, given the constraint $\cup_3(X, Y, Z)$, X, Y, and Z have the same color. Finally, a few non-deterministic choices dealing with c^{of} are added to the single rule of not_union and not_disj. (Complete constraint handling algorithms, as well as the colors procedure, can be found in [8].)

These extensions allow us finally to obtain the same results of Theorem 5.2 (correctness and completeness of $SAT_{\mathcal{SET}}$) and Theorem 5.3 (termination of $SAT_{\mathcal{SET}}$), but relaxing the restriction to non-colored sets.

To conclude this section, we point out that the $ACI1$ unification problem of Example 2.1, $X_1 \cup X_2 \cup X_3 = \{a, b\}$, as well as other similar unification problems, can be written as a conjunction of primitive constraints:

$$\cup_3(X_1, X_2, X) \wedge \cup_3(X, X_3, \{a, b\}).$$

The execution of $SAT_{\mathcal{SET}}$ on this constraint will return the desired answers.

6 Conclusions

In this work we have compared existing proposals for handling finite sets in CLP languages, and proposed a novel technique, that captures the benefits of the existing ones. The new representation scheme uses $\{\cdot \mid \cdot\}$ as set-constructor and $\cup_3$ as basic constraint predicate. We have described the syntactic and semantics components of the language and presented sound and complete operational semantics and constraint handlers.

Acknowledgements

We wish to thank Klaus U. Schulz for his kindness in suggesting interesting references and results, Alberto Policriti and Desh Ranjan for the comments in Footnotes 6 and 3, respectively. A. Dovier is partially supported by MURST project: *Tecniche formali per la specifica, l'analisi, la verifica, la sintesi e la trasformazione di sistemi software*. E. Pontelli is partially supported by NSF grants HRD 93-53271, INT 95-15256, and CCR 96-25358. The work is partially supported by CNR Grant 97.02426.CT12.

References

[1] P. Arenas-Sánchez and A. Dovier. A Minimality Study for Set Unification. *J. of Functional and Logic Programming*, No. 7, Volume 1997.

[2] F. Baader and W. Büttner. Unification in commutative and idempotent monoids. *Theoretical Computer Science*, 56:345–352, 1988.

[3] F. Baader and K. U. Schulz. Unification in the Union of Disjoint Equational Theories: Combining Decision Procedures. *J. of Symbolic Computation*, 21(2):211–243, 1996.

[4] C. Beeri, S. Naqvi, O. Shmueli, and S. Tsur. Set Constructors in a Logic Database Language. *J. of Logic Programming*, 10(3):181–232, 1991.

[5] W. Büttner. Unification in the Data Structure Sets. In J. K. Siekmann, ed., *Proc. of CADE'86*, vol. 230, 470–488. Springer-Verlag, 1986.

[6] A. Dovier. *Computable Set Theory and Logic Programming.* PhD thesis, Università degli Studi di Pisa, March 1996. TD–1/96.

[7] A. Dovier, E. G. Omodeo, E. Pontelli, and G. Rossi. {log}: A Language for Programming in Logic with Finite Sets. *J. of Logic Programming*, 28(1):1–44, 1996.

[8] A. Dovier, C. Piazza, E. Pontelli, and G. Rossi. On the Representation and Management of Finite Sets in CLP-Languages. NMSU-CSTR-97-18, Department of Computer Science, Las Cruces, New Mexico, USA, December 1997.

[9] A. Dovier, A. Policriti, and G. Rossi. Integrating lists, multisets, and sets in a logic programming framework. In F. Baader and K. U. Schulz, eds., *Proc. of FROCOS'96*, vol. 3 of *Applied Logic*, 213–229. Kluwer A. P., 1996.

[10] A. Dovier and G. Rossi. Embedding Extensional Finite Sets in CLP. In *Proc. of ILPS'93*, 540–556. The MIT Press, 1993.

[11] F. Fages and G. Huet. Complete sets of unifiers and matchers in equational theories. *Theoretical Computer Science*, 43:189–200, 1986.

[12] C. Gervet. Conjunto: Constraint Logic Programming with Finite Set Domains. In *Proc. of ILPS'94*, 339–358. The MIT Press, 1994.

[13] P. Hill and J. Lloyd, *The Gödel Programming Language.* The MIT Press, 1994.

[14] J. Jaffar and M. J. Maher. Constraint Logic Programming: A Survey. *J. of Logic Programming*, 19–20:503–581, 1994.

[15] B. Jayaraman and D. A. Plaisted. Programming with Equations, Subsets and Relations. In *Proc. of NACLP'89*, 1051–1068. The MIT Press, 1989.

[16] D. Kapur and P. Narendran. Complexity of Unification Problems with Associative-Commutative Operators. *J. of Automated Reasoning*, 9:261–288, 1992.

[17] G. M. Kuper. Logic Programming with Sets. *J. of Computer and System Science*, 41(1):44–64, 1990.

[18] J. L. Lassez, M. J. Maher, and K. Marriot. Unification revisited. In *LNCS*, vol. 306, 1986.

[19] B. Legeard and E. Legros. Short overview of the CLPS system. In J. Maluszynsky and M. Wirsing, eds., *Proc. of PLILP'91*, vol. 528 of *LNCS*, 431–433. Springer-Verlag, 1991.

[20] P. Lincoln and T. Christian. Adventures in associative-commutative unification. *J. of Symbolic Computation*, 8(1,2):217–240, 1989.

[21] M. Livesey and J. Siekmann. *Unification of Sets and Multisets.* Technical report, Institut für Informatik I, Universität Karlsruhe, 1976.

[22] A. Martelli and U. Montanari. An efficient unification algorithm. *ACM Transactions on Programming Languages and Systems*, 4:258–282, 1982.

[23] E. G. Omodeo and A. Policriti. Solvable set/hyperset contexts: I. Some decision procedures for the pure, finite case. *Communication on Pure and Applied Mathematics.* 9–10:1123–1155, 1995.

[24] C. Piazza. Analisi e Definizione di Linguaggi di "Set Constraint". *Master Thesis*, Università di Parma, Dip. di Matematica, `http://prmat.math.unipr.it/~gianfr/tesi/union.ps.gz`.

[25] O. Shmueli, S. Tsur, and C. Zaniolo. Compilation of Set Terms in the Logic Data Language (LDL). *J. of Logic Programming*, 12(1):89–120, 1992.

[26] F. Stolzenburg. Membership-Constraint and Complexity in Logic Programming with Sets. In *Proc. of FROCOS'96*, vol. 3 of *Applied Logic*, 285–302. Kluwer A. P., 1996.

Meta Linear Constraints in Constraint Logic Programming

Philippe Refalo[1]
ILOG, S.A.
9, rue de Verdun - BP 85
94253 Gentilly, France
refalo@ilog.fr

Abstract

This article introduces meta linear constraints in constraint logic programming and addresses the related problem of incremental entailment of linear constraint. We present first the syntax and semantics of our meta-constraints. After a brief overview of linear constraint solving, two forms for ask constraints are introduced that simplify the entailment test. Some properties and entailment algorithms are then described. Meta linear constraints have been integrated to the CLP language `Athena`. Practical experiments with optimization problems show a substantial reduction of the search tree and of the computation time.

Keywords : meta linear constraints, linear constraint entailment, linear constraint solving, constraint logic programming.

1 Introduction

Meta constraints such as the cardinality operator [21], blocking implication [22] and the possibility of expressing boolean relations on numerical constraints [2, 6] are widely used in constraint programming. Those constraints are defined over finite domain constraints or interval constraints. The goal of this work is to show how to define and to solve meta linear constraints over real numbers in a constraint logic programming language.

In addition to classical linear constraints built with the relation symbols $=$, $\leq$, $<$ and $\neq$, we introduce two kind of meta linear constraints. The first one is of the form

$$y_1 = [x_1 + x_2 = 3]$$

Informally speaking, this constraint associates the truth value of the expression $x_1 + x_2 = 3$ to the real variable y_1 : if one of the constraints $x_1 + x_2 = 3$ or $x_1 + x_2 \neq 3$ is always satisfied (or *entailed* by classical constraints), then this constraint is reduced respectively to $y_1 = 1$ or $y_1 = 0$. Conversely, if one of the equations $y_1 = 0$ or $y_1 = 1$ is always verified, then this meta constraint is reduced respectively to $x_1 + x_2 = 3$ or $x_1 + x_2 \neq 3$. This constraint is available over intervals in the language `CLP(BNR)` [2], in the language `Prolog IV` [6], and in `Ilog Solver` [18] The second meta linear constraint introduced is

$$[x_1 - x_2 \leq 1] \rightarrow [x_1 - x_2 \neq 0]$$

If the constraint $x_1 - x_2 \leq 1$ is always verified, this expression is reduced to the constraint $x_1 - x_2 \neq 0$. This constraint is similar to the blocking implication over

[1]A part of this work was done when the author was in Laboratoire d'informatique de Marseille, Faculte des sciences de Luminy, 13009 Marseille - France

finite domains included in the `cc(FD)` language [22]. This constraint is also defined, still over finite domains, in `clp(FD)` [4] and `AKL(FD)` [3].

Our language can be seen as a simplified instance of the concurrent constraint languages scheme [17], where the set of classical constraints is called the *constraint store*, and the constraints appearing in square brackets are called *ask* constraints. The meta constraints introduced are expressive enough to express the cardinality operator [21] or the **if_then_else** operator of **CHIP** [7] over linear constraints.

Solving meta constraints is based on constraint entailment. To handle meta constraints over intervals and finite domains the entailment test is approximated. The set of solutions is usually approximated by an n-dimensional box or a Cartesian product of domains. The entailment test is thus efficient but incomplete. Such an approximation is not applicable to linear constraints over the reals because practical experience shows that, in this case, the approximation is usually far from the set of solutions. On the other hand efficient and complete algorithm to solve linear constraints are used in many CLP languages such as `PrologIII`, [5] `CLP(`$\mathcal{R}$`)` [10] and **CHIP** [7] and it is worth using them for linear constraint entailment to provide a complete entailment test.

Linear constraints has not really been considered for entailment. The work of Lassez *et al.* has led to interesting theoretical results like the *subsumption cone* [12] which allows entailment to be decided very efficiently but whose computation is exponential.

The starting point of this work on entailment of linear constraints is the canonical form introduced by [13] and the solved forms for linear constraints used in the languages mentioned above. A *dereferenced form* and a *partial precise form* are introduced for linear constraints, properties of these forms are stated, and we show how to maintain constraints incrementally in these forms. We also describe the entailment algorithm for each type of classical linear constraints. For shortness, proofs of the properties are not given. They can be found in [15]. The algorithms have been implemented in the CLP language **Athena** [16] and we present practical results showing that our algorithm improves the naive entailment test (i.e., S entails c iff $S \cup \{\neg c\}$ is unsolvable) and that a substantial reduction of the search space and of the computation time is achieved in comparison with standard backtracking.

The rest of this paper is organized as follows: the syntax and semantics of our meta constraints are defined in section 2. In section 3 the normal form for classical linear constraints is described. The dereferenced form is introduced in section 4. Then it is applied to the entailment of an equation (section 5) and of an inequation (section 6). The partial precise form for entailment of disequations is defined in section 7. Entailment on a strict inequality is presented in section 8. Some optimizations of the algorithms are described in section 9. The evaluation of our approach on practical problems is given in section 10.

2 Meta Linear Constraints

First, let us define the syntax and semantics of our constraints

2.1 Syntax

Let $\mathcal{R}$ be the set of real numbers and V be an infinite and countable set of variables.

A *term* represents an element of $\mathcal{R}$ and a constraint represents the properties that those elements must satisfy.

A *constraint* is an expression of the form $t_1 = t_2$, $t_1 \leq t_2$, $t_1 < t_2$, $t_1 \neq t_2$, $t_1 \rightarrow t_2$ where t_i are terms. Those constraints are named respectively *equation, inequation, strict inequation, disequation* and *blocking implication*. A *term* is an expression of the form α, αx, $t_1 + t_2$ or $[t_1 \diamond t_2]$ where α is a real number, x is a variable of V, the t_i are terms and $t_1 \diamond t_2$ is a constraint. The meta level of our constraints appears here: constraints can be written inside terms.

A *linear constraint* is a particular case of our constraints. It is built with one of the symbols $=$, $\leq$, $<$, $\neq$ and does not contain any term constructed with symbols [and]. These constraints are also named *generalized linear constraints* [13].

An *atomic constraint* is a constraint of the form

$$t_1 \diamond t_2$$
$$x_i \rightarrow x_j$$
$$x_k = [t_1 \diamond t_2]$$

where x_i, x_j and x_k are either variables or real numbers and where $t_1 \diamond t_2$ is a linear constraint. Later, we will see that solving our constraints amounts to solving atomic constraints.

A *constraint system* is a finite set of constraints. A variable has an *occurrence* in a constraint if it appears with a non zero coefficient in the constraint.

Particular constraints are also distinguished. A *unary constraint* is a constraint containing one occurrence of a variable. A *trivial constraint* is a constraint having no occurrence of any variable.

In the following, matrix notations are used. If A is a matrix, a is a row vector of real numbers, x a column vector of variables, b a column vector of real numbers and β a real number, the expression $ax \leq \beta$ represents an inequality and the expression $Ax = b$ represents a set of equations. We implicitly assume compatibility of the sizes of matrices and vectors when they are multiplied. Matrices are denoted by upper case letters, vectors by lower case letters, and real numbers by Greek symbols.

2.2 Semantics

To determine the semantics of our constraints we define an assignment of variables and then the solution of a constraint.

An *assignment* is a mapping from set V to set $\mathcal{R}$ which assigns a value to each variable of V. An assignment can be extended naturally to a mapping from the set of terms to $\mathcal{R}$. It is defined as follows

$$\begin{aligned}
\sigma(\alpha) &= \alpha \\
\sigma(\alpha x) &= \alpha\, \sigma(x) \\
\sigma(t_1 + t_2) &= \sigma(t_1) + \sigma(t_2) \\
\sigma([t_1 \diamond t_2]) &= \begin{cases} 1 & \text{if } \sigma(t_1) \diamond \sigma(t_2) \\ 0 & \text{otherwise} \end{cases}
\end{aligned}$$

where $t_1 \diamond t_2$ is a linear constraint.

A *solution* of a constraint is an assignment σ such that σ is a solution of the constraint $t_1 \diamond t_2$ if $\sigma(t_1) \diamond \sigma(t_2)$ where $\diamond \in \{=, \leq, <, \neq\}$ and σ is a solution of $t_1 \rightarrow t_2$ if $(\sigma(t_1), \sigma(t_2)) \neq (1, 0)$.

An assignment is a solution of a constraint system if it is a solution of each constraint of this system. A system having at least one solution is *solvable* otherwise it is *unsolvable*.

Two systems of constraints are *equivalent* if they have the same set of solutions.

A variable is *fixed* for a constraint system S, if every solution of this system assigns the same value to the variable.

Let S be a solvable system of constraints and c be a constraint. If every solution of S is a solution of c then S *entails* c, which is denoted by $S \models c$. When there exists a solution of S that is not a solution of c, then S does not entail c. This is denoted by $S \not\models c$.

An inequation $t_1 \leq t_2$ from a constraint system S is an *implicit equality* if every solution of S is a solution of $t_1 = t_2$.

Finally, the expression $\{x \mid S\}$ represents the set of solutions of a system S on a vector of variables x.

2.3 Solving Meta Linear Constraints

Solving a constraint system S means determining its set of solutions. This set is generally infinite, so it is preferable to simplify this system to an equivalent one, where solutions of S are more "visible". In particular, if S is unsolvable, the simplified system should be reduced to the singleton $\{0 \neq 0\}$.

This goal is difficult to reach with meta constraints. In practice, the solving algorithm is incomplete with respect to the algebraic structure implicitly defined above. To define precisely the capabilities of the solving algorithm, we give the properties that it guarantees [6].

Let R be a constraint system. By adding a sufficient number of variables it is possible to transform this system into a system of atomic constraints T equivalent to R (the solutions of both systems coincide on variables of R).

Our algorithm performs this basic transformation and then decomposes the system of atomic constraints into two subsystems

$$T = S \cup C$$

where S is the system of linear constraints of T (having the form $t_1 \diamond t_2$ where $\diamond \in \{=, \leq, <\neq\}$) and where C is the set of remaining (meta) constraints (having the form $x_i \rightarrow x_j$ or $x_k = [t_1 \diamond t_2]$). The solving algorithm guarantees the four following properties :

1. S is solvable;
2. every variable x_i of S that is fixed to a value α appears in an equation of S having the form $x_i = \alpha$;
3. for each constraint of the form $x_i \rightarrow x_j$ from C, if $x_i = 1 \in S$ then $x_j = 1 \in S$;
4. for each constraint of the form $x_k = [t_1 \diamond t_2]$ from C we have
   - $\{0 \leq x_k, x_k \leq 1\} \subset S$,
   - $x_k = 1 \in S$ iff $S \models t_1 \diamond t_2$,
   - $x_k = 0 \in S$ iff $S \models \neg(t_1 \diamond t_2)$.

Here, x_i, x_j and x_k are variables, and $t_1 \diamond t_2$ is a linear constraint.

This set of properties is an interesting compromise between the efficiency of the solving algorithm and the relevance of the simplification. In particular, if T contains only linear constraints, one can see that our algorithm is complete and shows explicitly all fixed variables.

In constraint programming, constraint solving is incremental. It consists of adding a constraint c to a constraint system T that satisfies the four properties above, to obtain a new system T' that satisfies the same properties and that is equivalent to $T \cup \{c\}$.

Incremental solving of meta constraints is mainly based on the following items:

- **[incremental solving]** Let S be a solvable system of linear constraints and t a linear constraint. Decide if the system $S \cup \{t\}$ is solvable and determine all fixed variables of this system.

- **[incremental entailment]** Let c and t be two linear constraints and S be a system of linear constraints such that $S \not\models c$, decide if $S \cup \{t\} \models c$.

The first item has been studied for some time in the area of constraint programming. A normal form that guarantees the solvability of a linear constraint system is presented in the next section.

The rest of this paper is devoted to the second item which is the main problem to be addressed when handling meta linear constraints.

3 Normal Form

The normal form is a way of writing a constraint system to guarantee the solvability of the system and to show explicitly every fixed variable. The one briefly presented here is close to the one used in languages such as CLP($\mathcal{R}$) [10] or CHIP [7].

Each inequality is of the form

$$l_i \leq x_i \text{ or } x_i \leq u_i$$

where l_i can be $-\infty$ and u_i can be ∞.

Each equation expresses a variable (v_j) called a *basic variable* with respect to other variables $(x_1, \ldots, x_n)$:

$$v_j = a_1 x_1 + \cdots + a_n x_n$$

where $j \notin \{1, \ldots, n\}$.

Those equations that contain only bounded variables (i.e. variables x_i for which $\langle l_i,\ u_i \rangle \neq \langle -\infty,\ \infty \rangle$) must be solvable together with inequations. Moreover, this set must not contain implicit equalities (i.e. implicit equalities of the form $l_i \leq x_i$ and $x_i \leq u_i$ are replaced respectively by $x_i = l_i$ and $x_i = u_i$).

Finally, each disequation does not contain variables that appear on the left hand side of equations.

More formally, a system in normal form is a system

$$S = \left\{ \begin{array}{ll} y = Mz + M'x + f & (S_A) \\ v = Ax + b, \quad l \leq v \leq u, \quad l' \leq x \leq u' & (S_K) \\ d \neq Qz + Q'x & (S_D) \end{array} \right. \tag{1}$$

where y and z are vectors of unbounded variables and v and x are a vectors of bounded variables and

- S_K is solvable and does not contain implicit equalities;

- S_D does not contain a constraint of the form $0 \neq 0$.

Without going into details, it is important to note that this form can be computed incrementally.

- The form of equations is computed by Gaussian elimination [9, 15].
- The solvability of the subsystem S_K is usually decided with an incremental simplex method [10] or revised simplex method [16].
- For the incremental search of implicit equalities, several methods have been proposed [19, 15]. The one we use is based on the quasi dual formulation of the system S_K [11].

Finally, note that the (revised) simplex method computes a solution of the system S_K. This solution is called the *current solution* of S_K and will be used for simplifying our algorithms for entailment.

4 Linear Constraint Entailment

4.1 Two Approaches

According to the definition of entailment given in section 2.2, proving that $S \models c$ is equivalent to prove the unsolvability of $S \cup \{\neg c\}$.

Let S be a system in normal form. Let c be a linear constraint such that $S \not\models c$ and let t be a linear constraint. If $S \cup \{t\}$ can be mapped to a normal form S', then $S' \models c$ if and only if $S' \cup \{\neg c\}$ cannot be mapped to normal form. This is the *naive method.*

The *incremental method* maintains, for each ask linear constraint c_i a system in normal form Q_i equivalent to $S \cup \{\neg c_i\}$. If $S \cup \{t\}$ can be mapped to a normal form S', then $S' \cup \{t\} \models c_i$ if and only if the system $Q_i \cup \{t\}$ cannot be mapped to normal form. If it can, the system obtained is reused for constraints added to S' later on. This method is incremental in that the constraint addition to a normal form is incremental.

From the time complexity standpoint, these two methods are equivalent. The major drawback of the naive method is that it decides solvability for the system $S \cup \{t, \neg c_i\}$ while ignoring that the system $S \cup \{\neg c_i\}$ is already solvable. This information is used by the incremental method but it does not exploit the fact that the Q_i systems are very close (they are different in one constraint only). Consequently, similar operations are repeated. Moreover, the space complexity of this method is high since a system in normal form is maintained for each ask constraint.

The dereferenced form introduced below combines the advantages of the two methods without having their drawbacks. It has the space complexity of the naive method and several properties for entailment.

4.2 Dereferenced Form

After the definition of the dereferenced form, two general properties of this form are given.

Definition 1 (Dereferenced Form) *A linear constraint is in* dereferenced form *for a system in normal form if the constraint does not contain an occurrence of a basic variable of this system.*

Each ask constraint is maintained in dereferenced form. This form has several properties, the more general ones are given here. More specific properties are given in following sections.

The following property establishes a syntactic criterion on the form of some constraints that are not entailed. This enables discarding some constraints from an entailment test.

Property 4.1 *Let S be a system in normal form and c be an equation, an inequation or a strict inequation in dereferenced form for S. If c contains an occurrence of unbounded variables then S does not entail c.*

When the normal form contains only equations, the following property enables the immediate determination of constraints that are entailed.

Property 4.2 *Let S be a system of equations in normal form and c be a linear constraint in dereferenced form for S. The system S entails c if and only if c is trivial and solvable.*

These two properties are used for deciding linear constraint entailment. In the following, additional properties as well as algorithms are given for deciding entailment of each type of constraint. The proofs of those results are not detailed; they can be found in [15].

5 Entailment of an Equation

According to Property 1, an equation in dereferenced form that contains an occurrence of an unbounded variable is not entailed. However, the dereferenced form has a stronger property that simplifies the entailment test of an equation.

Property 5.1 *Let S be a system in normal form and c be an equation in dereferenced form, S entails c if and only if c is trivial and solvable.*

Deciding entailment of an equation amounts to checking if the equation has the form $\alpha = \alpha$. This is due to the absence of implicit equalities in the normal form.

6 Entailment of an Inequation

Consider now an inequation in dereferenced form. It is not entailed if it is trivial and unsolvable or if it contains an occurrence of unbounded variable (property 1).

The only inequations that can be entailed are the ones that do not verify these two conditions. Deciding entailment of an inequation is simplified thanks to the constraint propagation theorem given by Lassez and McAloon [13]. The following property is an extension of this result to our normal form.

Property 6.1 *Let S be a system in normal form 1 and c be an inequation in dereferenced form for S and containing only bounded variables, then $S \models c$ if and only if $S_K \models c$.*

For an efficient entailment test it is essential to note that

$$S_K \models ax \leq \beta$$

is equivalent to verifying that

$$\max\{ax \mid S_K\} \leq \beta \tag{2}$$

More generally, deciding entailment of an inequation is polynomially equivalent to solving a linear program. This linear program can be solved with the simplex method for example. Note that the simplex iterations can be stopped as soon as a solution of $S_K \cup \{\beta < ax\}$ is reached.

7 Entailment of a Disequation

The dereferenced form is of little relevance for deciding the entailment of a disequation efficiently. Lassez and McAloon have proposed in [13] a precise form for particular disjunctions of linear disequations. This form has interesting properties for entailment. However, for reasons that are explained below, we introduce a partial precise form for deciding entailment of a disequation.

7.1 Precise Form

The precise form of a disequation is a representation of the affine hull of solutions that this disequation excludes.

Definition 2 (Precise Form) *Let S be a system of linear constraints of the form $\{y = Mx + m, Ax \leq b\}$. The* precise form *of a disequation $ax \neq \beta$ is the expression $\{Cx = d\}$ where $S \cup \{Cx = d\}$ is solvable and where $\{x \mid Cx = d\}$ is the affine hull of the set $\{x \mid Ax \leq b,\ ax = \beta\}$.*

The affine hull of a system of linear constraints is the smallest affine space containing the solution of the system. It is characterized by the set of implicit inequalities of this system. Here the affine space defined by $\{x \mid Cx = d\}$ is excluded by the disequation $ax \neq \beta$.

This representation has a nice property for entailment: Let S be a system of equations and inequations, let $D = \{d_1, \ldots, d_n\}$ be a set of disequations in precise form for S and let c be a disequation in precise form for S. We have $S \cup D \models c$ if and only if there exists a disequation d_i from D such that $\{d_i\} \models c$ (see [13]).

However, the precise form has two drawbacks. First, it has the space complexity of the incremental method. It is also difficult to maintain incrementally. Each time a constraint is introduced in the system S we have to recompute a representation of the affine hull of excluded solutions for each disequation.

This is why we introduce the partial precise form. It is easier to compute and to maintain incrementally, it has the space complexity of a linear constraint and has interesting properties for deciding entailment.

7.2 Partial Precise Form

Like the precise form, the partial precise form of a disequation is a representation of the affine hull of the solutions that are excluded. But this representation is more compact.

The partial precise form of a disequation $ax \neq \beta$ only maintains implicit equalities of the system $S_K \cup \{ax = \beta\}$ which are sufficient to characterize the affine hull of excluded solutions.

Definition 3 (Partial Precise Form) *Let S be a system in normal form 1 and $ax \neq \beta$ be a disequation in dereferenced form for S such that $S \cup \{ax = \beta\}$ is solvable. Let $E = \{ux_F \leq v\}$ be the set of implicit equalities of the system $S_K \cup \{ax = \beta\}$. Here F is a set of indices and x_F is a vector composed of elements of x having their index in F. The* partial precise form *of $ax \neq \beta$ for S is the expression*

$$\begin{array}{ll} \overline{\{ax = \beta\}} & \text{if } E = \emptyset \\ \overline{\{x_F = w\}} & \text{if } E \neq \emptyset, \text{ where } w_i = v_i/u_i,\ i \in F \end{array}$$

The space complexity of this form is the one of a linear constraint (i.e. $O(n)$ if n is the number of variables of the normal form). Note that a disequation that cannot be mapped to partial precise form is entailed. Here is the essential property of this form:

Property 7.1 *Let S be a system in normal form 1, and let $ux \neq \xi$ be a disequation. Let us consider the partial precise form of this disequation for S :*

1. *if it is $\overline{\{x_F = w\}}$, then $S \models ux \neq \xi$ if and only if there exists a disequation $ex \neq \gamma$ from S_D such that $S \cup \{x_F = w\} \models ex = \gamma$;*
2. *if it is $\overline{\{ax = \beta\}}$, then $S \models ux \neq \xi$ if and only if there exists a disequation $ex \neq \gamma$ from S_D such that $a = \frac{\beta}{\gamma}.e$.*

This property shows the efficiency of the entailment test for disequations. It amounts to deciding entailment of an equation, which is very simple (see property 5.1), or to deciding the colinearity of two vectors.

7.3 Computing Partial Precise Form

Let $ax \neq \beta$ be a disequation in dereferenced form for a system S in normal form 1. The two main steps to map this disequation to partial precise form are

1. decide the solvability of the system $S_K \cup \{ax = \beta\}$;
2. compute the set of implicit equalities $E = \{ux_F \leq v\}$ of $S_K \cup \{ax = \beta\}$.

For the first step, the current solution of S_K is used. If this solution satisfies the expression $\beta < ax$, then finding a solution of $S_K \cup \{ax = \beta\}$ amounts to finding a solution of $S_K \cup \{ax \leq \beta\}$ and thus solving the linear program

$$\gamma = \min\{ax \mid S_K\} \tag{3}$$

for trying to give the term ax the value β (the case where the solution satisfies the expression $ax < \beta$ is symmetric). Note that γ can be equal to $-\infty$. The result of this minimization is then analyzed according to the value of γ :

- $\gamma > \beta$, the disequation is entailed by S_K;
- $\gamma = \beta$, the system $S_K \cup \{ax = \beta\}$ contains implicit equalities that must be computed to obtain the partial precise form;
- $\gamma < \beta$, the partial precise form is $\overline{\{ax = \beta\}}$.

For the second step, note that S_K does not contain implicit equalities. The search for implicit equalities can thus be performed incrementally (cf section 3). In particular, the system $S_K \cup \{ax = \beta\}$ does not contain any implicit equality if the constraint $ax = \beta$ contains an unbounded variable.

The partial precise form for disequations has the advantage that it can be maintained incrementally when a new constraint is introduced in the normal form. A disequation of the form $\overline{\{ax = \beta\}}$ has no particular structure, and the method described above is applied to it when a new constraint is introduced in the normal form. For a disequation of the form $\overline{\{x_F = w\}}$, since w_i is equal to one of the bounds of x_i in the system S, searching for a solution of the system $S_K \cup \{x_F = w\}$ is equivalent to searching a solution of the system $S_K \cup \{fx_F \leq fw\}$ with $f_i = 1$ (if $w_i = l_i$) or $f_i = -1$ (if $w_i = u_i$) for $i \in F$, assuming that S is in normal form 1 (cf [15]). The search for a solution is thus equivalent to solving the linear program $\min\{fx_F \mid S_K\}$.

For searching implicit equalities in the system $S_K \cup \{fx_F \leq fw\}$ an incremental method such as the one cited in section 3 can be used since S_K does contains implicit equalities. However to avoid discovering again the implicit equalities that were used for the actual form, they are searched in the system S_K where bounds have been modified such that $l_i = u_i = w_i$, for $i \in F$.

8 Entailment of a Strict Inequation

Entailment of a strict inequation $ax < \beta$ by a system S in normal form is equivalent to the entailment of both the inequation $ax \leq \beta$ in dereferenced form for S and the disequation $ax \neq \beta$ in partial precise form.

However such a decomposition in not efficient and can be improved. If the strict inequality does not contains any unbounded variable, then entailment can be decided by solving the following linear program

$$\gamma = \min\{ax \mid S_K\}$$

This leads to the three following cases:

- $\gamma < \beta$, the constraint $ax < \beta$ is not entailed;
- $\gamma > \beta$, the constraint $ax < \beta$ is entailed (in this case both $ax \leq \beta$ and $ax \neq \beta$ are entailed);
- $\gamma = \beta$, the entailment of the constraint $ax < \beta$ is equivalent to the entailment of the disequation $ax \neq \beta$.

The last condition is the only one where the entailment of a disequation has to be considered.

9 Optimizations

The forms and properties that were introduced previously lead to algorithms that improve the naive method and the incremental method.

However, for every new constraint introduced in the subsystem S_K of the solved form, a linear program must be solved to decide entailment or to maintain the partial precise form.

The ideal method would consider a number of ask constraints which depends on the number of entailed constraints and not on the total number of ask constraints. In practice we try to determine, with an easily verifiable criterion, the greatest possible number of constraints that are clearly *not* entailed.

This criterion is stated like this: if $S \not\models c$, then it is possible to compute a solution σ of the system $S \cup \{\neg c\}$. When a new constraint t is added to the normal form S, if σ is still a solution of t, then it is clear that $S \cup \{t\} \not\models c$.

To apply this criterion we associate a solution to every ask constraint over bounded variables. Here are, for a (strict) inequation and for a disequation, descriptions of the solution to associate and the ways to use them.

(Strict) Inequation The solution associated to an inequation $ax \leq \beta$ or a strict inequation $ax < \beta$ is a solution of the system $S_K \cup \{\beta < ax\}$. This solution is available as the current solution of S_K once the linear program 2 is solved. The (strict) inequation must be reconsidered when a constraint introduced in S_K excludes this solution.

Disequation The solution associated to a disequation in partial precise form, denoted generically by $\overline{\{Cx = d\}}$ is a solution of $S_K \cup \{Cx = d\}$. It is available once the linear program 3 is solved. The two following optimizations are then possible:

- the addition of a constraint $ax \diamond \beta$ to the system S_K does nor modify the partial precise form whose associated solution is a solution of $ax \diamond \beta$ without being a solution of $ax = \beta$;
- let $ex \neq \gamma$ a disequation of S_D, if the associated solution is a solution of $ex \neq \gamma$ the $\{ex \neq \gamma\} \not\models \overline{\{Cx = d\}}$.

To prove the first statement, consider the addition of an inequation $ax \leq \beta$. If σ is a solution of $ax \leq \beta$ without being a solution of $ax = \beta$, it is thus a solution of $S_K \cup \{Cx = d, ax < \beta\}$. From the definition of the partial precise form, the system $S_K \cup \{Cx = d\}$ does not contain implicit equalities, and thus the system $S_K \cup \{Cx = d, ax < \beta\}$ does not contain implicit equalities either. So the partial precise form of $\overline{\{Cx = d\}}$ is unchanged.

The second statement is easily proved: observe that the associated solution is a solution of $\{Cx = d,\ ex \neq \gamma\}$. Thus $\{Cx = d\} \not\models ex = \gamma$ and consequently $\{ex \neq \gamma\} \not\models \overline{\{Cx = d\}}$.

Associating a solution to an ask constraint reduces the number of applications of our algorithms. The impact of this association on the solving of meta linear constraints is evaluated in the following section.

	Naive Method		Dereferenced Form		Solution		
Problems	Pivot	Time (N)	Pivot	Time	Pivot	Time (S)	N / S
Bridge	322512	3706.2	114038	1749.3	13380	221.7	16.7
CNET	14010	385.1	13852	378.2	8751	159.5	2.4
Circuit	520	312.2	236	102.3	47	38.5	8.1
HSP1	18117	401.0	11258	250.2	6541	119.8	3.3
HSP2	25108	682.2	18523	510.3	11736	192.3	3.5
Ar. Mean							6.8

Table 1: Time Requirement for Entailment.

10 Applications

The entailment algorithms described in the previous section have been integrated to the CLP language **Athena** [16] whose linear constraint solver is based on an incremental revised simplex method over rational numbers.

Various problems from operation research and electrical engineering have been solved with this system. The **Bridge** problem is an optimization problem with disjunctive constraints whose first CLP solution appears in [20]. The disjunctive constraints states that two tasks T_1 and T_2, whose starting dates are t_1 and t_2 and whose durations are d_1 and d_2 cannot overlap. This is stated with the following constraint:

$$[t_2 + d_2 \leq t_1] + [t_1 + d_1 \leq t_2] = 1$$

The **CNET** problem [14] is a 0-1 mixed integer optimization problem for selecting the position of the concentrators on a network to minimize the distances between concentrators and plugs and the number of concentrators. The 0-1 constraint over a variable x_i is expressed as follows

$$0 \leq x_i \leq 1, \ [x_i > 0] \rightarrow [x_i = 1], \ [x_i < 1] \rightarrow [x_i = 0]$$

The **Circuit** problem [8] is a simulation of the temporal behavior of a hybrid circuit containing electro-mechanical and digital control devices. The behavior of these devices is easily represented by the high level operators using the implication operator.

Finally, the hoist scheduling problem (**HSP**) is a cyclic scheduling problem with disjunctive constraints [1]. Two instances of this problem from industrial applications have been considered.

In all these problems the presence of meta linear constraints simplifies the statement but does not avoid the use of enumeration for finding a solution or the optimal solution.

The search strategy that is used is an extension to the *first-fail* principle: in order to reduce the search space, it tries to satisfy first the constraints that are unlikely to be satisfied. For instance, consider the disjunction $[t_2+d_2 \leq t_1]+[t_1+d_1 \leq t_2] = 1$. For selecting the next constraint to branch on, the current solution of the system S_K is used. We only branch on those ask constraints that are not satisfied for this solution. Additionally, for each unsatisfied ask constraint $ax \Diamond \ \beta$, the distance to satisfaction is computed (i.e. the euclidean distance of the current solution to the hyperplane $\{x \mid ax = \beta\}$). The ask constraint that is chosen is the one that has the greatest distance since it is a priori the one that is harder to satisfy.

		Standard Backtracking		Meta Constraints		
Problems	Ask Cons.	Back.	Time (SB)	Back.	Time (M)	SB / M
Bridge	154	8948	221.7	436	205.0	1.08
CNET	20	173	159.5	45	280.2	0.56
Circuit	46	289	38.5	11	13.4	2.87
HSP1	348	965	119.8	52	14.5	8.26
HSP2	602	1750	192.3	89	21.2	9.07

Table 2: With and Without Meta Linear Constraints

Table 1 presents the number of pivoting operations and the time (in seconds on a Sun Sparc 10) required for the naive method, for using the dereferenced form and for associating a solution to each ask constraint. The dereferenced form always improves the number of pivots and the time requirement. The association of a solution to each ask constraints improves the naive algorithm by a factor of 6 on the average and up to a factor of 16 for the Bridge problem.

The results presented in table 2 show that a significant reduction of the search tree and of the computation time can be obtained when using meta linear constraints. On the other hand, entailment over linear constraints is computationally difficult. As a consequence, meta linear constraints should not be used systematically for solving any combinatorial linear constraint problem. The usefulness of their use must be evaluated because not every problem can benefit of them. For instance, for the CNET problem the reduction of the search space does not compensate for the cost of reducing it.

11 Conclusion

Solving meta linear constraints is related to deciding linear constraint entailment. Two forms were presented for this purpose: the dereferenced form and the partial precise form. The properties of these forms gives an efficient entailment test for a linear constraint.

The practical results shows that a substantial reduction of the search space and of the computation time can be obtained when expressing problems with meta linear constraints. They also show that a complete test of linear constraint entailment is computationally expensive.

As a future work, it would be interesting to study the cooperation between the algorithms presented herein and an interval constraint solver. Since interval-based solvers are sound, they can prove easily that some constraints are entailed (in linear time w.r.t. the number of variables). At the end, the entailment of some constraints would be decided by the interval approximation, the non entailment of some other constraints would be decided by the associated solution, and our algorithms were only applied to the remaining constraints.

12 Acknowledgments

The author is grateful to Pascal Van Hentenryck for many valuable comments and suggestions on a previous version of this work. This research was partially supported by the ESPRIT project ACCLAIM-7195.

References

[1] P. Baptiste, B. Legeard, and C. Varnier. Hoist scheduling problem : an approach based on constraint logic programming. In *Proceedings of the 1992 IEEE International Conference on Robotics and Automation*, pages 1139–1144, Nice, France, May 1992.

[2] F. Benhamou and W. Older. Applying Interval Arithmetic to Real, Integer and Boolean Constraints. *Journal of Logic Programming*, 32(1):1–24, July 1997.

[3] B. Carlson, M. Carlson, and D. Diaz. Entailment of finite domain constraints. In *Proceedings of the Eleventh International Conference on Logic Programming*. MIT Press, 1994.

[4] P. Codognet and D. Diaz. Boolean constraint solving using `clp(FD)`. In *Proceedings of the International Logic Programming Symposium*, 1993.

[5] A. Colmerauer. An introduction to Prolog III. *Communications of the ACM*, 33(7):69–91, July 1990.

[6] A. Colmerauer. Spécifications de Prolog IV. Technical report, Laboratoire d'Informatique de Marseille, 1996.

[7] M. Dincbas, P. van Hentenryck, and H. Simonis. The constraint logic programming langage CHIP. In *Proceedings of the International Conference on Fifth Generation Computer Systems*, pages 693–702, Tokyo, Japan, 1988.

[8] T. Graf, P. Van Hentenryck, C. Pradelles-Lasserre, and L. Zimmer. Simulation of hybrid circuits in constraint logic programming. *Computers Math. Applic.*, 20(9–10):45–56, 1990.

[9] J.-L. Imbert and P. van Hentenryck. On the handling of disequations in CLP over linear rational arithmetic. In Frederic Benhamou and Alain Colmerauer, editors, *Constraint Logic Programming: Selected Research*, pages 49–72. MIT Press, 1993.

[10] J. Jaffar, S. Michaylov, P. Stuckey, and R.H.C. Yap. The CLP($\mathcal{R}$) language and system. *Transactions on Programming Languages and Systems*, 14(3), July 1992.

[11] J-L Lassez. Parametric queries, linear constraints and variable elimination. In *DISCO 90, LNCS 429*, pages 164–173. Springer-Verlag Lecture Notes in Computer Science, 1990.

[12] J-L Lassez. Querying constraints. In *Proceedings of the ACM Conference on Principles of Database Systems*, Nashville, 1990.

[13] J-L Lassez and K. McAloon. A canonical form for generalised linear constraints. *Journal of Symbolic Computation*, (1):1–24, 1992.

[14] G.A. Narboni. Optimization of concentrator positioning in the design of private data networks. In *Conference on the Practical Applications of Prolog*, 1994.

[15] P. Refalo. *Resolution et implication de contraintes lineaires en programmation logique par constraintes*. Ph.D Thesis. Laboratoire d'informatique de Marseille, 1997.

[16] P. Refalo and P. van Hentenryck. CLP($\mathcal{R}_{lin}$) revised. In *Proceedings of the Joint International Conference and Symposium on Logic Programming*, pages 1–14, Bonn, Germany, 1996.

[17] V. A. Saraswat. *Concurent Constraint Programming Langages.* MIT Press, Cambridge, Mass., 1993.

[18] Ilog Solver 4.0. *User Manual.* ILOG, S.A., Gentilly, France, April 1997.

[19] P. J. Stuckey. Incremental linear constraint solving and implicit equalities. *ORSA Journal of Computing*, 3(4):269–274, 1991.

[20] P. van Hentenryck. *Constraint Satisfaction in Logic Programming.* MIT Press, Cambridge, Mass., 1989.

[21] P. van Hentenryck and Y. Deville. The cardinality operator: A new logical connective for constraint logic programming. In Frédéric Benhamou and Alain Colmerauer, editors, *Constraint Logic Programming: Selected Research*, pages 49–72. MIT Press, 1993.

[22] P. van Hentenryck, H. Simonis, and M. Dincbas. Constraint satisfaction using constraint logic programming. *Artificial Intelligence*, 58(1–3):113–159, 1992.

A High-Level Intermediate Language and the Algorithms for Compiling Finite-Domain Constraints[1]

Neng-Fa Zhou
Faculty of Computer Science and Systems Engineering
Kyushu Institute of Technology
680-4 Kawazu, Iizuka, Fukuoka 820, Japan
zhou@mse.kyutech.ac.jp
http://www.cad.mse.kyutech.ac.jp/people/zhou

Abstract

In this paper, we present a high-level intermediate language, called *delay-Prolog*, for implementing CLP(FD), the constraint language over finite-domains. Delay-Prolog has a much stronger description power than *indexicals*, the intermediate language widely used in current finite-domain constraint compilers. It is powerful enough for describing all kinds of constraint propagation procedures, which by now have been mostly written in low level languages. And, most importantly, delay-Prolog opens new ways to compiling constraints. Besides the *indexical* algorithm that compiles constraints into indexicals, we implemented two new algorithms: the *wait* algorithm that compiles a constraint as whole into a propagation procedure without splitting it into small pieces, and the *incremental simplification* algorithm that incrementally simplifies constraints into smaller ones. The results are noteworthy: The wait algorithm generates the fastest code, while the widely used indexical algorithm generates code that is about 3 times slower than that generated by the wait algorithm. The wait algorithm is adopted in the latest version of B-Prolog. The experimental results show that B-Prolog is comparable in performance with the fastest CLP(FD) systems, although it is an emulated system.

1 Introduction

CLP(FD) [7][2], the constraint logic programming language over finite domains, has been proved effective for solving a large number of real-life optimization problems. The key operation employed in CLP(FD) is called *constraint propagation*, which uses constraints actively to prune search spaces as follows: whenever a variable changes, i.e., the variable has been instantiated or its domain has been updated, the domains of all the remaining variables are filtered to contain only those values that are consistent with this variable. Like compiling unification is important for improving the performance of Prolog, compiling constraint propagation is a key to improving the performance of CLP(FD).

In early CLP(FD) systems, such as in the CHIP system [5], constraints are interpreted rather than compiled: constraints are first transformed into canonical-form

[1]This research was supported by a grant (No.09780298) from the Ministry of Education, Science, and Technology of Japan.

[2]In this paper, we use CLP(FD) as the name for the class of constraint languages over finite domains and clp(FD) to refer to the system developed at INRIA.

terms and are then executed by an interpreter that performs, among other things, constraint propagation. The propagation procedure adopted is general enough for handling all types of constraints. Learning from the experience of compiling Prolog programs into the Warren Abstract Machine (WAM), several researchers have extended the WAM for compiling CLP(FD). In the CHIP compiler [1], constraints are compiled into low level instructions such that different specialized propagation procedures can be used for different types of constraints. This compiler is called a *CISC* and a *black-box* compiler because it is based on a complex abstract machine and the constraint solver is not open to the users.

Recently, an intermediate language, called *indexical*, has been widely used for compiling finite-domain constraints [8, 2]. An indexical is a primitive constraint in the form of X *in* r, where X is a domain variable and r specifies the range for X. For each indexical, a propagation procedure specific to it is adopted. In contrast to the CHIP compiler, these compilers are called *RISC* and *glass-box* compilers because the underlying abstract machines are much simpler than that adopted in the CHIP compiler and the intermediate language is open to the users. However, indexical is very limited in description power because the delay mechanism is embedded in the language. It can be used to compile arithmetic as well as Boolean constraints[3], but is too week to be used to implement other types of constraints. In addition, the compilation from constraints into indexicals is so straightforward that it is impossible to try some new compilation algorithms and optimization techniques.

In this paper, we present a high-level intermediate language, called *delay-Prolog*, for implementing finite-domain constraints. Delay-Prolog extends Prolog in that it supports *domain variables* and a delay mechanism, called *delay clause*, that has the functionality of describing delay conditions on goals, triggering times for delayed goals, and actions taken after goals are delayed. Delay-Prolog will be defined in Section 3.

Delay-Prolog is a nice implementation language for programming constraint propagation. We will show in Section 4 how to program constraint propagation for various constraints including *reification* and the global constraint `all_distinct(L)`. Delay-Prolog has a much stronger description power than indexical, and opens new ways to compiling constraints. Besides the *indexical* algorithm, we will describe in Section 5 two new algorithms: the *wait* algorithm that compiles each constraint as a whole into a propagation procedure without splitting it into small pieces, and the *incremental simplification* algorithm that incrementally simplifies constraints into smaller ones. We will also analyze these algorithms and clarify their advantages and disadvantages.

We have implemented all the algorithms in B-Prolog and compared their performance for several benchmark programs. The results, which will be given in Section 6, are noteworthy: The wait algorithm is the best algorithm which generates code that is 3 times faster than that generated by the indexical algorithm. The wait algorithm is used in the latest version of B-Prolog (Version 3.0). The experimental results also show that B-Prolog is comparable in performance with, and sometimes faster than SICStus-Prolog and clp(FD), although it is an emulated system.

The advantages of delay-Prolog have not yet been explored thoroughly. In Section 7, we will propose two important optimization techniques.

The reader is assumed to be familiar with logic programming and constraint satisfaction, but no knowledge about abstract machines is assumed. In Section 2, we define some preliminary terms about CLP(FD) and constraint propagation. For detailed description, the reader may consult [7] and [9].

2 Preliminaries

2.1 CLP(FD)

In general, a CLP(FD) program is composed of three parts: the first part, called *variable generation*, generates variables and specifies their domains; the second part, called *constraint generation*, specifies constraints over the variables; and the final part, called *labeling*, instantiates the variables by doing enumeration.

The domain of a variable is defined as follows:

```
Vars in D
```

where `Vars` is a variable or a list of variables, and `D` is a list of integers or a range between two integers $l..u$ which denotes the set of integers $\{l, l+1, \ldots, u\}$.

A basic constraint is a call in the form $E_1\ R\ E_2$ where E_1 and E_2 are two arithmetic expressions and R is a relation symbol in {`#=`, `#\=`, `#>`, `#>=`, `#<`, `#=<`} which is self-explainable. There are several other primitives available for describing other types of constraints, choosing variables, instantiating variables, and finding optimal solutions with respect to some criteria.

2.2 Constraint propagation

Constraint Propagation (CP) is a basic operation employed in CLP(FD) systems for solving constraints. It uses constraints actively to exclude no-good values from the domains of variables. Many algorithms can be derived from this idea depending on when and to what level CP is applied. The following table illustrates how domains in `X#=Y+1` (`X,Y` $\in$ 1..5) are updated by four different algorithms. The *consistency checking* algorithm performs CP when constraints are generated. The *forward checking* algorithm, besides doing consistency checking, also invokes CP when a domain variable is instantiated. The *partial look-ahead* algorithm, besides doing forward checking, also invokes CP when a bound of a domain is updated. The *full look-ahead* algorithm, besides doing partial look-ahead, also invokes CP when an intermediate element is excluded from a domain.

Algorithm	Time	Effect
Consistency checking	generated	$X \in 2..5, Y \in 1..4$
Forward checking	$X = 3$	$X = 3, Y = 2$
Partial look-ahead	$X \neq 5$	$X \in 2..4, Y \in 1..3$
Full look-ahead	$X \neq 4$	$X \in [2,3,5], Y \in [1,2,4]$

3 Delay-Prolog

3.1 Domain variables

A domain variable is represented internally just like a suspending variable of Prolog, but there is more information associated with it (see the table below).

type	type of the domain
min	minimum element
max	maximum element
size	number of elements in the domain
ins_cs	list of constraints to be executed when the variable is instantiated
min_cs	list of constraints to be executed when the low bound is updated
max_cs	list of constraints to be executed when the upper bound is updated
dom_cs	list of constraints to be executed when any element is excluded
elms	data structure that stores the elements

The information about a domain variable can be accessed and/or updated through a group of primitives. The expression `min(X)` denotes the minimum element, `max(X)` the maximum element, `dom(X)` the list of elements, and `size(X)` the size of the domain of `X`. The primitive `exclude(X,E)` excludes the element `E` from the domain of `X`, and the primitive `elm(X,E)` checks whether `E` is an element in the domain of `X`.

A failure occurs when the domain of a variable becomes empty. When the domain of a variable becomes a singleton, then the variable will be bound to the element.

An update of a domain variable is called a *trigger* and the variable is called a *triggering variable*. There are four kinds of triggers. The trigger `ins(X)` is on when `X` is bound to any term; `min(X)` is on when the low bound of `X` is updated; `max(X)` is on when the upper bound of `X` is updated; and `dom(X)` is on when any change happens to `X`. There are four lists of constraints associated with a domain variable, each of which stores the constraints to be executed when the corresponding trigger is turned on.

3.2 Delay clauses

In this subsection, we describe the syntax and semantics of delay clauses. Examples that illustrate their usage will be given in the next Section.

A delay clause takes the following form:

```
delay Head :- Condition : [{Triggers}] Action.
```

where `Condition` is a sequence of in-line tests, `Triggers` is a sequence of trigger declarations, and `Action` is a sequence of arbitrary calls.

For any call to the predicate of `Head`, if it matches `Head` (*i.e.,* the call is an instance of `Head`) and `Condition` is satisfied, then the call delays and `Action` is executed. Since one-directional matching rather than full-unification is used to match the call against `Head` and `Condition` is composed of only in-line tests, the call will be kept unchanged before `Action` is executed. If the call does not match `Head` or `Condition` fails, then the next clause will be tried. If `Action` fails, then the original predicate call will fail. Notice that delay clauses are different from guarded clauses in concurrent languages. After a delay clause is chosen, the predicate can be reentered and the remaining clauses can be retried later.

The sequence of trigger declarations `Triggers`, which is optional, declares when the clause should be re-executed. The trigger declaration `ins(X)` means the time when the variable `X` is instantiated; `min(X)` (`max(X)`) means the time when the the low (upper) bound of `X` is updated; and `dom(X)` means the time when any change happens to `X`. When no trigger declaration is given, the compiler automatically generates a trigger `ins(X)` for each variable occurring in `Condition`.

A delay clause is executed in a event-driven manner. At the entry and exit points of every predicate, the system checks to see whether or not there is trigger that has been turned on. If so, then the current procedure is interrupted and control is moved to the lists of constraints associated with the trigger. When a delay clause is re-entered, the execution starts from different points depending on the type of the trigger. If the trigger is `ins(X)`, then the execution starts from the condition; otherwise, the execution starts from the action. This optimization technique avoids testing of the condition redundantly because the triggers `min(X)`, `max(X)`, and `dom(X)` do no affect the satisfiability of the condition. After the constraints finish their execution, the interrupted procedure will resume its execution. The implementation details can be found in [13].

Delay clauses defined here are much more powerful than other delay constructs available in different Prolog systems. It extends delay clauses proposed by Meier [10] which are unable to describe triggers and actions. All other constructs, such as *freeze* in Prolog-II and *when declarations* in NU-Prolog, can be implemented very easily by using delay clauses.

4 Programming Constraint Propagation

In this section, we show three examples that illustrate how to programming constraint propagation in delay-Prolog.

4.1 Indexical

Indexical, which is adopted by many CLP(FD) compilers for compiling constraints, can be implemented easily with delay-Prolog. Consider the indexical

```
X in min(Y)+min(Z)..max(Y)+max(Z).
```

This indexical is a primitive constraint that excludes no-good values from the domain of `X` that do not lie in the range of `min(Y)+min(Z)..max(Y)+max(Z)`. This constraint is reconsidered whenever a bound of `Y` or `Z` is updated. The following procedure implements the indexical:

```
delay 'V in V+V'(X,Y,Z):-dvar(X) :
      {ins(Y),min(Y),max(Y),ins(Z),min(Z),max(Z)},
      X in min(Y)+min(Z)..max(Y)+max(Z).
'V in V+V'(X,Y,Z):-true : X >= min(Y)+min(Z), X=< max(Y)+max(Z).
```

The predicate call `'V in V+V'(X,Y,Z)` propagates changes from `Y` and/or `Z` to `X`.

4.2 Reification

One well used technique in FD constraint programming is called *reification*, which uses a new Boolean variable `B` to indicate the satisfiability of a constraint `C`. `C` must be satisfied if and only if `B` is equal to `1`. This relationship is denoted as:

```
C <=> (B #= 1)
```

Reification is useful for implementing various global constraints, such as cardinality constraints [8].

It is straightforward to implement reification in delay-Prolog. Consider, as an example, the reification:

```
(X #= Y) <=> (B #= 1)
```

where X and Y are domain variables, and B is a Boolean variable. The following procedure describes the relationship:

```
delay reification(X,Y,B):-
      dvar(B),dvar(X),X\==Y : {ins(X),ins(Y),ins(B)}.
delay reification(X,Y,B):-
      dvar(B),dvar(Y),X\==Y : {ins(Y),ins(B)}.
reification(X,Y,B):-dvar(B) : (X==Y -> B=1; B=0).
reification(X,Y,B):-true : (B==0 -> X #\= Y; X #= Y).
```

Curious readers might have noticed that ins(Y) is a trigger in the first clause but ins(X) is not a trigger in the second clause. The reason is simply that ins(Y) affects the condition of the first clause but ins(X) has no effect on the condition of the second clause. X is guaranteed to be an integer when the condition of the second clause is satisfied.

4.3 all_distinct(L)

Besides arithmetic constraints, a constraint system usually offers the functionality for describing and solving symbolic constraints. Delay-Prolog is also a nice language for implementing symbolic constraints. We consider, as an example, how to implement all_distinct(L).

The constraint all_distinct(L) holds if variables in L are pair-wisely different. One naive way of implementing this constraint is to generate binary inequality constraints between all pairs of variables in L. This implementation has two problems: First, the space required to store the constraint is quadratic in the number of variables in L; Second, splitting the constraint into small granularity ones may lose possible propagation opportunities. The second problem has been pointed out before by other researchers (e.g., [11], [12]).

To solve the space problem, we define all_distinct(L) in the following way:

```
all_distinct(L):-all_distinct(L,[]).

all_distinct([],Left).
all_distinct([X|Right],Left):-
      outof(X,Left,Right),
      all_distinct(Right,[X|Left]).

delay outof(X,Left,Right):- dvar(X) : {ins(X)}.
outof(X,Left,Right):-true : outof(X,Left),outof(X,Right).
```

For each variable X, let Left be the list of variables to the left of X and Right be the list of variables to the right of X. The predicate call outof(X,Left,Right) holds if X appears in neither Left nor Right. Instead of generating inequality constraints between X and all the variables in Left and Right, the call outof(X,Left,Right) delays until X is instantiated. After X becomes an integer, the calls outof(X,Left) and outof(X,Right) exclude X from the domains of the variables in Left and Right. It is not difficult to understand that this implementation only consumes linear space.

In terms of the propagation ability, the second implementation is the same as the first one. In some systems, consistency checks are done to detect failure as early as possible. It is very easy to introduce consistency checks into the implementation. To do so, we only need to define `outof(X,Left,Right)` as follows:

```
delay outof(X,Left,Right):- dvar(X) : {dom(X)},
      consistency_check(X,Left,Right).
outof(X,Left,Right):-true : outof(X,Left),outof(X,Right).
```

where `consistency_check(X,Left,Right)` does the consistency check. There are many possible algorithms. The one implemented in B-Prolog is as follows: Let n be the size of the domain of `X`, and m be the number of variables in `Left` and `Right` whose domains are subsets of that of `X`. If $m + 1 > n$, then fails; otherwise, if $m + 1 = n$, then for each value v in `X`'s domain, exclude v from the domains of all the variables whose domains are not subsets of that of `X`. The soundness of the algorithm is obvious: If $m + 1 > n$, then it is impossible to assign n different values to $m + 1$ variables, and if $m + 1 = n$, then no value in the domain of `X` can be assigned to other variables except `X` and the m variables.

5 Compiling Arithmetic Constraints

In this section, we show that delay-Prolog can serve as an excellent intermediate language for compiling constraints. For each constraint, the compiler generates a constraint propagator tailored to the source constraint. We only consider linear arithmetic constraints.

Definition 1 (Canonical-form) *A constraint E_1 R E_2 is said to be in canonical-form if E_1 and E_2 are expressions in the following form: T_1+T_2+...+T_n where $T_i(i = 1, \ldots, n)$ is either a domain variable or a domain variable proceeded by a positive coefficient.*

For each constraint, the compiler first translates it into a canonical-form and then generates a constraint propagator for it. It is usually impossible to know the run-time properties of the variables in an expression at compilation time. A variable may be a constant, a domain variable, or even a complex expression at execution time. To invoke the propagator, the variables must be first checked at runtime. If they are domain variables or integers, then execute the specialized propagator; otherwise, call the constraint interpreter.

5.1 Compiling low-degree constraints

We first consider how to compile constraints that contains three or less variables. As *unary* constraints, i.e., constraints containing only one variable, can be translated into appropriate primitives on domain variables, we only need to consider constraints that contains two or three variables.

5.1.1 Compiling constraints into indexicals

We have shown in the previous section how to implement indexicals. With indexicals, we can compile constraints in the same way as many other compilers do. Consider, for example, the constraint `X #= Y+Z`. This constraint is replaced by the following three indexicals:

```
'V in V+V'(X,Y,Z),
'V in V-V'(Y,X,Z),
'V in V-V'(Z,X,Y).
```

This algorithm has both advantages and disadvantages. On one hand, indexicals themselves are specialized code that contains no redundancy. For example, when a bound of `X` is updated, the indexicals `'V in V-V'(Y,X,Z)` and `'V in V-V'(Z,X,Y)` will be triggered but the indexical `'V in V+V'(X,Y,Z)` will not be triggered. On the other hand, the granularity of indexicals is very small and the cost for executing them is usually high because space is required for storing the constraints and the execution context, i.e., some of the registers of the abstract machine, has to be switched frequently.

5.1.2 Compiling constraints into delay predicates

Another algorithm is to compile each constraint into one delay predicate without splitting it into smaller pieces. The delay predicate contains clauses for different modes of the constraints, starting from the mode where all the variables are free to the mode where all the variables are instantiated. The delay predicates for *binary constraints* (i.e., constraints having two variables) look like:

```
delay p(X,Y,C):-dvar(X),dvar(Y) : {Triggers}, Actions.
p(X,Y,C):-dvar(X) : solve the unary constraint over X.
p(X,Y,C):-dvar(Y) : solve the unary constraint over Y.
p(X,Y,C):-true : test the ground constraint.
```

The contents of `Triggers` and `Actions` are determined based on the type of the constraint.

For example, the constraint `X #\= Y` is compiled into the following predicate:

```
delay neq(X,Y):-dvar(X),dvar(Y): {ins(X),ins(Y)}.
neq(X,Y):-dvar(X) : exclude(X,Y).
neq(X,Y):-dvar(Y) : exclude(Y,X).
neq(X,Y):-true : X=\=Y.
```

No action will be taken when both `X` and `Y` are uninstantiated. As another example, consider the equality constraint `X #= Y+C`. The compiled predicate is as follows:

```
delay 'X=Y+C'(X,Y,C):-dvar(X),dvar(Y) :
      {ins(X),min(X),max(X),ins(Y),min(Y),max(Y)},
      X in min(Y)+C..max(Y)+C.
      Y in min(X)-C..max(X)-C.
'X=Y+C'(X,Y,C):-dvar(X) : X is  Y+C.
'X=Y+C'(X,Y,C):-true : Y is X-C.
```

This predicate is a little different from the skeleton we mentioned above: The last clause takes care of both of the cases when `Y` is a variable and when `Y` is an integer.

Compared with the scheme of compiling constraints into indexicals, this scheme does not have the small granularity problem. One constraint is compiled into only one predicate and thus only one frame is enough for storing the constraint. On the other hand, the code for reducing domains is not as specialized as in indexicals. Executing `X in min(Y)+C..max(Y)+C` is redundant if the constraint is triggered by changes to `X`. Experiments show that there is no big difference between these two schemes.

5.2 Compiling high-degree constraints

There are many ways for compiling n-ary constraints where n is greater than 3. We describe three algorithms.

5.2.1 The explosive examination algorithm

The first algorithm is to compile all constraints in the same way as that for compiling low-degree constraints: generate a clause for each mode of a constraint. We call this the *explosive examination* algorithm. This algorithm has the advantage that specific code for reducing domains can be generated for different modes of a constraint. However, for an n-ary constraint, there are 2^n clauses in the generated predicate. This algorithm is obviously not practical for compiling constraints with large n.

5.2.2 The split algorithm

The second algorithm is to split an n-nary constraint into a sequence of three-tuple constraints each of which contains at most three variables. We call this algorithm *split* algorithm. This algorithm is adopted by many compilers, such as SICStus-Prolog and clp(FD). It does not have the size-explosion problem of the explosive examination algorithm and can take advantage of the constraint library which is usually implemented in low-level languages and are well tuned. In addition, this algorithm, as described in [2], can restrict value propagation within small constraints as long as the shared variables do not change. The disadvantages of this algorithm are that new domain variables have to be introduced and the granularity of constraints becomes smaller.

5.2.3 The simplification algorithm

The third algorithm is to incrementally simplify n-ary constraints to lower degree ones. The generated predicate for an n-ary constraint looks like:

```
delay c(X1,X2,...,Xn,I):-
    dvar(X1),...,dvar(Xn) :
    {Triggers}
    reduce domains of X1,...,Xn.
c(X1,X2,...,Xn,I):-
    integer(X1) :
    I1 is a new constant,
    c1(X2,...,Xn,I1).
    ...
c(X1,X2,...,Xn,I):-
    integer(Xn) :
    In is a new constant,
    cn(X1,...,Xn-1,In).
```

When the reduced constraints c_1, c_2, ..., and c_n have the same structure, then only one predicate is adequate to define the propagation procedure for them. The simplification process is repeated until the simplified constraints have no more than three variables. We call this algorithm *incremental simplification* algorithm. This algorithm has the advantage that specific code is used to reduce domains. The disadvantages are that: there are a lot of argument passing involved in the execution, and the compiled code takes at least $O(n^3)$ space and thus cannot be applied to large constraints.

For example, the constraint `X1+X2+X3+X4 #= 34` is translated into a call

```
vvvv_eq_c(X1,X2,X3,X4,34)
```

which is defined as follows:

```
delay vvvv_eq_c(X1,X2,X3,X4,C):-
    dvar(X1),dvar(X2),dvar(X3),dvar(X4) :
    {ins(X1),min(X1),max(X1),...,ins(X4),min(X4),max(X4)},
    reduce domains of X1,X2,X3,and X4.
vvvv_eq_c(X1,X2,X3,X4,C):-
    integer(X1) :
    NewC is C-X1,
    vvv_eq_c(X2,X3,X4,NewC).
    ...
vvvv_eq_c(X1,X2,X3,X4,C):-
    integer(X4) :
    NewC is C-X4,
    vvv_eq_c(X1,X2,X3,NewC).
```

5.2.4 The wait algorithm

The fourth algorithm is to compile an n-ary constraint into:

```
delay c(X1,X2,...,Xn):-
    (dvar(X1);dvar(X2);...;dvar(Xn)) :
    {Triggers},
    reduce domains of X1,...,Xn.
c(X1,X2,...,Xn):-true : do the test.
```

The constraint is delayed until it becomes ground. We call this *wait* algorithm. This algorithm is simple and generates linear-size code. However, the code for reducing domains does not take the modes of constraints into account and is thus inefficient.

In the current implementation of delaying, no constraint can be delayed after it becomes ground. In other words, ground constraints will possibly become garbage to be collected by the garbage collector. By taking advantage of this feature, we can simplify the predicate to:

```
delay c(X1,X2,...,Xn):-
    true : {Triggers},
    reduce domains of X1,...,Xn.
```

It does not test the instantiation state of the constraint, but relies on the system to do the test.

6 Experimental Results

All the algorithms described in this paper have been implemented in B-Prolog. In this section, we first compare the performance of the four compilation algorithms and then compare the best one with other three CLP(FD) systems.

Table 1: Comparison of four compilation algorithms (SPARC-2, milliseconds)

Program	Wait	Split1	Split2	Simplify
magic4	33 (1)	83 (2.52)	66 (2.00)	33 (1.00)
eq10	100 (1)	700 (7.00)	665 (6.65)	116 (1.16)
eq20	256 (1)	1466 (5.73)	1950 (7.61)	333 (1.30)
crypta	83 (1)	300 (3.61)	300 (3.61)	83 (1.00)
alpha-ff	167 (1)	400 (2.40)	483 (2.89)	200 (1.20)

6.1 Comparing different compilation algorithms

Table 1 compares the execution time (on a SPARC-2) of the code generated by the four compilation algorithms: `Wait` is the algorithm that delays constraints until they become ground; `Split` is the algorithm that splits n-ary constraints into three-tuple ones; and `Simplify` is the algorithm that incrementally simplifies n-ary constraints into lower degree ones. For `Split`, the two algorithms for compiling small constraints are tested: `Split1` compiles constraints into indexicals and `Split2` compiles constraints into delay predicates. Each program was run five times and the minimal time was taken. There is no big difference between `Split1` and `Split2`. Based on the results, we can rank the algorithms as follows:

Wait > Simplify > Split

The `Wait` algorithm is the best. The generated code by `Wait` is 2 to 7 times as fast as that generated by the `Split` algorithm.

The cost of executing a constraint program comes mainly from three sources: delay-condition tests, domain reduction, and context switching. The `Wait` algorithm is the best in terms of the costs of delay-condition tests and context switching, but the worst in terms of the cost for domain reduction. The `Split` algorithm is the best in terms of the cost for reducing domains because value propagation can be restricted to small constraints as long as the temporary variables that connect them with others do not change. Nevertheless, the `Split` algorithm is the worst in terms of the cost for context switching. For an n-ary constraint, a change to one variable in it may trigger as many as $n-1$ three-tuple constraints in the worst case. The `Simplify` algorithm is better than `Wait` in terms of the cost for reducing domains, but has to pay the cost for passing arguments.

In B-Prolog, all propagation procedures are encoded in Prolog which are compiled to byte code that is interpreted by an emulator. In many systems, propagation procedures for small granularity constraints are written directly in C and are well tuned. If small constraints are handled in the same way, then the results for the `Split` algorithm will certainly become better. However, the same thing can be done to the `Wait` and `Simplify` algorithms. We have noticed that the code for reducing domains involves a lot of arithmetic computations. If it is compiled into C, then a great speed-up is expectable because the overhead of interpreting byte code is gone and the data involved in the computation can be untagged.

Through this experiment, we found that the `Wait` algorithm should be chosen. As a side result, we found that compiling constraints into small granularity ones is not a good idea.

Table 2: Comparison of four systems (SPARC-2)

Program	BP	SICS	clp(FD)	Eclipse
magic4	33 (1)	50 (1.52)	45 (1.36)	233 (7.06)
eq-10	100 (1)	120 (1.20)	80 (0.80)	416 (4.16)
eq-20	256 (1)	200 (0.78)	120 (0.50)	867 (3.39)
crypta	83 (1)	110 (1.33)	80 (0.96)	366 (4.41)
alpha	24,550 (1)	34,600 (1.41)	8,045 (0.33)	201,433 (8.21)
queens-16	914 (1)	2,290 (2.50)	1,553 (1.70)	12,084 (13.22)

6.2 Comparing B-Prolog with three other constraint systems

Table 2 compares the CPU times required to execute the benchmark programs by four systems: B-Prolog[14] version 3.0 (BP), SICStus-Prolog[11] version 3.0 #6 (SICS), clp(FD)[4] version 2.21, and Eclipse [6] version 3.5.2. For all the programs, variables are instantiated in the given order from left to right.

The constraints in `queens-16` are compiled by hand into efficient forms for running in `BP`, `SICS`, and `clp(FD)`. Therefore, this comparison is a little unfair to `Eclipse`. On average, `clp(FD)` is the fastest and `Eclipse` is the slowest system. `BP` and `SICS` lie in between, but `BP` is a little faster than `SICS`.

The systems compared are very different. `clp(FD)` compiles programs into C, `SICS` compiles programs into native code, and `BP` and `Eclipse` are emulated. In addition, `Eclipse` uses a general data structure, called meta-terms, to represent domain variables, while the other three systems use a special data structure for representing domain variables.

The results are very encouraging for us. Except for `eq-20` and `alpha`, `BP` has a comparable performance with `clp(FD)`, the fastest finite-domain constraint solver available now. If constraint propagation procedures are translated into C as done in `clp(FD)`, then a great speed-up is expectable because the overhead of byte-code interpretation and many low-level operations such as tagging and untagging can be eliminated. Therefore, delay-Prolog is not only a good programming language for programming constraint propagation, but also an efficient intermediate language for compiling constraints.

7 Improvements

As we mentioned before, the cost of executing a constraint program comes from mainly three sources: delay-condition tests, domain reduction, and context switching. All these three operations can be optimized.

7.1 Improving domain reduction

The code for reducing domains can become much faster if value propagation is done only when necessary. By profiling program executions of the benchmark programs, we found that more than 80% of the primitives of `X in L..U` are fruitless because the range `L..U` is bigger than or equal to the domain of `X`. To avoid executing this kind of useless primitives, we can do similar things done in the indexical compilation algorithm and split constraints into three-tuple ones by introducing temporary variables and connect these constraints into a loop chain. As long as the connecting variable changes, the code for the next three-tuple constraint in the chain will be executed. For each triggering variable in the constraint, there is a re-entry point that indicates the code of the three-tuple constraint to be executed first when the constraint is triggered by the variable. When registering the constraint into the corresponding constraint list of the triggering variable, we also register the re-entry point.

Let us take the constraint `X+Y+Z #= U` as an example to illustrate the idea. The constraint is split into two small ones: `X+Y #= T` and `T+Z #= U`. Notice here that the temporary variable `T` is not a domain variable. No event happens when temporary variables are updated, and for a temporary variable, we only need to store its low and upper bounds. The code for reducing domains looks like:

```
X_updated: Y in min(T)-max(X)..max(T)-min(X), %X+Y = T
           T in min(X)+min(Y)..max(X)+max(Y),
           if (updated(T)) goto T1_updated else continue,
Y_updated: X in min(T)-max(Y)..max(T)-min(Y),
           T in min(X)+min(Y)..max(X)+max(Y),
           if (updated(T)) goto T1_updated else continue,
T2_updated:X in min(T)-max(Y)..max(T)-min(Y),
           Y in min(T)-max(X)..max(T)-min(X),
           continue,
T1_updated:U in min(T)+min(Z)..max(T)+max(Z), %T+Z = U
           Z in min(U)-max(T)..max(U)-min(T),
           continue,
Z_updated: U in min(T)+min(Z)..max(T)+max(Z),
           T in min(U)-max(Z)..max(U)-min(Z),
           if (updated(T)) goto T2_updated else continue,
U_updated: T in min(U)-max(Z)..max(U)-min(Z),
           Z in min(U)-max(T)..max(U)-min(T),
           if (updated(T)) goto T2_updated else continue.
```

For each variable `V` in the original constraint, the label `V_updated` indicates the re-entry point from where the execution starts when the constraint is triggered by an update of `V`. For each temporary variable `T`, there are two labels that indicate, respectively, the two points to go when the two occurrences of the temporary variable is updated. The code has the advantages of indixicals but does not have the problems because no new domain variables are introduced and the granularity of constraints never become smaller.

7.2 Increasing the granularity of constraints

Increasing the granularity of constraints is an important technique for reducing the number of delay-condition tests and context switching. To do so, we combine multiple constraints and compile them into a bigger propagation procedure.

For several constraints, if they share the same set of variables, then combing them is quite straightforward. Consider, for example, the three constraints taken from the queens program:

```
X #\= Y, X+C #\= Y, X-C #\= Y
```

where `C` is an integer, and `X` and `Y` are domain variables. As the constraints share the same set of variables, they can be compiled as a whole into the following propagation procedure:

```
delay noattack(X,Y,C):-dvar(X),dvar(Y) : {ins(X),ins(Y)}.
noattack(X,Y,C):-dvar(X) :
      exclude(X,Y), exclude(X,Y-C), exclude(X,Y+C).
noattack(X,Y,C):-dvar(Y) :
      exclude(Y,X), exclude(Y,X-C), exclude(Y,X+C).
noattack(X,Y,C):-X=\=Y, X+C=\=Y,X-C=\=Y.
```

When `X` or `Y` is instantiated, context switching is done only once rather than three times, and thus the delay-condition tests against `X` and `Y` need not be done separately three times.

For constraints that do not have the same set of variables but share some variables, we can also increase the granularity by combining them. Let $\overline{X}$, $\overline{Y}$, and $\overline{Z}$ be three disjoint sets of variables. Suppose there are two constraints $c_1(\overline{X},\overline{Y})$ and $c_2(\overline{X},\overline{Z})$. We generate three propagation procedures, one called $p(\overline{X},\overline{Y})$ for c_1 which is triggered only when some change happens to variables in $\overline{Y}$, one called $q(\overline{X},\overline{Z})$ for c_2 which is triggered only when some change happens to variables in $\overline{Z}$, and the third called $pq(\overline{X},\overline{Y},\overline{Z})$ for both c_1 and c_2 which is triggered only when some shared variable in $\overline{X}$ changes. The two constraints is translated into the following three calls:

$$p(\overline{X},\overline{Y}), q(\overline{X},\overline{Z}), pq(\overline{X},\overline{Y},\overline{Z})$$

The procedure $p(\overline{X},\overline{Y})$ is defined as follows:

`delay` $p(\overline{X},\overline{Y})$ `:-`
    `delay condition tests over variables in` $\overline{Y}$ `:`
    `declare variables in` $\overline{Y}$ `as triggering variables,`
    `reduce domains of the variables in` $\overline{X}$ `and` $\overline{Y}$`.`
    ...

The procedure $q(\overline{X},\overline{Z})$ is similar, but only variables in $\overline{Z}$ become triggering variables. The procedure $pq(\overline{X},\overline{Y},\overline{Z})$ is defined as follows:

`delay` $pq(\overline{X},\overline{Y},\overline{Z})$ `:-`
    `delay condition tests over variables in` $\overline{X}$ `:`
    `declare variables in` $\overline{X}$ `as triggering variables,`
    `reduce domains of the variables in` $\overline{X}$, $\overline{Y}$, `and` $\overline{Z}$`.`
    ...

When a shared variable in $\overline{X}$ changes, only the propagator pq will be triggered.

8 Concluding Remarks

we presented a high-level intermediate language, called *delay-Prolog*, for programming constraint propagation and compiling finite-domain constraints. Delay-Prolog has a much stronger description power than indexical and opens new ways to compiling constraints. We tried four compilation algorithms and found that the wait algorithm is the best algorithm and that splitting constraints into small pieces has the worst performance. We also showed that B-Prolog, which employs the wait compilation algorithm, is already comparable in performance with the fastest finite-domain constraint systems available now. We further proposed two techniques for improving the compilation algorithm. A great speed-up of the generated code is expected after the techniques are implemented.

References

[1] Abderrahmane Aggoun and Nicolas Beldiceanu: Overview of the CHIP Compiler System, In *Proceedings of the 8th International Conference on Logic Programming*, pp.775-789, MIT Press, 1991.

[2] Philippe Codognet and Daniel Diaz: Compiling Constraints in clp(FD), *Journal of Logic Programming*, pp.185-226, 1996.

[3] Philippe Codognet and Daniel Diaz: A Simple and Efficient Boolean Solver for Constraint Logic Programming, *Journal of Automated Reasoning*, 17, pp.97-128, 1996.

[4] Daniel Diaz: *clp(FD) 2.21 User's Manual*, INRIA Rocquencourt, 1994.

[5] M. Dincbas, P. Van Hentenryck, H. Simonis, A. Aggoun, T. Graf, and F. Berthier: The Constraint Logic Programming Language CHIP, In *Proceedings of the Fifth Generation Computer Systems*, pp.693-702, ICOT, 1988.

[6] Eclipse 3.5 Extensions User Manual, ECRC Common Logic Programming System, 1995.

[7] Pascal Van Hentenryck: *Constraint Satisfaction in Logic Programming.* MIT Press, 1989.

[8] Pascal Van Hentenryck, Vijay Saraswat, and Yves Deville: Design, Implementation, and Evaluation of the Constraint Language cc(FD), Technical Report No.CS-93-02, Brown University, 1993.

[9] Vipin Kumar: Algorithms for Constraint Satisfaction Problems: A Survey. *AI Magazine*, 32–44, 1992,.

[10] Micha Meier: Better Late Than Never, *Implementations of Logic Programming Systems*, E. Tick and G. Succi, Eds., Kluwer Academic Publishers, 1994.

[11] *SICStus Prolog User's Manual*, Programming Systems Group, Swedish Institute of Computer Science, 1997.

[12] Gert Smolka: Constraint Programming in Oz, *Proc. 1997 International Symposium on Logic Programming*, pp.37-38.

[13] Neng-Fa Zhou: A Novel Implementation Method of Delay. In *Proceedings of Joint International Conference and Symposium on Logic Programming*, pp.97-111, MIT Press, 1996.

[14] Neng-Fa Zhou: *B-Prolog User's Manual, Version 3.0*, Kyushu Institute of Technology, 1998.

Distance: a New Metric for Controlling Granularity for Parallel Execution

Kish Shen*
IC-PARC
Imperial College
SW7 2AZ, U.K.
k.shen@icparc.ic.ac.uk

Vítor Santos Costa
DCC-FC & LIACC,
Univ. do Porto
150 Porto, Portugal
vsc@ncc.up.pt

Andy King
Computing Laboratory
Univ. of Kent
CT2 7NF, U.K
a.m.king@ukc.ac.uk

Abstract

Granularity control is a method to improve parallel execution performance by limiting excessive parallelism. The general idea is that if the gain obtained by executing a task in parallel is less than the overheads required to support parallel execution, then the task is better executed sequentially. Traditionally, in logic programming, task size is estimated as the sequential time-complexity of evaluating the task. Tasks are only executed in parallel if task size exceeds a pre-determined threshold.

We argue in this paper that the estimation of task complexity, on its own, is not an ideal metric for improving the performance of parallel programs through granularity control. We present a new metric for measuring granularity, based on a notion of *distance*. We present some initial results with two very simple methods of using this metric for granularity control. We then discuss how more sophisticated granularity control methods can be devised using the new metric.

1 Introduction

Granularity control is a method to improve parallel execution performance by limiting excessive parallelism. The general idea is that if the gain obtained by executing a task in parallel is less than the overheads required to support parallel execution, then the task is better executed sequentially [6]. Granularity control have been recently applied to Prolog/Logic Programming [18, 9, 8] and to Functional Programming [7]. In logic programs, a "task" is considered to be a goal or an alternative to be executed in parallel, and "useful work" the amount of computation performed to solve the goal or try the alternative. Granularity control in most of these systems thus boils down to a two-phase process. At compile-time, a global analysis system calculates an upper or lower bound on the time-complexity of a potentially parallel goal. At run-time, a pre-determined threshold for time-complexity of the whole task is used to determine if a task is to run in parallel or not: if its time-complexity is less than the threshold, it will not be executed in parallel. Results for small benchmark type programs have shown that these methods can and do increase performance of parallel logic programming systems.

The key motivation for controlling grain size is to reduce overheads. *Direct parallel task execution overheads* correspond to the cost of creating and maintaining a parallel task. These overheads usually include the cost of scheduling the task for parallel execution, the cost of initialising the new parallel task, and hardware related costs such as interprocess communication and locking. Up to a first approx-

*Work carried out while this author was at: Dept. of Computer Science, University of Manchester, Manchester M13 9PL, U.K.

imation, direct overheads are either fixed, such as publishing a task, or proportional to task size, such as the interprocess communication overheads, and are therefore proportional to the goal's time complexity for sizeable tasks. Furthermore, in many systems, as long as there is parallel execution, the direct overheads probably do not usually vary greatly from program to program, so the constant of proportionality would not change greatly between programs. Task size, as estimated by using a goal's time complexity, is therefore a suitable metric for accounting this source of overheads across a wide range of programs.

However, in many parallel systems, including most parallel logic programming systems, tasks can and do create other potentially parallel tasks dynamically. Subtask creation adds to the available parallelism, but it also adds to total overheads, which are not measured by the direct parallel task execution overheads. Instead, these new overheads should be considered a separate class, the *indirect parallel execution overheads*. Indirect overheads can contribute significantly to the total overhead. Indeed, and as shall be discussed later, experimental results from [8] strongly suggest that, at least for those two configurations and programs studied, the major factor for the increase in performance of the programs with granularity control is avoiding the indirect overheads associated with creating largely superfluous parallel work, which the system does not have the resources to exploit.

In contrast to direct overheads, indirect overheads may not be very dependent on the size of the task being executed in parallel and, in addition, may vary greatly from programs to programs. We thus believe that using task size as the metric is not sufficient in general to capture the full complexities of overheads in parallel execution. We would instead prefer a more robust metric, one that is generally applicable, and could apply to cases where it is hard to estimate time-complexity, and to cases where work creation is balanced unevenly.

Towards this goal, we propose in this work a different metric for measuring "granularity", the *distance metric*, defined as the amount of work performed between successive points at which major parallel overheads are incurred. Figure 1 shows this metric, along with the difference from the conventional complexity metric. Figure 1a illustrates a task executing sequentially, without any overheads. Figure 1b shows the conventional view of granularity. The same task is executed in parallel, with initialisation and termination overheads explicit. Moreover, the task itself takes somewhat longer to execute due to run-time parallel overheads. Together these form the direct parallel execution overheads. Figure 1c shows the situation assuming dynamic creation of parallel work. Overheads arise at several points in the execution. These overheads add to the cost of executing the task in parallel, and are unfortunately unaccounted for by the conventional view of granularity control. Note that in the general case these creation points occur at irregular intervals.

Figure 1c also shows the new distance metric. The metric measures distances (amounts of work performed) between points of major parallel overheads, such as parallel work creation, task creation and termination.

The above general description applies to any parallel system in which creation of parallel work incurs overheads. For example, in a conventional parallel programming environment, the parallel work creation overheads might correspond to the creation of a process. With parallel Prolog, for traditional or-parallel systems such as Aurora [10], Muse [1] and PEPSys [2], a task corresponds to the complete execution of a new alternative, and the overhead for creating parallel work

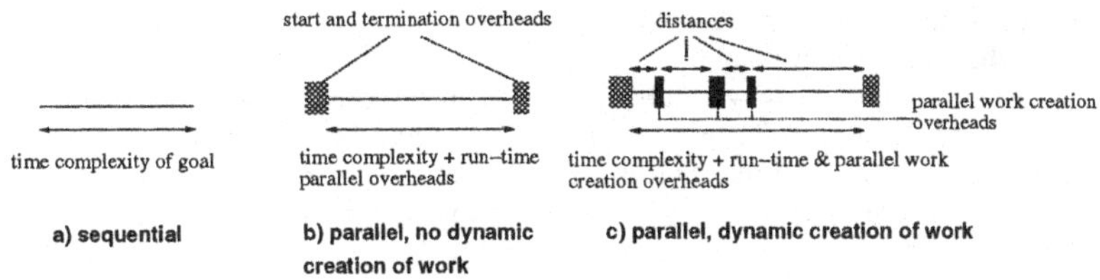

Figure 1: The "Distance" Metric

corresponds to the overhead for creating an or-node which allows or-parallelism to be exploited (sometimes referred to as a branch-node). For independent and-parallel (IAP) systems such as &-Prolog [5] and &ACE [11], a task corresponds to an and-goal, the overhead for creating parallel work corresponds to the overhead of handling CGEs, hence "distance" corresponds to the distance between successive CGEs. For concreteness, in the rest of this paper, we will discuss the issues within the context of IAP. This allows us to use specific examples for illustration and, as we have ready access to an IAP system (the IAP part of DASWAM [12]), this allows us to perform experiments.

There are several important considerations when using the distance metric. Firstly, if the creation of parallel work occurs at irregular intervals directed by the program, then the individual distances between such creation points can vary considerably. Therefore, it should be the *average* distance over the whole program (or over parts of the program in which granularity control is applied) that should be considered.

A second consideration is that, to achieve the best execution time for a particular configuration, the amount of parallelism produced should be just sufficient to keep the processors in the system as busy as possible doing useful work, while minimising the amount of parallel overheads. This is difficult to achieve, as it depends on a large number of factors, many of which cannot be known with high precision before runtime (for example, the ideal amount of parallelism can vary for different queries to the same program [8]). In addition, different sources of parallelism (points where parallel work are created) can lead to very different amounts of parallelism. The point is that for a given average distance, the amount of parallelism that is available can differ significantly, depending on which actual sources are removed. We would want to remove the "worst" sources of parallelism, that is, those that lead to the least amount of parallelism, first.

This ideal is almost certainly impossible to achieve in practice, but a system which seeks to perform close to the ideal would require both run-time and compile-time controls. On the one hand, the "worth" of a particular source of parallelism is only available after the execution of the particular task, not before, when the granularity control system actually needs it. On the other hand, it is impossible to determine at compile-time what the ideal amount of parallelism should be, because the query (and indeed the load and even the configuration of the parallel system) is usually not known. Thus, a good granularity control system should try to determine at run-time the actual amount of parallelism that should be made available, guided by information generated by compile-time analysis as to the best sources of parallelism to make available.

Such a sophisticated system has not yet been designed. However, and as a first step towards using the distance metric for controlling granularity and studying its usefulness, we will consider two simple schemes, one compile-time and the other run-time. These metrics do not take the quality of parallelism into account, i.e. they simply try to increase the distance between *individual* sources of parallelism by removing those sources when distances are considered too small.

The amounts and distributions of the various types of overheads will of course vary with different machines. This will have an impact on granularity control. For example, for distributed non-shared memory machines or networks, the direct parallel execution overheads would be much more significant, and although it is more appropriate to ignore indirect parallel overheads in such cases, using the distance measure is still appropriate as it represents a more accurate picture of the overheads. In addition, it will apply in situations where it is difficult to estimate the complexity of a goal.

2 The New Granularity Control Methods

We next discuss and compare the two simple methods for increasing grain-size as estimated by measuring distances between points of creation of work. The first method uses a simple source-to-source transformation to increase distance between CGEs. The second uses a run-time counter to estimate the distance between CGEs.

2.1 The Compile-Time Method

This method tries to determine the (average) distances between run-time CGEs (the sources of parallelism in a goal-level and-parallel Prolog scheme) at compile-time, and if the distance is too small, it increases the distance by source-to-source transformations that remove CGEs. In many cases, the distance between CGEs can be easier to determine than the time-complexity of a goal: e.g. if no recursive goals are executed sequentially between successive CGEs, as is the case for every example program in [8] except quick-sort, then the distance can simply be calculated by counting the number of resolutions between successive CGEs. As we already stated, we do not believe that these simple methods would lead to the best results, and our interest here is simply to study the effectiveness of distance as a granularity control metric in order to guide our development of more sophisticated methods. Therefore, we would not consider the exact method that would be needed to determine the distance.

To explain the compile-time method, consider first the Boyer benchmark as ported to Prolog by Tick [16]. This program has significant amounts of (non-strict) IAP. Most of the parallelism arises from parallel execution of term rewrite rule, that is a part of the `rewrite_args` procedure (following &-Prolog, & indicates a parallel conjunction):

```
rewrite_args(0,_,_) :- !.
rewrite_args(N,Old,Mid) :-
        arg(N,Old,OldArg),
        arg(N,Mid,MidArg),
```

```
        N1 is N-1,
        (rewrite(OldArg,MidArg0)
          &
         rewrite_args(N1,Old,Mid)),
        MidArg0 = MidArg.
```

Experience has shown that this program has very small granularity by the distance measure, because successive CGEs occur very close together at run-time. This results in a very significant overhead for running Boyer with the parallel annotation on a single worker versus running it without annotations – on the DASWAM running on a Sequent Symmetry, it is 43% slower, the largest such overhead for any IAP program examined in [12]. Moreover, the program is not suitable for the granularity control based on time-complexity analysis as described in [8, 9], because of the difficulties of deriving a relationship between input arguments and the complexity. The distance metric, however, suggests a very simple way to increase the distance, by performing a source-to-source transformation on the program such that and-parallelism is generated only for every second call to `rewrite_args/3`. We show the modification for `rewrite_args`:

```
rewrite_args(0,_,_) :- !.
rewrite_args(N,Old,Mid) :-
        arg(N,Old,OldArg),
        arg(N,Mid,MidArg),
        N1 is N-1,
        (rewrite1(OldArg,MidArg0)
         &
         rewrite_args1(N1,Old,Mid)),
        MidArg0 = MidArg.

rewrite_args1(0,_,_) :- !.
rewrite_args1(N,Old,Mid) :-
        arg(N,Old,OldArg),
        arg(N,Mid,MidArg),
        N1 is N-1,
        rewrite(OldArg,MidArg),
        rewrite_args(N1,Old,Mid).
```

This simple transformation reduces the number of CGEs allocated by half, regardless of what query is run.

2.1.1 Evaluation

To evaluate the impact of this method, we experimented with the original and the transformed program in several parallel machines. The results are shown in Table 1. The '#w' column shows the number of workers for each row. We present results for 'ideal', giving the 'ideal' amount of parallelism as obtained from the DASWAM simulator [12]; 'sun', giving results for a 10 processor SPARCcenter-2000 running Solaris; 'chal' for a 10 processor Silicon Graphics Challenge running IRIX; and 'pc' for a 4 processor PC with 200MHz Pentium Pros, running Linux. The '(g)' column indicates cases with granularity control, and the '(no-g)' without. All times are in seconds. The timings measure the duration from the start of query execution to the production of the (single) solution, and are the best of at least 5 executions. DASWAM is compiled with `gcc` (except for the Challenge, where it was compiled with MIPS' `cc`, because that resulted in faster code), with optimisation turned on. Note the extremely low speedup obtained for 2 workers on the Challenge for the granularity controlled case: this problem seem to be isolated to 2 workers on some programs (note for example the problem does not occur for the non-controlled case) on this particular machine; another SGI Challenge that we have access to (with 4 slower processors) does not appear to have this problem. For the SPARCcenter, there is a known problem with the cache on some of the processors, which results in slower performances when these particular processors are used. Also, we had no control over who else was using the Challenge and the SPARCcenter, and in particular the SPARCcenter was heavily loaded very frequently, and thus the results presented throughout the paper were obtained under varying loads. These factors all have impacts on the results in detail, although we do not believe that they affected the general conclusions we draw. Also, note that we experimented on several parallel machines in order to show that the methods are applicable to different machines, and the purpose is not to make any sort of comparison between the various machines used.

#w	ideal		sun		chal		pc	
	(no-g)	(g)	(no-g)	(g)	(no-g)	(g)	(no-g)	(g)
1	–	–	10.951 (1.00×)	9.034 (1.00×)	6.189 (1.00×)	5.051 (1.00×)	2.494 (1.00×)	2.025 (1.00×)
2	1.99×	1.98×	6.039 (1.81×)	4.787 (1.89×)	3.588 (1.73×)	4.389 (1.15×)	1.354 (1.84×)	1.074 (1.89×)
3	2.98×	2.93×	4.329 (2.53×)	3.466 (2.61×)	2.514 (2.46×)	1.955 (2.58×)	0.971 (2.57×)	0.777 (2.63×)
4	3.95×	3.85×	3.276 (3.34×)	2.862 (3.16×)	1.959 (3.16×)	1.547 (3.27×)	0.799 (3.12×)	0.608 (3.33×)
5	4.92×	4.74×	2.804 (3.91×)	2.251 (4.01×)	1.641 (3.77×)	1.312 (3.85×)		
6	5.87×	5.58×	2.426 (4.51×)	1.978 (4.57×)	1.436 (4.31×)	1.151 (4.39×)		
7	6.82×	6.39×	2.088 (5.25×)	1.811 (4.99×)	1.285 (4.82×)	1.064 (4.75×)		
8	7.76×	7.16×	1.997 (5.48×)	1.660 (5.44×)	1.187 (5.21×)	0.976 (5.18×)		
9	8.69×	7.86×	1.823 (6.01×)	1.574 (5.74×)	1.112 (5.57×)	0.928 (5.44×)		
10	9.60×	8.58×	1.732 (6.32×)	1.537 (5.88×)	1.020 (6.07×)	0.894 (5.65×)		

Table 1: Compile-time granularity control results for Boyer

Granularity control is effective if it gives better performances than the non-granularity controlled program. The ideal columns show that, as expected, granularity control reduces the amount of available parallelism. Thus, in the absence of overheads, performance should be better without granularity control. Instead, the results show that this form of granularity control gives better execution times, and is indeed effective in all cases. The main component that leads to the increased performance is clearly the removal of parallel creation overheads, as shown by the difference in performances between the one worker cases with and without control. Even so, and for all these systems, the *speedup* (which is relative to their respective one worker case) is better for the lower number of workers for the granularity controlled cases. The better speedups show that the granularity control was able not only to remove the parallel creation overheads (cost of allocating CGEs), but also some direct parallel task execution overheads, especially for the faster machines.

The major weakness of this method is that the reduction in parallelism can become quite significant with larger numbers of workers. It should be possible to achieve better performance if a more selective way is found to remove CGEs, but this would need some form of analysis (at compile-time) to determine the 'worth' of the CGEs. In addition, the method is quite a blunt instrument in that it applies to all CGEs, thus not allowing any form of control at the individual CGE level. Finally, this purely compile-time transformation does not take into account run-time situations: for example, with smaller number of workers, better results can be achieved by producing less CGEs.

The example for boyer transformed the program to create and not create CGEs alternately, thus reducing the number of CGEs generated at run-time by about half. One can of course reduce the numbers of CGEs by a greater or lesser amount by transforming the program to generate CGEs more or less often.

2.2 The Run-Time Method

This second granularity control method uses a simple counter in order to decide whether a CGE should be allocated or not. The counter measures the work done since the last CGE was allocated. If its value is below a pre-determined threshold, then the new CGE would not be allocated, and the goals in the CGE will be run sequentially instead. Conceptually, this method can be thought of as:

```
(above_threshold(Counter) -> reset(Counter), g1(...) & ... gn(...)
                            ; g1(...), ... gn(...))
```

The actual implementation of this method is at the abstract machine level. Due to lack of space, details of this scheme will not be given here. The reader is referred to [14] for a discussion of the implementation. The key idea is that, instead of counting unifications as a measure of work, we count the number of abstract machine instructions. The threshold is set by special abstract machine instructions which would be supplied at compile-time. The scheme is supported at a very low level, and the overheads for using the scheme are not high. In fact even for the (near) worst case of boyer where the threshold is 0, giving a very short distance between CGEs, the total overhead was only about 2%.

One more thing to be noted is that in parallel execution the number of CGEs that will be sequentialised is non-determinate for a given threshold. This is due to the fact that the threshold is counted from the start of a new and-goal. The goals which are selected for parallel execution can vary, and hence the distance and the number of sequentialised CGEs can also vary. Our results suggest that this variation is relatively small, and that as more tasks are actually executed in parallel, the number of sequentialised CGE would increase slightly.

2.2.1 Performance

Table 2 shows the results of using the runtime method on boyer, with the threshold set at 64, 80, and 96 abstract machine instructions. These particular thresholds were chosen because the implementation allowed the threshold to be set in increments of 16 units only. Again, the results are the best timings of at least 5 runs. The system was run on the 10 processor SGI Challenge. The numbers in brackets in the one worker case are the number of CGEs in each of the one worker case. The bracketed numbers in the other cases are the speedups relative to their respective one worker case.

As the machine was loaded at the time the experiments were performed, no results were gathered beyond 7 workers, because the system did not have the resources to allow DASWAM to utilize these processors. The results for no_gran, the case with no granularity, is taken from the experiment with the compile-time method presented in Table 1, when the machine was not busy. Thus, the results should favour no_gran. The results for 2 workers are not included because of the same problem as discussed previously.

#w	no_gran	64	80	96
1	6189 (94056)	5456 (48511)	5370 (44104)	5040 (32230)
3	2514 (2.46×)	2158 (2.53×)	2099 (2.56×)	1920 (2.63×)
4	1959 (3.16×)	1717 (3.18×)	1651 (3.25×)	1514 (3.33×)
5	1641 (3.77×)	1492 (3.66×)	1444 (3.72×)	1301 (3.87×)
6	1436 (4.31×)	1347 (4.05×)	1292 (4.16×)	1168 (4.32×)
7	1285 (4.82×)	1242 (4.39×)	1190 (4.51×)	1083 (4.65×)

Table 2: Run-time granularity control for boyer

Even with a bias towards no_gran, the results shows that the granularity control can improve the performance. Base speed (performance on one worker) improves, as one would expect. Speedups are quite close to the no_gran version. Interestingly, the improvements becomes greater with the higher thresholds, probably indicating that more direct parallel execution overheads were being reduced. Further experiments with even larger thresholds are necessary.

#w	no_gran	96
1	7893 (2100)	8034 (2100)
2	4062 (1.94×)	4074 (1.97×)
4	2035 (3.88×)	2063 (3.89×)
8	1053 (7.50×)	1060 (7.58×)
10	835 (9.45×)	859 (9.35×)

Table 3: Run-time granularity control for orsim

Table 3 shows a worst-case program for traditional granularity analysis. The program is orsim [15, 13]. This is quite a complex program that is very difficult to analyse. The program has quite high granularity, hence does not need granularity control. We obtained the results on a the SGI Challenge when it was lightly loaded. Times are in milliseconds, and are again the best of at least 5 timings. One advantage of the run-time method is that it does not require any analysis, and the overhead of using it is very small, so that in this case where no CGEs are sequentialised, the performance of the program with granularity control is quite close to the original performance.

3 Discussion

The average distance between CGEs is a good metric to explain the effectiveness of granularity analysis on programs such as boyer, as studied in [8]. Table 4 shows the average distances for these programs with no granularity control as a function of abstract machine instructions: i.e. the average number of instructions executed per CGE.

prog	Σinst	ΣCGE	av. distance
boyer	5106759	94056	**54.3**
hanoi(10)	47083	1023	**46.0**
hanoi(16)	3014635	65535	**46.0**
fib(17)	95593	2583	**37.0**
fib(19)	250290	6764	**37.0**
qs(300)	55452	300	**184.9**
qs(3200)	823168	3200	**257.2**
orsim	9069226	1200	**7557.7**

Table 4: Average distances

The average distances clearly show that all the programs except quick-sort and orsim have very small average distances: there are only about 3 to 5 unifications between each CGE (using the approximation that each unification approximately corresponds to 10 abstract machine instructions). We would expect that in these cases granularity control would be very effective in reducing the parallel overheads. On the other hand, we would expect that granularity control to be less effective for quick-sort. This is indeed the case from experimental results [8, 9].

The reason that quick-sort, running in IAP, has a large average distance is because the partition predicate is executed between successive CGEs:

```
qsort([], Rest, Rest).
qsort([X|Unsorted], Sorted, Rest) :-
   partition(Unsorted, X, Smaller, Larger),
   (qsort(Smaller, Sorted, [X|Sorted1]) &
    qsort(Larger, Sorted2, Rest)),
   Sorted2 = Sorted1.
```

The partition predicate is recursive and does not contain any CGEs. Analysis should be able to determine that it is likely that this predicate will perform a significant amount of work, thus making the distance between CGEs large on average. Such an analysis would decide not to add compile-time granularity control in this case.

It is interesting to compare the new methods with granularity-based approaches. Tables 5, 6 and 7 show the effect of the using granularity controls on qs(3200), hanoi(16), and fib(23) respectively. The programs are taken from [8], with 23 used as the parameter for fib to get results that would take over a second to execute on the Challenge. The results are again in milliseconds, the best of at least 5 executions. The qs(3200) query was performed on a 10 processor Sequent Symmetry, while hanoi(16) and fib(23) were performed on the SGI Challenge. We present the compile-time and run-time control methods, along with the traditional complexity threshold methods. The results for the complexity threshold method of qs(3200) are taken from [8], and are average timings, rather than the best times, but in the context of these experiments, the differences from best times are small. For the run-time control method, thresholds of 64, 80 and 96 abstract machine instructions were used. These are shown in the column with the threshold as the headings. The 'compile-time' columns are for the program transformed to call CGE only on alternate recursive calls, which reduces the CGEs by half for qs(3200) and fib(23), and by two-thirds for hanoi(16). The reduction is two-thirds for hanoi(16) because many of the calls terminates in the base case, and generate no CGEs. The results for the complexity method are show in the columns with headings of size(X), where X is the size threshold, measured in resolution steps.

The programs have quite different characteristics. As explained before, qs(3200) has a high average distance, and relatively low parallelism. The hanoi(16) and fib(23) queries have very low average distances and significant parallelism. The size of the two goals that are run in parallel in a CGE are identical for hanoi(16), but are slightly less well balanced for fib(23), where one goal is about 60% larger than the other. Another difference is that CGEs occurs regularly and at constant distances for hanoi(16) and fib(23), but irregularly for quick-sort. Note that although the compile-time transformation was applied to quick-sort, in actual use, no control would be applied because the analysis would have concluded that the average distance is sufficiently large and the query does not need granularity control. The results are presented here mainly to show the effect of an inappropriate application of the method.

We shall first discuss and compare the results obtained from the two new methods, and then compare them to the more traditional complexity-based approach.

3.1 Run-Time versus Compile-Time Methods

Table 5 shows the results for quick-sort. The run-time control removes some CGEs resulting in slight improvement in execution times for one worker. These differences are not very significant, because the original average distance was relatively large. In addition, and because in this benchmark CGEs occurs between recursive partitions of the list, each successive CGE distance must be smaller than the last (because smaller and smaller lists are partitioned). Sequentialising CGEs with small distances therefore removes those CGEs that result in small tasks, and does not significantly affect the available parallelism, and so the speedups were only reduced very slightly. When compared to no_gran, the slight reduction of speedups with run_time control tends to cancel out the slight decrease in overhead, but nevertheless, small improvements were still being obtained up to the 9 workers.

#w	no_gran	64	80	96	compile-time	size(16)	size(64)
1	13486 (3200)	13377 (2462)	13298 (2093)	13232 (1724)	13035 (1601)	14084 (2093)	13197 (557)
2	7453 (1.81×)	7399 (1.81×)	7376 (1.80×)	7364 (1.80×)	8151 (1.60×)	7701 (1.83×)	7338 (2.77×)
4	4818 (2.80×)	4767 (2.83×)	4762 (2.79×)	4818 (2.75×)	7091 (1.83×)	4926 (2.86×)	4772 (2.77×)
9	3722 (3.62×)	3699 (3.62×)	3703 (3.59×)	3698 (3.58×)	6988 (1.87×)	3767 (3.74×)	3742 (3.53×)

Table 5: Granularity control for qs(3200) on a Sequent

On the other hand, the compile-time approach shows that an inappropriate application of the CGE removal transformation can have negative impact on the performance. In fact, the speedup was greatly reduced, and the parallel performance is significantly worse than the other cases. Another point illustrated by the results is the importance of removing the right CGEs. Whereas the number of CGEs for the 96 run-time threshold case is only slightly more than the compile-time transformation case, the speedup obtained from the 96 threshold case is significantly better, because only the CGEs that produced the least parallelism were removed. A final point to note about the results is that the one worker case for the compile-time transformation are noticeably better than the other cases. We believe this is because the compile-time transformation carries no run-time overheads as the parallelism is removed at compile-time.

#w	no_gran	64	80	96	compile-time	size(16)	size(256)
1	2745 (65535)	2325 (34952)	2190 (26760)	2073 (21536)	1857 (21845)	1646 (8191)	1374 (256)
2	1671 (1.64×)	1276 (1.82×)	1176 (1.86×)	1097 (1.89×)	1012 (1.83×)	836 (1.97×)	676 (2.03×)
4	939 (2.92×)	703 (3.31×)	637 (3.44×)	591 (3.51×)	542 (3.43×)	434 (3.79×)	338 (4.07×)
9	567 (4.84×)	376 (6.18×)	337 (6.50×)	313 (6.62×)	278 (6.68×)	201 (8.19×)	157 (8.75×)

Table 6: Granularity control for hanoi(16) on a SGI Challenge

Table 6 shows results for the hanoi(16) query. Both compile-time and run-time methods were effective in increasing execution efficiency and, in fact, their improvements are quite significant. Part of this can be attributed to the use of the Challenge, which is a much faster machine than the Sequent, and therefore the parallel execution overheads are more significant. The compile-time method is more effective in this case, because again there is less overhead to pay for using the compile-time control.

#w	no_gran	64	80	96	compile-time	size(16)	size(1024)
1	1939 (46367)	1578 (20735)	1355 (14674)	1303 (13928)	1586 (23184)	1379 (10945)	945 (232)
2	1190 (1.63×)	820 (1.92×)	732 (1.85×)	710 (1.84×)	870 (1.82×)	722 (1.91×)	474 (1.99×)
4	671 (2.89×)	446 (3.54×)	391 (3.47×)	387 (3.37×)	463 (3.43×)	376 (3.67×)	235 (4.02×)
9	405 (4.79×)	254 (6.21×)	265 (5.11×)	282 (4.62×)	251 (6.32×)	179 (7.70×)	107 (8.83×)

Table 7: Granularity control for fib(23) on a SGI Challenge

The results for the Fib benchmark, as shown in Table 7, are similar to the ones for Hanoi, although the increase in performance is somewhat less, and the reduction in speedups is more marked, especially when the distance threshold is set high. The result is that the best run-time method performance for 9 workers is obtained for the lowest threshold value of 64, although the performance is better in the higher thresholds for smaller number of workers. The compile-time method removes slightly less CGEs than the 64 threshold case. Performance in terms of speedups and actual execution times are similar, although again the performance on one worker is slightly better in the compile-time method, even though it retains somewhat more parallel CGEs. At least for these cases where CGEs occurs regularly, neither the compile-time nor run-time methods are better at removing the "right" CGEs.

3.2 Distance-Based versus Task Complexity-Based Methods

We have seen that choosing the "right" CGEs can have very profound impact on how many CGEs can be removed without decreasing parallel speedups. The results obtained for the task complexity granularity method illustrates this point even more dramatically: there has been a great reduction in the number of parallel CGEs in all three programs (but most especially for Hanoi), but the resulting speedups are not greatly affected. Our previous results [8] on using task complexity analysis for granularity control illustrates this point for a larger set of programs and query sizes.

size	fib(17)	fib(19)	hanoi(10)	hanoi(16)	qs(300)	qs(3000)
0	2583 (8.4×)	6764 (8.7×)	47083 (8.3×)	65535 (8.9×)	300 (3.3×)	3200 (3.6×)
16	986 (8.4×)	4180 (8.7×)	127 (8.2×)	8191 (9.0×)	124 (3.3×)	2093 (3.7×)
64	376 (8.5×)	986 (8.7×)	31 (7.7×)	2047 (8.9×)	63 (3.2×)	557 (3.5×)
256	88 (8.4×)	232 (8.7×)	7 (7.6×)	511 (9.0×)		
1024	20 (6.8×)	54 (8.1×)	1 (2.0×)	127 (8.6×)		

Table 8: Number of CGEs with task complexity granularity control

Table 8 shows the number of CGEs remaining after performing the task complexity granularity control with the various granularity thresholds for the various programs. The mean speedup obtained for 9 workers on a Sequent Symmetry is shown in brackets. The results again show that although the number of CGEs was drastically reduced, in most cases the available parallelism is not greatly reduced. This is because the CGEs that are removed are the ones that do not contribute much extra parallelism with the relatively small number of workers used. However, results for the hanoi(10) query show that this is not always the case: if the parallelism is constrained to be less than what the processor resource can exploit, there can be a dramatic effect on the speedup. This again illustrates the importance of run-time considerations. As the query is not known at compile-time, run-time information is needed to ensure good performances in these cases.

The reason for the much better performance of the task complexity based method than the two distance methods for the Hanoi and Fib benchmark can be attributed to the great reduction in CGEs with granularity control. These two programs are ideal for the task complexity method because the and-goals in the CGEs are highly recursive and the two goals in each CGE would both lead to significant parallelism if they are sufficiently large. In addition, the distances between successive CGEs are very small. Thus, using even small complexity thresholds, a very large number of CGEs are removed, and those are precisely the CGEs which lead to least parallelism. Very few CGEs are needed to keep the workers busy, because the parallel tasks are large and well balanced in size. Thus, even though CGEs were not considered by the method, nevertheless a "side-effect" is the removal of many less useful CGEs. However, because CGEs are not directly considered, this method would not work as well for several classes of programs, such as programs with other distributions of CGEs, for example where the sizes of the goals in a CGE are less well balanced, or programs where the average distance is larger, as it is the case for quick-sort. In this case, although the proportion of removed CGEs for the 16 and 64 resolution steps are similar to the Fib benchmark, the positive impact is much less. In fact, there was a negative impact on the 16 resolution steps threshold case, because the gain from reducing CGEs cannot compensate the cost of the relatively expensive list length threshold test.

A different problem with using the task complexity threshold is that it relies on being able to derive a relationship between the input arguments' sizes and the resulting task complexity. Such a relationship does not always exist, and in cases where it does, it may not always be easy to derive. Even where it can be estimated, we have seen it might require relatively large run-time overheads to determine the size parameter, as in the case for quick-sort.

4 Improvements and Extensions

The quick-sort example showed a situation where the compile-time method (when applied blindly) performed worse than the run-time method because it removed "good" CGEs. There are cases where the run-time method can also remove "good" CGEs. As an example, consider the case where, early in the execution, a program creates several pieces of parallel work of significant size in quick succession, and then stops creating parallel work. In this case (which does occur in the bt_cluster benchmark first used by Andorra-I [17]), the actual distances between each CGE will be short, but the average distance (defined as the ratio of total work per number of CGEs) would be much larger. The CGEs should therefore not be sequentialised.

This situation illustrates a weakness of any purely run-time scheme. These methods cannot look ahead into what may happen further into the execution. In this case, when and where new CGEs will be created, and how much parallelism they might provide. Of course, more sophisticated run-time systems than the very simple counter method can be designed, for example, systems which takes into account if the workers are currently busy or not; and heuristics based on the execution history to try and anticipate future behaviour [4]. For example, a more sophisticated run-time scheme can only start to sequentialise CGEs when all the workers are busy *and* the distance is below the threshold. However, and as we have seen even for the simple scheme presented here, any run-time scheme does carry some overheads: the more sophisticated the scheme, the more expensive the overhead. In the end, run-time systems will always suffer from not having specific information about the execution still to come. This information can only be provided by compile-time analysis. On the other hand, a compile-time only method cannot take into account run-time conditions such as the load of the machine, and furthermore there will probably always be programs that cannot be analysed.

The ideal distance also needs to be adjusted for different parallel systems and machines, as system architecture would affect the relative importance of various sources of overheads. In fact, distributed network systems, where Debray et al. [3] have recently shown some promising results with task complexity-based granularity control, would require larger average distances than shared-memory machines in order to obtain performance improvements. Moreover, the penalty for parallelising the "wrong" CGE may be very high, suggesting that they may require more sophisticated distance granularity control schemes than the two we presented here. We believe that the notion of distance, under the appropriate granularity control scheme, will be a suitable basis for novel granularity control methods.

We would also like to extend granularity analysis to dependent and-parallelism. In a previous working paper [14], we described some initial experimentations with DAP granularity control. Our results showed that granularity control for DAP is more complicated than for IAP. the definition of distance needs to be modified to take into account such overheads as task suspension and, in addition, the actual time a task spends suspended would also need to be considered.

5 Conclusions

In this paper, we presented a new metric — distances between sources of parallelism — for measuring granularity, and explained how this metric can be used to control granularity to improve parallel execution performance. We presented results for two very simple schemes that make use of this metric, one run-time based and the other compile-time based. Results show that the new metric is quite promising. In fact, the two distance-based methods were able to obtain significant performance improvements in complex programs that are hard to improve with traditional, task complexity based, systems. Initial results suggest that even the simple run-time method can obtain surprisingly good performance for some of the benchmarks, even though no consideration has been given to the "worth" of CGEs being sequentialised. On the other hand, better performance requires compile-time analysis in order to remove the "correct" CGEs. This point was demonstrated by the fact that a task complexity based system could outperform the new methods for benchmarks that create parallelism regularly, frequently, and have well balanced parallel tasks, as in such cases it was able to greatly increase the average distance through removing the "correct" CGEs.

We believe that to fully make use of this distance metric, combined run-time and compile-time granularity control scheme will be needed. Hard problems are still open, such as how to best set thresholds, how to more efficiently combine run-time and compile-time techniques, how to combine the task complexity based and the distance based metrics, and how to use these principles to improve execution for other parallel systems. We are actively researching ways to achieve these goals.

Acknowledgements

The authors would like to acknowledge and thank for the contribution and support that Manuel V. Hermenegildo and Pedro López-García gave to this work, including the use of several multiprocessors. Kish Shen would like to thank the department of Computer Scinece at Manchester for the use of their computer facilities and office space after the end of his employment there. Vítor Santos Costa has been supported by the PRAXIS PROLOPPE project, the JNICT MELODIA project, and by the NATO MAPLE project.

References

[1] K. A. M. Ali and R. Karlsson. The Muse Approach to Or-Parallel Prolog. Technical Report SICS/R-90/R9009, Swedish Institute of Computer Science, 1990.

[2] U. C. Baron, J. Chassin de Kergommeaux, M. Hailperin, M. Ratcliffe, P. Robert, J.-C. Syre, and H. Westphal. The Parallel ECRC Prolog System PEPSys: An Overview and Evaluation Results. In *Proceedings of the International Conference on Fifth Generation Computer Systems 1988, Volume 3*, pages 841–850, 1988.

[3] S. K. Debray, P. López-García, and M. V. Hermenegildo. Lower Bound Cost Estimation for Logic Programs. In J. Małuszyński, editor, *Logic Programming: Proceedings of the 1997 International Symposium*, pages 291–306. The MIT Press, 1997.

[4] I. Dutra. Strategies for Scheduling And and Or Work in Parallel Logic Programming Systems. In *Logic Programming: Proceedings of 1994 Internation Symposium*. The MIT Press, 1994.

[5] M. V. Hermenegildo and K. J. Green. &-Prolog and its Performance: Exploiting Independent And-Parallelism. In D. H. D. Warren and P. Szeredi, editors, *Logic Programming: Proceedings of the Seventh International Conference*, pages 253–268. The MIT Press, 1990.

[6] R. W. Hockney and C. R. Jesshope. *Parallel Computers 2*. Adam Hilger, 1988.

[7] L. Huelsbergen, J. R. Larus, and A. Aiken. Using the Run-Time Sizes of Data Structures to Guide Parallel-Thread Creation. In *LFP'94*. ACM Press, 1994.

[8] A. King, K. Shen, and F. Benoy. Lower-bound Time-complexity Analysis of Logic Programs. In J. Małuszyński, editor, *Logic Programming: Proceedings of the 1997 International Symposium*, pages 261–276. The MIT Press, 1997.

[9] P. López-García, M. V. Hermenegildo, and S. K. Debray. A Methodology for Granularity Based Control of Parallelism in Logic Programs. *Journal of Symbolic Computing, Special Issue on Parallel Symbolic Computation*, 11(3–4):217–242, 1996.

[10] E. L. Lusk, R. Butler, T. Disz, R. Olson, R. A. Overbeek, R. Stevens, D. H. D. Warren, A. Calderwood, P. Szeredi, S. Haridi, P. Brand, M. Carlsson, A. Ciepielewski, and B. Hausman. The Aurora Or-Parallel Prolog System. In *Proceedings of the International Conference on Fifth Generation Computer Systems 1988, Vol. 3*, pages 819–830. Institute for New Generation Computer Technology, 1988.

[11] E. Pontelli, G. Gupta, and M. Hermenegildo. &ACE: A High-Performance Parallel Prolog System. In *International Parallel Processing Symposium*. IEEE Computer Society Technical Committee on Parallel Processing, IEEE Computer Society, April 1995.

[12] K. Shen. Overview of DASWAM: Exploitation of Dependent And-parallelism. *Journal of Logic Programming*, 29(1–3):245–293, Oct.–Dec. 1996.

[13] K. Shen and M. V. Hermenegildo. A Simulation Study of Or- and Independent And-parallelism. In V. Saraswat and K. Ueda, editors, *Logic Programming: Proceedings of 1991 International Symposium*, pages 135–151. The MIT Press, 1991.

[14] K. Shen, V. Santos Costa, and A. King. A New Metric for Controlling Granularity for Parallel Execution. In *1997 Post ILPS Workshop on Parallelism and Implementation Technology for (Constraint) Logic Programming*, 1997.

[15] K. Shen and D. H. D. Warren. A Simulation Study of the Argonne Model for Or-Parallel Execution of Prolog. In *Proceedings of the Fourth Symposium on Logic Programming*. Computer Society Press of the IEEE, Sept. 1987.

[16] E. Tick. Memory Performance of Lisp and Prolog Programs. In E. Shapiro, editor, *Third International Conference on Logic Programming*, pages 642–649. Springer-Verlag, 1986. Published as Lecture Notes in Computer Science 225.

[17] R. Yang, A. J. Beaumont, I. Dutra, V. Santos Costa, and D. H. D. Warren. Performance of the Compiler-based Andorra-I System. Technical report, Department of Computer Science, University of Bristol, 1993.

[18] X. Zhong, E. Tick, S. Duvvuru, L. Hansen, A. V. S. Sastry, and R. Sundararajan. Towards an Efficient Compile-Time Granularity Analysis Algorithm. In *Proceedings of the International Conference on Fifth Generation Computer Systems 1992, Volume 2*, pages 809–816. Institute for New Generation Computing, June 1992.

VisAll: A Universal Tool to Visualise the Parallel Execution of Logic Programs

Nuno Fonseca and Vítor Santos Costa
LIACC and DCC/FCUP
Porto, Portugal
{nf,vsc}@oat.ncc.up.pt

Inês de Castro Dutra
COPPE Sistemas/UFRJ
Rio de Janeiro, Brasil
ines@cos.ufrj.br

Abstract

One of the most important advantages of logic programming systems is that they allow the transparent exploitation of parallelism. The different forms of parallelism available and the complex nature of logic programming applications present interesting problems to both the users and the developers of these systems. Graphical visualisation tools can give a particularly important contribution, as they are easier to understand than text based tools, and allow both for a general overview of an execution and for focusing on its important details.

Towards these goals, we propose *VisAll*, a new tool to visualise the parallel execution of logic programs. VisAll benefits from a modular design centered in a graph that represents a parallel execution. A main graphical shell commands the different modules and presents VisAll as an unified system. Several input components, or translators, support the well-known VisAndor and VACE trace formats, plus a new format designed for independent and-parallel plus or-parallel execution in the SBA. Several output components, or visualisers, allow for different visualisations of the same execution.

1 Introduction

One of the most important advantages of logic programming systems is that they allow the transparent exploitation of parallelism. Several forms of parallelism can be exploited in logic programming systems. The major forms are or-parallelism (ORP), independent and-parallelism (IAP) and dependent and-parallelism (DAP). IAP was exploited in systems such as &-Prolog [11] and &-Ace [10, 9], ORP in systems such as Aurora [12] and Muse [1], and DAP in systems such as KLIC [20], Parlog [3], and DASWAM [18]. More recently, parallel logic programming systems have been developed to exploit a combination of these forms of parallelism. These include Andorra-I [16], ACE [9], SBA [2], Penny [13], ParAKL [14] and the EAM [22]. These systems have demonstrated the usefulness of parallel logic programming for non-trivial applications.

The different forms of parallelism available and the complex nature of logic programming applications present interesting problems to both the users and the developers of these systems. From the developer's point of view, designing and implementing a parallel logic programming system is a complex task. In order to obtain a correct and efficient implementation one must address problems such as synchronisation and dynamic distribution of varied sized work among processors. Moreover, debugging parallel programs is not simple. These are complex systems operating on a parallel environment where the response time is non-deterministic due to the interference of operating system operations. And even when the system is found to be working correctly, it may not perform well.

The evolution of parallel logic programming research and the more sophisticated computer architecture models further amplify these problems.

In order to alleviate the developers job, parallel systems must provide a set of tools that can utilise data extracted from execution (actual or simulated) and present it in a form that allows for qualitative reasoning. Graphical visualisation tools can give a particularly important contribution, as they are easier to understand than text based tools, and allow both for a general overview of an execution and for focusing on its important details.

It is therefore unsurprising that since early on most parallel logic programming systems have included a related visualisation tool. Examples include Aurora and WAMtrace [5], Muse and Must [19], &-Prolog and Visandor [7], or ACE and VACE [21]. These systems have been very important in the development of parallel logic programming.

The aim of this work is to design a general visualisation tool that addresses the problems mentioned thus far. We would like (i) to support the visualisation of all kinds of parallelism in logic programming, and (ii) to support different visualisation paradigms in the same framework. The resulting system should not be overly dependent on functionality from a single technology, such as a graphical toolkit, and should not depend on a specific parallel system.

We propose *VisAll*, as a *flexible* and *universal* visualisation tool that achieves these goals. To do so, VisAll relies on a simple idea, *the representation of parallel execution as a graph*. This graph is the cornerstone of the system.

VisAll is the subject of this paper. We first present the general structure of the system. Next we concentrate on the main implementation issues, concerning the structure and characteristics of the execution graph, how to design the filters that translate from external formats, and what visualisation paradigms are currently supported. We next present some examples of VisAll visualisation, comparing them throughout with other well-known visualisation tools. Finally, we give the conclusions and discuss future work.

2 System Design

VisAll was initially designed as a tool to support the development and the utilisation of the SBA [2], a parallel logic programming system that exploits both IAP and

ORP. The SBA is a system in continuous development, and soon it became clear that the visualiser would require extensibility as new components of the SBA are being developed and introduced to the system. Moreover, our experience with other systems motivated us in designing VisAll to be an universal system, one that should be used with both previous and novel parallel logic programming systems.

In order to obtain a general and flexible system, VisAll is based on the key idea of an *event graph*. VisAll assumes that the input to the visualisation process is a *trace-file*, consisting of a sequence of *events*. Each event includes a *timestamp*. One can say that the events form a graph, where edges represent direct dependencies between events. Usually, this graph of events is a directed acyclic graph.

VisAll makes no assumptions regarding how events were generated. Events may have been generated by actual execution on a parallel system, or by execution on some simulator, and we have in fact used trace-files originating from both forms of execution. As most other visualisers, the current VisAll implementation works off-line, meaning that it does assume execution has completed and the trace-file is closed when the visualisation process starts. With current technology, off-line execution is necessary for detailed and accurate visualisation.

VisAll does not impose any specific trace format for visualisation. On the contrary, from early on it became clear that VisAll would only benefit if it would understand the common trace formats, such as VisAndor's or VACE's format. To do so, we separate between an external trace-file, with the events generated by the system, and the internal representation. Internal nodes and events have semantics that are understood by the *visualisers*. *Translators*, or filters, translate from an external trace format to this internal graph representation.

One should remark that in general, and for completeness sake, we would prefer for the internal representation to be at least as general as any external representation accepted by the system. By doing so we never lose information. Alternatively, one could accept more general external trace formats and only process a projection that can be understood by VisAll.

A main graphical program commands the visualisers. The system has been designed to present a simple interaction to external users, and presents itself as a single, integrated, system. The *event configurer* currently allows users to associate symbols with events.

We next describe the individual components in detail.

2.1 The Structure of the Graph

The major VisAll component is the graph representing execution. This graph representation is generated from a trace-file format. An example of a trace format used to visualise the SBA execution is shown in Table 1. This format is based on the VisAndOr format [7], one of the most popular for parallel logic programming.

Each node contains information on **(i)** the timestamp, ie., the point in time where the node was generated; **(ii)**, an event code, that determines the type of the node; **(iii)**, a unique identifier; **(iv)** an or-branch number corresponding to an edge connecting the node to the node that started the current or-branch, for ORP

TS	Ev	NId	Br#	C-Node	#Goals	CGE#	goal#	PID	Info

Table 1: The SBA node format

support; **(v)**, a C-Node number for the support of the recomputation based models for ORP/IAP [8]; **(vi)**, the number of and-parallel goals from the current CGE (Conditional Graph Expression representing a conjunction that can be executed in parallel [4]); **(vii)**, a CGE-number connecting the node to the parent CGE, for the support of IAP; **(viii)**, a goal number connecting the node to the CGE branch, also for support of IAP; **(ix)**, a worker id, corresponding to the worker (or agent, or processor) that generated the event; and **(x)**, a fragment of text with information on the node. This fragment of text can contain information such as the name of a goal, the number of goals in a CGE, or the reason for a worker to have chosen a certain alternative.

Note that this format generalises the VisAndOr format in that it includes (1) new fields to visualise icons related to new forms of parallelism (**v** to support ORP/IAP); and (2) a string field used to store source program information or the behaviour of the parallel system (field **x**).

Event	Description
Start Time	Start the execution of a program
End Time	End the execution of a program
Create C-Node	C-Node was created (to support IAP)
Create CGE	New alternative to C-Node (to support IAP)
Start Goal	Parallel goal started execution
Finish Goal	Parallel goal completed
Join	Parallel conjunction completed (to support IAP)
Start_Busy	Worker joins a new team (to support dyn. sch.)
Stop_Busy	Worker leaves its team (to support dyn. sch.)
Make Public	Or-node available to other teams (to support ORP)
Start Branch	Branch in or-node taken (to support ORP)
Succ Branch	Branch finished successfully (to support ORP)
Suspend Branch	Team left non-completed branch (to support ORP)
Resume Branch	Team returns to completed branch (to support ORP)

Table 2: Main SBA Events

The event code field is particularly important in that it describes the type of event to visualise. The main events for the SBA trace closely follow the Visandor's events and are described in table 2.

Arguably, the simplest form of representing the graph would be to represent it as an ordered sequence of events in ASCII text. Instead, and for efficiency reasons,

VisAll uses a rather different strategy. The original execution graph is manipulated within the translator, and the translator is responsible for generating coordinates that can be used by a graphical tool. The resulting representation is organised as two components: (1) a sequence of events, represented as a line with an event number and skeletal information on the event, and (2) a sequence of graph building commands. Graph building commands use a simple language of the form *Command: Fields*, where the number of fields depends on the commands.

One major contribution of VisAll is representing the parallel execution graph as a list of commands. These commands do not just describe how the graph is composed, they actually *do indicate how to build the graph*, that is, how to physically place the nodes and edges of the graph. This greatly facilitates the implementation of the graphical components.

Three major commands are available. The *addInfo* command gives detailed information on a node. The *addNode* command describes how to place a node in the graph. The *addEdge* command describes how to place an edge of the graph, and gives information on its type.

The current implementation makes the system more efficient by combining in the translator two different components, actual translation and graph representation. In fact, the components do pursue separate goals and have been developed separately, as explained in the next section.

2.2 The Translators

Translators take a trace from an external format and create a VisAll style internal file. Translators include a format dependent component, the *trace module*, that converts from an external representation to VisAll's internal representation, and a format independent component that actually builds the graph, the *graph module*. The two modules are managed by common code that provides control and are responsible for the general look of the visualisation graph.

Input trace-files consist of lists of events. Most external formats are text based, such that each line in the trace-file line must refer to a single event, and has to be ordered chronologically (by a timestamp). Differently from other systems, VisAll accepts several events with the same timestamp.

Current translators are written in `C`. Translators have been written for the SBA visualisation format, for the VisAndor format, and for the VACE format. The trace module is the component concerned with the external trace format and with the conversion to the internal representation. The translator inputs the trace-file line by line. For each line, or in other words, each event, the translator calls an *event specific function* that depends on its type.

The graph module that defines the graph is essentially implemented as a series of rules, one for each kind of event. These rules then introduce the nodes and edges to the graph. This way one can generate different graphs supporting different visualisation paradigms just by rewriting this module. The rules are implemented through the `addNode` interface function. This function is called from the top level of the translator after a new event is read and translated from the input graph. The function receives a full description of the event and starts visualisation dependent rules defined for this type of event. In a second stage, after all events are loaded, the X and Y coordinates of the nodes (events) and edges of the graph must be calculated. The Y values can be obtained either from the timestamp field or from the event order, and the X values are obtained from an algorithm designed to balance the graph width. If necessary, the algorithm adjusts the Y coordinates in order to prevent icons from overlapping. By default, each unit of time will correspond to one pixel on the screen, which makes the visualisation accurate in terms of time.

Each edge has an associated *type* and *color*. The types are either dotted or full line. The color indicates the worker that generated that event. Black lines show relations between events, while color lines show working agents.

2.3 Visualisation

We have decided to implement the visualisation program with the `Tcl/Tk` language and toolkit. These graphical systems provide great flexibility, are portable, and allow for easily building nice-looking graphical systems. They do have worse performance than `C` or `C++`, but this is not a problem in our case as most heavy processing is performed by the translator.

Figure 1 shows the standard main VisAll interaction window. The top pane gives the standard control options. As usual this includes loading the visualisation graph from a file, saving it to a postscript file, or exiting. The interface accepts both external and translator processed trace-files. The load status bar is useful during loading of a new trace-file, as it informs how much of the file has been loaded so far. The icon to the right is the VisAll icon.

The bottom pane presents the standard static based form of visualisation. The main subwindow, to the right, displays the dependency graph contained in a VisAll file and shows the execution graph with information on each node (event). This information includes a user specified icon for each type of event and a tag with a string of text, if available from the original trace. The tool also displays execution time for each processor. As in other tools, it is possible to zoom in and out of the graph. In the example, the graph is zoomed and cannot fit the window, so scrollbars are used to navigate through the graph. VisAll uses the standard `Tcl/Tk` facilities to implement this functionality.

Control over the visualisation process is provided by a secondary pane to the left of the main visualisation window. The whole graph is reduced and shown in the small picture bottom-left. This picture also includes a small box indicating the part that is being visualised in the larger image. A zoom button controls the level of detail one wants to see in the main window. Last, on the left hand side top corner of the graph, VisAll shows detailed information about each event (node). It is sufficient to click on any node to obtain the information that corresponds to that event.

VisAll was designed from the beginning to allow several graphical interaction tools. VisAll supports a processor activity map, as shown in Figure 4.This tool works from the same graph, but only displays the points in time where each worker was active. VisAll provides as standard functionality the ability to jump between several sub-tools. In this case, one can just click on a worker bar in order to obtain the position where the worker is in the tree, and vice-versa.

The third tool currently supported in VisAll is the animated execution tool. The tool is activated from the main VisAll window using the "Animation Controls" bar shown in Figure 1. The bar includes a start button, a step-by-step button, a pause button and a stop button. Last it allows controlling execution speeding and auto-scrolling. Figure 7 shows an example of the animated execution tool in action. Note that the modular structure of VisAll allows having different animation tools for the same trace-file. The one we currently have implemented uses a VACE-like approach to represent the dynamics of building execution trees.

3 VisAll In Operation

VisAll was designed and built so that it could visualise traces of different parallel systems. This includes both visualising traces from well known logic programming systems, and visualising synthetic trace files that can be used to predict the performance of parallel systems not yet implemented. To achieve this goal, VisAll is distributed with several filters that can translate from the formats used in other tools to VisAll's internal graph representation.

In the following sections we show how the current implementation of VisAll visualises the major forms of parallelism and how it compares with other parallel logic programming visualisers.

3.1 Visualising ORP

Or-parallel execution can be described through or-trees. VisAll can display, but is not limited to, parallel execution of the Muse [1] and Aurora [12] or-parallel systems.

Implementors of or-parallel systems have experimented with very different approaches to problems such as work distribution or side-effects in Prolog programs, that require sequentialised execution of parts of the program. Thus, execution trees for the same problem from different systems may look quite different.

Figure 1 shows how VisAll visualises the parallel execution of the all-solutions queens problem, as run in Muse with four processors for a 8x8 board size. The small picture to the bottom left shows the whole picture of the parallel execution, and gives the structure of the search tree. The main picture shows the zoomed part of the execution tree. The triangles represent events associated to branches. An upwards pointing triangle (▲) indicates that a branch has been completed successfully, while a downwards pointing triangle (▼) represents the start of a branch. The downwards pointed stripped triangle represents branch suspension while an upwards pointing triangle after a suspension indicates resumption of the suspended branch.

One of the applications for our tool can be immediately identified in this picture. By observing Figure 1, one can see that for this execution too many suspen-

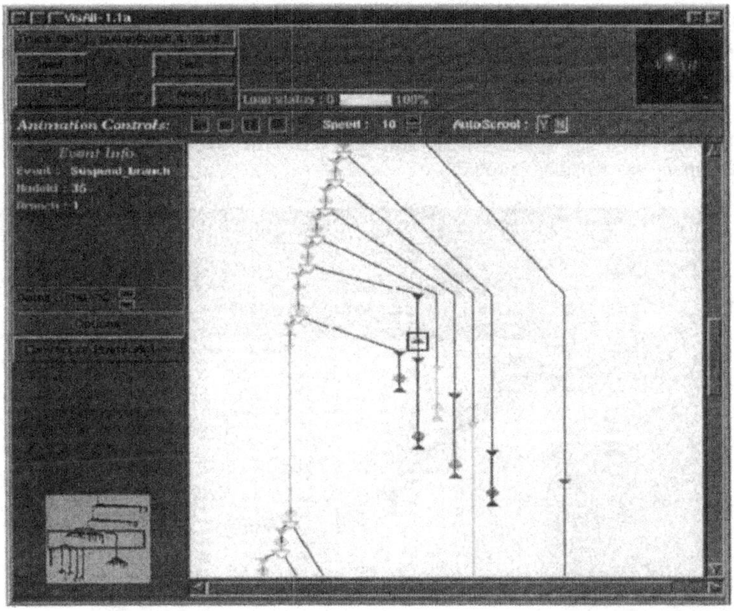

Figure 1: ORP: the 8-queens problem in Muse by VisAll

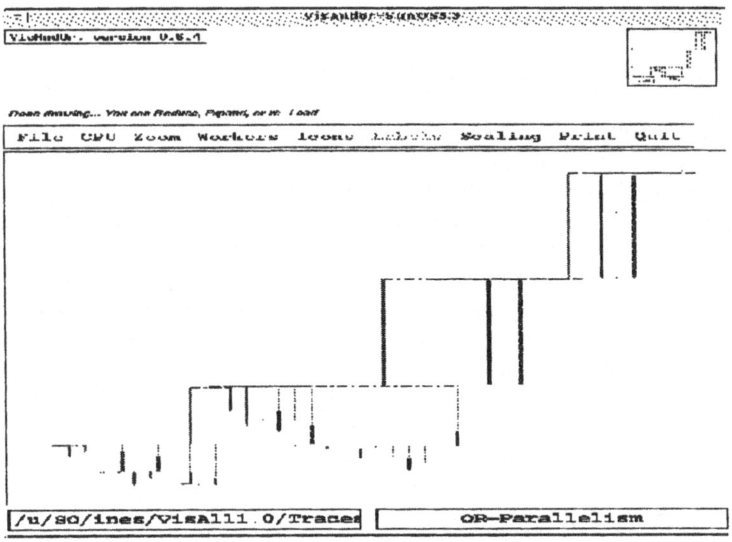

Figure 2: ORP: the 8-queens problem in Muse by VisAndOr

sions were made in very short intervals right after starting alternatives. This may indicate that Muse is being too eager to suspend branches and seek for better (less speculative) work in the tree, resulting in fine-grained work.

Figure 2 shows the same trace-file as visualised by VisAndOr. VisAndOr shows the same kind of tree, but does not show details. It is therefore harder to spot the "too many suspensions" problem.

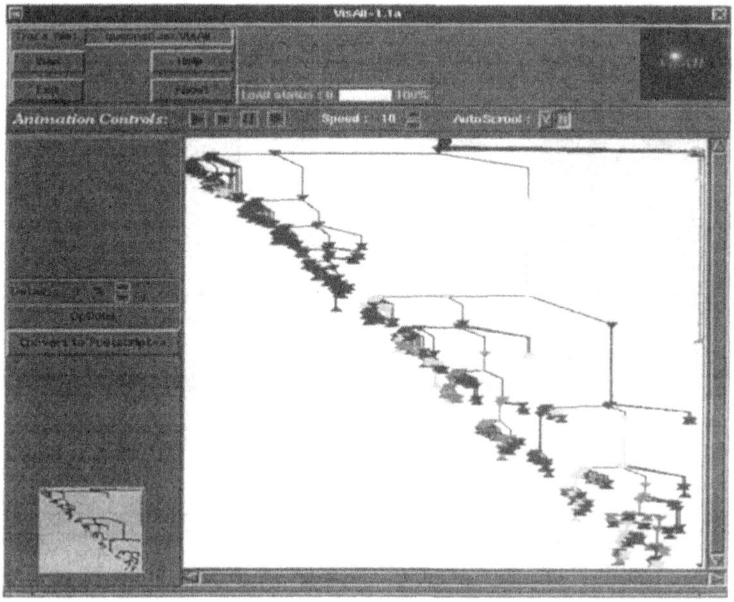

Figure 3: ORP: the 8-queens problem in Aurora by VisAll

Aurora [12], as Muse, exploits ORP in logic programming applications. Although both systems are based on SICStus Prolog, Aurora and Muse have major differences in their design. In particular, they use different data structures to manage conditional bindings and use different or-scheduling techniques. Using different data structures to manage or-parallel bindings does not necessarily make the execution trees look different, but different scheduling strategies definitely will. Figure 3 shows the all-solution parallel execution of the eight queens problem with four processors, in Aurora.

VisAll clearly shows how the execution trees of Muse and Aurora are quite different. Aurora tends to concentrate workers on the left hand side of the search tree. In contrast, Muse spreads workers evenly across branches, suspending work in a given branch from time to time in order to seek for better sources of work.

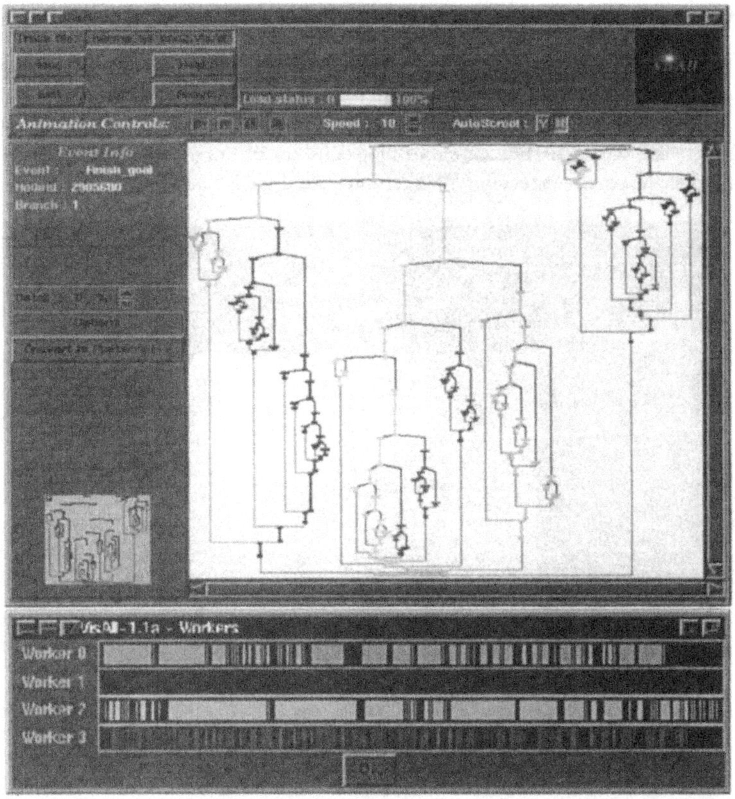

Figure 4: &-Prolog according to VisAll

3.2 Visualising And-parallelism

VisAll can visualise parallel execution of systems that exploit DAP and IAP. Figure 4 shows an execution for the &-Prolog IAP system. The trace-files generated by &-Prolog use the VisAndOr format and can be converted to the VisAll format. In Figure 4 we present the visualisation of a parallel execution of the quicksort program run in &-Prolog with four workers. Notice that work always *forks* from a conjunction, is run in parallel by the individual workers, and at the end *joins* to provide a partial solution. This is the *fork-join* structure typical of IAP. Although the structure of the execution is quite regular, tasks at the same level have quite different execution times, showing the need for good load-balancing.

Figure 4 also shows the VisAll's *activity map* for each processor allowing for easy investigation of the points at which workers became idle for longer time, and vice-versa.

3.3 Visualising DAP plus ORP

Andorra-I [16, 23, 6] is a system that exploits both ORP and *determinate and-parallelism*. By determinate and-parallelism we mean that the system only allows parallel execution of goals when they match at most one clause in the database. This makes the parallel execution tree looks like an or-tree with some "bushes" that indicate the parallel execution of determinate and-goals in a branch.

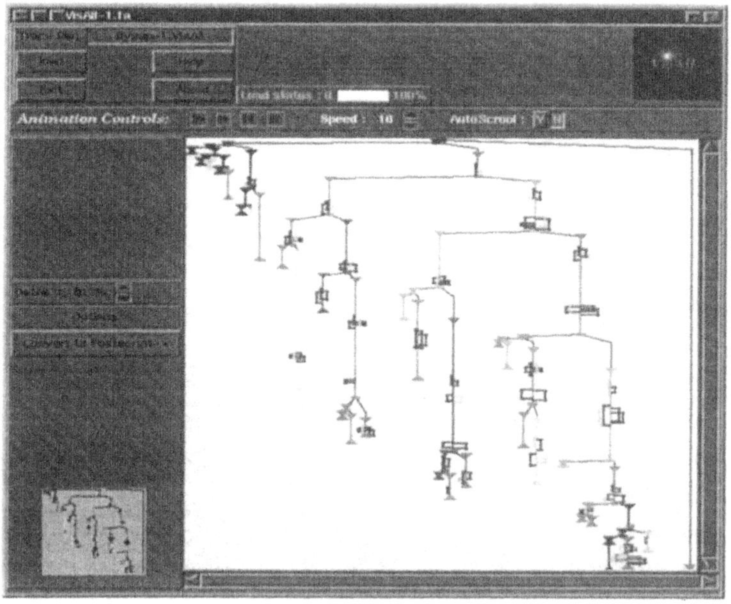

Figure 5: VisAll Visualisation of an Andorra-I Benchmark

Figure 5 shows the last phase of the parallel execution of a flight allocation program run in Andorra-I.

And-parallelism is depicted by parallel coloured lines that join in a same main branch of the execution tree. The top figure seems to indicate lack of sufficient work to sustain eight workers. The search tree is pretty small, and workers are quite often idle or jumping to find work in other branches.

3.4 Visualising IAP plus ORP

A different approach for combining different kinds of parallelism in logic programs is to support both ORP and IAP. Examples include ACE [9] and the SBA [2]. One of the major goals of VisAll is to visualise execution of SBA. Since the system is not fully implemented, VisAll can only visualise *synthetic* trace files for the SBA style of execution.

Figure 6 shows the visualisation of a synthetic trace-file of the SBA model, as visualised by VisAll.

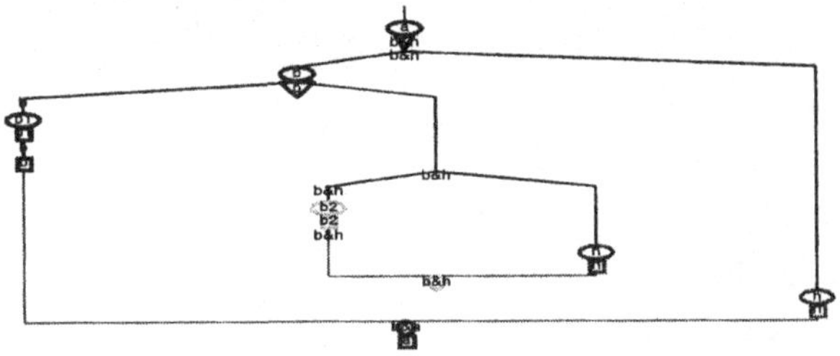

Figure 6: VisAll representation of IAP and ORP

The synthetic traces include information on the name of goals. A goal a unfolds in `b & h`. A C-node is created for this goal just at the top of the figure. The C-node has two alternatives. The first is obtained by taking `b1` and running `h` in parallel. The second by taking `b2` and running `h` in parallel.

Alternatively, VisAll allows the visualisation of VACE trace files. The VACE trace format is based on the VisAndOr trace format, to which it adds extensions deemed necessary to support IAP and ORP through copying.

Figure 7 shows the execution of a small ACE program. Note that the VACE format also includes a field for procedures names. This field is understood by the translator, allowing the display of procedure names.

The top sub-figure shows the static execution. ACE workers are grouped into *teams*. These teams execute in and-parallel, until they run out of and-goals to execute. When this happens, they ask other teams for work. VisAll represents all the elements of a team with the same colour. Copying is represented as a light blue line. A copying operation consists of a set of light blue lines all terminating at approximately the same point in time. Note that colours are very important in VisAll to express several kinds of visualisations such as number of copies made by teams of workers, amount of and-parallel execution exploited by a team, or exchange of signals between workers. As the text is black and white, those details are only visible through actual demonstrations of the software.

Execution under ORP plus IAP can arguably be rather more complex than just ORP or IAP. VisAll's animated execution window is particularly useful to understand these cases. The lower window in Figure 7 shows a snapshot of this tool. The window shows how teams move in the search tree and is particularly useful in recognising how teams work together in exploring the search tree.

4 Conclusions and Future Work

This work presented **VisAll**, a flexible and universal tool to visualise the parallel execution of logic programs. VisAll is capable of visualising several kinds of parallelism, such as IAP, DAP, and ORP. It can display traces of execution statically and

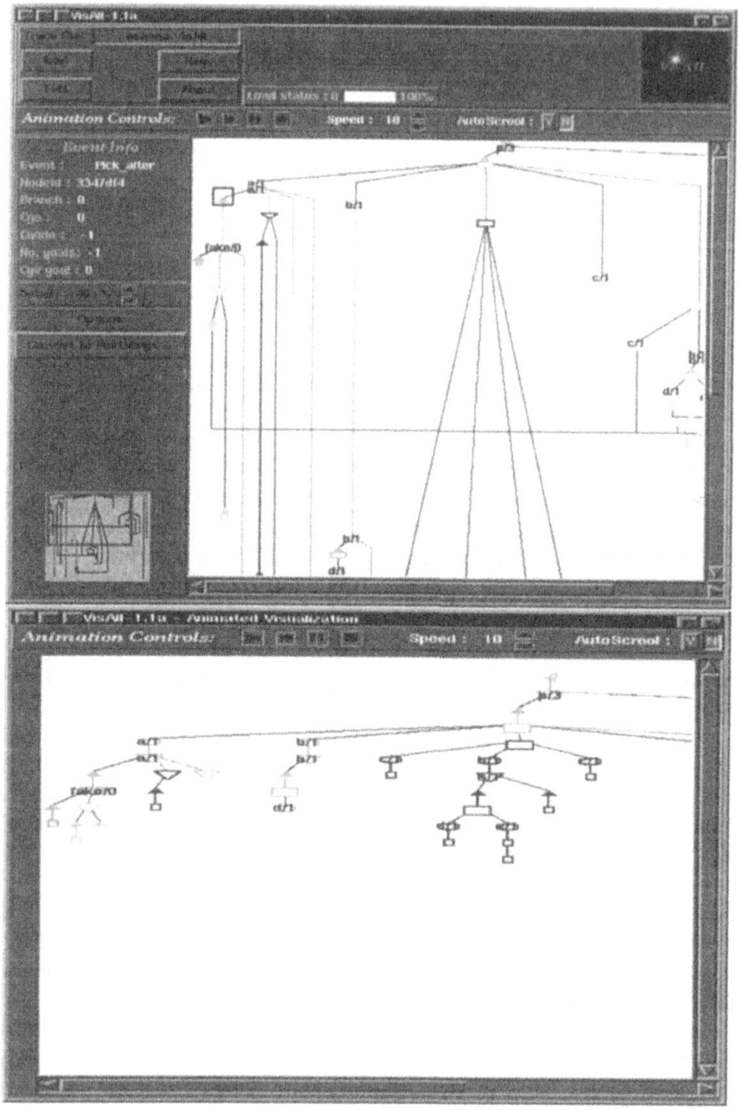

Figure 7: VisAll representation of an ACE program

dynamically, while also displaying individual processor activity maps. All these components work together, in an integrated fashion. VisAll allows users to zoom in and out at parts of the execution tree, to see dynamic execution, and to obtain information about the logic program source. Moreover, VisAll was designed so that it can visualise traces of different parallel logic programming systems, even if those traces were obtained for other visualisation tools, and currently supports the VisAndor and Vace input trace formats.

Development of VisAll continues active. In the future, we plan to add new forms of parallelism, namely non-determinate dependent and-parallelism, in collaboration with Shen [17], and Pontelli and Gupta [15]. Moreover, we would like to extend the tool to give more detailed information about the system, such as why a processor (or worker) suspended, why it is positioned somewhere in the tree, and where in the source program it is executing code. We are particularly interested in finding what kinds of information are of interest to parallel logic programming system designers. We are also starting research into using 3D visualisation for visualising the complex execution of AND-OR systems such as SBA or ACE.

So far, the development of VisAll has been directed towards the needs of parallel logic programming system developers. As parallel logic programming systems mature, systems like VisAll will be more and more important for developing and testing applications in parallel systems. We believe the modular structure of our system is ideal towards directing our tool towards the requirements of application developers.

Acknowledgments

This work has been supported by the PRAXIS Proloppe project, PRAXIS/3/3.1/-TIT/24/94. Vítor Santos Costa would like to acknowledge support from the JNICT Melodia project. Inês Dutra would like to acknowledge support from the PROTEM Appelo project. Nuno Fonseca would like to acknowledge support from the Subprograma Ciência e Tecnologia do 2º Quadro Comunitário de Apoio.

References

[1] Khayri A. M. Ali and Roland Karlsson. The Muse or-parallel Prolog Model and its Performance. In *Proceedings of the 1990 North American Conference on Logic Programming*, pages 757–776. MIT Press, October 1990.

[2] Manuel Eduardo Correia, Vítor Santos Costa, and Fernando Silva. The SBA: Exploiting Orthogonality in AND–OR Parallel Systems. In *ILPS'97, Port Jefferson, NY, USA,*, 1997.

[3] J. A. Crammond. The Abstract Machine and Implementation of Parallel Parlog. Technical report, Dept. of Computing, Imperial College, London, June 1990.

[4] Doug DeGroot. Restricted And-Parallelism. In Hideo Aiso, editor, *Proceedings of the 1984 International Conference on Fifth Generation Computer Systems*, pages 471–478. Institute for New Generation Computing, Tokyo, 1984.

[5] Terrence Disz and Ewing Lusk. A Graphical Tool for Observing the Behavior of Parallel Logic Programs. In *Proceedings of the 1987 International Logic Programming Symposium*, pages 46–53, 1987.

[6] I. C. Dutra. Strategies for Scheduling And- and Or-Work in Parallel Logic Programming Systems. In *Proceedings of the 1994 International Logic Programming Symposium*, pages 289–304. MIT Press, 1994. Also available as technical report CSTR-94-09, from the Department of Computer Science, University of Bristol, England.

[7] Luis Gómez, Manuel Carro, and Manuel Hermenegildo. Some Paradigms for Visualising Parallel Execution of Logic Programs. In *Proceedings of the Tenth International Conference on Logic Programming*, pages 184–202, 1993.

[8] Gopal Gupta, M. Hermenegildo, and V. Santos Costa. And-Or Parallel Prolog: A Recomputation based Approach. *New Generation Computing*, 11(3,4):770–782, 1993.

[9] Gopal Gupta, M. V. Hermenegildo, E. Pontelli, and V. Santos Costa. ACE: And/Or-parallel Copying-based Execution of Logic Programs. In *Proceedings of the Eleventh International Conference on Logic Programming*, Italy, June 1994.

[10] Gopal Gupta, Enrico Pontelli, and Manuel Hermenegildo. &ACE: A High Performance Parallel Prolog System. In *Proceedings of the First International Symposium on Parallel Symbolic Computation, PASCO'94*, 1994.

[11] M. V. Hermenegildo and K. Greene. &-Prolog and its Performance: Exploiting Independent And-Parallelism. In *Proceedings of the Seventh International Conference on Logic Programming*, pages 253–268. MIT Press, June 1990.

[12] Ewing Lusk, David H. D. Warren, Seif Haridi, et al. The Aurora Or-parallel Prolog System. *New Generation Computing*, 7(2,3):243–271, 1990.

[13] Johan Montelius. *Penny, A Parallel Implementation of AKL*. PhD thesis, Swedish Institute for Computer Science, SICS, Sweden, May 1997.

[14] Remco Moolenaar and Bart Demoen. Hybrid tree search in the Andorra Model. In Pascal Van Hentenryck, editor, *Proceedings of the Eleventh International Conference on Logic Programming*, pages 110–123. MIT Press, June 1994.

[15] E. Pontelli and G. Gupta. Non dependent and-parallelism revisited. Technical Report 1, Laboratory for Logic, Databases and Advanced Programming, New Mexico State University, Las Cruces, New Mexico, USA, February 1996.

[16] V. Santos Costa, D. H. D. Warren, and R. Yang. Andorra-I: A Parallel Prolog System that Transparently Exploits both And- and Or-Parallelism. In *Third ACM SIGPLAN Symposium on Principles & Practice of Parallel Programming*, pages 83–93. ACM press, April 1991. SIGPLAN Notices vol 26(7), July 1991.

[17] Kish Shen. Exploiting And-parallelism in Prolog: the Dynamic Dependent And-parallel Scheme (DDAS). In *Logic Programming: Proceedings of the Joint International Conference and Symposium on Logic Programming*, pages 717–731, 1992.

[18] Kish Shen. Memory Management and Goal Scheduling for Parallel Execution Revisited. Internal Report, Bristol University, 1993.

[19] J. Sunberg and C. Svensson. Muse trace: A graphic tracer for or-parallel prolog. Technical report, SICS, 1990.

[20] T. Chikayama, T. and Fujise, and H. Yashiro. A Portable and Reasonably Efficient Implementation of KL1. In *Proceedings of the Eleventh International Conference on Logic Programming*, June 1993.

[21] Rick Vaupel, Enrico Pontelli, and Gopal Gupta. Visualization of And/Or-Parallel Execution of Logic Programs. In *Proceedings of the Fourteenth International Conference on Logic Programming*, pages 271–285, 1997.

[22] David H. D. Warren. The Extended Andorra Model with Implicit Control. Presented at ICLP'90 Workshop on Parallel Logic Programming, Eilat, Israel, June 1990.

[23] Rong Yang, Tony Beaumont, Inês Dutra, Vítor Santos Costa, and David H. D. Warren. Performance of the Compiler-Based Andorra-I System. In *Proceedings of the Tenth International Conference on Logic Programming*, pages 150–166. MIT Press, June 1993.

Proof-Theoretic Foundation of Compilation in Logic Programming Languages

Iliano Cervesato
Department of Computer Science
Stanford University
Stanford, CA 94305-9045
iliano@cs.stanford.edu

Abstract

Commercial implementations of logic programming languages are engineered around a compiler based on Warren's Abstract Machine (WAM) or a variant of it. In spite of various correctness proofs, the logical machinery relating the proof-theoretic specification of a logic programming language and its compiled form is still poorly understood. In this paper, we propose a logic-independent definition of compilation for logic programming languages. We apply this methodology to derive the first cut of a compiler and the corresponding abstract machine for the language of hereditary Harrop formulas and then for its linear refinement.

1 Introduction

Compiled logic programs run over an order of magnitude faster than their interpreted source and constitute therefore a key step to combining the advantages of the declarative nature of logic programming with the efficiency requirements of full-scale applications. For this reason, commercial implementations of logic programming languages come equipped with a compiler to translate a source program into an intermediate language, and an abstract machine to execute this compiled code efficiently. Most systems are based on *Warren's Abstract Machine* (WAM) [1, 22], first developed for *Prolog*. The WAM has now been adapted to other logic programming languages such as *CLP*($\mathcal{R}$) [10] and *PROTOS-L* [2]. Extensions to λ*Prolog* [14] are under way [12, 16, 17], but no similar effort has been undertaken for other advanced logic programming languages such as *Lolli* [9] or *Elf* [20].

Warren's work appears as a carefully engineered construction, but, for its very pioneering nature, it lacks any logical status. This contrasts strongly with the deep roots that the interpretation semantics of logic programming has in logic and proof-theory [15]. Indeed, the instruction set of the WAM hardly bears any resemblance to the connectives of the logic underlying *Prolog* and seems highly specialized to this language. As a result, the WAM "resembles an intricate puzzle, whose many pieces fit tightly together in a miraculous way" [3], understanding it is complex in spite of the availability of excellent presentations [1], and designing WAM-like systems for other languages is a major engineering project. Several authors have proved the correctness of the WAM with respect to specifications of *Prolog*'s interpretation semantic [3, 21]. However, these results shed very little light on the logical reading of the WAM since they start from highly procedural presentations of the semantic of Horn clauses, as SLD-resolution for example. Adaptations of these proofs to the aforementioned extensions of the WAM to other logic programming languages [2, 4] suffer from the same problem. Therefore, differently from the case of functional programming for example [13, 18], there is no logical account of compilation for logic programs.

In this paper, we give a general definition of compilation that parallels and extends the notion of abstract logic programming language [15]. More specifically, we propose a proof-theoretic characterization of the compilation process based on the duality between left and right rules in a sequent calculus presentation of a logic. In doing so, we do not commit to any particular logic but consider any formalism whose proof theory obeys a minimal set of properties [15]. We use the logic of hereditary Harrop formulas [15] and its linear variant [9] as examples. The high-level rules of an abstract logic programming language leave several implementation choices open, such as the order in which conjunctive goals should be solved and how to instantiate variables. The same will happen in the compiled language. However, similarly to the case of abstract logic programming languages, our abstract compilation scheme can be refined to adopt specific strategies (e.g. left-to-right subgoal selection rule and unification). Modularity is achieved in this way.

The main contributions of this paper are: (1) the individuation of the logic underlying the WAM and a logical justification of the compilation process, (2) the definition of an abstract, logic-independent and modular notion of compilation for logic programming languages, and possibly (3) the first steps toward a logic-based theory of compilation for logic programming languages. We also hope that our approach will help make compilation an integral part of the design of new logic programming languages rather than the collateral engineering task it is now.

This paper is organized as follows. In Section 2, we recall the definition of abstract logic programming language and introduce the logic of hereditary Harrop formulas as an example. We describe our abstract notion of compilation in Section 3, apply it to our case study and prove correctness results. In Section 4, we further exemplify our approach on a logic programming language based on linear logic. Section 5 outlines directions of future work.

2 Abstract Logic Programming Languages

Computation in logic programming is achieved through proof search. Given a *goal* A to be proved in a *program* Γ, we want to be able to interpret the connectives of A as *search directives* and the *clauses* in Γ as specifications

Uniform provability

$$\frac{\Gamma, A, \Gamma' \xrightarrow{u} A \gg a}{\Gamma, A, \Gamma' \xrightarrow{u} a}\ \text{u\_Atom} \qquad \frac{}{\Gamma \xrightarrow{u} \mathbf{t}}\ \text{u\_True} \qquad \frac{\Gamma \xrightarrow{u} A_1 \quad \Gamma \xrightarrow{u} A_2}{\Gamma \xrightarrow{u} A_1 \wedge A_2}\ \text{u\_And}$$

$$\frac{\Gamma, A_1 \xrightarrow{u} A_2}{\Gamma \xrightarrow{u} A_1 \supset A_2}\ \text{u\_Imp} \qquad \frac{c \text{ ``new''} \quad \Gamma \xrightarrow{u} [c/x]A}{\Gamma \xrightarrow{u} \forall x.\, A}\ \text{u\_Forall}$$

Immediate entailment

$$\frac{}{\Gamma \xrightarrow{u} a \gg a}\ \text{i\_Atom} \qquad \text{(No rule for } \mathbf{t}\text{)}$$

$$\frac{\Gamma \xrightarrow{u} A_1 \gg a}{\Gamma \xrightarrow{u} A_1 \wedge A_2 \gg a}\ \text{i\_And}_1 \qquad \frac{\Gamma \xrightarrow{u} A_2 \gg a}{\Gamma \xrightarrow{u} A_1 \wedge A_2 \gg a}\ \text{i\_And}_2$$

$$\frac{\Gamma \xrightarrow{u} A_1 \gg a \quad \Gamma \xrightarrow{u} A_2}{\Gamma \xrightarrow{u} A_2 \supset A_1 \gg a}\ \text{i\_Imp} \qquad \frac{\Gamma \xrightarrow{u} [t/x]A \gg a}{\Gamma \xrightarrow{u} \forall x.\, A \gg a}\ \text{i\_Forall}$$

Figure 1: Uniform Deduction System for $\mathcal{L}_{HH}$.

of how to continue the search when the goal is atomic. These desiderata are given without mentioning the logic the program and the goal belong to.

A proof in any logic is *goal-oriented* if every compound goal is immediately decomposed and the program is accessed only after the goal has been reduced to an atomic formula. A proof is *focused* if every time a program formula is considered, it is processed up to the atoms it defines without need to access any other program formula. A proof having both these properties is *uniform*, and a formalism such that every provable goal has a uniform proof is called an *abstract logic programming language*, abbreviated *ALPL* [15]. An ALPL is conveniently described as a pair $(\mathcal{L}, \longrightarrow)$ consisting of a language $\mathcal{L}$ and an associated notion of (uniform) derivability $\longrightarrow$.

The language of *hereditary Harrop* formulas, abbreviated $\mathcal{L}_{HH}$, is the largest freely generated fragment of intuitionistic logic that passes the above ALPL test [15]. It is the logic underlying the programming language *λProlog* [14] and embeds the language of Horn clauses on which *Prolog* is based. Formulas and programs are defined by means of the following grammar:

Formulas: $A ::= a \mid \mathbf{t} \mid A_1 \wedge A_2 \mid A_1 \supset A_2 \mid \forall x.\, A$

Programs: $\Gamma ::= \cdot \mid \Gamma, A$

where a ranges over atomic formulas. We shall treat programs as sequences and omit the leading "$\cdot$" whenever a program is not empty. Moreover, we write t to indicate terms and denote the capture avoiding substitution of a term t for x in a formula A as $[t/x]A$. Notice that we do not specify the underlying language of terms. This is irrelevant to our development: it can be first-order, higher-order as in *λProlog*, or be based on any equational theory (which would yield corresponding *constraint logic programming languages*). Propositional $\mathcal{L}_{HH}$ can be handled as well once we omit the quantifiers $\forall x.\, A$. However, we do not admit quantification over atomic formulas.

Syntactically richer definitions of the logic of hereditary Harrop formulas exist [14, 15]. They are obtained by allowing the language of programs to be different from the language of goals. The former differs in minor points from the grammar displayed above. The latter is extended with numerous other logical operators. It is not a coincidence that these additional constructs correspond to the connectives and quantifiers into which program formulas will be compiled in the next section. This syntactic extension does not however alter the expressiveness of this logic.

Figure 1 displays the traditional sequent calculus rules for $\mathcal{L}_{HH}$ written in such a way that every proof is uniform. The specification of the *uniform provability* judgment, written $\Gamma \xrightarrow{u} A$, includes all the right sequent rules for this logic and calls the *immediate entailment* judgment $\Gamma \xrightarrow{u} A \gg a$ when the goal is atomic. Immediate entailment isolates a clause and decomposes it as prescribed by the left sequent rules of $\mathcal{L}_{HH}$ until an axiom applies. The cut-elimination theorem and simple permutations of inference rules suffice to show that any sequent derivation can be transformed into a uniform proof that uses only these rules [15]. Therefore $\mathcal{L}_{HH}$ is an ALPL.

The rules in Figure 1 present three main forms of non-determinism. First, the order in which the two premises of rules **u_And** and **i_Imp** should be proved is left unspecified (*conjunctive non-determinism*). Second, no criterion is given to select the program formula in rule **i_Atom** nor to choose among rules **i_And$_1$** and **i_And$_2$** (*disjunctive non-determinism*). Third, no strategy is specified to construct the term t in rule **i_Forall** (*existential non-determinism*). A concrete implementation must resolve these points.

3 Abstract Compilation

The search for a uniform proof consists of the alternation of two distinct phases: *goal decomposition*, where right sequent rules are applied according to the structure of the goal, and, once the goal is atomic, *clause decomposition* where left sequent rules are systematically used on the selected formula in the program. These two operational modes are clearly distinguished in $\mathcal{L}_{HH}$ by means of the two forms of judgments that describe its semantics (Figure 1). From a logic programming perspective, the connectives appearing in the goal are search directives and therefore goal decomposition is where the bulk of the action takes place. Clause decomposition can instead be viewed as a preparatory phase.

The objective of compilation is to separate these two phases so that all the preparatory steps are performed *before* any search begins [11]. An *abstract logic programming compilation system*, *ALPCS* for short, consists therefore of a *source ALPL* $(\mathcal{L}, \longrightarrow)$, an *intermediate language* $\mathcal{L}^c$ which is itself an ALPL with the characteristic that its notion of derivability $\xrightarrow{c}$ consists of right sequent rules only, and a *compilation function* $\gg$ that maps programs and goals in $\mathcal{L}$ to *compiled programs* and *compiled goals* in $\mathcal{L}^c$, respectively.

The intermediate ALPL $(\mathcal{L}^c, \xrightarrow{c})$ and the compilation function can be determined systematically from the source language and its derivability rules. First, since provable goals in the source language should have a derivation in the intermediate ALPL, the goal language of $\mathcal{L}$ must be a sublanguage of $\mathcal{L}^c$.

We get rid of every left-introduction rule **r** of $\longrightarrow$ by devising a dual rule $\mathbf{r}^c$ with an identical structure, but that operates on the right of the sequent arrow. In particular, the number of premises, the way other clauses are propagated to them, and possible interactions of the selected formula with the atomic goal of **r** should be preserved in $\mathbf{r}^c$. We should clearly rename the connective or quantifier introduced in **r** in order not to alter its search semantics. Although systematic, the process of transforming a left rule into an equivalent right inference figure may appear to step out of logic since we are required to invent new syntactic constructs. However, the source logic $(\mathcal{L}, \longrightarrow)$ is almost invariably a fragment of some larger logic (generally not an ALPL) that exhibits the very same duality principles we just described, but in a native form. Therefore, it will suffice to adopt these operators as the dual constructs of the program connectives of the source language, giving in this way a strong logical reading to the intermediate language. It is easily seen that this process preserves points of non-determinism.

The last question to answer is what to do when the search in $\mathcal{L}^c$ produces an atomic goal a. As in any ALPL, we want to consult the (compiled) program for indications on how to continue the search. Since the appropriateness of a program formula for this purpose should depend on a, we perform a *parametric compilation* of program formulas that keeps the atom they should resolve unspecified. Then, when an atomic formula a is produced, the computation proceeds by picking a (parametric) compiled clause, instantiating it with a and processing it as a goal.

We will now apply the methodology we just informally described to the language of hereditary Harrop formulas, $\mathcal{L}_{HH}$, discussed in Section 2. In order to construct the associated intermediate ALPL $(\mathcal{L}^c_{HH}, \stackrel{c}{\longrightarrow})$, we are going to look for connectives in general intuitionistic logic whose right rules are the dual of the immediate entailment rules from Figure 1.

The easiest operator to process in this way is **t**, which has no immediate entailment rule. The only construct in intuitionistic logic that does not have a right sequent rule is falsehood, **f**. We adopt it as the dual of **t**.

Next, we consider conjunction. This connective has two left introduction rules that differ only by the conjunct that is kept when reading them from the conclusion to the premises. The only construct whose right sequent rules behave in this manner is disjunction ($\vee$), as we can clearly see by placing corresponding rules next to each other:

$$\frac{\Gamma \stackrel{u}{\longrightarrow} A_i \gg a}{\Gamma \stackrel{u}{\longrightarrow} A_1 \wedge A_2 \gg a}\,\mathsf{i\_And}_i \qquad\qquad \frac{\Gamma \longrightarrow A_i}{\Gamma \longrightarrow A_1 \vee A_2}$$

for $i = 1, 2$. Therefore, we use disjunction to compile a conjunction appearing in a program position.

There is one immediate entailment rule for implication, it has two premises which each process one of its two subformulas. The right sequent rule for conjunction is structured in a similar way:

$$\frac{\Gamma \xrightarrow{u} A_1 \gg a \quad \Gamma \xrightarrow{u} A_2}{\Gamma \xrightarrow{u} A_2 \supset A_1 \gg a}\,\textbf{i\_Imp} \qquad \frac{\Gamma \longrightarrow A_1 \quad \Gamma \longrightarrow A_2}{\Gamma \longrightarrow A_1 \wedge A_2}$$

Consequently, we compile occurrences of implication in a program position as conjunctions. Notice that the left premise of rule **i_Imp** prescribes further clause decomposition, while its right premise sets up a goal for search. This distinction does not appear in the right introduction rule for $\wedge$. However, this is exactly what we are after since we want to be able to process every compiled clause as a goal, after instantiation.

The immediate entailment rule for the universal quantifier instantiates the embedded clause with some term t for further decomposition. The existential quantifier $\exists$ performs the same step, but on the right of the sequent arrow:

$$\frac{\Gamma \xrightarrow{u} [t/x]A \gg a}{\Gamma \xrightarrow{u} \forall x.\, A \gg a}\,\textbf{i\_Forall} \qquad \frac{\Gamma \longrightarrow [t/x]A}{\Gamma \longrightarrow \exists x.\, A}$$

We therefore compile each clause occurrence of $\forall$ to an existential quantifier in a goal position.

The only remaining immediate entailment rule is **i_Atom**, which applies once the selected clause has been decomposed to an atomic formula. Then, it checks whether this atom is the same as the (atomic) goal. We are therefore looking for a binary connective operating on atomic formulas and whose only right introduction rule has no premise. No construct in intuitionistic logic behaves in this way. We can however enrich this formalism with a logical operator that checks that two atomic formulas are syntactically equal. We denote syntactic equality has $\doteq$. The rule defining its semantics is displayed below on the right:

$$\frac{}{\Gamma \xrightarrow{u} a \gg a}\,\textbf{i\_Atom} \qquad \frac{}{\Gamma \longrightarrow a \doteq a}$$

Then, we compile program clauses parametrically with respect to the atomic goal they are expected to match. In particular, we associate to an atomic clause a the compiled goal $a \doteq \alpha$, where α is a *parameter*. When a generic clause is used to continue the search for some atomic goal a', we replace its parameter α with a' and use the resulting expression as a goal.

We are now in a position to bundle up this intuition into a formal definition. The intermediate language corresponding to $\mathcal{L}_{HH}$, that we denote $\mathcal{L}^c_{HH}$, is given by the following grammar:

$$\begin{array}{rrcl}
\textit{Goals:} & G & ::= & a \mid \mathbf{t} \mid G_1 \wedge G_2 \mid (\Lambda\alpha.\, C) \supset G \mid \forall x.\, G \\
\textit{C-Goals} & R & ::= & a_1 \doteq a_2 \mid \mathbf{f} \mid R_1 \vee R_2 \mid R \wedge G \mid \exists x.\, R \\
\textit{Clauses:} & C & ::= & a \doteq \alpha \mid \mathbf{f} \mid C_1 \vee C_2 \mid C \wedge G \mid \exists x.\, C \\
\textit{Programs:} & \Psi & ::= & \cdot \mid \Psi, \Lambda\alpha.\, C
\end{array}$$

In order to make the discussion fully precise, we distinguish the *goals* inherited from $\mathcal{L}_{HH}$, that we denote with the letter G, from the goal constructions

Goals

$$\frac{\Psi, \Lambda\alpha.\, C, \Psi' \xrightarrow{cg} [a/\alpha]C}{\Psi, \Lambda\alpha.\, C, \Psi' \xrightarrow{c} a}\ \textbf{c\_Atom} \qquad \frac{}{\Psi \xrightarrow{c} \mathbf{t}}\ \textbf{c\_True} \qquad \frac{\Psi \xrightarrow{c} G_1 \quad \Psi \xrightarrow{c} G_2}{\Psi \xrightarrow{c} G_1 \wedge G_2}\ \textbf{c\_And}$$

$$\frac{\Psi, \Lambda\alpha.\, C \xrightarrow{c} G}{\Psi \xrightarrow{c} (\Lambda\alpha.\, C) \supset G}\ \textbf{c\_Imp} \qquad \frac{c \text{ “new”} \quad \Psi \xrightarrow{c} [c/x]G}{\Psi \xrightarrow{c} \forall x.\, G}\ \textbf{c\_Forall}$$

Compilation goals

$$\frac{}{\Psi \xrightarrow{cg} a \doteq a}\ \textbf{cg\_Eq} \qquad \text{(No rule for } \mathbf{f}\text{)}$$

$$\frac{\Psi \xrightarrow{cg} R_1}{\Psi \xrightarrow{cg} R_1 \vee R_2}\ \textbf{cg\_Or}_1 \qquad \frac{\Psi \xrightarrow{cg} R_2}{\Psi \xrightarrow{cg} R_1 \vee R_2}\ \textbf{cg\_Or}_2$$

$$\frac{\Psi \xrightarrow{cg} R \quad \Psi \xrightarrow{c} G}{\Psi \xrightarrow{cg} R \wedge G}\ \textbf{cg\_And} \qquad \frac{\Psi \xrightarrow{cg} [t/x]R}{\Psi \xrightarrow{cg} \exists x.\, R}\ \textbf{cg\_Exists}$$

Figure 2: Search Semantics of $\mathcal{L}^c_{HH}$.

resulting from the compilation of a program formula. We call them *compilation goals*, or *c-goals*, and use the letter R for them.

We write $\Lambda\alpha.\, C$ to denote a *compiled clause* with parameter α. We view Λ as an operator that binds every free occurrence of α in C. When using this notation, we shall assume that C does not contain free parameters besides α so that $\Lambda\alpha.\, C$ is a closed expression. Moreover, we require every clause C to mention at most one free parameter. We denote the instantiation of a clause C with parameter α by means of an atomic formula a as $[a/\alpha]C$. A c-goal is then a clause whose (free) parameter has been replaced with an atomic formula (we omit the formal statement and its proof).

The antecedent of an implication goal is a compiled clause since solving the overall goal has the effect of extending the program with this subformula as an extra clause. Observe also that the right conjunct of a c-goal $R \wedge G$ is a goal. This is a consequence of the structure of rule **i_Imp**.

We report the inference rules defining the semantics of $\mathcal{L}^c_{HH}$ in Figure 2. Notice that only right introduction rules are mentioned. In order to achieve simple proofs of soundness and completeness, we distinguish the rules for goals from those applying to c-goals by means of the judgments $\Psi \xrightarrow{c} G$ and $\Psi \xrightarrow{cg} R$, respectively. Notice that they present the same non-deterministic behaviors as the rules for $\mathcal{L}_{HH}$ in Figure 1.

The compilation of the various linguistic entities of $\mathcal{L}_{HH}$ into $\mathcal{L}^c_{HH}$ is presented as a deductive system in Figure 3. Since clauses contain embedded goals and vice-versa, the judgments compiling these expressions, $A \gg \alpha \setminus C$ and $A \gg G$, have a mutually recursive definition. Compiling a program, denoted $\Gamma \gg \Psi$, reduces to compiling its clauses and collecting them. It can be easily shown that the compilation rules in Figure 3 specify a bijective function between $\mathcal{L}_{HH}$ and the fragment of $\mathcal{L}^c_{HH}$ that satisfies our restrictions.

Programs

$$\frac{}{\cdot \gg \cdot}\ \text{pc\_empty} \qquad \frac{\Gamma \gg \Psi \quad A \gg \alpha \backslash C}{\Gamma, A \gg \Psi, \Lambda\alpha.\, C}\ \text{pc\_clause}$$

Clauses

$$\frac{}{a \gg \alpha \backslash a \doteq \alpha}\ \text{cc\_Atom} \qquad \frac{}{\mathbf{t} \gg \alpha \backslash \mathbf{f}}\ \text{cc\_True} \qquad \frac{A \gg \alpha \backslash C_1 \quad B \gg \alpha \backslash C_2}{A \wedge B \gg \alpha \backslash C_1 \vee C_2}\ \text{cc\_And}$$

$$\frac{B \gg \alpha \backslash C \quad A \gg G}{A \supset B \gg \alpha \backslash C \wedge G}\ \text{cc\_Imp} \qquad \frac{A \gg \alpha \backslash C}{\forall x.\, A \gg \alpha \backslash \exists x.\, C}\ \text{cc\_Forall}$$

Goals

$$\frac{}{a \gg a}\ \text{gc\_Atom} \qquad \frac{}{\mathbf{t} \gg \mathbf{t}}\ \text{gc\_True} \qquad \frac{A \gg G_1 \quad B \gg G_2}{A \wedge B \gg G_1 \wedge G_2}\ \text{gc\_And}$$

$$\frac{A \gg \alpha \backslash C \quad B \gg G}{A \supset B \gg (\Lambda\alpha.\, C) \supset G}\ \text{gc\_Imp} \qquad \frac{A \gg C}{\forall x.\, A \gg \forall x.\, C}\ \text{gc\_Forall}$$

Figure 3: Compilation of $\mathcal{L}_{HH}$.

As an example, we consider the familiar (Horn) clauses computing the concatenation (or non-deterministic splitting) of two lists. We write "nil" for the empty list and $x :: l$ for a list with head x and tail l. For the sake of readability, we use $A_2 :- A_1$ as an alternate notation for $A_1 \supset A_2$.

$$\forall l.\, \text{append nil}\, l\, l$$
$$\forall k.\, \forall l.\, \forall m.\, \forall x.\, \text{append}\, (x :: k)\, l\, (x :: m) \ :- \ \text{append}\, k\, l\, m$$

Applying the compilation process we just described yields the following compiled clauses.

$$\Lambda\alpha.\, \exists l.\, (\text{append nil}\, l\, l) \doteq \alpha$$
$$\Lambda\alpha.\, \exists k.\, \exists l.\, \exists m.\, \exists x.\, (\text{append}\, (x :: k)\, l\, (x :: m)) \doteq \alpha \ \wedge \ (\text{append}\, k\, l\, m)$$

We can procedurally interpret the equality test in any compiled clause as a request to unify the head of the original clause ("append nil l l" for example), with the *current* (atomic) goal represented by the parameter α: in an unoptimized WAM, α corresponds to the register ($\texttt{A}_1$) holding the atomic formula being called. The conjunction introduced in the second clause can similarly be interpreted as a sequencing operator. Therefore, an operational reading of this clause specifies to allocate space for the local variables k, l, m and x, unify the current goal with "append $(x :: k)\ l\ (x :: m)$" and then call "append $k\ l\ m$" in case of success.

We have written a compiler and the corresponding abstract machine along the guidelines in this section for the language *LF* [19], a type theory closely related to $\mathcal{L}_{HH}$. By choosing appropriate names and spacing in order to print compiled clauses and no further processing, we could obtain the following WAM-like pseudo-code for the "append" program.

```
append1: ALLOCATE L
         UNIFY    append nil L L
```

```
append2: ALLOCATE K
         ALLOCATE L
         ALLOCATE M
         ALLOCATE X
         UNIFY    append (cons X K) L (cons X M)
         CALL     append K L M
```

The "real" WAM program is much more detailed since it provides code to handle the various forms of non-determinism we discussed in Section 2. However, its high-level structure is the same.

Compilation for first- and higher-order hereditary Harrop formulas has been extensively studied by Nadathur *et al.* [12, 16, 17] with the aim of building an abstract machine for λ*Prolog* [14]. Their work has focused on devising and optimizing a concrete WAM-like instruction set for this language.

We conclude this section by proving the soundness and completeness of the compilation process for $\mathcal{L}_{HH}$. An important fact to notice is the elegance and simplicity of these proofs (whose details are omitted for space reasons): they rely on nothing more than structural inductions. This contrasts greatly with the complexity of the hefty proofs of soundness and correctness currently available for the WAM [3, 21]. We do not believe that this huge difference depends solely on the fact that we are treating the compilation process at a very high abstraction level. We have furthermore transcribed our proofs in the *Elf* [20] implementation of the logical framework *LF* [19] and let this system check their validity. This contrasts again with the proofs in [3, 21], which have not been mechanically checked and should therefore be considered informal.

The soundness theorem states that whenever a goal is derivable from a program in $\mathcal{L}_{HH}$, then the compiled goal is derivable from the compiled program in $\mathcal{L}^c_{HH}$. A close analysis of the proof reveals that not only derivability but also actual derivations are preserved, so that it is possible to extract a function that maps derivations in the source ALPL to derivations in $\mathcal{L}^c_{HH}$.

Theorem 3.1 (*Soundness of the compilation of* $\mathcal{L}_{\mathrm{HH}}$)

i. If $\Gamma \xrightarrow{u} A$, $\Gamma \gg \Psi$ *and* $A \gg G$, *then* $\Psi \xrightarrow{c} G$.
ii. If $\Gamma \xrightarrow{u} A \gg a$, $\Gamma \gg \Psi$ *and* $A \gg \alpha \backslash C$, *then* $\Psi \xrightarrow{cg} [a/\alpha]C$.

Proof. By simultaneous induction of the structure of the given derivations. ☑

Completeness implies that it is not the case that a compiled goal is provable when the corresponding source goal is not. Again, the proof is constructive and a function mapping derivations in $(\mathcal{L}^c_{HH}, \xrightarrow{c})$ to derivations in $(\mathcal{L}_{HH}, \xrightarrow{u})$ can easily be extracted.

Theorem 3.2 (*Completeness of the compilation of* $\mathcal{L}_{\mathrm{HH}}$)

i. If $\Psi \xrightarrow{c} G$, $\Gamma \gg \Psi$ *and* $A \gg G$, *then* $\Gamma \xrightarrow{u} A$.

Uniform provability

$$\frac{\Delta \overset{?}{;} \Delta' \xrightarrow{u} A \gg a}{\Delta \hat{;} A \overset{?}{;} \Delta' \xrightarrow{u} a}\ \textsf{lu\_LinAtom} \qquad \frac{\Delta, A \overset{?}{;} \Delta' \xrightarrow{u} A \gg a}{\Delta, A \overset{?}{;} \Delta' \xrightarrow{u} a}\ \textsf{lu\_IntAtom}$$

$$\frac{}{\Delta \xrightarrow{u} \top}\ \textsf{lu\_Top} \qquad \frac{\Delta \xrightarrow{u} A_1 \quad \Delta \xrightarrow{u} A_2}{\Delta \xrightarrow{u} A_1 \,\&\, B_2}\ \textsf{lu\_With}$$

$$\frac{\Delta \hat{;} A_1 \xrightarrow{u} A_2}{\Delta \xrightarrow{u} A_1 \multimap A_2}\ \textsf{lu\_Lolli} \qquad \frac{\Delta, A_1 \xrightarrow{u} A_2}{\Delta \xrightarrow{u} A_1 \supset A_2}\ \textsf{lu\_Imp}$$

Immediate entailment

$$\frac{}{!\Delta \xrightarrow{u} a \gg a}\ \textsf{li\_Atom} \qquad \text{(No rule for } \top\text{)}$$

$$\frac{\Delta \xrightarrow{u} A_1 \gg a}{\Delta \xrightarrow{u} A_1 \,\&\, A_2 \gg a}\ \textsf{li\_With}_1 \qquad \frac{\Delta \xrightarrow{u} A_2 \gg a}{\Delta \xrightarrow{u} A_1 \,\&\, A_2 \gg a}\ \textsf{li\_With}_2$$

$$\frac{\Delta_1 \xrightarrow{u} A_1 \gg a \quad \Delta_2 \xrightarrow{u} A_2}{\Delta_1 \bowtie \Delta_2 \xrightarrow{u} A_2 \multimap A_1 \gg a}\ \textsf{li\_Lolli} \qquad \frac{\Delta \xrightarrow{u} A_1 \gg a \quad !\Delta \xrightarrow{u} A_2}{\Delta \xrightarrow{u} A_2 \supset A_1 \gg a}\ \textsf{li\_Imp}$$

Figure 4: Uniform Deduction System for $\mathcal{L}_{LHH}$.

ii. If $\Psi \xrightarrow{og} R$, $\Gamma \gg \Psi$, $R = [a/\alpha]C$ *and* $A \gg \alpha \backslash C$, *then* $\Gamma \xrightarrow{u} A \gg a$.

Proof. By mutual induction on the structure of the given derivations. ☑

4 Adding Linearity

The language of *linear hereditary Harrop* formulas [9], denoted $\mathcal{L}_{LHH}$, is the largest freely-generated fragment of intuitionistic linear logic with the properties satisfying the definition of an ALPL. Its operators are similar to the constructs of $\mathcal{L}_{HH}$ which can be viewed as a fragment of $\mathcal{L}_{LHH}$, modulo a simple encoding. $\mathcal{L}_{LHH}$ is the logic underlying the logic programming language *Lolli* [9]. The syntax of $\mathcal{L}_{LHH}$ is given by the following grammar.

$$\begin{array}{rl} \textit{Formulas:} & A ::= a \mid \top \mid A_1 \,\&\, A_2 \mid A_1 \multimap A_2 \mid A_1 \supset A_2 \mid \forall x.\, A \\ \textit{Contexts:} & \Delta ::= \cdot \mid \Delta, A \mid \Delta \hat{;} A \end{array}$$

As for $\mathcal{L}_{HH}$, we shall consider this definition independent from the language of terms. The assumptions contained in a context Δ are now distinguished in *linear* and *intuitionistic*; they are introduced by the constructors "$\hat{;}$" and ",", respectively. We write "$\overset{?}{;}$" as an abbreviation of "$\hat{;}$" or ",". We moreover write $!\Delta$ for a context from which all linear assumptions have been deleted, and $\Delta_1 \bowtie \Delta_2$ the result of the order-preserving merge of the linear assumptions in the contexts Δ_1 and Δ_2, which are assumed to contain identical intuitionistic assumptions [6]. We will omit discussing the universal quantifier since it is handled as in the non-linear case.

Figure 4 displays a deduction system for $\mathcal{L}_{LHH}$ set up in such a way that only uniform derivations are constructed. The involved judgments are similar to the non-linear case. A proof that $\mathcal{L}_{LHH}$ is an ALPL can be found in [9]. This result shows that a presentation similar to ours is sound and complete with respect to the usual rules for intuitionistic linear logic, as soon as $A_1 \supset A_2$ is expanded as $!A_1 \multimap A_2$ and every intuitionistic assumption A is replaced with $!A$.

Observe that rule **li_Lolli** displays a form of non-determinism not present in $\mathcal{L}_{HH}$: in order to implement this language, we must provide a strategy to partition the linear assumptions in the context Δ in the conclusion of this rule into the subcontexts Δ_1 and Δ_2 used in the premises, so that $\Delta = \Delta_1 \bowtie \Delta_2$ [5, 9].

An intermediate ALPL $(\mathcal{L}^c_{LHH}, \xrightarrow{c})$ for $\mathcal{L}_{LHH}$ with right introduction rules only is devised similarly to the case of hereditary Harrop formulas treated in Section 3: we consider constructs from full intuitionistic linear logic whose right rules have the same structure as the immediate entailment rules of $\mathcal{L}_{LHH}$. The only complication derives from the constraints linear logic imposes on the ways the context can be manipulated. It is easy to check that the correct choices for $\top$, & and $\multimap$ are $\mathbf{0}$, $\oplus$ and $\otimes$, respectively. Notice that, differently from $\mathcal{L}_{HH}$, $\multimap$ is mapped to multiplicative conjunction $\otimes$ and not to its additive counterpart &, which belongs to $\mathcal{L}_{LHH}$. As in the non-linear case, atomic clauses are rendered by adding a syntactic equality connective $\doteq$.

The only connective that we still need to analyze is intuitionistic implication, $\supset$. The immediate entailment rule for this connective has two premises and it prescribes that the program be integrally propagated to its left-hand branch, while only its intuitionistic assumptions should be forwarded to the right premise. Therefore, we are apparently compelled to invent a new connective, $\odot$ say, together with the desired right-introduction rule. This is a reasonable approach: it would simply have the effect of adding one more connective to linear logic. However, in this particular case, we can do better by observing that the right-introduction rule for the exponential operator ! is applicable only when its linear context is empty. The synergetic action of this connective and $\otimes$ achieve the desired effect:

$$\frac{\Delta \xrightarrow{u} A_1 \gg a \qquad !\Delta \xrightarrow{u} A_2}{\Delta \xrightarrow{u} A_2 \supset A_1 \gg a}\ \mathbf{li\_Imp} \qquad\qquad \frac{\Delta \longrightarrow A_1 \qquad \dfrac{!\Delta \longrightarrow A_2}{!\Delta \longrightarrow !A_2}}{\Delta \longrightarrow A_1 \otimes !A_2}$$

Therefore, if A_1 and A_2 are compiled into the clause C and the goal G respectively, the implication $A_1 \supset A_2$ is translated as $C \otimes !G$.

These considerations summon us to consider the language $\mathcal{L}^c_{LHH}$ defined by the following grammar as the intermediate language of $\mathcal{L}_{LHH}$.

$$\begin{array}{llcl} \textit{Goals:} & G & ::= & a \mid \top \mid G_1 \,\&\, G_2 \mid (\Lambda\alpha.\,C) \multimap G \mid (\Lambda\alpha.\,C) \supset G \mid \forall x.\,G \\ \textit{C-Goals} & R & ::= & a_1 \doteq a_2 \mid \mathbf{0} \mid R_1 \oplus R_2 \mid R \otimes G \mid R \otimes !G \mid \exists x.\,R \end{array}$$

Goals

$$\frac{\Psi \hat{;} \Psi' \xrightarrow{cg} [a/\alpha]C}{\Psi \hat{;} \Lambda\alpha.\, C \hat{;} \Psi' \xrightarrow{c} a}\ \text{lc\_LinAtom} \qquad \frac{\Psi, \Lambda\alpha.\, C \hat{;} \Psi' \xrightarrow{cg} [a/\alpha]C}{\Psi, \Lambda\alpha.\, C \hat{;} \Psi' \xrightarrow{c} a}\ \text{lc\_IntAtom}$$

$$\frac{}{\Psi \xrightarrow{c} \top}\ \text{lc\_Top} \qquad \frac{\Psi \xrightarrow{c} G_1 \quad \Psi \xrightarrow{c} G_2}{\Psi \xrightarrow{c} G_1 \,\&\, G_2}\ \text{lc\_With}$$

$$\frac{\Psi \hat{;} \Lambda\alpha.\, C \xrightarrow{c} G}{\Psi \xrightarrow{c} (\Lambda\alpha.\, C) \multimap G}\ \text{lc\_Lolli} \qquad \frac{\Psi, \Lambda\alpha.\, C \xrightarrow{c} G}{\Psi \xrightarrow{c} (\Lambda\alpha.\, C) \supset G}\ \text{lc\_Imp}$$

Compilation goals

$$\frac{}{!\Psi \xrightarrow{cg} a \doteq a}\ \text{lcg\_Eq} \qquad \text{(No rule for } \mathbf{0}\text{)}$$

$$\frac{\Psi \xrightarrow{cg} R_1}{\Psi \xrightarrow{cg} R_1 \oplus R_2}\ \text{lcg\_Plus}_1 \qquad \frac{\Psi \xrightarrow{cg} R_2}{\Psi \xrightarrow{cg} R_1 \oplus R_2}\ \text{lcg\_Plus}_2$$

$$\frac{\Psi_1 \xrightarrow{cg} R \quad \Psi_2 \xrightarrow{c} G}{\Psi_1 \bowtie \Psi_2 \xrightarrow{cg} R \otimes G}\ \text{lcg\_Times} \qquad \frac{!\Psi \xrightarrow{c} G}{!\Psi \xrightarrow{cg} !G}\ \text{lcg\_Bang}$$

Figure 5: Search Semantics of $\mathcal{L}^c_{LHH}$.

$$\begin{array}{lrcl} \textit{Clauses:} & C & ::= & a \doteq \alpha \mid \mathbf{0} \mid C_1 \,\&\, C_2 \mid C \otimes G \mid C \otimes !G \mid \exists x.\, C \\ \textit{Programs:} & \Psi & ::= & \cdot \mid \Psi, \Lambda\alpha.\, C \mid \Psi \hat{;} \Lambda\alpha.\, C \end{array}$$

The terminology, remarks, and conventions made in the non-linear case in Section 3 apply in the current setting.

The operational semantics of this language is given in Figure 5. Observe that it consists only of right-introduction rules. The above considerations about how to compile an intuitionistic implication in a program position lead to two alternative presentations of the search semantics of a c-goal of the form $R \otimes !G$. The simplest, displayed in Figure 5, views ! as an independent construct and relies on its right-introduction rule. Another possibility arises by observing that ! can only occur as the topmost operator of the right conjunct of $\otimes$. We could therefore have devised a rule specialized to this case:

$$\frac{\Psi \xrightarrow{cg} R \quad !\Psi \xrightarrow{c} G}{\Psi \xrightarrow{cg} R \otimes !G}\ \text{lcg\_TimesBang}$$

This is exactly the right sequent rule for the hypothetical connective $\odot$ we discussed earlier.

The rules describing the compilation of an expression in $\mathcal{L}_{LHH}$ into an object in $\mathcal{L}^c_{LHH}$ are given in Figure 6. Similarly to the non-linear case in Section 3, we can prove that they specify a bijection between $\mathcal{L}_{LHH}$ and $\mathcal{L}^c_{LHH}$, modulo obvious syntactic restrictions. The soundness and completeness for the compilation process of $\mathcal{L}_{LHH}$ is proved similarly to the non-linear case. We expect these proofs to be amenable to a direct encoding in the linear logical framework *LLF* [6]. We omit their statement for space reasons.

Programs

$$\frac{}{\cdot \gg \cdot}\ \text{lpc\_empty} \qquad \frac{\Delta \gg \Psi \quad A \gg \alpha \backslash C}{\Delta, A \gg \Psi, \Lambda\alpha. C}\ \text{lpc\_clause}$$

Clauses

$$\frac{}{a \gg \alpha \backslash a \doteq \alpha}\ \text{lcc\_Atom} \qquad \frac{}{\top \gg \alpha \backslash \mathbf{0}}\ \text{lcc\_Top} \qquad \frac{A_1 \gg \alpha \backslash C_1 \quad A_2 \gg \alpha \backslash C_2}{A_1 \,\&\, A_2 \gg \alpha \backslash C_1 \oplus C_2}\ \text{lcc\_With}$$

$$\frac{A_1 \gg \alpha \backslash C \quad A_2 \gg G}{A_2 \multimap A_1 \gg \alpha \backslash C \otimes G}\ \text{lcc\_Lolli} \qquad \frac{A_1 \gg \alpha \backslash C \quad A_2 \gg G}{A_2 \supset A_1 \gg \alpha \backslash C \otimes !G}\ \text{lcc\_Imp}$$

Goals

$$\frac{}{a \gg a}\ \text{lgc\_Atom} \qquad \frac{}{\top \gg \top}\ \text{lgc\_Top} \qquad \frac{A_1 \gg G_1 \quad A_2 \gg G_2}{A_1 \,\&\, A_2 \gg G_1 \,\&\, G_2}\ \text{lgc\_With}$$

$$\frac{A_1 \gg \alpha \backslash C \quad A_2 \gg G}{A_1 \multimap A_2 \gg (\Lambda\alpha. C) \multimap G}\ \text{lgc\_Lolli} \qquad \frac{A_1 \gg \alpha \backslash C \quad A_2 \gg G}{A_1 \supset A_2 \gg (\Lambda\alpha. C) \supset G}\ \text{lgc\_Imp}$$

Figure 6: Compilation of $\mathcal{L}_{LHH}$.

5 Conclusion and Future Work

In this paper, we have proposed an abstract, logic-independent and modular definition of the notion of compilation for logic programming languages, founded on proof-theory. We have described an effective method based on the duality between left and right sequent rules in order to find an intermediate language and to construct a compiler and a matching abstract machine from any abstract logic programming language. We have applied it to define abstract compilation systems for the language of hereditary Harrop formulas and for its linear refinement. We have furthermore sketched soundness and completeness proofs for the first of these examples.

Our compiled programs are clearly closer to the WAM than their sources, but there is still a wide gap to bridge in order to achieve the efficiency expected from compilation. We observed however that many of the optimizations found in the WAM can be achieved by proof-theoretic principles. In particular, it is easy to refine our system so that only pertinent clauses are selected (e.g., only those clauses defining atoms with the same predicate symbol as the goal). In a non-propositional setting, we can unfold the appropriate definition of $\doteq$ in a manner that is very reminiscent of the term instructions of the WAM. By systematically applying further simple logical manipulations, we obtain the following code in the case of "append" for example:

$$\begin{aligned}&\text{append} : \Lambda\alpha_1. \Lambda\alpha_2. \Lambda\alpha_3. \\ &\quad (\exists l.\, \text{nil} \doteq \alpha_1 \ \wedge\ l \doteq \alpha_2 \ \wedge\ l \doteq \alpha_3) \\ &\quad \vee (\exists k. \exists l. \exists m. \exists x. (x :: k) \doteq \alpha_1 \ \wedge\ l \doteq \alpha_2 \ \wedge\ (x :: m) \doteq \alpha_3 \ \wedge\ (\text{append}\, k\, l\, m))\end{aligned}$$

Observe that this corresponds exactly to the *Clark completion* [8] of the original clauses for "append": just prefix "(append $\alpha_1\ \alpha_2\ \alpha_3$) $\equiv$" in the scope of the abstractions. We indeed noticed that, in the case of *Prolog*, intermediate levels of compilation correspond to Clark completions of logic programs.

The approach described in this paper has been applied in a new implementation of the logical framework *LF* [19] as the constraint higher-order logic programming language *Twelf*, a successor to *Elf* [20]. In addition to constructs discussed in this paper, this formalism is characterized by (dependent) types and proof-terms. Handling the former is straightforward. Representing the latter in a *spine calculus* [7] enables an elegant treatment in our framework. At the time of writing, statistics to evaluate the benefits of compilation are not available, although *Twelf* has been observed to run significantly faster than the interpreted *Elf*. Indeed, it is not possible to measure the effects of compilation alone since *Twelf* is the result of a thorough redesign of its predecessor.

We intend to develop this research by showing that specific strategies to handle non-deterministic choices can be included in our compilation scheme and apply them to *Twelf*. We also intend to use the above techniques in order to compile *LLF* [6], a linear refinement of *LF*.

Acknowledgements

This research was supported by ONR grant N00014-97-1-0505. The author would like to thank Frank Pfenning for inspiring this work and for his comments on earlier versions of this paper.

References

[1] Hassan Aït-Kaci. *Warren's Abstract Machine: a Tutorial Reconstruction.* MIT Press, 1991.

[2] Christoph Beierle and Egon Börger. Correctness proof for the WAM with types. In E. Börger, G. Jäger, H. Kleine Büning, and M. M. Richter, editors, *Proceedings of the Fifth Workshop on Computer Science Logic — CSL'91*, pages 15–34. Springer-Verlag LNCS 626, 1992.

[3] Egon Börger and Dean Rosenzweig. The WAM — definition and compiler correctness. In C. Beierle and L. Pluemer, editors, *Logic Programming: Formal Methods and Practical Applications*, volume 11 of *Computer Science and Artificial Intelligence*, pages 21–90. North-Holland, 1995.

[4] Egon Börger and Rosario F. Salamone. CLAM specification for provably correct compilation of CLP programs. In E. Börger, editor, *Specification and Validation Methods*, pages 97–130. Oxford University Press, 1995.

[5] Iliano Cervesato, Joshua S. Hodas, and Frank Pfenning. Efficient resource management for linear logic proof search. In R. Dyckhoff, H. Herre, and P. Schroeder-Heister, editors, *Proceedings of the 5th International Workshop on Extensions of Logic Programming*, pages 67–81, Leipzig, Germany, March 1996. Springer-Verlag LNAI 1050.

[6] Iliano Cervesato and Frank Pfenning. A linear logical framework. In E. Clarke, editor, *Proceedings of the Eleventh Annual Symposium on Logic in Computer*

Science, pages 264–275, New Brunswick, New Jersey, July 1996. IEEE Computer Society Press.

[7] Iliano Cervesato and Frank Pfenning. A linear spine calculus. Technical Report CMU-CS-97-125, Department of Computer Science, Carnegie Mellon University, Pittsburgh, PA, April 1997.

[8] K.L. Clark. Negation as failure. In H. Gallaire and J. Minker, editors, *Logic and Databases*. Plenum Press, 1978.

[9] Joshua Hodas and Dale Miller. Logic programming in a fragment of intuitionistic linear logic. *Information and Computation*, 110(2):327–365, 1994. A preliminary version appeared in the Proceedings of the Sixth Annual IEEE Symposium on Logic in Computer Science, pages 32–42, Amsterdam, The Netherlands, July 1991.

[10] Joxan Jaffar, Spiro Michaylov, Peter Stuckey, and Roland Yap. An abstract machine for $CLP(\mathcal{R})$. In *Proceedings of the SIGPLAN'92 Conference on Programming Language Design and Implementation — PLDI'92*, San Francisco, CA, 1992.

[11] Ulrik Jørring and William L. Scherlis. Compilers and staging transformations. In *Thirteenth Symposium on Principles of Programming Languages*, pages 86–96. ACM, January 1986.

[12] Keehang Kwon, Gopalan Nadathur, and Debra Sue Wilson. Implementing polymorphic typing in a logic programming language. *Computer Languages*, 20(1):25–42, 1994.

[13] Peter J. Landin. The mechanical evaluation of expressions. *Computer Journal*, 6:308–320, 1964.

[14] Dale Miller. Lambda Prolog: An introduction to the language and its logic. Current draft available from `http://cse.psu.edu/~dale/lProlog`, 1996.

[15] Dale Miller, Gopalan Nadathur, Frank Pfenning, and Andre Scedrov. Uniform proofs as a foundation for logic programming. *Annals of Pure and Applied Logic*, 51:125–157, 1991.

[16] Gopalan Nadathur, Bharat Jayaraman, and Keehang Kwon. Scoping constructs in logic programming: Implementation problems and their solution. *Journal of Logic Programming*, 25(2):119–161, 1995.

[17] Gopalan Nadathur, Bharat Jayaraman, and Debra Sue Wilson. Implementation considerations for higher-order features in logic programming. Technical Report CS-1993-16, Department of Computer Science, Duke University, June 1993.

[18] Simon L. Peyton Jones. *The Implementation of Functional Programming Languages*. Prentice Hall, 1987.

[19] Frank Pfenning. Logic programming in the LF logical framework. In Gérard Huet and Gordon Plotkin, editors, *Logical Frameworks*, pages 149–181. Cambridge University Press, 1991.

[20] Frank Pfenning. Elf: A meta-language for deductive systems. In A. Bundy, editor, *Proceedings of the 12th International Conference on Automated Deduction*, pages 811–815, Nancy, France, June 1994. Springer-Verlag LNAI 814. System abstract.

[21] David M. Russinoff. A verified Prolog compiler for the Warren abstract machine. *Journal of Logic Programming*, 13:367–412, 1992.

[22] David H. D. Warren. an abstract Prolog instruction set. Technical Note 309, SRI International, Menlo Park, CA, October 1983.

Abstract compilation of λProlog

Frédéric Malésieux
École des Mines de Nantes, 4, rue Alfred Kastler, BP 20722,
F-44307 NANTES cedex03, France
`Frederic.Malesieux@emn.fr`

Olivier Ridoux
IRISA, Campus universitaire de Beaulieu,
F-35042 RENNES cedex, France
`Olivier.Ridoux@irisa.fr`

Patrice Boizumault
École des Mines de Nantes, 4, rue Alfred Kastler, BP 20722,
F-44307 NANTES cedex03, France
`Patrice.Boizumault@emn.fr`

Abstract

We propose a static analysis method for λProlog programs using a technique of abstract compilation that has already been applied to Prolog by Codish and Demoen. The method features two phases: program abstraction and goal abstraction. Since these phases require *normalized* programs as inputs, we present procedures for both the normalization of λProlog programs and their abstraction. The analysis of λProlog programs is more complex than for Prolog because the language include universal and existential quantifications, implication and λ-terms (higher-order). The principal difficulty is with higher-order because a static analysis must not only discover the properties of λ-terms but also how λ-terms propagate them. The propagation is described by *transfer functions*. We apply this method to groundness analysis.

1 Introduction

To compile more efficiently or to detect errors in programs requires to be able to analyze them before executing them. This is called static analysis.

In this article, we apply the technique of abstract compilation. It consists in translating a source program into an abstract program whose denotation is computed according to its concrete semantics. This can be compared with abstract interpretation, where a source program is evaluated with respect to an abstract semantics. Abstract compilation has been presented by Hermenegildo *et al.* [HWD92] and by Boucher *et al.* [BF96] and applied by Codish and Demoen to the groundness analysis of Prolog programs [CD95].

We transpose the abstract compilation technique to λProlog programs, and we apply it to the property of groundness. λProlog [MN86] extends

Prolog with λ-terms, and with the ability to use implication and explicit quantifications (either universal or existential) in clause bodies. The static analysis of λProlog programs can be studied according to two directions. On the one hand, the computation of properties that are classically studied for Prolog (groundness, mode, etc) can be extended to λProlog. On the other hand, the characteristics of this language require the specification of new properties such as β-normality or the fact that a term is a combinator or not. But, whatever the property studied, the main difficulty is to abstract higher-order.

We briefly present λProlog in Section 2. In Section 3, we expose the static analysis and abstract compilation of Prolog with Codish and Demoen's method. In Section 4, we propose a normalization of λProlog programs. It allows us to explain in Section 5 a proposition for abstracting λProlog programs with respect to groundness. Then, we illustrate our method on two examples of λProlog programs in Section 6.

2 λProlog

λProlog, designed by Dale Miller and Gopalan Nadathur [MN86], is a language which has features of both logic and higher-order functional programming, and still preserves some interesting logic and computation properties [MNS87]. In fact, λProlog can be described as a double extension of Prolog: one concerns terms and the other concerns the formulas.

λProlog terms are the simply typed λ-terms. Simple types, $\mathcal{T}$, are first-order terms built from a collection of type constants, a collection of type variables and one dedicated binary type constant, ->. The type of truth value is the type constant *o*. The arrow, ->, is right associative. This makes many brackets unnecessary: for instance, *(int->(int->int))* denotes the same type as *(int->int->int)* does.

Simply typed λ-terms are built from a collection of constants, $\mathcal{C}$, a collection of variables, $\mathcal{V}$, a collection of unknowns (logic variables), $\mathcal{U}$, and two construction rules: λ-abstraction[1], $\lambda x(E)$, and application, $(E\ F)$. Each constant must be declared with the *'type'* directive, specifying the type of a constant: for instance, *type + int->int->int* declares + as a constant of type *int->int->int*. λProlog allows polymorphic types: *type cons A->(list A)->(list A)*.

Three rewriting rules are defined on the set of terms. *α-Conversion* amounts to consistently renaming variables. So, a term λxM can be α-converted to $\lambda yM[x \leftarrow y]$ if y has no occurrence in M. The two terms are said to be *α-equivalent*. *β-Reduction* corresponds to a consistent parameter passing. The term $(\lambda xM\ N)$ β-reduce into $M[x \leftarrow N]$. The two terms are said to be *β-equivalent*. Here, "consistent" means that a precondition of

[1]We will consistently use "abstraction" for the abstraction as in static analysis and "λ-abstraction" for the abstraction as in the λ-Calculus.

β-reduction is that no free variable of N is bound in M. *η-Reduction* formalizes extensionallity of λ-defined functions. Thus, term $\lambda x(Mx)$ is η-reduced into M if x is not free in M. The two terms are said to be *η-equivalent.* A term is said to be in β-normal form if it contains no β-redex (subterms like $(\lambda xM\ N)$).

In the same way as Prolog's answer substitutions are produced *via* first-order unification, λProlog's answer substitutions are produced *via* higher-order unification [Hue75]. This is unification where the equality theory is based on α-, β-, and η-equivalence. Higher-order unification can be defined as well without η-equivalence, but η-equivalence is part of the logic of λProlog and must be coped with. This is a semi-decidable and infinitary problem: no unification procedure is certain to halt when an input problem has no solution, and there may be infinitely many most general solutions that can be enumerated by a non-deterministic algorithm.

A λProlog program is a set of declarations and an ordered set of clauses. As in Prolog, the constructor of non-unit clause is *':-'* and the conjunction constructor is *','*. The novelty of λProlog is in the goal language: explicit quantifications (universal and existential, written respectively "*pi*" and "*sigma*") and implications (written "=>") may occur in goals. Formulas generated this way are called *hereditary Harrop formulas.*

The word "scope" sums-up the new constructs of λProlog. λ-Abstraction limits the scope of variables in terms. Quantifications limit the scope of variables in formulas. And the deduction rules for universal quantification and implication limit the scope of constants and clauses, respectively, in the proof process.

The two following examples illustrate several features of λProlog: type definition, quantifications and implications.

Example 2.1 *type fnrev ((list A) -> (list A)) -> ((list A) -> (list A)) -> o.*
fnrev z\z z\z.
fnrev z\[A | (L z)] z\(R [A | z]) :- fnrev L R.

This example [BR91] defines the functional naive reverse predicate which is used to reverse functional lists (lists represented by functions). For example, the list *[1,2,3]* is represented by *z\[1,2,3|z]*. The second clause uses higher-order unification to split a list and to construct another one.

Example 2.2 *type abs (l_term -> l_term) -> l_term.*
type app l_term -> l_term -> l_term.
type typing l_term -> simple_type -> o.
typing (app X Y) B :- typing X (A -> B) , typing Y A.
typing (abs E) (A -> B) :- pi x\(typing x A => typing (E x) B).

This second example [BBR94] defines the well-typing relation by induction on a meta-level representation of λ-terms (the constructors of type *l_term*). It is a classic example of an important application domain of λProlog which is the manipulation of *higher-order abstract syntax* [PE88]. Using this representation, a term $\lambda x(x)$ is represented by *(abs x\x)*, and a term

$\lambda xy(x(xy))$ is represented by *(abs x\(abs \y(app x (app x y))))*. The clause for *app* is a pure Prolog clause, but the treatment of *abs* belongs to λProlog. A universal quantification *(pi x\)* introduces a universal variable of type *l_term*, which is the type on which the induction operates. So, one must augment the inductive definition in the scope of the universal quantification by using an implication. Here, clause *(typing x A)* is added to the program. It contains a free logical variable A that forces all the occurrences of x to have the same type.

In the domain of the static analysis of λProlog programs, some work on local analysis (clause level) has already been done [BR92] (detection of combinators or η-redexes). However, no work on global analysis has ever been done.

3 Static compilation of Prolog

One of the several techniques for doing static analysis is abstract compilation [HWD92, BF96]. The application of this technique to Prolog is presented by Codish and Demoen [CD95].

In logic programming, one says that a set of substitutions *Sub grounds* a variable x if each substitution in *Sub* instantiates x to a term containing no variables. So, the aim of groundness analysis is to determine which logic variables of which program atoms are always instantiated to ground terms during the program computation. Groundness is one of the most widely studied property on logic programming [JS87]. Codish and Demoen apply their method to this property, and so we will do in the sequel.

3.1 Codish and Demoen's method

Figure 1 represents Codish and Demoen's method. P^a and G^a are the abstract program and goal. P^a_m and G^a_m are the results of applying the so-called "magic" transformation [BMSU86, Ram91] to the abstract program and the abstract goal.

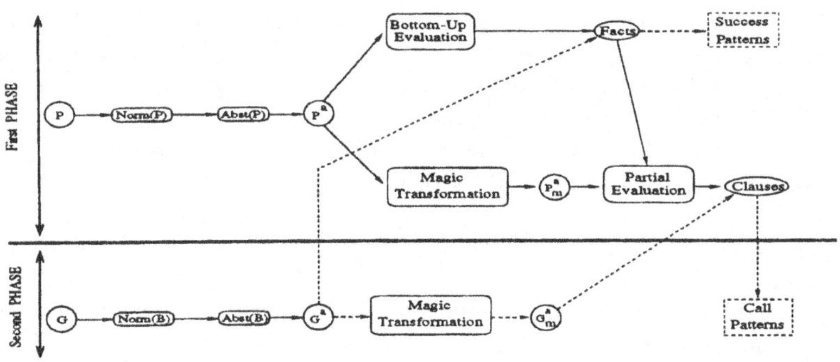

Figure 1: Codish and Demoen's analyzer

Their method provides two types of informations: *success patterns* and *call patterns*. Success patterns constitute an approximation of a program's non-ground minimal model. Call patterns describe the set of calls which arise in the computations of a goal G with a program P.

Before computing success-patterns and call-patterns, programs and goals must be normalized and then abstracted. Success patterns and call patterns are obtained in two phases. The first phase is independent from a query, and computes success patterns as the minimal model, $M(P^a)$, of the abstract program, P^a. The production of success patterns does not take into account the selection strategies (clauses and goals). Another task of the goal independent phase is to produces "call dependencies" that represent the fact that a predicate is called with some pattern if some other predicate has been successfully called with some other pattern. This takes into account the selection strategies by making them explicit *via* the "magic" transform. The "magically" transformed abstract program, P^a_m, is partially evaluated with respect to $M(P^a)$. The second phase depends on an input query. Success patterns can be used to characterize the answer substitutions of any initial query. Call patterns are computed by solving the "magically" transformed abstract query, G^a_m, with the call-dependency rules.

In the rest of this article, we focus on what happens between P and P^a (also G and G^a of course).

Normalization is independent of the analyzed property. It puts programs in a form such that each of the atoms and built-in predicates occurring in a program clause is either of the form $p(x_1, \ldots, x_n)$, $x = y$ or $x = f(y_1, \ldots, y_n)$ where x, x_i's, y and y_i's are distinct variables. The purpose of normalization is to make every unification step explicit, and that every goal corresponds to a single unification step. So, there must be at most one constant in every goal, and all variables of a goal must be different.

The abstraction of a normalized program is obtained by replacing every built-in predicate by a corresponding propositional predicate. Abstraction depends on the analyzed property because it describes the relation that exists between the arguments of a successful call to the built-in predicate. The equality predicate *=/2* introduced by normalization is always used in goals of the form $X = t$ where $vars(t) = X_1, \ldots, X_n$. For the groundness property, such a goal is abstracted into a goal *iff*$(X, X_1, \ldots, X_n)$.

A goal *iff*$(X, X_1, \ldots, X_n)$ is true if and only if $X \Leftrightarrow (X_1 \wedge \ldots \wedge X_n)$. In particular, *iff*$(X)$ is logically equivalent to X=*true*. The abstract program must include definitions for all of those *iff/n* predicates introduced by the abstraction. For groundness analysis, *iff*$(X, X_1, \ldots, X_n)$ can be read as X is bound to a ground term if and only if X_1, …, X_n are bound to ground terms.

The neat result of all this is that no functional symbols remains in the abstract program. More precisely, the abstract program is a Datalog program [Bid92] the domain of which is the *Pos* theory. The domain *Pos* [MS93], first called *Prop* [MS89, MS90] and further studied by Cortesi *et al.* [CFW91]

append(Xs, Ys,Zs) :- Xs=[], Ys=Zs.	*append(Xs, Ys,Zs) :- iff(Xs), iff(Ys,Zs).*
append(Xs, Ys,Zs) :- Xs=[X|Xs1], Zs=[X|Zs1], append(Xs1, Ys,Zs1).	*append(Xs, Ys,Zs) :- iff(Xs,X,Xs1), iff(Zs,X,Zs1), append(Xs1, Ys,Zs1).*
reverse(Xs, Ys) :- Xs=[], Ys=[]	*reverse(Xs, Ys) :- iff(Xs), iff(Ys).*
reverse(Xs, Ys) :- Xs=[X|Xs1], reverse(Xs1, Ys1), A=[X], append(Ys1,A, Ys).	*reverse(Xs, Ys) :- iff(Xs,X,Xs1), reverse(Xs1, Ys1), iff(A,X), append(Ys1,A, Ys).*

Figure 2: Normal form and abstraction of predicates *append* and *nrev*

consists of equivalence classes of propositional formulae constructed using the connectives $\Leftrightarrow$, $\wedge$ and $\vee$ ordered by implication (value *false* is added). Recent works have shown the optimality of domain *Pos* for analyzing Prolog groundness, and how it derives *naturally* from the specification of the groundness property [GS97, Sco97]. Computing all the answers of a Datalog program is a decidable problem. This is a crucial property for the abstract compilation technique: the language of the abstract programs must be a decidable language.

3.2 An example

Let P be the following Prolog program:

append([], L, L). *append([X|L], S, [X|R]) :- append(L, S, R).*
reverse([], []). *reverse([X|L], R) :- reverse(L, S), append(S, [X], R).*

The normal form of P (on the left) and its abstract form P^a (on the right) are as in Figure 2. Evaluating P^a yields the set $M(P^a)$ of all success patterns: *append(true,true,true)*, *append(true,false,false)*, *append(false,true,false)*, *append(false,false,false)*, *reverse(true,true)*, *reverse(false,false)*.

Let B be the goal *reverse([1],L)*. The abstract goal B^a is: *X=[Y|Z], Y=1, X=[], reverse(X,L)*. An approximation of the answer set is now computed by executing B^a on $M(P^a)$: {*reverse(true,true)*}. This result expresses that all answers to goal *reverse([1],L)* are ground.

4 Normalization of λProlog programs

We present a normalization procedure for λProlog programs. The purpose of the normalization of λProlog programs is the same as for Prolog: to make unification steps explicit. However, λ-terms make the details slightly more complex. We propose that in a normalized λProlog program every goal is either of the form[2] $p\ \overline{X_n}$, $X{=}Y$ or $X{=}\lambda\overline{x}(\Phi\ (X_1\ \overline{x})\ \ldots\ (X_m\ \overline{x}))$ where Φ can be either a constant, a λ-variable (one of the $\overline{x}$), or a logical variable, and the X_i's are distinct logical variables. In particular, Φ cannot be an application. We follow this convention in the sequel of this article. Moreover, all terms are η-expanded, so that the number of arguments of Φ reflects its type.

[2]In the sequel, we will write $\overline{x}$ for a finite sequence of x_i of undetermined length ($i \in [1\ldots]$), and $\overline{x_n}$ for a sequence of x of length n ($i \in [1\ n]$).

$$
\begin{array}{l}
Norm_{\mathcal{D}}\ [\![\forall x\ B]\!] \equiv \forall x(Norm_{\mathcal{D}}\ [\![B]\!]) \\
Norm_{\mathcal{D}}\ [\![p\ \overline{t_m}\ \text{:-}\ Body]\!] \equiv \forall \overline{X_m}(p\ \overline{X}\ \text{:-}\ Norm_{\mathcal{G}}\ [\![X_1{=}t_1\ ,\ \ldots\ ,\ X_m{=}t_m\ ,\ Body]\!]). \\
Norm_{\mathcal{G}}\ [\![p\ \overline{t_m}]\!] \equiv \exists \overline{X_m}(Norm_{\mathcal{G}}\ [\![X_1{=}t_1\ ,\ \ldots\ ,\ X_m{=}t_m]\!]\ ,\ p\ \overline{X}) \\
Norm_{\mathcal{G}}\ [\![A\ ,\ B]\!] \equiv Norm_{\mathcal{G}}\ [\![A]\!]\ ,\ Norm_{\mathcal{G}}\ [\![B]\!] \\
Norm_{\mathcal{G}}\ [\![A\ ;\ B]\!] \equiv Norm_{\mathcal{G}}\ [\![A]\!]\ ;\ Norm_{\mathcal{G}}\ [\![B]\!] \\
Norm_{\mathcal{G}}\ [\![\forall x\ B]\!] \equiv \forall x(Norm_{\mathcal{G}}\ [\![B]\!]) \\
Norm_{\mathcal{G}}\ [\![\exists x\ B]\!] \equiv \exists x(Norm_{\mathcal{G}}\ [\![B]\!]) \\
Norm_{\mathcal{G}}\ [\![C \Rightarrow B]\!] \equiv (Norm_{\mathcal{D}}\ [\![C]\!]) \Rightarrow (Norm_{\mathcal{G}}\ [\![B]\!]) \\
Norm_{\mathcal{G}}\ [\![F{=}\lambda\overline{x_n}(\Phi\ \overline{t_m})]\!] \equiv \exists \overline{X_m}(\ F{=}\lambda\overline{x_n}(\Phi\ (X_1\ \ \overline{x_n})\ \ldots\ (X_m\ \ \overline{x_n}))\ , \\
\qquad\qquad\qquad\qquad\qquad Norm_{\mathcal{G}}\ [\![X_1{=}\lambda\overline{x_n}\ t_1\ ,\ \ldots\ ,\ X_m{=}\lambda\overline{x_n}\ t_m]\!])
\end{array}
$$

Figure 3: Normalization of λProlog programs

The normalization procedure is presented in Figure 3. It has been implemented in λProlog. It consists in two sub-procedures, $Norm_{\mathcal{D}}$ and $Norm_{\mathcal{G}}$, for normalizing definite clauses and goals respectively. Note that we have handled all quantifications explicitly. This is almost useless in Prolog where everything boils down to essentially existential quantifications. However, this is crucial in λProlog because there may be universal quantifications in goals or in implied clauses: quantifications from the original program and quantifications introduced in its normal form must be properly scoped.

The second and third rules transform the atomic formulas of the program. The last rule normalizes program terms. The intuition of this rule is as follows. Let $F{=}\lambda\overline{x}(\Phi\ \overline{t})$ be a goal, then F and $\lambda\overline{x}(\Phi\ \overline{t})$ are functions, and $F{=}\lambda\overline{x}(\Phi\ \overline{t})$ implies $\forall\overline{x}[F\ \overline{x}{=}(\lambda\overline{x}(\Phi\ \overline{t}))\ \overline{x}]$. β-Reduction yields $\forall\overline{x}[F\ \overline{x}{=}(\Phi\ \overline{t})]$. In order to extract arguments $\overline{t}$ of the function, new existential variables, the $\overline{X}$, are introduced. They must be dependent of the universal quantified variables $\overline{x}$. This is the reason why the quantification of $\overline{X}$ is included in the quantification of $\overline{x}$: $\forall\overline{x}[\exists\overline{X}(F\ \overline{x}{=}(\Phi\ \overline{X}),(X_1{=}t_1),\ldots,(X_m{=}t_m))]$. Using skolemization, the existential quantification is put in front of the formula, while still keeping a trace of the fact that existential variables $\overline{X}$ may depend on universal variables $\overline{x}$. Thus, variables $\overline{X}$ are replaced by new variables $\overline{X'}$: $\exists\overline{X'}\forall\overline{x}[F\ \overline{x}{=}(\Phi\ (X'_1\ \overline{x})\ldots(X'_m\ \overline{x})),(X'_1\ \overline{x}{=}t_1),\ldots,(X'_m\ \overline{x}{=}t_m)]$. η-Equivalence yields the procedure's definition:

$\exists\overline{X'}[F{=}\lambda\overline{x}(\Phi\ (X'_1\ \overline{x})\ldots(X'_m\ \overline{x})),X'_1{=}\lambda\overline{x}t_1,\ldots,X'_m{=}\lambda\overline{x}t_m]$

To conclude, the normalization procedure that we propose for λProlog programs has the same result as the normalization of Prolog programs: it makes unification steps explicit.

5 Abstract compilation of λProlog programs

We describe a technique for abstracting λProlog programs with respect to the groundness property. The goal of groundness analysis is to determine which logic variables of which atoms are always instantiated to ground terms when the program is executed. In the case of λProlog this definition must be slightly modified because unification is done modulo λ-equivalence. The new definition is: groundness analysis is to determine which logic variables of which atoms are always instantiated to terms that are λ-equivalent to ground terms when the program is executed.

To abstract λProlog programs, we use a typed variant (overloading is forbidden in λProlog) of predicate *iff* defined as follows:

```
type iff bool -> (list bool) -> o.
iff true [].
iff false [false|_].
iff X [true|L] :- iff X L.
```

We study separately the abstract compilation of λ-terms and the abstract compilation of formulas.

5.1 Abstract compilation of λ-terms

A λ-term is ground if it contains no free variable. If it is ground, then its λ-normal form is also ground because λ-reduction does not introduce fresh variables (the only necessary renamings concern bound variables). However, if it is not ground, its λ-normal form may still be ground if its non-ground parts are dropped by λ-reduction (see Example 5.1). So, a λ-terms has two roles with respect to some property: it may satisfy the property, and it propagates the properties of its arguments to its λ-normal form. This feature is common to every attempt for analyzing higher-order programs. In order to illustrate this observation, let us take two examples.

Example 5.1 *Let* First = λxy(x) *be a λ-term.* (First 1 B) *β-reduces to a ground term even if* B *is not ground, because* First *only uses its first argument, which is ground.*

Example 5.2 *Let* F = λxyz(G x z), *and* G = λuv(v). (F A B C) *β-reduces to a ground term if and only if* C *does so.*

These examples show that the way a λ-term propagates the analyzed property must be represented somehow. We call it the *transfer function* of a λ-term. In the first example, *First* is ground but this does not say anything on how *First* propagates groundness. So, we have to associate with *First* a transfer function which says that the first argument is propagated but not the second. Such a transfer function can be represented by a boolean vector that says which arguments are actually used or not. For reasons of convenience in a logic programming setting, we will code these boolean vectors as boolean lists. So doing, the transfer function of term *First* is represented by *[true,false]*, meaning that its first argument is propagated but not the second. The transfer function of a given term is also used to compute the transfer functions of other terms in which it occurs. This part of the analysis bears similarities with strictness analysis in functional languages [Myc81].

Since abstraction is only applied on normalized programs, the form of every λ-term is $F{=}\lambda\overline{x_n}(\Phi\ (X_1\ \overline{x_n})\ \ldots\ (X_m\ \overline{x_n}))$ where Φ is either a constant (for instance *add*), a λ-variable (for instance x_i), or a non-instantiated variable. So, the property of F is a combination of the property of Φ and of the properties of the X's filtered by the transfer function of Φ. The properties of F, Φ, and X's are truth values (type *bool*). Similarly, the transfer function of F with respect to the x's is a combination of the transfer function of Φ with respect to the x's and of the transfer functions of the X's filtered by the transfer function of Φ with respect to the X's. So, one distinguishes the transfer function of Φ with respect to the X's (Φ_{tf_X}, or how Φ propagates the X's), and the transfer function of Φ with respect to the x's (Φ_{tf_x}, or how Φ propagates the x's). The transfer functions of F and of the X's are always boolean lists of length n. The transfer function of Φ with respect to the X's is a boolean list of length m, whereas the transfer function of Φ with respect to the x's is a boolean list of length n.

Definition 5.1 *(Higher-order disjunction) (ho_disj F_{tf} Φ_{tf_x} Φ_{tf_X} Xs_{tf_x})* $\stackrel{def}{=}$ *F_{tf} is a transfer function such that F_{tf_i} is true iff $\Phi_{tf_{x_i}}$ is true or the i-th element of some $Xs_{tf_{x_j}}$ marked true in Φ_{tf_X} is true.*

In other words, the *transfer function* of F with respect to the x's is built using a disjunction between the *transfer function* of Φ with respect to the x's and the *transfer function* of the X's that are propagated by Φ. This requires to elaborate the *transfer function* of Φ with respect to the X's.

Predicate *ho_disj* can be written in λProlog as follows:

```
type ho_disj (list pos)->(list pos)->(list pos)->(list(list pos))->o.
ho_disj L L [] [].
ho_disj Res G [true|Ls] [L|LL] :- ho_disj Res1 G Ls LL , disj Res L Res1.
ho_disj Res G [false|Ls] [_|LL] :- ho_disj Res G Ls LL.
```

where predicate *disj* specifies the disjunction between two transfer functions (the result is the first argument):

```
type disj (list bool) -> (list bool) -> (list bool) -> o.
disj [] [] [].
disj [true|Lz] [true|Lx] [_|Ly] :- disj Lx Ly Lz.
disj [true|Lz] [_|Lx] [true|Ly] :- disj Lx Ly Lz.
disj [false|Lz] [false|Lx] [false|Ly] :- disj Lx Ly Lz.
```

Remark 5.1 *ho_disj F G [] []* $\equiv$ *F=G*

Let us consider the second example again. The normalized form of F is $F{=}\lambda xyz(G\ (E_0\ xyz)\ (E_1\ xyz))$, $E_0{=}\lambda xyz(x)$, $E_1{=}\lambda xyz(z)$. Intuitively, F β-reduces to a ground term iff G is ground and all E_i with a corresponding "true" in the *transfer function* of G β-reduce to a ground term. The properties of every λ-term are represented by boolean values which are calculated with predicate *ho_iff* defined as follows:

Definition 5.2 *(ho_iff F_p Φ_p Φ_{tf} Xs_p)* $\stackrel{def}{=}$ *F_p is true iff Φ_p is true and all members of Xs_p with a corresponding "true" in Φ_{tf} are true.*

In other words, F has a certain property if Φ has this property and if all its arguments ($X1 \ldots Xm$) modulo the transfer function Φ_{tf} have the same property. Predicate *ho_iff* is defined as follows:

type ho_iff pos -> pos -> (list pos) -> (list pos) -> o.
ho_iff true true [] [].
ho_iff false false _ _.
ho_iff false true [true|_] [false|_].
ho_iff X true [true|Fs] [true|Ls]:- ho_iff X true Fs Ls.
ho_iff X true [false|Fs] [_|Ls]:- ho_iff X true Fs Ls.

In the rest of this section, $item^{(k)}$ denotes k copies of *item* in a list.

Remark 5.2 $ho\_iff\ F\ G\ []\ [] \equiv iff\ F\ [G]$
$ho\_iff\ F\ G\ [false^{(m)}]\ X \equiv iff\ F\ [G]$
$ho\_iff\ F\ G\ [true^{(m)}]\ X \equiv iff\ F\ [G|X]$
$ho\_iff\ F\ true\ [true^{(m)}]\ X \equiv iff\ F\ X$
$ho\_iff\ F\ G\ [false^{(i-1)},true,false^{(m-i)}]\ X \equiv iff\ F\ [G,X_i]$

We present now the complete procedure for abstracting the λ-terms.

Definition 5.3 $Abstr\ [\![F = \lambda\overline{x_n}(\Phi\ (X1\ \overline{x_n}) \ldots (Xm\ \overline{x_n}))]\!] \equiv$
$ho\_iff\ F_p\ \Phi_p\ \Phi_{tf}\ [X1_p, \ldots, Xm_p],$
$ho\_disj\ F_{tf}\ \Phi_v\ \Phi_{tf}\ [X1_{tf}, \ldots, Xm_{tf}]$

- *If* Φ *is a constant:* Φ_p=*true*, $\Phi_{tf}=[true^{(m)}]$, $\Phi_v=[false^{(n)}]$
- *If* Φ *is a* λ*-variable:*
  Φ_p=*true*, $\Phi_{tf}=[true^{(m)}]$, $\Phi_v=[false^{(i-1)},true,false^{(n-i)}]$
- *If* Φ *is an unknown:* $\Phi_v=[false^{(n)}]$, Φ_p *and* Φ_{tf} *are unknowns.*

Remark 5.3 $Abstr\ [\![F = f\ (X1 \ldots Xm)]\!] \equiv$
$ho\_iff\ F_p\ true\ [true^{(m)}]\ [X1_p, \ldots, Xm_p]$,
$ho\_disj\ F_{tf}\ []\ [true^{(m)}]\ [[], \ldots, []]$.

If the transfer functions *are never needed, as is the case in pure Prolog, the resulting abstraction is:*
$Abstr\ [\![F = f\ (X1 \ldots Xm)]\!] \equiv iff\ F_p\ [X1_p, \ldots, Xm_p],$
which is the abstraction rule proposed by Codish and Demoen for Prolog.

Remark 5.4 *There are two other frequently occurring special cases:*

- $Abstr\ [\![F = \lambda\overline{x_n}(x_i)]\!] \equiv$
  $ho\_iff\ F_p\ true\ []\ []\ ,\ ho\_disj\ F_{tf}\ [false^{(i-1)},true,false^{(n-i)}]\ []\ []$

hence, $Abstr\ [\![F = \lambda\overline{x_n}(x_i)]\!] \equiv F_p=true\ ,\ F_{tf}=[false^{(i-1)},true,false^{(n-i)}]$

- $Abstr\ [\![F = \lambda\overline{x_n}(E)]\!] \equiv ho\_iff\ F_p\ E_p\ []\ []\ ,\ ho\_disj\ F_{tf}\ [false^{(n)}]\ []\ []$

hence, $Abstr\ [\![F = \lambda\overline{x_n}(E)]\!] \equiv F_p=E_p\ ,\ F_{tf}=[false^{(n)}]$

Example 5.3 *A goal* F=λxy(x y) *is first normalized in*
F=λxy(x (X1 x y)) , X1=λxy(y).
It is then abstracted in
ho_iff F_p true [true] [$X1_p$] , ho_disj F_{tf} [true,false] [true] [$X1_{tf}$] ,
ho_iff $X1_p$ true [] [] , ho_disj $X1_{tf}$ [false,true], [] [] .
Using definitions 5.1 and 5.2, the abstract goal can be simplified into
$X1_{tf}$=[false,true] , $X1_p$=true , F_{tf}=[true,true] , F_p=true.

5.2 Abstract compilation of formulas

Atomic formulas are abstracted into atomic formulas of the corresponding abstract predicate with every variable replaced by its property and its transfer function. For convenience, we amalgamate the property and the transfer function in a single boolean list. Another solution would have been to double the parameters. An abstraction procedure operates on goals, $Abstr_{\mathcal{G}}$, and another on definite clauses, $Abstr_{\mathcal{D}}$.

Definition 5.4 $Abstr\ [\![p\ X1 \ldots Xn\ ]\!] \equiv p\ [X1_p \mid X1_{tf}] \ldots [Xn_p \mid Xn_{tf}]$

This applies to clause heads and atoms in bodies. So doing, a predicate p of arity n and type t is abstracted into a predicate p and arity n, but of a different type: *(list bool)->(list bool)->...->(list bool)->o.*

The implicit outermost universal quantifications are abstracted as quantifications of properties and transfer functions. An unknown is simply replaced by two unknowns that represent its property and its transfer function. Clause level quantifications are often ignored in Prolog, but this is no more possible in λProlog because there can be nested clauses (see Definition 5.7). Existential quantifications in goals are abstracted in the same way.

Definition 5.5 $Abstr_{\mathcal{D}}\ [\![\forall X\ D]\!] \equiv \forall X_p \forall X_{tf} (Abstr_{\mathcal{D}}\ [\![D]\!])$
$Abstr_{\mathcal{G}}\ [\![\exists X\ G]\!] \equiv \exists X_p \exists X_{tf} (Abstr_{\mathcal{G}}\ [\![G]\!])$

Universal quantifications in goals introduce universal variables, hence ground terms.

Definition 5.6 $Abstr_{\mathcal{G}}\ [\![\forall x\ G]\!] \equiv (Abstr_{\mathcal{G}}\ [\![G[x \leftarrow c]]\!])$
where c is any constant of the appropriate type.

Abstraction of implications propagates abstraction on both sides of the connective ("=>" in goals or ":-" in clauses).

Definition 5.7 $Abstr_{\mathcal{G}}\ [\![D \Rightarrow G]\!] \equiv (Abstr_{\mathcal{D}}\ [\![D]\!]) \Rightarrow (Abstr_{\mathcal{G}}\ [\![G]\!])$
$Abstr_{\mathcal{G}}\ [\![H\ \text{:-}\ G]\!] \equiv (Abstr\ [\![H]\!])\ \text{:-}\ (Abstr_{\mathcal{G}}\ [\![G]\!])$

5.3 Discussion

The programs obtained using the abstraction procedure described in the previous sections are not Datalog programs for two reasons: some variables range on lists instead of on constants, and some clauses contain implications in goals.

Lists in abstract programs are not a real breach in the Datalog property. Remember that they are only an encoding for boolean vectors whose length is always known statically. There is always a finite number of such vectors, hence of the lists that are actually considered. Resolution strategies that are complete for finite domain Prolog programs [War92] are also complete for this concern.

```
fnrev U0 U1 :-
      U0=x\x,
      U1=x\x.
fnrev U0 U1 :-
      U0=x\[(E0 x)|(E1 x)],

      E0=x\A,
      E1=x\(L(E2 x)),

      E2=x\x,
      U1=x\(R(E3 x)),

      E3=x\[(E4 x)|(E5 x)],

      E4=x\A,
      E5=x\x ,
      fnrev L R.
```

```
fnrev [U0_p|U0_tf] [U1_p|U1_tf] :-
      ho_iff U0_p true [] [], ho_disj U0_tf [true] [] [],
      ho_iff U1_p true [] [], ho_disj U1_tf [true] [] [].
fnrev [U0_p|U0_tf] [U1_p|U1_tf] :-
      ho_iff U0_p true [true,true] [E0_p,E1_p],
      ho_disj U0_tf [false] [true,true] [E0_tf,E1_tf],
      ho_iff E0_p A_p [] [], ho_disj E0_tf [false] [] [],
      ho_iff E1_p L_p L_tf [E2_p],
      ho_disj E1_tf [false] L_tf [E2_tf],
      ho_iff E2_p true [] [], ho_disj E2_tf [true] [] [],
      ho_iff U1_p R_p R_tf [E3_p],
      ho_disj U1_tf [false] R_tf [E3_tf],
      ho_iff E3_p true [true,true] [E4_p, E5_p],
      ho_disj E3_tf [false] [true,true] [E4_tf,E5_tf],
      ho_iff E4_p A_p [] [], ho_disj E4_tf [false] [] [],
      ho_iff E5_p true [] [], ho_disj E5_tf [true] [] [],
      fnrev [L_p|L_tf] [R_p|R_tf] .
```

Figure 4: Normal form and abstraction of predicates *fnrev*

Implications in goals are more profound. They are a real breach in the Datalog property in that no decision procedure known for Datalog applies directly to Datalog with implications in goals, Datalog$_{\Rightarrow}$. However, the decision in Datalog$_{\Rightarrow}$ has already been studied [Bon90]. The fragment Datalog$_{\Rightarrow}$ of predicate logic is still a decidable fragment, and so it makes sense to use it as the target of an abstract compilation method.

Note that the language of the abstract programs depends on the analysed property. It may be that for another property universal quantifications in goals remain in abstract programs. This will be still a greater breach because Datalog$_{\Rightarrow\forall}$ is undecidable in general [BMV89]. However, this may not be a real problem because if the allowed combinations of $\Rightarrow$ and $\forall$ are restricted, one gets a decidable fragment again.

6 Groundness analysis: examples

6.1 Functional naive reverse predicate

Let *fnrev* be a predicate which reverses a functional list.

```
fnrev z\z z\z.
fnrev z\[A | (L z)] z\(R [A | z]) :- fnrev L R .
```

• Goal independent analysis. The normal form (on the left) and the abstraction (on the right) of this program are given in Figure 4. Success patterns are *fnrev [true,true] [true,true]* and *fnrev [false,true] [false,true]*.

• Goal dependent analysis: let *fnrev x\[2,3|x] FL* be a goal. The normal form and the abstraction of this goal are given in Figure 5. Using the remarks of the previous section, the abstract goal can be simplified into *fnrev [true,true] FL*. The corresponding success pattern is *fnrev [true,true] [true,true]*. This says that if predicate *fnrev* is called with its first argument ground, its second argument will be ground when the execution finishes.

```
U0=x\[(E0 x)|(E1 x)],

E0=x\2,
E1=x\[(E2 x)|(E3 x)],

E2=x\3,
E3=x\x,
fnrev U0 FL
```

```
ho_iff U0_p true [true,true] [E0_p, E1_p],
ho_disj U0_tf [false] [true,true] [E0_tf,E1_tf],
ho_iff E0_p true [] [], ho_disj E0_tf [false] [] [],
ho_iff E1_p true [true,true] [E2_p, E3_p],
ho_disj E1_tf [false] [true,true] [E2_tf,E3_tf],
ho_iff E2_p true [] [] , ho_disj E2_tf [false] [] [],
ho_iff E3_p true [] [] , ho_disj E3_tf [true] [] [],
fnrev [U0_p|U0_tf] FL .
```

Figure 5: Normal form and abstraction of goal *fnrev x\[2,3|x] FL*

```
typing U0 B :-
      U0=app X Y,

      typing X E0,
      E0=A -> B,

      typing Y A.
typing U0 U1 :-
      U0=(abs E),

      U1=A -> B

      pi x\( pi E0\(
            typing E0 A :-
             E0=x)

        => (E1=(E E2),

            E2=x,

            typing E1 B)).
```

```
typing [U0_p|U0_tf] [B_p|B_tf] :-
      ho_iff U0_p true [true,true] [X_p, Y_p],
      ho_disj U0_tf [] [true,true] [[],[]],
      typing [X_p|X_tf] [E0_p|E0_tf],
      ho_iff E0_p true [true,true] [A_p, B_p],
      ho_disj E0_tf [] [true,true] [[],[]],
      typing [Y_p|Y_tf] [A_p|A_tf].
typing [U0_p|U0_tf] [U1_p|U1_tf] :-
      ho_iff U0_p true [true] [E_p],
      ho_disj U0_tf [] [true] [[]],
      ho_iff U1_p true [true,true] [A_p, B_p],
      ho_disj U1_tf [] [true,true] [[],[]],
      (     pi E0_p\(pi E0_tf\(
            typing [E0_p|E0_tf] [A_p|A_tf] :-
                  ho_iff E0_p true [] [] ,
                  ho_disj E0_tf [] [] []))
      => (ho_iff E1_p E_p E_tf [E2_p],
            ho_disj E1_tf [] E_tf [[]],
            ho_iff E2_p true [] [],
            ho_disj E2_tf [] [] [],
            typing [E1_p|E1_tf] [B_p|B_tf]).
```

Figure 6: Normal form and abstraction of predicate *typing*

6.2 Well-typing relation

Consider the predicate typing λProlog expressions. It features a combination of all the new capabilities of λProlog (λ-terms, universal quantifications and implications in goals).

typing (app X Y) B :- typing X (A -> B) , typing Y A.

typing (abs E) (A -> B) :- pi x\(typing x A => typing (E x) B).

The normal form and the abstraction of predicate *typing* are given in Figure 6. The evaluation of *typing* yields *typing [true] [true]* and *typing [true] [false]*.

7 Conclusion and further works

Codish and Demoen have proposed a method for the static analysis of Prolog programs which is based on abstract compilation. They apply their method to the analysis of the groundness property. We propose an extension of this method for the static analysis of λProlog programs.

The method involves several phases. First, λProlog programs must be normalized in order to make all unification problems explicit. Things are slightly more complicated than for Prolog because one has to cope with λ-terms and λ-equivalence. Second, λProlog programs are abstracted with respect to a given property (in this article, the groundness property). The difficulty in this phase is to represent properly how higher-order terms propagate the analysed property. This problem is common to the analysis of every higher-order language. Our abstract compilation scheme associates to every variable its property and a representation of its transfer function (how it propagates the property of interest).

The result of abstracting a λProlog program with respect to the groundness property is a $\text{Datalog}_{=>}$ program. This still falls in the realm of decidable fragments of the predicate calculus. Note however, that this may not be the case for other properties, and that the decidability of the language of the abstract programs must be assessed for every property of interest.

The static analysis of the groundness property of λProlog programs is only a first step. Indeed, other classical properties of Prolog are of interest for λProlog (e.g. modes), and the static analysis of properties that are specific to λProlog (e.g. λ-normality) is also required. These analyses may lead to a general purpose extension of Datalog, in which implications and universal quantifications in goals, and λ-terms would be allowed to occur in a disciplined way (let us call it λDatalog), so as to keep the decidability property.

References

[BBR94] C. Belleannée, P. Brisset, and O. Ridoux. A pragmatic reconstruction of λProlog. Number 2390. INRIA, Rennes, Octobre 1994.

[BF96] D. Boucher and M. Feeley. Abstract compilation: A new implementation paradigm for static analysis. In T. Gyimthy, editor, *CC*, volume 1060 of *LNCS*, pages 192–207, Linköping, Sweden, April 1996.

[Bid92] N. Bidoit. *Bases de Données déductives: Présentation de Datalog*. A. Colin, 1992.

[BMSU86] F. Bancilhon, D. Maier, Y. Sagiv, and J. Ullman. Magic sets and other strange ways to implement logic programs. In *Symp. on Principles of Database Systems*, pages 1–15, 1986.

[BMV89] A.J. Bonner, L.T. McCarty, and K. Vadaparty. Expressing database queries with intuitionistic logic. In E.L. Lusk and R.A. Overbeek, editors, *NACLP*, pages 831–850. MIT Press, 1989.

[Bon90] A.J. Bonner. Hypothetical datalog: Complexity and expressibility. *Theoretical Computer Science*, 76:3–51, 1990.

[BR91] P. Brisset and O. Ridoux. Naive reverse can be linear. In K. Furukawa, editor, *ICLP*, pages 857–870. MIT Press, 1991.

[BR92] P. Brisset and O. Ridoux. The architecture of an implementation of λProlog: Prolog/mali. In *Workshop on λProlog*, Philadelphia, PA, USA, 1992.

[CD95] M. Codish and B. Demoen. Analyzing logic programs using "Prop"-ositional logic programs and a magic wand. *Journal of Logic Programming*, 25(3):249–274, 1995.

[CFW91] A. Cortesi, G. Filé, and W. Winsborough. Prop revisited: Propositional formula as abstract domain for groundness analysis. In *SLCS*, volume CH3025-4, pages 322–327, Amsterdam - The Netherlands, 1991. IEEE.

[GS97] R. Giacobazzi and F. Scozzari. Intuitionistic implication in abstract interpretation. In H. Glaser, P. Hartel, and H. Kuchen, editors, *PLILP*, volume 1292 of *LNCS*, pages 175–189. Springer-Verlag, 1997.

[Hue75] G. Huet. A unification algorithm for typed λ-calculus. *Theoretical Computer Science*, (1):27–57, 1975.

[HWD92] M. Hermenegildo, R. Warren, and S. K. Debray. Global flow analysis as a practical compilation tool. *Journal of Logic Programming*, 13(3):349–366, 1992.

[JS87] N.D. Jones and H. Søndergaard. *Abstract Interpretation of Declarative Languages*, chapter A semantics-based framework for the abstract interpretation of PROLOG, pages 123–142. Ellis Horwood Ltd, 1987.

[MN86] D.A. Miller and G. Nadathur. Higher order logic programming. In E. Shapiro, editor, *ICLP*, pages 448–462. Springer-Verlag, 1986.

[MNS87] D.A. Miller, G. Nadathur, and A. Scedrov. Hereditary Harrop formulas and uniform proof systems. In D. Gries, editor, *SLCS*, pages 98–105, Ithaca, New York, USA, 1987.

[MS89] K. Marriott and H. Søndergaard. Notes for a tutorial on abstract interpretation of logic programs. In *NACLP*, Cleveland - Ohio, 1989.

[MS90] K. Marriott and H. Søndergaard. Abstract interpretation of logic programs : denotational approach. In A. Bossi, editor, *GULP*, Padova, 1990.

[MS93] K. Marriott and H. Søndergaard. Precise and efficient groundness analysis for logic programs. *ACM Letters on Programming Languages and Systems*, 2(1–4):181–196, 1993.

[Myc81] A. Mycroft. *Abstract Interpretation and optimising transformations of applicative programs*. PhD thesis, Edinburgh University, 1981.

[PE88] F. Pfenning and C. Elliot. Higher-order abstract syntax. In *PLDI*, pages 199–208. ACM Press, June 1988.

[Ram91] R. Ramakrishnan. Magic templates : A spellbinding approach to logic programs. *Journal of Logic Programming*, 11(3):189–216, 1991.

[Sco97] F. Scozzari. Logical optimality of groundness analysis. In P. Van Hentenryck, editor, *SAS*, volume 1302 of *LNCS*, pages 83–97. Springer-Verlag, 1997.

[War92] D.S. Warren. Memoing for logic programs. *Communications of the ACM*, 35(3):94–111, 1992.

Efficient Implementation of a Linear Logic Programming Language

Joshua S. Hodas and Kevin M. Watkins
Department of Computer Science
Harvey Mudd College
Claremont, CA 91711, USA
`hodas@cs.hmc.edu`, `kwatkins@cs.hmc.edu`

Naoyuki Tamura and Kyoung-Sun Kang
Department of Computer and Systems Engineering
Kobe University
Rokkodai, Nada, Kobe 657-8501, Japan
`tamura@kobe-u.ac.jp`, `kang@pascal.seg.kobe-u.ac.jp`

Abstract

A number of logic programming languages based on Linear Logic [3] have been proposed. However, the implementation techniques proposed for these languages have relied heavily on the copying and scanning of large data structures to ensure that linearity conditions have been met, and thus have been most suited to the creation of interpreters written in high-level languages. In this paper we present a new formulation of the logic of the language Lolli that is conducive to the creation of both more efficient interpreters, as well as compilers based on extensions of the standard WAM model. We present such an extension which implements a useful fragment of Lolli. Resource conscious algorithms executed using this system show significant performance advantages relative to their traditional Prolog implementations.

1 Introduction

Implementing logic programming languages based on Linear Logic [3] presents a number of problems, as the constraints on the use of assumptions must be carefully maintained. The issue of *resource management* has been discussed from the earliest proposals [8], and recently several papers have focused exclusively on these issues [2, 6, 4]. However, most of the methods proposed for controlling resource consumption have been specified in a manner that requires the manipulation of large structures. This makes them more suited to implementation by interpreters written in high-level languages, rather than by compilers. Indeed, all implementations of these languages to date have been interpreter-based.

In this paper we first introduce some of the basic concepts of linear logic programming. We discuss some of the basic issues in resource management, and then show how a recent treatment of the logic underlying the language Lolli can be reformulated to provide the foundations of a compiler for a fragment of the language. We present the specification of the compiler for the fragment, which we call LLP, to an extension of the Warren Abstract Machine (WAM). Finally, we show that, for the first time, the linear logic programming solution to a problem can be executed more efficiently than the traditional logic programming solution.

2 Linear Logic Programming

In linear logic the *structural rules* of weakening and contraction are available only for assumptions marked with the modal (or, as it is called in linear logic, *exponential*) "!". This means that, in general, a formula not thus marked can only be used once in a branch of the search for a proof.

2.1 Reasoning With Limited Resources

Limited-use formulas, which we will refer to as *linear resources* (we will refer to assumptions marked with the ! as *intuitionistic resources*) can represent limited resources in some domain. For example, in linear logic, the following formula (which is a tautology in traditional systems) would not be provable:

$$((dollar \supset pizza) \wedge (dollar \supset soda)) \supset (dollar \supset (pizza \wedge soda))$$

The reason is that the *dollar* assumption provided by the formula $(dollar \supset (pizza \wedge soda))$ cannot be used twice to drive both the rules on the left. The linear logic programming language Lolli [8] has been developed implements these constraints on the use of assumptions.

In many Prolog programs a list is used to store a set of resources on which the program relies, and this set is managed in a manner corresponding to the constraint on assumptions in linear logic. Consider the solution to the N-Queens problem given in The Art Of Prolog [10], which is shown on the left side of Figure 1. In this program, a list is used to store column positions corresponding to the rows of the chess board. For each row of the board, we `select` an unused column and test if it is safe to place the queen there. The list is managed to insure that each column is only used once.

The same basic technique is used in the Lolli program on the right side of Figure 1. The only difference is that resources are used to represent columns (`c/1`) and diagonals (`d/1` and `u/1`). This is done simply because it is easy to do in this setting.

2.2 The Operators of Linear Logic

In the absence of contraction and weakening, many of the logical operators split into two variants. For example, the conjunction operator splits into *tensor*, "$\otimes$", and *with*, "&". In proving a conjunction formed with $\otimes$, the

```
queen_all(N) :-queens(N, Q),fail.
queen_all(_).

queens(N, Qs) :- range(1, N, Ns),
                 queens(Ns, [], Qs).

queens([], Qs, Qs).
queens(UnplacedQs, SafeQs, Qs) :-
    select(Q,UnplacedQs,UnplacedQs1),
    \+ attack(Q,SafeQs),
    queens(UnplacedQs1,[Q|SafeQs],Qs).

select(X, [X|Xs], Xs).
select(X, [Y|Ys], [Y|Zs]) :-
    select(X, Ys, Zs).

attack(X, Xs) :- attack(X, 1, Xs).
attack(X, N, [Y|Ys]) :- X is Y + N ;
                        X is Y - N.
attack(X, N, [Y|Ys]) :-N1 is N + 1,
                        attack(X, N1, Ys).

range(M, N, [M|Ns]) :- M < N, M1 is M + 1,
                       range(M1, N, Ns).
range(N, N, [N]).
```

```
queen_all(N) :- queens(N, Q), fail.
queen_all(_).

queens(N, Q) :-n(N) -o result(Q) -o
                  rangeQueens(N).

rangeQueens(1) :-
    n(N),  (c(1),u(2),d(0)) -o
                solve(N, []).
rangeQueens(I) :-
   I > 1, I1 is I-1, U1 is 2*I,
   U2 is 2*I-1,D1 is I-1,D2 is 1-I,
   (c(I),u(U1),u(U2),d(D1),d(D2)) -o
        rangeQueens(I1).

solve(0, Q) :-result(Q), erase.
solve(I, Q) :-
   I > 0,c(J),U is I+J,u(U),
   solve(I1, [J|Q]).
```

Figure 1: **Left:** Resource-driven N-Queens program in Prolog from Art Of Prolog, Chap. 14. **Right:**Resource-driven N-Queens program in Lolli

current set of assumptions is split between the two conjuncts: those not used in proving the first conjunct must be used while proving the second. To prove a & conjunction, the set of assumptions is copied to both sides: each conjunct's proof must use all of the assumptions. In Lolli, the $\otimes$ conjunction is represented by the familiar "`,`". This is a natural mapping, as we expect the effect of a succession of goals to be cumulative. Each has available to it the resources not yet used by its predecessors. The & conjunction, which is less used, is written "`&`".

Though there are two forms of disjunction, only one, "$\oplus$" is used in Lolli. There are two forms of truth, $\top$, and **1**. The latter, which Lolli calls "`true`", can only be proved if all the assumptions have already been used. In contrast, the formula $\top$ is true even if some resources are, as yet, unused. This operator, which Lolli calls "`erase`", can be used to reintroduce a limited form of weakening. If a $\top$ occurs as one of the conjuncts in a $\otimes$ conjunction, then the conjunction may succeed even if the other conjuncts do not use all the linear resources. The $\top$ is seen to consume the leftovers.

A goal marked with the exponential "!" can be proved only if all the assumptions are intuitionistic, unlimited, ones. Rather than use a combination of this operator and a linear implication to load an intuitionistic resource, Lolli instead uses an unadorned resource, paired with the intuitionistic implication operator, $\Rightarrow$, depicted as "`=>`" to load unlimited resources.

It is beyond the scope of this paper to demonstrate the applications of all these operators. Many good examples can be found in the literature, particularly in the papers on Lygon and Lolli [5, 8].

3 The I/O Implementation Model

The management of resources during proof search is a serious problem for the implementor. A naive implementation of the rules for the linear logic operators would lead to a level of backtracking that would render the system useless. Consider, for example, the rule for proving the goal $G_1 \otimes G_2$:

$$\frac{\Delta_1 \longrightarrow G_1 \quad \Delta_2 \longrightarrow G_2}{\Delta_1, \Delta_2 \longrightarrow G_1 \otimes G_2} \otimes_R$$

When the system needs to use this rule during the bottom-up search for a proof, the assumptions have not yet been divided into sets Δ_1 and Δ_2. If the generate-and-test paradigm were used to find an appropriate partition of the assumptions, 2^n possibilities might need to be tested.

The solution, developed by Hodas and Miller in the first paper on Lolli [8], is to treat the management of resources lazily, allowing the conjuncts to determine the partition by their demand for resources. Hodas and Miller described the new execution model by reformulating the rules of linear logic so as to expose the intent of the model. For example, their rule for the $\otimes$ conjunction was:

$$\frac{I\{G_1\}M \quad M\{G_2\}O}{I\{G_1 \otimes G_2\}O} \otimes_R$$

in which the goal is bracketed and the context on the left is the *input context* and the context on the right is the *output context.* This formulation has come to be known as the I/O model for linear logic. Its system of rules is logically equivalent to the original rules: a formula is provable in a given context in the original system if an only if it is provable with that context as input, and with the empty context as output, in this system. However, the rules suggest a certain implementation method.

The I/O model has been refined several times, addressing various sources of non-determinism [7, 6, 2]. Recently, Cervesato, Hodas, and Pfenning have proposed a refinement, which they refer to as $\mathcal{RM}_3$ (for *resource management system 3*) which pays particular attention to the management of resources across a &. In the original I/O system, the rule for & was written:

$$\frac{I\{G_1\}O \quad I\{G_2\}O}{I\{G_1 \,\&\, G_2\}O} \&_R$$

which states that the conjuncts must use the same set of resources. (If the goal is the top-level goal, they must both use the entire context, leaving the output empty.) In a naive implementation the two conjunct are proved separately, and their outputs compared. This leads to unnecessary backtracking.

Cervesato, Hodas, and Pfenning reformulated the rule for & as two rules, differing in whether a $\top$ is seen in the first conjunct.

$$\frac{S|I\{G_1\}_0 O \quad (S, I-O)|[]\{G_2\}_v[]}{S|I\{G_1 \,\&\, G_2\}_0 O}\,\&_{0v} \qquad \frac{S|I\{G_1\}_1 M \quad (S, I-M)|M\{G_2\}_v O}{S|I\{G_1 \,\&\, G_2\}_v O}\,\&_{1v}$$

There are two main changes to the form of I/O rules. The flag appearing as the subscript on the right of the goal indicates whether a $\top$ was seen in the goal. The extra context added on the input side is the *strict* context. Resources in this context *must* be used in the proof of the goal. The other input context is now referred to as the *lax* context.

Thus, when the first conjunct does not encounter a $\top$, the second conjunct must consume all resources that the first had to (its strict context, S), as well as all the lax resources that the first did. All of these appear in the strict context of the second conjunct. The second conjunct has an empty lax context, since it may not consume anything the first did not. In the case where the first conjunct encounters a $\top$, the unconsumed part of the lax context is given as lax context to the second conjunct, since, if it chooses to use any of those formulas, they may be considered to have been also consumed in the first conjunct by the $\top$. The use of strict and *lax* contexts and the $\top$ flag, permeates the rest of $\mathcal{RM}_3$.

4 The $\mathcal{LRM}$ Level-Based Implementation Model

$\mathcal{RM}_3$ provides an efficient model of proof search for Lolli and related languages, at least as regards minimizing needless backtracking. However, the way in which it is formulated makes it best suited to implementation via interpreters written in high-level languages. In particular, the need to move formulas around between strict and lax contexts and perform operations such as intersection on contexts require manipulating large dynamic structures. While the authors remark that efficient implementation using such techniques as bit-vectors representing resource consumption should be possible, they supply no real guidance.

Tamura and Kaneda have suggested using a system of *level indices* to control the consumption of resources [11]. That system handled only a small fragment of linear logic, and was logically incomplete in its treatment of $\top$. In Figure 2 we present an enriched formulation of that system, which we call $\mathcal{LRM}$ for *Level-Based Resource Management System.* This system faithfully reproduces the logic and most of the search behavior of $\mathcal{RM}_3$. However, it is described so as to make the method of efficient implementation apparent.

The sequent system $\mathcal{LRM}$ makes use of two level indices, L and U, to manage consumption of resources. (These indices adorn the turnstile symbol, along with the $\top$-flag carried over from $\mathcal{RM}_3$.) L, a positive integer, is the *current consumption level.* At a given point in the proof tree, only resources labeled with that consumption level may be used. L is also used to set a deadline by which newly added resources must be used. U, a negative integer, is the *current consumption marker*. When a resource is used, its consumption level is changed to this value as an indicator of when it was consumed.

Each formula in the context is adorned with a super and subscript. The formulas can be classified by the values of these two fields: *Linear unconsumed* formulas have the form R_l^d, where l is the value of L at which the resource may be consumed, and d is the *smallest* value of L at which the resource may exist without having been consumed. If any resources exist with $d \geq L$ when it is time to decrement the proof level to $L - 1$, the solver will either backtrack (in the strict case) or consume those resources immediately (in the lax case). *Linear consumed* formulas have the form R_u^0, where u is the (negative) value of U at the time the resource was consumed. *Intuitionistic* formulas always take the form R_0^0.

The **pickR** rule handles the selection of clauses for backchaining. The relation $\texttt{pickR}_{L,U}(A, G, I, M)$ used in that rule is defined as a relation between an input list and atom, I and A, and an output list and G-formula, M and G. The relation selects an available (i.e. linear unconsumed, or intuitionistic) clause from the list I matching the atom A. The output goal G is the body of the clause (or **1** if the clause is atomic). The output list M is the same as I, but with the selected clause marked as linear consumed (with $u = U$) if it was linear unconsumed.

The two $\mathcal{RM}_3$ rules for & are split into four rules in $\mathcal{LRM}$, due to the need for different bookkeeping depending on whether $\top$ is seen in the right conjunct. Three relations define the "side conditions" used in the rules for &. Each can be implemented destructively in one pass through the context in an actual implementation:

- Let L be a positive integer. Then $\texttt{consumed}_L$ is a predicate on a list of R-formulas that is true if none of the R-formulas in the list have L as their deadline.
- Let L and L' be integers. Then $\underset{L \to L'}{\texttt{change}}$ is a relation between an input and output list of R-formulas that modifies the input list so that any R-formula in the list with its level, l, set to L has the level changed to L' in the output.
- Let L, L', D, and D' be integers. Then $\underset{(L,D)\to(L',D')}{\texttt{changepair}}$ is a relation between an input and output list of R-formulas that modifies the input list so that any R-formula in the list with its level, l, set to L and its deadline, d, set to D, has the level changed to L' and its deadline changed to D' in the output.

We will not present a detailed discussion of the rules here. The system has, however, been proved to be logically equivalent to $\mathcal{RM}_3$ [9]. The behavior of the rules can be understood by a careful reading of the description of their implementation in Section 6, below.

$$\frac{}{\vdash^0_{L,U} I\{\mathbf{1}\}I}\ \mathbf{1} \qquad \frac{}{\vdash^1_{L,U} I\{\top\}I}\ \top \qquad \frac{\vdash^v_{L+1,U-1} I\{G\}O}{\vdash^0_{L,U} I\{!G\}O}\ !$$

$$\frac{\vdash^{v_1}_{L,U} I\{G_1\}M \quad \vdash^{v_2}_{L,U} M\{G_2\}O}{\vdash^{v_1\, or\, v_2}_{L,U} I\{G_1 \otimes G_2\}O}\ \otimes \qquad \frac{\mathbf{pickR}_{L,U}(A,G,I,M) \quad \vdash^v_{L,U} M\{G\}O}{\vdash^v_{L,U} I\{A\}O}\ \mathbf{pickR}$$

$$\frac{\begin{array}{ll} \vdash^0_{L,U-1} I\{G_1\}M & \mathbf{changepair}_{(U-1,0)\to(L+1,L+1)}(M,M') \\ \vdash^0_{L+1,U} M'\{G_2\}O & \mathbf{consumed}_{L+1}(O) \end{array}}{\vdash^0_{L,U} I\{G_1 \,\&\, G_2\}O}\ \&_{00}$$

$$\frac{\begin{array}{ll} \vdash^0_{L,U-1} I\{G_1\}M & \mathbf{changepair}_{(U-1,0)\to(L+1,L+1)}(M,M') \\ \vdash^1_{L+1,U} M'\{G_2\}O' & \mathbf{changepair}_{(L+1,L+1)\to(U,0)}(O',O) \end{array}}{\vdash^0_{L,U} I\{G_1 \,\&\, G_2\}O}\ \&_{01}$$

$$\frac{\begin{array}{lll} \vdash^1_{L,U-1} I\{G_1\}M & \mathbf{changepair}_{(U-1,0)\to(L+1,L+1)}(M,M') & \mathbf{change}_{L\to L+1}(M',M'') \\ \vdash^0_{L+1,U} M''\{G_2\}O' & \mathbf{consumed}_{L+1}(O') & \end{array}}{\vdash^0_{L,U} I\{G_1 \,\&\, G_2\}O}\ \&_{10}$$

$$\frac{\begin{array}{lll} \vdash^1_{L,U-1} I\{G_1\}M & \mathbf{changepair}_{(U-1,0)\to(L+1,L+1)}(M,M') & \mathbf{change}_{L\to L+1}(M',M'') \\ \vdash^1_{L+1,U} M''\{G_2\}O'' & \mathbf{changepair}_{(L+1,L+1)\to(U,0)}(O'',O') & \mathbf{change}_{L+1\to L}(O',O) \end{array}}{\vdash^1_{L,U} I\{G_1 \,\&\, G_2\}O}\ \&_{11}$$

$$\frac{\vdash^v_{L,U} [R^L_L|I]\{G\}[R^0_U|O]}{\vdash^v_{L,U} I\{R \multimap G\}O}\ \multimap \qquad \frac{\vdash^1_{L,U} [R^L_L|I]\{G\}[R^L_L|O]}{\vdash^1_{L,U} I\{R \multimap G\}O}\ \multimap_1 \qquad \frac{\vdash^v_{L,U} [R^0_0|I]\{G\}[R^0_0|O]}{\vdash^v_{L,U} I\{R \Rightarrow G\}O}\ \Rightarrow$$

Figure 2: $\mathcal{LRM}$: A resource management system with deadlines

5 LLP: A Compiled Linear Logic Programming Language

While $\mathcal{LRM}$ can serve as the foundation of a Lolli interpreter, the design of the system was undertaken with a greater goal in mind: the creation of a compiler for a significant fragment of Lolli. That goal has been met in LLP.

5.1 The Definition of LLP

LLP is based on the following fragment of linear logic (where A is an atomic formula):

$$\begin{array}{lcl} C & ::= & !\forall\vec{x}.A \mid !\forall\vec{x}.(G \multimap A) \\ G & ::= & \mathbf{1} \mid \top \mid A \mid G \otimes G \mid G \,\&\, G \mid G \oplus G \mid\, !G \mid R \multimap G \mid R \Rightarrow G \mid \exists\vec{x}.A \\ R & ::= & A \mid R \,\&\, R \end{array}$$

The sets of allowed clauses and goals are subsets of the allowed formulas of Lolli. The principal limitations relative to the full language of Lolli are:

- The clauses of the initial program, denoted by the set C, are all !'ed. That is, the program may not contain any linear clauses.
- The resources added dynamically with the $\multimap$ and $\Rightarrow$ operators are either atomic formulas, or products (formed with &) of atomic formulas. Lolli allows arbitrary clause formulas to be added.
- Lolli allows nested quantification and the use of L_λ higher-order quantification and unification of λ-terms.

In spite of these limitations, the fragment covered by LLP is large enough to cover a broad and important class of Lolli programs. In particular, programs like the N-Queens solution presented in Section 2, in which the linear context is used simply to store data values being manipulated by the rest of the program, are included in the fragment covered by LLP.

Note that, as an informal extension to this language, we will allow a $\otimes$-product of multiple R-formulas to appear on the left of either implication operator. Such a formula is treated as though it were written with successive uses of the implication operator loading each individual R-formula.

6 The LLPAM Abstract Machine

LLP is implemented as a compiler to the LLP Abstract Machine (LLPAM), an extension of the Warren Abstract Machine (WAM) [12, 1]. All the data and control structures of the WAM are retained. Further, when executing LLP programs that do not make use of the resource management features of the language, at worst a small constant factor overhead is incurred by the new structures. This because the only added work in such a case is to record four new registers in each choicepoint, and to confirm on predicate dispatch that there are no relevant resources in the (always empty) resource table.

6.1 New Registers

The LLPAM has four new registers: `R`, `L`, `U`, and `T`:

- `R` is a non-negative integer index indicating the current top of the resource table, a new data area which is described below. The value of `R` increases as resources are added to the table by implicational goals, and decreases on backtracking. Its initial value is 0.
- `L` holds the current value of L as used in $\mathcal{LRM}$. It indicates the current consumption level in the proof tree. Its initial value is 1.
- `U` holds the current value of U as used in $\mathcal{LRM}$. This is the value assigned to resources as they are consumed. Its initial value is -1.
- `T` is a boolean flag indicating whether $\top$ has been seen as a subgoal at the current level. Its initial value is false.

6.2 New Data Areas

The LLPAM has three new data areas: RES, HASH, and SYMBOL:

6.2.1 The Resource Table

RES is used to store the formulas added to the program dynamically with implicational goals. It grows when resources are added by $\multimap$, or $\Rightarrow$, and shrinks on backtracking. An entry in RES can represent either a linear resource, or an unlimited one, depending on which implication operator was used to load it. Each entry corresponds to a single R-formula: either an atom, or a &-product of atoms. Note that by representing all the subformulas in a compound resource formula by a single resource table entry, the exclusivity of their consumption is maintained. If one of the atoms is used, the entry is so marked and the other atoms &'ed to it become unavailable.

RES is an array of records with the following structure.

```
record
  head: term;
  level: integer;
  deadline: integer;
  out_of_scope: Boolean;
end;
```

The fields of the record are assigned as follows:

- The atoms in the resource formula to which this entry in RES corresponds are stored as a list of terms on the HEAP. The field head contains a pointer to that structure.
- The fields level and deadline correspond to the l and d values attached to resources in $\mathcal{LRM}$. For linear resources the initial values of both fields are taken from the value of the L register. For exponential (unlimited use) resources, the two fields are set to 0.
- The out_of_scope bit is initially false. It is set to true when the goal underneath the implication that loaded this resource is completed, and the resource, therefore, goes out of scope. This flag is used because the resource table shrinks only on backtracking.

6.2.2 The Hash and Symbol Tables

Two additional structures are maintained to speed access to the resources in RES. HASH is a hash table of the resources added to RES. The entries are hashed on the predicate name/arity, and the first argument.

We cannot always rely on the hash table for access to the resources. When the goal atom has a logic variable in the first argument position, we must access all entries for the given predicate symbol, regardless of first argument. Similarly, those resources in which the first argument is a logic variable must be examined for every call on that predicate symbol. Therefore the entry for a predicate symbol in the symbol table, `SYMBOL`, contains a list of pointers to all resources with that predicate name/arity, and a list of pointers to all resources with that predicate name/arity and an unbound logic variable as its first argument.

Note that, in the case of an entry in `RES` corresponding to a &-product of atoms, multiple entries in `HASH` and `SYMBOL` will point to that entry in `RES`.

6.3 LLPAM Code Generation

The code generated for each operator in a goal represents an imperative implementation of the declarative $\mathcal{LRM}$ rule (or rules) for the operator. In each case the relationship between code and rule should be clear. The code for head unification remains the same as in the WAM, though some steps are added between the point that a `call` is issued, and the point that the block for the predicate is entered. These changes will be discussed below.

6.3.1 Code for $G_1 \otimes G_2$

The tensor product, $\otimes$, takes the place of "ordinary" conjunction in this setting. In accordance with the $\mathcal{LRM}$ rule for $\otimes$, the effect of the two conjuncts on the resource table and the T-flag is merely the accumulation of their individual effects. Therefore, the code generated for $G_1 \otimes G_2$ is simply:

Code for G_1
Code for G_2

6.3.2 Code for $R \multimap G$ or $R \Rightarrow G$

An implicational goal, $R \multimap G$ or $R \Rightarrow G$, requires adding the resource R to the resource table and then executing the goal G in the augmented context. Further, if the $\multimap$ implication is used, then the resource R must be used during the proof of G.

The following new instructions are used in the LLPAM in the code generated for an implication of the form $R \multimap G$ or $R \Rightarrow G$:

- **`begin_imp Yi`**: Stores the current value of register `R` in a new permanent variable $\mathtt{Y}_i$.
- **`add_res Ai`**: Used when the implication operator is $\multimap$. Adds a record for a primitive resource of the form A or $A_1 \mathbin{\&} \ldots \mathbin{\&} A_n$ as a new entry at the top of the resource table, `RES`. `Ai` is a pointer to a structure previously built on the heap holding a (possibly singleton) list of the individual atoms in the product. The value of register `L` is stored in the `level` field and the `deadline` field, the `out_of_scope` flag is set to false, and the register `R` is incremented.

- **add_exp_res Ai**: Used when the implication operator is $\Rightarrow$. Behaves the same as **add_res**, except that the **level** and **deadline** fields are set to zero.
- **mid_imp Yj,Yk**: Used between the code that loads the resource, R, and the code for the subgoal, G. Stores the current values of register R (the top of the resource table) and T (the current value of the top flag) to the permanent variables Yj and Yk, respectively.
- **end_imp Yi,Yj,Yk**: Used after the code for the subgoal, G, when the implication operator is $\multimap$. If there are any resources in positions from Yi to Yj$-$1 that have not been consumed, fail. Otherwise, set the **out_of_scope** flags of all records from Yi to Yj$-$1 to true (trailing the changes), and set the register T to Yk $\vee$ T.
  In order to account for the use of $\top$ at the top level of the subgoal, G, the check for unconsumed resources is made as follows:
  - If T is false, the **level** and **deadline** of each resource should be U and 0 respectively. Otherwise, the resource is unused.
  - If T is true, the **level** and **deadline** of each resource should be either U and 0, or L and L respectively. Otherwise, the resource is unconsumed.
- **end_exp_imp Yi,Yj,Yk**: Used after the code for the subgoal, G, when the implication operator is $\Rightarrow$. The added resource entries need not be examined. Just set the **out_of_scope** flags of all records from Yi to Yj$-$1 to true (trailing the changes), and set register T to Yk $\vee$ T.

The code generated for the goal $(p(1) \otimes (p(2) \,\&\, p(3))) \multimap G$ is:

```
begin_imp Y1
put_str p/1, A2        % put [p(1)] to A1
set_int 1
put_list A1
set_val A2
set_con []
add_res A1             % add linear [p(1)]
put_str p/1, A2        % Begin: put [p(2),p(3)] to A1
set_int 2
put_str p/1, A4
set_int 3
put_list A3
set_val A4
set_con []
put_list A1
set_val A2
set_val A3             % End: put [p(2),p(3)] to A1
add_res A1             % add linear [p(2),p(3)]
mid_imp Y2, Y3
Code for G
end_imp Y1, Y2, Y3
```

If the goal used $\Rightarrow$ rather than $\multimap$, then the code would have uses of **add_res** and **end_imp** replaced by **add_exp_res** and **end_exp_imp**, respectively.

6.3.3 Code for $G_1 \& G_2$

The code for a goal of the form $G_1\&G_2$ is, structurally, quite simple, however the semantics of each instruction is relatively complex, in order to match with the behavior defined in the corresponding $\mathcal{LRM}$ rules.

```
begin_with Yi
Code for G1
mid_with Yj
Code for G2
end_with Yi,Yj
```

- **begin_with** Yi: Decrement U so that we can tell which resources are consumed in G_1. Store the current value of T in a new variable Yi and set T to false.
- **mid_with** Yj: Perform $\underset{(U,0)\rightarrow(L+1,L+1)}{\texttt{changepair}}$. This marks all of the resources that were used in the left conjunct so that they can, and must, be used in the right conjunct. If the value of T is true, then perform $\underset{L\rightarrow L+1}{\texttt{change}}$ (making resources that were available but not used, but which $\top$ could have used, available in the second conjunct). Increment L and U. Store the current value of T in a new variable Yj. Set T to false.
- **end_with** Yi, Yj: Decrement L. If the value of T is true, then perform $\underset{(L+1,L+1)\rightarrow(U,0)}{\texttt{changepair}}$ ($\top$ was seen in this conjunct, so we can set all the resources that should have been consumed, but weren't, as though they were). Otherwise, perform $\texttt{consumed}_{L+1}$ to check whether all the resources that should have been consumed, were. If this fails, fail. Otherwise, if Yj is true, then perform $\underset{L+1\rightarrow L}{\texttt{change}}$ (Those resources that were made available to the second conjunct because the first conjunct included a $\top$, but weren't used in the second conjunct either, are put back to their original level). Set T to Yi $\vee$ (Yj $\wedge$ T).

The code generated for the goal $p \& (q \otimes (r \& s))$ is:

```
begin_with Y1
call p/0
mid_with Y2
call q/0
begin_with Y3
call r/0
mid_with Y4
call s/0
```

```
end_with Y3, Y4
end_with Y1, Y2
```

6.3.4 Code for $!G$

In the execution of $!G$, only exponential resources can be used. The following instructions are used for $!G$.

- `begin_bang Yi`: Increment `L`. (It is now higher than the `level` field of all resources, so they are all unavailable.) Store the value of `T` in a new variable `Yi`.
- `end_bang Yi`: Decrement `L`. Reset the value of the register `T` from the variable `Yi`.

The code generated for the goal $!(p \otimes q)$ is:

```
begin_bang Y1
call p/0
call q/0
end_bang Y1
```

6.3.5 Code for $\top$

The use of $\top$ as a goal (which is written `erase`) is compiled to the instruction:

- `top`: Set the register `T` to true.

6.4 Code for Atomic Goals

The execution of a `call` to an atomic goal A proceeds as follows:

1. Extract a list of pointers to possibly unifiable resources in the resource table, `RES`, by reference to `HASH` and `SYMBOL`.
2. For each `RES` entry R in the extracted list, attempt the following:
   (a) If R is out of scope, or is linear and has been consumed, fail.
   (b) For each term in the list pointed to by the `head` field R, Attempt to unify A with the term. If successful, proceed. If not, backtrack.
   (c) Mark the entry R as consumed (set `level` to the current value of `U`, and `dealine` to 0).
3. After the failure of all trials, `call` the ordinary code for predicate A.

6.5 Backtracking

In order to be able to recover the correct state on backtracking:

- The values of registers `R`, `L`, `U`, and `T` are stored in choice-point frames.
- Changes to the `HASH` table should be trailed.
- Moving entries in `RES` out of scope, and changing their `level` or `deadline` should be trailed.

N	# Runs Avged.	SICStus	LLPAM 0.42	% Δ	LLPAM Prolog
8	10	158 ms	140 ms	11%	327 ms
9	10	740 ms	608 ms	18%	1527 ms
10	5	3638 ms	2663 ms	27%	7443 ms
11	5	21264 ms	12939 ms	39%	41927 ms
12	5	123124 ms	68697 ms	44%	458333 ms
13	5	668336 ms	410267 ms	39%	1356277 ms
14	3	4222190 ms	2857655 ms	32%	8669450 ms

Figure 3: Comparison of results for LLPAM 0.42 vs SICStus 2.1

7 Performance and Conclusion

For several years the advocates of logic programming languages based on richer logics than Horn clauses have argued that the naturalness of programming in these more expressive logics would balance any loss of efficiency due to the added expense of proof search. Some took a bolder stance, however: that with appropriate implementation techniques, these logics could yield solutions to some problems whose performance would be better than the traditional solutions. The LLPAM is the first system to fulfill that promise.

The standard solution of the N-Queens problem as given in Figure 1 makes natural use of resources. Because these resources are managed in a list structure, there is little the compiler can do to optimize resource management. The rendition of this problem in Lolli as given in Figure 1 makes similar conceptual use of resources. However, because the resources are managed at the clause level, rather than at the term level, the compiler may bring various techniques to bare, in particular hashed access to the resource list.

The result of this shift is that the Lolli solution, executed under LLP 0.42[1] has superior performance compared to the traditional solution compiled under SICStus 2.1 "compact code" WAM compiler. Figure 3 compares the performance of the two programs finding all solutions for various values of N. All times were collected on a Sparcstation 20 running SunOS 4.1.4. As the reliance on resource management increases due to the increased number of queens being managed, the performance of LLP versus Prolog becomes more pronounced. Preliminary tests of other (admittedly simple) benchmarks such as knight's tour have confirmed these results.

In order to show the true nature of the speedup, the final column shows the time to execute the Prolog version of the program as compiled by our system and executed on the LLPAM emulator. Comparing this result to the performance of the SICStus version might seem to bely our claim that the

[1]LLP 0.42 is actually based on the earlier version of the LLPAM which handled a smaller fragment of Lolli than the LLPAM described here. (That version of the LLPAM is described in [11], and is available from `http://bach.seg.kobe-u.ac.jp/llp/`.) We do not, however, expect any slowdown from implementing the version described here.

new structures incur only a small overhead. We believe, however, that that disparity is more likely due to the difference between a modern optimizing Prolog compiler, and our relatively naive compiler.

References

[1] Hassan Aït-Kaci. *Warren's Abstract Machine.* The MIT Press, 1991.

[2] Iliano Cervesato, Joshua S. Hodas, and Frank Pfenning. Efficient resource management for linear logic proof search. In editors, *Proceedings of the Fifth Workshop on Extensions of Logic Programming*, 1996.

[3] Jean-Yves Girard. Linear logic. *Theoretical Computer Science*, 50:1–102, 1987.

[4] James Harland and David Pym. Resource distribution via boolean constraints. In editor, *Proceedings of the Fourteenth International Conference on Automated Deduction*, 1997.

[5] James Harland, David Pym, and Michael Winikoff. Programming in Lygon: An overview. In *Algebraic Methodology and Software Technology*, 1996.

[6] James Harland and Michael Winikoff. Implementing the linear logic programming language Lygon. In *Proceedings of the 1995 International Logic Programming Symposium*, 1995.

[7] Joshua S. Hodas. *Logic Programming in Intuitionistic Linear Logic: Theory, Design and Implementation.* PhD thesis, University of Pennsylvania, Department of Computer and Information Science, 1994.

[8] Joshua S. Hodas and Dale Miller. Logic programming in a fragment of intuitionistic linear logic. *Information and Computation*, 110(2):327–365, 1994. Extended abstract in the Proceedings of the Sixth Annual Symposium on Logic in Computer Science, 1991.

[9] Joshua S. Hodas, Kevin Watkins, Naoyuki Tamura, and Kyoung-Sun Kang. Efficient implementation of a linear logic programming language. An extended, journal version of this paper. In preparation.

[10] Leon Sterling and Ehud Shapiro. *The Art of Prolog: Advanced Programming Techniques.* MIT Press, Cambridge MA, 1986.

[11] Naoyuki Tamura and Yukio Kaneda. Extension of WAM for a linear logic programming language. In *Proceedings of the Second Fuji International Workshop on Functional and Logic Programming*, 1996.

[12] David H. D. Warren. An abstract Prolog instruction set. Technical Note 309, SRI International, October 1983.

Normal Forms for Defeasible Logic

G. Antoniou, D. Billington and M.J. Maher
CIT, Griffith University
Nathan, QLD 4111, Australia
ga,db,mjm@cit.gu.edu.au

Abstract

Defeasible logic is an important logic-programming based nonmonotonic reasoning formalism which has an efficient implementation. It makes use of facts, strict rules, defeasible rules, defeaters, and a superiority relation.

Representation results are important because they can help the assimilation of a concept by confining attention to its critical aspects. In this paper we derive some representation results for defeasible logic. In particular we show that the superiority relation does not add to the expressive power of the logic, and can be simulated by other ingredients in a modular way. Also, facts can be simulated by strict rules. Finally we show that we cannot simplify the logic any further in a modular way: Strict rules, defeasible rules, and defeaters form a minimal set of independent ingredients in the logic.

1 Introduction

Normal forms play an important role in computer science. Examples of areas where normal forms have proved fruitful include logic [10], where normal forms of formulae are used both for the proof of theoretical results and in theorem proving, and relational databases [5], where normal forms have been the driving force in the development of database theory and principles of good data modeling.

There are several potential benefits of normal forms. For example, they can be instrumental in the implementation of a logic because assuming that formulae have a specific form can actually simplify and facilitate the development of algorithms (see resolution [15]). Normal forms can help to classify objects according to some criteria; for example, in relational database theory, a normal form characterizes those databases that don't allow specific kinds of anomalies. But perhaps the main benefit from normal forms is that they can help the assimilation of a concept by confining attention to its critical aspects.

It is the third kind of benefit that we expect from the results of this paper. We will prove some representational results for Defeasible Logic [11, 12], following the presentation of [4].

Defeasible Logic is an approach to nonmonotonic reasoning [1] that has a very distinctive feature: It was designed to be easily implementable right from the beginning, unlike most other approaches. In fact it has an implementation as a straightforward extension of Prolog [6]. For a long time research in this particular approach has been mostly neglected, but practical difficulties with other approaches have recently refocused some attention to this logic.

There are five kinds of features in Defeasible Logic: facts, strict rules, defeasible rules, defeaters, and a superiority relation among rules. Essentially the superiority relation provides information about the relative strength of rules, that is, it provides information about which rules can overrule which other rules.

Our first result presents a normal form for defeasible theories in which there are no facts, strict rules are separated almost completely from defeasible rules, and strict rules are not subject to overruling.

Defeasible Logic expresses sceptical reasoning, in that a conclusion is only drawn when all reasons for the contrary conclusion have been definitely invalidated. It is here that the superiority relation comes into play: Even if a rule r contradicts the conclusion of rule r', we can still use r' to draw a conclusion if r' overrules r. This idea is applied in a recursive way.

Our second result is surprising: the superiority relation does not add to the expressive power of the formalism. To be more precise, for every defeasible theory T with a superiority relation we can construct a defeasible theory T' with an empty superiority relation such that T and T' support the same conclusions in the logical language of T.

The main tools that we use are modular transformations, that is, transformations that apply to each unit of information, independent of its context. Such transformations are valuable, since they can be the basis of the compilation of a defeasible theory into a more efficiently executable form. It is here that the modular nature of the transformations is important, since modifications to the original theory do not require the recompilation of the entire theory – only an incremental change needs to be made to the compiled theory.

Finally, we show that strict rules, defeasible rules, and defeaters constitute a minimal set of necessary ingredients of defeasible logic. More precisely, we prove that there is no modular way of eliminating strict rules, defeasible rules or defeaters while preserving the expressive power.

2 Basics of Defeasible Logic

2.1 Informal presentation

We begin by presenting the basic ingredients of Defeasible Logic. A defeasible theory[1] consists of five different kinds of knowledge: facts, strict rules,

[1] a knowledge base in Defeasible Logic

defeasible rules, defeaters, and a superiority relation.

Facts denote simple pieces of information that are deemed to be true regardless of other knowledge items. A typical fact is that Tweety is a bird: $bird(tweety)$.

Strict rules are rules in the classical sense: whenever the premises of a rule are given, we are allowed to apply the rule and get a conclusion. Often they are statements that are true by definition or fiat. An example of a strict rule is "Emus are birds". Written formally:

$$emu(X) \rightarrow bird(X).$$

Defeasible rules are rules that can be defeated by contrary evidence. An example of such a rule is "Birds typically fly"; written formally:

$$bird(X) \Rightarrow flies(X).$$

The idea is that if we know that something is a bird, then we may conclude that it flies, *unless there is other evidence suggesting that it may not fly.*

Defeaters are rules that cannot be used to draw any conclusions. Their only use is to prevent some conclusions. In other words, they are used to defeat some defeasible rules by producing evidence to the contrary. An example is "If a bird is wounded, it may not fly". Formally:

$$wounded(X) \leadsto \neg flies(X)$$

The main point is that a wound is not sufficient evidence to conclude that the bird cannot fly. It is only evidence that the bird *may* be not be able to fly.

The *superiority relation* among rules is used to define priorities among rules, that is, where one rule may override the conclusion of another rule. For example, given the defeasible rules

$$\begin{array}{rrl} r: & republican & \Rightarrow \neg pacifist \\ r': & quaker & \Rightarrow pacifist \end{array}$$

which contradict one another, no conclusive decision can be made about the pacifism of a person who is both a republican and a quaker. But if we introduce a superiority relation $>$ with $r > r'$, then we can indeed conclude $\neg pacifist$.

It turns out that we only need to define the superiority relation over rules with contradictory conclusions. Also notice that a cycle in the superiority relation is counter-intuitive. In the above example, it makes no sense to have both $r > r'$ and $r' > r$. Consequently, the defeasible logic we discuss requires an acyclic superiority relation.

Using these elements it is straightforward to express knowledge in the form of defeasible theories. A series of examples in Defeasible Logic can be found in [13, 6].

2.2 Technical details

In this paper we restrict attention to propositional defeasible logic, and assume that the reader is familiar with the notation and basic notions of propositional logic. If q is a literal, $\sim q$ denotes the complement of q (if q is a positive literal p then $\sim q$ is $\neg p$; and if q is $\neg p$, then $\sim q$ is p).

A *rule* r consists of its *antecedent* $A(r)$ (written on the left) which is a finite set of literals, an arrow, and its *consequent* $C(r)$ which is a literal. There are three kinds of rules: *Strict rules* are denoted by $A \rightarrow p$, *defeasible rules* by $A \Rightarrow p$, and defeaters by $A \leadsto p$. When A is empty we will omit it in stating rules. Given a set R of rules, we denote the set of all strict rules by R_s, and the set of strict and defeasible rules in R by R_{sd}. R_d is the set of defeasible rules and R_{dft} is the set of defeaters in R. $R[q]$ denotes the set of rules in R with consequent q.

A *superiority relation on* R is an acyclic relation $>$ on R (that is, the transitive closure of $>$ is irreflexive). When $r_1 > r_2$, then r_1 is called *superior* to r_2, and r_2 *inferior* to r_1. A rule is called *inferior* iff it is inferior to another rule.

A *defeasible theory* T is a triple $(F, R, >)$ where F is a finite set of literals (called *facts*), R a finite set of rules, and $>$ a superiority relation on R. A *conclusion* of T is a tagged literal and can have one of the following four forms:

- $+\Delta q$, which means that q is strictly provable in T, that is, is provable using only strict rules and facts from T.
- $-\Delta q$, which means that we have proved that q is not strictly provable in T.
- $+\partial q$, which means that q is defeasibly provable in T.
- $-\partial q$ which means that we have proved that q is not defeasible provable in T.

We refer to conclusions of the form $+\Delta q$ or $-\Delta q$ as *definite conclusions*, since they are not defeatable, even when information is added to T. Conclusions of the form $+\partial q$ or $-\partial q$ are called *defeasible conclusions*, since they can be defeated if new information is added to T. Provability is defined below. It is based on the concept of a proof in $T = (F, R, >)$. A *proof* or *derivation* is a finite sequence $P = (P(1), \ldots P(n))$ of tagged literals satisfying the following conditions ($P(1..i)$ denotes the initial part of the sequence P of length i):

$+\Delta$: If $P(i+1) = +\Delta q$ then either
  $q \in F$ or
  $\exists r \in R_s[q]\ \forall a \in A(r) : +\Delta a \in P(1..i)$

$-\Delta$: If $P(i+1) = -\Delta q$ then

$q \notin F$ and
$\forall r \in R_s[q]\ \exists a \in A(r) : -\Delta a \in P(1..i)$

$+\partial$: If $P(i+1) = +\partial q$ then either
(1) $+\Delta q \in P(1..i)$ or
(2) (2.1) $\exists r \in R_{sd}[q]\ \forall a \in A(r) : +\partial a \in P(1..i)$ and
(2.2) $-\Delta \sim q \in P(1..i)$ and
(2.3) $\forall s \in R[\sim q]$ either
(2.3.1) $\exists a \in A(s) : -\partial a \in P(1..i)$ or
(2.3.2) $\exists t \in R[q]$
$\forall a \in A(t) : +\partial a \in P(1..i)$ and
$t > s$

$-\partial$: If $P(i+1) = -\partial q$ then
(1) $-\Delta q \in P(1..i)$ and
(2) (2.1) $\forall r \in R_{sd}[q]\ \exists a \in A(r) : -\partial a \in P(1..i)$ or
(2.2) $+\Delta \sim q \in P(1..i)$ or
(2.3) $\exists s \in R[\sim q]$ such that
(2.3.1) $\forall a \in A(s) : +\partial a \in P(1..i)$ and
(2.3.2) $\forall t \in R[q]$ either
$\exists a \in A(t) : -\partial a \in P(1..i)$ or
not $t > s$

The elements of a proof are called *lines* of the proof. We say that a tagged literal L is *provable* in $T = (F, R, >)$, denoted $T \vdash L$, iff there is a proof P in T such that L is a line of P.

Even though the definition seems complicated, it follows ideas which are intuitively appealing. For example, the condition $+\partial$ states the following: One way of establishing that q is defeasibly provable is to show that it is definitely provable. The other way is to find a rule with conclusion q, all antecedents of which are defeasibly provable. In addition, it must be established that $\sim q$ is not definitely provable (to do otherwise would be counterintuitive – to derive q defeasibly, although there might be a definite reason against it), and for every rule s which might prove $\sim q$ defeasibly, either one of its antecedents is provably not derivable, or there is a rule with conclusion q which is stronger than s and can be applied (that is, all its antecedents are defeasibly provable). Essentially the rules with head q form a *team* which tries to counterattack any rule with head $\sim q$. If the rules for q win then q is derived defeasibly; otherwise q cannot be derived in this manner.

3 A Normal Form for Defeasible Logic

We propose a normal form for defeasible theories. The main purpose of this normal form is to provide a separation of concerns, within a defeasible theory, between definite and defeasible conclusions. In defeasible logic, a strict rule may participate in the superiority relation. This participation has no effect on the definite conclusions of the theory, but can affect the defeasible conclusions. We consider theories where this occurs to be somewhat misleading, and propose a normal form in which definite and defeasible reasoning are separated as much as is practicable.

Definition 3.1 *We call a defeasible theory $T = (F, R, >)$* normalized *(or in* normal form *iff the following three conditions are satisfied:*

(a) Every literal is defined either solely by strict rules, or by one strict rule and other non-strict rules.

(b) No strict rule participates in the superiority relation $>$.

(c) $F = \emptyset$

Every defeasible theory can be transformed into normal form. This establishes that facts are not needed in the formulation of defeasible logic, and that the misleading theories we discussed above are unnecessary. We now define this transformation explicitly. Following that we outline the proof that the transformation preserves the conclusions in the language of T.

Definition 3.2 *Consider a defeasible theory $T = (F, R, >)$. Let Σ be the language of T. We define $normal(T) = (\emptyset, R', >)$, where R' is defined below.*

Let $'$ be a function which maps propositions to new (previously unused) propositions, and rule names to new rule names. We extend this, in the obvious way, to literals and conjunctions of literals.

$R' = R_d \cup R_{dft} \cup$
$\{\rightarrow f' \mid f \in F\} \cup$
$\{r' : A' \rightarrow C' \mid r : A \rightarrow C \text{ is a strict rule in } R\} \cup$
$\{r : A \Rightarrow C \mid r : A \rightarrow C \text{ is a strict rule in } R\} \cup$
$\{p' \rightarrow p \mid p \text{ is a literal from } \Sigma\}$

The rules derived from F and rules $p' \rightarrow p$ are given distinct new names.

It is clear from the transformation described above that $normal(T)$ is normalized (i.e. satisfies conditions (a)–(c)). Notice that strict rules have been altered to become defeasible rules, although their names are unchanged. Thus although $>$ is unchanged, it now no longer concerns any strict rule.

It is easy to see that, for every literal p, $T \vdash +\Delta p$ iff $normal(T) \vdash +\Delta p$ and $T \vdash -\Delta p$ iff $normal(T) \vdash -\Delta p$, since the structure of the strict rules remains the same and the superiority relation does not affect the proof of definite conclusions.

Also notice that the structure (including the superiority relation) of defeasible rules and defeaters in R' is identical with the structure of all rules in R. Thus, when deriving a defeasible conclusion concerning a literal from

T (i.e. not involving a new proposition), the only difference between T and T' is the presence of rules $p' \rightarrow p$.

The remainder of the proof is a detailed verification that the defeasible conclusions of T and $normal(T)$ are the same. We prove by induction on the length of proofs that every defeasible Σ-conclusion of a proof in T is also a conclusion of a proof in $normal(T)$, and vice versa, where Σ is the language of T. Hence, we have

Theorem 3.1 *For every defeasible theory T in the signature Σ we can effectively construct a normalized defeasible theory T', such that T and T' have the same conclusions in Σ.*

Programs in normal form can use a simpler form of the proof conditions given in Section 2. Specifically, we can omit mention of F from both the $+\Delta$ and $-\Delta$ conditions, and we can omit clause (2.2) from both the $+\partial$ and $-\partial$ conditions.

4 Simulating the Superiority Relation

In this section we show that the superiority relation does not contribute anything to the expressive power of defeasible logic. Of course it does allow one to represent information in a more natural way.

We define below a transformation *trans* that eliminates all uses of the superiority relation. For every rule r, it introduces a positive literal denoted by $inf(r)$. Intuitively, $inf(r)$ expresses that r is overruled by a superior rule.

Definition 4.1 *Let $T = (F, R, >)$ be a defeasible theory. Define $trans(T) = (F, R', \emptyset)$, where*

$$
\begin{aligned}
&R' = \\
&\{A(r_1) \cup \{\neg inf(r_1)\} \rightarrow inf(r_2) \mid r_1 > r_2\} \cup \\
&\{A(r) \rightarrow \neg inf(r) \mid r \in R\} \cup \\
&\{\neg inf(r) \rightarrow C(r) \mid r \textit{ is a strict rule }\} \cup \\
&\{\neg inf(r) \Rightarrow C(r) \mid r \textit{ is a defeasible rule }\} \cup \\
&\{\neg inf(r) \leadsto C(r) \mid r \textit{ is a defeater }\}.
\end{aligned}
$$

For example, consider the defeasible theory

$f1$: sh	*Nanook is a Siberian Husky*
$r1$: $sh \rightarrow d$	*Siberian Huskies are dogs.*
$r2$: $sh \Rightarrow \neg b$	*Siberian Huskies usually don't bark.*
$r3$: $d \Rightarrow b$	*Dogs usually bark.*
$r2 > r3$	

According to the construction above, the theory is replaced by:

$$\begin{array}{lrl} f1: & sh & \\ r1a: & sh & \rightarrow \neg inf(r1) \\ r1b: & \neg inf(r1) & \rightarrow d \\ r2a: & sh & \rightarrow \neg inf(r2) \\ r2b: & \neg inf(r2) & \Rightarrow \neg b \\ r3a: & d & \rightarrow \neg inf(r3) \\ r3b: & \neg inf(r3) & \Rightarrow b \\ r3c: & sh, \neg inf(r2) & \rightarrow inf(r3) \end{array}$$

Consider $r3$, the only inferior rule. We break $d \Rightarrow b$ into two rules by inserting a literal between d and b to give $d \rightarrow \neg inf(r3)$ and $\neg inf(r3) \Rightarrow b$. These two rules mimic $d \Rightarrow b$. This intermediate literal has the meaning "$r3$ is not inferior to an applicable rule". The intermediate literal should be unprovable if the antecedent of $r2$ is provable and $r2$ is not, itself, inferior to an applicable rule. These aims are accomplished by adding the rule $sh, \neg inf(r2) \Rightarrow inf(r3)$. Independently, a similar construction is given in [9] for eliminating priorities among defeasible rules in an abstract credulous argumentation framework.

The following result shows that if we restrict attention to conclusions in the old signature Σ (that is, if we disregard the new inf-symbols), then T and $trans(T)$ are equivalent.

Theorem 4.1 *Let $T = (F, R, >)$ be a defeasible theory in the signature Σ. Then T and $trans(T)$ allow the same conclusions in the signature Σ.*

Based on Theorem 4.1, the two cases for defeasible provability in a normalized and transformed theory can be simplified as shown below. This definition will be used in the rest of the paper. Note that clauses (2.2) have been omitted, in accordance with the comment at the end of the previous section, but the numbering of clauses has not been altered, to retain consistency with the conditions in Section 2.

$+\partial$: If $P(i+1) = +\partial q$ then either
(1) $+\Delta q \in P(1..i)$ or
(2) (2.1) $\exists r \in R_{sd}[q]$ such that $\forall a \in A(r) : +\partial a \in P(1..i)$ and
(2.3) $\forall s \in R[\sim q]\ \exists a \in A(s) : -\partial a \in P(1..i)$

$-\partial$: If $P(i+1) = -\partial q$ then
(1) $-\Delta q \in P(1..i)$ and
(2) (2.1) $\forall r \in R_{sd}[q]\ \exists a \in A(r) : -\partial a \in P(1..i)$ or
(2.3) $\exists s \in R[\sim q]\ \forall a \in A(s) : +\partial a \in P(1..i)$

5 A Minimal Set of Ingredients

As a result of the discussion so far, a defeasible theory can be viewed as a finite set of rules. There are three kinds of rules: strict, defeasible, and defeaters. In this section we show that it is impossible to simulate any of these types by the other two in a modular way. First we show this for strict rules.

Proposition 5.1 Let $A \rightarrow p$ be a strict rule. Then, in general, there is no defeasible theory R' without strict rules, such that for all defeasible theories R, $R \cup \{A \rightarrow p\}$ and $R \cup R'$ allow the same conclusions in the signature Σ (where Σ is the signature of $R \cup \{A \rightarrow p\}$).

Proof: Suppose that there was such an R' for the strict rule $\rightarrow p$, and let $R = \emptyset$. We have $\{\rightarrow p\} \vdash +\Delta p$. But since there is no strict rule in R', $R' \not\vdash +\Delta p$, which gives us a contradiction to the statement of the Proposition. ■

Proposition 5.2 Let $A \Rightarrow p$ be a defeasible rule. Then, in general, there is no defeasible theory R' without defeasible rules, such that for all defeasible theories R, $R \cup \{A \Rightarrow p\}$ and $R \cup R'$ allow the same conclusions in the signature Σ (where Σ is the signature of $R \cup \{A \Rightarrow p\}$).

Proof: Suppose there was such an R' for the defeasible rule $\Rightarrow p$, and consider $R = \emptyset$. Then $\{\Rightarrow p\} \vdash +\partial p$. According to the claim of the Proposition $R' \vdash +\partial p$. But R' consists only of strict rules and defeaters. Inspection of the definition of a proof (defeaters can never support a conclusion) shows that then also $R' \vdash +\Delta p$. But $\{\Rightarrow p\} \not\vdash +\Delta p$, so we have a contradiction. ■

Both previous results were quite trivial. The following theorem is more difficult to prove, and states that we cannot simulate defeaters in a modular way using strict and defeasible rules. It constitutes the third main result of this paper.

Theorem 5.1 *Let $A \leadsto p$ be a defeater. Then, in general, there is no defeasible theory R' without defeaters, such that for all defeasible theories R, $R \cup \{A \leadsto p\}$ and $R \cup R'$ allow the same conclusions in the signature Σ (where Σ is the signature of $R \cup \{A \leadsto p\}$).*

Proof: Suppose there was such an R' for the defeater $\leadsto p$. We will consider three different sets R:

1. $R = \emptyset$. Since R' behaves the same as $\{\leadsto p\}$ we have:

$R' \vdash -\partial p$, and
$R' \vdash -\partial \neg p$.

2. $R = \{\Rightarrow p\}$. Since $R' \cup \{\Rightarrow p\}$ behaves the same as $\{\leadsto p, \Rightarrow p\}$ we have:

$R' \cup \{\Rightarrow p\} \vdash +\partial p$, and
$R' \cup \{\Rightarrow p\} \vdash -\partial \neg p$.

3. $R = \{\Rightarrow \neg p\}$. Since $R' \cup \{\Rightarrow \neg p\}$ behaves the same as $\{\leadsto p, \Rightarrow \neg p\}$ we have:

$R' \cup \{\Rightarrow \neg p\} \vdash -\partial p$, and
$R' \cup \{\Rightarrow \neg p\} \vdash -\partial \neg p$.

Let us first consider $R' \cup \{\Rightarrow p\}$. Consider a proof P in $R' \cup \{\Rightarrow p\}$ of length $i+1$, such that $+\partial p$ is its last line, and $+\partial p$ does not occur in $P(1..i)$. By condition (2.3) in the definition of a proof[2], for every rule r with consequent $\neg p$ there is a $b \in A(r)$ such that $-\partial b \in P(1..i)$.

Now we ask the following question: Can we regard $P(1..i)$ as a proof in R'? The only difference is that now the rule $\Rightarrow p$ is missing. What is the contribution of this rule in $P(1..i)$? Inspection of the definition of a proof shows that the rule is only used to add a line containing either p or $\neg p$. In our particular case, given that only $+\partial p$ and $-\partial \neg p$ are derivable[3] and given that $+\partial p$ doesn't appear in $P(1..i)$, the only possible contribution of the rule $\Rightarrow p$ is to derive $-\partial \neg p$ somewhere in $P(1..i)$. Now we proceed as follows:

Case 1: $-\partial \neg p$ doesn't occur in $P(1..i)$. Then it can be shown by a simple induction on the length of P that $P' = P$ is also a proof in R'.

Case 2: $-\partial \neg p$ occurs in $P(1..i)$. Then define P' as follows: We know that $-\partial \neg p$ is derivable in R'. Take such a proof P''. Concatenate P'' and P to construct P'[4]. Again it can be easily proven by induction on the length of proof that P' is a proof in R'. Intuitively what we did was the following: The missing rule $\Rightarrow p$ may only cause problems in deriving $-\partial \neg p$ in P. But already we know that $-\partial \neg p$ is derivable in R', so we establish this conclusion first and then proceed as in $P(1..i)$.

In both cases we get a proof P' in R' with the following property:

($*$) For every rule $r \in R'[\neg p]$ there is a $b \in A(r)$ such that $R' \vdash -\partial b$.

[2] Note that $\{\leadsto p, \Rightarrow p\} \not\vdash +\Delta p$, thus $+\Delta p \notin P(1..i)$.

[3] As [4] shows, it is impossible to derive both $+\partial p$ and $-\partial p$.

[4] As [4] shows, by concatenating two proof of a defeasible theory T one gets another proof in T.

Now we turn our attention to $R' \cup \{\Rightarrow \neg p\}$. Despite the presence of $\Rightarrow \neg p$ which has no antecedents, $-\partial\neg p$ is derivable. Let P be a proof of length $i+1$ with last line $-\partial\neg p$, such that $-\partial\neg p$ does not occur in $P(1..i)$. By the definition of a proof, there exists a rule r in $R'[p]$ such that for all $a \in A(r)$ $+\partial a \in P(1..i)$.

Using the same argument as before[5], we can transform $P(1..i)$ to a proof P' in R', such that there exists a rule s in $R'[p]$ such that for all $a \in A(s)$ $+\partial a \in P'$. Thus we have:

(**) There exists a rule s in $R'[p]$ such that for all $a \in A(s)$, $R' \vdash +\partial a$.

Obviously $R' \vdash -\Delta\neg p$ because $\{\leadsto p\} \vdash -\Delta\neg p$. Properties (*) and (**), together with the condition $+\partial$ in the definition of a proof, show that $R' \vdash +\partial p$. But also $R' \vdash -\partial p$ because $\{\leadsto p\} \vdash -\partial p$. [4] has shown that it is impossible to derive both together. Thus we have a contradiction. ∎

6 Discussion

As discussed earlier, a cyclic superiority relation is nonsensical in a defeasible theory. Nevertheless, for completeness, we briefly explore the effect of this possibility on our results. Certainly Theorem 3.1 continues to hold, even if the superiority relation is cyclic. Its proof is independent of the form of the superiority relation.

However Theorem 4.1 does not extend to cyclic defeasible theories. Consider the theory T:

$$\begin{array}{ll} r_1: & \Rightarrow p \\ r_2: & \Rightarrow \neg p \end{array}$$

$r_1 > r_2, r_2 > r_1$

In this case the proof theory concludes both $+\partial p$ and $+\partial\neg p$. As shown by Billington [4], this situation arises only when the superiority relation is cyclic. Thus $trans(T)$ does not have this property, and consequently does not have the same conclusions as T.

The minor results in section 5 continue to hold when superiority relation is cyclic. However the proof of Theorem 5.1 relies on Theorem 4.1. Thus currently it is unclear whether Theorem 5.1 can be extended to cyclic defeasible theories.

7 Comparison to other default reasoning approaches

In this section we summarize results on the relationship of defeasible logic to other default reasoning approaches. So far we have mostly concentrated

[5] Essentially we are faced with the same situation: $P(1..i)$ is a proof in $R' \cup \{\Rightarrow \neg p\}$, we remove the rule $\Rightarrow \neg p$, and $-\partial\neg p$ doesn't occur in $P(1..i)$. So the only possible contribution of $\Rightarrow \neg p$ is to help derive $-\partial p$. But $-\partial p$ is already derivable in R'.

on approaches that are logic programming based and make use of an explicit priority relation, the only other approach considered being default logic. A full exposition of these results will be included in a future paper.

Defeasible logic is a strictly sceptical reasoning approach. This should be contrasted with other approaches in which sceptical reasoning is realized using the intersection of credulous reasoning chains. For example, in default logic [14] sceptical reasoning is obtained by considering the intersection of all extensions. The two fundamental approaches lead to different behaviours, as pointed out by [16] in their "clash of intuitions" paper. For example, in default logic ambiguity in one predicate may be propagated to other predicates, but in defeasible logic this is not true.

Priority logic [17, 18] is a knowledge representation language where a theory consists of logic programming-like rules, and a priority relation among them. The meaning of the priority relation is that once a rule r is included in an argument, all rules inferior to r are automatically blocked from being included in the same argument.

Priority logic is a general framework with many instantiations, and supports both credulous and sceptical reasoning. To allow a fair comparison to defeasible logic, one has to make some assumptions including restriction to rules, restriction of the priority relation to rules with complementary heads. Under these restrictions, the difference between priority logic and defeasible logic is the same as that between default and defeasible logic mentioned above: Priority logic is extension based, thus it propagates ambiguity.

Courteous logic programs were introduced recently in [8] as a simple and efficient form of default reasoning, to be used as the reasoning basis for intelligent agents. The approach shares some basic ideas of defeasible logic. In particular, it is logic programming based, implements sceptical reasoning, and is based on competing teams of rules, and a priority relation. One difference appears to be that courteous logic programs allow the use of negation as failure. But we have shown that this is unnecessary, in fact negation as failure can be simulated easily, using rules without negation as failure, and the priority relation. Using this observation we showed that courteous logic programs are strictly a special case of defeasible logic.

LPwNF was introduced in [7] as an approach to default reasoning in which negation as failure is simulated by the use of a priority relation $>$. The paper introduced a proof theory and a corresponding argumentation framework. LPwNF can support both credulous and sceptical reasoning.

Even though the approaches seem very similar, a careful comparison reveals an important difference: *LPwNF argues on the basis of individual rules*, whereas *defeasible logic argues on the basis of teams of rules with the same head*. As a consequence, defeasible logic allows more "arguments" to be accepted, because it makes the counterattack of counterarguments easier. For example, in case two (applicable) rules r_1 and r_2 have head p and two (applicable) rules r_3 and r_4, and given that we have the priority information $r_1 > r_3$ and $r_2 > r_4$, defeasible logic allows the derivation of p whereas

LPwNF does not. On the other hand, we have shown that everything that can be proven in LPwNF is provable in defeasible logic.

8 Conclusion

Defeasible logic is a non-monotonic logic, one of many in the literature. The several features of defeasible logic provide for a very natural expression of many of the standard examples used to motivate other non-monotonic logics [12, 3].

Non-monotonic behaviour occurs only when a theory is altered by, for example, adding new facts. In such situations, we should not think of a theory as a stand-alone representation of knowledge, but rather as a module to which rules can be added (or deleted). Thus, when looking to simplify defeasible theories, the modularity of the simplification is essential.

We have shown the following results concerning modular simplification of defeasible theories.

- Facts can be eliminated, without loss of expressive power.
- The superiority relation can be eliminated, without loss of expressive power.
- Strict rules can be separated, almost completely, from the defeasible rules.
- Strict rules, defeasible rules, and defeaters cannot be eliminated without a loss in expressive power.

The main consequence of these results is that we can study, without loss of generality, a simpler form of defeasible logic. Deeper results on a semantics for defeasible logic and the relationship between defeasible logic and other non-monotonic formalisms now become more accessible.

Acknowledgements

This research was supported by an ARC Large Research Grant.

References

[1] G. Antoniou. *Nonmonotonic Reasoning.* MIT Press 1997.

[2] G. Antoniou, D. Billington and M.J. Maher. *Representation results in defeasible logic.* Technical Report, CIT, Griffith University 1997.

[3] G. Antoniou, D. Billington and M.J. Maher. *Sceptical logic programming without negation as failure.* Technical Report, CIT, Griffith University 1997.

[4] D. Billington. Defeasible Logic is Stable. *Journal of Logic and Computation* 3 (1993): 370–400.

[5] E.F. Codd. Further Normalization of the Data Base Relational Model. In *Data Base Systems, Courant Computer Science Symposia Series 6*, Prentice Hall 1972.

[6] M.A. Covington, D. Nute and A. Vellino. *Prolog Programming in Depth*. Prentice Hall 1997.

[7] Y. Dimopoulos and A. Kakas. Logic Programming without Negation as Failure. In *Proc. ICLP-95*, MIT Press 1995.

[8] B.N. Grosof. Prioritized Conflict Handling for Logic Programs. In *Proc. Int. Logic Programming Symposium*, J. Maluszynski (Ed.), 197–211. MIT Press, 1997.

[9] R.A. Kowalski and F. Toni. Abstract Argumentation, *Artificial Intelligence and Law Journal* 4(3-4), Kluwer Academic Publishers 1996.

[10] E. Mendelson. *Introduction to mathematical logic, 3rd edition*. New York, NY: Van Nostrand Reinhold 1987.

[11] D. Nute. Defeasible Reasoning. In *Proc. 20th Hawaii International Conference on Systems Science*, IEEE Press 1987, 470–477.

[12] D. Nute. Defeasible Logic. In D.M. Gabbay, C.J. Hogger and J.A. Robinson (Eds.): *Handbook of Logic in Artificial Intelligence and Logic Programming Vol. 3*, Oxford University Press 1994, 353-395.

[13] D. Nute. A decidable quantified defeasible logic. In D. Prawitz, B. Skyrms and D. Westerstahl (Eds.): *Logic, Methodology and Philosophy of Science IX*, Elsevier 1994, 263 – 284.

[14] R. Reiter. A logic for default reasoning. *Artificial Intelligence* 13 (1980): 81–132.

[15] J.A. Robinson. A machine oriented logic based on the resolution principle. *Journal of the ACM* 12,1, 1965, 23–41.

[16] D. Touretzky, J.F. Horty and R.H. Thomason. A clash of intuitions: The current state of nonmonotonic multiple inheritance systems. In *Proc. IJCAI-87*, 476-482, Morgan Kaufmann 1987.

[17] X. Wang, J. You and L. Yuan. Nonmonotonic reasoning by monotonic inferences with priority constraints. In *Nonmonotonic Extensions of Logic Programming*, J. Dix, P. Pereira, and T. Przymusinski (eds), LNAI 1216, Springer 1997, 91-109.

[18] X. Wang, J. You and L. Yuan. Logic programming without default negation revisited. In *Proc. IEEE International Conference on Intelligent Processing Systems*, IEEE 1997.

Regular Extension Semantics and Disjunctive Eshghi-Kowalski Procedure

Jia-Huai You, Li Yan Yuan, Randy Goebel

Department of Computing Science
University of Alberta, Edmonton, Alberta, Canada T6G 2H1

Abstract

Can the elegant abductive proof procedure by Eshghi and Kowalski be extended to answer queries for disjunctive logic programs? If yes, what is the semantics that such an extended procedure computes? Several years ago, in an unpublished manuscript Dung specified a proof procedure that embeds a form of linear resolution into the Eshghi-Kowalski procedure [3]. More recently, You et al. defined the regular extension semantics for disjunctive programs [19], which was strongly motivated by the observation that some forms of extended Eshghi-Kowalski procedure could be used to answer queries under this semantics. This paper reports the finding that a variant of the procedure specified by Dung computes the regular extension semantics.

1 Introduction

Logic programming has been considered by many as providing a suitable framework for abductive reasoning. Namely, default negations in the form of not_ϕ are treated as *abducibles*, and an explanation of an observation is a set of abducibles that, along with the given program, derives the observation while satisfying some desired integrity constraints.

The insight into this connection between abduction and default negation was first observed by Eshghi and Kowalski [5], who showed an abductive interpretation of negation-as-failure. A number of authors subsequently investigated abductive semantics for normal programs [4, 11]. A more comprehensive exploration of abductive logic programming was presented in [10].

Independently, the *regular model semantics* was formulated using a three-valued logic, and it was shown that, for normal programs, this semantics coincides with a number of independently proposed semantics [21]. This provides an abductive, argumentation interpretation and an alternating fixpoint characterization for the regular model semantics (see [1, 4]). More important, the Eshghi-Kowalski (EK) procedure, enhanced by positive loop checking, is known to be sound and complete (for ground programs) for these equivalent semantics (cf. [8]).

Recently, disjunction has been considered an important addition to logic programming based knowledge representation systems. Theoretically, the class of disjunctive programs is strictly more expressive than that of normal programs. Practically, many problem solutions can be expressed, naturally, using disjunction (see e.g. [7, 12]).

The question of abductive logic programming in the presence of disjunction has been pursued by Dung [2] where he shows that for the class of acyclic (i.e. head-cycle free and stratified negation) disjunctive programs, the EK procedure can be used to answer queries for the stable model semantics. Dung uses the technique of *shifting* to show that this class of disjunctive programs reduce to normal programs. However, it is known that the technique of shifting in general does not preserve even the stable model semantics. Then in [3], Dung specifies a disjunctive EK procedure. But the semantics of what the procedure computes is left unanswered.

More recently in [19], in showing that the stable model semantics for disjunctive programs can be understood as selecting monotonic inferences, using a language with priority, a new semantics for disjunctive programs was discovered, which extends the stable model semantics for disjunctive programs in the same way as regular/preferential semantics extends stable semantics for normal programs. The semantics is called *regular extension semantics.*[1] The semantics was strongly motivated by its natural form of abductive reasoning and the observation that some forms of extended EK procedure could be used to answer queries under this semantics. But the exact form of such a procedure was not totally clear. The primary goal of this paper is to report the finding that a variant of Dung's procedure computes the regular extension semantics. It is sound and complete for finite, ground disjunctive programs. This seems to be the first time that a suitable semantics for disjunctive programs is shown to possess an elegant top-down proof procedure. Since logic programming has been identified with a goal-oriented programming paradigm, the existence of an elegant top-down proof procedure is undoubtedly a significant feature for any semantics.

The semantics of disjunctive programs has been studied by a number of authors. The stable model semantics (as well as the answer set semantics) in principle does not possess a top-down proof procedure, since the semantics relies on global information in its semantic definition. Sakama and Inoue in [9] show a transformation from abductive programs, in the sense of [11], to extended disjunctive programs based on answer sets.

However, since regular extension is a weaker notion of stable model (in that every stable model is a regular extension but the reverse is not true in general), the proof procedure given in this paper is applicable to those programs whose stable models coincide with its regular extensions. For normal programs, a criterion to guarantee such coincidence is well-known; namely, no odd negative dependency loops are present in a program (see, for

[1] It was called partial stable semantics earlier in [19], which may be confused with many other uses of "partial stable" in the literature. The regular *extension* semantics differ from the regular *model* semantics for disjunctive programs as defined in [20]. Although a regular model always exists and the semantics based on it is more expressive than that of stable model, a number of authors have argued that no model theory can capture the intended meaning of disjunction in the presence of default negation.

example, [20]). This criterion can be extended to disjunctive programs. In this sense, the procedure described in this paper is also an abductive proof procedure for the stable model semantics of disjunctive programs.

The static semantics [15] is not designed to be capable of abductive reasoning. Almost all its implementations reply on a bottom-up generation of minimal models. It is unclear what a top-down proof procedure for the semantics would be.

The paper is organized as follows. In the next section we re-formulate the regular extension semantics, independently of the priority framework in which it was first formalized in an indirect, somewhat complex way. Then we present the disjunctive EK procedure, and show it computes the regular extension semantics. The version of disjunctive EK procedure presented here is modified from that of Dung's to ensure the soundness of the procedure for the regular extension semantics.

2 Regular Extension Semantics for Disj. Programs

Let L be a first order language, where for each *ordinary* predicate atom $\phi = p(t_1, ..., t_n)$, there is a predicate not_ϕ and the corresponding atom is $not\_p(t_1, ..., t_n)$.

A *disjunctive program* is a first order theory consisting of the clauses:

$$\alpha_1 \vee ... \vee \alpha_k \leftarrow \beta_1, ..., \beta_m, not\_\gamma_1, ..., not\_\gamma_n \tag{2.0}$$

where α_i's and β_i's are atoms, and not_γ_i's are called *assumptions*. Assumptions are used as *abducibles* in abductive logic programming.

We may denote a clause by $A \leftarrow B, not\_C$ where A is the set of the atoms in the head of the clause, B the set of the atoms in the body, and not_C the set of the assumptions in the body.

A disjunctive program is *positive* if no clause involves any assumptions.

Suppose ϕ is an (ordinary) atom. $\neg\phi$ is called a *negated atom*. Further, ϕ, $\neg\phi$, and not_ϕ are all called *literal.*

In the literature, disjunction is sometimes expressed by $|$, which is sometimes called *epistemic disjunction.* The intuitive meaning of epistemic disjunction is that it be interpreted as *exclusive as possible.* In the case of positive disjunctive programs, such a semantics coincides with the minimal model semantics. Here we replace it by classic disjunction $\vee$. Its intended meaning is enforced by the underlying semantics.

It is important to note that since such a clause is just a first order formula, the first order derivation relation $\vdash$ applies. E.g., with P consisting of

$$a \vee b \leftarrow not\_c$$
$$a \leftarrow b$$
$$b \leftarrow a$$

we have $P \vdash a \leftarrow not\_c$, $P \cup \{not\_c\} \vdash a$, etc.

One of the key ideas in the regular extension semantics is to augment the standard first order derivation relation by a resolution-like inference rule.

Rule of Assumption Commitment (RAC):

$$\frac{\begin{array}{l} not\_\phi \\ \phi_1 \vee \ldots \vee \phi_n \end{array}}{\sigma(\phi_1 \vee \ldots \vee \phi_{i-1} \vee \phi_{i+1} \vee \ldots \vee \phi_n)}$$

where ϕ is an atom, ϕ_j's are literals, and ϕ and ϕ_i are unifiable with m.g.u. σ. When $n = 1$, the resolvent is $\perp$.

This inference rule allows one to commit not_ϕ to $\neg\phi$ to force a stronger derivation relation. This implements the meaning of epistemic disjunction as exclusive as possible. E.g., with $a \vee b$, using RAC to augment the standard derivation we can derive a if we can prove not_b by negation-as-failure.

We will use $\vdash_d$ to denote the standard first order derivation relation augmented by RAC. Note that $\vdash_d$ is a monotonic relation.

In the sequel, for the sake of convenience, our technical exploration will be based on ground programs.

The regular extension semantics, initially formulated in the context of "priority logic" [19], is based on the notion of *alternating fixpoint*, first used by Van Gelder [6], and later by a number of authors (cf. [1, 6, 14, 21]) to define and study the semantics of normal programs and default theories. The interest in this technique is that the regular model semantics for normal programs, and all the semantics equivalent to it, can be expressed by maximal normal alternating fixpoints.

First let us define a function F_P over sets S of assumptions as:

$$F_P(S) = \{not\_\phi \ : \ \phi \text{ is an ordinary atom such that } P \cup S \not\vdash_d \phi\}.$$

It is easy to check that this function has the following property, called *anti-monotonicity*: $S_1 \subseteq S_2 \Rightarrow F_P(S_2) \subseteq F_P(S_1)$. This holds because the derivation relation $\vdash_d$ is monotonic; more information that we have, less information we do *not* derive. Then, the composite function that applies F_P twice, denoted F_P^2, is monotonic. That is,

$$S_1 \subseteq S_2 \Rightarrow F_P^2(S_1) \subseteq F_P^2(S_2).$$

Hence according to the fixpoint theory, commonly referred to as the Tarski-Knaster fixpoint theorem, F_P^2 possesses a least fixpoint, a maximum fixpoint, and possibly some others over the domain of a complete lattice.

A fixpoint of the function F_P^2 is called an *alternating fixpoint* of F_P (or simply, P). An alternating fixpoint S is said to be *normal* if $S \subseteq F_P(S)$. For normal programs, the least alternating fixpoint corresponds to the well-founded model [1, 6] and the maximal normal alternating fixpoints correspond to regular models/preferential extensions. Here we use maximal normal alternating fixpoints to define a credulous semantics for disjunctive programs.

Definition 2.1 (regular extension)
A regular extension *of a disjunctive program P is a maximal normal alternating fixpoint of P.*

Example 2.1 Suppose P consists of

$$a \vee b \leftarrow not\_a, not\_b$$
$$c \leftarrow not\_d$$

It is easy to show that $S = \{not\_d\}$ is a maximal normal alternating fixpoint. First, $F_P(S) = \{not\_d, not\_a, not\_b\}$. Then, $F_P^2(S) = \{not\_d\}$. Further, $S \subseteq F_P(S)$. Thus, S is a normal alternating fixpoint.

In addition, it is easy to see that S is the only normal alternating fixpoint. For example, $S' = \{not\_d, not\_a\}$ is not an alternating fixpoint, since $F_P(S') = \{not\_d, not\_a, not\_b\}$ and $F_P^2(S') = \{not\_d\}$. Further, though $S'' = \{not\_d, not\_a, not\_b\}$ is an alternating fixpoint (in fact, the maximum alternating fixpoint), it is not normal. Thus, S is trivially maximal.

By the equivalence results given in [21], we know for normal programs, the regular extension semantics reduces to the regular model semantics. In addition, stable models of a disjunctive program can be described by the fixpoints of F_P; i.e., any assumption set S such that $F_P(S) = S$ corresponds to a stable model, and vice versa.

The use of the inference rule RAC may be viewed as *semantically* shifting disjunctive clauses in a program P. Recall that the idea of *shifting* a clause $A \leftarrow B, not\_C$ (e.g. see [2, 7]) is to syntactically transform such a clause to a set of normal clauses where, for each atom ϕ in A there is a normal clause with ϕ as the head and any other atom ξ in A is removed to the body as not_ξ. This technique is too strong to capture even the minimal model semantics of positive disjunctive programs (cf. [7, 16]).

Example 2.2 Programs with *head-cycles* are often used to illustrate the difficulties with syntactically shifting a program. Consider P:

$$a \vee b \vee c \leftarrow$$
$$a \leftarrow b$$
$$b \leftarrow a$$

The program has a head-cycle between a and b. In terms of stratification, a should be one level higher than b (by the second clause) and b should be one level higher than a (by the third clause); but a and b also appear in the same head of a clause; hence the term *head-cycle*.

The program has two stable models (which are just minimal models), $\{c\}$ and $\{a, b\}$. However, the shifted normal program P_{shift} below dose not have any stable model.

$$\begin{array}{l} a \leftarrow not\_b, not\_c \\ b \leftarrow not\_a, not\_c \\ c \leftarrow not\_a, not\_b \\ a \leftarrow b \\ b \leftarrow a \end{array}$$

The idea of representing the epistemic disjunction by the classic disjunction combined with shifting does not work, either. In this case the program to be considered is $P' = P \cup P_{shift}$ where $\vee$ denotes the classical disjunction. However, $\{not\_c\}$ is not a fixpoint of the operator: $\mathcal{F}_{P'}(S) = \{not\_\phi :$ ϕ is an ordinary atom such that $P' \cup S \not\vdash \phi\}$. That is, the original stable model $\{a, b\}$ is lost.[2]

2.1 Regular extensions constitute an abductive semantics

The regular extension semantics can also be defined in an abductive framework more directly with the following integrity constraints:

$$IC = \{\bot \leftarrow (\phi_1 \vee ... \vee \phi_n), not\_\phi_1, ..., not\_\phi_n \mid n \geq 1\}.$$

Given a program P, a set of assumptions S is said to be $\bot$-*consistent* if $P \cup S \cup IC \not\vdash_d \bot$.

The following definition is essentially the same as that of Dung [4] except that the underlying derivation relation is augmented by RAC.

Definition 2.2 Let P be a disjunctive program. An assumption not_ϕ is said to be *acceptable* w.r.t. an assumption set S if for any assumption set S' such that $P \cup S' \vdash_d \phi$, we have $P \cup S \vdash_d \xi$, for some $not\_\xi \in S'$.

A *preferred extension* E is a maximal assumption set that is $\bot$-consistent, and for every $not\_\phi \in E$, not_ϕ is acceptable w.r.t. E.

The following theorem can be proved in a way similar to proving it for normal programs (see, e.g. [18], where the only difference is the underlying derivation relation which affects no derivation in such a proof).

Theorem 2.1 *For any disjunctive program P, a preferred extension of P is a regular extension of P, and vice versa.*

There are potential applications of abductive reasoning with disjunctive programs. For example, in AI planning and scheduling, in general we are interested in whether there is a plan that achieves the goal, and whether there is a schedule that satisfies the specified constraints. Such a solution

[2]The authors thank C. Sakama for pointing this out and providing this example. The problem is related to the following question: though it is known that disjunctive default logic falls into the same complexity level as default logic, so far no polynomial transformation has been found. Sakama suspects that such a transformation may have to be non-modular.

corresponds to an explanation (abducibles in a plan, for example) to an observation (the goal to be achieved) in abduction.[3] Here let us use a simple example to explain the notion of abductive solution.

Example 2.3 Consider the following disjunctive program P, extended from a normal program given in [4]:

$$shave(bob, x) \leftarrow not\_shave(x, x)$$
$$pay\_cash(y, x) \lor pay\_by\_credit(y, x) \leftarrow shave(x, y)$$
$$accepted(x, y) \leftarrow pay\_cash(x, y)$$
$$accepted(x, y) \leftarrow pay\_by\_credit(x, y)$$

This program intuitively says that *bob* shaves those who do not shave themselves; If x shaves y then y pays x by cash or by credit; either way is accepted.

Assume there is another person, called *greg*. Then clearly, we should conclude *bob* shaves *greg*, and *greg* pays *bob* by cash or by credit, either way is accepted. However, the program has no stable models in this case. But it has two regular extensions, both containing $not\_shave(greg, greg)$.

Suppose we observe $pay\_cash(greg, bob)$. Then the following set of abducibles (in the premise), along with the program, explains this observation:

$$P \cup \{not\_shave(greg, greg), not\_pay\_by\_credit(greg, bob)\} \vdash_d pay\_cash(greg, bob).$$

3 Disjunctive EK Procedure

The disjunctive EK procedure combines the EK procedure with a sound and complete linear resolution procedure, augmented by the inference rule RAC. The linear resolution procedure is adopted from [12].

Because of the restriction to ground programs, we can omit *factoring* used in linear resolution to preserve its completeness.

It is convenient to assume that subgoal selection is from the left to right, and a goal is written as $\leftarrow l, N$ where l is the current subgoal to be resolved, and N is the collection of the rest subgoals.

A *general goal* (a *goal* for short) is of the form

$$\leftarrow l_1, ..., l_k, not\_\phi_{k+1}, ..., not\_\phi_m$$

where each l_i is either an atom or a negated atom, and each not_ϕ_i is an abducible.

An empty clause (goal) is denoted by $\Box$.

For a set of atoms S, we define $\neg S = \{\neg\xi \ : \ \xi \in S\}$.

[3] An example of relating AI planning with logic programming semantics is [17], where nondeterminism is coded into a normal program. Their solution may be improved using disjunction so that, for example, the concept that either action a or action b can achieve a goal can be expressed. This differs from nondeterministically performing action a or action b.

Resolution is an inference rule for first order clause theories. For disjunctive programs, we only need to use it in three specific ways: *goal resolution*, *ancestor resolution*, and *body literal resolution*. For presentation purposes, we introduce each at a time.

Goal resolution is between the current goal and a program clause. Goal resolution is completely goal oriented – it focuses only on the current goal and uses program clauses to resolve it.

Definition 3.1 (goal resolution)
Let P be a disjunctive program, $G :\leftarrow l, N$ be a goal where l is an ordinary atom and N denotes the rest subgoals. The goal resolution *of G on l is with a program clause $A \leftarrow B, not\_C \in P$, where $l \in A$, and generates the resolvant goal $\leftarrow \neg(A - \{l\}), B, not\_C, N$.*

For example, when goal $\leftarrow a$ is resolved with clause $a \vee b \leftarrow not\_c$, we get resolvant goal $\leftarrow \neg b, not\_c$.

Goal resolution alone is incomplete for positive disjunctive programs.

Example 3.1 Consider

1. $p \vee r$
2. $r \leftarrow p$
3. $p \leftarrow q$
4. $q \leftarrow r$

It is easy to verify that goal resolution alone cannot resolve the goal $\leftarrow r$ to an empty clause. A goal should be allowed to resolve with a previous goal:

5.	$\leftarrow r$	resolve with 2
6.	$\leftarrow p$	resolve with 1
7.	$\leftarrow \neg r$	resolve with 5
8.	$\square$	

The last resolution step is called *ancestry resolution* in the literature.

Definition 3.2 (ancestry resolution)
Let P be a disjunctive program, $G :\leftarrow l, N$ be a goal where l is an ordinary or a negated atom. The ancestry resolution *of G on l is with a goal $G' :\leftarrow l', M$ before G on the* same *derivation where $\neg l' = l$, and yields the resolvant goal $\leftarrow N, M$.*

A negated atom in a goal can be proved by negation-as-failure for abductive reasoning. This would implement the inference rule RAC.

Example 3.2 Consider $P = \{a \vee b\}$, and the derivation

$$\leftarrow a$$
$$\leftarrow \neg b$$

If we can show not_b, then with the inference rule RAC, this hypothesis along with the program explains a. That is, $P \cup \{not\_b\} \vdash_d a$.

Goal resolution and ancestry resolution together still fails to yield a complete proof procedure.

Example 3.3 Consider program P

1. $a \vee b$
2. $c \leftarrow a$
3. $c \leftarrow b$

and a proof

4.	$\leftarrow c$	resolve with 2
5.	$\leftarrow a$	resolve with 1
6.	$\leftarrow \neg b$	resolve with 3
......		

In this case, a proof of *not_b* could be used to show the goal $\leftarrow \neg b$ under RAC. For this example, it is possible to prove *not_b*, such that $P \cup \{not\_b\} \vdash_d c$ in one proof, and *not_a* in another proof.

However, there are examples where resolving with a *body literal* is necessary.

Example 3.4 Consider adding two more clauses to the program in Example 3.3 above:

1. $a \vee b$
2. $c \leftarrow a$
3. $c \leftarrow b$

4. $a \leftarrow not\_a$
5. $b \leftarrow not\_b$

The clauses 4 and 5 above prevent generating *not_a* or *not_b* in any consistent proof. But a refutation exists:

6.	$\leftarrow c$	resolve with 2	(goal resolution)
7.	$\leftarrow a$	resolve with 1	(goal resolution)
8.	$\leftarrow \neg b$	resolve with 3	(body literal resolution)
9.	$\leftarrow \neg c$	resolve with 6	(ancestor resolution)
10.	$\square$		

Definition 3.3 (body literal resolution)
Let P be a disjunctive program, $G :\leftarrow \neg\phi, N$ be a goal where ϕ is an ordinary atom and N denotes the rest subgoals. The body literal resolution *of G on $\neg\phi$ is with a program clause $A \leftarrow B, not\_C \in P$, where $\phi \in B$, and generates the resolvant goal $\leftarrow \neg A, B - \{\phi\}, not\_C, N$.*

We are now ready to give the complete description of the disjunctive EK procedure.

The Disjunctive EK Procedure (DEKP)

An *abductive derivation* from (G_1, H_1) to (G_n, H_n) is a sequence

$$(G_1, H_1),\ (G_2, H_2),\ \dots,\ (G_n, H_n)$$

where each G_i, $0 < i < n$, has the form $\leftarrow l, N$ where l is the selected literal, N is the set of the rest subgoals, H_i is a set of hypotheses, and (G_{i+1}, H_{i+1}) is obtained from (G_i, H_i) as

AD1) if l is either an ordinary atom, or a negated atom $\neg\phi$ with $not\_\phi \notin H_i$, then

$$G_{i+1} = C \quad \text{and} \quad H_{i+1} = H_i,$$

where C is the resolvant of G_i, either by goal resolution or by body literal resolution with some program clause on the selected literal l, or by ancestor resolution with a previous goal G_j, $j < i$;

AD2) if l is a negated atom $\neg\phi$ or an abducible atom not_ϕ, and $not\_\phi \in H_i$, then

$$G_{i+1} = \leftarrow N \quad \text{and} \quad H_{i+1} = H_i;$$

AD3) if l is a negated atom $\neg\phi$ or an abducible atom not_ϕ, $not\_\phi \notin H_i$, and there is a consistency derivation from $(\{\leftarrow \phi\}, H_i \cup \{not\_\phi\})$ to $(\emptyset, H')$, where $\emptyset$ denotes an empty set of goals, then

$$G_{i+1} = \leftarrow N \quad \text{and} \quad H_{i+1} = H'.$$

An *abductive refutation* is an abductive derivation from (G, H_1) to $(\Box, H_n)$.

A *consistency derivation* from (F_1, H_1) to (F_n, H_n) is a sequence

$$(F_1, H_1),\ (F_2, H_2),\ \dots,\ (F_n, H_n)$$

such that for each i, $0 < i < n$, F_i has the form $\{\leftarrow l, N\} \cup F_i'$ where, without loss of generality, the goal $\leftarrow l, N$ has been chosen, and (F_{i+1}, H_{i+1}) is obtained from (F_i, H_i) as

CO1) if l is an ordinary atom, then

$$F_{i+1} = G \cup F_i' \quad \text{and} \quad H_{i+1} = H_i,$$

where G is the set of all resolvant goals from $\leftarrow l, N$, either by goal resolution with some program clause on l, or by ancestry resolution with a previous goal on the *same derivation branch*[4], and $\Box \notin G$;

[4]Since each goal is resolved by all applicable clauses or previous goals, a consistency derivation is a derivation tree. We use the term a *derivation branch* to mean a sequence of resolution steps in a branch of such a tree.

CO2) if l is a negated atom $\neg\phi$ such that the set of new resolvant goals is non-empty,[5] then

$$F_{i+1} = G \cup F_i \quad \text{and} \quad H_{i+1} = H_i,$$

where G is the set of all new resolvant goals from $\leftarrow l, N$, either by body literal resolution with some program clause on l, or by ancestry resolution with a previous goal on the same derivation branch;

CO3) if (l is a negated atom $\neg\phi$ and CO2 generates no new goals) or an abducible atom not_ϕ, $not\_\phi \in H_i$, and N is non-empty, then

$$F_{i+1} = \{\leftarrow N\} \cup F_i' \quad \text{and} \quad H_{i+1} = H_i;$$

CO4) if (l is a negated atom $\neg\phi$ and CO2 generates no new goals) or an abducible atom not_ϕ, and $not\_\phi \notin H_i$, then
if there is an abductive derivation from $(\{\leftarrow \phi\}, H_i)$ to $(\Box, H')$, then

$$F_{i+1} = F_i' \quad \text{and} \quad H_{i+1} = H'$$

else if N is non-empty then

$$F_{i+1} = \{\leftarrow N\} \cup F_i' \quad \text{and} \quad H_{i+1} = H_i.$$

Consistency derivations are augmented by positive loop checking. The following rule should be applied immediately when it is possible:

CO5) if l is an atom and there is a previous goal $\leftarrow l, M \in F_j$, $j < i$, on the same derivation branch, then

$$F_{i+1} = F_i' \quad \text{and} \quad H_{i+1} = H_i. \qquad \Box$$

Here are some technical remarks on the procedure.

Abductive derivations are relatively straightforward: find one way of proving a goal, including showing a subgoal of the form $\neg\phi$ by negation-as-failure, which corresponds to the semantic commitment of RAC.

Consistency derivations are more involved.

Recall in Theorem 2.1, in order to show not_ϕ, each way of defeating not_ϕ (i.e. deriving ϕ) should be shown counter-attacked. Thus, CO1 and CO2 expand the current set of goals to include all possible ways of defeating not_ϕ (note that CO2 keeps the goal being resolved upon), and in CO3 and CO4, the negated atom $\neg\phi$ is treated the same way as not_ϕ. This provides a rather direct implementation of RAC.

We now show some examples. In drawing these proofs, we use `\O` for empty set $\emptyset$, `[]` for empty clause $\Box$, and `-a` for negated atom $\neg a$.

[5]A resolvant goal is *new* in a consistency derivation if it has never appeared in any set of goals in the derivation.

Example 3.5 Let $P = \{a \vee b\}$. *not_b* may be abduced to conclude a:

```
-------------------------------------------------------------
|  <- a                                                    {}
|  <- -b                      % by AD1
|        (AD3) -----------------------------------------------
|        ! { <- b}                                   {not_b}
|        ! { <- -a}           % by C01
|        !                    (C04)---------------------------
|        !                    | <-a                    {not_b}
|        !                    | <- -b        % by AD1
|        !                    | []           % by AD2  {not_b}
|        !                    |-------------------------------
|        ! \O                                        {not_b}
|        !--------------------------------------------------
| []                                                 {not_b}
|------------------------------------------------------------
```

Example 3.6 Recall the program $P = \{a \vee b \vee c \leftarrow;\ a \leftarrow b;\ b \leftarrow a\}$, in Example 2.2 to show the failure of *shifting*. Here is a proof that a is true in one regular extension that contains *not_c*. Effectively, it shows that a is true in one minimal model where c is false.

```
-------------------------------------------------------------
|  <- a                                                    {}
|  <- -b, -c
|  <- -a, -c                  % by body literal resolution
|  <- -c                      % by ancestry resolution
|       (AD3)------------------------------------------------
|       ! {<- c}                                     {not_c}
|       ! {<- -a, -b}
|       ! {<- -a, -b; <- -b, -b}   % by C02
|       !       (C04)---------------------------------------
|       !       | <- a                               {not_c}
|       !       | ...          % steps omitted
|       !       | []
|       !       ---------------------------------------------
|       ! {<- -b}
|       !       (C04)---------------------------------------
|       !       | <- b                               {not_c}
|       !       | ...          % steps omitted
|       !       | []
|       !       ---------------------------------------------
|       ! /O                                         {not_c}
|       !---------------------------------------------------
| []                                                 {not_c}
-------------------------------------------------------------
```

For any program whose stable models coincide with regular extensions, DEKP can be used to answer queries for the stable model semantics.

Example 3.7 Consider $\{a \vee b \leftarrow not\_a;\ \ c \leftarrow a;\ \ c \leftarrow b\}$. There is precisely one regular extension, which is just a stable model, in which c is concluded. Here is a proof.

```
-------------------------------------------------------------
|  <- c                                                   {}
|  <- b
|  <- -a, not_a
|  <- not_a                 % simplified from above
|       -----------------------------------------------------
|       ! { <- a}                                   {not_a}
|       ! { <- -b, not_a}
|       ! { <- -b, not_a; <- -c, not_a}
|       !       ---------------------------------------------
|       !       | <- b                              {not_a}
|       !       | <- -a, not_a
|       !       | []                                {not_a}
|       !       |--------------------------------------------
|       ! { <- -c, not_a}
|       !       % by C04, details omitted
|       ! /0                                        {not_a}
|       !----------------------------------------------------
| []                                                {not_a}
-------------------------------------------------------------
```

4 Soundness and Completeness

Theorem 4.1 *Let P be a disjunctive program.*
(Soundness) For any abductive refutation $(\leftarrow \phi, \emptyset), \ldots, (\Box, H)$, there is a regular extension E such that $H \subseteq E$ and $P \cup E \vdash_d \phi$.
(Completeness) For any finite regular extension E and any literal ϕ such that $P \cup E \vdash_d \phi$, there is an abductive refutation $(\leftarrow \phi, \emptyset), \ldots, (\Box, H)$, such that $H \subseteq E$.

Embedding linear resolution into a negation-as-failure procedure is by no means a problem with an obvious or easy solution. For example, the semantics of Dung's original version is not very clear; at least it is unsound for the regular extension semantics.

Essentially, Dung's procedure is more liberal in justifying the defeat of an attack: not being able to resolve a negated atom $\neg\phi$ in a goal of a consistency derivation is a *sufficient* reason for a failure to prove. In the current version this has to be proved by a derivation of ϕ.

Example 4.1 Consider

$$P = \{a \leftarrow not\_b;\ b \vee c \vee d \leftarrow;\ p \leftarrow c;\ p \leftarrow;\ c \leftarrow not\_c;\ d \leftarrow not\_d\}$$

The question is whether a should be concluded in a semantics. If we conclude a, we must have not_b. To prove not_b, every possible way of deriving b should be shown defeated. To derive b we assume c and d to be false, but the last two clauses prevent them from being false.

Using Dung's procedure, we get

```
-------------------------------------------------------------
|  <- not_b
|          ----------------------------------------------------
|          ! { <- b}                                    {not_b}
|          ! { <- -c, -d}
|          ! { <- -p, -d}
|          ! /O
|          !---------------------------------------------------
| []                                                    {not_b}
-------------------------------------------------------------
```

The consistency derivation reduces to $\emptyset$ because the only goal in it cannot be resolved by any clause. Using our procedure, we will get the set of goals `{<- -c, -d; <- -p, -d}` in the consistency derivation, where there is no abduction refutation for either `<- c` or `<- d`. The inclusion of the first goal is due to the fact that $P \cup \{not\_c, not\_d\} \vdash_d b$, and thus the defeat of either not_c or not_d has to be established.

The behavior of Dung's proof procedure for this example is more like that of O-semantics [13], which is defined only on top of the well-founded semantics for normal programs.

References

[1] C. Baral and V. Subrahmanian. Stable and extension class theory for logic programs and default logic. *JAR*, pages 345–366, 1992.

[2] P. Dung. Acyclic disjunctive logic programs with abductive procedures as proof procedure. In *Proc. 1992 Fifth Generation Computer Systems*, pages 555–561, 1992.

[3] P. Dung. An abductive procedure for disjunctive logic programs. Unpublished manuscript, 1993.

[4] P. Dung. An argumentation theoretic foundation for logic programming. *J. Logic Programming*, 22:151–177, 1995. A short version in *ICLP'91*.

[5] K. Eshghi and R.A. Kowalski. Abduction compared with negation by failure. In *Proc. 6th ICLP*, pages 234–254. MIT Press, 1989.

[6] A. Van Gelder. The alternating fixpoint of logic programs with negation. *JCSS*, pages 185–221, 1993. A short version appeared in *PODS '89*.

[7] M. Gelfond, V. Lifschitz, H. Przymusinska, and M. Truszczynski. Disjunctive defaults. In *Proc. KR '91*, pages 230–237, 1991.

[8] L. Giordano, A. Marteli, and M. Sapino. A semantics for eshghi and kowalski's abductive procedure. In *Proc. 10th ICLP*. MIT Press, 1993. The full paper appears in JLP 26(1), 1996.

[9] K. Inoue and C. Sakama. Transforming abductive logic programs to disjunctive programs. In *Proc. 10th ICLP*. MIT Press, 1993.

[10] A. Kakas, R. Kowalski, and F. Toni. The role of abduction in logic programming. In *Handbook of Logic in Artificial Intelligence and Logic Programming*. Oxford University, 1995.

[11] A. Kakas and P. Mancarella. Generalized stable models: a semantics for abduction. In *Proc. 9th ECAI*, 1990.

[12] J. Lobo, J. Minker, and A. Rajasekar. *Foundations of Disjunctive Logic Programming*. MIT Press, 1992.

[13] L. Pereira, J. Alferes, and J. Aparicio. Adding closed world assumptions to well founded semantics. *Theoretical Comp. Sci.*, 122:49–68, 1994.

[14] H. Przymusinska and T.C. Przymusinski. Stationary default extensions. Technical report, California State Polytechnic and University of California at Riverside, 1991.

[15] T. C. Przymusinski. Static semantics for normal and disjunctive logic programs. *Annals of Mathematics and Artificial Intelligence*, 1995.

[16] C. Sakama and K. Inoue. Relating disjunctive logic programs to default theories. In *Proc. LPNMR*, pages 266–282. MIT Press, 1993.

[17] V.S. Subrahmanian and C. Zaniolo. Relating stable models and ai planning domains. In *Proc. 12th ICLP*, pages 233–248, 1995.

[18] J. You, R. Cartwright, and M. Li. Iterative belief revision in extended logic programming. *Theoretical Comp. Science*, 170(1-2):383–406, 1996.

[19] J. You, X. Wang, and L. Yuan. Disjunctive logic programming as constrained inferences. In *Proc. 14th ICLP*. MIT Press, 1997.

[20] J. You and L. Yuan. A three-valued semantics for deductive databases and logic programs. *J. Computer and System Sciences*, 49:334–361, 1994. A short version appeared in *Proc. PODS '90*.

[21] J. You and L. Yuan. On the equivalence of semantics for normal logic programs. *J. Logic Programming*, 22(3):211–222, 1995.

Beyond Success and Failure

Sandro Etalle
Dept. of Computer Science, Universiteit Maastricht
P.O. Box 616, 6200 MD Maastricht, The Netherlands
etalle@cs.unimaas.nl

Femke van Raamsdonk
CWI
P.O. Box 94079, 1090 GB Amsterdam, The Netherlands
femke@cwi.nl

Abstract

We study a new programming framework based on logic programming where success and failure are replaced by predicates for adequacy and inadequacy. Adequacy allows to extract a result from a partial computation, and inadequacy allows to flexibly constrain the search space. In this parameterized setting, the classical result of independence of the selection rule does not hold. We show that, under certain conditions, whenever there exists an adequate derivation there is one in which only so-called needed atoms are selected. This result is applied in a practical setting where adequacy is expressed using a notion of request.

1 Introduction

In logic programming, success and failure determine when the computation should stop and return the result and when it should start backtracking. In this sense, success and failure form the cornerstones of control. In the traditional approach, a resolution sequence is considered to be successful if it ends in the empty query, and failing if the resulting query is non-empty but no clause can be applied to the selected atom. In the present paper we propose to take a more general point of view by parameterizing over notions of success and failure, which we then call *adequacy* and *inadequacy*.

The important point of using adequacy is that it permits to extract a result from an incomplete computation, which is particularly useful in the presence of potentially infinite data structures. As an example we consider the following program, which computes the list of Fibonacci numbers.

$$\begin{array}{rcl} fib([x_n, x_{n+1}, x_{n+2}|l]) & \leftarrow & x_{n+2} \; is \; x_n + x_{n+1}, \\ & & fib([x_{n+1}, x_{n+2}|l]). \end{array}$$

Suppose we are interested in computing the fifth Fibonacci number. Then we start computing in the query $fib([0, 1, \_, \_, x|l])$ and specify that a computation is adequate if it computes the value of x. The derivation

$$fib([0,1,\_,\_,x|l]) \Rightarrow^* fib([1,1,\_,x|l]) \Rightarrow^* fib([1,2,x|l]) \Rightarrow^* fib([2,3,l]).$$

instantiates x to 3 and is hence considered to be adequate, although it is not successful in the traditional sense.

The inadequacy predicate can be used to cut away an infinite branch never leading to an adequate state. Consider for instance the program defined by the following clauses:

$$\begin{aligned} p(f(y)) &\leftarrow . \\ p(a) &\leftarrow . \\ q &\leftarrow q. \end{aligned}$$

Consider the query $p(x), q$ and suppose that a derivation is considered to be adequate if it computes the value of x. Consider the derivation

$$\langle p(x), q; \epsilon\rangle \Rightarrow \langle q; x \mapsto f(y)\rangle.$$

It is clear that there is no way to extend this derivation to an adequate one, because y will never be instantiated and the only possible extension is to enter the one-step loop $\langle q; x \mapsto f(y)\rangle \Rightarrow \langle q; x \mapsto f(y)\rangle$. At this point it becomes extremely useful to be able to backtrack instead of entering an infinite branch. This is possible by specifying an inadequacy predicate as follows: the inadequacy predicate $\mathcal{I}$ holds for a state $\langle Q; \sigma\rangle$ if $x\sigma$ is not ground and the variables in $x\sigma$ do not occur in Q.

It is easy to see that in this general setting independence of the selection rule does not hold. Hence it is important to investigate when appropriate selection rules can be devised. Following the approach initiated by Huet and Lévy in [5] in the context of rewriting, we introduce needed atoms, and we show that, under certain conditions, whenever there is an adequate derivation, there is one in which only needed atoms are selected. This result is obtained in a quite abstract setting. We then introduce for logic programs with guards and delay declarations the notion of request, which allows to formulate a notion of adequacy that is useful in practice, and we formulate conditions that permit to apply the result concerning needed atoms.

The remainder of the paper is organized as follows. In the next section we fix the notation. In Section 3 we discuss our approach of parameterizing over success and failure by means of predicates for adequacy and inadequacy. In Section 4 the notion of needed atoms is introduced, and we show that, under certain conditions, there is an adequate derivation in which only needed atoms are selected whenever there is an adequate derivation. Section 5 is concerned with logic programming with guards and delay declarations enriched with requests. Finally we discuss some other possible uses of the (in)adequacy predicates.

2 Preliminaries

We assume a set $\mathcal{V}$ of infinitely many *variables* written as $x, y, z, \ldots$. We write *function symbols* as $f, g, a, b, \ldots$ and *relation symbols* as $p, q, \ldots$. Sometimes we use more suggestive notation. Both function and relation symbols are supposed to have a fixed arity. If $\mathcal{F}$ is a set of function symbols, then *terms* over $\mathcal{F}$ are built from variables and function symbols in $\mathcal{F}$ in the usual way. If in addition $\mathcal{R}$ is a set of relation symbols, then *atoms* over $\mathcal{F}$ and $\mathcal{R}$ are built from terms over $\mathcal{F}$ and relation symbols in $\mathcal{R}$ in the usual way. Terms are written as $s, t, \ldots$ and atoms as $A, B, H, \ldots$. In the sequel, we won't specify the sets of function and predicate symbols if no confusion can arise. A *query* is defined as a finite sequence of atoms. Queries are denoted by $Q, \ldots$ or by specifying a finite sequence of atoms. A sequence of atoms $A_1, \ldots, A_n$ with $n \geq 0$ is often abbreviated to $\vec{A}$. The empty query is denoted by $\Box$. A *substitution* is a mapping from variables to terms, written as $\sigma, \tau, \ldots$, that is extended to terms and atoms homeomorphically. The identity substitution is denoted by ϵ. We will consider pairs consisting of a query and a substitution, written as $\langle Q; \sigma \rangle$, and call such pairs *states*. Instead of states one often considers queries only. The dynamics of logic programming is defined using clauses. A *clause* is an expression of the form $H \leftarrow B_1, \ldots, B_m$ with $H, B_1, \ldots, B_m$ atoms. A set of clauses is also called a *program*.

3 Success and Failure Revisited

In the approach we propose, the control part of a logic program is specified by two *control predicates:* one for *adequacy* and one for *inadequacy*. The adequacy predicate is used to express that a computation has yield sufficient information, and the inadequacy predicate to express that it is no use to continue the computation under consideration. Before we discuss the meaning and use of these predicates, we first need to introduce some more notions.

In logic programming languages with a dynamic selection rule there is often a way to express whether an atom can be selected. This can for instance be done by means of delay declarations, or, somewhat more implicitly, using guards. These two concepts will be considered in Section 5. Until then, it is sufficient to consider an abstract predicate for selectability.

Definition 3.1 Let a program $\mathcal{P}$ be given. A predicate $\mathcal{S}$ defined on atoms is said to be a *selectability predicate* if it satisfies the following requirements:

1. if $\mathcal{S}(A)$ holds then for every clause $H \leftarrow \vec{B}$ in $\mathcal{P}$ it is decidable whether A and H unify,
2. if $\mathcal{S}(A)$ holds then $\mathcal{S}(A\sigma)$ holds for every substitution σ. $\Box$

The first requirement makes sense for instance when considering guarded unification; note further that the selectability predicate is required to be monotonic.

A *selection rule* is a mapping that given a state returns a selectable atom in that state whenever the state contains a selectable atom, and returns δ otherwise.

In the following we will consider predicates $\mathcal{A}$ for adequacy and $\mathcal{I}$ for inadequacy. These predicates depend on the program and the selection rule under consideration; note that the latter in its turn depend on the selectability predicate. In the notation these parameters are suppressed: we denote by $\mathcal{A}(\langle Q;\sigma\rangle)$ that a state $\langle Q;\sigma\rangle$ is adequate and by $\mathcal{I}(\langle Q;\sigma\rangle)$ that it is inadequate. The (in)adequacy predicates are subject to the following three assumptions. We will suppose that

1. *(in)adequacy predicates are invariant under renaming,*
2. *there is no state in which both $\mathcal{A}$ and $\mathcal{I}$ hold,*
3. *if there is no clause the head of which unifies with the selected atom, then $\mathcal{I}$ holds.*

If a state is neither adequate nor inadequate and applying the selection rule to it yields δ, then we say that it is in *deadlock*. Note that it can be the case that inadequacy is defined to hold if the selection rule yields δ; in that case no state is in deadlock. By definition, adequacy, inadequacy and deadlock are mutually exclusive.

Now the dynamics are defined as follows.

Definition 3.2 Let $\mathcal{P}$ be a program. Suppose that

1. $\langle Q;\sigma\rangle$ is a state that is neither adequate, nor inadequate, nor in deadlock,
2. $Q = A_1,\ldots,A_{m-1},A_m,A_{m+1},\ldots,A_n$ with A_m the selected atom,
3. $c = H \leftarrow \vec{B}$, is a suitable renaming of a clause in $\mathcal{P}$,
4. τ is a most general unifier of A_m and H.

Then we have a *derivation step*

$$\langle Q;\sigma\rangle \overset{\tau}{\underset{c}{\Longrightarrow}} \langle Q';\sigma\tau\rangle$$

with $Q' = (A_1,\ldots,A_{m-1},\vec{B},A_{m+1},\ldots,A_n)\tau$.

We say that the clause c is *applied* to A_m in $\langle Q;\sigma\rangle$. For every $i \in \{1,\ldots,m-1,m+1,\ldots,n\}$, the atom $A_i\tau$ in Q' is said to be the *descendant* of the atom A_i in the query Q. The atoms $\vec{B}\tau$ in Q' are said to be *created* in the derivation step. □

We omit the labels specifying the most general unifier and/or the clause whenever possible. Further, we usually specify only the relevant part of a substitution in a state. A sequence of derivation steps is called a *derivation*. Derivations can be finite or infinite. The definition of descendant is extended in a natural way to derivations consisting of more than one derivation step. We make use of the following terminology.

Definition 3.3 Let $\mathcal{P}$ be a program and let an adequacy predicate $\mathcal{A}$ and an inadequacy predicate $\mathcal{I}$ be given. Let

$$\xi : \langle Q_1; \sigma_1 \rangle \Rightarrow^* \langle Q_m; \sigma_m \rangle$$

be a finite derivation.

1. ξ is said to be *adequate* if $\mathcal{A}(\langle Q_m; \sigma_m \rangle)$ holds.

2. ξ is said to be *inadequate* if $\mathcal{I}(\langle Q_m; \sigma_m \rangle)$ holds.

3. ξ is said to *deadlock* if $\langle Q; \sigma \rangle$ is in deadlock. □

The standard approach to logic programming is obtained by specifying that $\mathcal{A}$ coincides with the usual notion of *success*, that is, it holds for $\langle Q; \sigma \rangle$ and $\mathcal{P}$ if and only if $Q = \Box$, and that $\mathcal{I}$ coincides with the usual notion of *failure*, that is, it holds for $\langle Q; \sigma \rangle$ and $\mathcal{P}$ if and only if $Q \neq \Box$ and no clause in $\mathcal{P}$ can be applied to the selected atom. The general, parameterized, setting permits however to express many more notions of (in)adequacy, as discussed in the introduction.

Non-determinism. As is well-known, a derivation step is subject to four dimensions of non-determinism (c.f. Section 3.5 of [2]):

1. the choice of a renaming of the program clause used,

2. the choice of a most general unifier,

3. the choice of an atom,

4. the choice of a program clause.

Since (in)adequacy predicates are supposed to be invariant under renaming, it follows as for the classical approach to logic programming that neither the choice of a renaming of a clause nor the choice of a most general unifier is relevant. Further, the choice of a program clause yields non-determinism as in the classical approach.

The essential difference with the classical approach lies in the third dimension of non-determinism, the choice of an atom. In the classical approach, an important result is the independence of the selection rule. More precisely, it is shown (see [2]), that for every successful derivation ξ and for every selection rule R, there exists a derivation that is via R, successful, has the same length as ξ and that yields the same computer answer substitution as ξ. This result fails in the present, generalized setting. Consider for instance the program defined by the following clauses:

$$\begin{array}{rcl} q & \leftarrow & q. \\ p(a) & \leftarrow & . \end{array}$$

Suppose that we specify our adequacy condition to hold if and only if x is instantiated to a ground term. Then

$$\langle q, p(x); \epsilon \rangle \Rightarrow \langle q; x \mapsto a \rangle$$

is an adequate derivation, but there is no adequate derivation using the leftmost selection rule.

4 Call by Need

In the light of the negative result concerning independence of the selection rule, it is important to identify useful selection rules. Our approach is inspired by a line of research initiated by Huet and Lévy in [5] (for more recent contributions concerning also notions of partial result see for instance [6, 4]). They show in [5] that in an orthogonal term rewriting system, every term not in normal form contains a needed redex, and that repeatedly contracting needed redexes yields a rewrite sequence ending in normal form, whenever the initial term has a normal form. Intuitively speaking, the contraction of a needed redex cannot be avoided and needed rewriting is normalizing. Needed redexes are not computable.

In this section we define needed atoms as atoms that must be resolved in order to obtain an adequate state. We identify conditions on the selectability predicate and the (in)adequacy predicates that guarantee that if a state admits an adequate derivation, then it admits one in which only needed atoms are selected. We call such a derivation a *call by need* derivation. Note that due to the fourth dimension of non-determinism (the choice of the program clause), we cannot hope that every derivation via the call by need selection rule is adequate.

Needed atoms. Needed atoms are defined using the notion of descendant (see Definition 3.2).

Definition 4.1 Let $\mathcal{P}$ be a program and let $\mathcal{A}$ be an adequacy predicate. An atom A in a state $\langle Q; \sigma \rangle$ is *needed* with respect to $\mathcal{A}$ if for every adequate derivation $\langle Q; \sigma \rangle \Rightarrow^* \langle Q'; \sigma' \rangle$ we have that Q' does not contain a descendant of A. □

Note that in a state that is not the starting point of an adequate derivation, every atom is needed.

Example 4.2

1. If we take for adequacy the traditional notion of success, then in any state $\langle Q; \sigma \rangle$ every atom in Q is needed.
2. If $\mathcal{A}(\langle A; \sigma \rangle)$ does not hold, then A is needed. □

The first part of the previous example reveals that needed atoms are simply not interesting in the traditional approach to logic programming.

Requirements. What we aim at now, is to identify requirements that guarantee the following property to hold: if there is an adequate derivation, then there is one in which only needed atoms are selected. This is not the case in general. It can be the case that needed atoms do not exist. Moreover, problems occur when atoms that are not needed can make needed atoms available. This can happen in three ways: by creating an atom (in the sense of Definition 3.2), by turning an atom that is not needed into a needed one, and by turning a non-selectable needed atom into a selectable one. This is illustrated in the following example.

Example 4.3

1. Consider the program $\mathcal{P}$ defined by the clauses

$$\begin{array}{lcl} a & \leftarrow & c \\ b & \leftarrow & c \end{array}$$

Let the adequacy predicate $\mathcal{A}$ be defined as follows: $\mathcal{A}(\langle Q; \sigma \rangle)$ holds if and only if Q contains an atom c. Consider the state $\langle a, b; \epsilon \rangle$. Neither a nor b is a needed atom, since both $\langle a, b; \epsilon \rangle \Rightarrow \langle c, b; \epsilon \rangle$ and $\langle a, b; \epsilon \rangle \Rightarrow \langle a, c; \epsilon \rangle$ are adequate derivations. Hence the state $\langle a, b; \epsilon \rangle$ does not contain a needed atom.

2. Consider the program $\mathcal{P}$ defined by the clauses

$$\begin{array}{lcl} a & \leftarrow & a' \\ a' & \leftarrow & a'' \\ b & \leftarrow & b' \\ b' & \leftarrow & b'' \end{array}$$

Let the adequacy predicate $\mathcal{A}$ be defined as follows: $\mathcal{A}(\langle Q; \sigma \rangle)$ holds if and only if $Q \in \{(a'', b), (a, b'')\}$. Then the state $\langle a, b; \epsilon \rangle$ does not contain a needed atom, since we have adequate derivations $\langle a, b; \epsilon \rangle \Rightarrow \langle a', b; \epsilon \rangle \Rightarrow \langle a'', b; \epsilon \rangle$ and $\langle a, b; \epsilon \rangle \Rightarrow \langle a, b'; \epsilon \rangle \Rightarrow \langle a, b''; \epsilon \rangle$. Note that in this case resolving an unneeded atom creates a needed atom.

3. Consider the program defined by the clauses

$$\begin{array}{rl} q(a, b) & \leftarrow \\ q(a', b') & \leftarrow \\ p(a) & \leftarrow \\ p'(a') & \leftarrow \end{array}$$

Suppose that $\mathcal{S}(q(s,t))$ holds only if s is a ground term. Suppose further that a derivation starting in $\langle p(x), p'(x), q(x,y); \epsilon\rangle$ is adequate only if y is instantiated to a ground term. The query $p(x), p'(x), q(x,y)$ does not contain a needed atom, essentially because there is more than one way to make a descendant of $q(x,y)$ selectable. □

This example motivates the following two definitions; the first one concerns the predicates for (in)adequacy and the second one concerns the selectability predicate.

In the rest of this section we refer to an fixed unspecified program $\mathcal{P}$ and set of queries $\mathcal{Q}$, which we assume to be *closed* with respect to $\mathcal{P}$, i.e. that for every derivation step $\langle Q; \sigma\rangle \Rightarrow \langle Q'; \sigma\tau\rangle$, using a clause of $\mathcal{P}$ we have that $Q \in \mathcal{Q}$ implies $Q' \in \mathcal{Q}$.

Definition 4.4 (In)adequacy predicates $\mathcal{A}$ and $\mathcal{I}$ are said to be *serializable* if for each $Q \in \mathcal{Q}$ the following conditions are satisfied.

1. If $\xi = \langle Q; \sigma\rangle \Rightarrow \langle Q'; \sigma'\rangle$ is a derivation step with $\mathcal{A}(\langle Q'; \sigma'\rangle)$ and not $\mathcal{A}(\langle Q; \sigma\rangle)$, then the atom selected in ξ is needed.
2. Let $\xi = \langle Q; \sigma\rangle \Rightarrow \langle Q'; \sigma'\rangle$ be a derivation step in which the selected atom is not needed, and suppose that $\langle Q'; \sigma'\rangle$ admits an adequate derivation. Then all needed atoms in $\langle Q'; \sigma'\rangle$ are descendants of needed atoms in $\langle Q; \sigma\rangle$. □

Definition 4.5 A selectability predicate $\mathcal{S}$ is said to be *serializable* if for every $Q \in \mathcal{Q}$ the following requirement is satisfied. Let $\xi = \langle Q; \epsilon\rangle \Rightarrow \langle Q'; \sigma'\rangle$ be a derivation step with selected atom A, and let B be an atom in Q that is not selectable in $\langle Q; \epsilon\rangle$, but which descendant B' is selectable in $\langle Q'; \sigma'\rangle$. Then for every derivation $\langle Q; \epsilon\rangle \Rightarrow^* \langle Q''; \sigma''\rangle$ such that the descendant of B is selectable in $\langle Q''; \sigma''\rangle$, we have that Q'' does not contain a descendant of A. □

Call by need is adequate. Now we have the following result.

Theorem 4.6 *If the (in)adequacy predicates $\mathcal{A}$ and $\mathcal{I}$ and the selectability predicate $\mathcal{S}$ are serializable, then for each $Q \in \mathcal{Q}$.*

1. *if a state $\langle Q; \sigma\rangle$ is not adequate then it contains a needed atom,*
2. *if there is an adequate derivation starting in $\langle Q; \sigma\rangle$ consisting of n derivation steps, then there is an adequate derivation starting in $\langle Q; \sigma\rangle$ in which only needed atoms are selected and which does not contain more than n steps.*

Proof. Let

$$\xi \equiv \langle Q; \sigma\rangle = \langle Q_0; \sigma_0\rangle \Rightarrow^* \langle Q_n; \sigma_n\rangle$$

be an adequate derivation of n steps starting in $\langle Q;\sigma\rangle$. We proceed by induction on n.

1. Suppose that ξ consists of one step: $\xi \equiv \langle Q_0;\sigma_0\rangle \Rightarrow \langle Q_1;\sigma_1\rangle$. By the first property, we have that the selected atom in ξ is needed.

2. Suppose that $\xi \equiv \langle Q_0;\sigma_0\rangle \Rightarrow \langle Q_1;\sigma_1\rangle \Rightarrow^* \langle Q_n;\sigma_n\rangle$ consists of more than one step. By the induction hypothesis, there is a call by need derivation ξ_1 issuing from $\langle Q_1;\sigma_1\rangle$ that is adequate. Let A_0 be the atom that is selected in the first step of ξ. Two cases are distinguished.

   (a) A_0 is needed. Then the derivation step $\xi_0 \equiv \langle Q_0;\sigma_0\rangle \Rightarrow \langle Q_1;\sigma_1\rangle$ followed by ξ_1 is an adequate call by need derivation.

   (b) A_0 is not needed. We construct a call by need derivation that is adequate, using serializability.

This result is quite abstract. In the following section we discuss a concrete application.

5 Using (In)adequacy Predicates

In this section we consider logic programs with guards and delay declarations. We extend the language with so-called *requests*, which permits to formalize a simple notion of adequacy which is useful practice. The first subsection contains preliminaries, in the second subsection the notion of request is introduced.

5.1 Guards and Delay Declarations

Guards. We roughly follow the approach described by Shapiro in [8]. A *guard* is a conjunction of atoms built from function symbols and *guard relation symbols*, which possibly don't coincide with the relation symbols used in the program. Guards are written as $G_1, \ldots, G_k$, which can be abbreviated to $\vec{G}$. A *guarded clause* is an expression of the form

$$H \leftarrow G_1, \ldots, G_k \mid B_1, \ldots, B_n.$$

We assume that it is decidable whether a ground instance of a guard holds. The operational semantics as given in Definition 3.2 changes as follows. Let A be the selected atom in some query and let τ be a most general unifier of the head of a clause $c = H \leftarrow \vec{G} \mid \vec{B}$ and A. If $\vec{G}\tau$ is ground and holds, then c can be applied to A. If $\vec{G}\tau$ is ground and does not hold, then the computation fails. If $\vec{G}\tau$ is not ground, then the computations suspends. As in the case without guards, with classical notions of success and failure, the computations also fails if A does not unify with the head of any clause of the program.

Delay Declarations. Logic programming languages which employ a dynamic selection rule need a mechanism for determining when an atom is selectable. Here we use delay declarations as introduced by Naish in [7]. We roughly follow the approach described by Apt and Luitjes in [1]. A *delay condition* is a conjunction built from delay base conditions of the following form:

- *ground*(s), which holds iff s is a ground term,
- *nonvar*(s), which holds iff s is a non-variable term

A difference with the delay declarations as in [1] is that we do not consider delay conditions that are disjunctions.

Now a *delay declaration* for a relation symbol p is an expression of the form

delay A until c

with A an atom with relation symbol p and c a delay condition. We suppose that a program is equipped with delay declarations. We admit the possibility that there is more than one delay declaration for a relation symbol; in this respect our approach differs from the one in [1].

Delay declarations influence the operational semantics as follows. An atom B is said to be *delay-safe* if for every delay declaration *delay A until c* and for every substitution σ we have that $A\sigma = B$ implies that $c\sigma$ holds. In this setting we make use of the following notion of selectability: $\mathcal{S}(A)$ iff A is delay-safe. Note that this selectability predicate is monotonic. Now in order for the first requirement of Definition 3.1 to hold, we assume the following relation between guards and delay declarations:
for every delay-safe atom A and every guarded clause $H \leftarrow \vec{G} \mid \vec{B}$ of $\mathcal{P}$ we have that if A and H have a most general unifier θ then $\vec{G}\theta$ is ground.

Natural Programs. A *moding* is a function assigning to every argument of a predicate symbol *In* or *Out*. In the first case an argument is said to be *input* and in the second case it is said to be *output*. In the remainder of this paper we assume every predicate symbol to have a unique moding. An argument of a predicate symbol occurring in a clause (query) is said to be *producing* either if it occurs in the head and is input or if it occurs in the body and is output. An argument of a predicate symbol is said to be *consuming* otherwise.

Definition 5.1

1. A clause is said to be *natural* if the family of terms in its producing positions is linear, i.e. no variable appears more than once. A program is *natural* if every clause is natural.

2. A delay declaration *delay A until c* is *natural* if every variable of c occurs in an input position of A, and moreover A has only fresh distinct variables in its output positions. □

In the remainder of this section we consider natural programs with guards and delay declarations as described in this subsection.

5.2 Requests

In the examples we have seen that some reasonable notions of (in)adequacy depend not only on the program and the state under consideration, but also on the the degree of instantiation of the variables of the initial state. This is for instance the case if we start computing the list of prime numbers with the aim to find only the first one (or the first few ones). Then we would like to start in $\langle prime(x); \epsilon\rangle$ and specify the adequacy predicate to hold on $\langle Q; \sigma\rangle$ and $\mathcal{P}$ if the first element of $x\sigma$ is specified. In this subsection we introduce a way to formalize such notions of (in)adequacy by means of requests.

A *request condition* or shortly a *request* is a conjunction built from the following request base conditions:

- $Val(x)$, which holds in a state $\langle Q; \sigma\rangle$ if $Var(x\sigma) \cap Var(\vec{A}) = \emptyset$,
- $Root(x)$, which holds in a state $\langle Q; \sigma\rangle$ if either $x\sigma$ is not a variable or $Var(x\sigma) \cap Var(\vec{A}) = \emptyset$,

Definition 5.2 A *request configuration* is an expression of the form r : $\langle Q; \sigma\rangle$ with r a request.

The definition of a derivation step is extended to request configurations as follows: if $\langle Q; \sigma\rangle \Rightarrow \langle Q'; \sigma'\rangle$, then $r : \langle Q; \sigma\rangle \Rightarrow r : \langle Q'; \sigma'\rangle$. A request configuration $r : \langle Q; \sigma\rangle$ is natural if $\langle Q; \sigma\rangle$ is natural. □

Other notions concerning derivations are extended in the natural way.

Natural request configurations are closed under resolution with natural clauses.

In this setting we will consider the following notion of adequacy (now defined on a request configuration and a program): $\mathcal{A}(r : \langle Q; \sigma\rangle)$ holds if and only if r holds in $\langle Q; \sigma\rangle$. We take for inadequacy the usual notion of failure.

Example 5.3 The following program implements the sieve of Eratosthenes.

$$
\begin{array}{rcl}
primes(x) & \leftarrow & from(2, y), sieve(y, x). \\
from(x, y) & \leftarrow & from(x + 1, z), y = [x|z]. \\
sieve([x|y], [x|z]) & \leftarrow & filter(x, y, u), sieve(u, z). \\
filter(x, [y|z], u) & \leftarrow & div(x, y) \mid filter(x, z, u). \\
filter(x, [y|z], u) & \leftarrow & nondiv(x, y) \mid filter(x, z, u'), u = [y|u'].
\end{array}
$$

We have the following derivation:

$$\begin{array}{rl} Val(x) : \langle primes([x|xs]); \epsilon\rangle & \Rightarrow \\ Val(x) : \langle from(2,y), sieve(y,[x|xs]); \epsilon\rangle & \Rightarrow \\ Val(x) : \langle from(3,z), y = [2|z], sieve(y,[x|xs]); \epsilon\rangle & \Rightarrow \\ Val(x) : \langle from(3,z), sieve([2|z],[x|xs]); \epsilon\rangle & \Rightarrow \\ Val(x) : \langle from(3,z), filter(2,z,u), sieve(u,xs); x \mapsto 2\rangle & \end{array}$$

This derivation is adequate because in the last request configuration the request is satisfied. □

5.3 Call by need

The aim of the present subsection is to apply Theorem 4.6 in the practical setting of logic programs with guards and delay declarations, with the notion of request as defined above. So we need to show that the adequacy predicate using requests and the selectability predicate using delays are serializable. This can be shown provided we impose one further requirement on the programs we consider; this requirement is defined as follows.

Definition 5.4 We say that $\mathcal{P}$ is *non-destructive* if for every selectable atom A, for every clause $H \leftarrow \vec{G} \mid \vec{B}$ in $\mathcal{P}$ and for every most general unifier σ of H and A, we have that $A\sigma$ is in its input positions a variant of A. □

Thus, a non-destructive program is a program which never instantiates the input positions of the selected atoms. A large class of programs satisfies this requirement, as is argued in [3].

Assuming programs to be non-destructive, we can show that the selectability predicate and the (in)adequacy predicates of the present setting are serializable. Hence we have the following corollary of Theorem 4.6

Corollary 5.5 *Let $\mathcal{P}$ be a natural and non-destructive program. Every request configuration that is not adequate contains a needed atom, and if a request configuration admits an adequate derivation of length n then it admits an adequate call by need derivation of length not more than n.*

Finding needed atoms. We now discuss how to find needed atoms.

Definition 5.6 Let $r : \langle Q; \sigma\rangle$ be a request configuration.

1. If $r = Val(x)$, then we say that r *demands* an atom B in Q if a variable in $x\sigma$ occurs in a producing position of B.
2. If $r = Root(x)$ then we say that r *demands* an atom B in Q if $x\sigma$ is a variable occurring in a producing position of B.

3. If $r = r_1 \wedge r_2$, then we say that r *demands* an atom B in Q either if r_1 demands B or if r_2 demands B. □

We need one last concept.

Definition 5.7 Let A be an atom and $x \in Var(A)$. We say that A *is locked on* x if for every ground substitution σ not having x in its domain, we have that $A\sigma$ is not selectable. □

It can be proven that if A is not selectable then there is a variable x in its input positions such that A is locked on x. There might be more than one such variable.

Definition 5.8 (Demanded Atom) Let $r : \langle \vec{A}; \sigma \rangle$ be a request configuration. The set of *demanded atoms* is the minimal subset of $\vec{A}$ such that the following conditions are satisfied.

- if $r\sigma$ demands x and x occurs in an output position of A_i, then A_i is demanded,
- if A_i is demanded and it is locked on a variable x, and x occurs in an output position of A_j, then A_j is demanded. □

Now we have the following result.

Theorem 5.9 *In a natural and non-destructive program, demanded atoms are needed. Moreover, every state that is not adequate contains a demanded atom.*

Example 5.10 Consider the program quicksort using difference lists:

$$
\begin{array}{rcl}
qsort(x, y) & \leftarrow & qsort\_dl(x, y, []). \\
qsort\_dl([x|x'], y, z) & \leftarrow & partition(x', x, ls, bs), \\
 & & qsort\_dl(ls, y, [x|y']),\ qsort\_dl(bs, y', z). \\
partition(x, [y|ys], [y|ls], bs) & \leftarrow & x \geq y \mid partition(x, ys, ls, bs). \\
partition(x, [y|ys], ls, [y|bs]) & \leftarrow & x < y \mid partition(x, ys, ls, bs). \\
partition(x, [\,], [\,], [\,]). & & \\
qsort\_dl([], x, x). & &
\end{array}
$$

Let l be a ground list. Using the specification of the adequacy predicate as above, the request configuration

$Val(x) : \langle qsort(l, [x|x']); \epsilon \rangle$

is the starting point of an adequate derivation that ends in a request configuration in which the value of the first element of l is known. It is important to observe that in order to obtain the desired result the computation does *not* have to order the whole list, and it will not do so, provided that the selection rule is sufficiently "intelligent", which is the case if a call-by-need selection rule is employed; in this case it is worth noticing that the above request configuration generates a derivation in which only half of the atoms of the form $qsort\_dl(xs, ys, zs)$ which are introduced along the derivation will eventually be resolved. □

6 Concluding remarks

In this section we discuss some possible other uses of the parameterization over success and failure.

Interactive Computing

The computation with requests can be extended such that one is allowed to add requests on the fly. In this way we obtain in a very natural way a notion of interactive computing. The interaction then is between a *requesting* and a *resolving* agent. The requesting agent specifies a request of the form $r_0 : \langle Q; \epsilon \rangle$. Then it is the turn of the resolving agent, who will try to construct a derivation ending in a state that is adequate with respect to the request r_0. Having reached this point, it is again the turn of the requesting agent, who might decide either to be satisfied, or to add another request r_1. One can for instance think of a computation that is supposed to yield an infinite list; first one asks for the first value and having got that one, one may decide to ask in addition for the second one.

Expert Systems

As yet we did not fully exploit the possibility to specify an inadequacy predicate other than the usual notion of failure in logic programming. A domain where it is useful is in that of expert systems. Suppose we are in presence of a diagnosis system based on backward chaining. Then we can be interested in knowing whether the system, in order to provide a certain explanation δ, has been used a certain information (or inference rule) *inf* (or, equivalently, if the explanation δ would hold also if *inf* was not present). Generally, this can be done by removing *inf* from the knowledge base; in our framework this can be simply achieved by specifying together with the query an appropriate inadequacy predicate which triggers every time that some information in *inf* is being used. This has the advantage of not requiring internal modifications. Furthermore, it could allow arbitrarily sophisticate control over the inference mechanism, by forbidding certain "undesired" forms of reasoning.

Acknowledgments

We thank Krzysztof Apt for feed-back.
This research was supported by NWO/SION project number 612-33-003, entitled 'Parallel declarative programming: transforming logic programs to lazy functional programs'. The first author was working at the faculty of mathematics, computer science, physics, and astronomy of the University of Amsterdam when this research was initiated.

References

[1] K. R. Apt and I. Luitjes. Verification of logic programs with delay declarations. In A. Borzyszkowski and S. Sokolowski, editors, *Proceedings of the Fourth International Conference on Algebraic Methodology and Software Technology, (AMAST'95)*, Lecture Notes in Computer Science, pages 1–19, Berlin, 1995. Springer-Verlag.

[2] K.R. Apt. *From Logic Programming to Prolog.* Prentice-Hall, 1997.

[3] K.R. Apt and S. Etalle. On the unification free prolog programs. In A. Borzyszkowski and S. Sokolowski, editors, *Proceedings of the Conference on Mathematical Foundations of Computer Science (MFCS '93)*, number 711 in Lecture Notes in Computer Science, pages 1–19, Gdańsk, Poland, 1993. Springer Verlag.

[4] J. Glauert and Z. Khasidashvili. Relative normalization in orthogonal Expression Reduction Systems. In N. Dershowitz and N. Lindenstrauss, editors, *Proceedings of the 4th International Workshop on Conditional and Typed Rewriting Systems (CTRS '94)*, number 968 in Lecture Notes in Computer Science, pages 144–165, Jerusalem, Isreal, 1994. Springer Verlag.

[5] G. Huet and J.-J. Lévy. Computations in orthogonal rewriting systems, I and II. In Jean-Louis Lassez and Gordon Plotkin, editors, *Computational Logic: Essays in honor of Alan Robinson*, pages 395–443. MIT Press, Cambridge, Massachusetts, 1991.

[6] A. Middeldorp. Call by need computations to root-stable form. In *Proceedings of the 24th Symposium on Principles of Programming Languages (POPL '97)*, pages 94–105, Paris, France, January 1997. ACM Press.

[7] L. Naish. An introduction to mu-prolog. Technical Report 82/2, The University of Melbourne, 1982.

[8] E. Y. Shapiro. The family of concurrent logic programming languages. *ACM Computing Surveys*, 21(3):412–510, 1989.

Source-to-source Prolog program compression

Philippe Devienne, Anne Parrain
Laboratoire d'Informatique Fondamentale de Lille
Université des Sciences et Technologies de Lille
59655 Villeneuve d'Ascq - France
{devienne,parrain}@lifl.fr

Patrick Taillibert, Serge Varennes
Dassault Electronique
55 quai Marcel Dassault
92214 Saint-Cloud - France
{Serge.Varennes,Patrick.Taillibert}@dassault-elec.fr

Abstract

Partial evaluation is usually devoted to program specialisation, in order to improve the speed-up. Generally, the price to pay is measured in term of unreadability and size of the code produced, especially for real Prolog programs. Moreover, it is often difficult to ensure an improvement on the space complexity which is a crucial point in industrial program development where size of the stack during execution can exceed 15 MegaBytes. To focus on the problem of readability in this context, we propose a transformation which aims, *a contrario*, to "simplify" programs, that is to say which tends to make code compression.

We will first give the theoretical motivations of this purpose by making some links with the Kolmogorov complexity. Then, we will present our transformation, and an application to the reduction of predicate's arity. These technics permit to combine gains in terms of code size (and then in the WAM stacks), and in terms of readability. This clearly illustrates the William of Ockham's principle (what is called Ockham's razor [1]): *compression = understanding* and shows the classical program transformations in a new light.

1 Introduction

Program transformations in logic programming are mainly devoted to program specialisation, in order to improve the speed-up. One of the principles is that propagation of information may suppress some resolution steps ([5] for example) and shorten the length of non-successful finite derivations ([7]). The price to pay is generally measured in term of size and unreadability of the program specialised.

In industry, space complexity is a crucial problem. Prolog programs developed at Dassault Electronique are big ones: 10000 lines of code is frequent, some of them exceed 50000. During execution of some applications, global stack reaches 15 MegaBytes, and garbage collection is not unfrequent. In this context, the transformation that we propose aims to simplify programs, that is to say tends to make code and stack compression. An application of this transformation (by composition with classical transformations) is the reduction of predicate's arity. This allows to obtain smaller programs, and also more readable programs: the lack of global variables in logic programming makes predicates having naturally a big arity, and the incremental life cycle of software emphasizes the problem. Reducing predicate's arity, that is, aggregating strongly connected arguments, enlights the meaning of the program.

Reducing size of a program is obviously not just a syntactic operation. It refers to the notion of smallest program described by Kolmogorov complexity. Let us cite V. Uspensky [12] to describe Andrey Nikolayevich Kolmogorov's ideas on complexity:

The idea is very simple and reduces the notion of complexity of an object to the notion of size, though not of the object itself but of some description of that object. An object is complex if all its descriptions are large, and it is simple if at least one of its description is small. Hence it is natural to define the complexity *of an object as the minimal size of a description of this object.*

Moreover, the invariance theorem shows that, to express an algorithm succinctly in a program, it does not matter which programming language we use (up to a fixed additive constant that depends only on the two programming languages compared). In other words, the Kolmogorov complexity of an object is a form of absolute information of the individual object. This is not possible to do by C.E. Shannon's information theory. Nevertheless, the Kolmogorov complexity is not computable, hence for any program P, the smallest program P_0 equivalent to it is not computable.

Another point is that the smallest program in the sense of Kolmogorov is not unique. But the number of shortest descriptions of any object is bounded by a universal constant [4], so it is still relevant to try to approach such a program.

Even if this framework seems to be quite theoretical, this work has been indeed initiated from quite pragmatic point of view about the updating and execution of very large Prolog programs.

The following section describes our framework. Section 3 presents the simplification, which is the keystone of our transformations. Simplification is compared with other well-known similar transformations. In section 4 and 5, the interest of folding/unfolding is evaluated. Section 6 is the main section, it is concerned with the application to the reduction of predicate's arity.

2 Some definitions

We are interested in the operational behaviour of Prolog programs (intending to test our transformations on industrial programs). We will consider usual operational equivalence preserved by automatic partial evaluators: in the following, a SLD-tree denotes a SLD-tree via the leftmost selection rule, and the resolution strategy chosen is the standard depth-first (and leftmost) strategy. To avoid unnecessary technical remarks, we are only considering definite logic programs in a first step.

Definition 1 *Let* (P_1, G_1) *and* (P_2, G_2) *be two pairs (logic program, goal).* (P_1, G_1) *and* (P_2, G_2) *are said operationally equivalent (under the standard resolution strategy) if and only if*

- (P_1, G_1) *and* (P_2, G_2) *produce the same answer-substitutions in the same order;*
- (P_1, G_1) *halts if and only if* (P_2, G_2) *halts.*

This natural definition has been used in [10] for example. Some works have been done ([8]) to consider a more restrictive form of operational equivalence, including the preservation of all infinite derivations. Transformations presented here can easily been extended to this case, but we preferred to focus on a simpler definition of equivalence.

Usually, terms are represented by trees, and their size is the number of nodes of the corresponding tree[1]. This definition can be extended to clauses and programs. Each clause of a program can be represented by a tree, and the size of a program is the sum of the size of all its clauses.

Definition 2 *Let* P_1 *be a logic program and* G_1 *be a goal, the complexity of* (P_1, G_1)*, denoted* $K(P_1, G_1)$*, is the size of the smallest* (P_2, G_2) *which is operationally equivalent to* (P_1, G_1).

In order to take into account also the size of the WAM code, we have to consider the more general program w.r.t. to the subsumption.

Example 1 *The three following Horn clauses:*

1. `p(X,Y).`
2. `p(X,X).`
3. `p(a,a).`

have the same size, but not the same WAM complexity. Let $KW(P)$ *denote the size of the code WAM representing* P*. We have*

$$KW(p(X,Y).) < KW(p(X,X).) < KW(p(a,a).)$$

It is the reason why a more general clause must be analysed as a smaller clause. If the unification process is more complex, the WAM code will be too. The subjacent notion is subsumption. Intuitively, we can say that a clause C_1 contains less information (i.e. less constraints) than another clause C_2 if C_1 subsumes[2] C_2, that is, if C_1 is more general than C_2. Let us recall the definition of the subsumption:

Definition 3 *[6] Let* C_1 *and* C_2 *be the definite clauses* $A \leftarrow B_1, \ldots B_n$ *and* $G \leftarrow D_1, \ldots D_m$ *respectively.* C_1 *is subsumed by* C_2 *if there is a substitution* θ *such that* $A = \theta(G)$ *and* $\{\theta(D_1), \ldots \theta(D_m)\} \subseteq \{B_1, \ldots B_n\}$.

[1] We do not consider here directed acyclic graphs (which are a more compact representation) because the Warren Abstract Machine [14] is based on structure copying rather than sharing.

[2] Subsumption was first defined by [2]. We restrict here our attention to the θ-subsumption, which is commonly used in logic programming.

We extend this definition to programs. Let P_1 and P_2 be two logic programs. P_1 subsumes P_2 if every clause of P_2 is subsumed by some clause of P_1. Since we are in the case where P_1 and P_2 have the same size, the only θ-subsumptions that we are interested in are flat substitutions, that is, whose image is a set of variables and constants :

$$\forall X \in Dom(\theta), \theta(X) \text{ is a variable or a constant}$$

So in case of equality of the size between two clauses, subsumption can be tested by the number of distinct variables in each clause.

Theorem 2.1 *Let P be a logic program. The smallest program operationally equivalent to P is noncomputable.*

Proof As already seen, this is just a consequence of the Noncomputability Theorem of the Kolmogorov complexity. But it is easy to give an intuitive idea by another proof. Any non-productive (i.e. without solution) and non-halting program can be replaced by the following program:

$$again \leftarrow again.$$

as well as any non-productive halting program can be replaced by $\perp$ (empty program). This is equivalent to decide the halting and the existence of solutions of a program, which is undecidable. □

Example 2 *There is a natural morphism between automata and Prolog programs. This gives to us a class of smallest Prolog programs associated with the class of minimal automata. For instance, let $\{a,b\}$ be an alphabet, the set of words containing an even number of b is computing by the smallest definite logic program :*

$$\begin{cases} p([],0,1). \\ p([a|W],Q1,Q2) \leftarrow p(W,Q1,Q2). \\ p([b|W],Q1,Q2) \leftarrow p(W,Q2,Q1). \\ \leftarrow p(W,0,1). \end{cases}$$

Since the point of view is only syntactic, we may extend these notions to Prolog programs, that is, which contain extra-logical predicates. In this case, because of their expressive power (cut, bagof, ...), it is clear that, in general, the smallest Prolog programs will contain also such predicates.

We obviously apply "Ockham [3] 's razor" which states that "Entities are not to be, multiplied without necessity", or "It is vain to do with more what can be done with fewer". Then we are going to show that this approach can underline two advantages on readability and space complexity of Prolog programs for quite pragmatic problems.

[3]William of Ockham (1285-1349), the last of the great scholastics, is best known for what is called "Ockham's razor" which said that "plurality should not be assumed without necessity". That is to say, if everything in some science can be interpreted without assuming a complicated hypothesis, there is no ground for assuming it.

3 Prolog program's simplification

The idea underlying the previous section is "more general is a clause, smaller is its size". The simplification transformation permits to generalize a clause wherever information stated explicitly in its instantiated form is redundant w.r.t. the rest of the program.

We discuss this transformation versus other well-known transformations at the end of the section.

3.1 Simplification transformation

For any term t, we denote by $var(t)$ the set of all the variables of t and $term(t)$ the set of all the subterms of t (including t). For θ a substitution ($\theta : Dom(\theta) \mapsto Image(\theta)$), θ is said to be ***without overlapping*** if $\forall X, Y \in Dom(\theta)$ s.t. $X \neq Y, \theta(X) \notin term(\theta(Y))$. As a consequence, $\theta^{-1}(t)$, the inverse substitution of θ on t, is unique.

Definition 4 *Let C be a clause in a logic program and A be its head part. Let θ be a substitution without overlapping. θ is C-uniform if*

- $Image(\theta) \subseteq term(A)$
- $var(\theta^{-1}(C)) \cap var(Image(\theta)) = \emptyset$
- $Dom(\theta) \cap var(C) = \emptyset$

The first condition represents a condition of *minimalism* of θ w.r.t. C, in the sense that we are only considering the subterms of the head part of C. The second condition is really a condition of uniformity : if a variable X occurs in some terms, say $t, t' \in Image(\theta)$, then X always appears in C in and only in t and t'. The third condition imposes fresh variables w.r.t. C for $Dom(\theta)$.

The last condition and the non-overlapping condition ensure that $\theta\theta^{-1}(C) = C$. Finally, first and third conditions imply that $Dom(\theta) \cap Image(\theta) = \emptyset$, that is, θ is idempotent.

Definition 5 Simplification transformation
Let P be a logic program. Let C be a clause of P, $A \leftarrow B_1, \ldots B_m$ whose head predicate is p. Let θ be a (non-renaming) substitution without overlapping, and $\mathcal{A}$ be the result of the anti-unification[4] of calls to p in P. If

- *θ is C-uniform*
- *$\theta^{-1}(A) \vee \mathcal{A} = A \vee \mathcal{A}$ ($\vee$ is the unification operator).*

Then C is replaced in P by $C' : \theta^{-1}(A \leftarrow B_1, \ldots B_m)$.

[4]Anti-unification is also known as *most specific generalisation (msg)*.

Example 3

$$\left\{\begin{array}{rcl} & \leftarrow & p(f(Z),g(Z)). \\ p(f(X),g(X)) & \leftarrow & q(f(X)),r(g(X)). \end{array}\right.$$

is simplified into (with $\theta = \{A/f(X), B/g(X)\}$*) :*

$$\left\{\begin{array}{rcl} & \leftarrow & p(f(Z),g(Z)). \\ p(A,B) & \leftarrow & q(A),r(B). \end{array}\right.$$

Note that the simplification transformation is modifying the result of the anti-unification of the calls to p in the program. This can reduce the scope of the simplification. To avoid this side-effect of the transformation, it is possible to compute once the anti-unification of the calls to p before applying eventually several times the simplification transformation. Simplification does not affect calls to p (it only removes redundant information), so this sequentiality remains correct. In order to maintain the program, it is possible to keep a history of the computed anti-unification, but we will discussed this point in section 6.

Proposition 1 *Let P be a logic program, G be a goal, and P' be a logic program obtained by simplification from $P$and G. Then (P,G) is operationaly equivalent to (P',G).*

Sketch of proof Let $\mathcal{A}$ be the result of the anti-unification of calls to p in P. Let ϕ be the mgu associated with the unification of A and $\mathcal{A}$ (which is the same as for $\mathcal{A} \vee \theta^{-1}A$). A more specific version (as described in [7]) of P is $P_1 = (P - \{C\}) \cup \{\phi(C)\}$ and of P' is $P_2 = (P' - \{C'\}) \cup \{\phi(C')\}$. These versions can be obtained too by a partial evaluation à la Lloyd and Shepherdson [5], but we shall discuss this point later. It is clear that (P,G) and (P_1,G) have the same SLD-tree[5], as (P',G) and (P_2,G), so that, they are equivalent in the sense of the strong operational equivalence. The rest of the proof shows that $P_1 = P_2$ for each of the three cases $A \geq \mathcal{A}$, $\mathcal{A} \geq A$ (then, $\exists\phi_1$, ϕ_2 s.t. $\phi_1(A) = \phi_2\theta^{-1}(A) = \mathcal{A}$) and $\exists\phi_1,\phi_2,\phi_3$ s.t. $\phi_1(\mathcal{A}) = \phi_2(A) = \phi_3\theta^{-1}(A)$. □

Proposition 2 *Let P be a logic program, and P' be a logic program obtained by simplification from P. Then P' is strictly smaller than P.*

Proof By definition of the simplification, P is more instantiated than P', that is, $P = \theta(P')$. According to our complexity measure, either θ is not flat then the Prolog code of P' is strictly smaller than that of P, or θ is a flat substitution then P and P' have the same Prolog size, but the WAM code of P' is smaller than that of P. □

[5]Note that we are considering SLD-tree via leftmost selection rule. In fact, they have the same SLD-tree for any selection rule only depending on the current goal.

3.2 Simplification v.s. [GB90]-transformation

Simplification can be relied with the work of Gallagher and Bruynooghe [3]. The purpose of their transformation is the same as us (removing redundant information), but the choice of the data to be simplified is different. For P a program and p a predicate, a description of all calls to p in P is derived, say $p(s)$, and then the definition for p is replaced with a definition for q, where q has as many arguments as $p(s)$ has distinct variables, and each atom in P $p(t) = \theta(p(s))$ is replaced by $\theta(q(x_1, \dots x_k))$. $p(s)$ is obtained by some global analysis, a kind of abstract interpretation, on P.

Our transformation is slightly different. First, the element taken into consideration is a clause, and not only a predicate. Secondly, it does neither create any new predicate symbol, nor remove any function symbol during resolution. Simplification only removes syntactical redundancies in a clause. Application of the GB-transformation on example 3 would give:

$$\left\{ \begin{array}{lcl} & \leftarrow & p(f(Z), g(Z)). \\ p(f(X), g(X)) & \leftarrow & pnew(X). \\ pnew(A) & \leftarrow & q(A), r(A). \end{array} \right.$$

Simplification is the minimal characterization of removing redundant information at our knowledge. Moreover, simplification can handle any extra-logical predicate: it does perform no unfolding; and does not modify even partial substitutions computed at each step of the resolution procedure.

3.3 Simplification v.s. [MNL90]-specialisation

The purpose of the simplification transformation is the inverse of the definition of the most specific logic programs in [7] (that we call MNL-specialisation[6] for short). In their paper, Marriott, Naish and Lassez propose to propagate information, computed by global analysis, through the whole program, in order to reduce sometimes the length of successful derivations, but mostly this of finite failure derivations. On the other hand, MNL-specialisation increases program size.

But these two transformations can be combined in order to make a compromise: keep advantages of MNL-specialisation, while improving locally the size of the program.

Example 4 *This example comes from [7].*

$$P_0 = \left\{ \begin{array}{l} goal(X) \leftarrow \mathbf{r}(\mathbf{X}). \\ \mathbf{r}(\mathbf{Y}) \leftarrow \mathbf{s}(\mathbf{X}, \mathbf{Y}), \mathbf{t}(\mathbf{Y}). \\ s(f(a), f(X)). \\ s(f(b), g(a)). \\ s(f(a), g(b)). \\ t(g(a)). \\ t(g(b)). \end{array} \right.$$

[6] Program specialisation refers to manifold technics in the partial evaluation community. We distinguish MNL-specialisation from specialisation in larger sense.

After MNL-specialisation, we obtain the most specific version of P_0:

$$P_1 = \begin{cases} goal(g(X)) \leftarrow \mathbf{r(g(X))}. \\ \mathbf{r(g(Y))} \leftarrow \mathbf{s(X, g(Y)), t(g(Y))}. \\ s(f(a), f(X)). \\ s(f(b), g(a)). \\ s(f(a), g(b)). \\ t(g(a)). \\ t(g(b)). \end{cases}$$

Then, a step of simplification is needed for cleaning up and P_2 is obtained:

$$P_2 = \begin{cases} goal(g(X)) \leftarrow \mathbf{r(g(X))}. \\ \mathbf{r(Y)} \leftarrow \mathbf{s(X, Y), t(Y)}. \\ s(f(a), f(X)). \\ s(f(b), g(a)). \\ s(f(a), g(b)). \\ t(g(a)). \\ t(g(b)). \end{cases}$$

4 Unfolding

The definition of the unfold transformation proposed by H.Tamaki and T.Sato [11] is quite simple: it is a derivation step in a SLD-tree, with respect to any literal in a clause, for any computation rule. A literal in a body part is replaced by the bodies of all the clauses of which head is unifiable with this literal. The size of the program can increase quickly.

In order to preserve the operational semantics of Prolog programs (order of solutions, infinite derivations, ...), some additional hypotheses are needed. Let B be a literal in a clause body and C be a pure clause (that is, without built-in predicates):

- either B is unifiable with only one head of clause (that is deterministic unfolding);
- or, let us call simple literal, any literal which unifies with only one fact, the unfolded literal must be the leftmost non-simple atom in the body part of the clause.

Since we are interested in compressing Prolog code, the scope of unfolding is rather limited in this context. In some sense, unfolding rhymes with uncompression, that is, the most interesting notion will be folding.

Even if one could think that folding means to add a derivation step, this transformation is usually indeed much more powerful that unfolding since it permits to extract compressed recursive schemes. The main difficulty which occurs in the logic program transformation systems is to determinate the judicious sequence of unfoldings which leads into a folding. This is, of course, much more difficult in the case of Prolog programs.

5 Folding

The definition of folding is a little bit more complex to avoid new infinite derivations (i.e. a clause folded with itself) and unjustified capture of variables. The definite logic program is split up into two sets of clauses : P_{old} and P_{new}. Roughly speaking, P_{new} is the set of the definition clauses, that is, the new clauses which are added and used for folding.

Definition 6 Definition clause
Let P be a Prolog program, $B_1, \ldots B_n$ be a sequence of pure literals, then C is said to be a definition clause:

$$C : p(X_1, \ldots, X_m) \leftarrow B_1, \ldots B_n.$$

where p is a new predicate name and $\{X_1, \ldots, X_m\}$ are the set of variables occurring in the literals B_i.

Definition 7 Folding
Let P be a Prolog program, θ be a substitution, and C be a clause :
$A \leftarrow B_1, \ldots B_{j-1}, \theta(B_j, \ldots B_{j+k}), B_{j+k+1}, \ldots B_n.$
and D be a pure clause of P_{new}
$G \leftarrow B_j, \ldots B_{j+k}.$
such that

1. *D is the only clause whose head is unifiable with $\theta(G)$,*
2. *θ maps each local variable of D to a fresh variable (which does not appear in $\{A, B_1, \ldots B_{j-1}, B_{j+k+1}, \ldots B_n, \theta G\}$).*

Then C is replaced by
$A \leftarrow B_1, \ldots B_{j-1}, \theta B, B_{j+k+1}, \ldots B_n.$

In the original definition, the sequence of literals in the folded clause is not supposed to be consecutive. This additional hypothesis is due to the use of extra-logical predicates.

For compressing the source code, it is easy to see that we only have to find shared sequences of literals (up to a substitution) and add a definition clause before applying foldings.

Definition 8 Compressing Folding
Let P be a Prolog program, C_1 and C_2 be two pure clauses of P, then C_1 and C_2 are compressible by folding if there exist θ_1, θ_2 two substitutions, and $B_1, \ldots B_n$ such that for $\theta_1(B_1, \ldots B_n)$ and $\theta_2(B_1, \ldots B_n)$ are consecutive sequences of C_1 and C_2 and the source code after adding the corresponding definition clause and folding has been reduced.

The goal is not to extract more compact recursive schemes, but instead to find generic sequences of computation. The strategy for compressing as much as possible computes the most compressing foldings in this order. This sequence of foldings is not confluent, but is, of course, finite since the size of the source code strictly decreases at each step.

6 Aggregation and arity's reduction

A major characteristic of logic programming is the lack of global variables, which forces passing data as arguments. This first point makes predicates naturally having a big arity. Adding to this, the life cycle of software is in general (particularly for prototypes) incremental and this emphasizes the problem of the arity. It is often the case when modifying a prototype that some extra datum, not related to any object of the application is needed in some predicate, requiring it to be transferred from predicate to predicate without any transformation or use. This transmission can be achieved thanks to some facilities like those described in P. Van Roy's thesis [13], nevertheless, automated or handmade, it usually leads to an increase of predicate arity which is paid in terms of memory (in particular the global stack) and execution time.

One could think that reducing arity to one is quite trivial by coding $p(t_1, t_2, \cdots, t_n)$ as $p([t_1, t_2, \cdots, t_n])$ (like in Prolog III). In fact, this rough transformation obviously increases the Prolog code and the WAM code, but also the speed-up of programs and the size of the stacks. It is easy also to realize that the WAM indexing would be no more possible.

Conversely, the intuitive idea is here to gather arguments which are *strongly connected*, i.e. arguments which are used together in the same predicates. As we will see later, this transformation does not much decrease the speed-up of programs, but lightens the code and reduces the size of the stacks during execution. The transformation is made in three steps. First, determine which arguments are strongly connected. Second, aggregate them together. Third, simplify the new obtained clauses. If these three steps can produce a smaller code, this means that a new hidden data structure has been identified. Different solutions are described in [9] for computing some hidden connection between data. We shall here present one which allows to reduce the predicate arity.

Definition 9 *A variable is said to be argument in a literal A (resp. a clause C) if it occurs only as argument in A (resp. C).*

A variable is said to be linear in a literal A (resp. a clause C) if it occurs at most once in A (resp. in all literal of C).

Definition 10 *Let C be a clause $A \leftarrow B_1, \ldots B_n$. An aggregating set S for C is a set of variables of A such that:*

- *all elements of S are arguments and linear in C;*
- $\forall i, 1 \leq i \leq n,$
  - *either $S \subseteq$ argument(B_i)*
  - *or $S \cap$ argument(B_i)$= \emptyset$*

Simplification allows to extend the scope of an aggregating set.

Example 5

$$\left\{ \begin{array}{rcl} & \leftarrow & p(f(X), Y, Y). \\ p(f(X), Y, Z) & \leftarrow & q(f(X), Y, U), \\ & & r(f(X), Y, U, Z). \end{array} \right.$$

After a step of simplification, we obtain:

$$\left\{ \begin{array}{lll} & \leftarrow & p(f(X),Y,Y). \\ p(A,Y,Z) & \leftarrow & q(A,Y,U), \\ & & r(A,Y,U,Z). \end{array} \right.$$

Then, $\{A,Y\}$ is an aggregating set for p.

An aggregating set for a predicate p defined by several clauses is an aggregating set common to all these clauses. Furthermore, there is a finite number of aggregating sets for a same predicate (partially ordered by $\subseteq$, which allows to define best aggregating sets). It is possible to use all the best aggregating sets of a predicate, by repeating the following aggregating transformation each time on a best aggregating set.

Now that we have defined the notion of a set of aggregating arguments, we can aggregate them by putting a new function symbol over these arguments.

Definition 11 Aggregating predicate
Let p be a predicate of arity n in a logic program P. Let $I = \{i_1, \ldots i_p\} \subseteq [1 \ldots n]$ and $J = \{j_1, \ldots j_k\} = [1 \ldots n]/I$. Then the aggregating predicate for p w.r.t I is the new predicate p':

$$C \; : \; p'(X_{j_1}, \ldots X_{j_k}, \mathbf{aggreg}(X_{i_1}, \ldots X_{i_p})) \leftarrow p(X_1, \ldots X_n).$$

where **aggreg** *is a new function symbol. C is added to P and to its set of definitions.*

Example 6 *For p a predicate of arity 3, and $I = \{1,3\}$, the aggregating predicate p' is defined by:*

$$p'(X_2, \mathbf{aggreg}(X_1, X_3)) \leftarrow p(X_1, X_2, X_3).$$

As an aggregating set for a predicate p is a subset of the arguments of a head clause, it can be represented by their argument's numbers. The previous definition allows to define an aggregating predicate w.r.t. an aggregating set.

The following algorithm allows to combine the aggregating definition, unfolding, folding and simplification transformations in order to obtain the desired simplified program as presented in the example 7.

Aggregation algorithm

Input: Let P be a logic program, and p a predicate. Each clause defining p is denoted by $C_i \; : \; A_i \leftarrow B_{i_1}, \ldots B_{i_{m_i}}$. Let

Output: The logic program P'

Initialisation

-1- Compute the anti-unification of the calls to p.
-2- Apply a simplification transformation on clauses defining p.
-3- Compute S an aggregating set for p,

and let $E = \{B_{i_j} \mid 1 \leq j \leq m_i, S \subseteq argument(B_{i_j})\}$.

-4- Compute the anti-unification of the calls to each predicate in E.

Aggregation

-5- Define an aggregating predicate for p and each atom in E w.r.t. S. Let $D_1, \ldots D_k$ denote these definitions.

-6- Unfold each clause D_i.

-7- Fold each atom B in a body part of a clause in P, if its predicate symbol either is p or appears in E, with its corresponding definition D_i.

Simplification

-8- Apply a simplification transformation on clauses defining the aggregating predicates.

Example 7 *This program P returns the number of points with integer coordinates (X, Y, Z) which are in some sphere. The sphere is described by its center's coordinates (Xo, Yo, Zo) and its radius R.* $P = \{C_1, C_2, C_3, C_4\}$.

$$\left\{\begin{array}{ll} C_1: & in\_sphere([], \_, \_, \_, \_, 0). \\ C_2: & in\_sphere([Pt|L], Xo, Yo, Zo, R, N) \\ & \quad \leftarrow test\_in(Pt, Xo, Yo, Zo, R, N1), \\ & \quad in\_sphere(L, Xo, Yo, Zo, R, N2), \\ & \quad N\ is\ N1 + N2. \\ C_3: & test\_in((X, Y, Z), Xo, Yo, Zo, R, 1) \\ & \quad \leftarrow X1\ is\ X - Xo, Y1\ is\ Y - Yo, Z1\ is\ Z - Zo, \\ & \quad (X1 * X1 + Y1 * Y1 + Z1 * Z1) =< R * R, !. \\ C_4: & test\_in(\_, \_, \_, \_, \_, 0). \end{array}\right.$$

The aggregating set for in_sphere is $S = \{Xo, Yo, Zo, R\}$). *The definitions for the aggregating predicates are :*

$$\left\{\begin{array}{ll} D_1: & in\_sphere'(X_1, \mathbf{sphere}(X_2, X_3, X_4, X_5), X_6) \\ & \quad \leftarrow in\_sphere(X_1, X_2, X_3, X_4, X_5, X_6). \\ D_2: & test\_in'(X_1, \mathbf{sphere}(X_2, X_3, X_4, X_5), X_6) \\ & \quad \leftarrow test\_in(X_1, X_2, X_3, X_4, X_5, X_6). \end{array}\right.$$

Now, $P = \{C_1, C_2, C_3, C_4, D_1, D_2\}$. *Let us unfold* D_1 *and* D_2 *:*

$$\left\{\begin{array}{ll} C_5: & in\_sphere'([], \mathbf{sphere}(\_, \_, \_, \_), 0). \\ C_6: & in\_sphere'([Pt|L], \mathbf{sphere}(Xo, Yo, Zo, R), N) \\ & \quad \leftarrow test\_in(Pt, Xo, Yo, Zo, R, N1), \\ & \quad in\_sphere(L, Xo, Yo, Zo, R, N2), \\ & \quad N\ is\ N1 + N2. \\ C_7: & test\_in'((X, Y, Z), \mathbf{sphere}(Xo, Yo, Zo, R), 1) \leftarrow \quad \ldots \\ C_8: & test\_in'(\_, \mathbf{sphere}(\_, \_, \_, \_), 0). \end{array}\right.$$

Now, $P = \{C_1, C_2, C_3, C_4, C_5, C_6, C_7, C_8\}$. *Let us make the step of foldings.* C_6 *is the only clause concerned and is replaced by :*

$$\left\{\begin{array}{ll} C_9: & in\_sphere'([Pt|L], \mathbf{sphere}(Xo, Yo, Zo, R), N) \\ & \quad \leftarrow test\_in'(Pt, \mathbf{sphere}(Xo, Yo, Zo, R), N1), \\ & \quad in\_sphere'(L, \mathbf{sphere}(Xo, Yo, Zo, R), N2), \\ & \quad N\ is\ N1 + N2. \end{array}\right.$$

Now, $P = \{C_1, C_2, C_3, C_4, C_5, C_9, C_7, C_8\}$. *The simplification transformation is applied on* C_5, C_9 *and* C_8. *It is not possible to perform it on* C_7.

$$\left\{\begin{array}{lll} C_{10}: & in\_sphere'([\,], \_, 0). & \\ C_{11}: & in\_sphere'([Pt|L], S, N) \leftarrow & test\_in'(Pt, S, N1), \\ & & in\_sphere'(L, S, N2), \\ & & N \; is \; N1 + N2. \\ C_7: & test\_in'((X, Y, Z), \mathbf{sphere}(Xo, Yo, Zo, R), 1) \leftarrow & \ldots \\ C_{12}: & test\_in'(\_, \_, 0). & \end{array}\right.$$

$P' = \{C_1, C_2, C_3, C_4, C_{10}, C_{11}, C_7, C_{12}\}$.

As usual in strategies of "Definition - Unfolding - Folding", it is necessary to clean up the program from definitions of old predicates (here, $C_1, \ldots C_4$), and eventually to add "bridge"-definitions reversed w.r.t. the definition of aggregating predicates. These bridge-definitions, instantiated w.r.t. the corresponding anti-unified computed at step 1 and 4, are the history of applied transformations. By adding them to the program, semantics of the program w.r.t. old predicates is preserved. It allows, for programmers, to maintain easily the program.

Note that although we process some unfoldings and create some definition clauses, this size overhead is removed from the final program. At the end, we get:

- at least one simplified predicate (i.e *in_sphere'*) strictly smaller than the original one (i.e *in_sphere*),
- the size of head parts of definitions for the other new predicates may be at worst increased by one (i.e. for *test_in'*, the size of its definition is increased by one in a clause, and decreased by 3 in the other clause);
- as it is the case for calls of all new predicates.

The aggregation algorithm returns a program easier to read and maintain, and for which the meaning has been strengthened. In this sense, the aggregation algorithm can be seen as a help for the methodology.

We have made some tests with our transformation. On the program 7, (whose tree size decreases from 82 nodes to 64 nodes) for a list of one thousand elements, we obtained a saving of 18% on the size of the global stack, and 1% on time[7]. The local stack was not modified. Tests with some other small classic programs gave us comparable results, until a 29% saving on the global stack, and a time variation from -3% to +3% w.r.t. the original program.

Although our aggregation transformation can be seen as a transformation dual to this proposed by J. Gallagher and M. Bruynooghe [3], these benchmarks give encouraging results. Furthermore, simplification is in some sense, an anti-specialization transformation: where partial evaluation ([5]), or more specific versions of programs ([7]) add syntactically (in a first step), any known

[7] Tests were made on a Sparc Ultra, under Solaris, with SICStus 3.5

information on the program, simplification "gums" syntactically redundant information. To summarize the relation with other works, let us consider the following example:

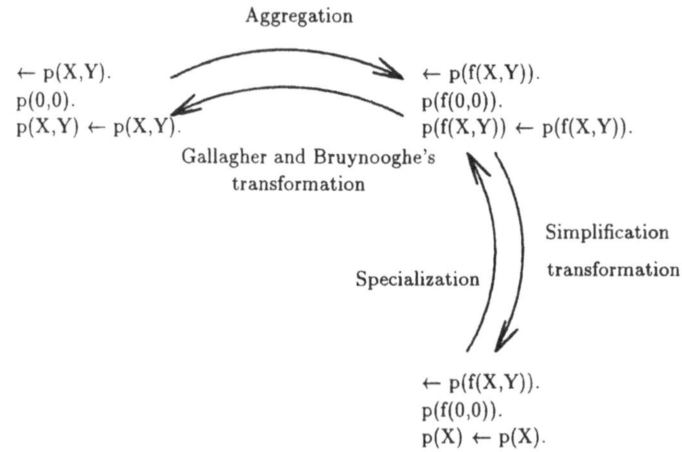

7 Conclusion and future works

As we are considering Prolog programs, we do not intend to modify too much the structure of programs. Our aim is to change data representation, by extracting some connection between data from the program, and then aggregating them. This is another kind of code compression w.r.t. classical transformations: data factorization versus calls (atoms) factorization.

Moreover we have shown that there is a link in practice between the size of the source code and space complexity. In industrial context, to compress Prolog code leads to a reduction of size of stacks. The transformations presented here (simplification, compressing folding and aggregation) can be easily controlled and can be applied on nonpure logic programs.

The easiest way to represent data connections through a Prolog program P is to abstract P in the form of a pure Datalog program where all arguments have been replaced by anonymous variables, except for the aggregatable variables. This abstract program clearly subsumes P and gives a compressed representation for evaluating and executing a sequence of aggregations. We are investigating good automatic strategies for computing a Prolog program as small as possible.

References

[1] P. Boehner. *Collected articles on Ockham.* Bonaventure, N.Y., 1956.

[2] C.-L. Chang and R.C.-T. Lee. *Symbolic Logic and Mechanical Theorem proving.* Academic Press, 1973.

[3] J. Gallagher and M. Bruynooghe. Some low-level source transformations for logic programs. *Proceedings of the second workshop on Meta-programming in Logic*, pages 229–244, Leuven, Belgium, April 1990.

[4] M. Li and P. Vitányi. *An introduction to Kolmogorov complexity and its applications*. Springer-Verlag, 1993.

[5] J.W. Lloyd and J.C. Shepherdson. Partial evaluation in logic programming. Technical Report 87-09, University of Bristol, December 1987.

[6] M.J. Maher. Equivalences of logic programs. In J.Minker, editor, *Foundations of Deductive Databases*, pages 627–658. Morgan Kaufmann, 1987.

[7] K. Marriott, L. Naish, and J.-L. Lassez. Most specific logic programs. *Annals of Mathematics and Artificial Intelligence*, 1:303–338, 1990.

[8] A. Parrain, Ph. Devienne, and P. Lebègue. Prolog program transformations and meta-interpreters. *Logic Program Synthesis and Transformation*, pages 238–251, Manchester, July 1991. Springer-Verlag.

[9] J.-F. Rabaute. Evaluation partielle de programmes PROLOG. Technical report, LIFL - Université de Lille 1, July 1997. in French.

[10] D. Sahlin. *An automatic partial evaluator for full Prolog*. PhD thesis, Swedish Institute of Computer Science, Stockholm, March 1991.

[11] H. Tamaki and T. Sato. Unfold/fold transformation of logic programs. *Second International Logic Programming Conference*, pages 127–138, Uppsala, 1984.

[12] V.A. Uspensky. Kolmogorov and mathematical logic. *The Journal of Symbolic Logic*, 57(2):385–412, June 1992.

[13] P. Van Roy. *Can Logic Programming execute as fast as Imperative Programming?* PhD thesis, UC Berkeley, December 1990.

[14] David H.D. Warren. An abstract Prolog instruction set. Technical report, SRI International, 1983.

Program Specialisation and Abstract Interpretation Reconciled

Michael Leuschel[1]
Department of Computer Science, K.U. Leuven, Belgium
DIKU, University of Copenhagen, Denmark

Abstract

We clarify the relationship between abstract interpretation and program specialisation in the context of logic programming. We present a generic top-down abstract specialisation framework, along with a generic correctness result, into which a lot of the existing specialisation techniques can be cast. The framework also shows how these techniques can be further improved by moving to more refined abstract domains. It, however, also highlights inherent limitations shared by all these approaches. In order to overcome them, and to fully unify program specialisation with abstract interpretation, we also develop a generic combined bottom-up/top-down framework, which allows specialisation *and* analysis outside the reach of existing techniques.

1 Introduction

At first sight *abstract interpretation* (see, e.g., [5, 3]) and *program specialisation* (see, e.g., [7]) might appear to be completely unrelated techniques: abstract interpretation focusses on *correct and precise* analysis, while the main goal of program specialisation is to produce more *efficient residual code* (for a given task at hand). Nonetheless, it is often felt that there is a close relationship between abstract interpretation and program specialisation and, recently, there has been a lot of interest in the integration of these two techniques (see, e.g., [16, 11, 22].

Indeed, for good specialisation to take place, program specialisers have to perform some form of analysis. For instance, the incomplete SLD-trees produced by *partial deduction* [20, 7] can be seen as complete (given the closedness condition of [20]) description of the top-down computation-flow.

In this paper we want to substantiate this intuition and make the link to abstract interpretation fully explicit. We therefore present a generic (augmented) top-down abstract interpretation framework in which most of the specialisation techniques (such as partial deduction [20, 7], ecological partial deduction [18, 13], constrained partial deduction [15], conjunctive partial deduction [17, 10]) can be cast. It also paves the way for more refined and

[1]The work was done while the author was Post-doctoral Fellow of the Belgian Fund for Scientific Research (F.W.O.-Vlaanderen). and visiting DIKU, University of Copenhagen. The author's present address is: Dept. of Electronics and Computer Science, University of Southampton, Southampton SO17 1BJ, UK. E-mail : mal@ecs.soton.ac.uk

powerful specialisation, by allowing more refined abstract domains and more refined "abstract unfolding" rules.

However, we will not stop there. The above formalisation will actually make two (additional) shortcomings of most earlier specialisation techniques apparent (already identified in, e.g., [16, 13]): the lack of *side-ways information passing* and of *inference of global success information*. Recent techniques [16, 23, 22] (as well as some earlier attempts such as [21] and [9, 6]) have tried to overcome these limitations by incorporating *bottom-up* abstract interpretation techniques. However, we feel that a fully satisfactory integration of program specialisation with abstract interpretation has not been achieved yet, and we strive to do so in this paper.

This integration is not solely beneficial for specialisation purposes. Indeed, as shown in [16, 13] (for one particular abstract domain), a full integration of abstract interpretation with program specialisation can yield *analysis* outside the reach of either method alone (and can even be used to perform inductive theorem proving or infinite model checking).

We thus present an augmented, combined top-down/bottom-up abstract specialisation framework in which all these earlier techniques (and more) can be cast, and provide the first "full-blown" integration of abstract interpretation and program specialisation, leading towards powerful specialisation *and* analysis beyond the reach of existing techniques.

2 Top-Down Abstract Partial Deduction

In this paper, we restrict ourselves to definite programs and goals (but possibly with declarative built-in's such as *is*, *call*, *functor*, *arg*, \==; this allows to express a very large number of interesting, practical programs; one can even implement and use certain higher-order features such as *map*/3).

An *expression* is either a term, an atom or a conjunction. We use $E_1 \preceq E_2$ to denote that the expression E_1 is an instance of the expression E_2. By $mgu(E_1, E_2)$ we denote a most general unifier and by $msg(E_1, E_2)$ a most specific generalisation of E_1 and E_2. Also, as common in partial deduction, the notion of SLD-trees is extended to allow *incomplete* SLD-trees which may contain leaves where no literal has been selected for further derivation.

2.1 The Abstract Domain

We denote by $\mathcal{Q}$ the set of all conjunctions. Our abstract domain $\mathcal{AQ}$ is then a set of *abstract conjunctions* equipped with a *concretisation function* $\gamma : \mathcal{AQ} \mapsto 2^{\mathcal{Q}}$, providing the link between the abstract and the concrete domain. We suppose that $\gamma(\mathbf{A})$ is always *downwards closed* ($Q \in \gamma(\mathbf{A}) \Rightarrow Q\theta \in \gamma(\mathbf{A})$), i.e. we restrict ourselves to "declarative" properties. Also, for reasons that will become clear below, we suppose that all conjunctions in $\gamma(\mathbf{A})$ have the same number of conjuncts and with the same predicates at the same position. Observe that this still admits the possibility of a bottom element $\perp$ whose concretisation is empty.

We will denote the fact that $\gamma(\mathbf{A_1}) \subseteq \gamma(\mathbf{A_2})$ by $\mathbf{A_1} \sqsubseteq \mathbf{A_2}$. We also sometimes use γ on sets of abstract conjunctions: $\gamma(S) = \{Q \mid Q \in \gamma(\mathbf{A}) \wedge \mathbf{A} \in S\}$. One particular abstract domain, which will often serve for illustration purposes, is the $\mathcal{PD}$-domain where $\mathcal{AQ} = \mathcal{Q}$ (i.e. the abstract conjunctions are the concrete ones) and $\gamma(Q) = \{Q' \mid Q' \preceq Q\}$ (i.e. an abstract conjunction denotes all its instances).

2.2 Abstract Unfolding

Program specialisation can achieve more efficient residual code — amongst others — by pre-computing certain operations at compile time (which then no longer have to be performed at run-time). In other words, one computation step in the residual program may actually represent an entire sequence of computation steps within the original program.

In the context of logic programming, this can be seen as producing a *residual* clause which, when resolved against, has the same effect as a sequence of resolution steps in the original program. Partial deduction, for example, produces these clauses by *unfolding* an atom A, thereby producing an SLD-tree τ for $P \cup \{\leftarrow A\}$. Every non-failing branch of τ is translated into a residual clause by taking the *resultant* of the derivation.[2] These resultants can then be used in a sound manner for any concretisation of A (i.e., any instance of A) in the sense that resolution will lead to computed answers and resolvents which can also be obtained in the original program. But actually the use by partial deduction algorithms of these resultants is not limited to code generation. Take, e.g., the resultant $p(f(X)) \leftarrow q(f(X))$. When resolving a particular runtime call $p(\bar{t})$ with that resultant we will obtain resolvents which are instances of $\leftarrow q(f(X))$. Partial deduction therefore also analyses (and specialises) the atom $q(f(X))$. In other words, the body of the residual clause is used for the flow analysis as a representative of all possible resolvents. This multiple use of the residual clauses relies on using an abstract domain identical to the concrete domain.

In the more general setting we endeavour to develop, these two roles of unfolding will have to be separated out (as the residual program has to be expressed in the concrete domain). In other words, to specialise an abstract conjunction $\mathbf{A}$ we generate:

- resultants $H_i \leftarrow B_i$, totally correct for the calls in $\gamma(\mathbf{A})$ and
- for each resultant $H_i \leftarrow B_i$ an abstract conjunction $\mathbf{A_i}$ approximating all the possible resolvent goals which can occur after resolving an element of $\gamma(\mathbf{A})$ with $H_i \leftarrow B_i$.

This leads to Definition 2.1 of abstract unfolding and resolution below. (Observe that the resultants $H_i \leftarrow B_i$ below are not necessarily Horn clauses. We will discuss the generation of Horn clause programs later in Section 2.4.)

[2] A resultant is a formula $H \leftarrow B$ where H and B are conjunctions of literals.

First, we introduce the following notations. Given an SLD-tree τ for $P \cup \{\leftarrow Q\}$ we denote by $Q \leadsto_{\tau}^{\theta} L$ the fact that a leaf goal L of τ can be reached via c.a.s. θ. Given a resultant $C_i = H_i \leftarrow B_i$ and a conjunction Q we denote by $Q \leadsto_{C_i}^{\theta} L$ the fact that $mgu(Q, H_i) = \theta'$ with $\theta' \mid_{vars(Q)} = \theta$ and $L = B_i\theta'$.[3]

Definition 2.1 An *abstract unfolding* operation *aunf*(.) maps abstract conjunctions to finite sets of resultants and has the property that for all $\mathbf{A} \in \mathcal{AQ}$ and $Q \in \gamma(\mathbf{A})$ there exists an SLD-tree τ for $P \cup \{\leftarrow Q\}$ such that:

$$Q \leadsto_{\tau}^{\theta} L \quad \Leftrightarrow \quad \exists C_i \in aunf(\mathbf{A}) \text{ s.t. } Q \leadsto_{C_i}^{\theta} L \tag{1}$$

An *abstract resolution* operation *ares*(.) maps an abstract conjunction $\mathbf{A}$ and a concrete resultant C_i to another abstract conjunction such that for all $Q \in \gamma(\mathbf{A})$: $Q \leadsto_{C_i}^{\theta} L \Rightarrow L \in \gamma(ares(\mathbf{A}, C_i))$.

The $\Rightarrow$ part of point 1 requests that the code generated by *aunf*(.) is *complete* while the $\Leftarrow$ part additionally requests *soundness* (as we want to have residual code which is *totally correct* and not just a safe approximation). We call an abstract unfolding rule *conservative* if the $\Leftarrow$ part of point 1 holds for all Q (and not just for $Q \in \gamma(\mathbf{A})$).

Example 2.2 Let P be the following program:

$eq([],[]) \leftarrow$
$eq([H|X],[H|Y]) \leftarrow eq(X,Y)$

Let $\mathbf{A} = eq([a|T], Z)$ in the $\mathcal{PD}$-domain. $aunf(\mathbf{A}) = \{H \leftarrow B\}$ and $ares(\mathbf{A}, H \leftarrow B) = eq(T,Y)$ where $H = eq(X,[a|Y])$ and $B = eq(X,Y)$ are correct. Also, both remain correct with $H = eq(H,[H|Y])$ but not with $H = eq(X,[b|Y])$. $H = eq([H],[H|Y])$ and $B = eq([],Y)$ is also incorrect.

Observe, that in Definition 2.1 above, nothing forces one to use the *same* structure (i.e. same selected literal positions, same clauses) for *all* the concretisations of $\mathbf{A}$. Indeed, this enables some very powerful optimisations not achievable within existing "classical" specialisation frameworks. For instance, in the example below we are able to completely eliminate a type-like check from the residual program.

Example 2.3 Let P be the program from Example 2.2 and $\mathbf{A}$ represent the set of all calls $eq(L, L)$ where L is a bounded (nil-terminated) list (this can obviously not be represented in the $\mathcal{PD}$-domain). Then $aunf(\mathbf{A}) = C_1 = \{eq(X,Y) \leftarrow\}$ and $ares(\mathbf{A}, C_1) = \square$ are correct according to the above definition ! One can thus generate the residual code:

$eq(X,Y) \leftarrow$

Observe that this abstract unfolding is, in contrast to Example 2.2, not conservative. In other words the residual code is only sound for concretisations of $\mathbf{A}$ but not, e.g., for the call $eq(a,[])$.

[3] If Q and H_i are atoms this is equivalent to saying that $\leftarrow Q$ resolves with the clause $H_i \leftarrow B_i$ via c.a.s. θ yielding $\leftarrow L$ as resolvent. Also observe that for any Q, C_i and there is at most one choice of θ and L such that $Q \leadsto_{C_i}^{\theta} L$.

Example 2.4 Let P be the following program:

$(C_1)\ p(a) \leftarrow$
$(C_2)\ p(f(X)) \leftarrow p(X)$
$(C_3)\ p(g(X)) \leftarrow p(X)$

Let $\mathbf{A}$ represent all calls $p(X)$ where X has type $\tau ::= a \mid g(\tau)$. Then $aunf(\mathbf{A}) = \{C_1, C_3\}$, $ares(\mathbf{A}, C_1) = \Box$ and $ares(\mathbf{A}, C_3) = \mathbf{A}$ is correct and by abstract unfolding we are able to safely remove the redundant clause C_2.

To more concisely express the flow analysis, we extend $aunf(.)$ so that it maps sets of abstract conjunctions to sets of abstract conjunctions in the following way: $aunf^*(S) = \{ares(\mathbf{A}, C) \mid C \in aunf(\mathbf{A})\}$.

2.3 Widening by Splitting

The computation flow aspect of program specialisation could now be performed by calculating $U \uparrow^\infty$, where $U(S) = S \cup aunf^*(S)$. However, it is obvious that, for but the simplest abstract domains, this construction will not terminate and that generalisation is required.

As usual in abstract interpretation, one could imagine to represent generalisation by a widening function $\omega : \mathcal{AQ} \mapsto \mathcal{AQ}$ such that $\forall \mathbf{A} \in \mathcal{AQ} : \mathbf{A} \sqsubseteq \omega(\mathbf{A})$. Unfortunately, this is not enough to be able to ensure termination of abstract interpretation in the present setting, because all concretisations of an abstract conjunction must have the same number of conjuncts. In other words, no terminating analysis could be produced for, e.g., a program containing the clause $p \leftarrow p, p$. This is why we need a more refined notion of widening, which involves splitting conjunctions into subconjunctions:

Definition 2.5 A sequence $\langle \mathbf{A_1}, \ldots, \mathbf{A_n} \rangle$ of abstract conjunctions is an *abstraction* of an abstract conjunction $\mathbf{A}$ iff $\gamma(\mathbf{A}) \subseteq \{Q_1 \wedge \ldots \wedge Q_n \mid Q_i \in \gamma(\mathbf{A_i})\}$.

Observe that for $i = 1$ this condition is equivalent to $\mathbf{A} \sqsubseteq \mathbf{A_1}$. Also observe that this splitting operation does not allow re-ordering of conjunctions. It is, however, straightforward to do so. One just has to be careful to use the *same* reordering for *all* concretisations (otherwise it will be impossible to synchronise the code generation with the flow analysis, cf. the next subsection).

We extend the abstraction concept to sets:

Definition 2.6 A set $\mathcal{A}'$ is called an *abstraction* of another set of abstract conjunctions $\mathcal{A}$, denoted by $\mathcal{A}' \sqsupseteq_{split} \mathcal{A}$, iff for all $\mathbf{A} \in \mathcal{A}$ there exists an abstraction $\langle \mathbf{A_1}, \ldots, \mathbf{A_n} \rangle$ of $\mathbf{A}$ such that all $\mathbf{A_i} \in \mathcal{A}'$.

For example, in the $\mathcal{PD}$-domain, $\langle p(X) \wedge q(X), p(b) \rangle$ is an abstraction of $p(b) \wedge q(b) \wedge p(b)$ and we have thus, for example, $\{p(X) \wedge q(X), p(b)\} \sqsupseteq_{split} \{p(b) \wedge q(b) \wedge p(b), p(c) \wedge q(c)\}$.

We can now define a more refined *widening operator* to be a function[4] $\omega : 2^{\mathcal{AQ}} \mapsto 2^{\mathcal{AQ}}$ satisfying that $\omega(\mathcal{A}) \sqsupseteq_{split} \mathcal{A}$ for all $\mathcal{A}$.

By using appropriate widening operators it is now possible to ensure termination for any program (we refer the reader, e.g., to [18, 10, 13] on how to devise ω in the context of partial deduction).

We also say that a set $\mathcal{A}$ of abstract conjunctions is *covered* iff $\mathcal{A} \sqsupseteq_{split} aunf^*(\mathcal{A})$. Intuitively, this means that $\mathcal{A}$ is a complete description of the computation flow (induced by $aunf(.)$) for all concretisations of $\mathcal{A}$.

2.4 Generating Residual Code

Generating residual code from the resultants $H_i \leftarrow B_i$ produced by the abstract unfolding involves transforming them into Horn clauses. This can be achieved by mapping the abstract conjunctions produced by the flow analysis to atoms and then appropriately renaming the heads H_i and the bodies B_i.

We first introduce the following concepts. A *concrete dominator* of an abstract conjunction $\mathbf{A}$ is a concrete conjunction which is more general than all the concretisations of $\mathbf{A}$. A *skeleton* for an abstract conjunction $\mathbf{A}$ is a maximally general concrete dominator of $\mathbf{A}$. By our earlier assumption that all conjunctions in $\gamma(\mathbf{A})$ have the same predicates at the same position we know that a concrete dominator (and thus skeleton) exists for all abstract conjunctions. By $\lceil \mathbf{A} \rceil$ we denote some skeleton for $\mathbf{A}$.

We also require that for all $\mathbf{A} \in \mathcal{AQ}$ and $H_i \leftarrow B_i \in aunf(\mathbf{A})$ we have $H_i \preceq \lceil \mathbf{A} \rceil$. The requirement prevents garbage code (any $H_i \not\preceq \lceil \mathbf{A} \rceil$ can never unify with a concretisation of $\mathbf{A}$) and simplifies the construction below.

Definition 2.7 An *atomic renaming* $\rho_{\mathbf{A}}$ for an abstract conjunction $\mathbf{A}$ is an atom A such that $vars(\lceil \mathbf{A} \rceil) = vars(A)$. Also, for any $Q \preceq \lceil \mathbf{A} \rceil$ we define $\rho_{\mathbf{A}}(Q) = A\theta$ where θ is such that $Q = \lceil \mathbf{A} \rceil \theta$.

In the $\mathcal{PD}$-domain, we might have $\mathbf{A} = p(f(X)) \wedge q(Z)$, $\lceil \mathbf{A} \rceil = p(X) \wedge q(Y)$, $\rho_{\mathbf{A}} = pq(X,Y)$ and $Q = p(f(a)) \wedge q(b)$. In that case $\rho_{\mathbf{A}}(Q) = pq(f(a),b)$.

Observe that for all $Q \preceq \lceil \mathbf{A} \rceil$ we have $\rho_{\mathbf{A}}(Q\theta) = \rho_{\mathbf{A}}(Q)\theta$. Also, to avoid name clashes, we will always suppose that for any $\mathbf{A} \neq \mathbf{A}'$ the predicate symbols used by $\rho_{\mathbf{A}}$ and $\rho'_{\mathbf{A}}$ are different.

Given a resultant $H_i \leftarrow B_i \in aunf(\mathbf{A})$ we can now produce an actual Horn clause by renaming H_i and B_i. Renaming H_i is easy: we just calculate $\rho_{\mathbf{A}}(H_i)$ (which is always defined). If our flow analysis also contains $\mathbf{A_i} = ares(\mathbf{A}, H_i \leftarrow B_i)$ (and thus code for $\mathbf{A_i}$ will be generated) then renaming B_i is just as easy: we just calculate $\rho_{\mathbf{A_i}}(B_i)$. However, suppose that we have applied a widening step and that we actually did not analyse $\mathbf{A_i}$ but an abstraction $\langle \mathbf{G_1}, \ldots, \mathbf{G_n} \rangle$ of it. In that case B_i has to be chopped up

[4] It is of course possible to give extra parameters to ω, e.g., to take the specialisation history into account.

and then renamed using the renaming functions of the abstraction. We thus define $\rho_{\mathcal{A},\mathbf{A}}(B) = \rho_{\mathbf{G_1}}(B_1) \wedge \ldots \wedge \rho_{\mathbf{G_1}}(B_n)$ where $B = B_1 \wedge \ldots \wedge B_n$ and $\langle \mathbf{G_1}, \ldots, \mathbf{G_n} \rangle$ is an abstraction of $\mathbf{A}$ such that $\mathbf{G_i} \in \mathcal{A}$ and $B_i \preceq \lceil \mathbf{G_i} \rceil$. If no such partitioning exists then we leave $\rho_{\mathcal{A},\mathbf{A}}(B)$ undefined.

Definition 2.8 Let $\mathcal{A}$ be a covered set of abstract conjunctions. We then define an *abstract partial deduction of P wrt $\mathcal{A}$* to be the set of clauses:
$\{\rho_{\mathbf{A}}(H) \leftarrow \rho_{\mathcal{A},\mathbf{A}'}(B) \mid H \leftarrow B \in aunf(\mathbf{A}) \wedge \mathbf{A}' = ares(\mathbf{A}, H \leftarrow B) \wedge \mathbf{A} \in \mathcal{A}\}$.

It is easy to see that, because $\mathcal{A}$ be a covered, the renamings of the bodies B will always be defined.

Observe that, a skeleton always has distinct variables as its only terms. In other words, we perform no structure filtering (i.e. $p(f(a))$ might get renamed into $p'(f(a))$ but never into $p'(a)$ or p'). Filtering could be achieved by using a concrete dominator, ideally $msg(\gamma(\mathbf{A}))$, instead of the skeleton $\lceil \mathbf{A} \rceil$ for the definition of $\rho_{\mathbf{A}}$. This, however, makes the exposition more tricky and would detract from the main points of the paper. Anyway, one can always apply [8] (as well as RAF, see, e.g., [13]) as a post-processing.

2.5 A Generic Correctness Result and Algorithm

We can now present a very general correctness result.

Theorem 2.9 Let P' be an abstract partial deduction of P wrt a covered set of abstract conjunctions $\mathcal{A}$ and let $Q \in \gamma(\mathbf{A})$ with $\mathbf{A} \in \mathcal{A}$. Then $P \cup \{\leftarrow Q\}$ has an SLD-refutation with c.a.s. θ iff $P' \cup \{\leftarrow \rho_{\mathbf{A}}(Q)\}$ has an SLD-refutation with c.a.s. θ.

Proofs can be found in the technical report [14]. In order to derive results about the preservation of finite failure we have to impose that the unfolding operation $aunf(.)$ is *fair*[5], i.e. when computing $aunf(\mathbf{A})$ it eventually selects every conjunct of $Q \in \gamma(\mathbf{A})$ in every non-failing branch. One can then prove (by reusing results from [17, 13]) that:

$P \cup \{\leftarrow Q\}$ has a finitely failed SLD-tree iff $P' \cup \{\leftarrow \rho_{\mathbf{A}}(Q)\}$ has.

Based upon the notions introduced above, we can now present a generic algorithm for top-down program specialisation in a very concise manner:

Algorithm 2.10 (Top-Down Abstract Partial Deduction)
Input: A program P and an abstract conjunction $\mathbf{A}$
Output: A specialised program P'
Initialise: $i = 0$, $\mathcal{A}_0 = \{\mathbf{A}\}$
  repeat
    let $\mathcal{A}_{i+1} := \omega(\mathcal{A}_i \cup aunf^*(\mathcal{A}_i))$; **let** $i := i + 1$;
  until $\mathcal{A}_{i-1} = \mathcal{A}_i$
  Let P' be an abstract partial deduction wrt $\mathcal{A}_i$

[5]Or even better weakly fair, see [17, 13].

The differences over "traditional" top-down abstract interpretation methods for logic programs (like, e.g., the top-down component of [3]) are:
1) abstract *conjunctions* instead of abstract atoms are used, 2) widening can generalise by "going up the lattice" *and* by splitting, 3) a *full abstract unfolding* (which can do, e.g., deforestation) is used instead of just a single abstract resolution step, and 4) there is no sideways information passing between abstract conjunctions (but perfect [16] sideways propagation within each abstract conjunction).

2.6 Expressing Existing Partial Deduction Techniques

Classical partial deduction [20, 7] can be seen as an instance of the above generic framework by taking

- the $\mathcal{PD}$-domain (i.e. the concrete domain is the abstract domain and an abstract element represents all its instances),
- abstract unfolding performs concrete resolution steps,
- ω will only produce sets of atoms and the initial abstract conjunction $\mathbf{A}$ is an atom.

To represent *conjunctive* partial deduction [17, 10, 13] we just have to drop the last requirement. *Ecological* partial deduction [18, 13] can be seen as an instance of the above generic framework by taking

- $\mathcal{AQ} = (\mathcal{A}, T)$, where $\mathcal{A}$ is the set of atoms and T is the set of characteristic trees.
- $\gamma((A,\tau)) = \{A'' \mid A'' \preceq A' \preceq A \wedge A'$ has characteristic tree τ $\}$,
- $aunf((A,\tau))$ is based on using the SLD-tree τ (see [18, 13]).

Similarly, *constrained* partial deduction [15] can be cast into the present framework , and its correctness results are a special case of the ones above.

The present framework can now be used to easily extend both methods to handle conjunctions or even to integrate all of these methods into one powerful top-down specialisation method.

2.7 Future Prospects

Improved Generalisation A lot of existing specialisation techniques (see, e.g., [18, 10]) ensure termination by using refined methods, such as homeomorphic embedding $\trianglelefteq$, to detect "dangerous" growth of structure. However, once such a growth has been detected these techniques still have to rely on rather crude generalisation operators, such as more specific generalisation (*msg*), because the resulting generalisation (or part of it, as in [18]) has to be expressed in the $\mathcal{PD}$-domain. For instance, when a specialiser goes from $A_1 = p(a)$ to $A_2 = p(f(a))$ then the homeomorphic embedding $\trianglelefteq$ will signal danger ($A_1 \trianglelefteq A_2$) and will even pinpoint the extra $f(.)$ in A_2 as the potential source of non-termination. But the *msg* of A_1 and A_2 is just $p(X)$ and no use of the information provided by $\trianglelefteq$ was made (nor is it possible to do so in the $\mathcal{PD}$-domain). In the enriched context of abstract partial deduction, however, we can now derive, e.g., a (regular) *type* describing the growth detected by $\trianglelefteq$ and arrive at much more intelligent generalisation and much improved specialisation. For instance A_1 and A_2 can be abstracted by something like $p(X\!:\!\tau)$ where the type τ is defined as $\tau ::= a \mid f(\tau)$. Also, atoms such as $p([])$ and $p([H|T])$ can be abstracted by $p(X\!:\!\mathbf{list})$. The example worked out in [14] makes use of that possibility.

Improved Unfolding and Code Generation As already hinted at in Section 2.2, our enriched abstract unfolding operation allows us to generate much more efficient code. Given the simple program

$p([]) \leftarrow$
$p([H|T]) \leftarrow p(T)$

one can, e.g., use the information that a particular variable X is a list to abstractly unfold $p(X)$ into $p(Z) \leftarrow$, i.e. generate a single residual fact instead of the "usual" recursive definition. This is something that *no* other specialisation framework (we are aware of) can currently achieve. In languages like Mercury or Gödel such type information will even be explicitly given and does not have to be inferred. We believe that our framework(s) will be especially useful for these languages.

Improved Handling of Built-in's If we know that a given variable X represents an integer we can, e.g., specialise both $atomic(X)$ or $number(X)$ into $true$. One can imagine various other optimisations not possible in conventional techniques based upon the $\mathcal{PD}$-domain, like specialising arg or $functor$ calls based upon type information of the arguments. A similar idea has been used in [23] and [22] to remove groundness tests (controlling parallel execution) from the residual program.

3 A Bottom-Up Analysis

Although using refined abstract domains within Algorithm 2.10 can lead to major improvements over existing specialisation techniques, it is still not possible to achieve side-ways (between different abstract conjunctions) or bottom-up success information propagation. A (seemingly) simple way to add bottom-up success information propagation to our abstract partial deduction framework is to request point 1 only for $Q \in \gamma(\mathbf{A}) \cap SS_P$ (instead of $Q \in \gamma(\mathbf{A})$) in Definition 2.1 of $aunf(.)$, where SS_P is the success set of P. In practice this means that the operation $aunf(.)$ can make use of a *subsidiary* (bottom-up) abstract interpretation phase to approximate SS_P. In order to achieve some interaction between the top-down and bottom-up components, one could imagine that the abstract interpretation takes the unfoldings into account (this is an approach proposed in [22]). This, however, means that one has to re-analyse whenever a new unfolding has been performed and to re-specialise whenever a tighter success set has been derived. The precise details of this "co-routining" are non-trivial and one can hardly call the above an algorithm. Furthermore, there are a considerable number of tasks (see [16]) that such an approach simply cannot handle, because the specialisation and analysis components basically still work in isolation. In this paper, we will therefore first present a pure bottom-up analysis algorithm, but which we then *fully* integrate with Algorithm 2.10 in Section 4.

In a bottom-up setting we need, instead of an abstraction of the unfolding operation, an abstraction of the bottom-up T_P operator [1, 19], or better its non-ground version (to capture the C-semantics and thus the computed answers). The (non-ground) T_P operator maps interpretations to interpretations, where an interpretation is usually represented by a set of atoms. Each interpretation in turn can be seen as representing (an approximation to) the success set. One could thus define an abstract version of T_P which maps a set of atomic abstract conjunctions to a set of atomic abstract conjunctions such that $\gamma(AT_P(\mathcal{A})) \supseteq \{H\theta_1 \dots \theta_n \mid H \leftarrow B_1, \dots, B_n \in P \wedge A_i \in \gamma(\mathcal{A}) \wedge \theta_i = mgu(B_i\theta_1, \dots, \theta_{i-1}, A_i)\}$. However, in light of a full integration with the framework of Section 2 (and in order to be able to capture all the techniques of [21]), we will describe a more refined abstraction of T_P based on *conjunctions* (instead of just atoms) and *resultants* derived by $aunf(.)$ (instead of simply the clauses of the original program P).

Abstract T_P for Abstract Conjunctions

So, instead of just representing the success set for each predicate in general, we want to represent success sets for a given choice of abstract conjunctions $\mathcal{A} = \{\mathbf{A_1}, \dots, \mathbf{A_n}\}$. This is accomplished by the following definition.

Definition 3.1 An *abstracted interpretation* is a set $\{(\mathbf{A_1}, \mathbf{I_1}), \dots, (\mathbf{A_n}, \mathbf{I_n})\}$ of couples $(\mathcal{AQ}, \mathcal{AQ})$ such that $\mathbf{I_i} \sqsubseteq \mathbf{A_i}$ and $i \neq j \Rightarrow \mathbf{A_i} \neq \mathbf{A_j}$. We also define a projection for abstracted interpretations $\pi_1(\mathcal{I}) = \{\mathbf{A} \mid (\mathbf{A}, \mathbf{I}) \in \mathcal{I}\}$.

An abstracted interpretation $\mathcal{I}$ represents for each $\mathbf{A_i}$ a set of possible computed instances in the form of the abstract conjunction $\mathbf{I_i}$. Let us now formulate how the knowledge contained in $\mathcal{I}$ can be used to refine some abstract conjunction, say $\mathbf{A}$ (not necessarily identical to some $\mathbf{A_i}$), into another abstract conjunction $\mathbf{A'} \sqsubseteq \mathbf{A}$ approximating the success set of $\mathbf{A}$.

Definition 3.2 Let $\mathcal{I} = \{(\mathbf{A_1}, \mathbf{I_1}), \dots, (\mathbf{A_n}, \mathbf{I_n})\}$ be an abstracted interpretation. Let $\mathbf{A}$ be an abstract conjunction such that $\langle \mathbf{G_1}, \dots \mathbf{G_j}, \dots \mathbf{G_m} \rangle$ is an abstraction of $\mathbf{A}$. Also let $\mathbf{G_j} \sqsubseteq \mathbf{A_i}$ for some i. Then any abstract conjunction $\mathbf{A'} \sqsubseteq \mathbf{A}$ such that $\langle \mathbf{G_1}, \dots \mathbf{G_{j-1}}, \mathbf{I_i}, \mathbf{G_{j+1}}, \dots, \mathbf{G_m} \rangle$ is an abstraction of it, is called a *refinement of* $\mathbf{A}$ *under* $\mathcal{I}$. $\mathbf{A}$ itself, as well as any refinement of $\mathbf{A'}$, is also called a refinement of $\mathbf{A}$ under $\mathcal{I}$ (i.e. we take the transitive and reflexive closure). By $ref_{\mathcal{I}}(\mathbf{A})$ we denote some refinement of $\mathbf{A}$ under $\mathcal{I}$.

Example 3.3 In the $\mathcal{PD}$-domain let $\mathbf{A} = p(X) \wedge q(X)$ as well as $\mathcal{I} = \{(p(X), p(f(Y))), (q(f(Z)), q(f(a)))\}$. Then $\mathbf{A'} = p(f(V)) \wedge q(f(V))$ is a refinement of $\mathbf{A}$ under $\mathcal{I}$. Now $\mathbf{A}'' = p(f(a)) \wedge q(f(a))$ is in turn a refinement of $\mathbf{A}'$ (and thus also of $\mathbf{A}$) under $\mathcal{I}$. The previously inapplicable couple $(q(f(Z)), q(f(a)))$ became applicable for $\mathbf{A}'$ and allowed us to achieve further refinement.

We can now formulate an abstract bottom-up operator:

Definition 3.4 An *abstract bottom-up operator* $AT_P(.)$ is a function $\mathcal{AQ} \times 2^{\mathcal{AQ}\times\mathcal{AQ}} \mapsto \mathcal{AQ}$ such that, for every abstracted interpretation $\mathcal{I} = \{(\mathbf{A_1}, \mathbf{I_1}), \ldots, (\mathbf{A_n}, \mathbf{I_n})\}$, we have that if $H \leftarrow B \in \mathit{aunf}(\mathbf{A_i})$ and $\mathbf{B} = \mathit{ares}(\mathbf{A_i}, H \leftarrow B)$ then $B\theta \in \gamma(\mathit{ref}_{\mathcal{I}}(\mathbf{B})) \Rightarrow H\theta \in \gamma(AT_P(\mathbf{A_i}, \mathcal{I}))$.

Intuitively, the above states that if a runtime resolvent $(\leftarrow B\theta)$ of $\mathbf{A_i}$ may succeed given the abstracted interpretation $\mathcal{I}$ (i.e., $B\theta \in \gamma(\mathit{ref}_{\mathcal{I}}(\mathbf{B}))$) then the corresponding head $H\theta$ should potentially succeed in $AT_P(\mathbf{A_i}, \mathcal{I})$. In other words, $AT_P(\mathbf{A_i}, \mathcal{I})$ is a safe approximation of one concrete non-ground[6] bottom-up propagation step performed on the resultants of $\mathbf{A_i}$. We also define $AT_P(.)$ to work on abstracted interpretations: $AT_P(\mathcal{I}) = \{(\mathbf{A_1}, AT_P(\mathbf{A_1}, \mathcal{I})), \ldots, (\mathbf{A_n}, AT_P(\mathbf{A_n}, \mathcal{I}))\}$.

For an abstract domain with no infinite ascending chains, we can now formulate a terminating bottom-up analysis algorithm basically as calculating $AT_P \uparrow^{\infty} (\mathcal{I}_0)$ where $\mathcal{I}_0 = \{(\mathbf{A_1}, \bot), \ldots, (\mathbf{A_n}, \bot)\}$.

Exploiting Success Information for the Code Generation

The following shows how the information derivation by such an analysis can be exploited to derive a specialised program.

Definition 3.5 Let $\mathcal{I}$ be an abstracted interpretation. We then define an *abstract partial deduction of P wrt $\mathcal{I}$* to be the set of clauses:

$$\{\rho_{\mathbf{A}}(H\theta) \leftarrow \rho_{\mathbf{A},\mathbf{A}''}(B\theta) \mid H \leftarrow B \in \mathit{aunf}(\mathbf{A}) \wedge \mathbf{A} \in \pi_1(\mathcal{I}) \wedge \mathbf{A}'' = \mathit{ref}_{\mathcal{I}}(\mathit{ares}(\mathbf{A}, H \leftarrow B)) \wedge B\theta \text{ is a concrete dominator}^7 \text{ of } \mathbf{A}''\}$$

If for all $\mathbf{A}''$ we have that $\{\mathbf{A}''\} \sqsubseteq_{split} \pi_1(\mathcal{I})$ then we call $\mathcal{I}$ *covered* (and all renamings $\rho_{\mathcal{A},\mathbf{A}''}(B\theta)$ above are defined).

The big difference over Definition 2.8 is that the resultants get instantiated using the success information contained in $\mathcal{I}$ and that the notion of coveredness also takes the success information into account. Indeed, $\mathcal{I}$ might be covered even though $\pi_1(\mathcal{I})$ is not (we might have $\{\mathbf{A}'\} \not\sqsubseteq_{split} \pi_1(\mathcal{I})$).

Example 3.6 Let P be the program from Example 2.2 and $\mathcal{I} = \{(eq(X,Y), eq(X,X))\}$ in the $\mathcal{PD}$-domain. Also, let $\mathit{aunf}(eq(X,Y)) = \{C_1, C_2\}$ and $\mathit{ares}(eq(X,Y), C_2) = eq(X,Y)$ with $C_1 = eq([],[]) \leftarrow$ as well as $C_2 = eq([H|S],[H|T]) \leftarrow eq(S,T)$. Then, obviously, $eq(X,X)$ is a refinement of $eq(X,Y)$ and the following is an abstract partial deduction of P wrt $\mathcal{I}$ (using $\rho_{eq(X,Y)} = eq_1(X,Y)$):

---

[6] $H\theta$ and $B\theta$ are not necessarily ground.

[7] One could also allow a set of instantiations $\theta_1, \ldots, \theta_n$ such that all concretisations of $\mathbf{A}''$ are an instance of at least one atom in $\{B\theta_1, \ldots, B\theta_n\}$. This can lead to more instantiated resultants but might also lead to code duplication and considerable slow-downs.

$eq_1([],[]) \leftarrow$
$eq_1([H|T],[H|T]) \leftarrow eq_1(T,T)$

The main technique of [21] can be seen an instance of this analysis by: taking the $\mathcal{PD}$-domain and using a composition of predicate-wise *msg* with the non-ground T_P operator on conjunctions. However, only a simple one-step unfolding is performed in [21] and it is not allowed to further refine refinements (which can be crucial, see [16]).

Theorem 3.7 Let P' be an abstract partial deduction of P wrt $AT_P \uparrow^\infty (\mathcal{I})$. Let $Q \in \gamma(\mathbf{A})$, $\mathbf{A} \in \pi_1(\mathcal{I})$, $AT_P \uparrow^\infty (\mathcal{I})$ be covered and *aunf*(.) be conservative.[8] Then $P \cup \{\leftarrow Q\}$ has an SLD-refutation with c.a.s. θ iff $P' \cup \{\leftarrow \rho_{\mathbf{A}}(Q)\}$ has.

For finite failure we can also derive that, if *aunf*(.) is fair then if $P \cup \{\leftarrow Q\}$ has a finitely failed SLD-refutation then so does $P' \cup \{\leftarrow \rho_{\mathbf{A}}(Q)\}$ (but not necessarily the other way around).

One major problem is now of course how to find interesting sets of abstract conjunctions $\mathcal{A} = \{\mathbf{A}_1, \ldots, \mathbf{A}_n\}$ (this was left open in [21]) as well as how to to ensure that $AT_P \uparrow^\infty (\{(\mathbf{A}_1, \bot), \ldots, (\mathbf{A}_n, \bot)\})$ is covered. Here the top-down framework can help, which in turn can benefit from the information provided by the bottom-up phase. This full integration is developed in the next section.

4 A Combined Top-Down/Bottom-Up Framework

The idea of the following algorithm is to combine the top-down with the bottom-up approach so that the mutually benefit from each other:

- the top-down component can, in addition to propagating goal dependent information downwards, provide interesting sets of abstract conjunctions for the bottom-up phase and ensure coveredness.
- the bottom-up phase can give the top-down component information about the global success-patterns, allowing a more focussed unfolding, producing more instantiated resultants as well as achieving side-ways information passing.

As shown in [16], for a particular abstract domain, such an integration can achieve optimisation and analysis which cannot be derived by either approach alone, nor by combining them in a naive manner (i.e. running them successively in isolation, as, e.g., discussed at the beginning of Section 3).

To formalise the flow analysis component of our integrated algorithm we define a refined abstract unfolding and resolution operator, which takes the current success information into account: $aiunf^*(\mathcal{I}) = \{(\mathbf{L}', \bot) \mid (\mathbf{A}, \mathbf{I}) \in \mathcal{I} \wedge$

[8]The difference with Theorem 2.9 is that calls to predicates are no longer guaranteed to be concretisations of the abstract conjunctions from which their definition has been derived; only their success patterns are ! Therefore the code also has to be sound (but not complete) for calls which are not concretisations. An alternative is to allow non-conservative rules but use the refinements only in, e.g., a left-to-right fashion.

$H \leftarrow B \in aunf(\mathbf{A}) \wedge \mathbf{L}' = ref_{\mathcal{I}}(ares(\mathbf{A}, H \leftarrow B))\}$. We also extend ω to abstracted interpretations and request that $\pi_1(\omega(\mathcal{I})) \sqsupseteq_{split} \pi_1(\mathcal{I})$.

Algorithm 4.1 (Refined Abstract Partial Deduction)
Input: A program P and an abstract conjunction $\mathbf{A}$
Output: A specialised program P'
Initialise: $i = 0$, $\mathcal{I}_0 = \{(\mathbf{A}, \perp)\}$
  repeat
    let $j := i$; $\mathcal{I}_{i+1} := AT_P(\mathcal{I}_i)$; **let** $i := i + 1$;   /* one BUP step */
    repeat
      let $\mathcal{I}_{i+1} := \omega(\mathcal{I}_i \cup aiunf^*(\mathcal{I}_i))$; **let** $i := i + 1$;
    until $\mathcal{I}_{i-1} = \mathcal{I}_i$
  until $\mathcal{I}_j = \mathcal{I}_i$
  Let P' be an abstract partial deduction wrt P and $\mathcal{I}_i$

One can easily see that, once the algorithm has terminated, $\mathcal{I}_i$ is covered. In fact, the inner repeat-loop — performing top-down abstract partial deduction — ensures (refined) coveredness. Also, abstract unfolding is applied after every single bottom-up step, i.e. *before* the fixpoint of $AT_P(.)$ is reached. This is the important aspect which makes this algorithm more powerful than running the top-down and bottom-up components in isolation (see [13] for a fully worked out example in the $\mathcal{PD}$-domain).

The algorithm in [16, 13] is an instance of the above algorithm using the $\mathcal{PD}$-domain and where $AT_P(.)$ is the predicate-wise *msg* composed with the non-ground T_P operator. Algorithm 4.1 is also strictly more powerful than [9, 6] (which uses the analysis information just to remove redundant clauses, and not, e.g., to instantiate them) or [22] (which cannot perform deforestation or tupling as it is restricted to specialising atoms individually). One can actually also express techniques based upon tabling (OLDT [12] or even EOLDT [2]) in a slight extension of our framework. In other words, the reconciliation of bottom-up and top-down evaluation [4] is then just a special case of our reconciliation of specialisation and analysis.

In [14] the reader can find how the *reverse-last* open problem from [16, 13] can be solved in our framework in a rather straightforward manner. Being able to solve this example is of prime relevance, e.g., whenever a statically known value is stored in a dynamic accumulator (e.g., an environment of an interpreter or a substitution in an explicit unification algorithm). No existing analysis, specialisation or transformation technique we are aware of, was able to solve this problem.

It is also possible to use the same approach to prove inductive theorems in a much less ad-hoc (and more generally reusable manner) than, e.g., [24]. We also believe that automation of this approach is feasible and endeavour to incorporate these possibilities into the ECCE partial deduction system in the not too distant future. We believe that the improved specialisation capabilities conferred by our new framework will further extend the practical applicability of program specialisation.

5 Conclusion

In this paper we have presented a generic framework and algorithm for top-down program specialisation, which supersedes earlier top-down approaches in generality and power. We have established a *generic correctness result* and have shown how the additional power can be exploited in practice, for improved generalisation, unfolding and code-generation. We have also clarified the relationship of top-down partial deduction with abstract interpretation, establishing a *common basis* and terminology. This clarification allowed us to precisely pinpoint shortcomings both of existing top-down specialisation methods and of existing abstract interpretation techniques. We then proceeded to remedy these shortcomings by incorporating bottom-up success information propagation, thereby fully *reconciling program specialisation with abstract interpretation* and providing a *unifying framework* into which almost all existing specialisation techniques can be cast. This new integrated framework with its generic algorithm provides the foundation for new, powerful specialisation *and* analysis outside the scope of existing techniques.

Acknowledgements

Maurice Bruynooghe provided very valuable feedback this paper. The author also greatly benefited from discussions with Danny De Schreye, Neil Jones, Jesper Jørgensen, Bern Martens, Torben Mogensen, Morten Heine Sørensen, and comments of anonymous referees.

References

[1] K. R. Apt. Introduction to logic programming. In J. van Leeuwen, editor, *Handbook of Theoretical Computer Science*, chapter 10, pages 495–574. North-Holland Amsterdam, 1990.

[2] D. Boulanger and M. Bruynooghe. Deriving fold/unfold transformations of logic programs using extended OLDT-based abstract interpretation. *Journal of Symbolic Computation*, 15(5&6):495–521, 1993.

[3] M. Bruynooghe. A practical framework for the abstract interpretation of logic programs. *The Journal of Logic Programming*, 10:91–124, 1991.

[4] F. Bry. Query evaluation in recursive databases: bottom-up and top-down reconciled. *Data and Knowledge Engineering*, 5:289–312, 1990.

[5] P. Cousot and R. Cousot. Abstract interpretation and application to logic programs. *The Journal of Logic Programming*, 13(2 & 3):103–179, 1992.

[6] D. A. de Waal and J. Gallagher. The applicability of logic program analysis and transformation to theorem proving. In A. Bundy, editor, *Automated Deduction—CADE-12*, pages 207–221. Springer-Verlag, 1994.

[7] J. Gallagher. Tutorial on specialisation of logic programs. In *Proceedings of PEPM'93*, pages 88–98. ACM Press, 1993.

[8] J. Gallagher and M. Bruynooghe. Some low-level transformations for logic programs. In M. Bruynooghe, editor, *Proceedings of Meta90*, pages 229–244, Leuven, Belgium, 1990.

[9] J. Gallagher and D. A. de Waal. Deletion of redundant unary type predicates from logic programs. In K.-K. Lau and T. Clement, editors, *Proceedings of LOPSTR'92*, pages 151–167, 1992.

[10] R. Glück, J. Jørgensen, B. Martens, and M. H. Sørensen. Controlling conjunctive partial deduction of definite logic programs. In H. Kuchen and S. Swierstra, editors, *Proceedings of PLILP'96*, LNCS 1140, pages 152–166, September 1996. Springer-Verlag.

[11] N. D. Jones. Combining abstract interpretation and partial evaluation. In P. Van Hentenryck, editor, *Proceedings of SAS'97*, LNCS 1302, pages 396–405, 1997. Springer-Verlag.

[12] T. Kanamori and T. Kawamura. OLDT-based abstract interpretation. *The Journal of Logic Programming*, 15:1–30, 1993.

[13] M. Leuschel. *Advanced Techniques for Logic Program Specialisation*. PhD thesis, K.U. Leuven, May 1997.

[14] M. Leuschel. Program Specialisation and Abstract Interpretation Reconciled. Technical Report CW 259, K.U. Leuven, 1998.
Available at `http://www.cs.kuleuven.ac.be/~lpai`

[15] M. Leuschel and D. De Schreye. Constrained partial deduction and the preservation of characteristic trees. *New Generation Computing*. To Appear.

[16] M. Leuschel and D. De Schreye. Logic program specialisation: How to be more specific. In H. Kuchen and S. Swierstra, editors, *Proceedings of PLILP'96*, LNCS 1140, pages 137–151, September 1996. Springer-Verlag.

[17] M. Leuschel, D. De Schreye, and A. de Waal. A conceptual embedding of folding into partial deduction: Towards a maximal integration. In M. Maher, editor, *Proceedings of JICSLP'96*, pages 319–332, September 1996. MIT Press.

[18] M. Leuschel, B. Martens, and D. De Schreye. Controlling generalisation and polyvariance in partial deduction of normal logic programs. *ACM Transactions on Programming Languages and Systems*, 20(1):208–258, January 1998.

[19] J. W. Lloyd. *Foundations of Logic Programming*. Springer-Verlag, 1987.

[20] J. W. Lloyd and J. C. Shepherdson. Partial evaluation in logic programming. *The Journal of Logic Programming*, 11(3& 4):217–242, 1991.

[21] K. Marriott, L. Naish, and J.-L. Lassez. Most specific logic programs. *Annals of Mathematics and Artificial Intelligence*, 1:303–338, 1990. Preliminary version in *Proceedings of JICSLP'88*, pages 909–923, 1988. MIT Press.

[22] G. Puebla, J. Gallagher, and M. Hermenegildo. Towards integrating partial evaluation in a specialization framework based on generic abstract interpretation. In M. Leuschel, editor, *Proceedings of the ILPS'97 Workshop on Specialisation of Declarative Programs and its Application*, K.U. Leuven, Tech. Rep. CW 255, pages 29–38, October 1997.

[23] G. Puebla and M. Hermenegildo. Abstract specialization and its application to program parallelization. In J. Gallagher, editor, *Proceedings of LOPSTR'96*, LNCS 1207, pages 169–186, August 1996.

[24] V. F. Turchin. Metacomputation: Metasystem transitions plus supercompilation. In O. Danvy, R. Glück, and P. Thiemann, editors, *Proceedings of the 1996 Dagstuhl Seminar on Partial Evaluation*, LNCS 1110, pages 482–509, 1996. Springer-Verlag.

Termination analysis: some practical properties of the norm and level mapping space

Stefaan Decorte and Danny De Schreye
Department of Computer Science, K.U.Leuven, Belgium
e-mail: dannyd@cs.kuleuven.ac.be

Abstract

The notions of norm and level mapping play an important role in the context of termination analysis. The goal of this paper to provide some structure on the norm and level mapping space, to analyse that structure and to obtain some new insights in termination analysis.

Our motivation for this work is two-fold. First, we aim to obtain a better understanding of the notions of boundedness and rigidity which have been introduced to handle partially instantiated input. In this context we show that whenever a program is acceptable wrt a non-bounded level mapping, there always exists a bounded mapping for which the program is still acceptable.

Next, we relate level mappings and norms to their sets of bounded atoms and terms and we take advantage of the order on sets of atoms/terms. We show that this order can be easily expressed in terms of finite sets of argument positions. Maximal sets of bounded atoms (terms) correspond to minimal sets of predicate (functor) argument positions. We use this structure to identify sets of terminating queries for the program and we apply the results in off-line program specialisation to automatically generate termination tests.

1 Introduction

In the context of termination analysis of logic programs *norms* and *level mappings* usually fulfil a central role (see e.g. [4]). Norms are functions that map terms to elements of some well-founded ordered set. In the context of this paper we will restrict the attention to the set $\mathbb{N}, <$. Similarly, level mappings map atoms to elements of $\mathbb{N}, <$. The aim of this paper is to provide some structure on the norm (and level mapping) spaces, to analyse that structure and to exploit it to provide new insight in (applications of) termination analysis.

There are two fairly different lines of motivation for this work. In this introduction, we discuss both of them in some detail.

1.1 Boundedness and rigidity

A first motivation is to provide a better understanding of the role of the notions of *boundedness* and *rigidity* in termination proofs. Let $Term_P$ and $Atom_P$ denote the sets of all terms and all atoms in the language underlying some program of interest, P. A norm, $||.|| : Term_P \rightarrow I\!N$ (respectively level mapping $|.| : Atom_P \rightarrow I\!N$) is said to be rigid on $t \in Term_P$ (resp. $A \in Atom_P$), if for every substitution θ : $||t\theta|| = ||t||$ (resp.$|A\theta| = |A|$). Similarly, a norm, $||.||$ (resp. level mapping $|.|$) is said to be bounded on $t \in Term_P$ (resp. $A \in Atom_P$), if $\{||t\theta|| \mid \theta$ a (grounding[1]) substitution $\}$ (resp. $\{|A\theta| \mid \theta$ a (grounding[1]) substitution $\}$) is bounded in $I\!N$.

In most approaches to left-termination analysis (see e.g. [1], [2]), termination proofs are only obtained for those atoms that are bounded or rigid with respect to the considered level mapping. Intuitively, the reason for this is that the proposed termination conditions are expressed in terms of decreases of the level mapping *local within each clause*[2].

Let us clarify the point. In what follows, in order to simplify the issues, we restrict our attention to directly recursive programs only. In that restricted context, the acceptability condition of [1] requires the existence of a level mapping, $|.|$, and of a model of P, I, such that for each ground instance, say $A \leftarrow B_1, \cdots, B_n$, of a clause in P, and for each atom B_i:

$$\text{if } I \models B_1, \cdots, B_{i-1} \text{ then } |A| > |B_i|$$

As we indicated above, the main reason why such a condition only implies termination for those queries that are bounded with respect to the level mapping is that the condition is completely *local* to the clause level. It expresses well-founded decreases *within* each applied clause separately, but fails to capture the unification/resolution steps between the calls of one clause and the heads of others. Therefore, in order to ensure that the local decreases can be combined into finite sequences of decreases on the level of the derivation, the top-level goal needs to be bounded. Otherwise, an infinite sequence of local decreases (generating, in the limit, infinitely large terms in the top level goal) cannot be ruled out.

In [5] a non-local variant of acceptability was introduced. That variant does take the unification/resolution step into account in the imposed decrease. As such, it is less easy to reason about by programmers, but, on the other hand, turns out to be more easily combined within abstract interpretation analysis techniques (see e.g. [9]). For directly recursive programs, it is formalised as follows.

Definition 1.1 (call set, [5])
Let P be a definite program and S a set of atomic queries. The *call set*,

---

[1]Some definitions in the literature require the use of grounding substitutions only, others don't.

[2]Note that this facilitates very much the reasoning of the programmer on the termination of his program. Non-local conditions are much harder to verify manually.

$Call(P, S)$, is the set of all atoms A, such that a variant of A is a selected atom in some derivation for a pair (P, Q), for some $Q \in S$ and under the left-to-right selection rule.

Definition 1.2 **(acceptability wrt S, [5])**
Let S be a set of atomic queries and P a definite, directly recursive program. P is *acceptable wrt* S if there exists a level mapping $|.|$ such that

- for any $A \in Call(P, S)$
- for any clause $A' \leftarrow B_1, \cdots, B_n$ in P, such that $\text{mgu}(A, A') = \theta$ exists,
- for any atom B_i having the same predicate symbol as A
- for any computed answer substitution θ' for $\leftarrow (B_1, \cdots, B_{i-1})\theta$:

$$|A| > |B_i\theta\theta'|$$

The notion of acceptability wrt S relates to left-termination in the following way:

Proposition 1.3 **(see [5])**
A directly recursive program P terminates under the left-to-right selection rule for all queries in S iff P is acceptable wrt S.

Notice the complete absence of any boundedness or rigidity constraint. Also notice that this acceptability condition imposes a decrease between every call and its recursively descending next call to the same predicate. Thereby, it takes the unification step into account, making boundedness or rigidity constraints redundant.

In the context of this first motivation, our aim in this paper is to investigate the extent in which this absence of boundedness and rigidity constraints actually affects the power of the analysis. Note that, in principle, it could possibly have no effect at all. Namely, imagine that for each atom which is not bounded wrt the considered level mapping the acceptability condition systematically fails to hold. If that would be the case, then we would not be able to derive any new termination proofs at all. The following example shows that this is *not* the case.

Example 1.4 **(append)**
Consider the append program.

$$\begin{array}{ll} \text{append}(nil, L, L) & \leftarrow \\ \text{append}([H|T], Y, [H|S]) & \leftarrow \text{append}(T, Y, S). \end{array}$$

Let $||.||_t$ be the term-size norm (which counts the number of functors occurring in a term), let $|append(t_1, t_2, t_3)| = ||t_1||_t$, for any $t_1, t_2, t_3 \in Term_P$ and let S be $\{append(t_1, t_2, t_3) \mid t_1$ is a nil-terminated list and (t_1, t_3) is linear$\}$.

Note that $Call(P, S) = S$. Also, $|.|$ is not bounded on S (and therefore definitely not rigid on any non-ground term of S). Still, append is acceptable wrt S, for the given $|.|$.

Comparing with the standard acceptability notion of [1], there, using the same level mapping $|.|$, termination can only be proved for the elements of S that are bounded wrt $|.|$, namely $S' = \{append(t_1, t_2, t_3) \mid t_1$ is a ground nil-terminated list$\}$. Of course, termination for S itself can be obtained using acceptability too, by just switching to the level mapping $|.|_2$, with $|append(t_1, t_2, t_3)|_2 = ||t_1||_l$, where $||.||_l$ is the list-length norm. Yet another possibility is to use acceptability wrt S (Definition 1.2), but with the level mapping $|.|_2$ instead of $|.|$. Again, left-termination of append for S follows.

This brings us to a key question concerning the added value of being able to prove termination for terms which are not bounded wrt the level mapping. Is it the case that if a program is acceptable wrt S for some level mapping $|.|$, then there always exists another level mapping $|.|_2$, such that S is bounded wrt $|.|_2$ and P remains acceptable wrt S? If so, is it always the case that such a level mapping $|.|_2$ can easily be derived from $|.|$? We address these issues in Section 3.

1.2 Generating termination conditions for program specialisation

In [3] a new approach to program specialisation is introduced. In a preprocessing phase, a transformation is performed which makes the desired control for unfolding during specialisation explicit. As an example — using somewhat different terminology from [3] — the append program could be transformed into

$$
\begin{array}{l}
new\_append(nil, L, L) \leftarrow \\
new\_append([H|T], Y, [H|S]) \leftarrow \\
\quad (terminates(append([H|T], Y, [H|S])) \\
\quad\quad \rightarrow append([H|T], Y, [H|S]); \\
\quad safe\_unfoldable(append([H|T], Y, [H|S])) \\
\quad\quad \rightarrow new\_append(T, Y, S); \\
\quad memoise(new\_append([H|T], Y, [H|S])))
\end{array}
$$

If a call to append is guaranteed to terminate, just call the original program to execute the call, else, if it is safe to produce some unfolding steps (for instance, because some well-founded measure decreases) then perform these unfoldings, else memoise the call.

The approach is very appealing because it unifies off-line and on-line specialisation. In *on-line specialisation*, the various tests in the transformed program can be verified during specialisation. In *off-line specialisation*, a program analysis step should generate sufficient preconditions under which the tests hold. These should then replace the original tests and act as annotations for the off-line specialiser.

In this paper we concentrate on the analysis involved in the off-line case. More specifically, we restrict ourselves to the test *terminates*(.) for which we would like to propose sufficient conditions.

At first glance, this looks like something that could be done by direct application of termination analysis. However, in this particular context, we would like to be able to generate a precondition which is as weak as possible. More specifically: different choices for the norm and level mapping in our termination analysis will give rise to different sets of calls for which termination is proved. How can we structure and analyse the norm and level mapping spaces, so that this can provide us with the largest possible set of terminating queries.

In section 2, we introduce some preliminaries. Section 3 presents the results on the role of boundedness and rigidity. In section 4 we structure norm and level mapping spaces in view of the off-line specialisation approach. We adapt our constraints-based termination analysis of [6] to these results in section 5. We end with a discussion. Most of the proofs have been omitted. We refer to [7].

2 Preliminaries

The following definitions are inspired by [2]. They make use of the notions of the extended Herbrand Universe U_P^E and Herbrand Base B_P^E which were originally introduced in [8].

Definition 2.1 **(generalised level mapping)**
Let P be a directly recursive, definite program. A *generalised level mapping* for P is a function $|.| : B_P^E \rightarrow \mathbb{N}$.

With some abuse of notation, we will apply generalised level mappings directly on elements of $Atom_P$, omitting reference to the variant equivalence classes. We will also drop 'generalised' from our terminology.

In view of the condition of acceptability wrt a set of atoms, we need a more refined notion of rigidity of a level mapping, relative to the atoms involved.

Definition 2.2 **(rigidity)**
A level mapping $|.| : Atom_P \rightarrow \mathbb{N}$ is said to be *rigid on* $A \in Atom_P$ *wrt a set of atoms* $S \subseteq Atom_P$, if for every substitution $\theta : |A\theta| = |A|$ if $A\theta \in S$.
A level mapping is *rigid on an atom* A if it is rigid on A wrt $Atom_P$.

A similar notion exists for boundedness.

Definition 2.3 **(boundedness)**
A level mapping $|.|$ is said to be *bounded on* $A \in Atom_P$ *wrt a set of atoms* $S \subseteq Atom_P$, if $\{|A\theta| \mid \theta$ a substitution with $A\theta \in S\}$ is bounded in $\mathbb{N}$.
A level mapping is *bounded on* $A \in Atom_P$ if it is bounded on A wrt $Atom_P$.

By characterising termination, acceptability inherits the undecidability of the halting problem. In particular, the existence of the level mapping is the undecidable property here. To facilitate a more systematic search for such a level mapping, these are often expressed as a (positive) combination of norms.

$$\forall p/n \in Pred_P : |p(t_1, \cdots, t_n)| = \sum_{i \in I_p} ||t_i||$$

A norm is *trivial* if it is the constant zero-mapping. A particularly interesting set of norms is given under the form of semi-linear norms. For such norms, it can be syntactically verified whether or not a term is rigid (see [2]).

Definition 2.4 (semi-linear norm)
A norm $||.||$ is *semi-linear* if it can be recursively defined by means of the following schema:

$\|\|V\|\|$	$=$	0	if V is a variable, and
$\|\|f(t_1, ..., t_n)\|\|$	$=$	c_f+	with $c_f \in I\!N, c_f, i_1, ..., i_m$ only
		$\|\|t_{i_1}\|\| + ... + \|\|t_{i_m}\|\|$	dependent on f/n,and
			$1 \leq i_1 < ... < i_m \leq n$.

Notice that a semi-linear norm is trivial if for each functor f, the constant c_f is zero.

3 The role of rigidity

In this section, we provide answers to our first questions concerning the role of rigidity and boundedness. We first address the question whether there always exists a bounded level mapping implying acceptability wrt a set of atoms S whenever acceptability wrt S holds wrt an unbounded one.

In the following, we say that a level mapping $|.|$ is *monotonic* ([9]) on a set of atoms S if for any atom A of S and for any substitution θ such that $A\theta \in S$: $|A| \geq |A\theta|$. Clearly, monotonicity implies boundedness.

Proposition 3.1
Let P be a definite program, S a set of atomic queries and $|.|$ a level mapping such that P is acceptable wrt $|.|$ and S. Then there exists a level mapping $|.|_r$ such that P is acceptable wrt $|.|_r$ and such that $|.|_r$ is monotonic on the call set $Call(P, S)$.

Proof We first introduce the following notation. $Gen(A)$ stands for the set $\{B \mid B\theta = A \text{ and } B \in Call(P, S)\}$ of all call atoms that are more general than A. $Gen_{|.|}(A)$ will denote the set $\{|B| \mid B \in Gen(A)\}$.

Given $|.|$, let $|.|_r$ be defined as $|A|_r = \mathbf{min}\ Gen_{|.|}(A)$, for any A in $Call(P, S)$.

(1) $|.|_r$ *is monotonic on* $Call(P,S)$. Let $|A|_r = \min\ Gen_{|.|}(A)$ and $|A\theta|_r = \min\ Gen_{|.|}(A\theta)$. Obviously, the set $Gen(A)$ is a subset of $Gen(A\theta)$ as for any member B of $Gen(A)$ with $B\sigma = A$, there exists the substitution $\sigma\theta$ such that $B\sigma\theta = A\theta$. Thus, $Gen_{|.|}(A)$ is a subset of $Gen_{|.|}(A\theta)$, so that $|A|_r \geq |A\theta|_r$ follows.
(2) P *is acceptable wrt* $|.|_r$. Take any call $A \in Call(P,S)$ and any clause $H \leftarrow B_1, \cdots, B_{i-1}, B_i, \cdots$ of P, such that $\theta = mgu(A,H)$ exists and θ' is a computed answer for $\leftarrow (B_1, \cdots, B_{i-1})\theta$. Then the following decrease must hold: $|A|_r > |B_i\theta\theta'|_r$.

In other words, it must hold that for each $A_g \in Gen(A)$, there exists a $B \in Gen(B_i\theta\theta')$ such that $|A_g| > |B|$. Now, as A_g is more general than A, the $mgu(A_g, H) = \rho$ also exists and $(B_1, \cdots, B_{i-1})\rho$ is more general than $(B_1, \cdots, B_{i-1})\theta$. In that case, there exists a computed answer substitution ρ' for $(B_1, \cdots, B_{i-1})\rho$. Moreover, ρ' is such that $B\rho\rho'$ is more general than $B_i\theta\theta'$ and thus $B\rho\rho' \in Gen(B_i\theta\theta')$. Now, recall that P is acceptable wrt $|.|$ and S. As A_g is an element of $Call(P,S)$, $|A_g| > |B\rho\rho'|$. □

Example 3.2 Consider the append program and let it be queried as in Example 1.4, with its first argument a nil-terminated list. Its call set is : $\{\ append(t_1,t_2,t_3) \mid t_1$ is a nil-terminated list and (t_1,t_2,t_3) is linear$\}$. As stated in Example 1.4, append is acceptable wrt the level mapping $|append(t_1,t_2,t_3)| = ||t_1||_t$.

Then the monotonic norm corresponding to append is the norm $|append(t_1,t_2,t_3)|_r = ||t_1||_l$ considering the list-length of the first argument. It can be obtained by applying the above proposition. Take any $append(t_1,t_2,t_3)$ in the call set. We know that t_1 has the form $[s_1, \cdots, s_n]$. Then:

$$\begin{aligned} |append([s_1,\cdots,s_n],t_2,t_3)|_r = min\{\ & |append(u_1,u_2,u_3)| \mid \\ & append(u_1,u_2,u_3)\theta = append([s_1,\cdots,s_n],t_2,t_3), \\ & append(u_1,u_2,u_3) \in Call(P,S)\} \end{aligned}$$

That minimum is reached for a substitution mapping the first argument to a list of n variables, specifying that $|append([s_1,\cdots,s_n],t_2,t_3)|_r = n$, or, in a more familiar way, $|append(t_1,t_2,t_3)|_r = ||t_1||_l$.

In the following, we again assume that level mappings are defined on predicates as a positive combination of a semi-linear norm of some of the argument positions. An important question is then whether the monotonic level mapping $|.|_r$ can again be expressed as in terms of one semi-linear norm. The following observation from [2] for semi-linear norms is of great importance.

$$||t\theta|| = ||t|| + \sum_{V \in SREL(t)} ||V\theta||$$

where $SREL(t)$ is the multiset of all variables 'selected' by the norm.

For semi-linear norms, it implies that $||t|| \leq ||t\theta||$. In our context, it makes explicit that when searching for the minimum of a semi-linear norm on a set of terms, all instances of such terms may be discarded. Moreover, it clarifies that, for level mappings based on semi-linear norms, monotonicity collides with rigidity. In other words, the level mapping $|.|_r$ is rigid whenever it can be expressed in terms of a semi-linear norm.

Unfortunately, this level mapping can not always be defined in terms of one semi-linear norm, as the following example illustrates.

Example 3.3

$$p([H|T],[S|L]) \leftarrow p(T,L).$$

Let p be queried with atoms of the set $S = \{p(t_1, t_2) \mid t_1 \text{ or } t_2 \text{ is a nil-terminated list } \}$. Its call set is again the same set S. Then, the program is acceptable wrt S and the following level mapping

$$|p(t_1, t_2)| = ||t_1||_l + ||t_2||_l$$

However, there does not exist a rigid level mapping expressed in terms of one semi-linear norm. As $p(X, l)$ is in the call set for some variable X and any possible list l, it would require that for any substitution θ, for which $p(X, l)\theta$ is again in the call set, $|p(X, l)| = |p(X, l)\theta|$. Notice that $p(X, l)\theta \in Call(P, S)$ for any θ. Fixing l as the empty list, and expressing $|.|$ in terms of one norm, $||X|| = ||X\theta||$ must hold for all θ.

As such, the general conclusion is that, in the context of automatic termination analysis, where most often *only* semi-linear norms are considered, the ability to work with non-bounded level mappings *does* increase the power of the analysis.

4 Structuring the norm space

In this second part, we introduce some basic properties on the relations between different norms that will allow us to address our second motivation: inferring sufficient preconditions for termination in the context of off-line specialisation.

One aspect of this problem is completely different from the setting that we had in the previous section. In Section 3, we assumed that the set S of queries of interest was given. In this section — and the next — only the program is given. The problem is to find a set of queries S (preferably as large as possible), such that the program terminates for all these queries. This involves two sub-problems:

1. Given a fixed level mapping $|.|$, what is the set of queries S such that P is acceptable wrt S under $|.|$?

2. Based on this answer, find a level mapping that maximises the associated set S.

To answer the first question, we make use of the following definitions and proposition of [6].

Definition 4.1 (rigid acceptability wrt S)
Let S be a set of atomic queries and P a definite, directly recursive program. We say that P is *rigidly acceptable wrt* S if there exists a level mapping $|.|$ which is rigid on $Call(P, S)$ and a model I for P, such that

- for any clause $H \leftarrow B_1, \cdots, B_n \in P$, and
- for any atom B_i in its body which has the same predicate symbol as H,
- for any substitution θ such that $I \models (B_1 \wedge \cdots \wedge B_{i-1})\theta$:

  $|H\theta| > |B_i\theta|$,

Proposition 4.2 (see [6])
If P is rigidly acceptable wrt S for a level mapping $|.|$, then P is acceptable wrt S and $|.|$.

The relevance of this proposition in our current context is that it provides us with a practical constraint to propose candidate sets S for which P terminates according to $|.|$. Namely, consider only those queries which are rigid wrt $|.|$. Then select from those the ones that fulfil the rigid acceptability condition. The latter will be imposed as a set of additional constraints, using the constraint-based termination analysis of [6] (see Section 5).

Example 4.3 (append)
Given the append program and the level mapping $|append(t_1, t_2, t_3)| = ||t_1||_l$, the set of rigid atoms wrt $|.|$ is $S = \{append(t_1, t_2, t_3) \mid t_1$ is a nil-terminated list $\}$. The rigid acceptability condition will impose no further constraints on this set. So S will be inferred.

Note however that the rigidity constraint (as argued in the previous section) is in principle too strong. If in the example we would have selected the level mapping $|append(t_1, t_2, t_3)|' = ||t_1||_t$, the rigid atoms would be $S' = \{append(t_1, t_2, t_3) \mid t_1$ is a ground nil-terminated list $\}$. However, the constraint offers a practical way of proposing a sufficient precondition for termination. Therefore, we will apply it in this context.

In the remainder of this section we study the effect of the choice of the norm (and level mapping) on the size of the resulting set S.

In the following we denote by *bounded*$(||.||)$ the set of all terms that are bounded by a norm $||.||$, and by *rigid*$(||.||)$ the set of all terms which are rigid wrt $||.||$. The sets of terms that are bounded with respect to a norm, induce a natural partial order on all norms:

Definition 4.4 **(partial order on norms)**
$||.||_1 \leq ||.||_2$ if $bounded(||.||_1) \subseteq bounded(||.||_2)$.

Semi-linear norms can be completely characterised in terms of their argument positions.

Definition 4.5 **(functor and predicate arguments)**
The set of functor arguments, respectively predicate arguments associated to a program P are the sets

$$FunArgs_P = \{\ f_i \mid f/n \in Fun_P \wedge 1 \leq i \leq n\}.$$
$$PredArgs_P = \{\ p_i \mid p/n \in Pred_P \wedge 1 \leq i \leq n\}.$$

We release the subscript P when no confusion is possible.

In the next definitions, we assume the program P fixed. We also exclude the trivial norm from the class of semi-linear ones.

Definition 4.6 **(selected functor arguments)**
The *selected functor arguments* of a semi-linear norm $||.||$ is the set:

$$SFA(||.||) = \{\ f_k \in FunArgs \mid ||f(t_1, ..., t_n)|| \text{ is defined as } c_f + ||t_{i_1}|| + ... + ||t_{i_m}|| \wedge \exists j \in \{1, ..., m\} : k = i_j\ \}$$

From the above it must be clear that there is a direct correspondence between sets of functor arguments and semi-linear norms. Each set of arguments positions defines one semi-linear norm (up to the constants c_f) and vice versa.

In view of our goal, given a norm, it is particularly interesting to associate it with a (maximal) set of bounded terms. For semi-linear norms, this set of bounded terms can be iteratively constructed.

Consider the following operator $B_{||.||}$.

Definition 4.7 **($B_{||.||}$)**
Let S be any subset of U_P^E. Then

$$B_{||.||}(S) = S \cup \{f(t_1, \cdots, t_n) \in U_P^E \mid t_i \in S \text{ if } f_i \in SFA(||.||)\}$$

We can define powers of this operator as usual.

$$B_{||.||} \uparrow 0 = \emptyset$$
$$B_{||.||} \uparrow n+1 = B_{||.||}(B_{||.||} \uparrow n)$$
$$B_{||.||} \uparrow \omega = \cup_{i<\omega} B_{||.||} \uparrow i$$

Observe that the operator is continuous. As a result a least fixpoint exists.

Proposition 4.8
Let $||.||$ be a semi-linear norm. Then

$$B_{||.||} \uparrow \omega = rigid(||.||).$$

Proposition 4.9
For a semi-linear norm $||.||, rigid(||.||) = bounded(||.||)$.

Proposition 4.10
Let $||.||_1$ and $||.||_2$ be two semi-linear norms. Then

$$||.||_1 \leq ||.||_2 \text{ iff } SFA(||.||_1) \supseteq SFA(||.||_2).$$

Example 4.11 Consider the termsize and listlength norms and let the listconstructor be the only functor. They are ordered as $||.||_t < ||.||_l$ as $SFA(||.||_l) \subset SFA(||.||_t)$. $bounded(||.||_t)$ consists of all ground lists while $bounded(||.||_l)$ is, as expected, the larger set of all nil-terminated lists.

We now come back to the characterisation of level mappings as a sum of the norms of selected argument positions. Note that by associating a set of 'selected' argument positions I_p to each predicate symbol these level mappings can be completely characterised:

$$SPA(|.|) = \{p_i \mid p \in Pred_P \text{ and } i \in I_p\}$$

Conversely, any subset of $PredArgs$ identifies uniquely a level mapping by fixing all subsets I_p.

The definitions of the set of bounded and rigid terms inspire similar definitions for level mappings, which we overload as $bounded(|.|)$ and $rigid(|.|)$. Just as for norms, the set of bounded atoms induces a partial order on level mappings.
As a result, for level mappings expressed in terms of semi-linear norms, the operator $B_{||.||}$ can be used to characterise all bounded atoms:

$$bounded(|.|) = \{p(t_1, \cdots, t_n) \in B_P^E \mid t_i \in bounded(||.||) \text{ if } p_i \in SPA(|.|)\}$$

We are now able to formulate the main proposition of this section.

Proposition 4.12
Let $|.|_1$ and $|.|_2$ be two level mappings defined in terms of norms $||.||_1$ and $||.||_2$ respectively. Then

$$|.|_1 \leq |.|_2 \text{ iff } SFA(||.||_2) \subseteq SFA(||.||_1) \text{ and } SPA(|.|_2) \subseteq SPA(|.|_1)$$

Example 4.13 Again, suppose that there is only one functor, namely the list constructor. Consider the following level mappings, which we abbreviate l_0 till l_6.

$$|append(t_1, t_2, t_3)|_0 = 0$$
$$|append(t_1, t_2, t_3)|_1 = ||t_1||_l \qquad |append(t_1, t_2, t_3)|_2 = ||t_1||_t$$
$$|append(t_1, t_2, t_3)|_3 = ||t_3||_l \qquad |append(t_1, t_2, t_3)|_4 = ||t_3||_t$$
$$|append(t_1, t_2, t_3)|_5 = ||t_1||_l + ||t_3||_l \qquad |append(t_1, t_2, t_3)|_6 = ||t_1||_t + ||t_3||_t$$

Figure 1 expresses the relations that exist among these level mappings. An arrow from level mapping l_i to l_j expresses that $l_i > l_j$.

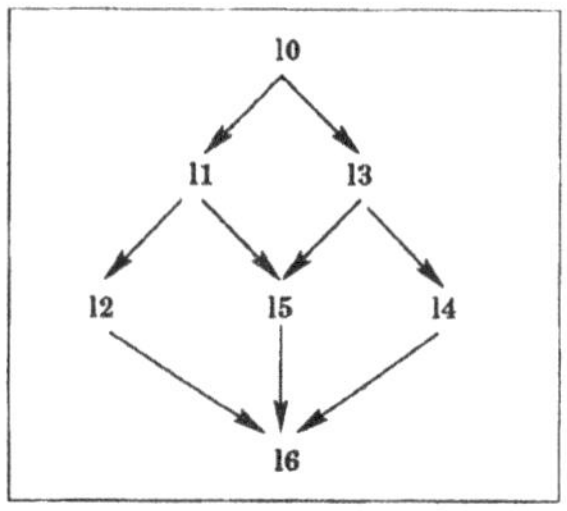

Figure 1: Part of the level mapping space for some well-known instances.

5 Synthesising terminating queries from programs

In this section we start from a constraint characterisation of level mappings and norms as presented in [6]. Applying the termination analysis of [6] will add sufficient constraints to select only those level mappings which fulfil the clausal condition in the definition of rigid acceptability. Then each level mapping which corresponds to a solution of this constraint system identifies a set of terminating queries. Our goal is then to identify a minimal subset of these solutions, covering a maximal set of terminating queries. In particular, identifying the union of all terminating queries is preferably.

We first propose a simplified (to our purpose) version of the level mapping characterisation in [6]. In the following, let C stand for $FunArgs \cup PredArgs \cup \{f_0 \mid f \in Fun_P\}$. This last component set associates with each functor a constant.

Definition 5.1 (symbol mapping)
A *symbol mapping* is a mapping $s : C \rightarrow \mathbb{N}$.

It is easy to see that each symbol mapping s characterises a level mapping $|.|$ and a norm $||.||$ by setting $SPA(||.||) = \{p_i \mid p_i \in C \text{ and } s(p_i) \neq 0\}$, and $SFA(||.||) = \{f_i \mid f_i \in C \text{ and } s(f_i) \neq 0\}$. Additionally, symbol mappings also fix the constants associated to each functor f as $s(f_0)$. In the following, we overload the notations SPA and SFA on symbol mappings. The level mapping (resp. norm) corresponding to any symbol mapping s will be denoted by $|.|^s$ (resp. $||.||^s$).

Definition 5.2 (acceptable symbol mapping)
s is called an *acceptable symbol mapping* wrt a definite program P if the clausal condition of rigid acceptability holds for P wrt $|.|^s$.

For such a level mapping $|.|^s$, the program P will be terminating wrt any set of queries such that $|.|^s$ is rigid on $Call(P, S)$. In [6], acceptable symbol mappings can be derived from the program P. The characterisation is in terms of constraint sets.

Definition 5.3 **(constraint set and solution)**
A *constraint set* is a set of equations and inequalities over the symbols in $\mathcal{C}$. A symbol mapping s is a *solution of a constraint set* S iff $\forall E \in S : s(E)$.

Example 5.4 **(append)**
An acceptable constraint set for the append program, obtained through the approach in [6] corresponds to the set

$$\{\bullet_0 = 1, \bullet_2 = 1, a_1 + a_3 > 0\}$$

where $\bullet$ stands for the list constructor and a_1 abbreviates $append_1$. The set characterises the level mappings $|.|_1$ till $|.|_6$ of Example 4.13.

[6] proposes a systematic approach for deriving constraint sets having only acceptable symbol mappings as solutions. Given now an 'acceptable' constraint set, probably characterising several acceptable level mappings, as our motivation consists in proposing an as large set of terminating queries as possible, the goal is to synthesise a set of minimal solutions, from which a maximal number of rigid queries can be derived. In other words, given a set of constraints on the symbols, find a minimal set of solutions covering a maximal number of atoms/terms. In Example 4.13, it corresponds to identifying both the level mappings l_1 and l_3.

First, notice that symbol mappings can be partially ordered by defining $s_1 \leq s_2$ if $SPA(s_1) \supseteq SPA(s_2)$ and $SFA(s_1) \supseteq SFA(s_2)$, and as a result of Proposition 4.10, $||.||^{s_1} \leq ||.||^{s_2}$.

Definition 5.5 **(minimal solution set)**
Let C be an acceptable constraint set for a program P. Then a set of norms N is a *minimal solution set* for C iff for each norm $||.||_C$ being a solution for C, $\exists n \in N : n \leq ||.||_C$.

Minimal solution sets are obtained by selecting those symbol mappings setting all free choices to 0, as this minimises the set of selected argument positions.

Example 5.6 **(append)**
The constraint set of Example 5.4 contains two minimal solution sets:

$$\left\{ \begin{array}{c} \bullet_0 = 1 \\ \bullet_2 = 1 \\ a_1 = 1 \end{array} \right\} \quad \text{and} \quad \left\{ \begin{array}{c} \bullet_0 = 1 \\ \bullet_2 = 1 \\ a_3 = 1 \end{array} \right\}$$

$\{\bullet_0 = 1, \bullet_2 = 1, a_1 = 1, a_3 = 1\}$ is another solution but is contained in our minimal solution set. Also, mapping any of the remaining constants like e.g. $\bullet_1$ to 1 corresponds to a non-minimal solution.

The set of rigid queries in this case consists of the set of atoms

$$\{append(t_1, t_2, t_3) \mid t_1 \text{ is nil-terminated or } t_3 \text{ is nil-terminated } \}$$

From both solution sets, we can now easily express the *terminates* test predicate for the *new_append* example of section 1.2. In general, each solution (as it identifies a set of terminating queries) provides on alternative definition. Consider the first solution set. Each predicate argument p_i results in an extra condition in the body, constraining argument position i for that predicate: $terminates(append(X, Y, Z)) \leftarrow bounded(X)$. Each functor position f_j causes a new condition on position j to be added to a clause testing for boundedness of f-terms: $bounded([X|Y]) \leftarrow bounded(Y)$.

As the functor constraints in both solutions are the same, namely $\bullet_2 = 1$, the same definition can be used in both *terminates* clauses. We then get:

$$terminates(append(X, Y, Z)) \leftarrow list\_bounded(X).$$
$$terminates(append(X, Y, Z)) \leftarrow list\_bounded(Z).$$

$$list\_bounded(X) \leftarrow var(X), fail.$$
$$list\_bounded(L) \leftarrow ground(L).$$
$$list\_bounded([X|Y]) \leftarrow list\_bounded(Y).$$

6 Conclusions

The notions of boundedness and rigidity have played an important role in the field of termination analysis. In the first part of this paper, the main result expresses that whenever a program is acceptable wrt a set of atoms for some (non-bounded) level mapping, there always exists a second bounded level mapping, for which the program is still acceptable wrt the same set of atoms. However, from a practical viewpoint, given a level mapping expressed in terms of a semi-linear norm, the bounded mapping can not always be expressed through the same scheme.

In a second part, we have ordered norms and level mappings by considering the sets of all atoms and terms for which they are rigid: a level mapping is larger than a second one if it is rigid on more atoms. By employing a characterisation of norms and level mappings in terms of sets of argument positions, we obtain an elegant reformulation of that order in terms of inclusion of finite sets of selected argument positions (of both the norm and the level mapping): a level mapping is larger than a second one if it considers less arguments.

We have applied these results in off-line program specialisation, with the eye towards deriving suffient termination conditions from a program. By using a constraint-based termination analysis on the program, we can identify in which part of the norm and level mapping space acceptable instances occur. The order relation on sets of argument positions allows to search that sub-space for those instances which are minimal. This guarantees that a maximal number of queries, for which the program is terminating, are covered. Both the constraint-based analysis and the search for minimal solutions can be fully automated.

References

[1] K.R. Apt and D. Pedreschi. Studies in pure Prolog: termination. In *Proceedings Esprit symposium on computational logic*, pages 150–176, Brussels, november 1990. Springer-Verlag.

[2] A. Bossi, N. Cocco, and M. Fabris. Norms on terms and their use in proving universal termination of a logic program. *Theoretical Computer Science*, 124(2):297–328, februari 1994.

[3] M. Bruynooghe, M. Leuschel, and K. Sagonas. A polyvariant binding-time analysis for off-line partial deduction. Technical report, Department Computer Science, K.U.Leuven, draft october 1997.

[4] D. De Schreye and S. Decorte. Termination of logic programs: the never-ending story. *Journal of Logic Programming*, 19 & 20:199–260, may/july 1994.

[5] D. De Schreye, K. Verschaetse, and M. Bruynooghe. A framework for analysing the termination of definite logic programs with respect to call patterns. In *Proc. FGCS'92*, pages 481–488, ICOT Tokyo, 1992. ICOT.

[6] S. Decorte and D. De Schreye. Demand-driven and constraint-based automatic termination analysis for logic programs. In L. Naish, editor, *Proc. 14th International Conference on Logic Programming*, pages 78–92, Leuven, Belgium, july 1997.

[7] S. Decorte and D. De Schreye. Termination analysis: some practical properties of the norm and level mapping space. Technical report, Department of Computer Science, K.U.Leuven, 1998.

[8] M. Falaschi, G. Levi, M. Martelli, and C. Palamidessi. Declarative modelling of the operational behaviour of logic languages. *Theoretical Computer Science*, 69(3):289–318, 1989.

[9] K. Verschaetse. *Static Termination Analysis for Definite Horn Clause Programs*. PhD thesis, Dept. Computer Science, K.U.Leuven, 1992. Accessible via `http://www.cs.kuleuven.ac.be/~lpai`.

On Logically Justified Updates [1]

Michael Dekhtyar
Dept. of CS, Tver State Univ.
3 Zheljabova str. Tver, Russia, 170013
Michael.Dekhtyar@tversu.ru

Alexander Dikovsky
Keldysh Institute for Applied Math.
4 Miusskaya sq. Moscow, Russia, 125047
dikovsky@spp.keldysh.ru

Nicolas Spyratos
Université de Paris-Sud, LRI, U.R.A. 410 du CNRS, Bât. 490
F-91405 Orsay Cedex, France
Nicolas.Spyratos@lri.fr

Abstract The Enforced Update Problem we investigate in this paper is as follows: given a theory T which formalizes integrity constraints, an initial state $I \models T$, and an external update Δ which specifies the facts D^+ to be added to I and the facts D^- to be deleted from it, one should introduce minimal changes $\Psi(I)$ in I, sufficient to accomplish Δ and to restore T if and when it is violated, i.e. to guarantee that $D^+ \subseteq \Psi(I), \Psi(I) \cap D^- = \emptyset$, *and* $\Psi(I) \models T$. We give an axiomatic description of such logically justified updates Ψ and describe their reasonable implementation.

1 Introduction

To put it very generally, a database (DB) or a knowledge base (KB) can be seen as a theory T whose models represent states (worlds). The difference between the two is that KBs T are supposed to be deductively closed, whereas this is not necessary of DBs. However in Deductive Data Bases (DDBs), similar to KBs, the *extensional* and *intensional* parts of states are distinguished. The first makes the explicit part of a state, whereas the other is available through its closure. In conventional DBs nothing but the extensional part exists. The difference between KBs and DBs becomes clearer in presence of *actions* changing their states. Speaking of DBs one has in mind a system of conditions on states, *integrity constraints* (IC), which should be preserved after changes. Meanwhile, the IC are optional for KBs. In KBs the actions incorporate some new knowledge into theories representing states, this being accompanied by subsequent logically justified changes. As

[1] This work was sponsored by the Russian Fundamental Studies Foundation (Grants 96-01-00395, 97-01-00973).

a result the theories evolve.

Two main approaches to modifying KB and DB states should be distinguished: *revisions* and *updates*. Loosely speaking the revision applies to the whole theory T in some constructive representation (formula, logic program, etc.) and to some new knowledge p and describes the resulting class of states (worlds) in terms of another theory T'. In other words the revision is theory oriented (cf. [23]). In contrast, the update applies simultaneously and independently to individual models of T and transforms them into some models of p. In other words it is pointwise model oriented.

The first effort to formalize the KB modifications was made by Gärdenfors and his colleagues [1, 11] who have proposed some philosophically founded set of postulates. Later Katsuno and Mendelzon [15] have refined these postulates in propositional case. They were first to point out the distinction between the notions of revision and update. Quite nonevidently the axioms of Katsuno and Mendelzon express a very important principle, that of a *minimal change* produced in initial models to obtain the resulting models. This principle was subsequently expressed by many authors through some explicit criterion of minimal difference between two models. The definitions as well as references can be found in the paper [9] where the computational complexity of revisions and updates is explored.

In 1st order case the definitions of DB and KB modifications are complicated by the absence of a satisfactory general constructive interpretation of negation. Various particular semantics were proposed since late seventies (see e.g. [6, 3, 13, 22]). Besides this, different theory interpretations exist: the classical *total* (2-valued) interpretations and the *partial* (3-valued) interpretations. Under total interpretations the truth of $\neg A$ in a model is *equivalent* to the absence of A in this model, whereas this is not the case in general in partial interpretations. Accordingly under total interpretations the models are sets of atoms, and under partial interpretations they are sets of literals. A particular type of interpretations $\mathcal{I}$ being fixed, an update Δ being applied to a KB or a DB specified by a logic program Φ, induces in general a nondeterministic update operator $\Psi_{\Phi,\Delta} : \mathcal{I} \mapsto 2^{\mathcal{I}}$. Sometimes Φ acts as an intensional program, in other cases as IC or even both. Rarely separate logic programs serve for specifying intensional knowledge and IC. There are different techniques of defining the resulting models $\Psi_{\Phi,\Delta}(I)$: sequential, which are based on some notion of a derivation or a computation, now frequently applied to active DBs [7], see e.g. [4, 5, 12, 17, 19, 21, 24], and various nonsequential, such as e.g. revision programming [16], inertia axioms [18, 2], and conflict resolution [14, 10, 8]. There is certain technical dissimilarity between the definitions of KB update operators $\Psi_{\Phi,\Delta}$ from those of DBs. The former generally use some default rule based semantics of negation (CWA [20], stable model semantics [13], etc.), whereas for the latter it is not natural: DB states are determined by actual data. The basic difference between the two is in the way they treat the new data (knowledge) Δ when it is not consistent with Φ. The result of a KB update $\Psi_{\Phi,\Delta}(I)$ in this case is a model of Δ whose deviation from the initial model I is "minimal" and justified by Φ (see [2]). In other words KBs adapt themselves to new knowledge. On the contrary, the result of a DB update $\Psi_{\Phi,\Delta}(I)$ is a model of Φ "minimally deviating" from the initial model I and incorporating a "maximal" part of Δ consistent with Φ. So DBs adapt new data to IC. In both cases the deviation of the resulting model from the initial one is justified by Φ.

This paper substantially extends our previous paper [8]. Here we present an axiomatic definition of DB update operators introducing into DB states minimal necessary changes (we call these operators *conservative*), whereas in [8] a particular algorithm implementing a conservative operator was described and verified. In [8] it is presumed that the external update does not contradict the IC. Here we consider the opposite case too. Besides this, in this parer both, the partial and the total interpretations are considered, whereas in [8] we consider only the partial ones.

This paper is organized as follows. Section 2 contains the basic notions. The axiomatic definition of the conservative update operators is given and discussed in section 3. In section 4 we describe quite a feasible implementation of conservative update operators in the class of partial interpretations, based on conflict resolution technique. In the last section we discuss their implementation in the class of total interpretations.

2 Basic notions and notation

We consider a first order signature $\mathbf{S}$ consisting of a set $\mathbf{C}$ of constants, a set $\mathbf{P}$ of predicates, and a set of variables $\mathbf{V}$. For a finite set of constants $C \subset \mathbf{C}$ in this signature $\mathbf{A}_C$ denotes the set of all atoms in $\mathbf{S}$ with variables in $\mathbf{V}$ and constants in C. $\mathbf{B}_C \subset \mathbf{A}_C$ denotes the set of all ground instances of atoms in $\mathbf{A}_C$ with respect to C. For an atom $a \in \mathbf{A}_C$ both a and $\neg a$ are *literals.* A pair of the form $(a, \neg a)$ or $(\neg a, a)$ is called a *contrary pair.* For a contrary pair (l_1, l_2) we write $l_1 = \neg.l_2$ and $l_2 = \neg.l_1$. The set of all literals over $\mathbf{V}$ and C is denoted by $\mathbf{L}_C$. For each $W \subseteq \mathbf{L}_C$ we denote by $\neg.W$ the set $\{a|\neg a \in W\} \cup \{\neg a|a \in W\}$. $\mathbf{LB}_C$ denotes the set $\mathbf{B}_C \cup \neg.\mathbf{B}_C$. Let Φ be a finite set of clauses of the form

$$r = (l \leftarrow l_1, ..., l_n)$$

where $n \geq 0$ and l, l_i are literals in $\mathbf{L}_C$. We call Φ *integrity constraints,* or simply *IC* and the clauses of Φ *constraints.* A constraint is *normal* if it has an atom in its head. Φ is *normal* if all its constraints are normal. We denote by $ground_C(\Phi)$ the set of all ground instances of constraints in Φ using constants in C. Finite subsets $I \subset \mathbf{LB}_C$ are called *partial interpretations.* For a partial interpretation I we set $I^+ = I \cap \mathbf{B}_C$ and $I^- = I \cap \neg.\mathbf{B}_C$. A partial interpretation I is *total* if $I^+ \cup \neg.I^- = \mathbf{B}_C$. So a total interpretation is completely defined by its positive part. Considering partial interpretations we shall regard them as *DB states*. In this context a DB state is *consistent* if it does not contain contrary pairs. Intuitively, in a consistent partial interpretation I the atoms in I^+ are regarded as true, the atoms in $\neg.I^-$ are regarded as false, and all others are regarded as unknown. Considering only total interpretations we shall call DB states their positive parts I^+. When it does not lead to a conflict, we name I^+ a total interpretation. A constraint $r = (l \leftarrow l_1, ..., l_n)$ is *valid in a DB state* I (denoted $I \models r$) if $I \models l$ whenever $I \models l_i$ for each $1 \leq i \leq n$. When partial interpretations are considered $I \models l$ means $l \in I$. When total interpretations are considered, then for a DB state I and for an atom a $I \models a$ means $a \in I$, and for a literal $l = \neg a$ $I \models l$ means $a \notin I$. Total interpretations are consistent by definition. IC Φ *are valid in a DB state* I if every constraint in Φ is valid in I. This is denoted by $I \models \Phi$. I is a *model* of Φ if it is consistent and $I \models \Phi$.

A pair $\Delta = (D^+, D^-)$ where D^+, D^- are finite subsets of $\mathbf{LB}_C$, and $D^+ \cap D^- = \emptyset$, is called an *update*. Intuitively, the literals of D^+ are to be added to I, and those of D^- are to be removed from I. In total interpretations both D^+ and D^- are sets of atoms. We say that $\Delta = (D^+, D^-)$ is *accomplished* in I if $D^+ \subseteq I$ and $D^- \cap I = \emptyset$.

An *implication tree* of a ground IC Φ for a literal l is a finite tree $T(l)$ whose nodes are labeled by ground literals with no contrary pair among them, the root is labeled by l, and a node v is labeled by a literal l_0 if and only if there is a constraint $r = (l_0 \leftarrow l_1, ..., l_n) \in \Phi$ such that if $n > 0$, then v has sons $v_1, \ldots, v_n$ labeled by $l_1, \ldots, l_n$ respectively. We denote by $cr(T)$ the *crown* of T, i.e. the set of all literals labelling the leaves of T. It is clear that the leaves are labelled by the literals l occurring in facts $l \leftarrow$ of Φ.

For some given Φ, Δ, and I let *con* be the set of all constants which occur in them. We consider below only the constants in *con*, i.e. only the sets $\mathbf{A}_{con}$, $\mathbf{B}_{con}$, $\mathbf{L}_{con}$, $\mathbf{LB}_{con}$, $ground_{con}(\Phi)$, etc., therefore the subscript *con* will be dropped in the sequel.

3 Conservative update operators enforcing IC

We consider the following problem which we call in [8] an *Enforced Update Problem* (*EUP*). Given a DB state I, an update $\Delta = (D^+, D^-)$, and an IC Φ one should find a consistent DB state I_1 such that

- $I_1 \models \Phi$,
- Δ is accomplished in I_1, and
- I_1 is as "*close*" to I as possible.

The first claim says that one needs to restore the IC Φ after the update. The second claim says that the update is enforced in the course of the transformation of the initial DB state. The third claim expresses the conservative nature of the change. It requires that only minimal necessary changes should be performed in the initial state in order to make the resulting DB state satisfy the first two claims.

The *EUP* was resolved in [14] for constraints of the form $l \leftarrow l_1$. The operators providing solutions to the general *EUP* can be naturally axiomatized. Before we proceed to their axiomatization we should introduce some additional notions and notation.

The claim of minimal changes included into the *EUP* should be formulated in terms of some criterion of "closeness" of DB states. We propose a new and very natural criterion, which is a combination of two independent criteria: that of maximal intersection with the initial DB state, and the other, of minimal symmetric difference with respect to this DB state. We proceed from the assumption that it is more important to keep as much initial facts as possible, than to add possibly fewer new facts. The criterion of minimal symmetric difference as a concept of closeness has been frequently used, see for example [15, 9, 16, 18, 14]. The complex criterion we use here is more precise. First it minimizes deletions of available data and then it minimizes insertions of new data. This is put in a precise form as follows.

Definition 1. *Let* I, I_1, I_2 *be three DB states. We say that* I_1 *is* intersection-closer *to* I *than* I_2 *(notation:* $I_1 \geq^I_{it} I_2$*) if* $I \cap I_2 \subseteq I \cap I_1$. *We write* $I_1 \equiv^I_{it} I_2$ *if* $I_1 \geq^I_{it} I_2$ *and* $I_2 \geq^I_{it} I_1$, *and we write* $I_1 >^I_{it} I_2$ *if* $I_1 \geq^I_{it} I_2$ *and* $I_2 \not\geq^I_{it} I_1$. I_1 *is* symmetric-difference-closer *to* I *than* I_2 *(notation:* $I_1 \geq^I_{sd} I_2$*) if* $I \nabla I_1 \subseteq I \nabla I_2$. *We write* $I_1 >^I_{sd} I_2$ *if* $I_1 \geq^I_{sd} I_2$ *and* $I_2 \not\geq^I_{sd} I_1$.

As we have already stressed, the DB states resulting from updates should satisfy the IC. Meanwhile, the update can contradict the IC in general. So we are to face two different situations. In the first situation the IC Φ and the update Δ are consistent. This property is easy to formalize.

Definition 2. *An update* $\Delta = (D^+, D^-)$ *is* consistent *with IC* Φ *if there exists a consistent DB state* I *such that*

- $I \models \Phi$ *and*
- Δ *is accomplished in* I.

In our language the consistency can be checked constructively.

Definition 3. *Let* Φ *be IC. For a given partial interpretation* I

$$cl(I) = \{l \mid \exists r = (l \leftarrow l_1, ..., l_n) \in \Phi \ \ (\bigwedge_{i=1}^{n} I \models l_i\ )\}.$$

A strong immediate consequence operator *is the total operator*

$$T_\Phi(I) = \begin{cases} cl(I) & : \ cl(I) \text{ is consistent} \\ \mathbf{LB} & : \ cl(I) \text{ is inconsistent.} \end{cases}$$

Let us denote this operator by $T^{\in}_\Phi$ *in the case of partial interpretations and by* $T^{\models}_\Phi$ *in the case of total interpretations.*

Several useful remarks can be made concerning $T_\Phi^\in(I)$.

1. In contrast to the classical positive Horn logic programs, an interpretation I such that $cl(I) \subseteq I$, is not always a model of Φ because it can be inconsistent. In the latter case $T_\Phi^\in(I) = \mathbf{LB}$. Let us call the interpretations with the property $T_\Phi^\in(I) \subseteq I$ *closed sets* or *c-sets* of Φ.

2. Evidently, $T_\Phi^\in$ is continuous, i.e. for any nondecreasing sequence of partial interpretations $I_1 \subseteq I_2 \subseteq \ldots$ $T_\Phi^\in(\bigcup_{i=1}^{\infty} I_i) = \bigcup_{i=1}^{\infty} T_\Phi^\in(I_i)$. Therefore the least fixed point of $T_\Phi^\in$ is defined as $lfp(T_\Phi^\in) = T_\Phi^\in\uparrow\omega = M_{min}(\Phi)$, where $M_{min}(\Phi)$ is the minimal c-set of Φ. If $M_{min}(\Phi)$ is consistent, then it is the minimal model of Φ.

3. The definition of consistency of IC Φ with an update $\Delta = (D^+, D^-)$ guarantees the existence of a *model* I of Φ in which Δ is accomplished. Hence, for such Φ and Δ there evidently exists the *minimal model* $M_{min}(\Phi \cup D^+)$ which is in fact the set of all ground consequences of the update Δ with respect to Φ. We denote this model by M_Δ. $M_\Delta = lfp(T_{\Phi \cup D^+})$, therefore it is constructed in time linear with respect to the summary size of $ground(\Phi)$ and Δ. Hence the consistency of Φ and Δ is recognized in the same time.

In the situation where Δ is consistent with Φ it must be accomplished completely. In the case of their inconsistency one should define some part of Δ, consistent with Φ, which should be accomplished. First we present an axiomatic definition of the operators resolving the *EUP* in the case of consistent IC and update.

Definition 4. **(Consistency case axioms AC** *) Let the given update Δ be consistent with IC Φ. In this case an operator $\Psi = \Psi[\Phi, \Delta]$ on the set of partial interpretations is a* conservative [IC enforcing] update operator *if for each I :*

(AC1) $\Psi(I)$ is a model of Φ,

(AC2) Δ is accomplished in $\Psi(I)$,

(AC3) $\Psi(I)$ is $\geq_{it}^I$-maximal with respect to the models of Φ in which Δ is accomplished,

(AC4) in the class of the models of Φ with accomplished Δ and $\equiv_{it}^I$-equivalent to $\Psi(I)$, this model is $\geq_{sd}^I$-maximal.

Our formalization of DB updates is not in the line of KB updates. The fundamental difference between the KB revisions and updates on the one hand and the DB updates on the other hand is that for the former the update Δ is taken for granted, and the theory Φ is changed when it contradicts Δ, whereas for the latter, just the opposite, the IC cannot be changed (point(AC1)) and the update should be reconciled to it in the case of contradictions. The idea behind this reconciliation is that a maximal in some sense part of Δ, consistent with Φ should be extracted and accomplished. Such a part can be defined in various ways. The simplest one is based on some priority relation on updates.

Let some linear order $\prec$ be given on pairs of sets of literals (D^+, D^-). For each $\Delta = (D^+, D^-)$ let us denote by $\Delta^{\prec}_{\Phi\Delta}$ the update $max_{\prec}\{(D^+_{\prec}, D^-_{\prec}) | D^+_{\prec} \subseteq D^+, D^-_{\prec} \subseteq D^-, \Phi$ *is consistent with* $(D^+_{\prec}, D^-_{\prec})\}$. In the general case where consistency of Δ and Φ is not presumed the axioms **AC** are revised as follows.

Definition 5. (**General case axioms** $AG^{\prec}$) *An operator* $\Psi = \Psi[\Phi, \Delta]$ *on the set of partial interpretations is a* conservative [IC enforcing] update operator *if for each* I *:*

(AG1) $\Psi(I)$ *is a model of* Φ,

(AG2) $\Delta^{\prec}_{\Phi\Delta}$ *is accomplished in* $\Psi(I)$,

(AG3) $\Psi(I)$ *is* $\geq^I_{it}$*-maximal with respect to the models of* Φ *in which* $\Delta^{\prec}_{\Phi\Delta}$ *is accomplished,*

(AG4) in the class of the models of Φ *with accomplished* $\Delta^{\prec}_{\Phi\Delta}$ *and* $\equiv^I_{it}$*-equivalent to* $\Psi(I)$, *this model is* $\geq^I_{sd}$*-maximal.*

These axioms do not guarantee that the update with maximal priority leads to the model closest to the initial one. The axioms only say that the resulting model is closest among those defined by $\Delta^{\prec}_{\Phi\Delta}$. It is clear that the axioms AC are a special case of $AG^{\prec}$.

The definitions 4 and 5 are based on no default rules outlining some class of "good" models. This leads to the following simple but important model completeness property of enforced updates:

Theorem 1. *(of model completeness)*
Let I_1, I_2 *be two different models of a program* Φ. *Then there exists an update* Δ_0 *consistent with* Φ *such that* $I_2 = \Psi[\Phi, \Delta_0](I_1)$.

Proof. We just set $\Delta_0 = (I_2 \setminus I_1, I_1 \setminus I_2)$. This update is accomplished in I_2.
1. Δ_0 is consistent with Φ because $I_2 \models \Phi$.
2. $\Psi(I_1) \cap (I_1 \setminus I_2) = \emptyset$, we have $\Psi(I_1) \cap I_1 \subseteq I_1 \cap I_2$.
3. As I_2 is also a model of Φ with accomplished Δ_0, $\Psi(I_1) \geq^{I_1}_{it} I_2$, i.e. $I_1 \cap I_2 \subseteq \Psi(I_1) \cap I_1$, therefore $\Psi(I_1) \equiv^{I_1}_{it} I_2$.
4. Now, as Δ_0 is accomplished in $\Psi(I_1)$, this implies $I_2 \setminus I_1 \subseteq \Psi(I_1)$, and therefore $I_2 \subseteq \Psi(I_1)$.
5. On the other hand, 3 implies that $\Psi(I_1) \geq^{I_1}_{sd} I_2$. Hence, $\Psi(I_1) \setminus I_1 \subseteq I_2 \setminus I_1$, and so finally, $\Psi(I_1) \subseteq I_2$. □

This fact implies in particular that the range of a conservative update operator Ψ related to Φ coincides with the set of all models of Φ. This is very natural for the data bases, because they do not propose any criteria for the choice between different models of a user view. Meanwhile, this is just not true for the default rule based operators like the revision in [16, 18], view update in [10], etc. which are more natural for knowledge bases.

Since we consider the EUP for finite IC Φ, updates Δ, and initial DB states I, the space of DB states which result from updates is finite as well. So there evidently exists a brute force algorithm which implements some conservative IC enforcing update operator. Given some Φ, Δ, and I it enumerates all DB states in order induced by our relation of closeness to I and checks for every DB state I' whether $I' \models \Phi$ and Δ is accomplished in I'. The first DB state which satisfies both conditions is the result of the update.

4 Principle-oriented algorithms

Conservative IC enforcing update operators can be quite reasonably implemented. We present below an implementing algorithm $\mathcal{A}$ based upon "oracles" who judge which choice is right when a conflict is encountered. We call such an oracle a preference strategy.

Definition 6. *A* preference strategy *is any function* ρ *which maps any contrary pair* $(l, \neg.l)$ *into one of the literals* $l, \neg.l$. *A strategy* ρ *and an update* Δ *are* compatible *if for all* $l \in M_\Delta$, $\rho(l, \neg.l) = l$ *and for all* $l \in D^-$, $\rho(l, \neg.l) = \neg.l$. *A DB state* I *and a strategy* ρ *are* compatible *if for all* $l \in I$, $\rho(l, \neg.l) = l$.

Another idea behind the algorithm $\mathcal{A}$ is that of a hitting set which cuts out all the choices contradicting a given preference strategy and so reconciles globally all the conflicts caused by the update to be accomplished.

Definition 7. *Let* $\mathcal{L} = (L_1, ..., L_k)$ *be a collection of finite sets of literals. A set* $H \subset \mathbf{LB}$ *is called a* hitting set *of* $\mathcal{L}$ *if* $H \cap L_i \neq \emptyset$ *for each* $1 \leq i \leq k$. H *is a minimal hitting set of* $\mathcal{L}$ *if it is a hitting set of* $\mathcal{L}$ *and no proper subset of* H *is a hitting set of* $\mathcal{L}$.

Algorithm $\mathcal{A}$ resolving the *EUP* for updates consistent with IC.

Input: a DB state I, an update $\Delta = (D^+, D^-)$, and IC Φ consistent with Δ. Let **lit** be the set of literals present either in I, or in Δ, or in $ground(\Phi)$.

Step 1.

Construct $ground(\Phi)$.

Construct M_Δ.

Eliminate from $ground(\Phi)$ every clause r such that for some l in its body $l \in D^-$ or $\neg.l \in M_\Delta$.

From the body of each remaining clause eliminate every $l \in M_\Delta$.

Let the resulting program be denoted by Φ_Δ.

Step 2.

Construct $\tilde{I} = ((I \cup M_\Delta) \setminus \neg.M_\Delta) \setminus D^-$.

Let $next(H)$ be the function which enumerates all subsets of $\tilde{I} \setminus M_\Delta$ in the lexicographic order.

Step 3.

Construct the set $\pi = \{(l, \mathcal{L}_l) \mid l \in \mathbf{LB},\ \mathcal{L}_l = \{c \mid c \subseteq \tilde{I}$ *and* $c = cr(T(l))$ *for some implication tree* $T(l)$ *of* $\Phi_\Delta \cup \tilde{I}\} \neq \emptyset\}$.

Step 4.

```
H := Ĩ \ M_Δ
FOR_ALL ρ compatible with M_Δ DO
    H_ρ := ∅ ; b := false
    WHILE ¬b DO
        b := true
        FOR_ALL l ∈ lit DO
            IF (ρ(l, ¬.l) = l & FOR_SOME c ∈ L_{¬.l}(c ∩ H_ρ = ∅))
            THEN H_ρ := next(H_ρ); b := false; BREAK
            END_IF
        END_FOR_ALL
    END_WHILE
    IF H_ρ ⊊ H
    THEN H := H_ρ
    END_IF
END_FOR_ALL
```

Step 5.

$I_1 := (\tilde{I} \setminus H) \cup \{l \mid (l, \mathcal{L}_l) \in \pi \text{ and } \exists\, c \in \mathcal{L}_l (c \cap H = \emptyset)\}$.

Output: I_1.

Algorithm $\mathcal{A}$ finds in the course of the outermost loop **FOR_ALL** at the step 4 a strategy ρ and a minimal hitting set H of

$$R(\rho) = \bigcup\{\mathcal{L}_{\neg.l} \mid (\neg.l, \mathcal{L}_{\neg.l}) \in \pi \;\&\; \rho(l, \neg.l) = l\}$$

which is optimal in the sense that for no subset $H' \subset H$ and for no preference strategy ρ' compatible with Δ, H' is a hitting set of $R(\rho')$. This optimal H is then used at the step 5 to construct the resulting DB state I_1.

Example 1. *Let* Φ *be defined as*

$$\Phi = \begin{cases} c & \leftarrow a, b \\ \neg c & \leftarrow d, f \\ e & \leftarrow d, b \\ \neg e & \leftarrow \end{cases}$$

$\Delta = (\{a, d\}, \emptyset)$, *and* $I = \{b.f, \neg e\}$. *Then* $M_\Delta = \{a, d, \neg e\}$, $\tilde{I} = \{b, f, \neg e, a, d\}$, $\pi = \{(c, \{a, b\}), (\neg c, \{d, f\}), (e, \{b, d\}), (\neg e, \{\neg e\})\}$, $\rho(c, \neg c) = \neg c$ *and* $\rho(e, \neg e) = \neg e$, $H = \{b\}$, *and the algorithm delivers the model* $I_1 = \{f, \neg e, a, d, \neg c\}$.

The following theorem shows that the algorithm $\mathcal{A}$ is correct.

Theorem 2. *Let* I_1 *be the DB state constructed by the algorithm* $\mathcal{A}$ *for IC* Φ, *a given DB state* I *and an update* $\Delta = (D^+, D^-)$. *Then*

1) Δ *is accomplished in* I_1;

2) I_1 *is consistent;*

3) $I_1 \models \Phi$;

4) For no DB state $I' \models \Phi$ *with accomplished* Δ, $I' >^I_{it} I_1$;

5) For no DB state $I' \models \Phi$ *with accomplished* Δ, *and such that* $I_1 \equiv^I_{it} I'$, $I' >^I_{sd} I_1$.

The proof of this theorem is close to the proof of correctness of the *EUP*-algorithm $\mathcal{A}$ in [8]. The algorithm we present here is much more optimal.

Corollary 1. *(of nondegeneracy and implementation)*

(1) For any IC Φ *and update* Δ *consistent with* Φ *there exists a conservative IC-enforcing update operator* $\Psi = \Psi[\Phi, \Delta]$.

(2) The algorithm $\mathcal{A}$ *implements some conservative IC-enforcing update operator.*

From the axioms $AG^{\prec}$ it follows that the *EUP* in general case is reduced to this problem in the case of consistent updates and IC, at the cost of an additional loop on subsets of Δ. Indeed, the maximal subset of Δ consistent with Φ always exists and is constructed by the evident algorithm. After $\Delta^{\prec}_{\Phi\Delta}$ is found the algorithm $\mathcal{A}$ for consistent update and IC is applied.

5 The Case of Total Interpretations

Now we consider the *EUP* in the case of total interpretations. We presume that update $\Delta = (D^+, D^-)$ and IC Φ are consistent. This means that the program $\Phi_1 = \Phi \cup D^+ \cup \neg.D^-$ has a total model. Moreover, the set of literals $M_\Delta = lfp(T^{\in}_{\Phi_1})$ is consistent (though its positive part should not necessarily be a model of Φ_1). Let $M_\Delta = M^+_\Delta \cup \neg.M^-_\Delta$, where $M^+_\Delta = M_\Delta \cap \mathbf{B}$ and $M^-_\Delta = M_\Delta \cap \neg.\mathbf{B}$. It is clear that if I is a total model of Φ such that Δ is accomplished in I, then $M^+_\Delta \subseteq I$ and $I \cap \neg.M^-_\Delta = \emptyset$.

In the algorithm to follow we use a particular order function *next*. Let $X \subseteq \mathbf{B}, Y \subseteq \mathbf{B}$. We consider the following partial order $\prec_Y$ on subsets of X: $X_1 \prec_{X,Y} X_2$ holds for some $X_1, X_2 \subseteq X$ iff $X_1 \cap Y \subsetneq X_2 \cap Y$ or $X_1 \cap Y = X_2 \cap Y$ and $X_2 \setminus Y \subsetneq X_1 \setminus Y$. Let $next^X_Y(Z)$ be a function which enumerates all subsets of X in any linear order compatible with $\prec_{X,Y}$. For example one can use the lexicographic enumeration on $Z \cap Y$ combined with antilexicographic enumeration on $Z \setminus Y$.

The algorithm $\mathcal{B}$ below implements a conservative update operator which resolves the *EUP* for total DB states. It resembles the algorithm $\mathcal{A}$ but in fact it differs from it substantially in the steps 3 and 4.

Algorithm $\mathcal{B}$ resolving the *EUP* for total interpretations

Input: a total DB state I, and some consistent update $\Delta = (D^+, D^-)$ and IC Φ.

Step 1.
Construct $ground(\Phi)$ and $M_\Delta = M_\Delta^+ \cup M_\Delta^-$.
Eliminate from $ground(\Phi)$ every clause r such that for some l in its body either $\neg.l \in M_\Delta^+$, or $l \in M_\Delta^-$.
Then eliminate all clauses with literals in M_Δ in their heads.
From the body of each remaining clause eliminate every $l \in M_\Delta$.
The resulting program is denoted by Φ_Δ.
Step 2.
Construct $\tilde{I} = ((I \cup M_\Delta^+) \setminus \neg.M_\Delta^-$.
Step 3.
Set $\bar{\mathbf{L}}_\Delta = \mathbf{lit} \setminus (M_\Delta \cup \neg.M_\Delta)$
and

$$\pi = \{(l, \mathcal{L}_l) \mid l \in \mathbf{lit},\ \mathcal{L}_l = \{c \mid c \subseteq \bar{\mathbf{L}}_\Delta \ and\ c = cr(T(l)) \\ for\ some\ implication\ tree\ T(l)\ of\ \Phi_\Delta \cup \bar{\mathbf{L}}_\Delta\} \neq \emptyset\}.$$

Construct the set of literals which contribute to producing conflicts:

$$K := \{a \in \mathbf{B} | \exists(\rho\ compatible\ with\ M_\Delta)\exists l(\rho(l, \neg l) = l \& (\neg.l, \mathcal{L}_{\neg.l}) \in \pi\ \& \\ \exists(c \in \mathcal{L}_{\neg.l})(a \in c \vee \neg a \in c))\}.$$

Step 4.
$H := K \cap I$
FOR_ALL ρ *compatible with* M_Δ **DO**
  $H_\rho := K \setminus I$; $b := false$
  WHILE $\neg b\ \&\ (H_\rho \prec_{K,I} H)$ **DO**
    $b := true$
    FOR_ALL $l \in \mathbf{lit} \setminus M_\Delta$**DO**
    IF $(\rho(l, \neg.l) = l\ \&$ **FOR_SOME** $c \in \mathcal{L}_{\neg.l}(c \cap (H_\rho \cup \neg.(K \setminus H_\rho)) = \emptyset))$
    THEN $H_\rho := next_I^K(H_\rho)$; $b := false$; *BREAK*
    END_IF
    END_FOR_ALL
  END_WHILE
  IF $H_\rho \prec_{K,I} H$
  THEN $H := H_\rho$
  END_IF
END_FOR_ALL
Step 5.
$I' := (\tilde{I} \setminus H) \cup (K \setminus H)$
$I_1^+ := I' \cup \{a \in \mathbf{B} \mid (a, \mathcal{L}_a) \in \pi\ \&\ (H \cup \neg.(K \setminus H))\ is\ not\ a\ hitting\ set\ of\ \mathcal{L}_a\}$.
Output: $I_1 = I_1^+ \cup \neg.(\mathbf{B} \setminus I_1^+)$.

It is easy to check that algorithm $\mathcal{B}$ has the following properties.

Lemma 1. *(i) After the step 3* $\{a \in \mathbf{B} \mid (a, \mathcal{L}_a), (\neg a, \mathcal{L}_{\neg a}) \in \pi\} = \mathbf{B} \setminus (M_\Delta^+ \cup \neg.M_\Delta^-)$. *Moreover, for any* $a \in \mathbf{B} \setminus (M_\Delta^+ \cup \neg.M_\Delta^-)$ $\{a\} \in \mathcal{L}_a$ *and* $\{\neg a\} \in \mathcal{L}_{\neg a}$.
(ii) After the step 4 $H \cap M_\Delta = \emptyset$ *and for any* $a \in \mathbf{B} \setminus (M_\Delta^+ \cup \neg.M_\Delta^-)$ $a \in H$ *or* $\neg a \in \neg.(K \setminus H)$.

(iii) After the step 5 $M_\Delta^+ \subseteq I_1^+$ *and* $\neg.M_\Delta^- \cap I_1^+ = \emptyset$*, hence the update* Δ *is accomplished in* I_1*.*

Lemma 2. $I_1 \models \Phi$.

Proof. Let $r = (l \leftarrow l_1, ..., l_k) \in ground(\Phi)$, $k \geq 0$ be such that $l_i \in I_1$ for all $1 \leq i \leq k$. If $l \in M_\Delta$ then by point (iii) of Lemma 1 $I_1 \models l$. Now suppose that $l \in \mathbf{LB} \setminus M_\Delta$ and let $r' = (l \leftarrow l'_1, ..., l'_{k_1})$ be the residue of rule r included into Φ_Δ. Then for every $1 \leq j \leq k_1$ $l'_j \notin M_\Delta$ and at the step 3 of $\mathcal{B}$ a set $\{l'_1, ..., l'_{k_1}\}$ is included in $\mathcal{L}_l$ and $(l, \mathcal{L}_l)$ is included in π. Since all $l'_j \in I_1$, then $\{l'_1, ..., l'_{k_1}\} \cap H = \emptyset$ and therefore $\rho(l, \neg.l) = l$ for that preference strategy ρ whose minimal H was found at the step 4. Then $l \notin H$ and $l \in I_1$. □

Using these lemmas it is easy to establish correctness of algorithm $\mathcal{B}$.

Theorem 3. *Let* I_1 *be the total DB state constructed by the algorithm* $\mathcal{B}$ *for some IC* Φ*, total DB state* I *and update* $\Delta = (D^+, D^-)$*. Then*

1) Δ *is accomplished in* I_1*;*

2) I_1 *is consistent;*

3) $I_1 \models \Phi$*;*

4) For no DB state $I' \models \Phi$ *with accomplished* Δ*,* $I' >^I_{it} I_1$*;*

5) For no DB state $I' \models \Phi$ *with accomplished* Δ*, and such that* $I_1 \equiv^I_{it} I'$*,* $I' >^I_{sd} I_1$*.*

The main problem with algorithm $\mathcal{B}$ is its complexity. Point (i) of lemma 1 shows that the conflict set at the step 3 includes contrary pairs for all literals (except those in M_Δ) independent of the initial DB state I. Therefore at the step 4 the number of considered different preference strategies is the same as the number of different models which should be considered by the straightforward brute force algorithm we mention in the previous section. We don't know whether the algorithm $\mathcal{B}$ can be so modified for general IC as to deal only with the conflicts produced by I or $\tilde{I}$. However it does so in a very special situation which is rather common in practice. In this situation there is an efficient algorithm resolving the *EUP*.

For a constraint $r = p(\bar{u}) \leftarrow \beta$ let us denote the predicate p by $def(r)$ and say that p is *defined* by r. Let $def(\Phi)$ denote the set of all predicates defined by constraints in Φ. For a literal $l = p(\bar{u})$ or $l = \neg p(\bar{u})$ $def(l) = p$. For an update Δ we denote by $def(\Delta)$ the set of predicates p such that $p = def(l)$ for some $l \in \Delta$.

Definition 8. *A normal IC* Φ *is* superstratified *if there exists a stratification* $def(\Phi) = \bigcup_{i=1}^{n} P_i, P_i \cap P_j = \emptyset, i < j \leq n$ *such that the following condition holds:*

- *Let* $r = h \leftarrow \beta_1, l, \beta_2$ *be a constraint in* Φ*,* $def(r) \in P_i$ *and* $def(l) \in P_j$*. Then* $j < i$*.*

The partition on $def(\Phi)$ induces the partition of Φ : $\Phi = \bigcup_{i=1}^{n} \Phi_i$, where Φ_i $(1 \le i \le n)$ is the set of constraints defining predicates in P_i. It is clear that superstratified IC are not recursive and that the constraints in Φ_1 are positive facts. The situation we consider is where Φ is superstratified and D^- does not affect the facts in Φ_1 and predicates in $P_i, i > 1$.

Algorithm $\mathcal{C}$
Input: a total DB state I, an update $\Delta = (D^+, D^-)$, a superstratified normal IC Φ with stratification $def(\Phi) = \bigcup_{i=1}^{n} P_i$, consistent with an update $\Delta = (D^+, D^-)$ such that $def(D^-) \cap P_i = \emptyset, 1 < i \le n$.
Step 1.
Construct $ground(\Phi)$.
Eliminate from $ground(\Phi)$ every clause $r \leftarrow \beta_1, l, \beta_2$ with $l \in (D^- \cup \neg.D^+)$.
From the body of each remaining clause eliminate every $l_1 \in D^+$ and every $\neg.l_2$, where $l_2 \in D^-$. Let $\Phi_\Delta = \bigcup_{i=1}^{t} \Phi_{\Delta,i}$ be the resulting superstratified program.
Step 2.
Construct $J_1 = (I \cup \Phi_{\Delta,1} \cup D^+) \setminus D^-$
Step 3.
Output: $I_1 = T^{\models}_{\Phi_{\Delta,t}} \uparrow \omega(...T^{\models}_{\Phi_{\Delta,2}} \uparrow \omega(T^{\models}_{J_1}(\emptyset))...)$
Since all conflicts are resolved at the step 2 the following fact holds.

Theorem 4.
(1) The algorithm $\mathcal{C}$ *implements a conservative IC-enforcing update operator on total DB states, normal IC* Φ *superstratified by* $def(\Phi) = \bigcup_{i=1}^{n} P_i$, *and consistent with* Φ *updates* $\Delta = (D^+, D^-)$ *such that* $def(D^-) \cap P_i = \emptyset, 1 < i \le n$.
(2) $\mathcal{C}$ *runs in polynomial time with respect to the summary size of* I, $ground(\Phi)$, *and* Δ.

Concluding Remarks

In this paper we present a formal framework for updating data bases with automatic restoration of integrity constraints. We distinguish such updates from the updates of knowledge bases, taking into account all models of integrity constraints, not only intended ones. We describe update operators axiomatically, and the only requirements we impose on them are: (1) accomplishing the maximal part of update consistent with IC, (2) restoring the IC, and (3) introducing minimal changes into the initial DB state, sufficient to achieve (1) and (2). The minimal change criterion combines two principles: that of maximal intersection and that of minimal symmetric difference. The so formalized *conservative* updates are complete in the sense that any correct DB state can be derived from any other correct DB state by some appropriate update. The conservative updates are quite reasonably implementable in the case of partial interpretations. We propose a principle-oriented algorithm computing the conservative updates, which is quite feasible in practical situations where a local change to a DB state does not introduce too many conflicts. On the other hand, in the case of total interpretations we can propose some principle-oriented algorithm only in a special class of normal stratified IC.

References

[1] Alchourón, C.E., Gärdenfors, P., and Makinson, D.: On the logic of theory change: partial meet contraction and revision functions. *J. Symbolic Logic.* **50** (1985) 510-530.

[2] Alferes, J.J.,Pereira, L.M.: Update-Programs Can Update Programs. In J.Dix, L.M. Pereira, T.C. Przymusinski, editors: *Second International Workshop, NMELP'96. Selected Papers.* LNCS **1216** (1996) 110-131.

[3] Apt, K.R., Bol, R.: Logic programming and negation: A survey. *Journal of Logic Programming.* **19-20** (1994) 9-71.

[4] Baral, C., Lobo, J.: Formal Characterization of Active Databases. In Pedreschi, D., Zaniolo, C., editors: *Logic in Databases. Intern. Workshop LID'96. Proceedings.* San Milano, Italy. (1996), 175-195.

[5] Baralis E., Ceri S., Paraboschi S.: Improved rule analysis by means of triggering and activation graphs. In T.Sellis, editor: *Rules in Database Systems,* LNCS **985** (1995) 165-181.

[6] Bidoit, N.: Negation in rule-based database languages: a survey. *Theoretical Computer Science.* **78** (1991) 3-83

[7] Dayal, U., Hanson,E., and Widom, J.: Active database systems. In: W. Kim, editor, *Modern Database Systems.* Addison Wesley (1995) 436-456.

[8] Dekhtyar, M., Dikovsky, A., Spyratos, N.: On Conservative Enforced Updates. In: Dix, J., Furbach, U., Nerode, A., editors: *Proceedings of 4th International Conference, LPNMR'97.* Dagstuhl Castle, Germany, LNCS **1265** (1997) 244-257.

[9] Eiter, T., Gottlob, G.: On the complexity of propositional knowledge base revision, updates, and counterfactuals. Artificial Intelligence **57** (1992) 227-270.

[10] Fernandez, J.A., Grant, J., Minker, J.: Model-Theoretic Approach to View Updates in Deductive Databases. *Journ. of Automated Reasoning,* **17**(1996) 171-197.

[11] Gärdenfors, P., Makinson, D.: Revisions of knowledge systems using epistemic entrenchment. In: *Proceedings of the Second Conference on Theoretical Aspects of Reasoning about Knowledge* , Pacific Grove, CA (1988) 83-95.

[12] Gottlob, G., Moerkotte, G., Subrahmanian, V.S.: The PARK semantics for active databases. In: *Proceedings of EDBT'96.* Avignon, France (1996).

[13] Gelfond, M., Lfschitz, V.: The stable semantics for logic programs. In: R.Kovalsky and K.Bowen, editors, *Proc. of the 5th Intern. Symp. on Logic Programming.* Cambridge, MA, MIT Press (1988) 1070-1080.

[14] Halfeld Ferrari Alves, M., Laurent, D., Spyratos, N., Stamate, D.: Update rules and revision programs. Rapport de Recherche Université de Paris-Sud, Centre d'Orsay, LRI **1010** (12 / 1995).

[15] Katsuno, H., Mendelzon, A. O.: Propositional knowledge base revision and minimal change. Artificial Intelligence **52** (1991) 253-294.

[16] Marek, V.W., Truszcińsky, M.: Revision programming, database updates and integrity constraints. In: *International Conference on Data Base theory, ICDT.* LNCS **893** (1995) 368-382.

[17] Picouet, Ph., Vianu, V.: Expressiveness and Complexity of Active Databases. In: Afrati, F., Kolaitis, Ph., editors, *6th Int. Conf. on Database Theory, ICDT'97.* LNCS **1186** (1997) 155-172.

[18] Przymusinski, T.C., Turner, H.: Update by Means of Inference Rules. In: V.W.Marek, A.Nerode, M.Truszczyński, editors, *Logic Programming and Non-monotonic Reasoning.* Proc. of the Third Int. Conf. LPNMR'95, Lexington, KY, USA (1995) 166-174.

[19] Raschid, L., Lobo, J.: Semantics for Update Rule Programs and Implementation in a Relational Database Management System. ACM Trans. on Database Systems **21** (December 1996) 526-571.

[20] Reiter, R.,: A logic for default reasoning. *Artificial Intelligence.* **13** (1980) 81-132.

[21] Schewe, K.-D., Thalheim, B.: Consistency Enforcement in Active Databases. In: Chakravarty, S., Widom, L., editors: *Research Issues in Data Engineering - Active Databases.* Proceedings. Houston, (1994).

[22] Van Gelder, A., Ross, K.A., and Schlipf, J.S.: The Well-Founded Semantics for General Logic Programs. Journal of the ACM **38** (1991) 620-650.

[23] Witteveen, C., van der Hoek, W.: A General Framework for Revising Non-monotonic Theories. In Dix, J., Furbach, U., Nerode, A., editors: *Proceedings of 4th International Conference, LPNMR'97.* Dagstuhl Castle, Germany, LNCS **1265** (1997) 258-272.

[24] Zaniolo, C.: Active database rules with transaction-consious stable-model semantics. In:*Proceedings of Fourth International Conference, DOOD'95.* LNCS **1013** (1995) 55-72

Iterated Logic Program Updates

João Alexandre Leite
Luís Moniz Pereira
{jleite|lmp}@di.fct.unl.pt
Centro de Inteligência Artificial (CENTRIA)
Departamento de Informática
Universidade Nova de Lisboa
2825 Monte da Caparica, Portugal

Abstract

The field of theory update has seen some improvement, in what regards updating, by allowing desired updates to be specified by update programs. The updating of models is governed by update rules, as well as by inertia applied to those literals not directly affected by the update program. Though this is important, it remains necessary to tackle too the updating of theories specified by programs. In this paper we explore logic program updates, namely how to exert inertia on program rules rather than on the literals of their models. We define program updates and characterize them semantically, both for the 2-valued and the 3-valued cases. We also define iterated logic program updating, a crucial notion inasmuch as it allows us to conceive what it is to successively update one program by another, and so to prescribe the evolution of knowledge bases by means of updates.

Keywords: Nonmonotonic reasoning, Updates

1 Introduction and Motivation

When dealing with modifications to a knowledge base represented by a propositional theory, two kinds of abstract frameworks have been distinguished both by Keller and Winslett in [8] and by Katsuno and Mendelzon in [7]. One, theory revision, deals with incorporating new knowledge about a static world. The other deals with changing worlds, and is known as theory update. In this work, we are concerned with theory update only, and, in particular, within the framework of logic programming.

A key insight into the issue of updating theories is due to Winslett [14], who showed that one must consider the effect of an update in each of the states of the world that are consistent with our current knowledge of its state. Following this approach, most of the work to date concerns the updating of models on a one by one basis [11][13][4]. The common intuition behind the update of a model has been based on what is referred to as the commonsense law of inertia, i.e. things do not change unless they are expressly made to, in this case that the truth value of each element of the model to be updated should remain the same unless explicitly changed by the update. Suppose, for example, that we have a model in which "sunshine" is true and "rain" is false; if later we receive the information that the sun is no longer shining, we conclude that "sunshine" is false, due to the update, and that "rain" is still false by inertia.

Suppose now that our vision of the world is described instead by a logic program and we want to update it. Is updating each of its models enough? Is all the information borne by a logic program contained within its set of models? The answer to both these questions is negative. A logic program encodes more than the set of its individual models. It encodes the relationships between the elements of a model, which are lost if we envisage updates simply on a model by model basis, as proposed in [7].

To show that a logic program encodes more than its set of models, consider the following situation:

Example 1 *Consider program P stating that someone is a pacifist and that a pacifist is a reasonable person:*

$$P : reasonable \leftarrow pacifist; \quad pacifist \leftarrow .$$

whose only stable model is $M = \{pacifist, reasonable\}$*. Later on, an update program (originally introduced in [11] under the name of* revision program*) states that we're at war, and that a state of war will make that person no longer a pacifist:*

$$U : out(pacifist) \leftarrow in(war); \quad in(war) \leftarrow .$$

According to [11] and model updating we obtain as the single update of M the model $M_U = \{war, reasonable\}$*, to the effect that, although we know that the person is not a pacifist, he/she is still considered a reasonable person. But looking at the program and at the update program, we arguably conclude that* M_U *doesn't represent the intended meaning of the update of P by U for a commonsensical reasoner: Since "*$reasonable$*" was true because "*$pacifist$*" was true, the removal of "*$pacifist$*" should make one expect "*$reasonable$*" to become false. The intended update model of the example presumably is* $M_U' = \{war\}$*.* ◇

Why are we obtaining this somewhat unintuitive result? To answer this question we must first consider the role of inertia in updates.

Newton's first law, also known as the law of inertia, states that: *"every body remains at rest or moves with constant velocity in a straight line, unless it is compelled to change that state by an unbalanced force acting upon it"* (adapted from [12]). One often tends to interpret this law in a commonsensical way, as things keeping as they are unless some kind of force is applied to them. This is true but it doesn't exhaust the meaning of the law. It is the result of all applied forces that governs the outcome. Take a body to which several forces are applied, and which is in a state of equilibrium due to those forces canceling out. Later one of those forces is removed and the body starts to move.

The same kind of behaviour presents itself when updating programs. Before obtaining the truth value, by inertia, of those elements not directly affected by the update program, one should verify whether the truth of such elements is not indirectly affected by the updating of other elements.

Going back to the example, before stating that "$reasonable$" is true by inertia, since it wasn't directly affected by the update program, we should verify that since the person is no longer a pacifist, there is no way to prove "$reasonable$" and therefore its truth value should no longer be 'true'.

Another way to view program updating, and in particular the role of inertia, is to say that the rules of the initial program carry over to the updated program, due to inertia, instead of the truth of literals, just in case they aren't overruled by the update program. Once again this should be so because the rules encode more information than their models.

This approach was first adopted in [10], under a two-valued semantics, where the authors present a program transformation which, given an initial program and an update program, produces an updated program obeying rule inertia.

In this paper we start by generalizing the transformation and semantical characterization of [10] to the case where the initial program is of the same kind as the update program i.e. capable of expressing negative information in rule conclusion. Then, in section 4, we introduce the notion of iterated update programming: Suppose knowledge is represented by an initial program (possibly empty) and a sequence of update programs. Iterated update programming allows us to represent the evolution of that knowledge, characterizing it after each update. In section 5, we extend logic program updating to the case where a partial stable semantics is used. Finally, in section 6, we conclude and elaborate on future developments.

2 Preliminary Definitions

The following definitions will be needed in the subsequent sections.

Definition 1 (Three-valued interpretation) *A three-valued interpretation M of a language $\mathcal{L}$ is any set*

$$T \cup not\ F$$

where T and F are disjoint subsets of $\mathcal{L}$.

The set T contains all ground atoms which are true in M, the set F contains all ground atoms which are false in M. The truth value of the remaining atoms is unknown (or undefined). Two-valued interpretations are a special case of 3-valued ones, for which $T \cup F = \mathcal{L}$ is further imposed. ◊

Proposition 1 *Any interpretation $M = T \cup not\ F$ can equivalently be viewed as a function $M : \mathcal{L} \to V$ where $V = \{0, \frac{1}{2}, 1\}$, defined by:*

$$M(A) = \begin{cases} 0 & \text{if } not\ A \in M \\ 1 & \text{if } A \in M \\ \frac{1}{2} & \text{otherwise} \end{cases} \quad \diamond$$

Based on this function we can define a truth valuation of formulae.

Definition 2 (Truth valuation) *If M is an interpretation, the truth valuation $\hat{M}$ corresponding to M is a function $\hat{M} : C \to V$ where C is the set of all formulae of the language recursively defined as follows:*

-if A is a ground atom then $\hat{M}(A) = M(A)$.

-if S is a formula then $\hat{M}(not\ S) = 1 - M(S)$.

-if S and V are formulae then:

- $\hat{M}((S,V)) = \min(\hat{M}(S), \hat{M}(V))$.
- $\hat{M}(L \leftarrow S) = 1$ *if* $\hat{M}(S) \leq \hat{M}(L)$, *and* 0 *otherwise.* ◊

As in [10], in order to translate update programs ([11]) written in a language $\mathcal{L}$ into logic programs, we extend $\mathcal{L}$ with explicit negation $\neg$. The next definition relates interpretations of this extended language with interpretations of $\mathcal{L}$.

Definition 3 (Interpretation Restriction) *Given a language $\mathcal{L}$ that does not contain explicit negation $\neg$, let $M_\neg = T_{M_\neg} \cup not\ F_{M_\neg}$*[1] *be an interpretation, of the*

[1] When dealing with total interpretations, M can be more simply represented by just the literals that are true in it.

language $\mathcal{L}_\neg$ *obtained by augmenting* $\mathcal{L}$ *with the set* $E = \{\neg A : A \in \mathcal{L}\}$. *We define the corresponding* restricted interpretation *as* $M = T_M \cup not\ F_M$, *of* $\mathcal{L}$, *where* $T_M = \{A : A \in T_{M_\neg}$ *and* $A \in \mathcal{L}\}$ *and* $F_M = \{A : A \in F_{M_\neg}$ *and* $A \in \mathcal{L}\}$. *Additionally we define an* objective literal *of* $\mathcal{L}_\neg$ *as being an atom* A *or its explicit negation* $\neg A$. ◇

The translation of update programs into extended logic programs follows:

Definition 4 (Translation of UPs into LPs) *Let* UP *be an update program (or revision program as designated in [11]) in the language* $\mathcal{L}$. *Its* translation into an extended logic program U *in the language* $\mathcal{L}_\neg$ *is obtained from* UP *by replacing each update rule (r) by the corresponding rule (r') where:*

- *If r is of the form* $in(p) \leftarrow in(q_1), ..., in(q_m), out(s_1), ..., out(s_n)$
  then r' is of the form $p \leftarrow q_1, ...q_m, not\ s_1, ..., not\ s_n$
- *If r is of the form* $out(p) \leftarrow in(q_1), ..., in(q_m), out(s_1), ..., out(s_n)$
  then r' is of the form $\neg p \leftarrow q_1, ...q_m, not\ s_1, ..., not\ s_n$ ◇

From now onwards, and unless otherwise stated, whenever we refer to an update program we mean its (reversible) translation into an extended logic program according to the previous definition. Notice that such programs do not contain explicitly negated atoms in the body of its rules. In fact, although defined in the language $\mathcal{L}_\neg$, the use of explicit negation in these programs is limited for we will be concerned only with the models of the restricted language $\mathcal{L}$. For this reason, we will dub these programs normal logic programs. Also, and to prepare for further generalization, we allow for the initial program to be of the same form of the translated update program. In [1] we defined iterative updates for programs under stable model semantics and allowing for default negation in heads of rules.

3 Updating Logic Programs under Answer-Set Semantics

To achieve the rule inertia mentioned in the Introduction, we start by defining the subprogram of the initial program containing the rules that persist in the updated program. We use this program together with the update program to characterize the desired models resulting from the update, i.e. the program-justified updates. Afterwards, we present a joint program transformation of the initial and update programs, which includes also inertia rules, to produce an updated program whose models are exactly the required program-justified updates. Answer-sets semantics of extended logic programs [6] will be used to define the models of programs.

3.1 <P,U>-Justified Updates

The <P,U>-justified updates are the set of interpretations that characterize the update of a normal logic program P by an update program U. To obtain them we start by defining a sub-program of the initial program.

Definition 5 (Inertial Sub-Program) *Let* P *be a normal logic program in the language* $\mathcal{L}_\neg$, U *an update program in the language* $\mathcal{L}_\neg$ *and* $M_\neg$ *an interpretation of* $\mathcal{L}_\neg$. *Let:*

$$Rejected(M_\neg, P, U) = \{L \leftarrow body \in P : \hat{M}_\neg(body) = 1 \text{ and } \exists \neg L \leftarrow body' \in U : \hat{M}_\neg(body') = 1\ \} \quad (1)$$

where L *is an objective literal. The* Inertial Sub-Program $P_{inertial}(M_\neg, P, U)$ *is:*

$$P_{inertial}(M_\neg, P, U) = P - Rejected(M_\neg, P, U) \ \Diamond \quad (2)$$

Intuitively, the rules that belong to $Rejected(M_{\neg}, P, U)$ are those that belong to the initial program but, although their body is still verified by the interpretation, there is an update rule that overrides them, by contravening their conclusion.

Definition 6 (<P,U>-Justified Updates) *Let P be a normal logic program and U an update program, both in the language $\mathcal{L}_{\neg}$. Let M be an interpretation of the language $\mathcal{L}$. M is a* <P,U>-Justified Update *of P updated by U, iff there is an interpretation $M_{\neg}$ of $\mathcal{L}_{\neg}$ such that $M_{\neg}$ is an answer-set of $\uplus(M_{\neg}, P, U)$, where*

$$\uplus(M_{\neg}, P, U) = P_{inertial}(M_{\neg}, P, U) + U \ \diamond \tag{3}$$

Notice that the new definition of program-justified update doesn't depend on any initial model. Once again this is because inertia applies to rules and not model literals.

The following example will illustrate the rôle played by $Rejected(M_{\neg}, P, U)$ when determining the <P,U>-Justified Updates.

Example 2 *Consider P and U from Example 1. Let's check whether $M'_U = \{war\}$ is a $<P,U>$-justified update. M'_U is the restriction of $M'_{\neg U} = \{war, \neg pacifist\}$. Since*

$$Rejected(M'_{\neg U}, P, U) = \{pacifist \leftarrow\}; \quad \uplus(M'_{\neg U}, P, U) = P + U - \{pacifist \leftarrow\}$$

$M'_{\neg U}$ is an answer-set of $\uplus(M'_{\neg U}, P, U)$ and so M'_U is a $<P,U>$-justified update.

The model $M_U = \{reasonable, war\}$, being an update of the only answer-set of P, determined according to interpretation updating, is not a $<P,U>$-justified update. Intuitively, it should not be one because the truth value of "reasonable" should be determined by the evaluation of rule $reasonable \leftarrow pacifist$, of P, on the strength of the truth of "$pacifist$" in the updated model, and therefore false. M_U is the restriction of $M_{\neg U} = \{reasonable, war, \neg pacifist\}$. We have that

$$Rejected(M_{\neg U}, P, U) = \{pacifist \leftarrow\}; \quad \uplus(M_{\neg U}, P, U) = P + U - \{pacifist \leftarrow\}$$

and $M_{\neg U}$ since not an answer-set of $\uplus(M_{\neg U}, P, U)$, M_U is not a $<P,U>$-justified update. $\diamond$

3.1.1 Properties of <P,U>-Justified Updates

Given the definition of <P,U>-justified updates we can demonstrate the following properties:

Theorem 1 *Let Q be a normal logic program in the language $\mathcal{L}_{\neg}$, and $\emptyset$ an empty program. Then the answer-sets of Q are exactly any of: the $<Q,\emptyset>$-justified updates; the $<\emptyset,Q>$-justified updates; the $<Q,Q>$-justified updates.* $\diamond$

Theorem 2 (Associativity of Updates) *Let P, Q and R be three normal logic programs in the language $\mathcal{L}_{\neg}$. Let $\uplus(M_{\neg}, P, U)$ be the program obtained as per Def.6, corresponding to the update of P by U given $M_{\neg}$, where $M_{\neg}$ is an interpretation of $\mathcal{L}_{\neg}$. If P updated by Q (resp. Q updated by R) has at least one $<P,Q>$-justified update (resp. $<Q,R>$-justified update) then $M_{\neg}$ is an answer-set of the program $\uplus(M_{\neg}, \uplus(M_{\neg}, P, Q), R)$ iff $M_{\neg}$ is an answer-set of the program $\uplus(M_{\neg}, P, \uplus(M_{\neg}, Q, R))$.* $\diamond$

3.2 Update Transformation of a Normal Program

Next we present a program transformation that produces an updated program from an initial program and an update program. The answer-sets of the updated program so obtained will be exactly the <P,U>-justified updates, according to Theorem 3 below. The updated program can then be used to compute them.

Definition 7 (Update transformation of a normal program) *Given an update program U in the language $\mathcal{L}_\neg$. For a logic program P in the language $\mathcal{L}_\neg$, its updated program P_U with respect to U , written in the extended language $\mathcal{L}_\neg + \{A', \neg\_A', A^U, \neg A^U : A \in \mathcal{L}\}$ is obtained via the operations:*

- All rules of U and P belong to P_U subject to the changes:

- *in the head of every rule of P_U originated in U replace objective literal L by a new objective literal L^U;*
- *in the head of every rule of P_U originated in P replace atom A (resp. $\neg A$) by a new atom A' (resp $\neg\_A'$);*

-Include in P_U, for every atom A in $\mathcal{L}$, the defining rules:

$$\begin{array}{ll} A \leftarrow A', not\ \neg A^U; & A \leftarrow A^U; \\ \neg A \leftarrow \neg\_A', not\ A^U; & \neg A \leftarrow \neg A^U. \ \diamond \end{array} \tag{4}$$

The above assumes that in the language $\mathcal{L}_\neg$ there are no symbols of the form A', $\neg\_A'$, A^U and $\neg A^U$. The defining rules establish that, after the update, a literal is either implied by inertia or forced by an update rule.

Example 3 *Consider the P and U of Example 2. The updated program P_U of P by U is (where the rules for A stand for all their ground instances):*

$$\begin{array}{lll} pacifist' \leftarrow; & war^U \leftarrow; & A \leftarrow A', not\ \neg A^U; \\ reasonable' \leftarrow pacifist; & A \leftarrow A^U; & \neg A \leftarrow \neg\_A', not\ A^U; \\ \neg pacifist^U \leftarrow war; & \neg A \leftarrow \neg A^U. & \end{array}$$

whose only answer-set (modulo A', A^U and explicitly negated atoms) is $M_1 = \{war\}$, coinciding with the only <P, U>-justified update determined in Example 2. $\diamond$

The following theorem establishes the relationship between the models of the update transformation of a program and its <P,U>-justified updates.

Theorem 3 (Correctness of the update transformation) *Let P be a normal logic program in the language $\mathcal{L}_\neg$ and U an update program in the language $\mathcal{L}_\neg$. Modulo any primed, L^U and explicitly negated literals, the answer-sets of the updated program P_U are exactly the <P, U>-Justified Updates of P updated by U.* $\diamond$

4 Iterated Updates

What happens if we want to update a program more than once? Since the definitions in the previous section apply only to programs without explicit negation in the body of their rules, and updated programs obtained via Def.7 include such negations in the body of inertia rules, those definitions cannot be used to update previously updated programs.

But if we take a closer look at the rôle of inertia rules, as well as the intuitive characterization of justified updates, we realize that inertia rules don't need to be updated. Indeed, given a sequence of update programs to be applied to an initial program (which, as we've seen in theorem 1, can itself be envisaged as an update program applied to the empty program), the justified updates should be answer-sets of a program composed of the rules of the last update program, together with some rules from each of the previous update programs, that haven't been overriden by a subsequent update. Equally, to construct a program whose answer-sets are the justified updates, we might just use the rules of each update program, together with some rules enacting inertia from one stage to the next.

In this section we will generalize the notions presented in the previous one to the case where we have a sequence of update programs. For this we start with a definition, allowing us to "time-stamp" updates.

Definition 8 (State Set) *Let the* State Set T *be an initial sequence of natural numbers* $T = \{0, 1, 2, ..., n\}$. *We call the members of* T *states, and the first element 0 the* initial state. ◇

4.1 S-justified Updates

We now characterize the set of interpretations that should be accepted as justified updates, at any given state, in a sequence of updates. They are called the S-justified updates. Like for <P,U>-justified updates, we start by defining the set of rules, of each update program, that should persist up to some state under consideration.

Definition 9 (Inertial Sub-Program of state t_1 at state t) *Consider an ordered sequence* $S = \{U_t : t \in T\}$, *indexed by* T, *of update logic programs* U_t *in the language* $\mathcal{L}_\neg$, *and* $M_\neg$ *an interpretation of* $\mathcal{L}_\neg$. *Let:*

$$Rejected(M_\neg, t_1, t) = \bigcup_{t_1 < t_2 \le t} Rejected_i(M_\neg, t_1, t_2) \tag{5}$$

$$\begin{aligned} Rejected_i(M_\neg, t_1, t_2) = \{ & L \leftarrow body \in U_{t_1} : \hat{M}_\neg(body) = 1 \\ & and\ \exists \neg L \leftarrow body' \in U_{t_2} : \hat{M}_\neg(body') = 1\} \end{aligned} \tag{6}$$

where L *is an objective literal. We then define the* Inertial Sub-Program of state t_1 at state t, $U^{inertial}(M_\neg, t_1, t)$ *as:*

$$U^{inertial}(M_\neg, t_1, t) = U_{t_1} - Rejected(M_\neg, t_1, t)\ \diamond \tag{7}$$

Note that $Rejected(M_\neg, t, t) = \{\}$ and so $U^{inertial}(M_\neg, t, t) = U_t$.

Intuitively, the rules for some literal L that belong to $Rejected(M_\neg, t_1, t)$ are those that belong to U_{t_1} and, although their body is still verified by the model, there is a rule of a subsequent update program that overrides them, by contravening their conclusion.

Definition 10 (S-Justified Updates at a given state t) *Consider an ordered sequence* $S = \{U_t : t \in T\}$, *indexed by* T, *of update logic programs* U_t *in the language* $\mathcal{L}_\neg$, *with smallest element* U_{t_0}, *and* M *an interpretation of* $\mathcal{L}$. M *is a* S-Justified Update at a given state t *iff there is an interpretation* $M_\neg$ *of* $\mathcal{L}_\neg$ *such that* $M_\neg$ *is an answer-set of* $\uplus_S(t)$, *where*

$$\uplus_S(t) = \bigcup_{t_i \le t} (U^{inertial}(M_\neg, t_i, t)) \tag{8}$$

and $t_i \in T$, *if there is a non-contradictory S-justified update at every state* t_i, $t_0 \le t_i \le t$. *Otherwise there is no S-justified update at state* t. ◇

Intuitively, if $M_\neg$ is an answer-set of the program consisting of the rules from the update program at state t, together with every rule belonging to a program of a previous state whose conclusion has not been contravened by a rule of a subsequent update program (up to t). The non-contradictoriness condition for every previous state ensures that we reached state t without passing a contradictory state. Addressing contradiction is beyond the scope of this work.

Note that if a rule is rejected by some rule, which itself is subsequently rejected, there is no need to reinstate the original rule because the rule rejecting the rejector rule takes it place.

Theorem 4 *Let $S = \{U_0, ..., U_n\}$ be an ordered sequence of update logic programs U_n in the language $\mathcal{L}_\neg$, with smallest element U_0. If there is at least one S-justified update at state $n-1$ then the S-justified updates at state n are exactly the $<\uplus_S(n-1), U_n>$-justified updates.* ◇

Corollary 1 (Generalization of <P,U>-justified updates) *Let P and U be update programs in the language $\mathcal{L}_\neg$. Let $T = \{0,1\}$ and $S = \{U_0, U_1\}$ such that $U_0 = P$ and $U_1 = U$. Then an interpretation M is an S-justified update at state 1 iff it is a $<P, U>$-justified update.* ◇

4.2 Iterated Update Transformation

Next we define a transformation which, given a sequence of update logic programs, produces a final logic program. It does so by introducing inertia rules to 'link' the intermediate programs in the given sequence. The final program, together with defining rules as will be seen below, has exactly as its models the S-justified Updates of the update sequence.

Definition 11 (Iterated Program Updates) *Let $S = \{U_t : t \in T\}$ be an ordered sequence of update logic programs U_t, indexed by T, in the language $\mathcal{L}_\neg$, with smallest element U_{t_0}. The* Iterated Update Program *P_S defined by S, in the extended language $\mathcal{L}^*_\neg = \mathcal{L}_\neg + \{A_t, \neg\_A_t, A^U_t, \neg\_A^U_t : A \in \mathcal{L}, t \in T\}$ is obtained via the operations:*

- All rules of $U_t \in S$ belong to P_S except that in the head of every rule one replaces atom A (resp. $\neg A$) by a new atom A^U_t (resp $\neg\_A^U_t$);

- Include in P_S, for every atom A of $\mathcal{L}$, and for any $t > t_0$, the defining rules:

$$\begin{array}{ll} A_t \leftarrow A_{t-1}, not\ \neg\_A^U_t; & A_t \leftarrow A^U_t; \\ \neg\_A_t \leftarrow \neg\_A_{t-1}, not\ A^U_t; & \neg\_A_t \leftarrow \neg\_A^U_t. \end{array} \tag{9}$$

- Include in P_S, for every atom A of $\mathcal{L}$, the rules:

$$A_{t_0} \leftarrow A^U_{t_0} \quad and \quad \neg\_A_{t_0} \leftarrow \neg\_A^U_{t_0} \ \Diamond \tag{10}$$

The above definition assumes that in the language $\mathcal{L}_\neg$ there are no symbols of the form A_t, $\neg\_A_t$, A^U_t and $\neg\_A^U_t$. Note that P_S does not contain any rules for atoms of $\mathcal{L}_\neg$, i.e. neither A nor $\neg A$ appear in the heads of the rules of P_S.

Now, to find out what is the result of the updates up to a given state t, we add the "current state" defining rules, to obtain the program at a given state t:

Definition 12 (Iterated Update Program at a current state t) *Consider a non-contradictory iterated update program P_S. The* Iterated Update Program at a given current state t $\in T$, $P_S(t)$, *is the program* P_S *augmented with the* current state *defining rules:*

$$A \leftarrow A_t \quad \text{and} \quad \neg A \leftarrow \neg\_A_t \tag{11}$$

for all $A \in \mathcal{L}$, *if* $P_S(r)$ *is non-contradictory for all* $r \in T, r < t$. *Otherwise* $P_S(t)$ *is not defined.* ◊

Example 4 *Let* $S = \{U_1, U_2, U_3\}$ *be an ordered sequence of programs such that:*

$$U_1 : pacifist \leftarrow; \quad reasonable \leftarrow pacifist. \qquad U_2 : \neg pacifist \leftarrow war; \quad war \leftarrow . \qquad U_3 : \neg war \leftarrow .$$

The iterated update program P_S *is the logic program (where the rules for A stand for all their ground instances and t=2,3):*

$$\begin{array}{lll} pacifist_1^U \leftarrow; & \neg\_war_3^U \leftarrow; & A_t \leftarrow A_{t-1}, not\ \neg\_A_t^U; \\ reasonable_1^U \leftarrow pacifist; & A_1 \leftarrow A_1^U; & \neg\_A_t \leftarrow \neg\_A_{t-1}, not\ A_t^U; \\ \neg\_pacifist_2^U \leftarrow war; & \neg\_A_1 \leftarrow \neg\_A_1^U; & A_t \leftarrow A_t^U; \\ war_2^U \leftarrow; & & \neg\_A_t \leftarrow \neg\_A_t^U. \end{array}$$

The iterated update program at a given current state t is P_S *together with the current state defining rules (11), so that* $P_S(1)$ *has the single answer-set* $M_1 = \{pacifist, reasonable\}$, $P_S(2)$ *has the single answer-set* $M_2 = \{war\}$, *and* $P_S(3)$ *has the single answer-set* $M_3 = \{pacifist, reasonable\}$ *(all answer-sets are modulo irrelevant elements). Note that since after* U_3 *there is no longer a state of war, the rule "*$\neg pacifist \leftarrow war$*" of* U_2 *has no effect and the truth value of "pacifist" is determined solely by the rule "*$pacifist \leftarrow$ *" of* U_1. ◊

The following theorem establishes that iterated program updates generalize program updates.

Theorem 5 (Generalization of Program Updates) *Let P and U be update programs in the language* $\mathcal{L}_\neg$. *Let* $T = \{0, 1\}$ *and let* $U_0 = P$ *and* $U_1 = U$. *Then the iterated update program* $P_S(1)$ *at state* $t = 1$ *is semantically equivalent to the updated program* P_U *of P by U, i.e. for every answer-set* $M_\neg$ *of* $P_S(1)$ *there is exactly an answer-set* $M'_\neg$ *of* P_U *such that* $M = M'$, *conversely, for every answer-set* $M'_\neg$ *of* P_U *there is exactly an answer-set* $M_\neg$ *of* $P_S(1)$ *such that* $M' = M$. ◊

The next theorem establishes the relationship between the iterated program and the S-justified updates at a given state t.

Theorem 6 (Correctness of the iterated UP at a state *t***)** *Given an ordered sequence* $S = \{U_t : t \in T\}$ *of update logic programs* U_t *in the language* $\mathcal{L}_\neg$, *with smallest element* U_{t_0}. *Restricted to* $\mathcal{L}$, *the answer-sets of the iterated update program at a given current state t, are exactly the S-justified updates at state t.* ◊

5 Updating Normal Logic Programs under Partial Stable Semantics

In this section we extend the notions of logic program updating to the case where a partial stable semantics is used. To bring out the implications of such an extension in a simple way, it will be just presented for the case of normal logic programs, and of a single update. The extension to the iterated case, is similar to the one presented in the previous section.

As will be seen, we need only extend the characterization of <P,U>-justified updates. The update transformation used before for normal logic programs is valid for the three-valued case simply by using the partial stable semantics to compute models. For simplicity, we represent 3-valued interpretations as sets of objective and default literals.

5.1 Three-valued <P,U>-Justified Updates

The characterization of <P,U>-justified updates will have to suffer a modification to allow for partial iterpretations and models. To better understand the need for such modifications, and the intuition behind them, consider a very simple example:

Example 5 *Initial program P and update program U (next to each rule of U we exhibit the original update rule):*

$$P : a \leftarrow . \quad U : \neg a \leftarrow c; \quad [out(a) \leftarrow in(c)]$$
$$c \leftarrow not\ c. \quad [in(c) \leftarrow out(c)]$$

Any 3-valued U-justified update (as in [4]) of $M = \{a\}$ should be a 3-valued <P,U>-justified update as well because P contains just facts. According to [4], $M = \{\}$ is the only 3-valued U-justified update i.e., both **a** *and* **c** *are undefined. Looking at the rules of both P and U we note the impossibility of having a partial stable model (PSM) where* **a** *is undefined, of a program composed of those rules. This is so because having* $\neg$**a** *undefined doesn't affect the truth value of* **a**. ◇

The previous example suggests that the characterization of 3-valued <P,U>-justified updates can no longer be made to depend on a composition of the rules of P and U alone. We will have, under certain conditions, to explicitly undefine some objective literals. Informally, this should be done whenever a literal L is true due to a rule of P but $\neg L$ is undefined due to a rule of U. Formally:

Definition 13 (Three-valued Inertial Sub-Program) *Let P be a normal logic program in the language $\mathcal{L}_\neg$, U an update program in the language $\mathcal{L}_\neg$ and $M_\neg = \langle T_{M_\neg}, F_{M_\neg}\rangle$ a 3-valued interpretation of $\mathcal{L}_\neg$. Let:*

$$\begin{aligned} Rejected(M_\neg, P, U) = \{ & L \leftarrow body \in P : \hat{M}_\neg(body) = 1 \\ & and\ \exists \neg L \leftarrow body' \in U : \hat{M}_\neg(body') \neq 0\ \} \end{aligned} \tag{12}$$

where L is an objective literal. We define Three-valued Inertial Sub-Program $P_{inertial}(M_\neg, P, U)$ *as:*

$$P_{inertial}(M_\neg, P, U) = P - Rejected(M_\neg, P, U)\ \diamond \tag{13}$$

Intuitively, the rules for some L that belong to $Rejected(M_\neg, P, U)$ are those that belong to the initial program but, although their body is still verified by the interpretation, there is an update rule that overrides them, by either truthifying or undefining its complementary literal.

Now we define the set of literals that are to be explicitly undefined:

Definition 14 (Undefining Rules) *Let P be a normal logic program in the language $\mathcal{L}_\neg$, U an update program in the language $\mathcal{L}_\neg$ and $M_\neg = \langle T_{M_\neg}, F_{M_\neg}\rangle$ a 3-valued interpretation of $\mathcal{L}_\neg$. The set of* Undefining Rules, $Undefining(M_\neg, P, U)$ *is:*

$$\begin{aligned} Undefining(M_\neg, P, U) = \{ & L \leftarrow \mathbf{u} : L \leftarrow body \in Rejected(M_\neg, P, U) \\ & and\ \nexists \neg L \leftarrow body' \in U : \hat{M}_\neg(body') = 1\ \}\ \diamond \end{aligned} \tag{14}$$

$Undefining(M_\neg, P, U)$ contains rules to undefine precisely those literals L such that there is an update rule undefining its complementary literal $\neg L$, and none truthifying it, which are required to reject rules for L. Recall that **u** stands for the propositional symbol with the property of being undefined in every interpretation. Finally, the three-valued <P,U>-justified updates are defined as:

Definition 15 (3-valued <P,U>-Justified Updates) *Let P be a normal logic program and U an update program, both in the language $\mathcal{L}_\neg$. Let M be a 3-valued interpretation of the language $\mathcal{L}$. M is a* 3-valued <P,U>-Justified Update *of P updated by U, iff there is an interpretation $M_\neg$ of $\mathcal{L}_\neg$ such that $M_\neg$ is a partial stable model of $\uplus(M_\neg, P, U)$, where*

$$\uplus(M_\neg, P, U) = U + P_{inertial}(M_\neg, P, U) + Undefining(M_\neg, P, U) \ \Diamond \qquad (15)$$

The next example shows the rôle played by $Undefining(M_\neg, P, U)$ when determining the 3-valued <P,U>-Justified Updates.

Example 6 *Consider the program P of the pacifist situation of Example 1 but where now the update U states that it is not clear whether we're at war or at peace, and that a state of war will make that person no longer a pacifist:*

$$\begin{array}{ll} P: pacifist \leftarrow; & U: \neg pacifist \leftarrow war; \\ \quad reasonable \leftarrow pacifist. & \quad peace \leftarrow not\ war; \\ & \quad war \leftarrow not\ peace. \end{array}$$

Intuitively, examining the two 2-valued <P,U>-justified updates:

$$M_1 = \{pacifist, reasonable, peace, not\ war\}$$
$$M_2 = \{not\ pacifist, not\ reasonable, not\ peace, war\}$$

one should expect the interpretation $M_3 = \{\}$ to be a 3-valued <P,U>-justified update. Let's check if it is so. M_3 is the restriction of $M_{\neg 3} = \{\}$. Since the truth value of war in the rule $\neg pacifist \leftarrow war$ is not false, we have that the rule $pacifist \leftarrow$ should be rejected, i.e.

$$Rejected(M_{\neg 3}, P, U) = \{pacifist \leftarrow\}$$

Now, we have to include an undefining rule for $pacifist$ just in case there aren't any rules in U for $\neg pacifist$ with a true body. Since that is the case we have

$$Undefining(M_{\neg 3}, P, U) = \{pacifist \leftarrow \mathbf{u}\}$$

and we obtain the program:

$$\begin{array}{ll} \uplus(M_{\neg 3}, P, U): pacifist \leftarrow \mathbf{u}; & \neg pacifist \leftarrow war; \\ \quad reasonable \leftarrow pacifist; & peace \leftarrow not\ war; \\ & war \leftarrow not\ peace. \end{array}$$

Since $M_{\neg 3}$ is a PSM of $\uplus(M_{\neg 3}, P, U)$, M_3 is a 3-valued <P,U>-justified update. $\Diamond$

The theorem below shows that the (2-valued) <P,U>-justified updates are a special case of the 3-valued <P,U>-justified updates:

Theorem 7 (Generalization of <P,U>-justified updates) *Whenever dealing with total interpretations, the 3-valued <P,U>-justified update definition reduces to that of (2-valued) <P,U>-justified update.* $\Diamond$

The 3-valued <P,U>-justified updates can be determined from the updated program constructed from the initial program and the update program, as per Def. 7, if we consider its partial stable models (or WFSX models[3]).

Example 7 *Take P and U of Ex.6. The updated program P_U of P by U is (where the rules for A stand for all their ground instances):*

$$\begin{array}{lll} pacifist' \leftarrow; & peace^U \leftarrow not\ war; & A \leftarrow A', not\ \neg A^U; \\ reasonable' \leftarrow pacifist; & war^U \leftarrow not\ peace; & \neg A \leftarrow \neg A', not\ A^U; \\ \neg pacifist^U \leftarrow war; & A \leftarrow A^U; & \neg A \leftarrow \neg A^U. \end{array}$$

whose partial stable models (modulo A', A^U and explicitly negated atoms) are:

$$\begin{array}{ll} M_1 = \{pacifist, reasonable, peace, not\ war\} & M_3 = \{\} \\ M_2 = \{not\ pacifist, not\ reasonable, not\ peace, war\} & \end{array}$$

coinciding with the three 3-valued $<P,U>$-justified updates determined in ex.6. ◇

The following theorem establishes the relationship between the partial stable models of the update transformation of a program and its 3-valued <P,U>-justified updates.

Theorem 8 (Correctness of the update transformation) *Let P be a normal logic program and U an update program, both in the language $\mathcal{L}_{\neg}$. Modulo any primed, L^U and explicitly negated literals, the partial stable models of the updated program P_U are exactly the 3-valued $<P,U>$-Justified Updates of P updated by U.* ◇

6 Conclusions and Future Work

Throughout this paper we have motivated and formalized the generalization of the notion of updates to the case where we want to update programs instead of just their models. We have shown that since a program encodes more information than a set of models, the law of inertia should be applied to rules instead of to model literals, as had been done so far. We presented a transformation which, given an initial program and an update program, generates the desired updated program. This was achieved both for the stable as well as for the partial stable semantics. Another important result set forth in this work is the extension to the case where we want to update a given program more than once, i.e. iterated updating. This is important inasmuch as it allows us to conceive what it is to successively update one program by another, and so to define the evolution of knowledge bases by means of updates[2].

Program updating is a new and crucial notion deserving future foundational work and opening up a whole new range of applications and problems such as:

Software specification: One of the major tasks in the software industry is the updating of software. This process would be made much easier if we could just simply specify the update i.e. the parts of the program specific to the new version, and automatically generate the updated version.

Generalize the scope of update rules: Just as interpretation updates were extended to updating by means of arbitrary inference rules [13], logic program updating should also be generalized, possibly using super logic programs [5].

[2]For a generalization of the results presented here for the case of extended (with explicit negation) logic programs, the reader is referred to [9].

Reasoning about the past: Since no information is lost during the update process, i.e. after any iteration we can still characterize any previous state, we can use this framework to reason about the past in various ways:

- The scope of update rules could be extended to allow for updates to depend on some past state. This would be done by allowing the body of update rules to refer to previous states, thus increasing the expressibility of updates.

- The iterated updated program at state t can be used to directly determine *what might have happened in the past with present knowledge.* This could be done by checking the truth value of atoms A_{t_1} and $\neg\_A_{t_1}$ where t_1 refers to the previous state we want reason about.

Self updates Throughout this work we assumed that updates were externally driven. This need not be so. We could allow for internal self updating. This would be of the form of update rules scheduled to be triggered at some state, under certain conditions. Informally, an example of such kind of self update rules would be:

$$up\,[in(L) \leftarrow in(L_1), out(L_2)] \leftarrow in(L_3), out(L_4)$$

with the intended meaning of: if at state t $in(L_3), out(L_4)$ is verified, perform the update $in(L) \leftarrow in(L_1), out(L_2)$ at state $t+1$.

Improved expressibility could be obtained by combining these self updates with the externally driven ones. A simple application example of this combination would be the modeling of an automata receiving external input by means of an update, changing its state by means of a self update, and performing some output. By allowing internal self update rules one opens up the concept of self-evolving programs, that could be used to model artificial life.

Dealing with contradiction: Contradiction may have its origin at several stages of the update process: both the program to be updated and the update program may be contradictory, and even if they are both non-contradictory, the updated program may be so. One might apply well known contradiction avoidance/removal techniques [2][3] to updates. Furthermore updates should be generalized to include integrity constraints.

Also updates could be used as a means to remove contradiction. Note that the update of a contradictory program need not necessarily be contradictory.

Reasoning about actions: Updates pave the way for the dynamics of logic programming as opposed to its statics which has received most attention till now. Areas such as temporal databases, production systems, event calculus and situation calculus can benefit and be fertilized by this updates theory.

Acknowledgements

This work was partially supported by PRAXIS XXI project MENTAL. The work of João Alexandre Leite was partially supported by PRAXIS XXI scholarship no. BD/13514/97. We thank the three anonymous referees for their helpful comments.

References

[1] J. J. Alferes, J. A. Leite, L. M. Pereira, H. Przymusinski and T. C. Przymusinski. *Dynamic Logic programming.* In Sixth International Conference on Principles of Knowledge Representation and Reasoning, KR'98, Morgan Kaufmann 1998.

[2] J. J. Alferes and L. M. Pereira. *Contradiction: when avoidance equals removal, I and II.* In Dyckhoff, editor, 4th ELP, volume 798 of LNAI. Springer-Verlag, 1994.

[3] J. J. Alferes and L. M. Pereira *Reasonning with Logic Programming.* LNAI 1111, Berlin. Springer-Verlag, 1996.

[4] J. J. Alferes and L. M. Pereira. *Update-programs can update programs.* In J. Dix, L. M. Pereira and T. Przymusinski, editors, Selected papers from the ICLP'96 ws NMELP'96, vol. 1216 of LNAI, pages 110-131. Springer-Verlag, 1997.

[5] S. Brass, J. Dix and T. Przymusinski. *Super Logic Programs.* In L. C. Aiello, J. Doyle, and S. C. Shaphiro, editors, Principles of Knowledge Representation and Reasoning, Proc. of the Third Int'l Conf (KR96), pages 529-541. San Francisco, CA, Morgan-Kaufmann, 1996.

[6] M. Gelfond and V. Lifschitz. *Logic Programs with classical negation.* In Warren and Szeredi, editors, 7th Int. Conf. on LP, pages 579-597. MIT Press, 1990.

[7] H. Katsuno and A. Mendelzon. *On the difference between updating a knowledge base and revising it.* In James Allen, Richard Fikes and Erik Sandewall, editors, Principles of Knowledge Representation and Reasoning: Proc. of the Second Int'l Conf., pages 230-237, Morgan Kaufmann 1991.

[8] A. Keller and M. Winslett Wilkins. *On the use of an extended relational model to handle changing incomplete information.* IEEE Trans. on Software Engineering, SE-11:7, pages 620-633, 1985.

[9] João A. Leite. *Logic Program Updates.* MSc dissertation, Universidade Nova de Lisboa, 1997.

[10] J. A. Leite and L. M. Pereira. *Generalizing updates: from models to programs.* In LPKR'97: ILPS'97 workshop on Logic Programming and Knowledge Representation, Port Jefferson, NY, USA, October 13-16, 1997.

[11] V.Marek and M. Truszczynski. *Revision specifications by means of programs.* In C. MacNish, D. Pearce and L. M. Pereira, editors, JELIA '94, volume 838 of LNAI, pages 122-136. Springer-Verlag, 1994.

[12] Isaaco Newtono. *Philosophiæ Naturalis Principia Mathematica.* Editio tertia aucta & emendata. Apud Guil & Joh. Innys, Regiæ Societatis typographos. Londini, MDCCXXVI. Original quotation:*"Corpus omne perseverare in statu suo quiescendi vel movendi uniformiter in directum, nisi quatenus illud a viribus impressis cogitur statum suum mutare."*.

[13] T. Przymusinski and H. Turner. *Update by means of inference rules.* In V. Marek, A. Nerode, and M. Truszczynski, editors, LPNMR'95, volume 928 of LNAI, pages 156-174. Springer-Verlag, 1995.

[14] M. Winslett. *Reasoning about action using a possible models approach.* In AAAI'88, pages 89-93, 1988.

Specialising The Other Way Around

Wim Vanhoof, Bern Martens,
Danny De Schreye, Karel De Vlaminck
Department of Computer Science, K.U.Leuven, Belgium
e-mail: {wimvh, bern, dannyd, kdv}@cs.kuleuven.ac.be

Abstract

In this paper, we present a program transformation based on bottom up evaluation of logic programs. We explain that using this technique, programs can be "specialised" w.r.t. a set of unit clauses instead of a query. Moreover, examples indicate that excellent specialisation can be obtained when this bottom up transformation is combined with a more traditional top down approach, resulting in conceptually cleaner techniques requiring a less complicated control than one overall approach.

1 Introduction

Basically, logic programs can be evaluated in two ways: *top down*, in which SLD-resolution is used to build a search tree with the query as its root, and *bottom up* in which, starting from the facts of the program, new facts are derived during subsequent iterations, and hence the success set of the program is computed (e.g. [12]). Both strategies have their merits and disadvantages: while in general top down evaluation is considered to be more efficient and seems to be the preferred evaluation technique for logic programs, for a lot of programs the evaluation does not terminate. Bottom up evaluation, on the other hand, can guarantee completeness and termination for a certain class of programs (datalog), which makes it suited for use in e.g. deductive databases [20]. While in general, this evaluation strategy tends to be less efficient, for some kinds of programs and queries it equals (and sometimes even outperforms) top down evaluation.

Program specialisation, in a logic programming setting also called partial deduction, is an important transformation technique capable of removing certain inefficiencies from programs [6, 13, 4]. The basic idea is, given a program and part of its input, to evaluate the program parts that depend on the known input, and generate a new program that computes its result using only the remainder of the input. Since this new program has less computations to perform, in general, it will be more efficient. To achieve this goal, a partial deducer is in essence an evaluator with extra control components imposed to assure termination of the specialisation process.

To the best of our knowledge, all general partial deducers for logic programs use a top down evaluation strategy, specialising a program with respect to a partially instantiated query representing the known input part. This technique is suited if the information with respect to which we want to specialise flows in a top down fashion into the program. However, information can also reside in (unit) clauses and flow bottom up into the program. Taking the latter into account can be very hard for an automatic top down specialiser, since it has to start from a very general query, requiring a sophisticated control mechanism to reach the interesting information and obtain a satisfactory degree of specialisation.

In Section 2 of this paper we give some examples where one would like to "specialise" a program w.r.t. a set of unit clauses instead of a partially instantiated query and discuss the basic problem top down specialisers have with these. In Section 3, we develop a dual transformation technique based on bottom up evaluation of logic programs which is capable of achieving the proposed specialisation. Section 4 shows how this technique can be integrated with a top down specialiser. We demonstrate that such a combination requires a less sophisticated control mechanism for the top down part in order to achieve the same amount of specialisation, possibly opening the way for more and more involved programs to be specialised well. A comparison with other work and some directions for future research can be found in Section 5. Throughout the paper, we only consider definite programs and goals.

2 Motivation and Top Down Specialisation

2.1 Some Motivating Examples

Consider the following implementation of *append*, in which an abstract data type (ADT) is used to represent lists.

Example 2.1

$append(X,Y,Y) \leftarrow nil(X).$
$append(X,Y,Z) \leftarrow not\_nil(X), head(X,H), tail(X,T),$
$\qquad append(T,Y,R), cons(H,R,Z).$

This *append* program can be seen as a very general program that can be run with a variety of different ADT-implementations. Such a specific ADT-implementation is represented as a set of unit clauses, for example:

$nil([]).$ $\quad head([X|X_s],X).$ $\quad cons(X,X_s,[X|X_s]).$
$not\_nil([X|X_s]).$ $\quad tail([X|X_s],X_s).$

From a software engineering point of view, the ability to give such an ADT as part of the "input" to a program might be worthwhile during its development. However, at a certain point in time, one might want to fix the representation, and "specialise" the general *append* program w.r.t. a specific ADT-implementation yielding (see also [9]):

$append([],Y,Y).$
$append([X|X_s],Y,[X|R]) \leftarrow append(X_s,Y,R).$

While this version of *append* will answer exactly the same queries as the previous version (and thus is not specialised in the classic sense), it is specialised in that it can no longer be run with a representation for lists in the form of an ADT as (part of its) input.

Another well-known example is the specialisation of a meta interpreter w.r.t. an object program. Consider the Vanilla meta interpreter (V):

Example 2.2
$solve(true).$
$solve((A, B)) \leftarrow solve(A), solve(B).$
$solve(A) \leftarrow clause(A, B), solve(B).$

The aim is to specialise V w.r.t. a given object program, represented by a number of *clause*-facts, e.g. the *reverse* program:

$clause(rev([], L, L), true).$
$clause(rev([X|X_s], L, R), rev(X_s, [X|L], R)).$

As a result, in essence, the original *reverse* predicate is expected.

2.2 Top Down Specialisation

The key idea in automatic (top-down) partial deduction consists of building a number of different SLD-trees that together cover the complete computation of a goal G in a program P and synthesise new program clauses from them.

To that end, the control of on-line partial deduction is conceptually divided into two levels [6, 16]: the first one, often referred to as the *local* control level, deals with constructing a finite, possibly incomplete SLD-tree for a certain atom. Specialisation is obtained since unfolding is guided by the (partial) input provided in the root atom and the appropriate input part is propagated down the tree.

An *unfolding criterion* decides whether or not a certain atom in a goal may be unfolded while not endangering termination of the process [15, 4, 6]. This decision is based on comparing the atom under consideration with atoms previously encountered in the derivation (i.e. the SLD-tree built so far). An atom B will not be unfolded if its arguments are in some way *growing* w.r.t. a previously unfolded atom A, in which case the relation $WHISTLE(A, B)$[1] holds. More formally:

Definition 2.3 A relation $\mathcal{R}$ on atoms over a finite alphabet is called a *WHISTLE* iff any infinite series of atoms $A_1, \ldots, A_i, \ldots$ over the given alphabet must contain two atoms A_i and A_j $(i < j)$ such that $\mathcal{R}(A_i, A_j)$.

In the sequel we use the general notation *WHISTLE* to denote such a whistle relation. In the examples throughout the remainder of this paper we use the *homeomorphic embedding* relation ($\trianglelefteq$)[18, 10] as a concrete, elegant and simple, instance of the *WHISTLE* relation.[2]

[1]Terminology taken from [18].

[2]Of course, other *WHISTLE* relations may also give good results [15]. See Section 5

Definition 2.4 Let X, Y range over variables, f over functors, and p over predicates. As usual, $e_1 \prec e_2$ denotes that e_2 is a strict instance of e_1. Define $\trianglelefteq$ on terms and atoms:

$$
\begin{array}{lll}
X \trianglelefteq Y & & \\
s \trianglelefteq f(t_1, \ldots, t_n) & \Leftarrow & s \trianglelefteq t_i \text{ for some } i \\
f(s_1, \ldots, s_n) \trianglelefteq f(t_1, \ldots, t_n) & \Leftarrow & s_i \trianglelefteq t_i \text{ for all } i \\
p(s_1, \ldots, s_n) \trianglelefteq p(t_1, \ldots, t_n) & \Leftarrow & s_i \trianglelefteq t_i \text{ for all } i \text{ and } p(t_1, \ldots, t_n) \not\prec p(s_1, \ldots, s_n)
\end{array}
$$

As shown in [10], the following property holds:

Proposition 2.5 For any given finite alphabet, $\trianglelefteq$ is a *WHISTLE* relation.

The *global* control level, on the other hand, concerns the set of atoms for which an SLD-tree is built. To ensure correctness [13] while producing a maximally precise partial deduction, basically, for atoms appearing in the leaf of a constructed SLD-tree, a fresh such tree needs to be built when there is not yet one with (a variant of) the given atom as its root. In this way, a set of partially deduced atoms and associated SLD-trees is produced. Without further measures, this set will often expand infinitely. Therefore, it is necessary to apply appropriate generalisations, again based on some *WHISTLE* relation, replacing two or more atoms by their most specific generalisation (*msg*).

For each constructed SLD-tree, a new predicate is generated; one clause per branch with the root of the tree as head and the leaves as body. Further details on correctness and control of on-line partial deduction can be found in [13] and e.g. [6, 10, 15, 16] respectively. Finally, it can be noted that partial deduction *automates* a *subset* of unfold/fold transformations [19]. Comments on the relationship can be found in [17] and [3].

2.3 The Problems That Be

An unfolding criterion based on the partial SLD-tree built so far works well if all information necessary to unfold deeply enough without endangering termination is present in that tree. For example, when building a derivation for the atom *append*([1, 2, 3], Y, Z), no sensible unfolding criterion will stop the derivation prematurely since subsequent atoms have an argument (the first one) that is shrinking in size.

$$
append([\mathbf{1}, \mathbf{2}, \mathbf{3}], Y, Z) \stackrel{Z=[1|Z_2]}{\longrightarrow} append([\mathbf{2}, \mathbf{3}], Y, Z_2) \rightarrow \ldots
$$

Consider the following, admittedly somewhat artificial, example. The predicate *make_list*(T, I, R) can be used to create a list of a fixed length (type T), with each element initialised with I. The result is returned in R.

Example 2.6

$fill\_list(L, T, I, L) \leftarrow type(T, L).$	$type(list1, [X])$
$fill\_list(L, T, I, R) \leftarrow fill\_list([I\|L], T, I, R).$	$type(list3, [X_1, X_2, X_3]).$
$make\_list(T, I, R) \leftarrow fill\_list([], T, I, R).$	

Example 2.6 represents a class of recursive predicates that build up some structure between calls before a base clause of the predicate (ending the recursion) is reached, depending on the structure built. Unfolding techniques are known to have problems with these, since it often cannot be derived from the SLD-tree built so far whether or not unfolding such a recursive call will eventually terminate. In Figure 1, e.g., a partial SLD-tree for *make_list*$(list3, a, R)$ is depicted. The only argument in which atom (2) dif-

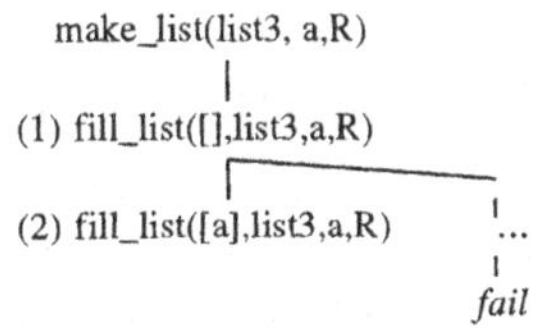

Figure 1: SLD-tree for *make_list*$(list3, a, R)$

fers from atom (1) is growing w.r.t. the latter and potential non-termination is concluded, although further unfolding will eventually lead to a successful derivation with R instantiated to $[a, a, a]$.

Reconsider Example 2.1. The aim of specialisation is to remove the calls to the ADT, and to propagate the concrete list representation into the *append* predicate. The only sensible query to start top down specialisation with is *append*(X, Y, Z). The absence of instantiated arguments in this query reflects the fact that the necessary information for specialisation is supplied elsewhere. Due to the simplicity of the example, most top down specialisers will not have any difficulties in obtaining the required specialisation. For Example 2.2 this is no longer true. As shown in [22], fully general and automatic top down specialisation of the vanilla meta interpreter requires a sophisticated control mechanism with interaction between the local and global control.

Apart from the fact that using an uninstantiated query to achieve specialisation with a system tuned to exploit information in the query seems strange, it will sometimes even be impossible. Reconsider once more the ADT of Example 2.1. Suppose we have a program that defines a library of distinct predicates $p_1, \ldots, p_n$ of which each uses the ADT for lists. Specialising this program w.r.t. the ADT will be impossible using a single query.

In the remainder of this paper, we develop a technique that can be used to specialise programs in the sense outlined above, when no partial information is given in the query (or no query at all is given). We first elaborate on the propagation of information in a bottom up fashion. Next, we show how the resulting transformation technique can be integrated to good effect with top down specialisation.

3 Bottom Up Specialisation

The ground consequence T_P-operator (see e.g. [12]) and its use in logic programming are well-known. In what follows, we define a T_P-like operator which, starting from a set of non-ground atoms, calculates new atoms (non-ground consequences) and arranges them in a *directed acyclic graph* or DAG. In Section 3.2, we subsequently show how a transformed program can be extracted from this DAG. For lack of space, all proofs are omitted.

3.1 From Bottom Up Evaluation to Specialisation

Definition 3.1 An *annotated* DAG is a DAG with atoms as nodes, connected by edges, carrying a substitution. Nodes are characterised as either *active* or *passive* and can have an additional annotation, saying that the node is *generalised*.

The characterisation of the nodes in the DAG provides a basis to keep the DAG finite: a node characterised as *passive* will not be used to compute new consequences, whereas an *active* node will. A node is annotated by *generalised* if its atom is not derived as a consequence of other atoms, but rather is a generalisation of such a consequence. Now we can define our DAG-building operator D_P.

Definition 3.2 For a program P, the operator $D_P(G)$ on a DAG G is defined as follows: For each standardised apart variant $H \leftarrow L_1, \ldots, L_m$ of a clause in P and for each set of active atoms $\{B_1, \ldots, B_n\}$ $(n \leq m)$ in G: let $\{C_1, \ldots, C_m\}$ be a set of atoms such that $\forall i \in \{1, \ldots, m\}, \exists j \in \{1, \ldots, n\}$: $C_i = B_j\gamma_j$, with γ_j a fresh variable renaming of B_j. If $\sigma = mgu((L_1, \ldots, L_m), (C_1, \ldots, C_m))$ then $H\sigma$ is an *immediate consequence* of $B_1, \ldots, B_n$ in P, and $H\sigma$ is entered in G. Moreover, $\forall i \in \{1, \ldots, m\}$, if $C_i = B_j\gamma_i$, an edge $B_j \overset{\gamma_i\sigma}{\rightarrow} H\sigma$ is added to G.

The operator D_P thus builds an annotated DAG in which an edge leaves an atom A only if A is characterised as active. Since $H\sigma$ is entered in the DAG, the substitution σ, labelling an edge $B_j \overset{\gamma_i\sigma}{\rightarrow} H\sigma$ can be restricted to the variables of B_j. Moreover, the variable renaming γ_i, labelling an edge $B_j \overset{\gamma_i\sigma}{\rightarrow} H\sigma$ can be discarded if B_j is used only once in the derivation of $H\sigma$. In the examples throughout the paper, atoms in the DAG are for simplicity reasons only renamed when strictly necessary. Moreover, edges are labelled only with the relevant part of the substitution, if any at all.

Example 3.3 Let P be the program of Example 2.2 and G a DAG containing only three *active*, unconnected atoms: the unit clauses of P. The result of $D_P(G)$ is then depicted in Figure 2.

The following definitions will be useful:

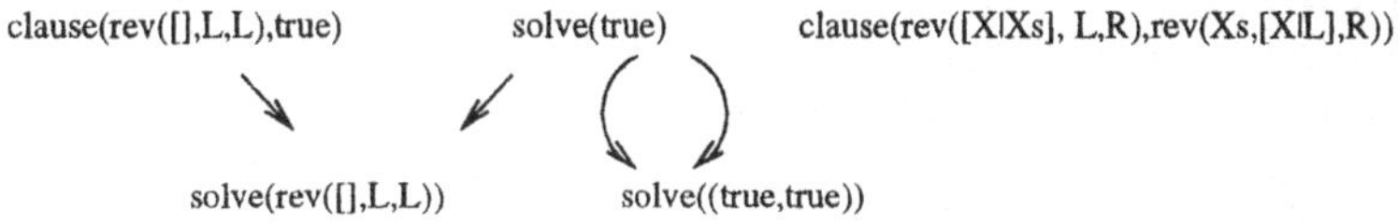

Figure 2: The result of applying $D_P(G)$

Definition 3.4 Consider a DAG G, and two nodes $A, B \in G$. There is a *path* from A to B in G, denoted by $A \Longrightarrow B$, if there is an edge $A \rightarrow B$ in G or there exists another node C in G such that $A \rightarrow C$ is an edge in G and there exists a path from C to B in G.

Definition 3.5 The *consequence sub*DAG of a node A in a DAG G, denoted by $CS(G, A)$, is the subDAG of G with as nodes $\mathcal{N} = \{B | \exists \text{ a path } A \Longrightarrow B \in G\}$ and all edges from G connecting nodes in $\mathcal{N}$.

The consequence subDAG $CS(G, A)$ denotes the part of G in which every atom was derived by D_P using (a consequence of) A.

Example 3.6 For the DAG G of Figure 2, $CS(G, \mathit{solve}(\mathit{true}))$ is depicted in Figure 3.

solve(rev([],L,L)) solve((true,true))

Figure 3: $CS(G, \mathit{solve}(\mathit{true}))$

As in top down specialisation [16, 10] we have to take care that the structure building process terminates: Naively applying D_P will often produce an infinite DAG. Abstraction is called for, replacing a possibly infinite number of atoms that can be derived by a single more general one. We need the following operations: $\mathit{make\_passive}(G, A)$ which changes the characterisation of a node A in G from *active* to *passive*, and $\mathit{generalise}(G, N_1, N_2)$, producing a DAG G' in which N_1, together with $CS(G, N_1)$, is "replaced" by a generalisation of N_1 and N_2.

Definition 3.7 Let N_1, N_2 be two nodes in an annotated DAG G. The DAG $\mathit{generalise}(G, N_1, N_2)$ is obtained from G as follows:

- Every node in $CS(G, N_1)$ is removed from G. Also, every edge $A \rightarrow B$ with A or $B \in CS(G, N_1)$ is removed from G.
- N_1 is characterised as *passive* and a new *active* node $M = \mathit{msg}(N_1, N_2)$ is entered in the DAG and annotated *generalised*. Furthermore, for every edge $B \stackrel{\sigma}{\rightarrow} N_1$ in the DAG, a new edge $B \stackrel{\{\}}{\rightarrow} M$ is added to G.

Algorithm 3.8
input: an annotated DAG G
output: an annotated DAG $Abstract(G)$
$G_0 := G; i := 0;$
repeat
 If $\exists$ a path $A \Longrightarrow B$ in G_i, with B an *active* node and $WHISTLE(A, B)$:
 then if $\exists$ a path $N \Longrightarrow B$ in G, N is generalised and $N\theta = B$ for a substitution θ
  then $G_{i+1} := make\_passive(G_i, B)$.
  else $G_{i+1} := generalise(G_i, A, B)$.
 $i := i + 1;$
until $G_i = G_{i-1};$
$Abstract(G) := G_i$

Proposition 3.9 Algorithm 3.8 terminates for any input DAG G.

Example 3.10 In the DAG $D_P(G)$ depicted in Figure 2, $solve(true) \trianglelefteq solve((true, true))$, so $WHISTLE$ holds between these atoms. The result of $Abstract(G)$ is depicted in Figure 4. Passive nodes are underlined, while nodes annotated *generalised* are italicised.

clause(rev([],L,L),true) *solve(X)* <u>solve(true)</u> clause(rev([X|Xs], L,R),rev(Xs,[X|L],R))

Figure 4: The result of applying *Abstract* on the DAG of Figure 2.

The bottom up specialisation algorithm then consists of alternating D_P with *Abstract* until a fixpoint is reached.

Algorithm 3.11
Consider a program P.
$i := 0;\ G_0 := \{\}.$
repeat
 $G_{i+1} := Abstract(D_P(G_i));$
 $i := i + 1;$
until $G_{i+1} = G_i$

Theorem 3.12 Algorithm 3.11 terminates for any program P.

Example 3.13
Applying algorithm 3.11 on the program of Example 2.2 yields the DAG depicted in Figure 5.

3.2 The Transformed Program

Generating a residual program from the annotated DAG is quite straightforward. For an atom A that is derived using only D_P steps (thus no generalised node occurs on any path to A), a new fact $A \leftarrow$ can be generated. (Instances of) other (generalised) atoms in the DAG are true iff particular instances of the generalised nodes they are consequences of can be proven. For each such atom, a program clause is generated.

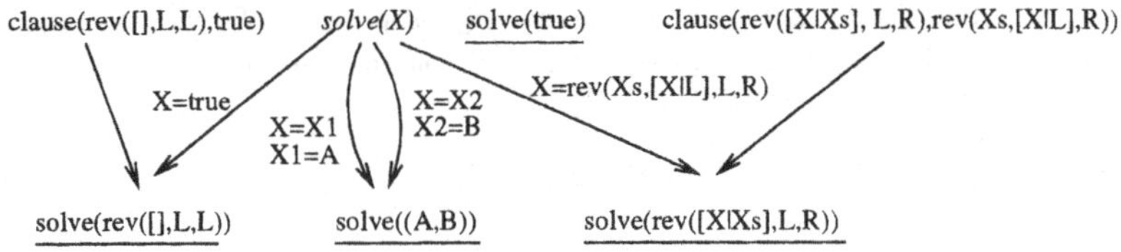

Figure 5: Applying algorithm 3.11 on the program of Example 2.2.

Definition 3.14 defines, for a given node N and DAG G, all the paths in G from a nearest generalised node to N together with the composed substitution along the path.

Definition 3.14 For a given DAG G and node $H \in G$, the set of *generalised predecessors* is defined as:
$GP(G,H) = \{(A,\sigma) \mid$ there exists a path $A \overset{\theta_1}{\to} N_1 \overset{\theta_2}{\to} \ldots \overset{\theta_{n-1}}{\to} N_{n-1} \overset{\theta_n}{\to} H$ in G where A is annotated *generalised*, no N_i is annotated *generalised* and $\sigma = \theta_1\theta_2 \ldots \theta_n.\}$

Observe that every node in a DAG has at most one generalised predecessor on every incoming path. These will exactly be the body atoms in the fresh clauses synthesised from the DAG.

Definition 3.15 The *residual program* for a DAG G can be defined as
$\{H \leftarrow A_1\sigma_1, \ldots, A_m\sigma_m \mid H \in G, H$ is not annotated as *generalised* and
$GP(G,H) = \{(A_1,\sigma_1), \ldots, (A_m,\sigma_m)\}\}$.

Theorem 3.16 For a program P, let P' be the program extracted according to Definition 3.15 from the DAG built by Algorithm 3.11.

- If $P \cup G$ has an SLD-refutation with computed answer substitution (c.a.s.) θ then so does $P' \cup G$.
- If $P' \cup G$ has an SLD-refutation with c.a.s. θ then $P \cup G$ has an SLD-refutation with c.a.s. γ such that there exists a substitution σ with $\theta = \gamma\sigma$ and $P \cup G\theta$ has an SLD-refutation (with empty c.a.s.).
- If $P \cup G$ has a finitely failed SLD-tree, so does $P' \cup G$.

So soundness and completeness of the transformation are ensured, but P' may, in some cases, render additional more specific answers than P. While Theorem 3.16 states that the bottom up transformation preserves finite failure, it may convert infinite failure into finite failure, as the following example shows.

Example 3.17

$P:$	$q(a).$	$P':$	$q(a).$
	$q(X) \leftarrow q(X).$		

The query $q(b)$ fails infinitely in the original program P, whereas it fails finitely in the transformed program P'. Of course, several other techniques achieve the same effect (see e.g. [6]).

Example 3.18 For the DAG G of Figure 5, the set of generalised predecessors is as follows.

$GP(G, clause(rev([], L, L), true)) = \{\}$
$GP(G, clause(rev([X|X_s], L, R), rev(X_s, [X|L], R))) = \{\}$
$GP(G, solve(true)) = \{\}$
$GP(G, solve(rev([], L, L))) = \{(solve(X), \{X = true\})\}$
$GP(G, solve((A, B))) = \{(solve(X), \{X = A\}), (solve(X), \{X = B\})\}$
$GP(G, solve(rev([X|X_s], L, R))) = \{(solve(X), \{X = rev(X_s, [X|L], R)\})\}$

The generated program is then:

$solve(true).$
$solve((A, B)) \leftarrow solve(A), solve(B).$
$solve(rev([], L, L)) \leftarrow solve(true).$
$solve(rev([X|X_s], L, R)) \leftarrow solve(rev(X_s, [X|L], R)).$
$clause(rev([], L, L), true).$
$clause(rev([X|X_s], L, R), rev(X_s, [X|L], R)).$

If the only queries of interest for the resulting program of Example 3.18 are queries having *solve* as predicate, the definition of the *clause* predicate can be removed. Since it is precisely this kind of information which is available to a top down specialiser, it seems natural to combine our bottom up transformation with a traditional top down specialisation phase.

4 Integration With Top Down

4.1 On The Control of Bottom Up Specialisation

The use of the *WHISTLE* relation to detect possible infinite paths allows consecutive facts of a recursive predicate to be derived as long as there is some structure that is not growing w.r.t. an earlier derived fact.

This allows the specialisation of program fragments like Example 2.6: Whereas it is hard to automatically allow unfolding $fill\_list([], list3, a, R)$ because the first argument is growing between successive recursive calls, that same argument is shrinking if successive consequences are derived in a bottom up fashion starting from the base case $fill\_list([X_1, X_2, X_3], list3, I, [X_1, X_2, X_3])$. The bottom up transformation for this example ends with the following unit clauses, which is precisely what we want:

$make\_list(list1, I, [I]).$
$make\_list(list3, I, [I, I, I]).$

On the other hand, most logic programs contain predicates processing structure that shrinks between successive recursive calls. An example is the parsing clause of the Vanilla meta interpreter:

$solve((A,B)) \leftarrow solve(A), solve(B).$

When this kind of clause is used the other way round during a bottom up derivation of consequences, the argument in the newly derived instance of the head is always growing w.r.t. the argument of the atoms unifying with the clause body, meaning that the former cannot be used for further derivations.

A possible solution to this problem is to design a more fine-grained bottom up control scheme, allowing structure to grow within certain bounds. For example: structure in an atom should be allowed to grow if the resulting atom can be used in the body of a rule that could not be used before.

On the other hand, this very problem is something top down techniques deal well with. Once more, this indicates possibilities for an integration of our bottom up transformation with a traditional, top down partial deducer.

4.2 Mixing Bottom Up and Top Down

In this section we consider specialisation of a given program P (completely with a set of unit clauses) and a query of interest Q. $\mathcal{B}(P)$ denotes the set of body atoms of P. As a working example, we extend Example 2.2.

Example 4.1 As a program P, we reconsider the Vanilla meta interpreter of Example 2.2 together with a representation of *reverse* with a type check on the accumulator. The query of interest $Q = solve(rev(X, Y, Z))$.

$solve(true).$
$solve((A,B)) \leftarrow solve(A), solve(B).$
$solve(A) \leftarrow clause(A,B), solve(B).$
$clause(rev([], L, L), true).$ $\quad$ $clause(ls([]), true).$
$clause(rev([X|X_s], L, R), (ls(L), rev(X_s, [X|L], R))).$ $\quad$ $clause(ls([X|X_s]), ls(X_s)).$

The residual program P' created from the DAG G generated by algorithm 3.11 is the following, together with the original definition of the *clause*-predicate from P:

$solve(true).$
$solve((A,B)) \leftarrow solve(A), solve(B).$
$solve(ls([])) \leftarrow solve(true).$
$solve(ls([X|X_s])) \leftarrow solve(ls(X_s)).$
$solve(rev([], L, L)) \leftarrow solve(true).$
$solve(rev([X|X_s], L, R)) \leftarrow solve((ls(L), rev(X_s, [X|L], R))).$

As a result of the bottom up propagation, the heads of the residual clauses are instantiations of heads of original clauses in P. The atoms of $\mathcal{B}(P')$ are instantiations of generalised nodes in G: They usually carry interesting structure. Therefore, it might be worthwhile to specialise the atoms in $\mathcal{B}(P') \cup Q$ top down. Since information has been propagated upwards in P', unfolding an atom in P' will need to be less sophisticated to reach the same amount of information as unfolding the same atom in the original program P.

Example 4.2 Consider P' from Example 4.1 with $solve(rev(X,Y,Z))$ as query. Using a very simple unfolding strategy – an atom is unfolded only if it matches a single clause head in the program (deterministic unfolding [8]) – produces the SLD-trees depicted in Figure 6.

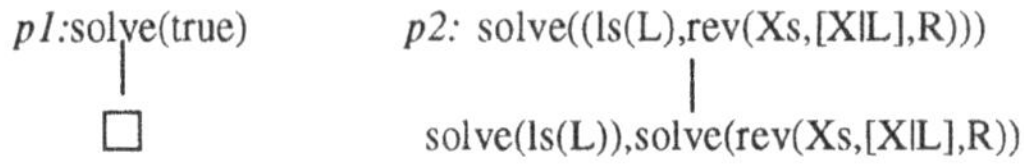

Figure 6: deterministic SLD-trees for the body atoms of P' (if any)

When the new predicates p_1 and p_2 are created, the residual program P'' looks as follows (after removing useless clauses):

$solve(ls([])) \leftarrow p_1.$
$solve(ls([X|X_s])) \leftarrow solve(ls(X_s)).$
$solve(rev([], L, L)) \leftarrow p_1.$
$solve(rev([X|X_s], L, R)) \leftarrow p_2(L, X, X_s, R).$
$p_1.$
$p_2(L, X, X_s, R) \leftarrow solve(ls(L)), solve(rev(X_s, [X|L], R)).$

As another consequence of the instantiations made by the bottom up propagation, the transformed program can be renamed, and structure can be filtered from it [7] (splitting a predicate definition in several new definitions according to the structure it handles).

Example 4.3 After renaming and structure filtering, P'' from Example 4.2 looks as follows:

$solve(rev(X,Y,Z)) \leftarrow solve_2(X,Y,Z).$
$solve_1([]) \leftarrow p_1.$
$solve_1([X|X_s]) \leftarrow solve_1(X_s).$
$solve_2([], L, L) \leftarrow p_1.$
$solve_2([X|X_s], L, R) \leftarrow p_2(L, X, X_s, R).$
$p_1.$
$p_2(L, X, X_s, R) \leftarrow solve_1(L), solve_2(X_s, [X|L], R).$

Another bottom up transformation step will propagate the definition of p_1 into P'' and leads to the removal of the superfluous call to p_2, resulting in an object program without any parsing overhead due to the original meta interpreter. This example suggests that the two transformation phases can be alternated to obtain programs in which information is maximally propagated. However, a fully automatic control (and thus termination) of such an alternation is not straightforward: If a program P'' is derived from a program P', the transformation cycle can be continued as long as the "quality" of P'' is significantly better than that of P'. While (automatically) determining a program's quality still is an open problem, the use of cost analysis (e.g. [5]) seems a promising direction for future research.

5 Discussion & Further Work

Bottom up evaluation of logic programs has perhaps been mostly studied in the field of deductive databases [20, 1]. The basic idea to propagate object clauses bottom up into meta-interpreters was proposed in [2] (and [21]). Apart from this, little is known concerning the use of bottom up evaluation in program specialisation and its relation to standard unfolding techniques.

In this paper, using a control adapted from top down techniques, a specialisation scheme based on bottom up evaluation is presented. Excellent specialisation can be obtained in combination with a more traditional top down approach. The importance of such a bottom up component is twofold: Firstly, it enables specialisation through evaluation of program fragments obtaining information that hardly can be obtained through unfolding alone due to some bottom up information flow (See Example 2.6). Secondly, since structural information is propagated upwards, a top down component needs to unfold less deeply in order to reach the same information (and thus specialisation) as would be the case without the propagation. This results in smaller, more concentrated SLD-trees which can be built using a less complicated unfolding rule.

Dividing the specialisation in bottom up and top down phases results in conceptually cleaner, less complicated techniques with which at least the same results can be obtained as with one overall approach, in general requiring a much more complicated control. A concrete example is the specialisation of Vanilla-like meta interpreters. As was demonstrated in [22], specialisation of non ground meta interpreters using completely general and fully automatic top down techniques still is a non trivial task. In that paper, a sophisticated approach is described based on extending a local unfolding rule by global information. Although the resulting technique is completely general and automatic, in spite of its complexity, it turns out to be not sufficiently effective when more involved meta interpreters are at hand. As is shown in this paper, the same results can be obtained by using a trivial unfolding rule in combination with a basic bottom up transformation phase. Moreover, ongoing research shows that the work presented in this paper provides an elegant and powerful basis for handling general meta programs. On the other hand, meta programs using a term representation of the object clauses may not contain any information to be propagated bottom-up. Clearly, in such cases, adding bottom up phases will not improve much over pure top down specialisation.

In [11] top down partial deduction is combined with a *more specific program* transformation [14] based on abstract interpretation: after unfolding, a non ground version of T_P is used to derive success information which is then imposed on the residual predicates. Consider e.g. the following predicate:

$q(a)$.
$q(X) \leftarrow q(X)$.

The technique of [11] will correctly deduce that the only answer substitution for $q(X)$ is $\{X = a\}$. However, due to the use of T_P with a rather general abstract domain (the predicate-wise *msg* of every derived consequence is taken in each T_P-step), if the example is extended with another base clause, $q(b)$ e.g., the algorithm will not be able to derive $\{q(a), q(b)\}$ as the only possible answers.

Our approach is quite different: consequences are computed and ordered in a structure, and a new program is generated from this structure (completely independently of any top down interference). Generalisation of two atoms is performed only if one atom is a consequence of the other. However, instead of a new program, success information could be derived from the DAG and imposed on a predicate, as is the case in [11]. In case of the example above, our technique would deduce $\{q(a), q(b)\}$. Of course, with a more precise abstraction, the technique of [11] might achieve the same result.

In future work, we will further tune the transformation so as to exactly preserve computed answer substitutions. We also plan to investigate more refined bottom up inference, guiding the search towards "interesting" atoms (possibly avoiding unnecessary generalisations) integrating e.g. *magic templates* [20] and other techniques to direct bottom up search towards known top down information. Furthermore, the precise impact of a bottom up transformation phase on the required control for top down specialisation needs to be scrutinised, together with a finer integration of the two. Since the presented technique seems especially apt to specialise meta interpreters, its effects on more involved (meta) programs will be studied in detail together with the impact of more powerful (bottom up as well as top down) control.

Acknowledgements

We thank anonymous referees for useful remarks. Wim Vanhoof is supported by a specialisation grant of the Flemish Institute for the Promotion of Scientific-Technological Research in Industry (IWT), Belgium. Bern Martens is partially supported by the Belgian GOA "Non-Standard applications of Abstract Interpretation" and Danny De Schreye is Senior Research Associate of the Belgian National Fund for Scientific Research.

References

[1] F. Bancilhon and R. Ramakrishnan. An amateur's introduction to recursive query-processing strategies. In *ACM SIGMOD Intl. Conf. on Management of Data*, pages 16–52, 1986.

[2] Y. Cosmadopoulos, M. Sergot, and R. W. Southwick. Data-driven transformation of meta-interpreters: A sketch. In H. Boley and M. M. Richter, editors, *Proceedings of the International Workshop on Processing Declarative Knowledge (PDK'91)*, volume 567 of *LNAI*, pages 301–308. Springer Verlag, 1991.

[3] D. De Schreye, R. Glück, J. Jørgensen, M. Leuschel, B. Martens, and M. H. Sørensen. Conjunctive partial deduction: Foundations, control, algorithms and experiments. 1998. Submitted for publication.

[4] D. De Schreye, M. Leuschel, and B. Martens. Tutorial on program specialisation (abstract). In J.W. Lloyd, editor, *Proceedings ILPS'95*, pages 615–616, Portland, Oregon, December 1995. MIT Press.

[5] S. Debray and N.-W. Lin. Cost analysis of logic programs. *ACM Transactions on Programming Languages and Systems*, 15(5):826–875, 1993.

[6] J. Gallagher. Specialisation of logic programs: A tutorial. In *Proceedings PEPM'93, ACM SIGPLAN Symposium on Partial Evaluation and Semantics-Based Program Manipulation*, pages 88–98, Copenhagen, June 1993. ACM Press.

[7] J. Gallagher and M. Bruynooghe. Some low-level source transformations for logic programs. In M. Bruynooghe, editor, *Proceedings Meta'90*, pages 229–244, Leuven, April 1990.

[8] J. Gallagher and M. Bruynooghe. The derivation of an algorithm for program specialisation. *New Generation Computing*, 9(3&4):305–333, 1991.

[9] H. J. Komorowski. Synthesis of programs in the partial deduction framework. In Michael R. Lowry and Robert D. McCartney, editors, *Automating Software Design*, pages 377–403. AAAI Press, 1991.

[10] M. Leuschel, B. Martens, and D. De Schreye. Controlling generalisation and polyvariance in partial deduction of normal logic programs. *ACM Transactions on Programming Languages and Systems*, 20(1), 1998.

[11] M. Leuschel and D. De Schreye. Logic program specialisation: How to be more specific. In H. Kuchen and S. Swierstra, editors, *Proceedings of the International Symposium on Programming Languages, Implementations, Logics and Programs (PLILP'96)*, pages 137–151, Aachen, Germany, September 1996. Springer-Verlag. LNCS 1140.

[12] J. W. Lloyd. *Foundations of Logic Programming.* Springer-Verlag, 1987.

[13] J. W. Lloyd and J. C. Shepherdson. Partial evaluation in logic programming. *Journal of Logic Programming*, 11(3&4):217–242, 1991.

[14] K. Marriot, L. Naish, and J.-L. Lassez. Most specific logic programs. In *Proceedings of the Joint International Conference and Symposium on Logic Programming*, pages 909–923, Seattle, 1988. IEEE, MIT Press.

[15] B. Martens and D. De Schreye. Automatic finite unfolding using well-founded measures. *Journal of Logic Programming*, 28(2):89–146, 1996.

[16] B. Martens and J. Gallagher. Ensuring global termination of partial deduction while allowing flexible polyvariance. In L. Sterling, editor, *Proceedings ICLP'95*, pages 597–611, Shonan Village Center, Kanagawa, Japan, June 1995. MIT Press.

[17] A. Pettorossi and M. Proietti. Transformation of logic programs: Foundations and techniques. *Journal of Logic Programming*, 19/20:261–320, 1994.

[18] M. H. Sørensen and R. Glück. An algorithm of generalization in positive supercompilation. In J.W. Lloyd, editor, *Proceedings ILPS'95*, pages 465–479, Portland, Oregon, December 1995. MIT Press.

[19] H. Tamaki and T. Sato. Unfold/fold transformation of logic programs. In S-Å. Tärnlund, editor, *Proceedings ICLP'84*, pages 127–138, Uppsala, July 1984.

[20] J. D. Ullman. *Database and Knowledge-Base Systems.* Computer Science Press, 1988, 1989.

[21] W. Vanhoof. Bottom up information propagation for partial deduction. In M. Leuschel, editor, *Proceedings of the International Workshop on Specialization of Declarative Programs and its Applications*, pages 73 – 82, Port Jefferson, Long Island N.Y. (USA), October 1997. Proceedings available as report CW255, Dept. of Computer Science, K.U.Leuven, Belgium.

[22] W. Vanhoof and B. Martens. To parse or not to parse. In N. Fuchs, editor, *Proceedings of LOPSTR'97*, Leuven, Belgium, July 1997. To appear in Lecuture Notes in Computer Science series (Springer-Verlag).

Greedy Algorithms in Datalog with Choice and Negation

Sergio Greco
Dip. Elettr. Informatica Sist.
Università della Calabria
87030 Rende, Italy
greco@si.deis.unical.it

Carlo Zaniolo
Computer Science Dept.
Univ. of California at Los Angeles
Los Angeles, CA 90024
zaniolo@cs.ucla.edu

Abstract

In the design of algorithms, the greedy paradigm provides a powerful tool for solving efficiently classical computational problems, within the framework of procedural languages. However, expressing these algorithms within the declarative framework of logic-based languages has proven a difficult research challenge. In this paper, we extend the framework of Datalog-like languages to obtain simple declarative formulations for such problems, and propose effective implementation techniques to ensure computational complexities comparable to those of procedural formulations. These advances are achieved through the use of the `choice` construct, extended with preference annotations to effect the selection of alternative stable-models and nondeterministic fixpoints. We show that, with suitable storage structures, the differential fixpoint computation of our programs matches the complexity of procedural algorithms in classical search and optimization problems.

1 Introduction

The problem of finding efficient implementations for declarative logic-based languages represents one of the most arduous and lasting research challenges in computer science. The interesting theoretical challenges posed by this problem are made more urgent by the fact that extrema and other non-monotonic constructs are needed to express many real-life applications, ranging from the 'Bill of Materials' to graph-computation algorithms.

Significant progress in this area has been achieved on the semantic front, where the introduction of the well-founded model semantics and stable-model semantics allows us to assign a formal meaning to most, if not all, programs of practical interest. Unfortunately, the computational problems remain largely unsolved: various approaches have been proposed to more effective computations of well-founded models and stable models [20, 7], but these fall well short of matching the efficiency of classical procedural solutions, such as, say, algorithms that find shortest paths in graphs. In general, it is known that determining whether a program has a stable model is NP-complete [14].

Therefore, in this paper we propose a different approach: while, at the semantic level, we strictly adhere to the formal declarative semantics of logic programs with negation, we also allow the use of extended non-monotonic constructs with first order semantics to facilitate the task of programmers and compilers alike. This entails simple declarative formulations and nearly optimal executions for large classes of problems, that are normally solved using greedy algorithms.

Greedy algorithms [15] are those that solve a class of optimization problems, using a control structure of a single loop, where, at each iteration some element judged the 'best' at that stage is chosen and it is added to the solution. The simple loop hints that these problems are amenable to a fixpoint computation. The choice at each step calls attention to mechanisms by which nondeterministic choices can be expressed in logic programs. This framework also provides an opportunity of making, rather than blind choices, choices based on some heuristic criterion, such as greedly choosing the least (or most) among the values at hand when seeking the global minimization (or maximization) of the sum of such values. Following these hints, this paper introduces primitives for choice, and greedy selection, and show that classical greedy algorithms can be expressed using them.

A significant amount of excellent previous work has investigated the issue of how to express in logic and compute efficiently greedy algorithms, and, more in general, classical algorithms that require non-monotonic constructs. An incomplete list include work by [19, 5, 18, 21, 6]. In this paper we introduce a treatment for greedy algorithms that is significant simpler and more robust than previous approaches (including that of Greco, Zaniolo and Ganguly [11]); it also treats all aspects of these algorithms, beginning from their intuitive formulation, and ending with their optimized expression and execution.

For space limitation the proofs of our results are omitted and they can be found in the full version of the paper [12].

2 Nondeterministic Reasoning

Say that, with relation `student(Name,Major,Year)`, our university database contains the relation `professor(Name,Major)`. In fact, say that our toy database contains only the following facts:

```
student('JimBlack', ee, senior).        professor(ohm, ee).
                                        professor(bell, ee).
```

Now, the rule is that the major of a student must match his/her advisor's major area of specialization. Then eligible advisors can be computed as follows:

```
elig_adv(S,P) ← student(S,Majr,Year), professor(P,Majr).
```

This yields

```
elig_adv('JimBlack',ohm).
elig_adv('JimBlack',bell).
```

But, since a student can only have one advisor, the goal `choice((S),(P))` must be added to force the selection of a unique advisor, out of the eligible advisors, for a student.

Example 1. *Computation of unique advisors by choice rules*

```
actual_adv(S,P) ← student(S,Majr,Yr), professor(P,Majr),
                  choice((S),(P)).
```

The computation of this rule gives for each student S a unique professor P □

The goal `choice((S),(P))` can also be viewed as enforcing a functional dependency (FD) $\mathtt{S} \rightarrow \mathtt{P}$; thus, in `actual_adv`, the second column (professor name) is functionally dependent on the first one (student name).

The result of executing this rule is *nondeterministic*. It can either give a singleton relation containing the tuple (`'JimBlack',ohm`) or that containing the tuple (`'JimBlack',bell`).

A program where the rules contain choice goals is called a *choice program*. The semantics of a choice program P can be defined by transforming P into a program with negation, $foe(P)$, called the *first order equivalent* of a choice program P. $foe(P)$ exhibits a multiplicity of stable models, each obeying the FDs defined by the choice goals. Each stable model for $foe(P)$ corresponds to an alternative set of answers for P and is called a *choice model* for P. $foe(P)$ is defined as follows:

Definition 1. The *stable version* $foe(P)$ of a choice program P is obtained by the following transformation. Consider a choice rule r in P:

$$r : A \leftarrow B(Z),\ choice((X_1),(Y_1)),\ \ldots,\ choice((X_k),(Y_k)).$$

where,

(i) $B(Z)$ denotes the conjunction of all the goals of r that are not choice goals, and

(ii) X_i, Y_i, Z, $1 \leq i \leq k$, denote vectors of variables occurring in the body of r such that $X_i \cap Y_i = \emptyset$ and $X_i, Y_i \subseteq Z$.

Then the original program P is transformed as follows:

1. Replace r with a rule r' obtained by substituting the choice goals with the atom $chosen_r(W)$:

   $$r' : A \leftarrow B(Z),\ chosen_r(W).$$

   where $W \subseteq Z$ is the list of all variables appearing in choice goals, i.e., $W = \bigcup_{1 \leq j \leq k} X_j \cup Y_j$.

2. Add the new rule

   $$chosen_r(W) \leftarrow B(Z),\ \neg diffChoice_r(W).$$

3. For each choice atom $choice((X_i),(Y_i))$ $(1 \leq i \leq k)$, add the new rule

   $$diffChoice_r(W) \leftarrow chosen_r(W'),\ Y_i \neq Y_i'.$$

   where (i) the list of variables W' is derived from W by replacing each $A \notin X_i$ with a new variable A' (i.e., by priming those variables), and (ii) $Y_i \neq Y_i'$ is true if $A \neq A'$, for some variable $A \in Y_i$ and its primed counterpart $A' \in Y_i'$.

The stable version of Example 1 is given in Example 2, which can be read as a statement that a professor will be assigned to each student if a different professor has not been assigned to the same student.

Example 2. The stable version of the rule in Example 1

```
actual_adv(S,P) ←       student(S,Majr,Yr), professor(P,Majr),
                        chosen(S,P).
chosen(S,P) ←           student(S,Majr,Yr), professor(P,Majr),
                        ¬diffChoice(S,P).
diffChoice(S,P) ←       chosen(S,P'), P ≠ P'.
```

In general, the program $foe(P)$ generated by the transformation discussed above has the following properties[8]:

- $foe(P)$ has one or more total stable models.
- The `chosen` atoms in each stable model of $foe(P)$ obey the FDs defined by the choice goals.

The stable models of $foe(P)$ are called *choice models* for P.

While the topic of operational semantics for choice Datalog programs will be further discussed in Section 4, it is clear that they can be implemented efficiently. Basically, the `chosen` atoms need to be produced one-at-a-time and memorized in a table. The `diffchoice` atoms need not be computed and stored; rather, the goal `¬diffchoice` can simply be checked dynamically against the table `chosen`. Since these are simple operations (actually quasi constant-time if an hash table is used), it follows that choice Datalog programs can be computed in polynomial time, and that rules with choice can be evaluated as efficiently as those without choice.

3 Computing with Choice

The introduction of choice in Datalog has a significant impact on the expressive power of the language, since it allows us to express *nondeterministic* queries that cannot be expressed in Datalog with stratified negation, and *deterministic* queries that could not be expressed otherwise [10, 8].

In fact, the expressive power of the choice construct has been studied in [9, 10], where it is shown that it is more powerful than other nondeterministic constructs, including the witness operator [2], and the original version of choice proposed in [13], which is called static-choice, to distinguish from the dynamic choice used here [8]). For instance, it has been shown in [8], that the task of ordering a domain or computing whether it contains an even number of elements (parity query) cannot performed by positive programs with static choice or the witness operator [2].

In the rest of the paper, we will concentrate on nondeterministic queries. In particular, our previous advisor example, can be modified using more sophisticated criteria are used to match students with candidate advisors. Say that the application of these criteria has yielded a relation `candidate(Student, Advisor, D)`, which for each new `Student` gives several professors suitable to become their advisors (with and additional column `D` denoting dates at which the new advisory engagement can be initiated—thus there might be several values of `D` for each student-professor pair.) Then our matching problem can be expressed as follows:

Example 3. *Matching in a directed graph*

```
advisor(St, Adv) ← candidate(St, Adv, D),
                   choice((St), (Adv)), choice((St), (D)).
```
□

By viewing candidate as a graph from `St` to `Adv` we immediately see that we have here an instance of a bi-partite graph-matching problem. This also defines the optimization problem discussed in Section 5, by requiring that the sum of all `Ds` be minimized or maximized[1].

Example 4. *Rooted spanning tree.* We are given an undirect graph where an edge joining two nodes, say x and y, is represented by means of two fact $g(x, y, c)$ and $g(y, x, c)$, where c is the cost. A spanning tree in the graph, starting from the source node `a`, can be expressed by means of the following program:

```
st(root, a, 0).
st(X, Y, C) ← st(_, X, _), g(X, Y, C), Y ≠ a,
              choice((Y), (X)), choice((Y), (C)).
```

[1]Given that the pair `St → Adv`, `St → D` is equivalent to `St → Adv,D`, the last rule could also have been written as:

```
advisor(St,Adv) ← candidate(St,Adv,D), choice((St),(Adv,D)).
```

To illustrate the presence of multiple total choice models for this program, take a simple graph consisting of the following arcs:

```
g(a, b, 1).   g(b, a, 1).
g(b, c, 2).   g(c, b, 2).
g(a, c, 3).   g(c, a, 3).
```

Several outcomes are possible for this program. For instance, after the exit rule adds `st(root, a, 0)`, the recursive rule could add `g(a, b, 1)` and `st(a, c, 3)` along with the two tuples `chosen(b, a, 1)` and `chosen(c, a, 3)` in the `chosen` table. No further arc can be added after those, since the addition of `st(b, c, 2)` or `st(c, b, 2)` would violate the FD that follows from `choice((Y), (X))` enforced through the `chosen` table. However, since `st(root, a, 0)`, was produced by the first rule (the exit rule), rather than the second rule (the recursive choice rule), the table `chosen` contains no tuple `(root, a)`. Therefore, to avoid the addition of `st(c, a, 3)` or `st(b, a, 1)`, the goal $\mathtt{Y} \neq \mathtt{a}$ was added to the recursive rule.

By examining all possible solutions, we conclude that this program has three different choice models, for which we list only the `st`-atoms, below:

```
1. st(a, b, 1).   st(b, c, 2).
2. st(a, b, 1).   st(a, c, 3).
3. st(a, c, 3).   st(c, b, 2).
```
□

Example 5. *Single-Source Reachability.* Given a direct graph where the arcs are stored by means of tuples of the form $g(x, y, c)$, the set of nodes reachable from a node a can be defined by the following program:

```
reach(a, 0).
reach(Y, C) ← reach(X, C1), g(X, Y, C2), Y ≠ a,
              C = C1 + C2, choice((Y), (C)).
```
□

Once the cost arguments are eliminated from these rules, we obtain the usual transitive-closure-like program, for which the fixpoint computation terminates once all nodes reachable from node a are found, even if the graph contains cycles. However, if the choice goal were eliminated, the program of Example 5 could become nonterminating on a cyclic graph. This illustrates a first useful application of the choice constraint.

In the next example, we have a complete undirected labeled graph G, represented by facts `g(x, y, c)`, where the label c typically represents the cost of the edge. A simple path of G is a path passing through each node at most once. A Hamiltonian path is a simple path reaching each node in the graph. Then, a simple path can be constructed as follows:

Example 6. *The Hamiltonian path problem.*

```
s-path(root, X, 0) ← g(X, _, _), choice((), X).
s-path(X, Y, C) ← s-path(_, X, _), g(X, Y, C), s-path(root, Z, _), Y ≠ Z,
                  choice((X), (Y)), choice((Y), (X)), choice((Y), (C)).
```
□

When G is a complete graph, the simple path produced by this program is Hamiltonian (i.e., touches all the nodes). In many applications, we need to find a minimum-cost Hamiltonian path; this is the Traveling Salesman Problem (TSP) discussed in Section 5.

4 Fixpoint Semantics for Choice Programs

Let I be an interpretation for a program P; the *immediate consequence operator* $T_P(I)$ is defined as the set containing the heads of each rule $r \in ground(P)$ s.t. all positive goals of r are in I, and none of the negated goals of r, is in I. For a choice program P, with first order equivalent $foe(P)$, let us denote by T_{P_C} the immediate consequence operator associated with the rules defining the predicate `chosen` in $foe(P)$ (these are the rules with the ¬`diffchoice` goals) and let T_{P_D} denote the immediate consequence for all the other rules in $foe(P)$ (for positive choice programs these are Horn clauses).

Therefore, we have that, for any interpretation I of $foe(P)$:

$$T_{foe(P)}(I) = T_{P_D}(I) \ \cup \ T_{P_C}(I).$$

Following [9] we can now introduce a general operator for computing the nondeterministic fixpoints of a choice program P. The stable models of $foe(P)$ are called *choice models* for P, and the choice goals define the functional dependencies FD_P:

Definition 2. Given a choice program P, its *nondeterministic immediate consequence operator* Ψ_P is a map from an interpretation of $foe(P)$ to a set of interpretations of $foe(P)$ defined as follows:

$$\Psi_P(I) = \{ \ T_{P_D}^{\uparrow\omega}(J) \mid \ J \in \Gamma_P(I) \ \} \tag{1}$$

where:

$$\begin{aligned} \Gamma_P(I) \ &= \ \{ I \cup \Delta I \ \mid \emptyset \subset \Delta I \subseteq T_{P_C}(I) \setminus I \text{ and } I \cup \Delta I \models FD_P \ \} \\ &\quad \cup \{ \ I \ \mid \ T_{P_C}(I) \setminus I = \emptyset \ \}. \end{aligned} \tag{2}$$

Where $I \cup \Delta I \models FD_P$ denotes that $I \cup \Delta I$ satisfies the dependencies in FD_P. □

Therefore, the Ψ_P operator, is basically the composition of two operators. Given an interpretation I, the first operator computes all the admissible subsets of $\Delta I \subseteq T_{P_C}(I)$, i.e., those where $I \cup \Delta I$ obeys the given FDs; the second operator derives the logical consequence for each admissible subset using the ω-power of T_{P_D}.

The definition of $\Gamma_P(I)$ is such that ΔI is not empty iff $T_{P_C}(I) \setminus I$ is not empty; thus, if there are possible new choices, then at least one has to be taken.

The Ψ_P operator formalizes a single step of an ideal bottom-up computation of a choice program. Instead of defining the powers of Ψ_P, it is technically more convenient to define directly the notion of a nondeterministic computation based on the Ψ_P operator.

Definition 3. *Given a choice program P, an* inflationary choice fixpoint computation *for P, is a sequence $\langle I_n \rangle_{n \geq 0}$ of interpretations such that:*

i. $I_0 = \emptyset$,

ii. $I_{n+1} \in \Psi_P(I_n)$, *for* $n \geq 0$. □

Inasmuch as every sequence $\langle I_n \rangle_{n \geq 0}$ is monotonic, it has a unique limit for $n \rightarrow \infty$; this limit will be called an *inflationary choice fixpoint* for the choice program P. Thus, we have the following result.

Theorem 1.[8] *Let P be a Datalog program with choice, and M a Herbrand interpretation for $foe(P)$. Then M is a choice model for P iff M is an inflationary choice fixpoint for P.* □

Moreover, the inflationary choice fixpoint is *sound* (every result is a choice model) and *complete* (for each choice model there is some inflationary choice fixpoint computation producing it). For logic programs with infinite Herbrand universe, an additional assumption of *fairness* is needed to ensure completeness [9]. As customary for database queries, computational complexity is evaluated with respect to the size of the database.

Theorem 2. [8] *Let P be a choice Datalog program. Then, the data complexity of computing a choice model for P is polynomial time.* □

Therefore, for a choice Datalog program, P, the computation of one of the stable models for $foe(P)$ can be performed in polynomial time using the Choice Fixpoint Computation. This contrast with the general untractability of finding stable models for general programs: in fact, we know that checking if a Datalog program with negation has a stable model is NP-complete [14].

Therefore the choice construct allows us to capture a special subclass of programs that have a stable model semantics but are amenable to efficient implementation and are appealing to intuition. Implementing these programs only requires memorization of the *chosen* predicates; from these, the *diffchoice* predicates can be generated on-the-fly, thus eliminating the need to store `diffchoice` explicitly. Moreover, the model of memorizing tables to enforce functional dependencies provides a simple enough metaphor for a programmer to make effective usage of this construct without having to become cognizant on the subtleties of non-monotonic semantics.

4.1 Greedy Choice

Definition 2 leaves quite a bit of latitude in the computation of Δ (Equation 2). This freedom can be used to select Δs that have additional properties. In particular, we want to explore specializations of this concept that trade nondeterministic completeness (which is only of abstract interest to a programmer) in return for very concrete benefits, such as expressive power and performance. For instance, in the specialization called *Eager Choice* [8], a maximal ΔI is used in Equation 2. This results in a significant increase in expressive power, as demonstrated by the fact that negation can be emulated by eager choice [8, 9].

In this paper, we introduce a new kind of specialization called *greedy choice*; this is motivated by the observation that it is frequently desirable to select a value that is the *least* (or the *most*) among the possible values and still satisfy the FDs defined by the choice atoms [11]. Therefore, with X denoting one or more variables of r, and C denoting one single variable ranging over an ordered domain, a goal `choice-least((X),(C))` in a rule r can be used to denote that the FD `choice((X),(C))` is to be satisfied using least values of `C`. Then we will write `choice-least((X),(C))` to denote this variation of choice (`choice-most((X),(C))` is the dual construct where the maximum available value of `C` is used at each step).

We can now define a choice-least rule as one that contains one choice-least goal (possibly with other choice goals). A program that contains one choice-least rule, and other rules with zero or more choice goals is called a *choice-least* program. The correct computation for `choice-least` program can be thus defined by specializing the nondeterministic immediate consequence operator of Definition 2 as follows.

Definition 4. *Least Immediate-Consequence Operator.*

Let P be a choice program and I an interpretation of P. Then $\Psi_{least(P)}(I)$ for P is defined as follows:

$$\begin{array}{lcl} \Theta_I & = & \{\delta \in T_{P_C}(I)\setminus I \mid I \cup \{\delta\} \models FD_P\} \\ \Gamma_{least(P)}(I) & = & \{I \cup \{\delta\} \mid \delta \in least_C(\Theta_I)\} \cup \{I \mid \Theta_I = \emptyset\} \\ \Psi_{least(P)}(I) & = & \{\, T_{P_D}^{\uparrow\omega}(J) \mid J \in \Gamma_{least(P)}(I)\,\} \end{array}$$

where $least_C(\Theta_I)$ denotes the subset of tuples of Θ_I which are minimal in the value of C. Ψ_{least} will be called the *Least Immediate-Consequence Operator.* □

Observe that Definition 4 is obtained from Definition 2 by letting $\Delta = \{\delta\}$ be a singleton set, and selecting out of all possible δs one that has the *least* value for the cost attribute C. Likewise, we have the dual definition of the *Most Immediate-Consequence Operator.*

Definition 5. Given a program P with choice and choice-least goals. An *inflationary least choice fixpoint computation* (LFC) for P, is a sequence $\langle I_n\rangle_{n\geq 0}$ of interpretations such that:

i. $I_0 = \emptyset$,

ii. $I_{n+1} \in \Psi_{least(P)}(I_n)$, for $n \geq 0$. □

Thus, all the tuples that do not violate the given FDs (including the FDs implied by least) are considered, and one is chosen that has the least value for the cost argument.

Theorem 3. *Let P be a Datalog program with choice and choice_least. Then,*

1. *every inflationary least choice fixpoint for P is a choice model for P.*

2. *every inflationary least choice fixpoint of P can be computed in polynomial time.* □

Therefore, the inflationary choice fixpoint computation restricted to making greedy selections is sound (i.e., produces only choice models) but no longer complete.

5 Greedy Algorithms

In a system that adopts a concrete semantics based on *least choice fixpoint*, a programmer will specify a `choice-least((X),(Y))` goal to ensure that only particular choice models rather than arbitrary ones are produced, through the greedy selection of the least values of `Y` at each step. Thus an optimal matching in a directed graph problem can be expressed as follows:

Example 7. *Optimal Matching in a directed graph*

```
best-advisor(St,Adv,D) ←  candidate(St,Adv,D),
                          choice((St),(Adv)),
                          choice-least((St),(D)).
```
□

Observe that this program is basically that of Example 1 after that the choice goal has been specialized to a choice-least goal.

The specialization of choice goals into `choice-least` or `choice-most`) goals yields a convenient and efficient formulation of many greedy algorithms, such as Dijkstra's shortest path and Prim's minimum-spanning tree algorithms are discussed next. (We assume that we have a undirected graphs where edges are labeled by their costs. Then, an edge between nodes `a` and `b` with cost 34 will be represented by the pair `g(a,b,34)` and `g(b,a,34)`.)

The algorithm for finding the minimum spanning tree in a weighted graph, starting from a source node `a`, can be simply derived from the program of Example 4 by replacing the goal `choice((Y),(C))` with `choice-least((Y),(C))` yielding the well-known Prim's algorithm.

Example 8. *Prim's Algorithm.*

```
st(root, a, 0).
st(X, Y, C) ← st(_, X, _), g(X, Y, C), Y ≠ a,
              choice((Y), (X)), choice-least((Y), (C)).
```
□

Example 9. *Dijkstra's algorithm.*

```
dj(a, 0).
dj(Y, C) ← dj(X, C1), g(X, Y, C2), Y ≠ a,
           C = C1 + C2, choice-least((Y), (C)).
```
□

Greedy algorithms often provide efficient approximate solutions to NP-complete problems; the following algorithm yields heuristically effective approximations of optimal solutions for the traveling salesperson problem [16].

Example 10. *Greedy TSP.*
Given a complete undirected graph[2], the exit rule simply selects an arbitrary node X, from which to start the search. Then, the recursive rule the greedily chooses an arc of least cost having X as its end node. In general, when the least cost arc from X to Y is selected, we must make sure that an arc with starting node Y had not been selected. The choice constraints, and the goal Y $\neq$ Z to avoid returns to the initial node, ensure that a Hamiltonian path is obtained.

```
s-path(root, X, 0) ← node(X), choice((), X).
s-path(X, Y, C) ←    s-path(_, X, _), g(X, Y, C),
                     s-path(root, Z, _), Y ≠ Z,
                     choice((X), (Y)), choice((Y), (X)),
                     choice-least((Y), (C)).
```
□

Observe that the program of Example 10 was obtained from that of Example 6 by replacing a choice goal with its choice-least counterpart. Therefore, a most encouraging conclusion emerges from the comparison of the algorithms of these section vis a vis those in Section 3. In fact, in Section 3, we formulated several graph problems using a transitive closure computation restricted by choice-enforced FD constraints, to ensure that the resulting graph has some topological properties (e.g., a tree, a path, a Hamiltonian cycle, etc.). In this section, we have shown that the specialization of the choice goal into a choice-least goal for the cost argument, turns the algorithms of Section 3, into the classical greedy algorithms of graph optimization problems. The TSP problem of Example 10 elucidates the role that the choice-least construct has in this regard. The solutions of many search problems rely on an heuristic guiding-function to prune the search and find an optimal or quasi-optimal solution quickly.

[2]Here every graph can be reduced to completed graph by simply adding edges of very high cost.

Here, we have seen that *choice-least* provides a very effective optimization heuristics for selecting between alternative choice models during the fixpoint computation. In fact, for the TSP problem choice-least is only guaranteed to deliver a polynomial-time approximation of the optimal solution requiring exponential time. However, for simpler problems, such as minimum spanning tree or single source shortest-path, the greedy heuristics is known to be optimal in most situations of practical interest (e.g., edges with positive costs). In conclusion, we have obtain a a framework for deriving and expressing greedy algorithms (such as Prim's algorithm) characterized by conceptual simplicity, logic-based semantics, and short and efficient programs.

6 Implementation and Complexity

A most interesting aspect of the programs discussed in this paper is that their stable models can be be computed very efficiently. Indeed, the exponential intractability of stable models is no longer an issue: our greedy fixpoint computations are always polynomial-time in the size of the database. Moreover, we obtain the same asymptotic complexity obtainable by expressing the algorithms in procedural languages, when comparable data structures are used.

In general computation computation consists of two phases: (i) compilation (ii) the execution phase. All compilation algorithms discussed here execute with time complexity that is polynomial in the size of the programs. Moreover, we will assume, as it is customarily done [22], that the size of the database dominates that of the program. Thus, execution costs dominate the compilation costs, which will then be disregarded in the derivation of the worst case complexities. We will use compilation techniques, such as the differential fixpoint computation, that are of common usage in deductive database systems [22]. Also we will employ suitable storage structures, such as hash tables to support search on keys, and priority queues to support choice-least and choice-most goals.

6.1 Implementation of Programs with Choice

Let us begin with the implementation of choice goals. As described in Section 4, all the arguments (variables or expressions) appearing in choice goals are stored in `chosen` tables. When a condition ¬`diffchoice` needs to be checked, it is checked directly against the `chosen` tables. No `diffchoice` atom is ever generated or stored.

Consider now, a choice rule from our recursive examples: for instance, take the following rule from Example 8.

$$\mathtt{st(X,Y,C)} \leftarrow \quad \mathtt{st(\_,X,\_)},\ \mathtt{g(X,Y,C)},\ \mathtt{Y} \neq \mathtt{a},$$
$$\mathtt{choice((Y),(X))},\ \mathtt{choice((Y),(C))}.$$

Since this is the only choice rule, and the set of arguments in the choice goals coincide with the head arguments, then, there is no need for a separate `chosen` rule and table; the `st` table which is used in the computation of the fixpoint can also play here the role of `chosen`. Thus, the `st` table that is used to memorize the `st`-tuples previously generated and discard duplicates in the fixpoint computation, can now be used to enforce the FD choice constraints as well. In our example, that means that `Y` (the second column of `st`) is a unique key, where no duplicate is allowed. The same observation holds for all the previous examples. The data structures needed to support search and insertion on keys are well-known. For main memory we can use hash tables, where searching for a key value, and inserting or deleting an entry can be considered constant-time operations.

Given this scenario, we can now determine the asymptotic complexity of the algorithms discussed in Section 3, under the assumption that the standard differential fixpoint techniques are used in the computation of recursive rules.

Complexity of rooted spanning-tree algorithm: Example 4

For each node `X` of the goal `st(_, X,)` this recursive rule finds the matching edges `g(X, Y, C)`, before the choice conditions are checked. We can assume that the growing relation `st` is only traversed once, since the new `st` tuples generated during the differential fixpoint computation can being appended to the end of the relation (as in fact it is done by most deductive systems). Now, given the FD constraints, the second column in `st` becomes a key for `st`; thus, all the nodes of the graph are visited exactly once, at a cost $O(n)$. Moreover, for each `X`, all matching edges `g(X, Y, C)` must be found and inserted in `st` while checking for key violations. For properly constructed hash tables, these operations have cost linear in the number of edges of `g` visited, where an edge is visited at most once during the computation. Thus the overall cost is $O(e)$, where e is the number of tuples in `g` (i.e., the edges in the graph).

Complexity of single-source reachability algorithm: Example 5

This case is very similar to the previous case. The size of `reach` is n, or less, and its nodes are visited sequentially at a cost $O(n)$. However, in the process of generating `reach`, all the edges reachable from the source node `a` are explored by the algorithm. Thus the worst case complexity is $O(e)$.

Complexity of Hamiltonian circuit: Example 6

Again, all the edges in the graph will be visited in the worst case, yielding complexity $O(e)$, where $e = n^2$, according to our assumption that the graph is complete.

Complexity of graph matching: Example 3

Consider now the problem of matching students and advisors. This is a simpler situation since it is expressed without recursive rules. A compiler that only relies on the memorization of previous choices will end-up visiting each professor for each student, and then rejects every choice but the first one (with cost proportional to the product of the number of students and professor). Intelligent backtracking techniques have bee proposed to stop the system for looking for additional professors after a student has been matched with a professor.

6.2 Implementation of Choice-least and Choice-most Programs

These programs can be implemented efficiently via a simple extension of the well-known differential fixpoint technique used in deductive databases. Consider for instance Prim's algorithm in Example 8, with recursive rule:

$$\begin{array}{ll} \mathtt{st(X,Y,C)} \leftarrow & \mathtt{st(\_,X,\_)},\ \mathtt{g(X,Y,C)},\ \mathtt{Y} \neq \mathtt{a}, \\ & \mathtt{choice((Y),(X))}, \mathtt{choice\text{-}least((Y),(C))}. \end{array}$$

And recall the definition the least choice operator:

$$\begin{array}{lcl} \Theta_I & = & \{x \in T_{P_C}(I) \setminus I \mid I \cup \{x\} \models FD_P\} \\ \Gamma_P(I) & = & \{I \cup \{\delta\} \mid \delta \in least_C(\Theta_I)\} \ \cup \ \{I \mid \Theta_I = \emptyset\}. \end{array}$$

Now, the Θ_I mapping, used in the choice fixpoint iteration, can be implemented by the following following *star rule*:

$$\mathtt{st^*(X,Y,C)} \leftarrow \ \mathtt{st(\_,X,\_)},\ \mathtt{g(X,Y,C)},\ \mathtt{Y} \neq \mathtt{a}, \neg\mathtt{st(X',Y,C')}.$$

where the FD enforcement performed by the choice and choice least goals in the recursive rule, is now performed in this non-recursive rule by the negated goal. Then Γ_P finds the tuple with the least value of C generated in the last step. This computation can be improved in two simple ways:

1. Using differential techniques to compute the new value of st* from the old value of the same
2. Combining the computation of Θ_I with that of $least_C(\Theta_I)$, by discarding tuples that have the same Y-value as another tuple, but the larger value for C.

With the symbolic differentiation techniques, such as those used in the seminaive fixpoint computation, we partition st* between old tuples old_st* and the new tuples δst*. Likewise, δst denotes st-tuple added in the last step. Then, by symbolic differentiation, we obtain:

$$\begin{array}{ll} \mathtt{new\_st^*(X,Y,C)} \leftarrow & \mathtt{old\_st^*(X,Y,C)}, \neg\delta\mathtt{st(X',Y,C')}. \\ \mathtt{new\_st^*(X,Y,C)} \leftarrow & \delta\mathtt{st(\_,X,\_)},\ \mathtt{g(X,Y,C)},\ \mathtt{Y} \neq \mathtt{a}, \neg\mathtt{st(X',Y,C')}. \end{array}$$

Thus, the computation of t*(X, Y, C) is now performed by (i) taking the old value of st* and deleting tuples where the Y-values conflict with the newly selected δst, and adding the new tuples implied by the addition of δst. As a result of this improvement, the arcs of our graph are not visited more than once. Thus, in a graph with e edges the overall cost of computing st* is $O(e)$.

Observe that that if st* contains two tuples with the same Y-value but different C-value, only the tuple with the smaller value will be selected in Γ, and the other will be ignored. Thus, when computing Θ_I we only need to keep those tuples that have a minimal value of C for the same value of Y. Thus, when a new tuple $t_2 = (\mathtt{X}_2, \mathtt{Y}_2, \mathtt{C}_2)$ is generated, the current content of this table is searched for any conflicting tuple $t_1 = (\mathtt{X}_1, \mathtt{Y}_1, \mathtt{C}_1)$, with $\mathtt{Y}_1 = \mathtt{Y}_2$ If no such t_1 is found, then t_2 is stored in st*. But, if such a tuple is found and $\mathtt{C}_2 < \mathtt{C}_1$ then t_1 is obliterated and t_2 is instead stored in its place; but if $\mathtt{C}_2 < \mathtt{C}_1$ then t_1 is left untouched and t_2 is discarded. Furthermore, we can also brake ties, i.e., $\mathtt{C}_1 = \mathtt{C}_2$, in an arbitrary non-deterministic way. It thus follow that no two tuples in st* will ever exist with identical Y-columns. Therefore, Y is a key for st*, which has maximum cardinality n (rather than e).

All is left to perform, therefore, is finding the least value of C in the relation st* incrementally computed as described above. When no priority queue is used the finding a least-cost tuple in st* is a $O(n)$ operation, since st* contains at most n tuples, where n is the number of nodes in the graph. Since this step is repeated n times the the overall cost of Prim's algorithm without priority queues is $O(n^2)$. If a priority queue is used to index the tuples in st*, then, the cost of finding the least value at each step is constant; thus it is $O(n)$ over n steps. However, including the cost of updating the priority queue, the maintenance of st* becomes the dominant cost. Basically, e entries might be added and deleted from the queue, which has maximum length n. Thus overall cost of $O(e \times log\ n)$. We can now apply a similar reasoning to determine the complexity of the Algorithms in Section 5.

Complexity of Prim's Algorithm: Example 8

As previously discussed the cost of the algorithm is $O(e \times log\ n)$ with a priority queue, and $O(n^2)$ without it.

Complexity of Dijkstra Algorithm: Example 9

Here too, while e additions might be made to dj*, its size never exceeds n. Thus, without a priority queue, the complexity is $O(n^2)$. With a priority queue, the worst case occurs when the queue must be update for each new edge visited. Then, the complexity is $O(e \times log\ e)$

Greedy TSP: Example 10

Assuming that we are dealing with a complete graph, then all edges are visited, and the cost is $O(n^2)$. Priority queues cannot improve this complexity.

Optimal Matching in a directed graph: Example 7

For each source node the least-cost sink node must be found. The overall cost is $O(n^2)$ without a priority queue and $O(n\ lg\ n)$ with one.

References

[1] Abiteboul S., R. Hull, V. Vianu. *Foundations of Databases.* Addison-Wesley. 1994.

[2] Abiteboul S. and V. Vianu. Datalog Extensions for Databases Queries and Updates. In *Journal of Computer and System Science*, 43, pages 62–124, 1991.

[3] Aho A.V., J.E. Hopcropt J.E., and J.D. Ullman, *The Design and analysis of Computer Algorithms.* Addison-Wesley, 1974.

[4] Apt K.R., H.A. Blair, and A. Walker. Towards a theory of declarative knowledge. In (Minker ed.) Foundations of Deductive Databases and Logic Programming, Morgan Kaufmann, 1988.

[5] S. W. Dietrich. Shortest Path by Approximation in Logic Programs. *ACM Letters on Programming Lang. and Sys.* Vol 1, No, 2, pages 119–137, June 1992.

[6] Ganguly S., S. Greco, and C. Zaniolo. Extrema Predicates in Deductive Databases. *Journal of Computer and System Science*, 1995.

[7] Gelfond M. and V. Lifschitz. The stable model semantics of logic programming. In *Proc. Fifth Intern. Conf. on Logic Programming*, 1988.

[8] Giannotti F., D. Pedreschi, D. Saccà, and C. Zaniolo. Nondeterminism in deductive databases. In *Proc. 2nd DOOD Conference*, 1991.

[9] Giannotti F., D. Pedreschi, C. Zaniolo, Semantics and Expressive Power of Non-Deterministic Constructs in Deductive, Tecnical Report C96-04, Cnuce-CNR, Pisa, 1996, (submitted for publication).

[10] Greco S., D. Saccà, and C. Zaniolo, DATALOG Queries with Stratified Negation and Choice: from P to D^P In *Proc. Fifth ICDT Conference*, 81-96, 1995.

[11] Greco S., C. Zaniolo, and S. Ganguly. Greedy by Choice. In *Proc. of the 11th ACM Symp. on Principles of Database Systems*, 1992.

[12] Greco S., and C. Zaniolo, Greedy Fixpoint Algorithms for Logic Programs with Negation and Extrema. Technical Report, 1997.

[13] Krishnamurthy R. and S. Naqvi. Non-deterministic choice in Datalog. In *Proc. of the 3rd International Conf. on Data and Knowledge Bases*, 1988.

[14] Marek W., M. Truszczynski. Autoepistemic Logic. *Journal of ACM*, 38(3):588–619, 1991.

[15] Moret B.M.E., and H.D. Shapiro. *Algorithms from P to NP.* Benjamin Cummings, 1993.

[16] Papadimitriou C., K. Steiglitz, *Combinatorial Optimization: Algorithms and Complexity.* Englewood Cliff, N.J., Prentice Hall.

[17] Przymusinski T., On the declarative and procedural semantics of stratified deductive databases. In Minker, ed., *Foundations of Deductive Databases and Logic Programming*, Morgan-Kaufman, 1988.

[18] K.A. Ross, and Y. Sagiv. Monotonic Aggregation in Deductive Databases. In *Proc. 11th ACM Symp. on Princ. of Database Systems*, pages 127–138, 1992.

[19] S. Sudarshan and R. Ramakrishnan. Aggregation and relevance in deductive databases. In *Proc. of the 17th Conference on Very Large Data Bases*, 1991.

[20] Van Gelder A., K.A. Ross, and J.S. Schlipf. The well-founded semantics for general logic programs. *Journal of ACM*, 38(3):620–650, 1991.

[21] Van Gelder A., Foundations of Aggregations in Deductive Databases In *Proc. of the Int. Conf. On Deductive and Object-Oriented databases*, 1993.

[22] Zaniolo C., S. Ceri, C. Faloutsos, V.S. Subrahmanian and R. Zicari, *Advanced Database Systems*, Morgan Kaufmann Publishers, 1997.

On the Optimality of Scheduling Strategies in Subsumption based Tabled Resolution

Prasad Rao*
C.R. Ramakrishnan
I.V. Ramakrishnan

Department of Computer Science
SUNY at Stony Brook
Stony Brook, NY 11794-4400
email: prasadr@bellcore.com, {cram, ram}@cs.sunysb.edu

Abstract

Subsumption-based tabled logic programming promotes more aggressive reuse of answer tables over variant-based tabling. However resolving subgoals against answers in tabled logic programming may require accessing incomplete answer tables (*i.e.*, more answers remain to be added). In subsumption-based tabling it is far more efficient to retrieve from completed tables. Scheduling strategies promote more frequent usage of such tables by exercising control over access to incomplete tables. Different choices in the control can lead to different sets of proof trees in the search forest produced by tabled resolution. The net effect is that depending on the scheduling strategy used, tabled logic programs under subsumption can exhibit substantial variations in performance. In this paper we establish that for subsumption-based tabled logic programming an optimal scheduling strategy *does not exist*— *i.e.*, they are all incomparable in terms of time and space performance.

Subsumption-based tabled resolution under *call abstraction* minimizes the set of proof trees constructed. In the presence of call abstraction, we show that there exists a family of scheduling strategies that minimize the number of calls that consume from incomplete answer tables produced by strictly more general calls.

1 Introduction

Tabled resolution for general logic programs [1, 10, 3] as embodied in the XSB system, introduces a new level of declarativeness over traditional (Prolog-like) logic programming systems. Availability of tabled logic programming systems makes it feasible to develop a larger class of efficient declarative solutions to complex applications than heretofore possible using traditional Prolog-based systems. (See [6] for example.)

At a high level, top-down tabling systems evaluate programs by recording subgoals (referred to as *calls*) and their provable instances (referred to as *answers*) in a table. Predicates are marked *a priori* as either *tabled* or *nontabled*. Clause resolution, which is the basic mechanism for program evaluation of a subgoal, proceeds as follows. For nontabled predicates the subgoal is resolved against program clauses. For tabled predicates, if the subgoal is "already present" in the table, then it is resolved against the answers recorded

*Currently at Bellcore, 445 South Street, Morristown, NJ 07960.

in the table; otherwise the subgoal is entered in the table, and its answers, computed by resolving the subgoal against program clauses, are entered in the table. For both tabled and nontabled predicates, program clause resolution is carried out using SLD. While SLD derivations can be captured as a proof *tree*, derivations using a tabled resolution strategy can be viewed as a *forest* of proof trees, with each proof tree corresponding to an answer table.

Following the original formulation of tabled resolution in [10], we say that a subgoal t_1 is present in the table if there already exists another subgoal t_2 in the table that *subsumes* t_1, *i.e.*, t_1 is an instance of t_2[1]. On the other hand one can also say, as is done in the XSB system, that a subgoal t_1 is present in the table only if the table contains a *variant* of t_1 *i.e.* t_2 is identical to t_1 up to renaming of their variables. Since in a subsumption-based system a new call α is resolved using the answers of an earlier call β *even when* α *is a proper instance of* β, subsumption-based tabling promotes more aggressive reuse of computations than variant-based tabling. Note that, in subsumption-based tabling, when a call α is resolved against the answers of a more general call β made earlier, only a subset of the answers in the answer table of β are relevant for α. Hence, we need mechanisms to quickly index into the answers of β that are relevant for α. We showed, via an implementation [8] that, with judicious choice of data structures for representing tables in a subsumption-based system, the aggressive reuse can result in considerable improvement in performance over any tabling system based solely on variant checks.

From a computational viewpoint, resolving subgoals against answers in tabled logic programming systems may require accessing *incomplete* answer tables, *i.e.*, tables where more answers remain to be added. In a subsumption-based system, when answer clause resolution is performed against incomplete tables, we need to retrieve a *subset* of answers from a dynamically growing set. However, answer clause resolution against *complete* tables— tables with no more answers to be added— selects a subset of a static set. The problem of indexing (selecting a subset of answers from) a dynamic set is inherently more expensive than indexing a static set, making incomplete table accesses considerably more expensive than complete table accesses (sometimes by a few orders of magnitude). Therefore, techniques that promote consumption from complete tables over consumption from incomplete tables are central to efficient implementation of subsumptive tabling.

In a tabling system, *scheduling strategies* determine the order in which proof trees of a forest are selected to be explored. (The search within a proof tree itself is determined by the resolution strategy.) Note that, while exploring a proof tree the corresponding answer table is incomplete. Hence we can use scheduling strategies to control access to incomplete tables, and consequently, promote use of complete tables over incomplete tables. In subsumption-based systems, different scheduling strategies can lead to construction of different sets of trees in the proof forest[2]. The net effect is that depending on the scheduling strategy used, tabled logic programs can exhibit substantial variations in performance. The interesting question is whether there exists a scheduling strategy that constructs the minimum number of proof trees for computing <u>all</u> answers to a query, while at the same time, promoting access to complete tables.

In this paper we first establish that for subsumption-based tabled logic programming an optimal scheduling strategy *does not exist— i.e.*, scheduling strategies are all incomparable in terms of time and space performance. In general, incomparability is primarily caused by lack of control over the number of trees that can be generated by a scheduling strategy. An intriguing question then is: if all scheduling strategies produce the same forest, then

[1]We say that t_1 strictly subsumes t_2 (t_2 is strictly more general than t_1) iff t_1 subsumes t_2 but is not its variant.

[2]Note that the forest generated by any scheduling strategy is *always* a subset of the forest generated by a variant engine.

are there nontrivial cost measures under which scheduling strategies can be compared. We show that this is indeed possible for tabling engines augmented with *call abstraction*. In tabled resolution under call abstraction, whenever a call c is encountered, we make a most general call c' such that c' will be eventually made, and let c consume from the the answer table of c'. Subsumption-based tabled resolution with call abstraction constructs the minimum set of proof trees, independent of scheduling strategies. For resolution under call abstraction, we describe a family of scheduling strategies that *minimize* the number of calls that consume from incomplete answer tables produced by strictly more general calls.

1.1 Overview of Proofs

We show that, given any two different scheduling strategies S_1 and S_2, neither is uniformly better (in terms of running time and table space used) than the other over all programs (see Definition 3.3). The above result is established as follows:

- ABSTRACT EXECUTION MODEL (Section 2): We first present a formal definition of a scheduling strategy, based on the development of an abstract execution model for subsumption-based tabling engines.
- EXECUTION TRACE (Section 3): In order to quantify the effect of a scheduling strategy, we develop the notion of an *execution trace*. The trace generated by a scheduling strategy while evaluating a query is simply the sequence of calls made to tabled predicates (see Definition 3.1). Two strategies S_1 and S_2 are deemed different if there is a program/query pair such that the execution trace generated by the two strategies is different. We show that there exist at least two scheduling strategies and a program/query pair such that these two strategies generate different execution traces (see Lemma 3.1).
- THE INCOMPARABILITY THEOREM (Section 3): Given a program/query pair $\langle P, q\rangle$ such that S_1 and S_2 generate traces T_1 and T_2 respectively, where $T_1 \neq T_2$, we derive P' from P such that evaluation of q in P' using S_2 takes longer time than the corresponding evaluation using S_1 (see Theorem 3.2).

  Specifically, suppose that the traces generated by S_1 and S_2 while evaluating q in P' are T_1' and T_2' respectively. By exploiting the properties of the abstract execution model, P' is so constructed that T_1' contains one additional call over T_1, while T_2' has arbitrarily many additional calls over T_2. By suitably adjusting the weight and number of the additional calls, execution of P' using S_2 can be made slower than the corresponding execution using S_1. Using the same proof strategy we can establish that the table space used is also larger.

  Note that, by symmetry, we can derive another program P'' such that evaluation using S_1 is slower (and uses more table space) than evaluation using S_2. Since there exist strategies with different traces (Lemma 3.1), this completes the proof for nonexistence of optimal scheduling strategies.
- SCHEDULING STRATEGIES UNDER CALL ABSTRACTION (Section 4): We first show that, under call abstraction, all scheduling strategies yield the same subgoal dependency graph for any program/query pair (Lemma 4.2). We introduce the concept of *needed subsumptive consumption from incomplete tables* based on the structure of subgoal dependency graphs. We then define *lazy* scheduling strategies that perform only the needed consumption, thereby minimizing the number of subsumptive consumers of incomplete tables.

Implications of the results of this paper are discussed in Section 5. A detailed illustration of the table access problem and the scheduling problem in a subsumption-based system appears in the appendix.

2 Abstract Model of Tabled Resolution

We now describe an abstract model for tabled resolution of positive logic programs based closely on SLG resolution [3].

Notational Conventions We assume familiarity with the standard logic programming definitions of terms, formulas, predicates, clauses, Horn-clause logic programs, mgu, substitution, unification and subsumption [5]. We use $t \uparrow t'$ to say that t and t' unify. For simplicity of exposition our technical development is based on definite Horn clause programs (*i.e.* no negative literals in clause bodies). We use the notation $\langle a_1, a_2, \ldots, a_n \rangle$ to denote the sequence of terms $a_1, a_2, \ldots, a_n$ and $A \cdot B$ denotes the concatenation of two sequences A and B.

Following Prolog convention we use uppercase letters to begin variable names and lowercase letters to begin names of constants. The symbol "_" stands for an anonymous variable. a:-$a_1; a_2; \ldots; a_n$ stands for the sequence of clauses a :- a_1. a :- a_2. ... a :- a_n.

Tabled Resolution: In tabled resolution, derivations are captured as a proof *forest*, with each tree in the forest corresponding to an answer table. The search for answers within each proof tree is controlled by the resolution strategy (*e.g.*, left-to-right literal selection order), whereas the *interleaving* of the searches among individual trees is controlled by the scheduling strategy. The model we present here abstracts away operational details that are irrelevant to the results of this paper. A more fine-grained abstract operational model of tabled resolution can be found in [9].

Tabled resolution associates a *unique* answer table with each tree in the proof forest. Given a program P and a query q, tabled resolution proceeds by building the proof forest using a sequence of the following four *tabling operations*, starting with a PROGRAM RESOLUTION operation for q.

PROGRAM RESOLUTION: A proof tree in the forest is extended by one step using OLD-resolution [10].

NEW SUBGOAL: This operation is applicable whenever a tabled subgoal g is encountered in the process of program clause resolution. Given a subgoal g, this operation creates a *consumer* node for g in the current proof tree, and if necessary, creates a new proof tree for computing the answers for g using program clause resolution. In a variant-based engine, a new proof tree is created for g whenever there is no proof tree for a variant of g at the time this operation is performed. In a subsumption-based engine, a new proof tree is created for g only when there is no proof tree for any g' such that g' subsumes g, at the time this operation is done. The root of a newly created proof tree is called the *producer* of the tree (and the associated answer table).

NEW ANSWER: Applicable whenever a new answer a has been computed for a tabled subgoal g (*i.e.*, whenever a success leaf is derived in the proof tree for g), this operation places a in the answer table for g.

ANSWER RESOLUTION: This operation is parameterized by an answer table t to consume from, a subgoal g, and a set of answers A from t that have been previously used for resolution of g. The operation becomes applicable whenever there is some answer a in t that is not in A; then a is resolved against g.

The construction of the proof forest terminates when none of the above operations can be applied. The above description of tabled resolution follows the development of the operational semantics of SLG resolution in [3, 2, 4]. Note that COMPLETION operation in tabled resolution does not lead to a growth in the forest of proof trees and hence is treated separately from the above four operations. COMPLETION can be considered simply as a marking scheme implemented in the tabling engine by which all mutually dependent subgoals are marked as complete when none of them have pending PROGRAM RESOLUTION or ANSWER RESOLUTION operations. The operation is formalized by first defining the notion of a subgoal dependency graph.

Definition 2.1 (Subgoal Dependency Graph) *The subgoal dependency graph for evaluating all answers to a query q over program P with a scheduling strategy is $G(q, P, S) = (V, E)$ such that:*

(a) V is the set of all subgoals g such that:

(i) a NEW SUBGOAL *for g was applicable during resolution (g is a* consumer*), or*

(ii) a proof tree with g as the root is constructed in the forest (g is a producer*).*

(b) E is the set of edges (g_1, g_2) satisfying one of the following conditions:

1. *g_1 is a producer subgoal and g_2 is a consumer node in g_1's proof tree* (i.e., NEW SUBGOAL *operation for g_2 became applicable when constructing g_1's proof tree).*
2. *g_1 is a consumer node in some proof tree, g_2 subsumes g_1 and answers to g_1 are computed by performing* ANSWER RESOLUTION *against g_2's answer table (due to subsumptive answer clause resolution).*
3. *g_1 is a consumer node in some proof tree and g_1 is a variant of g_2 such that answers to g_1 are computed by performing* ANSWER RESOLUTION *against g_2's answer table (due to variant answer clause resolution).*

We denote the edges that satisfy conditions (1), (2) and (3) above as type-1, type-2 and type-3 edges respectively.

The subgoal dependency relation *depends* is the path relation on the subgoal dependency graph. We denote the set of all subgoals that g depends on by $dep(g)$. We use $\mu(g)$ to represent the set of all subgoals g' that are mutually dependent on g, *i.e.*, $\mu(g) = \{g' \mid g' \in dep(g) \wedge g \in dep(g')\}$. Note that the set of mutually dependent subgoals form a strongly connected component of the subgoal dependency graph.

A subgoal g is deemed complete if no more answers can be added to its answer table. Formally,

Definition 2.2 (Complete) *An answer table for a subgoal g is* complete *iff there are no* PROGRAM RESOLUTION *or* ANSWER RESOLUTION *steps applicable for the proof tree of g, and all answer tables to subgoals in $dep(g)$ are complete. A producer subgoal is said to be complete if its associated answer table is complete.*

In order for the rest of the system to know whether an answer table is complete (so that future subgoals may use more efficient access algorithms to consume from complete tables), tabling engines implement a completion detection procedure that *marks* tables as complete. For efficiency, implementations of completion detection procedures perform the marking as soon as possible. However, for the results presented in this paper, we require that the completion detection procedure satisfies the following weaker property:

Proposition 2.1 *Suppose there are no non-*PROGRAM RESOLUTION *steps applicable for the proof tree of a tabled subgoal* p, *and suppose that* $\mathbf{dep}(p) = \phi$. *Then the answer table for* p *will be* marked *as complete as soon as the last* PROGRAM RESOLUTION *step applied to the proof tree of* p *fails.*

It should be noted that it is straightforward to design completion detection algorithms that satisfy the above requirement (see, *e.g.*, [9]).

2.1 Scheduling of Tabling Operations

Note that, in the above model to construct proof forests for tabled resolution, more than one resolution operation may be applicable at any step. In a sequential implementation of tabled resolution, the order in which these operations are done needs to be determined. Traditionally [11], a unique "active" tree is chosen, and is "grown" using PROGRAM RESOLUTION steps until no more such steps are applicable. Such a configuration is called a *decision point* of the proof forest construction procedure. At a decision point, another tree is selected as active (possibly after performing a tabling operation— *i.e.*, NEW SUBGOAL, NEW ANSWER or ANSWER RESOLUTION), and grown; these steps are repeated until no further operations are applicable. *Scheduling strategies* select the tabling operation to be performed at each decision point, and determine the order in which trees of the proof forest are grown, as described below.

Since we perform program clause resolution using OLD-resolution, there will be at most one PROGRAM RESOLUTION operation applicable for a given proof tree at any step. Moreover, the sequence of PROGRAM RESOLUTION steps either ends in a tabling operation or ends in failure (when there are no more PROGRAM RESOLUTION steps possible for the subgoal). The tabling operations may lead to switching between proof trees (making some other tree active). When a NEW SUBGOAL operation is selected, the next active tree is determined uniquely by the operation itself. After applying NEW ANSWER, however, we can choose to continue exploring the currently active tree (thereby attempting to generate more answers), or apply an ANSWER RESOLUTION operation (to consume the newly generated answer). When an ANSWER RESOLUTION operation is applicable, we can either perform the resolution or choose to generate more answers for some other subgoal (in an attempt to consume from complete tables as far as possible). However, once we choose to perform an ANSWER RESOLUTION operation, note that the active tree remains unchanged.

Scheduling strategies (deterministically) select the next tabling operation to perform, based only on the set of tabled operations on incomplete tables applicable at the current step, and the dependencies between these tables. We assume that complete tables can be treated the same way as static code (as is done in the XSB system where complete tables are "compiled" into WAM code). Hence scheduling strategies do not distinguish between PROGRAM RESOLUTION operations and ANSWER RESOLUTION operations that consume out of complete tables. Furthermore, scheduling strategies do not postpone a NEW SUBGOAL operation. If the NEW SUBGOAL operation creates a new producer, note that there is no information *before* applying the operation about the producer itself, and hence it is consistent with the view that the scheduling decisions be solely based on the current state of the incomplete tables. We concretize the notion of scheduling strategies below.

Definition 2.3 (Scheduling Strategies) *A scheduling strategy is a deterministic algorithm that selects both the tabling operation to be performed and the next active proof tree. The selection is based only on the set of applicable tabling operations, the corresponding proof trees and the dependencies between them. The selection algorithm is such that*

1. *A* NEW SUBGOAL *operation is performed whenever possible;*

2. *If an* ANSWER RESOLUTION *operation is applicable for the currently active tree, it is performed whenever the operation consumes out of a complete answer table and rule (1) is not applicable;*

3. *If a* NEW ANSWER *operation is selected, then the operation is performed and either*

   (a) *the current proof tree stays active, or*

   (b) *a proof tree with an applicable* ANSWER RESOLUTION *operation is made active;*

4. *If an* ANSWER RESOLUTION *operation is selected, then the corresponding proof tree is made active and the operation is performed.*

2.2 Properties of the Abstract Model

The abstract model presented above captures certain essential properties of tabled resolution that are independent of the scheduling strategy used. We formally state these properties as they will be used in our proofs.

First of all, from the definition of scheduling strategies, observe that there is no way to postpone program clause resolution for producers.

Proposition 2.2 *Program clause resolution for a producer is never postponed.*

Secondly, recall that decisions in scheduling strategy are based solely on the state of incomplete tables. Therefore, invoking a tabled subgoal that fails without performing any other tabling operations does not affect any scheduling decisions in the future. Formally,

Lemma 2.3 *Let r be a tabled predicate in a program P such that r does not depend on any tabled predicate (including itself) and r has no answers. Let θ be the sequence of SLG operations produced by a scheduling strategy S while resolving some query q against P such that θ contains* NEW SUBGOAL *for r. Let P' be a program obtained from P by replacing every occurrence of r in P by* `fail`. *Then the sequence of SLG operations θ' scheduled by S while resolving q against P', is identical to the sequence obtained by deleting the occurrence of* NEW SUBGOAL *for r from θ.*

Proof (Sketch): The sequences θ and θ' are clearly the same until the occurrence of NEW SUBGOAL for r. Let A be the set of applicable operations when NEW SUBGOAL of r was selected by S. Since r derives no new answers, the set of applicable operations after the failure of r is $A-$ { NEW SUBGOAL for r }, which is identical to the set of applicable operations had fail been called instead of r. From Proposition 2.1, r will be marked as complete upon failure. The rest of the proof follows from the fact that scheduling decisions are based only on the state of incomplete tables. ∎

3 Nonexistence of Optimal Scheduling Strategy

Using the properties of the abstract model developed in the previous section we now establish the main results of this paper. We first define the concepts used in the development of our main result.

3.1 Trace Equivalence and Optimality

We use the sequence of program clause resolution steps resulting from the evaluation of tabled predicates to distinguish between scheduling strategies.

```
Program P:
:- table p/2, q/1.
w(X) :- p(X,Y),q(a).
p(a,b).
p(a,c) :- q(b).
q(a).
```

$trace_1 = \langle p(X,Y), q(b), \ldots \rangle$
$trace_2 = \langle p(X,Y), q(a), \ldots \rangle$

Figure 1: Existence of strategies that are not trace equivalent.

Definition 3.1 (Trace) *The trace generated by a scheduling strategy S while evaluating query q using program P, denoted $trace_{\langle S,P,q \rangle}$, is an ordered sequence of producers $\langle p_0, p_1, \ldots, p_n \rangle$ where the call p_i is made before p_j for all i and j such that $i < j$.*

Intuitively, the trace of a program evaluation consists of all and only those subgoal invocations that are producers. We use traces to distinguish between scheduling strategies as follows.

Definition 3.2 (Trace Equivalence) *Let S and S' be two scheduling strategies. S and S' are* trace equivalent *iff for all programs P and for all queries q, $trace_{\langle S,P,q \rangle} = trace_{\langle S',P,q \rangle}$.*

We denote trace equivalence by $=_{trace}$, *i.e.*, $S =_{trace} S'$ means that S and S' are trace equivalent.

Lemma 3.1 *There exist at least two strategies that are not trace equivalent.*

Proof: Consider the evaluation of the program in Figure 1 for the query `w(X)`. A proof tree for `w(X)` is initially constructed and, when doing PROGRAM RESOLUTION for `w(X)`, NEW SUBGOAL for `p(X,Y)` is performed, resulting in a new proof tree for `p(X,Y)`. Now, when answer `p(a,b)` is generated by PROGRAM RESOLUTION of `p(X,Y)`, a NEW ANSWER operation becomes applicable. After placing the answer in `p(X,Y)`'s table we can choose to either (i) continue resolution of `p(X,Y)`, or (ii) perform ANSWER RESOLUTION in the proof tree for `w(X)` that has just become applicable. In case (i), the next NEW SUBGOAL operation will be for `q(b)`, while in case (ii) the next NEW SUBGOAL operation will be for `q(a)`. The two scenarios yield two different traces (see Figure 1). ■

The significance of the above lemma is that we can prove results based on trace equivalence without losing generality.

We shall compare two strategies based on the running time and the table-space used for evaluating all answers to a query. We shall use $time_{\langle S,P,q \rangle}$ to denote the time taken by strategy S for evaluating all answers to a query q using program P.

Definition 3.3 (Uniformly Faster) *We say that S is uniformly faster than S' if and only if for all programs P and queries q, $time_{\langle S,P,q \rangle} < time_{\langle S',P,q \rangle}$*

3.2 Formal Presentation of the Proof

Our proof relies on the properties of a predicate `f` defined in Figure 2. `g` is a non-tabled predicate whose rules are a database of facts. Let n_g denote the number of `g` facts. Let P be a tabled logic program that contains `f` and `g`.

```
:- table f/1.
f(X) :- g(Y),fail.
g(1).  g(2).  g(3).   ...g(n_g)
```

Figure 2: Program defining `f` and `g`

Note that every call to `f(X)` (`X` can be bound or free) has no answers. Hence, it follows from Lemma 2.3 that a call to `f(X)` (`X` either bound or free) does not affect any of the engine's subsequent scheduling decisions. Secondly, the program clause resolution for such a call completely backtracks through `g`'s database of facts. Let τ be the time taken to backtrack through this entire database of facts. τ is proportional to n_g. We can make τ as large as we want by suitably choosing n_g.

We are now ready to establish our main result. We show that if two strategies are not trace equivalent then neither of them can be uniformly faster than the other.

Theorem 3.2 (Incomparability Theorem for Time) *Let S_1 and S_2 be two scheduling strategies such that $S_1 \neq_{trace} S_2$. Then neither S_1 nor S_2 is uniformly faster than the other.*

Proof: Without loss of generality we prove that S_2 is not uniformly faster than S_1 since the other case is symmetric. Since $S_1 \neq_{trace} S_2$ we can find a program P and query q such that $trace_{\langle S_1,P,q\rangle} \neq trace_{\langle S_2,P,q\rangle}$. Either $time_{\langle S_1,P,q\rangle} < time_{\langle S_2,P,q\rangle}$ or $time_{\langle S_1,P,q\rangle} \geq time_{\langle S_2,P,q\rangle}$. In the former case we have nothing left to prove. Hence let us assume the latter, *i.e.*, $\forall P, q \quad time_{\langle S_1,P,q\rangle} \geq time_{\langle S_2,P,q\rangle}$ and prove the above theorem by arriving at a contradiction.

We proceed as follows: Let α and β be the calls where $trace_{\langle S_1,P,q\rangle}$ and $trace_{\langle S_2,P,q\rangle}$ first differ (α is in the trace generated by S_1 and β is in the trace generated by S_2). Let $A{\cdot}\langle\alpha\rangle{\cdot}B_1$ denote $trace_{\langle S_1,P,q\rangle}$. Similarly let $trace_{\langle S_2,P,q\rangle}$ be denoted by $A{\cdot}\langle\beta\rangle{\cdot}B_2$.

We transform P to P' by adding the rules for `f`, the database of facts for `g` and two new rules R_α (based on α) and R_β (based on β) to P such that $trace_{\langle S_1,P',q\rangle} = A{\cdot}\langle\alpha,$`f(_)`$\rangle{\cdot}B_1$ and $trace_{\langle S_2,P',q\rangle} = A{\cdot}\langle\beta,$`f(1), f(2), ...f(k-1)f(_)`$\rangle{\cdot}B_2$. Notice that the only changes in the trace are the addition of the calls to `f`. Intuitively this means that the computation not involving `f` is left unchanged.

R_α and R_β are so designed that when α is called, either R_α alone is triggered or R_α is triggered before R_β; similarly when β is called, R_β alone is triggered or R_β is triggered before R_α.

Let α' denote α in which all its variables are bound to new constants not in P (*i.e.* a ground instance of α). Similarly let β' denote a ground instance of β in which all its variables have been bound to constants not in P or α'. Let R_α be the clause α' `:- f(_)` and R_β be the clause β' `:- f(1);f(2);...;f(k-1);f(_).`

Observe that if α subsumes β then α' will not unify with β, but α unifies with β'. Symmetrically, if β subsumes α then β' will not unify with α but α' will unify with β. We add R_α, R_β and the clauses of `f` and `g` defined as in Figure 2 (`f` and `g` are assumed to be new symbols that do not occur in P) to the beginning of program P to get P'.

To trigger R_α and R_β in the right order we place R_β before R_α if β subsumes α, otherwise we place R_α before R_β. (Note that if α and β are incomparable under subsumption then the order of insertion does not matter.)

We will prove that

(a) $trace_{\langle S_1,P',q\rangle} = A{\cdot}\langle\alpha,$`f(_)`$\rangle{\cdot}B_1$

(b) $trace_{\langle S_2,P,q\rangle} = A{\cdot}\langle\beta,$`f(1), f(2), ..., f(k-1), f(_)`$\rangle{\cdot}B_2$.

(c) τ(the time taken to compute `f(_)`) can be made the dominating component in $time_{\langle S_1,P',q\rangle}$

(d) $k * \tau$ is the dominating component in $time_{\langle S_2,P',q\rangle}$

- Proof of (a): In S_1 the call α immediately triggers R_α. This results in a producer `f(_)` which is not postponed (by Proposition 2.2).

  The call `f(_)` fails without computing any answers and returns. Thus the rest of the proof for (a) follows directly from Lemma 2.3.

- Proof of (b): The details of this proof are similar to the proof of (a) and hence omitted.
- Proof of (c): We can choose n_g, the number of facts in the g's database, to make the evaluation of `f(_)` the dominant part in $time_{\langle S_1,P',q\rangle}$.
- Proof of (d): Observe that `f(1), f(2), ..., f(k-1), f(_)` are producers in $trace_{\langle S_2,P',q\rangle}$. Evaluation of each `f(i)` takes time τ and there are k such calls. Hence, $k * \tau$ is the dominating part of $time_{\langle S_2,P',q\rangle}$.

From (a), (b), (c) and (d) above, it follows that $time_{\langle S_2,P',q\rangle} > time_{\langle S_1,P',q\rangle}$, resulting in a contradiction. ■

We have shown that if two strategies are not trace equivalent then neither is better than the other. Now we can use Lemma 3.1 to show the generality of this result, namely:

Theorem 3.3 (Nonexistence of Time-Optimal Scheduling Strategy) *For evaluating definite logic programs using subsumption-based tabling, there exists no scheduling strategy S such that for all strategies S', if S and S' are different then evaluation under S is uniformly faster than evaluation under S'.*

Proof: By contradiction. Let us assume there exists a strategy S that is optimal. By Lemma 3.1 we can find S_2 that is not trace equivalent to S. If S is optimal then S is uniformly faster than S_2. However this contradicts Theorem 3.2. ■

We can immediately derive two results from the previous theorems. First of all, since the class of positive programs is a subset of the class of normal logic programs, non-existence of optimal strategies for positive programs clearly implies non-existence for the larger class also. Hence,

Corollary 3.4 *For evaluating normal logic programs using subsumption-based tabling, there exists no scheduling strategy S such that for all strategies S', if S and S' are different then evaluation under S is uniformly faster than evaluation under S'.*

Secondly, from the proof of Theorem 3.2 it is straightforward to show a similar result for table space. We denote the table space consumed by a strategy S for evaluating all answers to a query q using program P by $space_{\langle S,P,q\rangle}$. Then:

Theorem 3.5 (Nonexistence of Space-Optimal Scheduling Strategy) *For evaluating definite logic programs using subsumption-based tabling, there is no scheduling strategy S such that for all scheduling strategies S', if S and S' are different then $\forall P, q \quad space_{\langle S,P,q\rangle} < space_{\langle S',P,q\rangle}$.*

Proof: We use the transformation in the proof of this theorem to obtain P' from P. Observe that the call table that results when S_2 evaluates query q using program P' contains `f(1), f(2), ..., f(k-1)`. These calls are absent when S_1 is used for evaluation instead. ■

4 Minimizing Incomplete Table Accesses under Call Abstraction

Observe from the proof of Theorem 3.2 in Section 3 that incomparability of scheduling strategies in subsumption-based engines stems from lack of control over the sets of trees produced. Now suppose all scheduling strategies generate the same forest. Would it then be possible to compare them with respect to specific cost measures? We explore this question in this section. We show that under such conditions we can indeed devise a scheduling strategy to minimize the number of calls that consume out of incomplete answer tables produced by strictly more general calls.

The differences between the sets of proof trees constructed by different scheduling strategies in subsumption-based tabled resolution arises from the differences in the order in which specific and more general calls are made. To ensure that the same proof forest is constructed irrespective of the scheduling strategy, we can modify the construction process such that proof trees are built only for the most general calls. When the first NEW SUBGOAL operation for subgoal g is encountered, instead of starting a new proof tree for g and computing its answers by PROGRAM RESOLUTION, we build a proof tree for g' such that g' subsumes g and NEW SUBGOAL for g' will be encountered subsequently; we then compute answers for g by ANSWER RESOLUTION. The general subgoal g' is called an abstraction of g and is represented by $abs(g)$. We call this resolution strategy as *tabled resolution under call abstraction.* Note that in practice, $abs(g)$ may not be computable and can only be estimated, as discussed in Section 5.

Observe that the traces generated by scheduling strategies for any program/query pair in variant-based tabled resolution are permutations of one another. Moreover, the sets of calls in traces produced by any subsumption-based resolution are subsets of the set of calls in traces produced by variant-based resolution. This enables us to define $abs(g)$ as:

Definition 4.1 (Call Abstraction) *Let ω be trace produced by a variant tabling engine for a query q and program P. Let C be the set of calls c' such that c' subsumes c and there is no other call c'' in ω that subsumes c'. The abstraction of the call c in ω, denoted by $abs(c)$, is a call c' in C chosen* a priori, *independent of the scheduling strategy.*

We distinguish between two kinds of consumers from an answer table c depending upon the type of edge connecting the producer and consumer in the subgoal dependency graph. Whenever (c', c) is a type-2 edge, then c' is a *subsumptive consumer* of c; when (c'', c) is a type-3 edge, c'' is a *variant consumer* of c. Recall that our original motivation was to minimize the use of incomplete tables by subsumptive consumers, and hence we choose the set of subsumptive consumers to incomplete tables as our cost measure:

Definition 4.2 *The set of subsumptive consumers of incomplete tables is the set of calls c in a subgoal dependency graph G that consume answers out of incomplete tables c' such that (c, c') is a type-2 edge in G.*

Note that in any subgoal dependency graph, for any node c, either there is a single outgoing edge (c, c') of type-2 or type-3, or one or more outgoing edges of type-1. Furthermore, under call abstraction, program clause resolution is done only for the abstracted calls. Therefore,

Proposition 4.1 *Under call abstraction, the subgoal dependency graph for any given program P, query q and scheduling strategy S has the following property: If $abs(c)$ strictly subsumes c then there is a type-2 edge from c to $abs(c)$.*

From the above property, we can show that for any given program/query pair, all scheduling strategies under call abstraction yield the same subgoal dependency graph.

Lemma 4.2 *For any program P the subgoal dependency graph constructed while evaluating all answers to a query q using subsumption-based tabled resolution under call abstraction is independent of the scheduling strategy.*

Proof (Sketch): Let G_1 and G_2 be the subgoal dependency graphs produced by scheduling strategies S_1 and S_2 respectively. Since the subgoal dependency graphs are such that every node is reachable from initial query q, G_1 and G_2 are identical if for each path of length n from q in G_1, there is an identical path in G_2. We show this by induction on path length as follows.

The base case (for 0-length paths from q) trivially holds since both G_1 and G_2 contain q.

Assume, as induction hypothesis, that for every path of length n from q in G_1, there is an identical path in G_2.

Now let $q, p_2, \ldots, p_n, p_{n+1}$ be a path of length $n+1$ starting at q in G_1. From induction hypothesis, there exists a path $q, p_2, \ldots, p_n$ in G_2. We now have three cases, based on the relationship between p_n and p_{n+1}.

Case 1: (p_n, p_{n+1}) is a type-1 edge in G_1. Since type-1 edges correspond to dependencies due to PROGRAM RESOLUTION operations which are independent of scheduling strategies, there is a type-1 edge (p_n, p_{n+1}) in G_2 also.

Case 2: (p_n, p_{n+1}) is a type-2 edge in G_1. Due to call abstraction, $p_{n+1} = abs(p_n)$, and since p_n is in G_2, so is $abs(p_n)$. Hence, by proposition 4.1, there must be a type-2 edge from p_n and $abs(p_n)$ in G_2.

Case 3: (p_n, p_{n+1}) is a type-3 edge in G_1. Again, due to call abstraction, $p_n = abs(p_n)$, otherwise the edge will not be a type-3 edge. Moreover, p_n is a consumer node in G_1. Since there is a unique producer node for each proof tree, p_{n+1} is uniquely determined given p_n. Since $p_n = abs(p_n)$, there will be a producer corresponding to $abs(p_n)$ in G_2 also. Hence (p_n, p_{n+1}) is a type-3 edge in G_2.

Hence $q, p_2, \ldots, p_n, p_{n+1}$ is a path in G_2. ■

We can now characterize subsumptive consumers that always consume from incomplete tables, irrespective of the scheduling strategy. Observe, from Definition 2.2 that if c_1 and c_2 belong to the same SCC in the subgoal dependency graph, c_2 cannot complete unless c_1 has consumed all its answers. Formally,

Proposition 4.3 (Needed Consumption from Incomplete Tables) *For every type-2 edge (c_1, c_2) in the subgoal dependency graph such that $c_1 \in \mu(c_2)$, c_1 consumes out of c_2's incomplete table under any scheduling strategy.*

The above property leads to the definition of scheduling strategies that schedule only the *needed* subsumptive consumers to perform answer clause resolution against incomplete tables.

Definition 4.3 (Lazy Scheduling Strategies) *A scheduling strategy is* lazy *iff for every type-2 edge (c_1, c_2) in the subgoal dependency graph, c_1 consumes out of c_2's incomplete table only when $c_1 \in \mu(c_2)$.*

An immediate consequence of Proposition 4.3 and Definition 4.3 is:

Theorem 4.4 (Optimality of Lazy Scheduling Strategies) *Lazy scheduling strategies minimize the set of subsumptive consumers from incomplete tables.*

5 Discussion

Subsumption based evaluation of tabled logic programs has the potential to yield superior performance over variant engines since they reuse answers computed for more general calls instead of recomputing them for each specific call. To realize this potential, however, one must reduce the overheads associated with accessing answer tables, especially from incomplete tables. Hence scheduling strategies are devised to improve performance by controlling access to incomplete tables. We showed that for subsumption-based tabled resolution there is no scheduling strategy that is uniformly better than any other.

Our proof of non-existence of optimal scheduling strategies also applies to tabled resolution with backward subsumption. When resolving with backward subsumption, PROGRAM RESOLUTION of subgoal g is terminated when a more general subgoal g' is encountered; the remaining answers to g are then computed by ANSWER RESOLUTION, consuming out of the answer table of g'. Note that, the gadget `f/1` used in our proof is such that the particular calls are completed before the general call is made, and hence the proof is not affected by backward subsumption.

The incomparability of scheduling strategies in subsumption based engines arises due to lack of control over the sets of proof trees produced. By ensuring that all scheduling strategies produce the same forest via tabled resolution under call abstraction, we showed that lazy strategies can in fact minimize the set of subsumptive consumers of incomplete tables. Observe that our optimality result above is predicated on call abstraction, which is not computable in general. One can only hope to implement approximations of tabled resolution under call abstraction by using estimates of $abs(g)$ computed via program analysis. Subsumption-based tabled resolution under call abstraction has other significant applications. For instance, in a deductive database environment, due to the disk accesses involved, making a few calls that return a large number of answers is clearly more efficient than making a large number of more specific calls. Call abstraction can identify the set of most general calls. Hence, from the viewpoint of optimizing subsumption-based tabling engines, development of program analysis techniques for call abstraction is an important and worthwhile research endeavor.

Although scheduling strategies are in general incomparable, our optimality result for lazy strategies seems to indicate that by using tabled resolution under call abstraction scheduling strategies can be compared with respect to other cost measures also. Identifying such measures is an interesting avenue of research.

Finally some remarks are due about scheduling strategies for a variant tabling engine. Since the difference in cost between accessing complete and incomplete tables is insignificant in a variant engine (see [7] for details), minimizing incomplete table accesses does not appear to be a meaningful cost measure. Observe that, in variant-based tabled resolution, the traces generated by different strategies are permutations of one another. So scheduling strategies only control the order in which the search forest is explored. The operations underlying such a control do not lead to arbitrary slowdowns. Hence we strongly conjecture that scheduling strategies for variant-based tabled resolution differ in performance by at most a constant factor.

References

[1] R. Bol and L. Degerstadt. Tabulated resolution for well-founded semantics. In *Proc. of the Symp. on Logic Programming*, 1993.

[2] W. Chen, T. Swift, and D.S. Warren. Efficient implementation of general logical queries. *J. Logic Programming*, September 1995.

[3] W. Chen and D. S. Warren. Tabled evaluation with delaying for general logic programs. *JACM*, 43(1), 1996.

[4] J. Freire, T. Swift, and D.S. Warren. Taking I/O seriously: Resolution reconsidered for disk. In *Proc of Intl. Conf. on Logic Programming*, 1997.

[5] J. W. Lloyd. *Foundations of Logic Programming*. Springer, 1984.

[6] Y. S. Ramakrishna, C. R. Ramakrishnan, I. V. Ramakrishnan, S. A. Smolka, T. W. Swift, and D. S. Warren. Efficient model checking using tabled resolution. In *Proc. of the 9th Intl. Conf. on Computer-Aided Verification*, 1997.

[7] I.V. Ramakrishnan, P. Rao, K. Sagonas, T. Swift, and D.S. Warren. Efficient table access mechanisms for logic programs. In *International Conference on Logic Programming*, 1995.

```
:- table a/2, h/2.
a(X,Y) :- p(X,Y).

h(X,Y) :- a(A,X),a(A,Y), X ≠ Y.
p(1,2).  p(2,3).  p(1,4).
```

Figure 3: A Tabled Program

[8] P. Rao, C. R. Ramakrishnan, and I. V. Ramakrishnan. A thread in time saves tabling time. In *Proc. of the Joint Int'l Conf. and Symp. on Logic Programming*, 1996.

[9] Prasad Rao. *Efficient Datastructures for Tabled Resolution*. PhD thesis, SUNY at Stony Brook, 1997.

[10] H. Tamaki and T. Sato. OLDT resolution with tabulation. In *Third Int'l Conf. on Logic Programming*, pages 84–98, 1986.

[11] The XSB Group. The XSB tabled logic system v1.7.2, 1997. Dept. of Computer Science, SUNY at Stony Brook. Available by anonymous ftp from `http://www.cs.sunysb.edu/~sbprolog`.

Appendix

Problem Illustration

Consider evaluation of the call `h(X,Y)` made to the tabled predicate shown in Figure 3. Figures 4(a) and 4(b) show the sequence of calls made (a()'s and p()'s) and answers computed (the integers appearing singly or in pairs) by a tabling system for that call.

Note that each column represents a specific call made at a particular time followed by the sequence of answers computed for that call. For instance, in Figure 4(a) the second column represents the call `a(A,X)` (made at time t_2) and its answers `(1,2)`, `(2,3)`, `(1,4)` that were computed and recorded in the table at times t_3, t_6 and t_9 respectively. Observe that when the call `a(1,Y)` is made at time t_4, it is subsumed by the call `a(A,X)` made earlier. Rather than recomputing the answers for `a(1,Y)` through program clause resolution we now resolve it against the answers computed for the call `a(A,X)` (the second column). The only answer computed so far for `a(A,X)` is (1,2) and so we record the first answer `Y=2` for `a(1,Y)` in its answer table (third column) at time t_5. The rest of the entries in Figure 4(a) are computed similarly.

Observe that the set of answers to a subsumed call is a subsequence of the answers computed for the more general subsuming call. For instance, the answer (`Y=4`) to the call `a(1,Y)` is a subsequence of answers (`(1,2)`, `(1,4)`) for the call `a(A,X)`. Secondly, note that on invoking a subsumed call one can either resolve it immediately against the answers computed for the more general call (*i.e.* the answer tables are *eagerly* consumed) or we can choose to suspend it (resulting in *delayed* consumption). Figures 4(a) and 4(b) illustrate the sequence of calls and answers generated by the former and latter choices respectively.

A consequence of eager consumption is that incomplete answer tables may need to be accessed for performing answer resolution. For example, in Figure 4(a), at time t_3 only the first answer to the call `a(A,X)` has been computed. At time t_4 the call `a(1,Y)` has to access this incomplete table. Accessing incomplete tables is expensive since answers to a subsumed call are to be retrieved from a dynamically growing answer table associated with the general call. On the other hand if we postpone doing answer resolution of a subsumed call until the answer table for the general call is complete then we only need to retrieve

(a)

time					
t_1	h(X,Y)				
t_2		a(A,X)			
t_3		1, 2			
t_4			a(1,Y)		
t_5			2		
t_6		2, 3			
t_7				a(2,Y)	
t_8				3	
t_9		1, 4			
t_{10}					a(1,Y)
t_{11}					2
t_{12}	4, 2				
t_{13}			4		
t_{14}	2, 4				
t_{15}					4

(b)

time					
t_1	h(X,Y)				
t_2		a(A,X)			
t_3		1, 2			
t_4			a(1,Y)		
t_5		2, 3			
t_6				a(2,Y)	
t_7		1, 4			
t_8					a(1,Y)
t_9			2		
t_{10}			4		
t_{11}	2,4				
t_{12}				3	
t_{13}					2
t_{14}	4,2				
t_{15}					4

Figure 4: (a)Eager Consumption and (b) Delayed Consumption

```
:- table p/3.
p(A,B,C) :- body of p/3.
q(X,Y) :- p(1,X,Y),
   p(1,X,B),
   p(A1,A2,A3).
q(X,Y) :- p(2,X,Y).
.
.
q(X,Y) :- p(n,X,Y).
```

Figure 5: Illustrative Example

the answers from a static set.(In Figure 4(b) all the calls subsumed by `a(A,X)` consume answers from its answer table only after it is complete.) Hence delayed consumption can result in consuming answers from completed tables and thereby improve efficiency of table access.

Delayed consumption however can introduce new program resolution steps and easily offset these gains. For example, consider the calls resulting from the query `q(X,W), fail` made to the program in Figure 5. Assume that `p(1,X,Y)` succeeds with `X` bound to some constant α. Suppose we defer the consumption of answers until completion of `p(1,X,Y)`. Observe that we will end up exploring alternative paths of computation which will result in calls to `p(2,X,Y)`, `p(3,X,Y)`, ..., `p(n,X,Y)`. All of these calls are solved using program clause resolution. On the other hand by letting p(1,α,B) eagerly consume answers, `p(A1,A2,A3)` will be called next. All of the calls `p(2,X,Y)`, `p(3,X,Y)`, ..., `p(n,X,Y)` will be made later and will be solved by resolving against answers in the answer table of `p(A1,A2,A3)`. Thus by deferring consumption of answers until completion of the answer table, we have increased the number of program clause resolution steps which could have been avoided by eager consumption. In addition, we also created answer tables for `p(2,X,Y)`, `p(3,X,Y)`, ..., `p(n,X,Y)` and thus increased the *table space* for computing the query `q(X,W)`.

Admissible Graph Rewriting and Narrowing

Rachid Echahed and **Jean-Christophe Janodet**
Laboratoire LEIBNIZ, IMAG, CNRS
46, avenue Felix Viallet F-38031 Grenoble - France
Rachid.Echahed@imag.fr ; Jean-Christophe.Janodet@imag.fr

Abstract

We address the problem of graph rewriting and narrowing as the underlying operational semantics of rule-based programming languages. We propose new optimal graph rewriting and narrowing strategies in the setting of orthogonal constructor-based graph rewriting systems. For this purpose, we first characterize a subset of graphs, called *admissible graphs*. A graph is admissible if none of its defined operations belongs to a cycle. We then prove the confluence, as well as the confluence modulo bisimilarity (unraveling), of the admissible graph rewriting relation. Afterwards, we define a sequential graph rewriting strategy by using Antoy's definitional trees. We show that the resulting strategy computes only needed redexes and develops optimal derivations w.r.t. the number of steps. Finally, we tackle the graph narrowing relation over admissible graphs and propose a sequential narrowing strategy which computes independent solutions and develops shorter derivations than most general graph narrowing.

1 Introduction

Many efforts have been dedicated to investigate the integration of functional and logic languages during the last decade, see [11] for a survey and [18, 12] for recent language propositions. The underlying operational semantics of such languages is often based on *first-order term* rewriting and narrowing.

In practice, data structures are represented as (cyclic) graphs. There are many reasons that motivate the use of graphs. They actually allow sharing of subexpressions which leads to efficient computations. They also permit to go beyond the processing of first-order terms by handling efficiently real-world data structures. In this paper, we consider *graph* rewriting and narrowing as the underlying operational semantics of rule-based (functional and logic) programming languages.

Using a graph rewriting system (GRS) is not an easy task. Indeed, the classical properties of term rewriting systems (TRS) cannot be lifted without caution to GRSs. One of these properties is confluence. Let us consider the rule $F(a, a, x) \to x$ where a is a constant and x is a variable. This rule, which constitutes an orthogonal TRS, generates a confluent rewrite relation over (finite or infinite) terms whereas it generates a non confluent rewrite relation over graphs [15]. It is well-known that this source of nonconfluency of GRSs comes from the so-called "collapsing rules" in orthogonal GRSs. A rewrite rule is collapsing if its right-hand side is a variable. However, collapsing rules are very often used in programming and thus cannot be prohibited in any programming discipline. Most of access functions are defined by means of collapsing rules, e.g.,

```
car (cons (x,u)) -> x        left-tree (bin-tree (l,x,r)) -> l
cdr (cons (x,u)) -> u       right-tree (bin-tree (l,x,r)) -> r
```

In practice, many programming languages are constructor-based, i.e., operators called *constructors*, which are intended to construct data structures are distinguished from operators called *defined operators* which are defined by means of rewrite rules. In this paper, we follow this discipline and define a new class of GRSs which could be seen as a natural extension to graphs of the well known class of orthogonal constructor-based TRSs. We investigate the graph rewriting and narrowing relations over a particular subset of graphs called *admissible graphs.* An admissible graph is a graph whose cycles do not include defined operators. We give a sufficient (syntactic) condition which ensures that the set of admissible graphs is closed under rewriting. Then, we show the confluence of admissible graph rewriting relation even in the presence of an arbitrary amount of collapsing rules.

It is notorious that finite graphs represent rational terms. Sometimes, one would like to equate two graphs if they represent the same rational term. In this case we say that the two graphs are *bisimilar* (if we refer to the theory of concurrency). We show the confluence modulo bisimilarity of the considered GRSs.

The confluence of a rewrite relation allows to evaluate expressions in a deterministic and efficient way by using rewriting strategies. Such strategies have been well investigated in the setting of finite and infinite orthogonal TRSs (e.g., [19, 13, 16]). In [1], a strategy that computes outermost needed redexes based on definitional trees has been designed in the framework of orthogonal constructor-based TRSs. In this article, we show that Antoy's strategy can be extended to orthogonal constructor-based GRSs with the same nice properties. We particularly prove that the resulting strategy is c-hyper-normalizing on the class of admissible graphs and develops shortest derivations.

Narrowing [14] has been intensively investigated during the last decade in the framework of TRSs. An optimal narrowing strategy is presented in [2]. However, to our knowledge, only few studies considered the extension of narrowing to graphs [9, 21, 10]. In these papers the considered graphs are acyclic and the best known strategy is basic narrowing. In the present paper, we investigate most general narrowing on admissible (cyclic) graphs and establish its soundness and completeness. Furthermore, we extend the strategy presented in [2] to admissible graphs and provide a sequential graph narrowing strategy which computes independent solutions and develops narrowing derivations which are always shorter than most general derivations.

The rest of the paper is organized as follows. We recall briefly some preliminaries on graphs in the next section. In Section 3, we introduce the framework of constructor-based GRSs and exhibits the results concerning confluence and confluence modulo bisimilarity. We define our rewriting strategy in Section 4 and list its properties. Section 5 introduces admissible graph narrowing and states the completeness of most-general graph narrowing. In Section 6, we define a sequential narrowing strategy and list its properties. Due to lack of space, some detailed definitions and all the proofs are omitted from this paper. Precise definitions and proofs can be found in [7, 6].

2 Preliminaries

Many different notations are used in the literature to investigate graph rewriting [8, 22]. The aim of this section is to recall briefly some key definitions in order to make easier the understanding of the paper. We are mostly consistent with [5].

A *many-sorted signature* $\Sigma = \langle S, \Omega \rangle$ consists of a set S of sorts and an S-indexed family of sets of operation symbols $\Omega = \uplus_{s \in S} \Omega_s$ with $\Omega_s = \uplus_{(w,s) \in S^* \times S} \Omega_{w,s}$. We shall write $f : s_1 \dots s_n \to s$ whenever $f \in \Omega_{s_1 \dots s_n, s}$ and say that f is of *sort* s and *rank* $s_1 \dots s_n$. We consider a graph as a set of nodes and edges between the nodes. Each node is labeled with an operation symbol or a variable. Let $\mathcal{X} = \uplus_{s \in S} \mathcal{X}_s$ be an S-indexed family of countable sets of *variables* and $\mathcal{N} = \uplus_{s \in S} \mathcal{N}_s$ an S-indexed family of countable sets of *nodes*. We assume that $\mathcal{X}$ and $\mathcal{N}$ are fixed throughout the rest of the paper.

A *graph* g over $\langle \Sigma, \mathcal{N}, \mathcal{X} \rangle$ is a tuple $g = \langle \mathcal{N}_g, \mathcal{L}_g, \mathcal{S}_g, \mathcal{R}\text{oots}_g \rangle$ such that $\mathcal{N}_g$ is a set of nodes, $\mathcal{L}_g : \mathcal{N}_g \to \Omega \cup \mathcal{X}$ is a *labeling function* which maps to every node of g an operation symbol or a variable, $\mathcal{S}_g$ is a *successor function* which maps to every node of g a (possibly empty) string of nodes and $\mathcal{R}\text{oots}_g$ is a set of distinguished nodes of g, called its *roots*. We also assume three conditions of well definedness. (i) Graphs are well typed : a node n is of the same sort as its label $\mathcal{L}_g(n)$, and its successors $\mathcal{S}_g(n)$ are compatible with the rank of $\mathcal{L}_g(n)$. (ii) Graphs are connected : for all nodes $n \in \mathcal{N}_g$, there exist a root $r \in \mathcal{R}\text{oots}_g$ and a path from r to n. (iii) Let $\mathcal{V}(g)$ be the set of variables of g. For all $x \in \mathcal{V}(g)$, there exists one and only one node $n \in \mathcal{N}_g$ such that $\mathcal{L}_g(n) = x$.

A *term graph* is a (possibly cyclic) graph with one root denoted $\mathcal{R}\text{oot}_g$. Two term graphs g_1 and g_2 are *bisimilar*, denoted $g_1 \doteq g_2$, iff they represent the same (infinite) tree when one unravels them [3]. We write $g_1 \sim g_2$ whenever the term graphs g_1 and g_2 are equal up to renaming of nodes.

As the formal definition of graphs is not useful to give examples, we introduce a linear notation [5]. In the following grammar, the variable A

(resp. n) ranges over the set $\Omega \cup \mathcal{X}$ (resp. $\mathcal{N}$) :

GRAPH ::= NODE | NODE + GRAPH

NODE ::= n:A(NODE,...,NODE) | n

The set of roots of a graph defined with a linear expression contains the first node of the expression and all the nodes appearing just after a +.

Example 2.1 We define a first graph G which represents a cyclic list alternating the expressions `s(0)+s(0)` and `s(0)`. The term graph G is given by (i) $\mathcal{N}_G = \{\texttt{n1}, \ldots, \texttt{n5}\}$, (ii) $\mathcal{R}oot_G = \texttt{n1}$, (iii) $\mathcal{L}_G$ is defined by $\mathcal{L}_G(\texttt{n1}) = \mathcal{L}_G(\texttt{n5}) = \texttt{c}$, $\mathcal{L}_G(\texttt{n2}) = \texttt{+}$, $\mathcal{L}_G(\texttt{n3}) = \texttt{s}$ and $\mathcal{L}_G(\texttt{n4}) = \texttt{0}$ and (iv) $\mathcal{S}_G$ is defined by $\mathcal{S}_G(\texttt{n1}) = \texttt{n2.n5}$, $\mathcal{S}_G(\texttt{n2}) = \texttt{n3.n3}$, $\mathcal{S}_G(\texttt{n3}) = \texttt{n4}$, $\mathcal{S}_G(\texttt{n4}) = \varepsilon$ and $\mathcal{S}_G(\texttt{n5}) = \texttt{n3.n1}$. An equivalent description of G is `n1:c(n2:+(n3:s(n4:0),n3),n5:c(n3,n1))`. We define a second graph T with two roots {`l1`,`r1`} which represents the classical rewrite rule `s(u)+v` $\rightarrow$ `s(u+v)` : $T =$ `l1:+(l2:s(l3:u),l4:v)` + `r1:s(r2:+(l3,l4))`.

A *subgraph* of a graph g rooted by a node p, denoted $g_{|p}$, is built by considering p as a root and deleting all the nodes which are not accessible from p in g. The *sum* of two graphs g_1 and g_2, denoted $g_1 \oplus g_2$, is the graph whose nodes and roots are those of g_1 and g_2 and whose labeling and successor functions coincide with those of g_1 and g_2. The *replacement by a term graph u of the subgraph rooted by a node p in a term graph g*, denoted $g[p \leftarrow u]$, is built in three steps : (i) compute $g \oplus u$, (ii) redirect all the edges pointing on p to point on $\mathcal{R}oot_u$ in $g \oplus u$ and (iii) delete all the "uninteresting" nodes (garbage collection).

Example 2.2 Consider the graph G of Example 2.1. The subgraph $G_{|\texttt{n2}}$ is `n2:+(n3:s(n4:0),n3)`. Let $D =$ `r1:s(r2:+(n4:0,n3:s(n4)))`. $G \oplus D =$ `n1:c(n2:+(n3:s(n4:0),n3),n5:c(n3,n1))` + `r1:s(r2:+(n4,n3))`. We now compute $G[\texttt{n2} \leftarrow D]$, thus we redirect all edges pointing on `n2` to point on `r1` in the graph $G \oplus D$, and we obtain
`n1:c(r1:s(r2:+(n4:0,n3:s(n4))),n5:c(n3,n1))` + `r1` + `n2:+(n3,n3)`.
After a garbage collection, the resulting graph is
$G[\texttt{n2} \leftarrow D] =$ `n1:c(r1:s(r2:+(n4:0,n3:s(n4))),n5:c(n3,n1))`.

A *(rooted) homomorphism* h from a graph g_1 to a graph g_2, denoted $h : g_1 \rightarrow g_2$, is a mapping from $\mathcal{N}_{g_1}$ to $\mathcal{N}_{g_2}$ such that $\mathcal{R}oots_{g_2} = h(\mathcal{R}oots_{g_1})$ and for all nodes $n \in \mathcal{N}_{g_1}$, if $\mathcal{L}_{g_1}(n) \notin \mathcal{X}$ then $\mathcal{L}_{g_2}(h(n)) = \mathcal{L}_{g_1}(n)$ and $\mathcal{S}_{g_2}(h(n)) = h(\mathcal{S}_{g_1}(n))$ and if $\mathcal{L}_{g_1}(n) \in \mathcal{X}$ then $h(n) \in \mathcal{N}_{g_2}$. If $h : g_1 \rightarrow g_2$ is a homomorphism and g is a subgraph of g_1 rooted by p, then we write $h(g)$ for the subgraph $g_{2|h(p)}$. If $h : g_1 \rightarrow g_2$ is a homomorphism and g is a graph, $h[g]$ is the graph built from g by replacing all the subgraphs shared between g and g_1 by their corresponding subgraphs in g_2. We can prove that there exists a homomorphism $h' : g \rightarrow h[g]$. h' is called the *extension of h to g*.

Example 2.3 Consider the subgraph $G_{|\mathtt{n2}}$ of Example 2.2. Let $L =$ `l1:+(l2:s(l3:u),l4:v)` and μ the mapping from $\mathcal{N}_L$ to $\mathcal{N}_{(G_{|\mathtt{n2}})}$ such that $\mu(\mathtt{l1}) = \mathtt{n2}$, $\mu(\mathtt{l2}) = \mu(\mathtt{l4}) = \mathtt{n3}$ and $\mu(\mathtt{l3}) = \mathtt{n4}$. μ is a homomorphism from L to $G_{|\mathtt{n2}}$. On the other hand, let $R =$ `r1:s(r2:+(l3:u,l4:v))`. R and L share the subgraphs `l3:u` and `l4:v` whose images by μ are respectively `n4:0` and `n3:s(n4:0)`, thus $\mu[R] =$ `r1:s(r2:+(n4:0,n3:s(n4)))`. The extension of μ to R is the homomorphism $\mu' : R \to \mu[R]$ such that $\mu'(\mathtt{r1}) = \mathtt{r1}$, $\mu'(\mathtt{r2}) = \mathtt{r2}$, $\mu'(\mathtt{l3}) = \mathtt{n4}$ and $\mu'(\mathtt{l4}) = \mathtt{n3}$.

A term graph l matches a graph g at node n if there exists a homomorphism $h : l \to g_{|n}$. h is called a *matcher* of l on g at node n. Two term graphs g_1 and g_2 are *unifiable* if there exist two graphs G and H and a homomorphism $h : G \to H$ such that (i) g_1 and g_2 are both subgraphs of G and (ii) $h(g_1) = h(g_2)$. h is called a *unifier* of g_1 and g_2. If g_1 and g_2 are unifiable, we can prove that there exists a *most general unifier* (*mgu*) in the following sense : there exist a graph g and a homomorphism $h : (g_1 \oplus g_2) \to g$ such that $h(g_1) = h(g_2) = g$ and for all unifiers $h' : G \to H$, there exists a homomorphism $\phi : g \to h'(g_1 \oplus g_2)$.

Example 2.4 The homomorphism μ of Example 2.3 is a matcher of L on G at node n2. Let $H =$ `p1:c(p2:+(p3:x,p3),p4:c(p3,p1))`. The graphs $H_{|\mathtt{p2}}$ and L are unifiable. Indeed, let $H' =$ `q1:+(l2:s(l3:u),l2)` and v the homomorphism from $(H_{|\mathtt{p2}} \oplus L)$ to H' such that $v(\mathtt{p2}) = v(\mathtt{l1}) = \mathtt{q1}$, $v(\mathtt{p3}) = v(\mathtt{l2}) = v(\mathtt{l4}) = \mathtt{l2}$ and $v(\mathtt{l3}) = \mathtt{l3}$. The reader may check that $v(H_{|\mathtt{p2}}) = v(L) = H'$. Thus v is a unifier of $H_{|\mathtt{p2}}$ and L.

Independently of homomorphisms, we need substitutions in order to define solutions computed by narrowing. A *substitution* σ is a partial function from the set of variables $\mathcal{X}$ to a set of term graphs. $\mathcal{D}\sigma$ denotes the *domain* of σ, i.e., the set of variables x such that $\sigma(x)$ is not a graph reduced to a single node labeled with the variable x. The *restriction* of σ to a set V of variables is denoted $\sigma_{|V}$. $\mathcal{D}(\sigma_{|V}) = V \cap \mathcal{D}\sigma$ and $\sigma_{|V}(x) = \sigma(x)$ for all $x \in \mathcal{D}(\sigma_{|V})$. $\sigma(g)$ denotes the graph built from g by replacing all the variables $x \in \mathcal{D}\sigma$ by their images $\sigma(x)$. Given two term graphs g_1 and g_2, we write $g_1 \mathrel{\dot{\leq}} g_2$ iff there exists a substitution θ such that $\theta(g_1) \doteq g_2$. The *composition* of two substitutions σ_1 and σ_2 is the substitution $\sigma_2 \circ \sigma_1$ such that $\mathcal{D}(\sigma_2 \circ \sigma_1) = \mathcal{D}\sigma_1 \cup \mathcal{D}\sigma_2$ and $\sigma_2 \circ \sigma_1(x) = \sigma_2(\sigma_1(x))$ for all $x \in \mathcal{D}\sigma_1$ and $\sigma_2 \circ \sigma_1(x) = \sigma_2(x)$ for all $x \in (\mathcal{D}\sigma_2 - \mathcal{D}\sigma_1)$. Given two substitutions σ_1 and σ_2 and a set V of variables, we write $\sigma_1 \mathrel{\dot{\leq}} \sigma_2$ $[V]$ iff there exists a substitution θ such that $\theta \circ \sigma_1(x) \doteq \sigma_2(x)$ for all x in V. Given a homomorphism $h : g_1 \to g_2$, we define σ_h as the substitution such that for every x in $\mathcal{V}(g_1)$ which labels some node $n \in \mathcal{N}_{g_1}$, $\sigma_h(x) = g_{2|h(n)}$.

Example 2.5 Consider the homomorphism μ of Example 2.3. σ_μ is defined by $\sigma_\mu(\mathtt{u}) =$ `n4:0` and $\sigma_\mu(\mathtt{v}) =$ `n3:s(n4:0)`. The reader may check that

$\sigma_\mu(L) =$ `l1:+(l2:s(n4:0),n3:s(n4))` and that $\mu[L] = G_{|\texttt{n2}} =$ `n2:+(n3:s(n4:0),n3)`. We remark that $\mu[L]$ and $\sigma_\mu(L)$ are not equal up to renaming of nodes but bisimilar. Consider now the homomorphism υ of Example 2.4. σ_υ is defined by $\sigma_\upsilon(\texttt{u}) =$ `l3:u` and $\sigma_\upsilon(\texttt{x}) = \sigma_\upsilon(\texttt{v}) =$ `l2:s(l3:u)`. We can notice that $\sigma_\upsilon \dot{\leq} \sigma_\mu\ [\{\texttt{u},\texttt{v}\}]$.

3 Admissible graph rewriting systems

This section introduces the class of GRSs we consider. For practical reasons, many declarative languages use constructor-based signatures. A *constructor-based signature* Σ is a triple $\Sigma = \langle S, \mathcal{C}, \mathcal{D}\rangle$ where S is a set of sorts, $\mathcal{C}$ is an S-indexed family of sets of *constructor symbols*, $\mathcal{D}$ is an S-indexed family of sets of *defined operations* such that $\mathcal{C} \cap \mathcal{D} = \emptyset$ and $\langle S, \mathcal{C} \cup \mathcal{D}\rangle$ is a signature. In Example 2.1, `0`, `s` and `c` are constructor symbols and `+` is a defined operation.

In the rest of the paper, we investigate graph rewriting and narrowing for the class of what we call *admissible* term graphs (atgs). Roughly speaking, an atg corresponds to nested procedure (function) calls whose parameters are complex constructor graphs (classical data structures).

Definition 3.1 *Let g be a term graph over a constructor-based signature. A node $n \in \mathcal{N}_g$ is called a* defined node *(resp.* variable node*) if $\mathcal{L}_g(n)$ is a defined operation ($\in \mathcal{D}$) (resp. variable ($\in \mathcal{X}$)). g is an admissible term graph (atg) if there exists no path from a defined node of g to itself. An atg g is a* pattern *if g has a tree structure (i.e., linear first-order term) which contains one and only one defined operation at its root. A* constructor graph *is a graph which has no defined node. An atg is* operation-rooted *if its root is a defined node.*

The graph G of Example 2.1 is admissible, but `z:cdr(c(0,z))` and `z:+(z,z)` are not. `l1:+(l2:0,l3:0)` is a pattern, whereas `l1:+(l2:0,l2)` is not.

The next definition introduces the notion of admissible rewrite rule. Such rules are tailored so that the set of atgs is stable with respect to the rewrite relation induced by admissible rules (see (counter)Example 3.7).

Definition 3.2 *A* rewrite rule *is a graph with two roots, denoted $l \to r$. l (resp. r) is a term graph called the* left-hand side *(resp.* right-hand side*) of the rule. A rule $l \to r$ is* admissible *iff (i) l is a* pattern *(thus an atg), (ii) r is an atg, (iii) l is not a subgraph of r and (iv) $\mathcal{V}(r) \subseteq \mathcal{V}(l)$. A rule e' is a* variant *of another rule e if e and e' are equal up to renaming of nodes and variables and all the nodes and the variables of e' are new. Two admissible rules are* non-overlapping *if their left-hand sides are not unifiable.*

By the definition of graphs, the variables occurring in a rewrite rule are always shared between the left-hand side and the right-hand side. The graph T of Example 2.1 shows an example of an admissible rule.

Definition 3.3 *An* admissible graph rewriting system (AGRS) *is a pair* $SP = \langle \Sigma, \mathcal{R} \rangle$ *where* $\Sigma = \langle S, \mathcal{C}, \mathcal{D} \rangle$ *is a constructor-based signature and* $\mathcal{R}$ *is a set of admissible rules such that every two distinct rules in* $\mathcal{R}$ *are non-overlapping.*

Below, we recall the definition of a graph rewriting step [5].

Definition 3.4 *Let* $SP = \langle \Sigma, \mathcal{R} \rangle$ *be an AGRS,* g_1 *an atg,* g_2 *a graph,* $l \to r$ *a variant of a rewrite rule of* $\mathcal{R}$ *and* p *a node of* g_1. *We say that* g_1 rewrites to g_2 at node p using the rule $l \to r$ *and write* $g_1 \to_{[p,l\to r]} g_2$ *if there exists a homomorphism* $h : l \to g_{1|p}$ *(i.e.,* l *matches* g_1 *at node* p*) and* $g_2 = g_1[p \leftarrow h[r]]$. *In this case, we say that* $g_{1|p}$ *is a* redex *of* g_1 *rooted by* p. *An atg is in* normal form *if it has no redex.* $\overset{*}{\to}$ *denotes the reflexive and transitive closure of* $\to$.

Example 3.5 According to the Example 2.3, L matches G at node **n2** with homomorphism μ and $\mu[R]$ = `r1:s(r2:+(n4:0,n3:s(n4)))`. As $\mu[R]$ is equal to the graph D of Example 2.2, we infer that $G[$`n2` $\leftarrow \mu[R]] =$ `n1:c(r1:s(r2:+(n4:0,n3:s(n4))),n5:c(n3,n1))`. Let G' be this last graph. By Definition 3.4, $G \to_{[\mathbf{n2},L\to R]} G'$.

The following proposition states the stability of the set of admissible term graphs w.r.t. rewriting with admissible rules.

Proposition 3.6 *Let* $SP = \langle \Sigma, \mathcal{R} \rangle$ *be an AGRS,* g_1 *an atg and* $g_1 \to_{[p,l\to r]} g_2$ *a rewriting step. Then* g_2 *is an atg.*

Example 3.7 The rule `l1:+(l2:0,l3:x)` $\to$ `r1:+(l1,r2:0)` is not admissible since the root of its left-hand side is a node of its right-hand side, thus its left-hand side is a subgraph of its right-hand side, thus the Condition (iii) of Definition 3.2 is not fulfilled. By using this rule, the reader may check that the atg `x1:+(x2:0,x3:0)` rewrites to `r1:+(r1,r2:0)`. This last graph is not an atg, since there is a cycle on the defined operation `+`.

One of the main properties of GRSs is confluence. We have seen in Section 1 that the confluence of AGRSs is not a straightforward extension of the confluence of orthogonal TRSs. We establish below the confluence (modulo $\sim$ and $\doteq$) of the graph rewriting relation with respect to atgs.

Definition 3.8 *We say that the rewriting relation* $\to$ *is* confluent modulo renaming of nodes (resp. bisimilarity) w.r.t. atgs *iff for all atgs* g_1, g_2, g'_1 *and* g'_2 *such that* $g_1 \sim g_2$ *(resp.* $g_1 \doteq g_2$*),* $g_1 \overset{*}{\to} g'_1$ *and* $g_2 \overset{*}{\to} g'_2$*, there exist two atgs* g''_1 *and* g''_2 *such that* $g'_1 \overset{*}{\to} g''_1$, $g'_2 \overset{*}{\to} g''_2$ *and* $g''_1 \sim g''_2$ *(resp.* $g''_1 \doteq g''_2$*).*

Theorem 3.9 $\to$ *is confluent modulo* $\sim$ *and* $\doteq$ *w.r.t. atgs.*

4 An optimal rewriting strategy

In this section, we define an optimal rewriting strategy for atgs. A *(sequential) graph rewriting strategy* is a partial function $\mathcal{S}$ which takes an atg g and returns a pair (p, R) such that p is a node of g, R is a rewrite rule of $\mathcal{R}$ and g can be rewritten at node p with rule R. We denote by $g \to_{\mathcal{S}} g'$ the *$\mathcal{S}$-step* from g to g' such that $\mathcal{S}(g) = (p, R)$ and $g \to_{[p,R]} g'$. A derivation $g \overset{*}{\to}_{\mathcal{S}} g'$ is called an *$\mathcal{S}$-derivation.* A strategy $\mathcal{S}$ is *c-normalizing* iff for all atgs g and constructor graphs c such that $g \overset{*}{\to} c$, there exists a constructor graph c' such that $g \overset{*}{\to}_{\mathcal{S}} c'$ and $c' \sim c$. A strategy $\mathcal{S}$ is *c-hyper-normalizing* iff for all atgs g and constructor graphs c such that $g \overset{*}{\to} c$, every derivation starting with g which alternates $\mathcal{S}$-steps with some arbitrary reductions ends with a constructor normal form c' such that $c' \sim c$.

Definition 4.1 *Let $SP = \langle \Sigma, \mathcal{R} \rangle$ be an AGRS, g and g' two atgs and $B = g \overset{*}{\to} g'$ a rewriting derivation. A defined node q in g is* a residual node by B *if q remains a node of g'. We call* descendant of $g_{|q}$ *the subgraph $(g')_{|q}$. A redex u rooted by q in g is a* needed redex *iff in every rewriting derivation from g to a constructor normal form, a descendant of $g_{|q}$ is rewritten at its root q. A redex u rooted by q in g is an* outermost redex *iff $q = \mathcal{R}oot_g$ when g is a redex or else $\mathcal{S}_g(\mathcal{R}oot_g) = r_1 \ldots r_k$ and u is an outermost redex of $g_{|r_i}$ for some $i \in 1..k$. A node q is* the leftmost-outermost defined node *of g iff $q = \mathcal{R}oot_g$ when $\mathcal{R}oot_g$ is a defined node or else $\mathcal{S}_g(\mathcal{R}oot_g) = r_1 \ldots r_k$ and there exists $i \in 1..k$ such that q is the leftmost-outermost defined node of $g_{|r_i}$ and the subgraphs $g_{|r_j}$ are constructor graphs for all $j < i$.*

Example 4.2 Let $g =$ `x1:c(x2:*(x3:0,x4:+(x3,x3)),x5:c(x4,x1))`. The leftmost-outermost node of g is `x2`. $g_{|\texttt{x2}}$ and $g_{|\texttt{x4}}$ are outermost needed redexes (though there exists a path from `x2` to `x4`).

The notions of leftmost-outermost defined node and outermost redex are well-defined in the framework of atgs. Indeed, if p and q are two defined nodes of an atg such that there exists a path from p to q (i.e., p is *outer* than q), then there is no path from q to p.

Our graph rewriting strategy is based on definitional trees [1]. A definitional tree is a hierarchical structure whose leaves are the rules of an AGRS used to define a given operation. In the following definition, *branch* and *rule* are uninterpreted symbols, used to construct the nodes of a definitional tree.

Definition 4.3 *Let $SP = \langle \Sigma, \mathcal{R} \rangle$ be an AGRS. A tree $\mathcal{T}$ is a* partial definitional tree, *or* pdt, *with pattern π iff one of the following cases holds :*

- *$\mathcal{T} = rule(\pi \to r)$, where $\pi \to r$ is a variant of a rule of $\mathcal{R}$.*
- *$\mathcal{T} = branch(\pi, o, \mathcal{T}_1, \ldots, \mathcal{T}_k)$, where o is a variable node of π, o is of sort s, $c_1, \ldots, c_k$ $(k > 0)$ are different constructors of the sort s and for all $j \in 1..k$, $\mathcal{T}_j$ is a pdt with pattern $\pi[o \leftarrow p : c_j(o_1 : X_1, \ldots, o_n : X_n)]$,*

such that n is the number of arguments of c_j, $X_1, \ldots, X_n$ are new variables and $p, o_1, \ldots, o_n$ are new nodes.

We write pattern($\mathcal{T}$) to denote the pattern argument of a pdt. A definitional tree *$\mathcal{T}$ of a defined operation f is a* finite *pdt with a pattern of the form $p : f(o_1 : X_1, \ldots, o_n : X_n)$ where n is the number of arguments of f, $X_1, \ldots, X_n$ are new variables, $p, o_1, \ldots, o_n$ are new nodes, and for every rule $l \to r$ of $\mathcal{R}$, with l of the form $f(g_1, \ldots, g_n)$, there exists a leaf rule($l' \to r'$) of $\mathcal{T}$ such that $l' \to r'$ is a variant of $l \to r$. An AGRS is* inductively sequential *(IGRS) iff for every defined operation f, there exists a definitional tree of f.*

Example 4.4 Consider the following AGRS where 0 and s are constructors and p, q, r, u, v, w are variables.

```
(R0)  n1:f(n2:s(n3:p),n4:q) -> n3
(R1)  m1:f(m2:0,m3:r) -> m3
(R2)  l1:g(l2:w,l3:s(l4:u),l5:s(l6:v)) -> l2
```

The definitional trees $\mathcal{T}_{\mathtt{f}}$ and $\mathcal{T}_{\mathtt{g}}$ of the operations f and g are

$$\mathcal{T}_{\mathtt{f}} = \mathit{branch}(\ \mathtt{k1{:}f(\underline{k2{:}X1},k3{:}X2),k2},\ \mathit{rule}(\mathtt{m1{:}f(m2{:}0,m3{:}r)} \to \mathtt{m3}),\ \mathit{rule}(\mathtt{n1{:}f(n2{:}s(n3{:}p),n4{:}q)} \to \mathtt{n3}))$$

$$\mathcal{T}_{\mathtt{g}} = \mathit{branch}(\ \mathtt{k4{:}g(k5{:}X3,\underline{k6{:}X4},k7{:}X5),k6},\ \mathit{branch}(\ \mathtt{k8{:}g(k9{:}X6,k10{:}s(k11{:}X7),\underline{k12{:}X8}),k12},\ \mathit{rule}(\mathtt{l1{:}g(l2{:}w,l3{:}s(l4{:}u),l5{:}s(l6{:}v))} \to \mathtt{l2})))$$

We are ready to define our graph rewriting strategy Φ. The strategy Φ is a partial function that operates on atgs in the presence of IGRSs. $\Phi(g)$ returns, when it is possible, a pair (p, R) where p is a node of g and R is a rewrite rule such that g can be rewritten at node p with rule R. Φ uses an auxiliary function φ which takes two arguments : an operation-rooted atg and a pdt of this operation.

Definition 4.5 *Let $SP = \langle \Sigma, \mathcal{R} \rangle$ be an IGRS and g an atg. Φ is the partial function defined by $\Phi(g) = \varphi(g_{|p}, \mathcal{T})$, where p is the leftmost-outermost defined node of g and $\mathcal{T}$ is a definitional tree of the label of p.*
Let g be an operation-rooted atg and $\mathcal{T}$ a pdt such that pattern($\mathcal{T}$) matches g at the root. We define the partial function φ by :

$$\varphi(g, \mathcal{T}) = \begin{cases} (p, R) & \text{if } \mathcal{T} = \mathit{rule}(\pi \to r),\ p = \mathcal{R}oot_g \text{ and} \\ & \quad R \text{ is a variant of } \pi \to r \text{ ;} \\ \varphi(g, \mathcal{T}_i) & \text{if } \mathcal{T} = \mathit{branch}(\pi, o, \mathcal{T}_1, \ldots, \mathcal{T}_k) \text{ and} \\ & \quad \mathit{pattern}(\mathcal{T}_i) \text{ matches } g \text{ for some } i \in 1..k \text{ ;} \\ (p, R) & \text{if } \mathcal{T} = \mathit{branch}(\pi, o, \mathcal{T}_1, \ldots, \mathcal{T}_k), \\ & \quad \pi \text{ matches } g \text{ by a homomorphism } h : \pi \to g, \\ & \quad h(o) \text{ is labeled with a defined operation } f \text{ in } g, \\ & \quad \mathcal{T}' \text{ is a definitional tree of } f \text{ and} \\ & \quad \varphi(g_{|h(o)}, \mathcal{T}') = (p, R). \end{cases}$$

Example 4.6 Consider the AGRS defined in Example 4.4 and the atg $t_1 =$ `x1:g(x2:s(x2),x2,x3:f(x2,x2))`.

$$
\begin{aligned}
\Phi(t_1) &= \varphi(t_1, \mathcal{T}_{\mathtt{g}}) \\
&= \varphi(t_1, \mathit{branch}(\mathtt{k4{:}g(k5{:}X3,}\underline{\mathtt{k6{:}X4}}\mathtt{,k7{:}X5),k6,}\ldots)) \\
&= \varphi(t_1, \mathit{branch}(\mathtt{k8{:}g(k9{:}X6,k10{:}s(k11{:}X7),}\underline{\mathtt{k12{:}X8}}\mathtt{),k12,}\ldots))
\end{aligned}
$$

The pattern of *rule*(`l1:g(l2:w,l3:s(l4:u),l5:s(l6:v))` $\to$ `l2`) does not match t_1 because `l5` is labeled with `s` whereas `x3` is labeled with `f`. So $\Phi(t_1)$ recursively calls $\varphi(t'_1, \mathcal{T}_{\mathtt{f}})$ where $t'_1 = t_{1|\mathtt{x3}} =$ `x3:f(x2:s(x2),x2)`. The reader may check that $\Phi(t_1) = \varphi(t'_1, \mathcal{T}_{\mathtt{f}}) = (\mathtt{x3}, \mathtt{R0})$.

Below, we list some properties of Φ.

Proposition 4.7 *If $\Phi(g) = (p, R)$, then $g_{|p}$ is an outermost needed redex of g and g can be rewritten at node p with rule R. If $\Phi(g)$ is not defined, then g has no constructor normal form.*

Theorem 4.8 *Φ is c-hyper-normalizing (thus c-normalizing).*

Graph rewriting does not duplicate data. Thus the number of rewriting steps which are necessary to compute a constructor normal form may be optimized.

Theorem 4.9 *Let g be an atg and c a constructor graph such that there exists a rewriting derivation $g \overset{*}{\to} c$. Then there exists a constructor graph c' with $c' \sim c$ such that the length of the Φ-derivation $g \overset{*}{\to}_{\Phi} c'$ is less than (or equal to) the length of the derivation $g \overset{*}{\to} c$.*

5 Admissible graph narrowing

Besides rewriting, narrowing is the basis of many functional logic programming languages [11]. In this section we generalize narrowing to admissible term graphs.

Definition 5.1 *Let $SP = \langle \Sigma, \mathcal{R} \rangle$ be an AGRS, g_1 an atg, $l \to r$ a variant of a rewrite rule of $\mathcal{R}$, p a non variable node of g_1, $h : G \to H$ a homomorphism and g_2 a graph. We say that g_1* narrows to g_2 at node p using the rule $l \to r$ and the homomorphism h, *denoted $g_1 \leadsto_{[p, l \to r, h]} g_2$, if l and $g_{1|p}$ are unifiable, h is a unifier of l and $g_{1|p}$ and $g_2 = h[g_1][h(p) \leftarrow h[r]]$. A narrowing step is* most general *when the unifier, h, is an mgu.*

Example 5.2 In Example 2.4, $H_{|\mathtt{p2}}$ and L are unifiable with mgu v. The reader may check that $v(\mathtt{p2}) = \mathtt{q1}$, $v[R] =$ `r1:s(r2:+(l3:u,l2:s(l3))` and $v[H] =$ `p1:c(q1:+(l2:s(l3:u),l2),p4:c(l2,p1))`. Let $H_1 =$ $v[H][v(\mathtt{p2}) \leftarrow v[R]] =$ `p1:c(r1:s(r2:+(l3:u,l2:s(l3))),p4:c(l2,p1))`. By Definition 5.1, $H \leadsto_{[\mathtt{p2}, L \to R, v]} H_1$.

In general, the set of atgs is not stable w.r.t. narrowing.

Example 5.3 Let $g = \texttt{n1:f(n2:x)}$ and $R = l \to r$ a rule such that $l = \texttt{l1:f(l2:0)}$ and $r = \texttt{r1:g(r2:f(r3:0))}$. g and l are unifiable, say with $h : (g \oplus l) \to r_{|\texttt{r2}}$. Let $g' = h[g][h(\texttt{n1}) \leftarrow h[r]]$. We can show that $h[g] = r_{|\texttt{r2}}$, $h(\texttt{n1}) = \texttt{r2}$ and $h[r] = r$, thus $g' = \texttt{r1:g(r1)}$. By Definition 5.1, $g \rightsquigarrow_{[\texttt{n1}, R, h]} g'$. However, g is admissible whereas g' is not.

Under some technical assumptions on the unifiers detailed in [6], we can prove the following proposition.

Proposition 5.4 *Let $SP = \langle \Sigma, \mathcal{R} \rangle$ be an AGRS, g_1 an atg and $g_1 \rightsquigarrow_{[p, l \to r, h]} g_2$ a most general narrowing step. Then g_2 is an atg.*

Narrowing is used to solve goals. A solution of a goal is often represented by a substitution. A substitution computed by a narrowing derivation is defined as follows.

Definition 5.5 *Let g_1 and g_2 be two atgs and σ a substitution. We say that σ* is computed by a narrowing derivation from g_1 to g_2 *and write $g_1 \overset{*}{\rightsquigarrow}_\sigma g_2$, if there exists a derivation $g_1 \rightsquigarrow_{[p_1, l_1 \to r_1, h_1]} \cdots \rightsquigarrow_{[p_k, l_k \to r_k, h_k]} g_2$ and $\sigma = (\sigma_{h_k} \circ \ldots \circ \sigma_{h_1})_{|\mathcal{V}(g_1)}$.*

Example 5.6 Let $H \rightsquigarrow_{[\texttt{p2}, L \to R, v]} H_1$ be the narrowing step of Example 5.2. We saw in Example 2.5 that $\sigma_v(\texttt{x}) = \texttt{12:s(13:u)}$. Consider a second narrowing step starting with H_1 and the rule $L' \to R'$ where $L' = \texttt{15:+(16:0,17:w)}$ and $R' = \texttt{17:w}$. $H_{1|\texttt{r2}}$ and L' unify and an mgu is $v' : (H_{1|\texttt{r2}} \oplus L') \to H_1'$ with $H_1' = \texttt{q2:+(16:0,q3:s(16))}$. Therefore, $H_1 \rightsquigarrow_{[\texttt{r2}, L' \to R', v']} H_2$ where $H_2 = \texttt{p1:c(r1:s(q3:s(16:0)),p4:c(q3,p1))}$. From v', we deduce that $\sigma_{v'}(\texttt{u}) = \texttt{16:0}$. The reader may check that $\sigma = (\sigma_{v'} \circ \sigma_v)_{|\{\texttt{x}\}}$ is defined by $\sigma(\texttt{x}) = \texttt{12:s(16:0)}$. By Definition 5.5, σ is computed by the narrowing derivation from H to H_2.

We define below the notions of soundness and completeness of narrowing. These definitions do not consider narrowing as an inference rule for solving some particular goals but rather as a general computational model for arbitrary expressions (graphs). The traditional goals such as equations can be represented as boolean expressions.

Definition 5.7 *Let $SP = \langle \Sigma, \mathcal{R} \rangle$ be an AGRS. We say that a narrowing calculus is* sound *iff for all atgs g, constructor graphs c and substitutions θ such that $g \overset{*}{\rightsquigarrow}_\theta c$, there exists a constructor graph c' such that $\theta(g) \overset{*}{\to} c'$ and $c' \doteq c$. We say that a narrowing calculus is* complete *iff for all atgs g, constructor graphs c and constructor substitutions θ such that $\theta(g) \overset{*}{\to} c$, there exist a constructor graph c' and a substitution σ such that $g \overset{*}{\rightsquigarrow}_\sigma c'$, $c' \leq c$ and $\sigma \dot{\leq} \theta$ $[\mathcal{V}(g)]$.*

Theorem 5.8 *The most general narrowing is sound and complete.*

6 An optimal narrowing strategy

In this section, we define a sequential narrowing strategy Λ which generalizes the rewriting strategy Φ to narrowing. A *(sequential) graph narrowing strategy* is a partial function $\mathcal{S}$ which takes an atg g and returns a set of triples of the form (p, R, h) such that g is narrowable at node p using the rule R and homomorphism h. We denote by $g \rightsquigarrow_{\mathcal{S}} g'$ an $\mathcal{S}$-*step* from g to g' such that $\mathcal{S}(g) \ni (p, R, h)$ and $g \rightsquigarrow_{[p,R,h]} g'$. A derivation $g \overset{*}{\rightsquigarrow}_{\mathcal{S}} g'$ is called an $\mathcal{S}$-*derivation*.

Definition 6.1 *Let $SP = \langle \Sigma, \mathcal{R} \rangle$ be an IGRS and g an atg. Λ is the partial function such that $(n, R, h') \in \Lambda(g)$ iff there exists $(n, R, h) \in \lambda(g_{|p}, \mathcal{T})$, p is the leftmost-outermost defined node of g, $\mathcal{T}$ is a definitional tree of the label of p and h' is the extension of h to $g \oplus l$.*
Let g be an operation-rooted atg and $\mathcal{T}$ a pdt such that pattern($\mathcal{T}$) and g are unifiable. $\lambda(g, \mathcal{T})$ is a set of triples of the form (n, R, h), where n is a non variable node of g, R is a rewrite rule and h is a unifier of $g_{|n}$ and the left-hand side of R. $\lambda(g, \mathcal{T})$ is defined as the smallest set such that :

$$\lambda(g,\mathcal{T}) \supseteq \begin{cases} \{(p,R,h)\} & \text{if } \mathcal{T} = rule(\pi \to r),\ p = \mathcal{R}oot_g,\ R = \pi' \to r' \text{ is} \\ & \quad \text{a variant of } \pi \to r \text{ and } h \text{ is an mgu of } \pi' \text{ and } g\ ; \\ \lambda(g,\mathcal{T}_i) & \text{if } \mathcal{T} = branch(\pi, o, \mathcal{T}_1, \ldots, \mathcal{T}_k) \text{ and} \\ & \quad pattern(\mathcal{T}_i) \text{ and } g \text{ unify for some } i; \\ \{(p,R,h)\} & \text{if } (1)\ \mathcal{T} = branch(\pi, o, \mathcal{T}_1, \ldots, \mathcal{T}_k), \\ & \quad (2)\ g \text{ and } \pi \text{ are unifiable with} \\ & \quad\quad \text{most general unifier } \tau : (g \oplus \pi) \to g', \\ & \quad (3)\ \tau(o) \text{ is labeled with a defined operation } f, \\ & \quad (4)\ \mathcal{T}' \text{ is a definitional tree of } f, \\ & \quad (5)\ (p', R, h') \in \lambda(g'_{|\tau(o)}, \mathcal{T}'), \\ & \quad (6)\ p \text{ is the node of } g \text{ such that } \tau(p) = p', \\ & \quad (7)\ R \text{ is of the form } l \to r, \\ & \quad (8)\ h = h'' \circ \tau' \text{ where } h'' \text{ is the extension} \\ & \quad\quad \text{of } h' \text{ to } g' \oplus l \text{ and } \tau' \text{ is the extension} \\ & \quad\quad \text{of } \tau_{|\mathcal{R}oot_g} \text{ to } g \oplus l. \end{cases}$$

Example 6.2 Consider the AGRS defined in Example 4.4 and the atg s_1 = `y1:g(y2:s(y3:s(y2)),y4:z,y5:f(y6:x,y7:s(y8:y)))`. As the leftmost-outermost defined node of s_1 is its root `y1`, we infer that

$$\begin{aligned} \Lambda(s_1) &= \lambda(s_1, \mathcal{T}_{\mathtt{g}}) \\ &= \lambda(s_1, branch(\mathtt{k4{:}g(k5{:}X3,\underline{k6{:}X4},k7{:}X5),k6,\ldots})) \\ &= \lambda(s_1, branch(\mathtt{k8{:}g(k9{:}X6,k10{:}s(k11{:}X7),\underline{k12{:}X8}),k12,\ldots})) \end{aligned}$$

Let π = `k8:g(k9:X6,k10:s(k11:X7),k12:X8)`. s_1 and π are unifiable with most general unifier $\tau : (s_1 \oplus \pi) \to s'_1$ where
s'_1 = `p1:g(y2:s(y3:s(y2)),k10:s(k11:X7),y5:f(y6:x,y7:s(y8:y)))`. τ

is precisely defined by $\tau(\mathtt{y1}) = \tau(\mathtt{k8}) = \mathtt{p1}$, $\tau(\mathtt{y2}) = \tau(\mathtt{k9}) = \mathtt{y2}$, $\tau(\mathtt{y3}) = \mathtt{y3}$, $\tau(\mathtt{y4}) = \tau(\mathtt{k10}) = \mathtt{k10}$, $\tau(\mathtt{k11}) = \mathtt{k11}$, $\tau(\mathtt{y5}) = \tau(\mathtt{k12}) = \mathtt{y5}$, $\tau(\mathtt{y6}) = \mathtt{y6}$, $\tau(\mathtt{y7}) = \mathtt{y7}$ and $\tau(\mathtt{y8}) = \mathtt{y8}$. Notice that the variable `z` which labels the node `y4` in s_1 is assigned with the constructor graph `k10:s(k11:X7)` by σ_τ. s_1 does not unify with the pattern of $rule($`l1:g(l2:w,l3:s(l4:u),l5:s(l6:v))` $\rightarrow$ `l2`$)$. Indeed, `l5` is labeled with `s` whereas `y5` is labeled with `f`. So $\Lambda(s_1)$ recursively calls $\lambda(g_1, \mathcal{T}_{\mathtt{f}})$ where $g_1 = s'_{1|\tau(\mathtt{k12})} = s'_{1|\mathtt{y5}} = $ `y5:f(y6:x,y7:s(y8:y))`.

$$\begin{array}{rcl}\lambda(g_1, \mathcal{T}_{\mathtt{f}}) & = & \lambda(g_1, branch(\mathtt{k1:f(}\underline{\mathtt{k2:X1}}\mathtt{,k3:X2),k2,}\ldots))\\ & \supseteq & \lambda(g_1, rule(\mathtt{n1:f(n2:s(n3:p),n4:q)} \rightarrow \mathtt{n3}))\end{array}$$

Let l be the pattern of $rule($`n1:f(n2:s(n3:p),n4:q)` $\rightarrow$ `n3`$)$, i.e., the left-hand side of the rule `R0` defined in Example 4.4. g_1 and l are unifiable and a most general unifier is the homormophism $h' : (g_1 \oplus l) \rightarrow e$ where $e = $ `p2:f(n2:s(n3:p),y7:s(y8:y))`. The homomorphism h' is defined by $h'(\mathtt{y5}) = h'(\mathtt{n1}) = \mathtt{p2}$, $h'(\mathtt{y6}) = h'(\mathtt{n2}) = \mathtt{n2}$, $h'(\mathtt{n3}) = \mathtt{n3}$, $h'(\mathtt{y7}) = h'(\mathtt{n4}) = \mathtt{y7}$ and $h'(\mathtt{y8}) = \mathtt{y8}$. By the definition of λ, we conclude that $\lambda(s'_{1|\tau(\mathtt{k12})}, \mathcal{T}_{\mathtt{f}}) = \lambda(g_1, \mathcal{T}_{\mathtt{f}}) \supseteq \{(\mathtt{y5}, \mathtt{R0}, h')\}$. h' is a homomorphism from the graph $s'_{1|\tau(\mathtt{k12})} \oplus l$ to the graph e. We now compute the extension of h' to the graph $s'_1 \oplus l$. We thus obtain a homomorphism $h'' : (s'_1 \oplus l) \rightarrow e'$ where $e' = $ `p1:g(y2:s(y3:s(y2)),k10:s(k11:X7),p2:f(n2:s(n3:p),y7:s(y8:y)))` $+$ `p2` and h'' is defined by $h''(\mathtt{p1}) = \mathtt{p1}$, $h''(\mathtt{y2}) = \mathtt{y2}$, $h''(\mathtt{y3}) = \mathtt{y3}$, $h''(\mathtt{k10}) = \mathtt{k10}$, $h''(\mathtt{k11}) = \mathtt{k11}$, $h''(\mathtt{y5}) = h''(\mathtt{n1}) = \mathtt{p2}$, $h''(\mathtt{y6}) = h''(\mathtt{n2}) = \mathtt{n2}$, $h''(\mathtt{n3}) = \mathtt{n3}$, $h''(\mathtt{y7}) = h''(\mathtt{n4}) = \mathtt{y7}$ and $h''(\mathtt{y8}) = \mathtt{y8}$. Let τ' be the extension of $\tau_{|\mathcal{R}\mathrm{oot}_{s_1}}$ to $s_1 \oplus l$, i.e., τ' is the homomorphism from $s_1 \oplus l$ to $s'_1 \oplus l$ such that $\tau'(s_1) = s'_1$ and $\tau'(l) = l$. Let $h = h'' \circ \tau'$. h is a homomorphism from $s_1 \oplus l$ to e' such that $h(\mathtt{y1}) = \mathtt{p1}$, $h(\mathtt{y2}) = \mathtt{y2}$, $h(\mathtt{y3}) = \mathtt{y3}$, $h(\mathtt{y4}) = \mathtt{k10}$, $h(\mathtt{y5}) = h(\mathtt{n1}) = \mathtt{p2}$, $h(\mathtt{y6}) = h(\mathtt{n2}) = \mathtt{n2}$, $h(\mathtt{n3}) = \mathtt{n3}$, $h(\mathtt{y7}) = h(\mathtt{n4}) = \mathtt{y7}$ and $h(\mathtt{y8}) = \mathtt{y8}$. It appears that `y5` is the only node of s_1 such that $\tau(\mathtt{y5}) = \mathtt{y5}$. By the definition of Λ, we conclude that $\Lambda(s_1) \supseteq \{(\mathtt{y5}, \mathtt{R0}, h)\}$. The reader may check that s_1 narrows at node `y5` using the rule `R0` and the homomorphism h into the graph $s_2 = $ `p1:g(y2:s(y3:s(y2)),k10:s(k11:X7),n3:p)`.

In the following we list some properties of Λ.

Proposition 6.3 *Let g_1 be an atg such that $g_1 \leadsto_\Lambda g_2$. Then g_2 is an atg.*

Definition 6.4 *Let $SP = \langle \Sigma, \mathcal{R} \rangle$ be an AGRS and g and g' two atgs. A narrowing step $g \leadsto_{[p,R,h]} g'$ is* outermost needed *iff for all substitutions η such that $\sigma_h \leq \eta\ [\mathcal{V}(g)]$, $\eta(g_{|p})$ is an outermost needed redex of $\eta(g)$.*

Proposition 6.5 *If $\Lambda(g) \ni (p, R, h)$, then $g \leadsto_{[p,R,h]} g'$ is an outermost needed narrowing step. If $\Lambda(g)$ is not defined, then g cannot be narrowed into a constructor graph.*

Theorem 6.6 *The narrowing relation induced by Λ is sound and complete.*

Λ always computes independent substitutions, that is to say Λ never performs redundant calculus. We say that two substitutions θ and θ' are *independent* on a set V of variables iff there exists $x \in V$ such that $\theta(x)$ and $\theta'(x)$ are not unifiable.

Theorem 6.7 *Let g be an atg, c and c' two constructor graphs and $g \overset{*}{\rightsquigarrow}_{\sigma} c$ and $g \overset{*}{\rightsquigarrow}_{\sigma'} c'$ two distinct Λ-derivations. Then σ and σ' are independent on $\mathcal{V}(g)$.*

The restriction of Λ to first-order terms always develops shortest narrowing derivations [2]. This is not the case in our framework, as it is witnessed by the following (counter-)example.

Example 6.8 Consider the graph $g =$ `n1:f(n2:g(n3:x),n4:g(n3))` and the rules `l4:g(l5:w)` $\rightarrow$ `l5` and `l1:f(l2:u,l3:v)` $\rightarrow$ `r1:c(l2,l3)`. The following Λ-derivation is of length 3 : $g \rightsquigarrow_{\Lambda}$ `r1:c(n2:g(n3:x),n4:g(n3))` $\rightsquigarrow_{\Lambda}$ `r1:c(n3:x,n4:g(n3))` $\rightsquigarrow_{\Lambda}$ `r1:c(n3:x,n3)`. But arbitrary unifiers can collapse nodes labeled with defined operations. The following derivation is of length 2 : $g \rightsquigarrow$ `r1:c(r2:g(n3:x),r2)` $\rightsquigarrow$ `r1:c(n3:x,n3)`.

Nevertheless, the derivations developed by Λ are always shorter than those developed by most general narrowing.

Theorem 6.9 *Let g be an atg, σ and σ' two substitutions and c and c' two constructor graphs such that $A = g \overset{*}{\rightsquigarrow}_{\sigma} c$ is a Λ-derivation, $B = g \overset{*}{\rightsquigarrow}_{\sigma'} c'$ is a most general narrowing derivation and σ and σ' are equal up to renaming of nodes. Then the length of A is less than (or equal to) the length of B (and $c \sim c'$).*

7 Conclusion

We defined the class of admissible graph rewriting systems, AGRSs, and characterized a subset of graphs called admissible graphs for which graph rewriting is confluent (modulo renaming and bisimulation) even in the presence of collapsing rules. We defined a new sequential graph rewriting strategy for the class of inductively sequential AGRSs which is c-normalizing and optimal for the class of admissible graphs. The use of definitional trees allows to combine the elegance of neededness with an efficient implementation by pattern-matching. In [17], a lazy graph rewriting strategy close to ours is described, namely the annotated functional strategy, which combines the discriminating position strategy [20] and rewriting with priority [4]. To our knowledge, no formal result has been proved regarding this strategy. In addition, we considered the extension of narrowing to admissible graphs and established the completeness and the soundness of most general narrowing.

We also used definitional trees to define a sequential graph narrowing strategy which is complete and sound, computes only independent substitutions and develops derivations which are shorter than most general narrowing. As far as we are aware of, the graph narrowing strategies presented in this paper are the first ones that handle graphs with cycles.

Acknowledgements

The first author is very indebted to Sergio Antoy and Michael Hanus for the many fruitful discussions. We are also grateful to the anonymous referees for their helpful comments.

References

[1] S. Antoy. Definitional trees. In *ALP'92*, pages 143–157. LNCS 632.

[2] S. Antoy, R. Echahed, and M. Hanus. A needed narrowing strategy. In *POPL'94*, pages 268–279, Portland.

[3] Z.M. Ariola and J.W. Klop. Equational term graph rewriting. *Fundamenta Informaticae*, 26(3-4), 1996.

[4] J.C. Baeten, J.A. Bergstra, and J.W. Klop. Term rewriting systems with priorities. In *RTA'87*, pages 83–94, Bordeaux. LNCS 256.

[5] H. Barendregt, M. van Eekelen, J. Glauert, R. Kenneway, M. J. Plasmeijer, and M. Sleep. Term graph rewriting. In *PARLE'87*, pages 141–158. LNCS 259.

[6] R. Echahed and J.C. Janodet. Introducing graphs in functional logic programming languages. Technical report, IMAG, 1997. Available via URL : ftp://ftp.imag.fr/pub/LEIBNIZ/ATINF/c-graph-narrowing.ps.gz.

[7] R. Echahed and J.C. Janodet. On constructor-based graph rewriting systems. Technical report, IMAG, 1997. Available via URL : ftp://ftp.imag.fr/pub/LEIBNIZ/ATINF/c-graph-rewriting.ps.gz.

[8] H. Ehrig and G. Taentzer. Computing by graph transformation : A survey and annotated bibliography. *Bulletin of the EATCS*, 59:182–226, June 1996.

[9] A. Habel and D. Plump. Term graph narrowing. *Mathematical Structures in Computer Science*, 6:649–676, 1996.

[10] A. Habel and D. Plump. Completeness of narrowing in non-copying implementations. In *not yet published*, 1997.

[11] M. Hanus. The integration of functions into logic programming: From theory to practice. *Journal of Logic Programming*, 19&20:583–628, 1994.

[12] M. Hanus. Curry: An integrated functional logic language. Available at `http://www-i2.informatik.rwth-aachen.de/~hanus/curry`, 1997.

[13] G. Huet and J.-J. Lévy. Computations in orthogonal term rewriting systems. In J.-L. Lassez and G. Plotkin, editors, *Computational logic: essays in honour of Alan Robinson*. MIT Press, Cambridge, MA, 1991.

[14] J.-M. Hullot. Canonical forms and unification. In *CADE'80*, pages 318–334. LNCS 87.

[15] J. R. Kennaway, J. K. Klop, M. R. Sleep, and F. J. De Vries. On the adequacy of graph rewriting for simulating term rewriting. *ACM Trans. on Programming Languages and Systems*, 16(3):493–523, 1994.

[16] J. R. Kennaway, J. K. Klop, M. R. Sleep, and F. J. De Vries. Transfinite reduction in orthogonal term rewriting systems. *Information and Computation*, pages 18–38, 1995.

[17] P.W. Koopman, J.E. Smetsers, M.C. van Eekelen, and M.J. Plasmeijer. Graph rewriting using the annotated functional strategy. In [22], chapter 23, pages 317–332.

[18] J. W. Lloyd. Combining functional and logic languages. In *Proc. of Int. Logic Programming Symp.*, pages 43–57, 1994.

[19] M. O'Donnell. *Computing in Systems Described by Equations*. LNCS 58.

[20] R. Plasmeijer and M. van Eekelen. *Functional Programming and Parallel Graph Rewriting*. Addison-Wesley, 1993.

[21] M.R.K. Krishna Rao. Completeness results for basic narrowing in non-copying implementations. In *Proc. of Joint Int. Conf. and Symp. on Logic Programming*, pages 393–407. MIT press, 1996.

[22] M. R. Sleep, M. J. Plasmeijer, and M. C. J. D. van Eekelen, editors. *Term Graph Rewriting. Theory and Practice*. J. Wiley & Sons, Chichester, UK, 1993.

Poster Abstracts

Applications of Abductive Logic Programming

A.C. Kakas and A. Michael
Department of Computer Science, University of Cyprus,
P.O.Box 537, CY-1678 Nicosia, CYPRUS
Email: {antonis, antonia}@turing.cs.ucy.ac.cy

Two real-life applications of abduction within the framework of Abductive Logic Programming (ALP) [1, 2, 3] are studied: a university course time tabling problem for the University of Cyprus and a crew rostering problem for Cyprus Airways. Based on the experience of developing these applications some general methodological features have emerged that can be useful in other abductive applications. This work thus bridges the more theoretical work on abduction and its practice to real-life problems. It is an attempt to understand more generally the characteristics of solving real, complex problems under the ALP framework and to propose some general guidelines for the better development of abductive applications. In this short abstract we give a brief outline of these general characteristics of abductive applications. More information can be found in [4].

Abductive applications in ALP are based on the view that abduction generates solutions described in terms of the abducible predicates, rather than variable bindings alone, as it is usual in other (deductive) approaches to problem solving with logic. In other words, the solution carriers are not simply the general problem independent logical variables, but problem-specific application predicates - the abducible predicates.

The central characteristic of abductive applications is that an abductive framework (like that of ALP) offers the possibility for a **high-level representation** of the application domain, with the ability to model directly properties of the problem. The fact that now the solution carriers of our problem are directly represented by the abducible predicates allows us to express the natural structure of our problem and the properties of the required solution in a direct way from their natural specification. This in turn means that we can now model easily complex domains and more importantly we can accommodate the particular specialized requirements that a specific application might have. Hence when deciding whether an application is suitable or will benefit from the use of abduction one needs to look for the following characteristics: complex functionality with specialized needs which are not necessarily fixed but can change dynamically.

This high-level representation offered by abduction has two further advantages in the development of an application: (i) the development can be **modular** and (ii) the resulting solution is **flexible** under changes of the requirements. Let us analyze these a little further.

The main dimension of **modularity** in abductive applications comes form the fact that we can separate the issues of validity and optimality of the solution. We can improve the quality of the solution by incrementally refining the model of the problem, represented in the logic program P of the abductive theory T=<P, Ab, IC>, without affecting the validity of the solution which is ensured by the integrity constraints IC of the theory T. We can also experiment with different design alternatives adopting different strategies to improve the optimality of the solutions. On the other hand, we can change the requirements on the solution expressed by the integrity constraints IC, without affecting the way that the problem is modeled in P.

The basic model of the problem in P can be incrementally refined along two different but inter-related lines. The first possibility is to exploit incrementally natural characteristics of the problem in order to build in P a more informed model. This can result not only in improvements on the quality of the solution but also on the computational effectiveness of the solution. The second possibility refers to the high-level handle that we have on the solution through the abducible predicates and the choice of abducible that we build in the model P of our problem. This choice can be easily implemented to follow either some heuristics, priorities, or algorithm for optimality, thus directly controlling the quality of the solutions. With this we can also control the way a solution is found or build up, where for example we may want the choice of abducible to follow a least commitment principle or some particular order.

The other major advantage of abductive applications is the **flexibility** they offer under new or dynamically changing requirements. Once we have one complete representation of the problem we can easily experiment with different requirements on the solution, by changing the integrity constraints which specialize the general model to the needs and preferences of a particular case. Furthermore, the build-in characteristic of abduction to be able to reason with existing hypotheses/solutions facilitates the task of recomputing a solution, or more precisely the task of adapting an old existing solution to accommodate new requirements that appear in time (e.g. for the case of rescheduling). Such adaptations can be done in a natural way with minimal changes to the existing solution, preserving parts of the solution that should not be affected. Also natural requirements and strategies for the recomputation of the solution can easily be accommodate within the high-level modeling environment of abduction.

Finally, we emphasize that the role of abductive reasoning within the computation task should in general be seen as that of automatically translating or reducing the high-level representation that it allows, to lower-level computational problems (often independent of the particular problem domain). In this way it provides a bridge between the high-level problem domain properties and domain independent solving methods. It is thus important to allow abduction to cooperate with other solvers in a hybrid framework for a more effective computation of the solutions.

Acknowledgments

We would like to thank Cyprus Airways and the University of Cyprus support services for their collaboration in developing the applications. Part of this work has been carried out with financial help from the EU, KIT programme.

References

[1] M. Denecker and D. De Schreye. SLDNFA: an abductive procedure for abductive logic programs. Journal of Logic Programming, 1996.

[2] Tze Ho Fung and R.A. Kowalski. The IFF Proof Procedure for Abductive Logic Programming. Journal of Logic Programming, 1996.

[3] A.C. Kakas, R.A. Kowalski and F.Toni. Abductive Logic Programming. Journal of Logic and Computation, 2(6), 719-770, 1993.

[4] A.C. Kakas and A. Michael. Applications of Abductive Logic Programming. Technical Report, Dept. of Computer Science, University of Cyprus, 1997.

Relationships between Partial Consistencies over Continuous Domains

Hélène Collavizza, François Delobel, Michel Rueher
Université de Nice–Sophia-Antipolis — I3S
930, route des Colles - B.P. 145
ESSI
06903 Sophia-Antipolis, France

We investigates the relationships between different partial consistencies which have been proposed for pruning the domains of the variables in constraint systems over the real numbers. The focus is both on the capability of these partial consistencies for handling the so called dependency problem and on their ability to limit the drawbacks due to their local scope. We establish several properties of the filtering achieved by the algorithm based up[on partial consistencies.

We consider the following consistencies:

- *2B–Consistency* (or hull consistency), an approximation which only requires to check the arc consistency property at each bound of the intervals;
- *Box–Consistency*, a coarser approximation of arc consistency than 2B–Consistency. Roughly speaking, Box–Consistency consists in replacing all existentially quantified variables but one by their intervals in the definition of 2B–Consistency. The key point is that Box–Consistency generates univariate functions which can be tackled by numerical methods such as Newton, and which do not require any constraint decomposition;
- *3B–Consistency* an approximation of path consistency, a higher order extension of arc-consistency. The key point is that 3B–Consistency is no more a strict local property: roughly speaking, 3B–Consistency checks whether 2B–Consistency can be enforced when the domain of a variable is reduced to the value of one of its bounds in the whole system;
- *Bound-Consistency* which applies the principle of 3B–Consistency to Box–Consistency : Bound-Consistency checks whether Box–Consistency can be enforced when the domain of a variable is reduced to the value of one of its bounds in the whole system.

The relationships between these different partial consistencies and the dependency problem are analized. Let $\Phi_{cstc}(P)$ be the closure of a constraint system P computed by an algorithm ensuring consistency *cstc* and let P_{decomp} be a decomposition of P allowing 2B-consistency filtering, we prove that:

- 2B–Consistency algorithms actually achieves a weaker filtering than Box–Consistency especially when a variable occurs more than once in some constraint:

  $$\Phi_{2B}(P) \preceq \Phi_{Box}(P)$$

  ($\Phi_{2B}(P) \equiv \Phi Box(P)$ when no variable occurs more than once).

  This is due to the fact that 2B–Consistency algorithms require a decomposition of the constraints with multiple occurrences of the same variable. This decomposition increases the limitations due to the local nature of 2B–Consistency;

- Box–Consistency achieves a weaker filtering than the one computed by 3B–Consistency algorithms:

  $$\Phi_{3B}(P) \preceq \Phi_{Box}(P) \preceq \Phi_{2B}(P)$$

Moreover, we show that no order relationship between $\Phi_{3B}(P_{decomp})$ and Φ_{2B}(P) holds: neither $\Phi_{2B}(P) \preceq \Phi_{3B}(P_{decomp})$ nor $\Phi_{3B}(P_{decomp}) \preceq \Phi_{2B}(P)$ hold, even if only one variable occurs more than once in each constraint of P.

From a more practical point of view, 2B–Consistency is weakened by the decomposition required for computing the narrowing functions. On the other hand, the univariate functions generated by Box–Consistency can be handled by Newton-like methods very efficiently.

However, 2B–Consistency can be more more efficient than Box–Consistency in some cases, especially when the projection functions used in 2B–filtering give an immediate result wherever Newton-like method (Box) has to iterate to yield the same result.

References

[1] H. Collavizza, F. Delobel, M. Rueher. Research Report 97-25, October 1997 *Laboratoire I3S. Les Algorithmes/Bâtiment Euclide. 2000 route des Lucioles. 06410 SOPHIA-ANTIPOLIS, FRANCE, 15 pages*

Controlling Search in Functional Logic Programs

Michael Hanus **Frank Steiner**
RWTH Aachen, Informatik II, D-52056 Aachen, Germany
`{hanus,steiner}@i2.informatik.rwth-aachen.de`

Motivation. A distinguishing feature of logic languages is their ability to deal with non-deterministic computations via built-in search facilities. However, standard search methods like global backtracking are often not sufficient and a source of many programming errors. Therefore, we propose the addition of a single primitive to logic-oriented languages to control non-deterministic computation steps. Based on this primitive, a number of different search strategies can be easily implemented. These search operators can be applied if the standard search facilities are not successful or to encapsulate search. The latter is important if logic programs interact with the (non-backtrackable) outside world, like file accesses or Internet applications.

The basic setting. We propose a search control operator (a generalization of Oz's operator [4]) which might be integrated in a variety of (functional, constraint) logic languages based on a non-deterministic evaluation principle. To abstract from the concrete language, we only assume that a computation step reduces an expression to a disjunction consisting of pairs of substitutions and expressions,i.e, the *operational semantics of the base language* is defined by a one-step relation $e \Rightarrow \sigma_1, e_1 \mid \cdots \mid \sigma_n, e_n$ where $n \geq 0$, e, e_1,...,e_n are expressions and $\sigma_1, \ldots, \sigma_n$ are substitutions ($n = 0$ corresponds to a failure). In logic programming, e is a goal, $e_1, \ldots, e_n$ are all resolvents of this goal and $\sigma_1, \ldots, \sigma_n$ are the corresponding unifiers. All following examples are related to the functional logic language Curry [2] (with "$\Rightarrow$" defined in [1, 2]).

A search control primitive. Since search is used to find solutions to some constraint, we assume that search is always initiated by a constraint containing a *search variable* for which a solution should be computed.Thus, a *search goal* has the form `\`x`->`c (this is the notation for lambda abstractions, i.e., x is a variable occurring in c which is not visible outside the search goal), where c is the constraint to be solved and x is the search variable. For instance, if we are interested in values for the variable `X` such that the equation `append([1],X)=[1,2]` holds, then the corresponding search goal is `\X->{append([1],X)=[1,2]}`.

To control the non-deterministic steps performed by the base language to find solutions to constraints, we introduce the *search control operator* `try` which takes a search goal as an argument and produces a list of search goals as a result. `try` attempts to evaluate the constraint of the search goal until the computation finishes or yields a non-deterministic step. In the latter case, the computation is immediately stopped and the different constraints obtained by the non-deterministic step are returned. Thus, an expression of the form `try(\`x`->`c`)` can have the following outcomes:

`[]`: The empty list indicates that the constraint has no solution, i.e., c reduces to the empty disjunction in the base language.

`[\`x`->`c'`]`: A one-element list indicates that the search goal has a single solution represented by the solved constraint c'.

`[`g_1`,...,`g_n`]`, $n > 1$: If the result list contains more than one element, the evaluation of the search goal requires a non-deterministic computation step. The different alternatives immediately after this non-deterministic step are represented as elements of this list, where the different bindings of the search variable are added as constraints.

Search strategies. Based on the primitive operator `try`, one can implement powerful and easily applicable search strategies. For instance, the *depth-first search* strategy, which collects all solutions of a search goal in a list, can be defined as follows (here we use a functional notation as in Curry):

```
all(G) = collect(try(G))
     where collect([])          = []
           collect([G])         = [G]
           collect([G1,G2|Gs]) = concat(map(all,[G1,G2|Gs]))
```

Similarly, one can define many other search strategies, like depth-bounded search, breadth-first search, best solution search or negation-as-failure.

Exploiting laziness. The strategy `all` might compute an infinite list of solutions. This causes no problem if we are only interested in a finite number of them and use *lazy evaluation*. For instance, in Curry one can easily implement a Prolog-like top-level shell (where the next solution is only computed by a user request) which is parameterized by a search strategy. If this generic shell is instantiated with `all`, we obtain the standard Prolog shell, but we can also use it with depth-bounded, iterative deepening, or breadth-first search to obtain a system with a more powerful search strategy. Such a modular approach is not simply possible in eager languages like Prolog or Oz.

Final remarks. The introduction of a search operator contributes to an old idea of logic programming by separating logic and control: the specification of functions or predicates becomes more independent of their use since the same function can be used for evaluation (computing values) or for searching (computing solutions) with various strategies without the necessity to define them in different ways. More details about the search operator and its application can be found in [3].

[1] M. Hanus. A Unified Computation Model for Functional and Logic Programming. In *Proc. of the 24th ACM Symposium on Principles of Programming Languages (Paris)*, pp. 80–93, 1997.

[2] M. Hanus (ed.). Curry: An Integrated Functional Logic Language. Available at `http://www-i2.informatik.rwth-aachen.de/~hanus/curry`, 1997.

[3] M. Hanus and F. Steiner. Controlling Search in Functional Logic Programs. Technical Report, RWTH Aachen, 1998.

[4] C. Schulte and G. Smolka. Encapsulated Search for Higher-Order Concurrent Constraint Programming In *Proc. of the 1994 ILPS*, pp. 505–520, 1994.

A Solver Collaboration in BALI [1]

Eric Monfroy
CWI, Kruislaan 413, 1098 SJ Amsterdam, The Netherlands
email: eric@cwi.nl web: http://www.cwi.nl/~eric

The need for *solver collaboration*, i.e., that is solver combination and cooperation, has been by now well recognized: several solvers collaborate to process constraints that cannot be solved (or efficiently solved) by a single solver. We are concerned with the need of a general scheme for integration, and re-usability of heterogeneous solvers, together with some strategies and a language for realizing their collaborations. So far, systems based on cooperation either provide fixed cooperation mechanisms, are dedicated to a single constraint domain, impose the solvers to be homogeneous, or do not provide strategies for solver cooperations.

BALI [1] is an environment for solver collaboration that separates constraint programming from constraint solving. We here focus on constraint solving techniques, i.e., the constraint solver collaboration language of BALI. This domain independent language has been designed for realizing distributed solving mechanism in terms of solver collaborations with solving strategies. The basic objects handled by the language are heterogeneous solvers. They are used inside *collaboration primitives* that integrate several paradigms (such as sequentiality, parallelism and concurrency) commonly used in solver combination or cooperation. In order to write finer strategies, we have also introduced some *control primitives* (such as iterator, fixed-point and conditional) in the collaboration language. A prototype implementation, BALI showed the feasibility of our approach and its interest in practice as well. BALI allows us to describe solver collaborations with a high-level language, and automatically implements new prototypes of cooperative solvers.

We illustrate some of the collaboration primitives of BALI with the simulation of CoSAc [2], a CLP system for non-linear polynomial constraints [2]. In CoSAc five heterogeneous solvers cooperate through a client/server architecture: *chr_lin* for solving linear constraints, *gb* for computing Gröbner bases, *maple_uni* for computing roots of univariate polynomials, *maple_exp* for simplifying and transforming constraints, *maple_exp* for simplifying and transforming constraints, and *ecl* for testing closed inequalities. These solvers cooperate in three collaborations:

[1] Full version available at http://www.cwi.nl/~eric/Private/Papers/bali.ps.gz

[2] The host language with solving strategies described in [1] is used as the constraint programming language of the simulation of CoSAc.

S_{inc}, S_{fin} and S'_{fin}. S_{inc} is triggered each time the constraint store is modified: *maple_exp* transforms polynomials so *eq_lin* can propagate information and simplify the linear equations. S_{inc} is realized in **BALI** using the sequential primitive ";" (similar to composition of functions):

$$S_{inc} = maple\_exp \ ; \ eq\_lin$$

After Prolog resolution, S_{fin} is applied to the remaining constraints. They are simplified (*maple_exp*) before computing their Gröbner base. Then, variables are eliminated from univariate polynomials (*maple_uni*), solutions are propagated, and linearized equations are solved (*eq_lin*). This elimination-propagation process is repeatedly applied untill a fixed-point is reached: all variables have been eliminated or no more univariate polynomials remain in the store. Using "f_p", the fixed-point primitive of **BALI**, we can simulate S_{fin} with the following collaboration:

$$S_{fin} = maple\_exp \ ; \ gb \ ; \ \text{f\_p}(maple\_uni; eq\_lin)$$

S'_{fin} is an alternative to S_{fin} which is more efficient when eliminations of non-linear variables do not linearize any other constraints. In **BALI**, this collaboration is created by:

$$S'_{fin} = maple\_exp \ ; \ gb \ ; \ \text{f\_p}(maple\_uni); ecl$$

As soon as solvers are integrated (i.e., data converters) in **BALI** only two lines of code are required to create the collaborations. This is negligible compared to the thousands of lines of **CoSAc**, and the simulation of **CoSAc** in **BALI** is actually as efficient as **CoSAc** itself.

We improved **CoSAc** using the ψ_concurrent primitive which provides a non-deterministic choice upon which we can act by introducing methods (e.g., psi_c(ψ_{basic}, S_1, S_2) executes simultaneously S_1 and S_2, and the result is given by the first solver that terminates.). The first solvers of S_{fin} and S'_{fin} are "factorized", and we obtain $S''_{fin} =$ $maple\_exp; gb;$ psi_c(ψ_{basic}, f_p($maple\_uni; eq\_lin$), f_p($maple\_uni$); ecl) S''_{fin} is always as efficient as the most efficient of the two collaborations S_{fin} and S'_{fin}. Thus, the simulation of **CoSAc** with **BALI** becomes more efficient than **CoSAc** itself.

References

[1] E. Monfroy. *Collaboration de solveurs pour la programmation logique à contraintes.* PhD Thesis, Université Henri Poincaré-Nancy I, Nov. 1996. (also available in english).

[2] E. Monfroy, M. Rusinowitch, and R. Schott. *Implementing Non-Linear Constraints with Cooperative Solvers.* In Proc. of ACM SAC'96, pages 63–72, Feb. 1996.

Integration of CLP and Stochastic Optimisation Strategies

Alvaro Ruiz-Andino, Jose J. Ruz
Department of Computer Science, Universidad Complutense de Madrid

1 Introduction

Most Constraint Logic Programming (CLP) languages are based on a constraint propagation solver, incorporating a branch and bound algorithm to solve Constrained Optimisation Problems (COP). However, in real scale problems, the search space can be too large to use this kind of exhaustive bounded search. We present a hybridisation of a propagation solver and stochastic optimisation strategies, in order to improve CLP operational behaviour on real scale COPs, as an instance of a general model to approach COPs using a propagation solver. Stochastic optimisation permit to deal with large-scale search spaces, while constraint propagation allow handling of constraints. Previous related work was done by Stuckey [4] Kuchenhoff [2] and Paredis [3].

2 General Model for solving COPs

Solving a COP requires coming up with an instance for each of the following templates: a) A Propagation Solver, implementing a consistency maintenance technique. b) A Solution Generator (LCS-Generator), which searches for Local-Consistent (LC) solutions, sub-spaces of the search space whose local consistency is guaranteed by the propagation solver. c) An Optimizer, implementing an optimisation strategy.

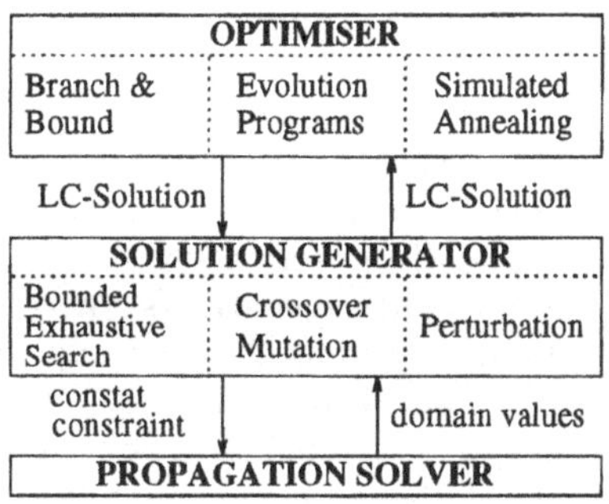

Figure 1: Model for COP solving techniques based on a propagation solver.

Our system, CSOS (Constrained Stochastic Optimisation System) pursuits tackling large-scale constrained optimisation problems, implementing instances for each of the three templates. CSOS' propagation solver is based in the indexical scheme [1]. Supported LC-Optimizer instances are a traditional Branch&Bound algorithm and two stochastic search strategies: evolution programs and simulated annealing. Crossover and mutation, for evolution programs, and perturbation, for simulated annealing, are instances of the LCS-Generator template.

3 Stochastic constrained optimisation

Representation and Evaluation of LC-Solutions. An LC-solution is represented as a list $[d_1, \cdots, d_n]$, where d_i is the finite domain associated with variable V_i. For evaluation purposes, an LC-solution has a related d_F, the pruned domain of function $\mathcal{F}$ (readily assimilated to a domain variable). *Fitness* value is computed as a normalised value of d_F with respect to the original domain of $\mathcal{F}$. But as we are dealing with non ground solutions, a *feasible* evaluation value is computed to indicate how much the domains of the variables have been pruned.

Crossover searches for a new LC-solution combining two randomly-biased chosen LC-solutions. Given two LC-solutions, $[a_i]$ and $[b_i]$, the crossover operator generates a mixture of both. K randomly chosen variables $V_{p(1)}$ through $V_{p(K)}$ are constrained to domains $a_{p(1)}$ through $a_{p(K)}$ from first parent. Remaining variables $V_{p(K+1)}$ through $V_{p(n)}$ are constrained, if possible, to second parent's domains, $b_{p(K+1)}$ through $b_{p(n)}$. If constraint posting leads to inconsistency, variable's domain is left unchanged, hence deep backtracking never occurs.

Mutation creates a new LC-solution by means of a small change in a LC-solution. Two LC-Generator instances are used: one of them randomly prunes a not completely ground solution, helping convergence towards ground solutions; the other one generates a not ground LC-solution from a ground solution, making possible the exploration of new areas of the search space.

Perturbation generates a neighbour LC-solution from a given LC-solution, $[a_i]$. First, K randomly chosen variables $V_{p(1)}$ through $V_{p(K)}$ are constrained to domains $a_{p(1)}$ through $a_{p(K)}$. Then, remaining variables $V_{p(K+1)}$ through $V_{p(n)}$ are randomly assigned. If assignment leads to inconsistency, the domain is left unchanged.

CSOS has been evaluated using a set of hardware design problems. Results point out that stochastic strategies scale much better than B&B in real-scale problems.

References

[1] P.V. Hentenryck, V. Saraswat, and Y.Deville. Design, Implementation and Evaluation of the Constraint Language cc(FD) *Draft*, 1993.

[2] V. Kuchenhoff. Novel search and constraints - an integration. *Technical Report IR-LP-92-16i, ECRC*, 1992.

[3] J. Paredis. Genetic State-Search for constrained Optimisation Problems. *13th Int. J. Conf. on Artificial Intelligence*, 1993.

[4] P. J. Stuckey and V. Tam. Models for using stochastic Constraint Solvers in Constraint Logic Programming. *Proc. of PLILP*, 1996.

A Generic Type System for CLP($\mathcal{X}$)

François Fages and Massimo Paltrinieri
CNRS-LIENS, Ecole Normale Supérieure, Paris, France
fages@dmi.ens.fr

Abstract

Inherited from the Logic Programming tradition, constraint logic programs generally have no static types or have a poor type structure. However, the structure $\mathcal{X}$ of interest is generally a quite complex combination of basic structures that may include integer arithmetic, real arithmetic, booleans, lists, Herbrand terms, infinite terms, feature structures, ..., with implicit coercions as in e.g. Prolog IV. Even the early CLP($\mathcal{R}$) system of [2] already combines Herbrand terms with arithmetic expressions in a non-symmetrical way: any arithmetic expression may appear under a Herbrand function symbol, e.g. in a list, but not the other way around. The framework of *many sorted logic* in [2] is not adequate for representing the type system underlying such a combination, as it forces Herbrand function symbols to have a unique type (e.g. over reals or Herbrand terms), whereas Herbrand functions can be used polymorphically (e.g. in `f(1)` and `f(f(1))`, or the list constructor in a list of list of numbers `[[3]]`). Making the underlying type system explicit is not of purely theoretical interest, as there is also a growing need for using a type system at compile-time for *detecting errors statically* in CLP($\mathcal{X}$) programs, instead of dynamically at run-time as in an untyped CLP system. The need for *a flexible type discipline* becomes even more accurate nowadays where CLP systems grow in size and various libraries and modules can be composed and re-used.

It is the purpose of a *prescriptive type system*, such as Mycroft-O'Keefe system, to impose type restrictions on programs with respect to type declarations, e.g. as in Gödel. The type system of Mycroft-O'Keefe is an adaptation to logic programs of the *parametric polymorphism* of ML. A *type inference algorithm* is given in [3]. In this system, types are first-order terms, type variables inside types, like α in $list(\alpha)$, express type parameters, so that programs defined over data structures of type $list(\alpha)$ can be used polymorphically over any list of elements of some type α. The flexibility of parametric polymorphism is however by far insufficient to handle properly coercions and complex structures in constraint logic programs.

A type system for CLP($\mathcal{X}$) should also support the meta-programming facilities of logic programming, through the ability to type meta-predicates such as `call(X)`, `setof(X,G,L)` or `arg(N,T,A)`. One way to acquire such a flexibility is to allow *subtypes*. A subtype relation between types $list(\alpha) <$

term allows to type the predicate $arg : nat \times term \times term \to bool$ so that, for instance, the atom $arg(1, [X|L], X)$ is well-typed although the second argument is a list. Similarly, we can type $call : bool \to bool$, $freeze : term \times bool \to bool$, $setof : \alpha \times bool \times list(\alpha) \to bool$, and the subtyping relation $bool < term$ allows to apply the *arg* predicate to atoms as well, whereas applying the `call` predicate to a list would raise a type error. Static types with subtyping relations between type constructors are also compatible with powerful forms of object-oriented programming in CLP over computation domains with inheritance hierarchies, such as feature structures.

Combining parametric polymorphism with subtyping in a static type system is thus a major issue. Several type systems combining parametric polymorphism with subtypes have been proposed for logic programs. However a number of problems still appear: except in a restricted case in [4], subtype relations between (parametric) type constructors are not allowed. That prevents subtype relations as $list(\alpha) < term$ and thus forbids to type meta-predicates. Furthermore, type inference algorithms have been shown to be incomplete in general [4] [1].

By abstracting from particular structures, as required in the CLP scheme, we study a *generic* static type system for CLP programs, independently of any specific computation domain $\mathcal{X}$. We present a type system that includes parametric polymorphism and subtype relations between constructors of different arities. We show that in this system the subject reduction property (i.e. goal resolution preserves static types) holds under the assumption that the type of predicates is definitional-generic in the sense of [3]. The type checking problem reduces in polynomial-time to the solving of subtype inequalities of some simple form, decidable in linear time. Type inference for variables and predicates reduces similarly in polynomial-time to the solving of general systems of subtype inequalities. We indicate that type inference for variables and predicates is possible in the universe of infinite types, but is an open problem in the universe of finite types.

References

[1] M. Hanus, Parametric Order-Sorted Types in Logic Programming, *Proc TAPSOFT'91*, LNCS 494:181–200, 1991.

[2] J. Jaffar, J.L. Lassez. Constraint Logic Programming. *Proc. of POPL'87, Munich*, 111–119, 1987.

[3] T.K. Lakshman, U.S. Reddy, Typed Prolog: A Semantic Reconstruction of the Mycroft-O'Keefe Type System, *ILPS'91, San Diego*, 1991.

[4] G. Smolka, Logic Programming with Polymprphically Order-Sorted Types, *Proc. ALP'88*, LNCS 343:53–70, 1988.

Implementing Randomised Algorithms in Constraint Logic Programming

N. Angelopoulos, A. Di Pierro and H. Wiklicky
Department of Computer Science
City University, London EC1V OHB
{nicos,adp,herbert}@cs.city.ac.uk

Synopsis

Algorithms where the flow of information is determined by an element of random choice (a "coin flipping" device), aka randomised algorithms, have known in the last decade a tremendous growth of interest, especially in the field of complexity theory.

Up to now such algorithms have been implemented mostly by means of probabilistic programs written in imperative languages. These programs have been analysed largely only by ad-hoc methods. However, real problems, and especially problems related to probabilistic concepts, are usually quite complicated and intuition is very likely to fail. Therefore, a formal deductive system would be much more handy.

In this paper, we propose a declarative-based implementation of randomised algorithms, which exploits the Concurrent Constraint Programming (CCP) paradigm for the formalisation of such algorithms. The main advantage in doing so is that we can rely on a sound and mathematically rigorous semantical framework, instead of on intuition, for tasks related to reasoning about probabilistic programs (analysis, synthesis, transformation and verification).

The foundations of such a semantical framework have been devised in previous papers [3, 2], where we introduce a probabilistic language based on CCP, namely Probabilistic CCP (PCCP), and provide it with an operational and a denotational semantics. In PCCP randomness is expressed by means of a construct for probabilistic choice, which replaces (or refines) nondeterminism, and allows the program to make stochastic moves during its execution.

In this work we concentrate on the implementation aspects of PCCP by designing a meta-interpreter for it. PCCP also includes synchronisation and concurrency aspects. However, for the time being, we put aside these aspects, by treating the parallel construct as a purely sequential one. As a consequence, the guarded choice, yet present in our language as a *global* choice (guards are not necessarily to be *true*), does not allow any synchronisation. From this point of view we effectively use here only the (probabilistic) Constraint Logic Programming (CLP) fragment of PCCP.

For the constraint solving, the meta-interpreter exploits existing constraint handling facilities (more concretely the SICStus 3.#6 system). This is possible because the design of PCCP does not require any additional structure on the underlying constraint system (e.g. fuzzy or belief systems). The current prototype consists basically of two phases: first PCCP agents and declarations are handled by a preprocessor that transforms them into an internal representation; this is then "executed" in a second phase. For more details we refer to [1]. In that paper, the capabilities of our system in implementing randomised algorithms are also demonstrated, by presenting an example of a generic randomised algorithm commonly used for combinatorial optimisation, namely Simulated Annealing, along with its application for solving specific NP-complete problems, like the travelling salesman problem.

These results show that the PCCP language is not only of theoretical interest, but can also be used for "real" applications. We do not claim that the examples we present are efficient implementations from the complexity-theoretic point of view – this is not our objective. However, our system offers all the advantages stemming from declarativity, like readability, flexibility, clarity of semantics, etc.

References

[1] N. Angelopoulos, A. Di Pierro, and H. Wiklicky. Randomised Algorithms and CLP. Technical Report 1998/02, Department of Computer Science, City University, 1998.

[2] A. Di Pierro and H. Wiklicky. A Banach Space Based Semantics for Probabilistic Concurrent Constraint Programming. In Xuemin Lin, editor, *Proc. 4th Australasian Theory Symposium, CATS'98*, volume 20 – 3 of *Australian Computer Science Communications*, pages 245–259, Singapore, 1998. Springer-Verlag.

[3] A. Di Pierro and H. Wiklicky. An Operational Semantics for Probabilistic Concurrent Constraint Programming. In Y. Choo P. Iyer and D. Schmidt, editors, *Proc. ICCL'98 – International Conference on Computer Languages*, IEEE Computer Society and ACM SIGPLAN, Chicago, 1998. IEEE Computer Society Press.

Horn Logic Denotations [1]

Gopal Gupta
Laboratory for Logic, Databases, and Advanced Programming
Department of Computer Science, New Mexico State University
Las Cruces, NM, USA 88003
email:gupta@cs.nmsu.edu; http://www.cs.nmsu.edu/lldap

Extended Abstract

While there has been decades of work in programming language semantics, the practical impact of this area has been very limited [6]. The reason is the different types of semantics that have been advocated—operational semantics, denotational semantics, and axiomatic semantics, etc.—that use different notations and that are designed for different types of users (language designers, implementors, programmers, etc.). Also, these different semantics are specified in a non-executable or only partially executable notation. Often, as Schmidt notes [6], formal semantics (especially denotational semantics) is mired in deep mathematics and lacks "calculational clarity." In this paper we present a simple solution to providing this missing "calculational clarity" to formal semantics. Our approach permits automatic derivation of efficient implementations and verification systems from semantic specifications.

In our approach [1] we advocate the use of Horn logic (and eventually constraint logic) as the language for specifying semantics, instead of the traditionally-used λ-calculus. Given that the syntax of a language, $\mathcal{L}$, can also be expressed as a Definite Clause Grammar the syntax and semantic specifications of $\mathcal{L}$ together trivially yield an interpreter for $\mathcal{L}$. Partial evaluation of this interpreter (using a partial evaluator such as Mixtus) w.r.t. to a given program, $\mathcal{P}$ (written in $\mathcal{L}$), yields "compiled code" for $\mathcal{P}$. Essentially, the valuation functions of $\mathcal{L}$ are compiled to the semantic algebras used in definition of $\mathcal{L}$. The switch from the Lambda calculus to Horn Logic has many other important implications: (i) Given the (Horn Logic) declarative denotational semantics various operational semantics can be obtained by choosing an appropriate Horn Logic selection function. (ii) A provably correct compiler can be obtained from the denotational description of the language with no extra effort (by using partial evaluation as described above). (iii) Given that axiomatic semantics of a program can be expressed in logic, it follows that all three semantics (operational, denotational, and axiomatic) are expressible in a common language. (iv) The postconditions

[1]Thanks to E. Pontelli and S. Akhter for discussions. Research partially supported by NSF grants CCR 96-25358, CDA 97-29848, HRD 96-28450, INT 95-15256.

and preconditions can be inserted in the compiled program (which is in Horn logic syntax) and evaluated; by choosing a precondition carefully, and turning it into a *generator* a deductive model-checker is immediately obtained for the program [1]. (v) By using evaluation engines other than Prolog, such as those that are tabling-based, and by choosing an abstract semantics, abstract interpreters for a language $\mathcal{L}$ can be automatically obtained from the abstract semantic specification of $\mathcal{L}$ [1]. (vi) Horn logic denotational semantics together with partial evaluation subsume evolving algebras, since the semantic algebra used in denotational definition can be further defined in terms of another algebra, and partially evaluated to obtain compilation of the program to this new algebra [1]. (vii) Expressing Horn logic denotations in terms of constructs of another language, a formal framework for *semantic porting* is obtained. Thus, if a language $\mathcal{L}_1$ is to be translated to language $\mathcal{L}_2$, then the denotational semantics of $\mathcal{L}_1$ can be given in terms of $\mathcal{L}_2$; the interpreter thus obtained is effectively a (provably correct) formal language translation system [1]. (viii) The specification of the input language of a software system $\mathcal{S}$ is a specification of $\mathcal{S}$. Thus, a Horn logic denotational specification of this input language yields an executable specification of $\mathcal{S}$ [5]. Efficient implementation and verifiers for this software system can be automatically obtained, as discussed above. By generalizing to constraint logic, timed languages (and, thus, real-time systems) can also be specified, and their verifiers obtained [2]. (ix) Semantics of parallel languages is easily given, as logic programs naturally encapsulate parallelism. Additionally, parallelizing compilers can be derived from the semantics specification [3].

References

[1] G. Gupta. Horn Logic Denotations and Their Applications. NMSU-CSTR-9719, Dec. 1997.

[2] G. Gupta, E. Pontelli. Constraint-based Approach for Specification & Verification of Real-time Systems. In *Proc. IEEE RTSS'97*, 230-239.

[3] G. Gupta, E. Pontelli, R. Cardenas, A. Lara. Automatic Generation of Provably Correct Parallelizing Compilers. NMSU-CSTR-9803. Jan. '98.

[4] G. Gupta, E. Pontelli, et al. Automatic Generation of a WAM-compiler and a Native Code Compiler for Prolog. Internal paper.

[5] G. Gupta, E. Pontelli. Logical Denotational Approach to Software Specification, Verification, Composition & Interoperation, Internal paper.

[6] D. Schmidt. *On the Need for a Popular Formal Semantics. Proc. ACM Conf. on Strategic Directions in Computing Research,* Cambridge, MA, June 1996. ACM SIGPLAN Notices 32-1 (1997) 115-116.

Towards Early Projection in CLP($\mathcal{R}$)

Andreas Fordan
GMD-FIRST, Berlin, Germany
`fordan@gmd.de`
Roland H.C. Yap
Department of Information Systems & Computer Science
National University of Singapore, Singapore
`ryap@iscs.nus.edu.sg`

Abstract

The execution of a constraint logic program (CLP) or logic program typically creates a number of local variables. After some point in the computation, these variables are no longer used in the computation, and hence are inaccessible or *dead*. In Prolog, and other programming languages, the data referenced by these dead variables can be removed automatically by garbage collection. In CLP, this situation can be more complex, since the dead variables are involved with constraints in the store and do not necessarily represent explicit data structures. The removal of these dead variables from the constraint store is tantamount to removing some existentially quantified variables from a set of constraints. This is referred to as *quantifier elimination* or *projection*. The projection problem arises in CLP systems such as CLP($\mathcal{R}$) and PROLOG III when the answer to a goal is desired. In CLP($\mathcal{R}$), the output module will project/remove the non-output (usually non-goal) variables from the answer constraints produced, when it can do so. Other techniques for projection in arithmetic constraints are described in [2, 3].

The primary use of projection in CLP systems has been as a mechanism for obtaining constraint output and answer constraints. In this poster, we propose the use of automatic projection during the execution of a CLP program. Dead variables can impose a number of overheads during execution:

- Space wastage due to the presence of dead variables involved with constraints in the store.
- Slowdown of the constraint solver due to the necessity of having to manipulate dead variables in the store.
- Slower projection given that there can be a substantial number of dead variables to remove.

Thus, it can be advantageous to remove dead variables during execution. A related piece of work is the identification of dead variables through the use of program analysis [5]. The optimizing compiler for CLP($\mathcal{R}$) described in [6] has dead variable removal as one of its optimizations. A major difference with the approach here is that the previous work only removes dead variables in arithmetic equations. Secondly, it relies on the accuracy of program analysis to perform dead variable removal. We propose instead, a general system architecture, for automatic early projection of linear constraints in CLP($\mathcal{R}$). This approach is runtime based and can either remove, more or less dead variables, as so desired. There would, of course, be tradeoffs in the benefits of removal versus the costs of the runtime removal.

The following simple example illustrates how removing dead variables can be beneficial:

```
p(0, X) :- X <= 1.
p(N, X) :- N > 0, p(N-1, Y), X <= Y.
```

The goal `:- p(500, X)` takes about 12 seconds to run in CLP($\mathcal{R}$) version 1.2 on a Sun 5 workstation. If a projection is enforced after every rule application, it becomes about 100 times faster. Experiments with the Can-Build problem [1] also show an improvement. A prototype implementation for automatic early projection in CLP($\mathcal{R}$) is currently under development.

References

[1] A. Fordan, U. Geske and A. Nareyek. Optimizing Constraint-Intensive Problems Using Early Projection. *JICSLP'96: Proc. of the 1996 Joint Intl. Conf. and Symp. on Logic Programming*, poster, 537, 1996.

[2] T. Huynh, C. Lassez and J-L. Lassez. Practical Issues on the Projection of Polyhedral Sets. *Annals of Mathematics and Artificial Intelligence*, 6:295–316, 1992.

[3] J-L. Imbert. Fourier's elimination: Which to choose? In *Principles and Practice of Logic Programming*, MIT Press, 1995

[4] J. Jaffar, M.J. Maher, P.J. Stuckey, R.H.C. Yap. Projecting CLP($\mathcal{R}$) constraints. *New Generation Computing*, 11(3&4):449–469, 1993.

[5] A.D. Macdonald, P.J. Stuckey and R.H. C. Yap. Redundancy of Variables in CLP($\mathcal{R}$). *ILPS'93: Proc. of the 3rd Logic Programming Symp.*, 73–93, 1993.

[6] A.D. Kelly, A. Macdonald, K. Marriott, P.J. Stuckey and R.H. C. Yap. Effectiveness of optimizing compilation for CLP($\mathcal{R}$). Proc. JICSLP'96: Joint Intl. Conf. on Logic Programming, 37–51, 1996.

Author Index

Logic Programming

Ehud Shapiro, editor
Koichi Furukawa, Jean-Louis Lassez, Fernando Pereira, and David H. D. Warren, associate editors

The Art of Prolog: Advanced Programming Techniques, Leon Sterling and Ehud Shapiro, 1986

Logic Programming: Proceedings of the Fourth International Conference (volumes 1 and 2), edited by Jean-Louis Lassez, 1987

Concurrent Prolog: Collected Papers (volumes 1 and 2), edited by Ehud Shapiro, 1987

Logic Programming: Proceedings of the Fifth International Conference and Symposium (volumes 1 and 2), edited by Robert A. Kowalski and Kenneth A. Bowen, 1988

Constraint Satisfaction in Logic Programming, Pascal Van Hentenryck, 1989

Logic-Based Knowledge Representation, edited by Peter Jackson, Han Reichgelt, and Frank van Harmelen, 1989

Logic Programming: Proceedings of the Sixth International Conference, edited by Giorgio Levi and Maurizio Martelli, 1989

Meta-Programming in Logic Programming, edited by Harvey Abramson and M. H. Rogers, 1989

Logic Programming: Proceedings of the North American Conference 1989 (volumes 1 and 2), edited by Ewing L. Lusk and Ross A. Overbeek, 1989

Logic Programming: Proceedings of the 1990 North American Conference, edited by Saumya Debray and Manuel Hermenegildo, 1990

Logic Programming: Proceedings of the Seventh International Conference, edited by David H. D. Warren and Peter Szeredi, 1990

The Craft of Prolog, Richard A. O'Keefe, 1990

The Practice of Prolog, edited by Leon S. Sterling, 1990

Eco-Logic: Logic-Based Approaches to Ecological Modelling, David Robertson, Alan Bundy, Robert Muetzelfeldt, Mandy Haggith, and Michael Uschold, 1991

Warren's Abstract Machine: A Tutorial Reconstruction, Hassan Aït-Kaci, 1991

Parallel Logic Programming, Evan Tick, 1991

Logic Programming: Proceedings of the Eighth International Conference, edited by Koichi Furukawa, 1991

Logic Programming: Proceedings of the 1991 International Symposium, edited by Vijay Saraswat and Kazunori Ueda, 1991

Foundations of Disjunctive Logic Programming, Jorge Lobo, Jack Minker, and Arcot Rajasekar, 1992

Types in Logic Programming, edited by Frank Pfenning, 1992

Logic Programming: Proceedings of the Joint International Conference and Symposium on Logic Programming, edited by Krzysztof Apt, 1992

Concurrent Constraint Programming, Vijay A. Saraswat, 1993

Logic Programming Languages: Constraints, Functions, and Objects, edited by K. R. Apt, J. W. de Bakker, and J. J. M. M. Rutten, 1993

Logic Programming: Proceedings of the Tenth International Conference on Logic Programming, edited by David S. Warren, 1993

Constraint Logic Programming: Selected Research, edited by Frédéric Benhamou and Alain Colmerauer, 1993

A Grammatical View of Logic Programming, Pierre Deransart and Jan Małuszyński, 1993

Logic Programming: Proceedings of the 1993 International Symposium, edited by Dale Miller, 1993

The Gödel Programming Language, Patricia Hill and John Lloyd, 1994

The Art of Prolog: Advanced Programming Techniques, second edition, Leon Sterling and Ehud Shapiro, 1994

Logic Programming: Proceedings of the Eleventh International Conference on Logic Programming, edited by Pascal Van Hentenryck, 1994

Logic Programming: Proceedings of the 1994 International Symposium, edited by Maurice Bruynooghe, 1994

Logic Programming: Proceedings of the Twelfth International Conference, edited by Leon Sterling, 1995

Logic Programming: Proceedings of the 1995 International Symposium, edited by John Lloyd, 1995

Inductive Logic Programming: From Machine Learning to Software Engineering, Francesco Bergadano and Daniele Gunetti, 1995

Meta-Logics and Logic Programming, Krzysztof Apt and Franco Turini, 1995

Logic Programming: Proceedings of the 1996 Joint International Conference and Symposium on Logic Programming, edited by Michael Maher, 1996

Logic Programming: Proceedings of the 14th International Conference on Logic Programming, edited by Lee Naish, 1997

Logic Programming: Proceedings of the 1997 International Symposium, edited by Jan Małuszyński, 1997

Logic Programming: Proceedings of the 1998 Joint International Conference and Symposium on Logic Programming, edited by Joxan Jaffar, 1998

Made in the USA
Coppell, TX
07 April 2026

75503277R00210